D1784382

BRITISH WILD
FLOWERS

VOLUME TWO

BRITISH WILD FLOWERS

VOLUME TWO

by

John Hutchinson

DAVID & CHARLES : NEWTON ABBOT

ISBN 0 7153 5553 8

First published by Penguin Books Limited 1945
First hardback edition, revised 1972
David & Charles (Publishers) Ltd

COPYRIGHT NOTICE
John Hutchinson 1945, 1972

All rights reserved. No part of this
publication may be reproduced, stored
in a retrieval system, or transmitted,
in any form or by any means, electronic,
mechanical, photocopying, recording or
otherwise, without the prior permission
of David & Charles (Publishers) Limited

Reproduced and printed in Great Britain by
Redwood Press Limited   Trowbridge & London

SEQUENCE OF FAMILIES IN THE TWO VOLUMES

(The numbers in brackets refer to the illustrations)

VOLUME I

KEY TO THE FAMILIES DESCRIBED AND ILLUSTRATED IN THE TWO VOLUMES

(The number in brackets refer to the illustrations)

Part 1. Ovules (potential seeds) not enclosed in an ovary; to this group belong only the three native Conifers, i.e. the Yew, Pine and Juniper . . . . **Gymnosperms (1–3)**

Part 2. Ovules (potential seeds) enclosed in an ovary which later develops into a fruit and contains the seed or seeds; all other native British flowering plants, except the three in part 1 above, belong here . . . . **Angiosperms (4–409)**

*

The families belonging to Part 2 (**Angiosperms**) are further subdivided into two groups called DICOTYLEDONS and MONOCOTYLEDONS, determined as follows:

Leaves usually with a net-like venation (such as that of a Birch or Oak leaf, a Buttercup, a Lime tree etc.; seedling with 2 seed-leaves; bundles in the stem arranged in a ring or rings (as seen in a cross-section of a Birch- or Oak-stem); sepals and petals usually 5 or 4 each . DICOTYLEDONS (4–709)

Leaves usually with nerves running parallel to the midrib (as in Grasses, Sedges, Lilies, etc.), often narrow with parallel margins; seedling with only 1 seed-leaf; bundles in the stem not in rings, but scattered; sepals and petals usually 6 or 3, or completely reduced

MONOCOTYLEDONS (710–809) (for key see p. xix)

*

The DICOTYLEDONS are divided into three groups as follows:

Petals present, free from each other . . . GROUP 1

Petals present, more or less united into a tube GROUP 2

Petals absent . . . . GROUP 3

GROUP 1

(PETALS PRESENT, FREE FROM EACH OTHER, RARELY MUCH REDUCED)

1 Carpels free from each other, sometimes crowded in or on a swollen receptacle (floral axis), more than 1; styles free from each other (to p. viii):

2 Leaves with stipules, these sometimes joined to the leaf-stalks; trees, shrubs or herbs:
  3 Carpels more than 2, or if few, then fruits with numerous hooks on the outside; leaves simple or more often pinnate, trifoliolate or 5-foliolate; calyx often with an epicalyx
Rosaceae (4–43)
  3a Carpels 2, often partially united below; herbs:
    4 Leaves pinnate . . . . . . **Rosaceae** (4–43)
    4a Leaves not pinnate . . . . **Saxifragaceae** (425–437)
2a Leaves without stipules; mostly herbs:
  5 Carpels not immersed in or enclosed by the floral axis:
    6 Herbs:
      7 Carpels usually numerous, or if few the petals often modified into tubes or spurs and the leaves much divided . . . . . **Ranunculaceae** ((223–241)
      7a Carpels few; petals never modified; leaves fleshy, undivided . . . . . **Crassulaceae** (421–424)
      7b Carpels 5; leaves twice divided **Paeoniaceae** (214)
7c Carpels several; leaves much divided **Helleboraceae** (215–222)
and **Podphyllaceae** (244)
      8 Flowers large and showy, solitary; aquatic plants
Nymphaeaceae (242, 243)
      8a Flowers very small in dense spike-like panicles
Rosaceae (4–43)
1a Carpels more or less united into a single ovary, or carpel 1 (as in the Pea family):
  9 Ovary not united to the sepals or calyx-tube (i.e. ovary completely superior or nearly so) (to p. xxii):
    10 Perfect stamens the same number as the petals and opposite to them:
      11 Sepals 3 or more:
        12 Anther opening by valves (flaps); style 1; petals with 2 large nectaries within the base; shrubs or herbs with prickly margined leaves or leaflets . . . . **Berberidaceae** (244–246)
        12a Anthers opening by a slit lengthwise;
          13 Sea-side herbs with pale blue flowers and basal rosette of leaves
Plumbaginaceae (379, 380)
          13a Inland shrubs or small trees, sometimes with thorny branches; flowers greenish
Rhamnaceae (195, 196)
      11a Sepals 2; petals widely notched at the apex
Portulacaceae (353, 354)

10a Perfect stamens as many as the petals and alternate with
   them, or more numerous or rarely fewer than the petals:
14 Flowers divisable into equal halves in more than one direction (i.e. flowers actinomorphic or regular) (to p. xi):
15 Filaments of the stamens more or less united into several
   separate bundles; leaves opposite, often gland-dotted
                              Hypericaceae (183–189)
15a Filaments of the stamens united into a single central tube
    around the ovary and styles; leaves often clothed with
    star-shaped hairs . .   .   .   . **Malvaceae (146–150)**
15b Filaments free or slightly united only at the base:
16 Stamens 6, four longer and two shorter (tetradynamous);
   sepals 4, petals 4, often clawed; ovary of 2 united carpels
   often divided by a thin false septum (Wallflower family)
                              Cruciferae (259–314)
16a Stamens and other floral parts not combined as above, if
    stamens 6 then more or less equal in length:
17 Leaves opposite or whorled (never all radical, i.e. direct
   from the root or base of the stem, (to p. x):
18 Stamens numerous (more than 10); shrublets clothed
   with star-shaped (stellate) hairs; petals soon falling
   off . . . . **Cistaceae (128, 129)**
18a Stamens not more than double the number of the
    petals:
19 Trees with flowers in pendulous racemes or cymes;
   leaves lobed; fruits with 2 widely spreading winged
   lobes . . . . **Aceraceae (198, 199)**
19a Trees with very small flowers in broad flat corymbs;
    leaves pinnate .   .   . **Caprifoliaceae (97–102)**
19b Woody shrubs or shrublets; fruits not winged as
    described above:
20 Ovules attached to the walls of the 1-locular ovary;
   fruit a capsule opening by valves; shrublet with small
   whorled or opposite leaves   **Frankeniaceae (140)**
20a Ovules attached to the central axis of the several-
    locular ovary:
21 Fruit a small black berry; shrublets with small heath-
   like leaves . . . . . . **Empetraceae (191)**
21a Fruit a capsule, 4-lobed, red to pink; seeds with
    a yellow aril . . . . . **Celastraceae (192)**
19c Herbs:
22 Ovary half-inferior (i.e. partly united to the calyx-
   tube; leaves deeply divided; flowers in a cluster
   on a common peduncle . . **Adoxaceae (438)**

22a Ovary completely superior (i.e. placed above the insertion of the sepals):
23 Ovary incompletely or not at all divided into loculi, with free-central or basal placentas
Caryophyllaceae (317–352)
23a Ovary completely divided into separate loculi:
24 Leaves with very conspicuous stipules, mostly with stalks of unequal length in each pair; sepals and petals 5 each
Geraniaceae (641–654)
24a Leaves without or with very minute stipules:
25 Stamens united into a short tube . **Linaceae (151, 153)**
25a Stamens not united:
26 Sepals and petals 3–4 each . . . **Elatinaceae (316)**
26a Sepals and petals more than 4 each:
27 Ovules several in each ovary . **Lythraceae (409, 410)**
27a Ovule 1 in each ovary. . **Illecebraceae (399–402)**
17a Leaves alternate or all radical (i.e. from the root or near the base of the stem):
28 Trees or shrubs with broadish elliptic rounded or cordate leaves:
29 Flowers with a large elongated bract partly attached to the peduncle (Lime tree family)
Tiliaceae (144,145)
29a Flowers without such a bract, arranged in slender racemes or on spiny branches or in clusters from scaly buds (Rose family) . **Rosaceae (4–43)**
29b Flowers without a bract as described above, arranged in umbels; climber with aerial roots and evergreen leaves . . . . **Araliaceae (103)**
28a Shrubs or shrublets with woody branches and very small leaves:
30 Tall sea-side shrubs with slender whip-like branches, minute leaves and slender racemes of pink flowers; fruit a capsule, the seeds crowned by a tuft of hairs . . . . **Tamaricaceae (141)**
30a Dwarf shrublet with small narrow leaves with rolled back margins; fruit a berry
Empetraceae (191)
28b Herbs, sometimes aquatic:
31 Stamens numerous, more than 10:
32 Stamens inserted below the ovary (hypogynous):
33 Sepals and petals 5 each
Ranunculaceae (223–241)
33a Sepals 2; petals 4 **Papaveraceae (249–256)**

32a Stamens inserted around the ovary (perigynous):
34 Terrestrial plants; petals 5   .   .   .   **Rosaceae (4–43)**
34a Aquatic plants, floating leaves and large yellow or white flowers; petals more than 5
Nymphaeaceae (242, 243)
31a Stamens 10 or fewer:
35 Leaves small and scale-like, yellowish; flowers pale yellow, a saprophyte on the roots of certain trees
Monotropaceae (181)
35a Leaves not like scales, more or less green; not saprophytic:
36 Anthers opening by a round terminal pore; leaves rounded, long-stalked; flowers in terminal racemes
Pyrolaceae (178–180)
36a Anthers opening by slits lengthwise:
37 Leaves with stipules:
38 Leaves trifoliaolate   .   .   .   .   **Oxalidaceae (655)**
38a Leaves not trifoliolate:
39 Ovary 5-locular; leaves more or less lobed or toothed   .   .   .   .   .   **Geraniaceae (641–654)**
39a Ovary 1-locular; leaves very small and entire
Illecebraceae (399–402)
37a Leaves without stipules:
40 Flowers with branched glandular staminodes alternating with the stamens
Saxifragaceae (425–437)
40a Flowers without staminodes:
41 Leaves densely sticky-glandular more or less all over or on the margin
Droseraceae (439–441)
41a Leaves not glandular as described above:
42 Leaves deeply divided
Ranunculaceae (223–241)
42a Leaves not divided:
43 Seed solitary in the fruit
Illecebraceae (399–402)
43a Seeds several in the fruit   **Linaceae (151–153)**
14a Flowers divisable into 2 equal halves only in vertical direction (flowers zygomorphic or irregular):
44 Ovary composed of 1 carpel with 1 style:
45 Petals not spurred, but often clawed; leaves mostly pinnate or trifoliolate; stamens united into a sheath often with one free from the rest (Pea family)
Papilionaceae (44–93)

45a Petals with a spur at the base; stamens free
         Ranunculaceae (223–241)
44a Ovary composed of more than 1 united carpels with more
 than 1 style or stigmas:
 46 Ovary 1–2-locular with the ovules inserted on the walls or
  at the apex of the loculi:
 47 Stamens free from each other:
  48 Anther-connective produced beyond the loculi; leaves
   stipulate . . . . . **Violaceae** (132–139)
  48a Anther-connective not produced; leaves not stipulate
          Resedaceae (315)
 47a Stamens connate into two bundles:
  49 Ovules on the walls of the ovary
         Fumariaceae (257, 258)
  49a Ovules at the apex of the ovary **Polygalaceae** (142)
 46a Ovary 5-locular, with the ovules arranged on the central
  axis; one sepal spurred and petaloid
         Balsaminaceae (656–658)
9a Ovary more or less united to the calyx-tube (ovary from ½ inferior to wholly inferior):
 50 Leaves alternate or rarely clustered:
  51 Flowers in umbels, usually very small (as in the Hemlock) or rarely in a dense head-like cluster (Sea-
   holly); leaves often very much divided:
  52 Herbs with more or less hollow ribbed stems,
   flowering in spring and summer
         Umbelliferae (442–485)
  52a Climber with aerial roots, flowering and fruiting in
   autumn; leaves evergreen (Ivy)
         Araliaceae (103)
  51a Flowers neither in umbels nor in head-like clusters,
   sometimes in corymbs:
  53 Stamens numerous; trees, shrubs or herbs; leaves
   usually with prominent stipules, entire, pinnate
   or toothed . . . . . **Rosaceae** (4–43)
  53a Stamens 10 or fewer:
  54 Ovary 1-locular with numerous ovules on 2
   parietal placentas; shrubs, branches armed
   with 3-forked spines . **Grossulariaceae** (94)
  54a Ovary 2-locular; dwarf herbs with small white
   or pink flowers . **Saxifragaceae** (425–437)
  54b Ovary 4-locular; herbs with pink, white or
   rarely large yellow flowers
         Onagraceae (411–418)

50a Leaves opposite or whorled:
55 Parasitic shrublet with minute flowers and round white
   berries (Mistletoe) . . . . . **Loranthaceae (193)**
55a Low cushion-like herbs with bluish-purple solitary flowers
   Saxifragaceae (425–437)
55b Shrubs or herbs not forming cushions:
56 Flowers in heads surrounded by a whorl of white bracts, or
   in terminal cymes without bracts . **Cornaceae (95, 96)**
56a Flowers not in heads or cymes:
57 Herbs with toothed leaves; style simple or divided only at
   the top . . . . **Onagraceae (411–418)**
57a Aquatic herbs with very minute flowers; styles or stigmas
   separate . . . . . . **Halorrhagaceae (419, 420)**

GROUP 2

(PETALS UNITED)

1 Ovary not united to the sepals or calyx-tube (i.e. ovary
   superior) (to p. xv):
2 Stamens the same number as the corolla-lobes and opposite to
   them; herbs often with a basal rosette of leaves;
3 Sepals or calyx-lobes 5 . . . **Primulaceae (464–378)**
3a Sepals 2 . . . . **Portulacaceae (353, 354)**
2a Stamens, if the same number as the corolla-lobes, then not
   opposite to them, sometimes more or few than the lobes:
4 Stamens not inserted on the corolla-tube; anthers mostly
   opening by a terminal pore, rarely by slits lengthwise:
5 Leaves mostly radical, long-stalked and orbicular or
   spoon-shaped . . . . . . **Pyrolaceae (78–80)**
5a Leaves not all radical, at most shortly stalked, often very
   small with rolled back margins, alternate or whorled or
   opposite . . . . **Ericaceae (164–174)**
4a Stamens inserted more or less on the corolla-tube; anthers
   usually opening by a slit lengthwise:
6 Stamens twice as many as the corolla-lobes; leaves orbicular, peltate . . . . **Crassulaceae (421–424)**
6a Stamens as many as or fewer than the corolla-lobes:
7 Stamens as many as the corolla-lobes (to p. xiv):
8 Leaves pinnate; shrub or small tree
   Caprifoliaceae (97–102)
8a Leaves pinnate; small herb, not aquatic
   Polemoniaceae (659)
8b Leaves trifoliolate or orbicular; aquatic plants
   Menyanthaceae (362, 363)

8c Leaves simple or toothed:
9 Leaves opposite:
10 Ovary deeply divided vertically with the style inserted between the lobes; herbs . . . . **Labiatae (678–709)**
10a Ovary not divided as above; style terminal on the ovary:
11 Herbs with leafy stems and sometimes also basal rosettes or leaves; flowers mostly blue
Gentianaceae (355–361)
11a Shrublet with decumbent or prostrate, wiry, leafy stems and solitary blue flowers . . . **Apocynaceae (202)**
9a Leaves alternate, or all radical or crowded into rosettes:
12 Ovary deeply lobed vertically into 4 parts, especially in fruit; style inserted between the lobes (gynobasic); plants often covered with rough bulbous-based hairs
Boraginaceae (660–677)
12a Ovary and style not as above:
13 Tree with evergreen prickly leaves, small white flowers and clusters of bright red berries
Aquifoliaceae (190)
13a Herbs or climbers or small cushion-like plants:
14 Ovary with not more than 2 ovules; twining or creeping plants with lovely broadly tubular flowers
Convolvulaceae (608–610)
14a Ovary with more than 2 ovules in each loculus:
15 Woody cushion plantlet found only in the Scottish mountains, with dense rosettes of small leaves and single stalked white flowers **Diapensiaceae (182)**
15a Habit not as above:
16 Corolla dry and scarious; herbs with radical leaves and flowers mostly in dense spikes
Plantaginaceae (381–384)
16a Corolla not dry and scarious:
17 Corolla-lobes contorted; leaves pinnate
Polemoniaceae (659)
17a Corolla-lobes imbricate or plicate; two very closely-related families
Solanaceae (601–607) and **Scrophulariaceae (611–636)**
7a Stamens fewer than the corolla-lobes:
18 Trees with pinnate opposite leaves: stamens 2; fruit winged (Ash tree) or a berry (Privet)
Oleaceae (200, 201)
18a Herbs:
19 Flowers actinomorphic (regular); ovary 1-locular with free placentation; sepals 2 **Portulacaceae (353, 354)**

19a Flowers more or less zygomorphic (irregular):
20 Ovary 1-locular with a free basal placenta; aquatic or bog plants, the latter with a rosette of broadish leaves
Lentibulariaceae (639, 640)
20a Ovary usually with more than 1 loculus and with axile placentas:
21 Ovules numerous in each loculus or ovary:
22 Ovules attached to the central axis of the 2-locular ovary; corolla sometimes spurred at the base; stamens 4 or 2
Scrophulariaceae (611–636)
22a Ovules attached to the walls of the ovary; stamens 4 in two pairs, anthers connivent **Orobanchaceae (637, 638)**
21a Ovule 1 in each loculus; corolla mostly very distinctly 2-lipped:
23 Ovary not lobed, with a terminal style
Verbenaceae (213)
23a Ovary deeply and vertically lobed with the style inserted between   .   .   .   .   **Labiatae (678–709)**
1a Ovary more or less united to the sepals or calyx-tube (i.e. ovary inferior):
24 Flowers in heads surrounded by an involucre of bracts (as in the Daisy, Dandelion, etc.):
25 Anthers united into a tube around the style; calyx of the small individual flowers representd by a pappus of bristles or bristle-like hairs, these rarely absent
Compositae (507–600)
25a Anthers not united as above; calyx not as above
Dipsacaceae (490–493)
24a Flowers not in heads as described above but sometimes in a dense cluster:
26 Leaves alternate or all radical (to p. xvi):
27 Anthers opening by pores at the top of the loculi
Vacciniaceae (175–177)
27a Anthers opening by slits lengthwise:
28 Corolla not spurred at the base:
29 Corolla actinomorphic (regular):
30 Climber with tendrils; leaves 5–7-lobed; flowers unisexual, yellowish-green
Cucurbitaceae (143)
30a Erect or decumbent herbs; flowers bisexual
Campanulaceae (479–504)
29a Corolla zygomorphic (irregular); stamens united into a column around the style
Lobeliaceae (505, 506)

28a Corolla spurred at the base . **Valerianaceae 486–489)**
26a Leaves opposite or whorled:
  31 Leaves stipulate or in whorls (the stipules the same or al-
    most the same as the leaves) . **Rubiaceae (203–21)**
  31a Leaves not whorled, simple or compound; no stipules:
    32 Ovary 1-locular with 1 pendulous ovule
                  Valerianaceae (486–489)
    32a Ovary more than 1-locular:
      33 Very small herb with deeply divided leaves and a
        terminal cluster of small greenish flowers
                    Adoxaceae (438)
      33a Shrubs scramblers or climbers
                Caprifoliaceae (97–102)

GROUP 3

(PETALS ABSENT, SOMETIMES THE CALYX PETALOID)

1 Flowers (at least the males) in catkins, very small:
  2 Ovary superior (i.e. not united to the sepals):
    3 Branches and leaves covered by silvery scales; sea-side shrub
    or small tree . . . . . **Elaeagnaceae (197)**
    3a Branches and leaves not covered by silvery scales; willows,
    birches, oaks, nettles, etc.:
      4 Ovules attached to the wall of the ovary; trees, shrubs or
      subherbaceous; willows and poplars
                Salicaceae (105–115)
      4a Ovules attached to the top or bottom of the ovary:
        5 Leaves alternate:
          6 Leaves stipulate; trees:
            7 Ovary superior . . . . . **Betulaceae (117, 118)**
            7a Ovary inferior . . . . . **Fagaceae (121, 122)**
          6a Leaves not stipulate; shrublets with glandular leaves
                Myricaceae (116)
        5a Leaves opposite; herbs with stinging hairs
                Urticaceae (124–126)
  2a Ovary inferior (i.e. united with the sepals or calyx-tube):
      8 Male flowers with a calyx; involucre not leafy and not
      jagged . . . . **Fagaceae (121, 122)**
      8a Male flowers without a calyx; fruits partially enclosed
      in a leafy jagged persistent involucre
                Corylaceae (119–120)
1a Flowers not in true catkins, but sometimes in clusters or heads
  or in slender spikes:

9 Ovary wholly superior (i.e. not united with the sepals or calyx-tube) (to p. xxviii):
10 Flowers enclosed in an involucre (called a cyathium), (see figs. 156–163), with large glands on the margin; stems often exuding milk-like sap when cut or bruised
Euphorbiaceae (154–163)
10a Flowers not arranged as above, but the females sometimes in a dense bracteate head:
11 Leaves opposite or verticillate, never all radical:
12 Leaves with stipules:
13 Ovary with free central placentation (i.e. crowded on the central axis without dividing walls)
Caryophyllaceae (317–352)
13a Ovary with axile, basal or apical placentation:
14 Flowers bisexual, very small   **Illecebraceae (399–402)**
14a Flowers unisexual:
15 Twiners with 3–5-lobed toothed leaves; female flowers with large bracts . . . . **Cannabinaceae (127)**
15a Erect herbs with stinging hairs; ovary with 1 ovule
Urticaceae (124–126)
15b Erect herbs but no stinging hairs; ovary with more than 1 ovule . . . **Euphorbiaceae (154–163)**
12a Leaves without stipules:
16 Shrubs or trees with hard wood:
17 Leaves undivided . . . . . . **Buxaceae (104)**
17a Leaves pinnate . . . . . . **Oleaceae (201)**
16a Herbs or soft-wooded climbers:
18 Climber with free carpels with long hairy tails in fruit leaves compound
Ranunculaceae (223–241)
18a Erect herbs:
19 Flowers bisexual:
20 Ovules numerous:
21 Placenta free basal . **Primulaceae (364–378)**
21a Placenta free central
Caryophyllaceae (317–352)
20a Ovule 1, pendulous from a basal placenta
Illecebraceae (399–402)
19a Flowers unisexual . **Chenopodiaceae (399–402)**
11a Leaves alternate or all radical:
22 Leaves stipulate:
23 Ovary 2- or more-locular, composed of united carpels:
24 Fruits not winged   **Euphorbiaceae (154–163)**
24a Fruits winged . . . . . . **Ulmaceae (123)**

23a Ovary 1-locular or carpels free:
   25 Stipules forming a sheath around the stem or attached
      to the leaf-stalk:
     26 Leaves entire . . . . . **Polygonaceae** (385–398)
     26a Leaves digitately lobed, trifolioate or simply pinnate
                                  Rosaceae (4–43)
   26b Leaves twice pinnate:
   26c Ovules several . . . . . **Helleboraceae** (215–222)
   26d Ovule 1 . . . . . **Ranunculaceae** (223–241)
  25a Stipules neither sheathing nor attached to the
     petiole:
    27 Flowers without staminodes
                        Chenopodiaceae (403–408)
    27a Flowers with staminodes between the fertile stamens
                        Illecebraceae (399–402)
22a Leaves without stipules:
   28 Stamens connate; leaves kidney-shaped
                        Aristolochiaceae (247–248)
   28a Stamens free from each other:
   29 Woody plants but sometimes shrublets:
     30 Leaves covered with silvery scales; sea-side shrub
       or small tree . . . . . **Elaeagnaceae** (197)
     30a Leaves not covered by silvery scales, sometimes
       glandular:
     31 Leaves gland-dotted, odorous when bruised
                        Myricaceae (116)
     31a Leaves not gland-dotted:
     32 Stamens perigynous; flowers bisexual, mostly
       sweet-scented; calyx green or coloured, tubular
                        Thymelaeaceae (130, 131)
     32a Stamens hypogynous; leaves very small and
       heath-like; dwarf shrublets with small
       crowded leaves and small inconspicuous
       flowers . . . . . **Empetraceae** (191)
  29a Herbs:
    33 Ovary of several separate free carpels
                        Ranunculaceae (214–241)
    33a Ovary of 1 carpel or united carpels
                        Chenopodiaceae (403–408)
9a Ovary inferior (more or less united with the calyx):
   34 Woody plants:
     35 Leaves covered with silvery scales; sea-side shrub or
       small tree   **Elaeagnaceae** (197)
     35a Leaves not covered with silvery scales:

36 Plants parasitic on trees; branches brittle (Mistletoe)
Loranthaceae (193)
34a Herbs:
　37 Leaves trifoliolate; carpels free or nearly so with separate
　　　styles . . . . **Rosaceae (4–43)**
　37a Leaves not trifoliolate:
　　38 Leaves alternate:
　　　39 Leaves kidney-shaped or cordate; calyx coloured; 3-
　　　　lobed or 2-lipped and tubular spoon-shaped
Aristolochiaceae (247, 248)
　　　39a Leaves lanceolate; calyx green　**Urticaceae (124–126)**
　　38a Leaves opposite:
　　　40 Ovules attached to the walls of the ovary; leaves
　　　　rounded; small herbs in wet places
Saxifragaceae (425–437)
　　　40a Ovules not attached to the walls of the ovary:
　　　　41 Aquatic or semiaquatic plants:
　　　　　42 Leaves in whorls . . . **Halorrhagaceae (419, 420)**
　　　　　42a Leaves opposite . . . . **Onagraceae (411–418)**
　　　　41a Not aquatics, leaves narrow . . **Santalaceae (194)**

MONOCOTYLEDONS

1 Ovary superior, i.e. not united to either the calyx or corolla
　(perianth) (to p. xxxi):
　2 Carpels free from each other or only one carpel with 1 stigma;
　　mostly aquatic or semi-aquatic plants:
　　3 Flowers bracteate:
　　　4 Flowers in simple umbels; carpels 6; ovules spread all over
　　　　the inside of the carpels . . . . **Butomaceae (710)**
　　　4a Flowers in panicles or compound umbels; ovules not
　　　　spread over the inner surface of the carpels:
　　　　5 Carpels 6 or more; leaves not ligulate
Alismataceae (714–717)
　　　　5a Carpels 4–3; leaves ligulate . . **Scheuchzeriaceae (718)**
　　3a Flowers without bracts:
　　　6 Terrestrial or marsh herbs with linear radical leaves and
　　　　leafless flowering stems bearing a slender raceme or
　　　　spike of greenish flowers . . **Juncaginaceae (719)**
　　　6a Fresh-water aquatics with floating leaves; flowers
　　　　bisexual; stamens 4 . . **Potamogetonaceae (720)**
　2a Carpels more or less completely united with usually more
　　than 1 stigma;

7 Perianth present:
8 Perianth of 2 separate and usually dissimilar whorls (calyx and corolla):
9 Flowers not in heads surrounded by bracts:
10 Low shrublet with leaf-like cladoiform branchlets; stamens united into a tube; flowers mostly unisexual

Ruscaceae (740)

10a Herb with a whorl of usually 4 obovate leaves subtending a single conspicuous flower; stamens free; anther-connective produced beyond the loculi

Trilliaceae (722)

10b Herb with a loose terminal raceme of small flowers

Scheuchzeriaceae (718)

9a Flowers in a head surrounded by bracts; leaves linear in a radical cluster . . . . . **Eriocaulaceae** (721)
8a Perianth of 1 whorl, each part more or less similar, mostly conspicuous and petaloid:
11 Flowers in an umbel or single but subtended by a spathaceous bract or bracts; rootstock a bulb

Amaryllidaceae (745–750)

11a Flowers not arranged as above:
12 Flowers in globose clusters, unisexual, the upper clusters male, the lower female

Sparganiaceae (744)

12a Flowers arranged on a spadix (dense spike), subtended by a large spathe, sometimes this narrow and leaf-like . . . . . . **Araceae** (742, 743)
12b Flowers not as above:
13 Branchlets modified and looking like leaves bearing the flowers on their surface; stamens united into a tube; flowers mostly unisexual

Ruscaceae (740)

13a Branchlets not modified as above; flowers bisexual:
14 Leaves in a whorl of 4, 5 or 6 subtending a single flower . . . . . . **Trilliaceae** (722)
14a Leaves not as above:
15 Flowers without bracts; ovary or 6–3 carpels

Juncaginaceae (719)

15a Flowers with bracts; ovary of 3 or 2 carpels:
16 Perianth petaloid . . . **Liliaceae** (723–739)
16a Perianth glume-like; plants grass-like

Juncaceae (779–784)

7a Perianth absent or represented by hypogynous scales or setae; flowers very small, arranged in spikelets in the axils of scaly bracts . . . . . . **Cyperaceae** (785–809)

1a Ovary inferior, i.e. united to the calyx or corolla (perianth):

17 Perianth composed of a distinct separate calyx and corolla:

18 Stamens 3 or more; flowers actinomorphic (regular):

19 Aquatics; ovules on the walls of the ovary or on intrusive placentas . . . **Hydrocharitaceae** (711–713)

19a Terrestrial plants; ovules on the inner angles of the loculi . . . . **Iridaceae** (751–754)

18a Stamens 2 or 1; ovary or pedicel or both often spirally twisted; flowers zygomorphic (irregular)
Orchidaceae (755–778)

17a Perianth-segments more or less alike and often petaloid, mostly 6, free or united at the base into a single tube, in orchids the third petal often often much modified into a lip:

20 Flowers more or less actinomorphic (regular), if less so then stamens 3 or more:

21 Ovules spread all over the walls of the ovary; aquatic plants . . . . . **Hydrocharitaceae** (711–713)

21a Ovules on the placentas in the inner angle of the loculi:

22 Stamens 6:

23 Inflorescence scapose, umbellate, subtended by an involucre of one or more spathaceous bracts, sometimes reduced to one flower; not climbing
Amaryllidaceae (745–750)

23a Inflorescence raceomose, axillary; climbers; flowers unisexual . . . . **Dioscoreaceae** (741)

22a Stamens 3; herbs, not climbing; flowers bisexual, showy . . . . . . **Iridaceae** (751–754)

20a Flowers very zygomorphic (irregular), the third petal often very different and modified into a lip; stamens 2 or 1; ovary and often the pedicel spirally twisted
Orchidaceae (755–778)

GLOSSARY OF BOTANICAL TERMS

Achene: a small, dry seed-like fruit.
acuminate: gradually pointed.
adnate: attached the whole length to another structure.
alternate: not opposite to something else.
annual: lasting only one year or season.
anther: portion of stamen bearing the pollen.
apiculate: with a little point.
aquatic: living in water.
aril: outgrowth from seed-stalk (common in *Euphorbia* family).
astringent: contracting or binding.
axil: the angle between leaf and branch or stem.
axillary: in the axil.

berry: succulent fruit with seeds immersed in the pulp.
biennial: lasting two years.
bisexual: having two sexes (i.e. stamens and pistil in the same flower).
bract: modified leaf at base of flower-stalk, or leaves around a flower-head.
bracteole: small bract on the flower-stalk.
bullate: blistered or puckered.

calcareous: chalky or limy.
calyx: outermost, usually green, floral envelope.
capitate: arranged in a head, or head-like.
capsule: dry fruit which opens.
carpel: one or more divisions of ovary or fruit.
caruncle: wart or protuberance near stalk of seed.

catkin: slender, often pendulous spike of flowers.
compound: formed of many similar parts.
concave: scooped out.
connate: united similar parts.
connective: portion of filament connecting lobes of the anther.
convex: humped.
cordate: heart-shaped.
corolla: collective name for the petals.
corymb: more or less flat-topped collection of flowers.
crenate: with blunt, curved teeth.
crenulate: diminutive of crenate.
cross-pollination: transference of pollen from one flower to stigmas of another.
cyme: an inflorescence repeatedly divided with the oldest flower in the middle of each fork.
cystoliths: mineral markings in the leaves as found in the Nettle family.

deciduous: falling off.
decumbent: lying on the ground.
decurrent: running down.
dentate: toothed.
dioecious: male and female flowers on different plants.
disk: a fleshy portion of floral axis, often secreting nectar.
disk-flower: flowers in the middle of a flower-head with rays.
drupe: stone fruit such as a plum.

elliptic: shaped like an ellipse.
endosperm: reserve food material in a seed.
entire: not divided or toothed.

epicalyx: collection of bracteoles like an extra calyx.

falcate: sickle-shaped.
female: the fruiting part of the flower (ovary or carpels).
filament: stalk of stamen.
fruit: the fertilized and mature ovary or carpel.

glabrous: not hairy.
glaucous: with a whitish-blue lustre like the 'bloom' of a grape.
globose: round like a globe.

hastate: like an arrow, but with the barbs turned outwards.

imbricate: overlapping, with one part wholly outside.
inferior: below.
inflexed: turned inwards.
inflorescence: collection of flowers on the shoot.
introrse: facing inwards.
involucre: a ring of bracts surrounding one or more flowers.
irregular: applied to a flower (like that of a pea) which cannot be divided into equal halves in more than one direction.

lanceolate: lance-shaped.
leaflet: unit of a compound leaf.
lenticels: corky spots on bark.
lobulate: divided into small lobes.
locular: divided into chambers.
loculus: a chamber or cavity of an ovary, fruit, or anther.
longitudinal: lengthwise.

male: a plant or flower which bears stamens.

monoecious: male and female flowers on the same plant.
mucronate: bearing a little tip.

nectary: organ in which nectar is secreted.
node: point of insertion of a leaf or leaves.
nutlet: little nut.

oblanceolate: reverse of lanceolate.
obovate: reverse of ovate.
opposite: inserted at same level, as leaves on a shoot.
orbicular: circular.
ovary: the female part of the flower, represented by the carpels.
ovate: egg shaped.
ovoid: ovate in outline.
ovule: the organ which after fertilization develops into a seed.

panicle: a branched raceme.
papillous: clothed with short, knob-like hairs.
pappus: modified calyx of the *Compositae.*
pectinate: divided like a comb.
pedicel: the ultimate flower-stalk.
peduncle: common stalk of several flowers.
peltate: attached in the middle (like the stalk of a mushroom).
pendulous: hanging down.
perennial: lasting more than two years.
perianth: the collective outer covering of the flower.
persistent: not falling off.
petal: the usually coloured inner part of the floral leaves.
petiolate: stalked leaves.
petiole: leaf-stalk.

pinnate: divided like a feather.

placenta: the part of the ovary or carpel which bears the ovules.

plumose: feather-like.

pollen: the fertilizing, dust-like powder in the anthers.

procumbent: lying down.

pubescent: hairy.

pustulate: covered with little warts.

raceme: unbranched inflorescence with individual flowers stalked.

radical: from the root.

ray-flower: marginal flower of the *Compositae.*

receptacle: floral axis.

reflexed: bent back.

regular: symmetrical.

reticulate: like a net.

rootstock: underground stem.

scabrid: rough.

segment: division of an organ.

self-pollination: pollen from the same flower.

serrate: with saw-like teeth.

serrulate: diminutive of serrate.

sessile: without a stalk.

spadix: spike with a fleshy axis (as in *Arum*).

spathe: envelope around the spadix.

spike: stiff unbranched inflorescence with the flowers not stalked.

stamen: the male organ of the flower.

stigma: tip of the style

stipule: appendage at base of leaf or leaf-stalk.

stolon: basal branch which roots.

style: narrow portion of pistil between ovary and stigma.

superior: placed above.

tendril: thread-like production.

terminal: at the top or end.

ternate: in threes.

tomentose: densely covered with short hairs.

truncate: cut off abruptly.

tuber: fleshy underground part of the stem.

tuberculate: with small outgrowths like warts.

umbel: inflorescence branched like the ribs of an umbrella.

unisexual: of one sex.

valve: portion into which a fruit or other organ separates or opens.

villous: with long shaggy hairs.

viscid: sticky.

vitta: oil tubes of fruits of *Umbelliferae.*

whorl: arranged in a circle around an axis.

Peplis portula L. (×⅔)

A creeping sometimes much-branched annual often forming wide patches in ditches and moist places, rooting at the lower nodes; stems glabrous, green or tinged with crimson; leaves opposite, shortly stalked, spoon-shaped, gradually narrowed to the base, rounded at the apex, glabrous, with 2–3 pairs of lateral spreading nerves; no stipules; flowers (A, ×6) very small in the axils of the leaves, scarcely stalked; calyx (B, ×8) widely bell-shaped, with 6 acutely triangular inner lobes and 6 awl-shaped outer lobes between; petals very minute and pink or often absent; stamens 6, inserted outside a thin nectar-secreting ring around the base of

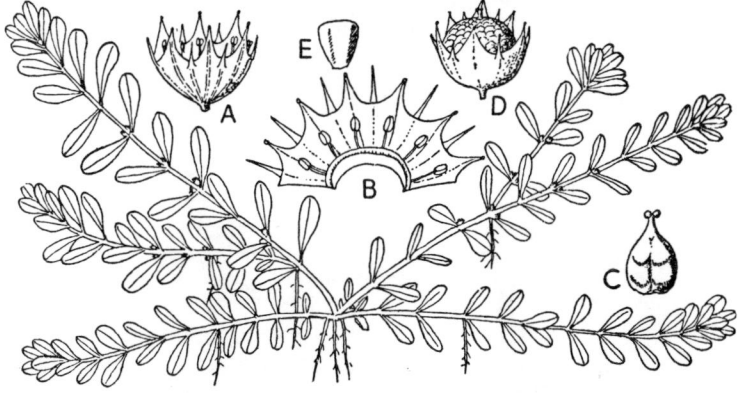

the ovary (C, ×8); style very short, with 2 rounded stigmas; fruit (D, ×4) a depressed-globose capsule girt by the calyx, with a very thin coat showing the shape of the numerous small broadly obovoid slightly angular seeds (E, ×8).

When growing partly in water, submerged flowers remain closed, and, since they contain air, are automatically self-pollinated. When mature in the open air the flowers are wide open and the six stamens are curved inwards, so that automatic self-pollination is also inevitable, especially when the flowers close and the anthers press against the stigma. Fruits are produced in great abundance.

The Water Purslane belongs to the family *Lythraceae*, which is very poorly represented in Britain, there being only three species, the one here shown, the handsome Purple Loosestrife shown on the next page, and the Hyssop, *Lythrum hyssopifolium* L., which has the upper leaves linear and alternate.

Lythrum salicaria L. ($\times\frac{1}{2}$)

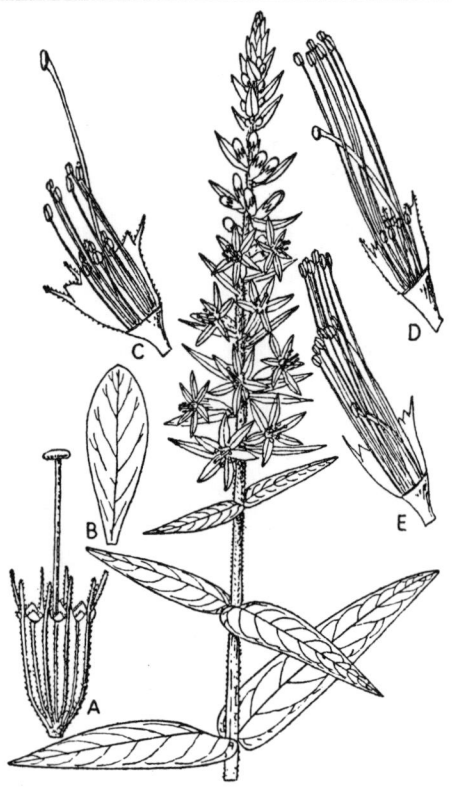

Perennial; stems erect, up to 3 ft. high, rather densely leafy, hairy; leaves opposite or 3 in a whorl, sessile and clasping the stem, lanceolate, rounded at the base, gradually acute at the apex, shortly hairy below, with prominently looped lateral nerves; flowers arranged in a dense terminal spike-like raceme leafy towards the base with smaller green leafy bracts throughout; calyx (A, ×3) tubular, usually with 6–8 short triangular lobes and as many subulate teeth between them; petals (B, ×2½) often 6, inserted at the top of the calyx-tube, reddish purple or pink with darker veins, oblanceolate; stamens about twice as many as the petals (see note on next page); ovary free within the calyx-tube, 2-locular; stigma head-like (capitate); fruit a capsule with several seeds; grows in wet ditches and by sides of ponds, rivers, etc., flowering during summer (family *Lythraceae*).

Darwin investigated very thoroughly the structure and function of the flowers of this species, which are of three forms (trimorphic), differing in the comparative length of the stamens and styles; this arrangement is of benefit to the species, because the reproductive organs, when of different length, behave to one another like different species of the same genus in regard to productiveness and character of the offspring. The diagrams in the sketch opposite show these different forms of flowers:

> C, *long-styled flowers*: style longer than the stamens; half of the latter are of medium length, half short.
> D, *medium-styled flowers*: style of medium length; half of the stamens longer than the style, half short.
> E, *short-styled flowers*: style short; half of the stamens long and the other half of medium length.

The anthers of the long stamens are green, and produce the largest pollen grains; the medium length and the short stamens are yellow, and have medium-sized and small pollen respectively. There are eighteen possible modes of pollination in this arrangement, but Darwin showed that only six lead to complete fertility, in which each length of style bearing the stigma receives pollen from anthers situated at a corresponding level. This is brought about by insects which visit the flower for the nectar secreted in the fleshy base of the calyx. The red inner surface of the calyx and the dark veins of the petals which point to the middle of the flower serves as guides to the nectar.

The most noteworthy visitor is a bee which sucks the nectar and gathers the pollen, and almost confines itself to this plant when it is in flower. When it thrusts into the calyx-tube it touches the shortest set of reproductive organs with the undersurface of its head, the next set with the ventral surface of its thorax, and the longest set with the ventral surface of its abdomen, the dimensions of the insect exactly suiting the flower.

Epilobium hirsutum L. ($\times \frac{2}{5}$)

Rank growing herb up to about 5 ft. high, softly hairy all over, by ditches and streams and in wet places; leaves opposite, lanceolate, acute, toothed, the teeth

pointed and curved upwards; lateral nerves several; upper leaves becoming alternate; flowers axillary in the upper leaves, those at the top forming a corymb with the unopened buds in the middle; buds (A, $\times 1\frac{1}{2}$) ellipsoid, with 4 slender tips; sepals (B, $\times 1\frac{1}{4}$) 4, slightly united at the base, narrowly oblong, hooded and shortly horned at the apex, not overlapping (valvate) in bud; petals (C, $\times 1\frac{1}{4}$) 4, mauve, deeply notched at the apex; stamens (D, $\times 2\frac{1}{2}$) 8, 4 long and 4 shorter; ovary inferior, elongated and rather like a flower-stalk, deeply 4-grooved, softly pubescent; style (E, $\times 2\frac{1}{2}$) stout, with 4 recurved stigmas far above the longer stamens; ovules numerous; fruit (F, $\times \frac{2}{5}$) long and slender, quadrangular, splitting into 4 slender recurved parts and releasing the numerous tiny seeds (G, $\times 1\frac{1}{2}$) which float away in the wind by means of a tuft of long fine white hairs at the top; flowers during summer (family *Onagraceae*.

Three types of flowers occur, but on separate plants; large flowers with long styles curved so that self-pollination is not possible; medium-sized flowers, with a straight style, and if cross-pollination fails the stigmas curve back so as to touch the anthers of the longest stamens; small flowers with the stigmas at the same level as the stamens, with inevitable self-pollination.

Perennial; stems up to about 2 ft. high, with a few withered leaves towards the base, rounded, minutely hairy; leaves alternate or opposite or both on the same stem, very shortly stalked, spreading horizontally, rather narrowly ovate, only half acute, rounded at the base, rather sharply and irregularly toothed (doubly dentate), 2–3 in. long, apparently smooth, but really very minutely hairy (pubescent); flowers stalked; sepals 4, at the top of the very long inferior ovary, shortly united

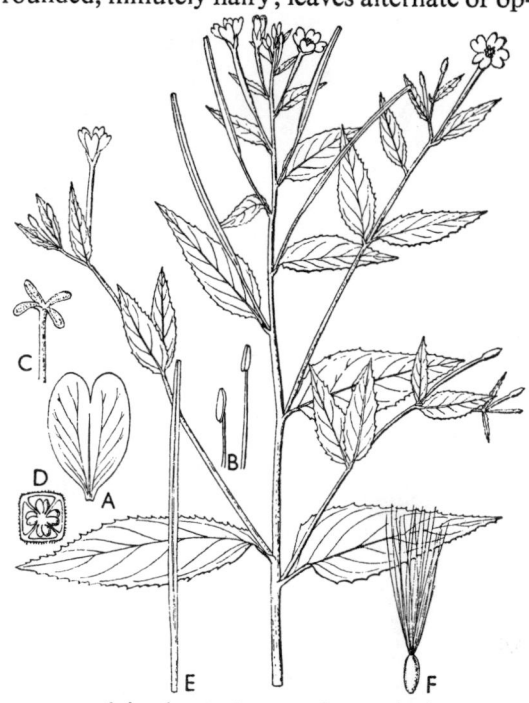

at the base, oblong, acute, ¼ in. long, 1-nerved; petals (A, ×1¼) 4 spirally arranged in bud, pink, and veiny, obovate, deeply 2-lobed; stamens (B, ×2) 8, alternately long and short; anthers attached at the back; style (C, ×2) white, with 4 thick spreading lobes; ovary (D, ×4) 4-locular and 4-angled, very shortly hairy; ovules numerous, in 2 rows in each compartment; fruit (E, ×⅓) a capsule 2–3½ in. long; seeds (F, ×3) tipped with a brush of long fine hairs (family *Onagraceae*).

On shady banks, old walls, and on roofs, and often a weed in shady garden borders; in autumn stolons covered with a rosette of scales; widely distributed into north and western Asia and as far south as the Himalayas. Insect visitors are very few, and self-pollination takes place through the anthers of the long stamens maturing at the same time as the stigmas. The anthers of the shorter stamens open later, and may effect cross-pollination.

Epilobium palustre L. ($\times\frac{1}{2}$)

Perennial with slender subterranean scaly stolons bearing in autumn scaly buds; stems slender, erect, rounded, more or less equally hairy all around, the hairs soft and short; leaves sessile, opposite, but the upper becoming alternate and bract-like, lanceolate to almost linear, apex obtuse, finely hairy, especially on the midrib below, lateral nerves few, ascending; flowers (A, $\times 1\frac{1}{2}$) few to solitary at the top of the stems, each subtended by a leafy bract, distinctly stalked, nodding in bud; ovary (inferior) resembling a thickened stalk and densely and softly pubescent; calyx shortly

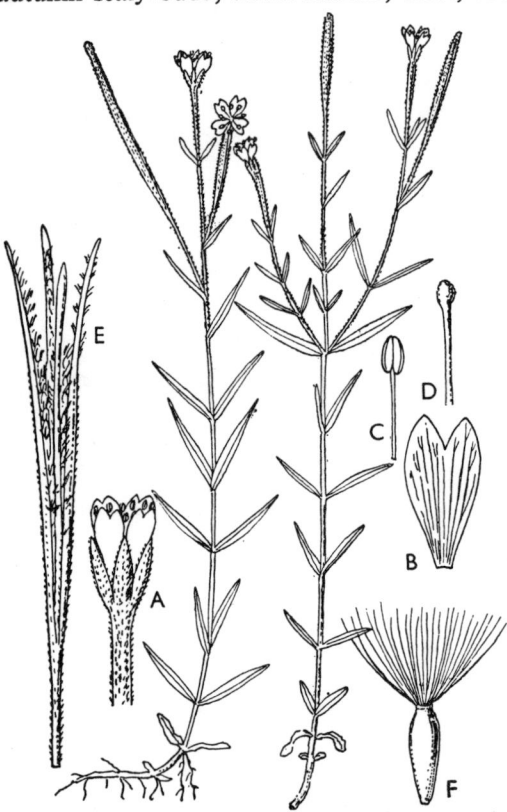

tubular 4-lobed, lobes oblong, hairy, margined with red; petals (B, $\times 2$) 4, rosy-lilac, $\frac{1}{4}$ in. long, deeply notched; stamens (C, $\times 2$) 8; anthers broadly ellipsoid; style (D, $\times 2$) with a club-shaped, entire stigma; capsule (E, $\times 2$) up to about 3 in. long, slender, splitting from the top downwards and releasing rows of superposed seeds (F, $\times 2\frac{1}{2}$), the latter smooth but crowned by a tuft of long silky hairs like the pappus of a thistle (family *Onagraceae*).

This is found in wet boggy places, and flowers in summer. It is widely distributed as far as Asiatic Russia and even into the arctic regions.

Epilobium parviflorum Schreb. (×⅔)

Perennial up to 1½ ft. high; stems reddish, covered with soft white hairs; leaves opposite or the upper alternate, those about the middle of the stem sessile, the others very shortly stalked, lanceolate, rounded at the base, very finely toothed, with about 5–6 pairs of lateral nerves, shortly and softly hairy on both surfaces; flowers axillary in the upper reduced leaves, distinctly stalked below the elongated slightly hairy ovary; buds with 4 short knobs at the tip; sepals (A, ×1½) 4, oblong-elliptic, reddish, nearly glabrous; petals (B, ×1½) 4, rosy, broadly obovate, deeply bilobed; stamens (C, ×4) 8; anthers broadly elliptic in outline; style (D, ×2) club-shaped

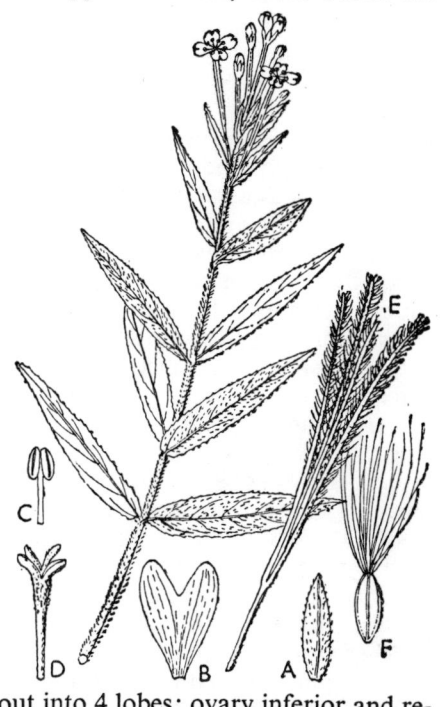

when young, but opening out into 4 lobes; ovary inferior and resembling a thickened stalk; fruit (E, ×2) elongated, splitting into 4 narrow recurved parts and releasing the numerous tiny seeds (F, ×8) with a tuft of silky hairs at the top; flowers in summer (family *Onagraceae*).

Grows in ditches and on river-banks, flowering in July and August; stolons are produced in the autumn, and have a bunch of nearly sessile leaves. It is widely distributed into north Africa and as far east as the Himalayas.

ROSE BAY

Chamaenerion angustifolium (L.) Scop. ($\times \frac{1}{2}$)

A very beautiful plant, but in some parts a troublesome weed; stems reddish, usually unbranched, up to about 4 ft. high, the base of the leaf forming a ridge for a short distance below the base, glabrous or minutely hairy; leaves numerous, alternate, ascending, narrowly lanceolate to almost linear, tapered at both ends, up to about 6 in. long, entire or with very minute and distant teeth, with very numerous nerves spreading at a right angle, looped and forming a wavy line well within the margin; flowers (A, $\times 1\frac{1}{2}$, petals removed) arranged in a very showy terminal raceme up to about a foot or more long; upper leaves gradually transformed into narrow bracts below each flower; flower-stalks up to $\frac{1}{2}$ in. long, hoary like the ovary and calyx above with very short mealy hairs; calyx above the ovary, with a little hump at the top in bud, lobes 4, spreading, lanceolate, $\frac{1}{2}$ in. long; petals (B, $\times 2$) 4, spreading, purplish red, obovate, narrowed into a slender claw, slightly notched at the top, veiny; stamens 8, nearly as long as the petals; anthers rather large, fixed to the back above the base; ovary inferior, 4-locular, long and narrow; style shorter than the stamens, with a deeply 4-lobed stigma; fruit (C, $\times 1$) about 2 in. long, splitting into 4 narrow divisions and releasing the very numerous tiny seeds (D, $\times 4$) clothed at one end with a tuft of long slender white hairs by means of which they float away in the wind (synonym *Epilobium angustifolium* L.) (family *Onagraceae*).

This is one of our most beautiful wild plants which flowers in summer and grows chiefly in light soil in moist open woods. The flowers open between 6 and 7 a.m., and the anthers are mature before the stigmas (protandrous), thus preventing self-pollination. The nectar is secreted by the fleshy green top of the ovary, and is protected from rain by the expanded bases of the filaments and hairs on the style just above them. In freshly-opened flowers the stamens serve as a landing place for insects, for the style is still short and the stigmas not receptive. The pollen grains, which are bound together by threads of viscin, are thus carried to another and older flower in which the stamens have curved downwards, and their place taken by the elongated style with its four spreading stigmas which in turn provide the only alighting place.

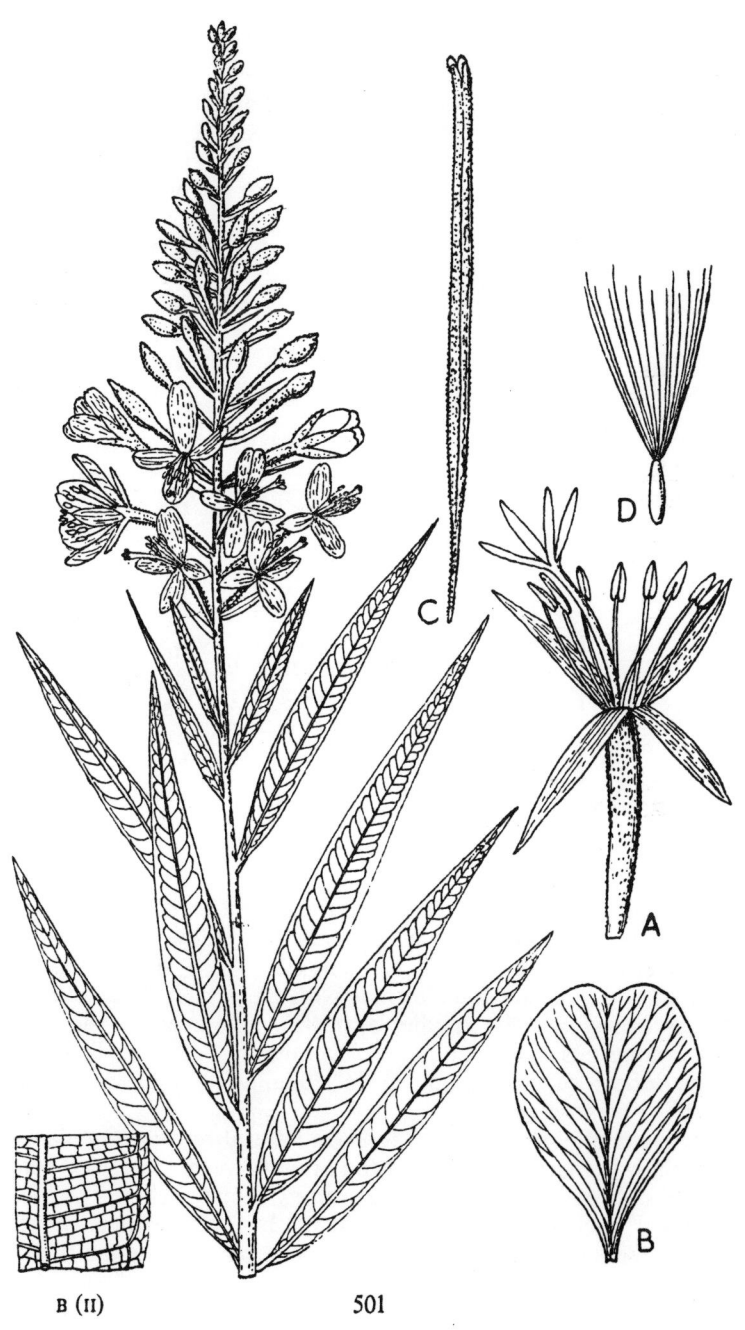

B (II)   501

Oenothera biennis L. ($\times\frac{1}{3}$)

Biennial herb up to 3 ft. high; stems full of pith, obtusely angular, green and often tinged with crimson, often with scattered bulbous-based hairs and numerous shorter gland-tipped hairs (F, ×4); leaves alternate, sessile, lanceolate, slightly toothed, about 4 in. long and $1\frac{1}{2}$ in. broad, midrib tinged with crimson, with about 6 pairs of lateral nerves, glabrous or nearly so below, minutely hairy on the midrib above; flowers (B, × $\frac{2}{3}$) opening in the evening, axillary, solitary, the lowermost well into fruit before the upper ones open; calyx in

bud (A, × $\frac{2}{3}$) with 4 free beaks at the apex (i.e. composed of 4 sepals), at length reflexed; petals 4, bright yellow, free, broadly obovate, about 1 in. broad; stamens (C, ×1) 8, inserted at the base of and opposite and alternate with the petals; anthers versatile, attached near the middle; ovary (D, ×1) inferior, 4-locular, with numerous ovules on axile placentas (E, × $2\frac{1}{2}$); style with 4 large lobes; capsule about $1\frac{1}{2}$ in. long, with numerous seeds (family *Onagraceae*).

A native of North America and now naturalized in many places, especially in maritime districts, and often in waste places and near gardens. The flowers open in the evening shortly before 7 o'clock (summertime); nectar is secreted at the base of the long slender calyx-tube and is protected by fine woolly hairs inside the tube.

Circaea lutetiana L. ($\times \frac{2}{3}$)

Perennial herb with a slender creeping rootstock; stems annual, up to about 2 ft. high, clothed with very short whitish hairs; leaves opposite, stalked ovate, rounded or slightly heart-shaped (cordate) at the base, rather broadly pointed at the apex, the few pairs of lateral nerves forming a distinct loop well within the margin, shortly toothed on the margin and very thin, slightly hairy below to glabrous, the stalk and midrib sometimes suffused with crimson; flowers (A, $\times 2$) in slender terminal and axillary racemes, sometimes these 3 together at the top, each flower becoming pendulous on opening; stalks slender; sepals 2, crimson, soon reflexed, inserted at the top of a short stalk on top of the inferior ovary; petals (B, $\times 4$) 2, white or pink, deeply

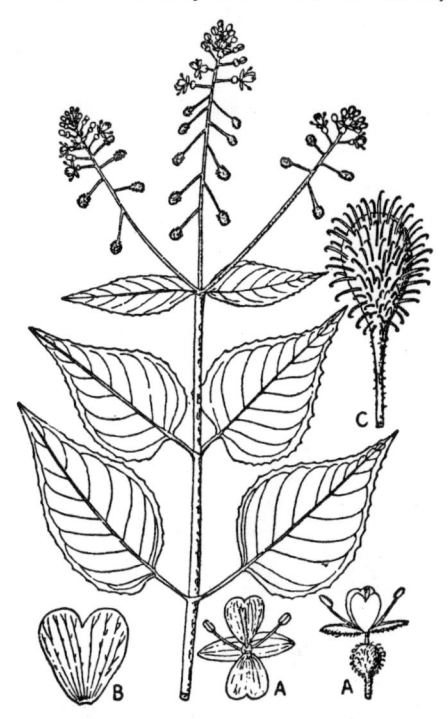

notched; stamens 2, opposite the sepals; ovary inferior, covered with hooked hairs; style with a 2-lobed stigma, girt at the base by a ring of nectar; fruits (C, $\times 4$) with deflexed stalks, club-shaped, covered with slender hooked bristles, containing 2 seeds; flowers during the summer and grows in woods and shady places, often in great abundance, but rare in Scotland, where, however, there is another species, *C. alpina* L., a much smaller plant and the fruit with usually only one seed; cross-pollination is brought about by hover flies which cling to the stamens and stigmas (family *Onagraceae*).

The hooked, slender bristles on the fruits account for the wide distribution of this plant, as they cling to the fur of animals.

MARSH LUDWIGIA
Ludwigia palustris (L.) Ell. (× ½)

Small annual herb the lower part of the glabrous stems creeping in mud or floating in water, rooting at the nodes; leaves opposite, petiolate, petiole winged, blade ovate, entire, the largest about 1 in. long and ¾ in. broad, with about 4 pairs of lateral nerves, glabrous; flowers solitary, axillary, nearly sessile, very small; calyx green, lobes 4, ovate; petals absent; stamens 4, opposite the

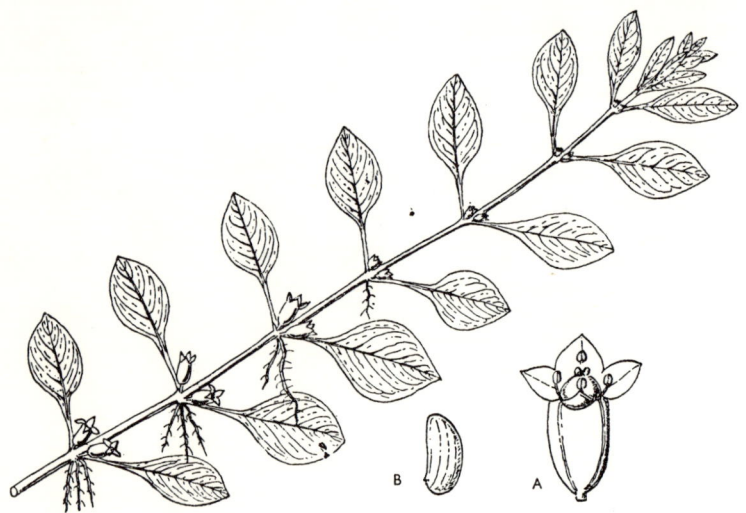

calyx-lobes, very short; anthers didymous; ovary inferior (adnate to the calyx-tube), 4-locular, with numerous ovules on axile placentas; fruit a capsule with 4 green spongy angles and crowned by the persistent stamens and short capitate style; seeds unilaterally ellipsoid, slightly lined, straw-coloured (family *Onagraceae*). – Synonym *Isnardia pallustris* L.

In the Channel Islands but formerly found in one or two southern counties of England.

Aquatic perennial with a creeping rootstock rooting at the bottom of the water; stems usually wholly immersed in the water except the flowering spikes, simple or branched; leaves whorled, usually in fours, distributed throughout the stem, pinnately divided to the midrib into fine thread-like segments; flowers unisexual and monoecious, the males (A, ×4) crowded and forming a continuous spike in the upper part, the females (D, ×6) spaced at intervals in whorls of four, each subtended by a small ovate toothed bract; male flowers with 4 conspicuous crimson sepals covering the six stamens; petals (B, ×8) very small and triangular, toothed; anthers (C, ×6) large, on short filaments attached at the base; no rudimentary ovary; female flowers (D, ×6) with the 4-grooved calyx adnate to the 4-locular ovary (E, ×6) and without lobes, with microscopic triangular petals between; stigmas 4, short and broad, with a broad brush-like top; fruit a globose or oblong capsule, each lobe separating into 1-seeded parts (family *Halorrhagaceae*).

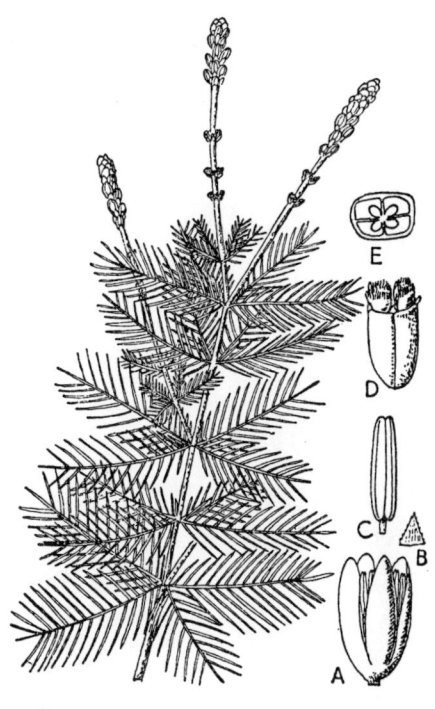

This plant grows in water in ditches and ponds and flowers most of the summer. The flowers are wind-pollinated, the anthers being large and containing abundant easily dispersed pollen, which is blown on to the stigmas, already well developed and receptive before the anthers open. The second British species, *M. verticillatum* L., is less common, and its flowers do not appear above the water, except when very shallow, but the bracts or floral leaves are then longer than the flowers.

MARESTAIL
Hippuris vulgaris L. ($\times\frac{1}{2}$)

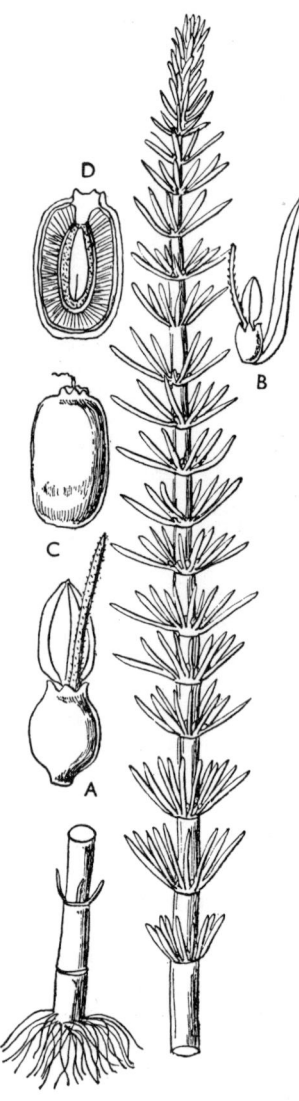

Aquatic perennial herb with a creeping rootstock very like an *Equisetum* (Horsetail); stem unbranched, the upper part rising above the water for about 1 ft. and bearing the flowers; leaves in whorls of 8–12, linear, entire, about $\frac{1}{2}$–$\frac{3}{4}$ in. long, glabrous; flowers (A, $\times 10$; B, $\times 6$) very small, sessile in the axils of the leaves; calyx very reduced at the top of the inferior ovary; stamen 1, at first sessile, at length on a filament; anther reddish, 2-locular; ovary 1-locular, with 1 pendulous ovule; style unbranched, hairy; fruit (C, D, $\times 10$) a very small ellipsoid nut with 1 seed, the latter with endosperm and a large straight embryo (family *Halorrhagaceae*).

In ponds and ditches throughout Britain, widely distributed in the north temperate zone; flowers from early June until late summer. This is one of the most highly evolved plants in the British flora, with whorls of small leaves, and extremely minute axillary flowers, having no petals, only 1 stamen, and a 1-locular inferior ovary with a single ovule; reduction could hardly go any farther.

These tiny flowers are wind-pollinated. They go through two distinct stages, firstly the female stage in which the style is prominent and the anther is sessile and still unopened, and secondly the male stage, with the style withered and the anther elevated on a slender filament and exposing its pollen to the wind.

Sempervivum tectorum L. ($\times \frac{1}{3}$)

This well known plant has some other rather delightful common names such as 'Jupiter's Beard', 'Jupiter's Eye', and 'Bullock's

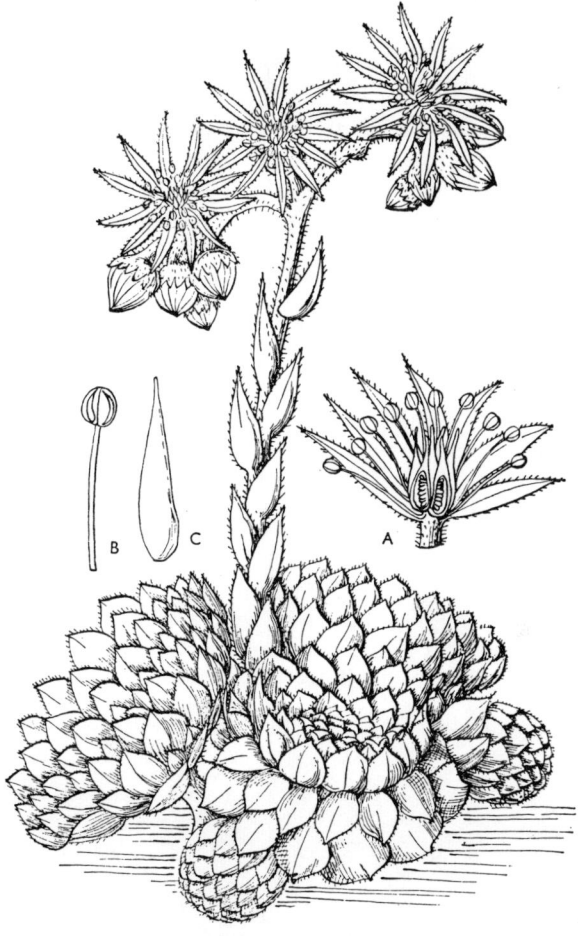

Beard', besides 'Welcome home husband, however drunk you be'. It is an introduced species from the continent of Europe and has been cultivated for a very long period, preferring the roofs of old farm-yard buildings and old walls (family *Crassulaceae*).

ENGLISH STONECROP
Sedum anglicum Huds. ($\times \frac{1}{2}$)

Small perennial herb up to about 3 in. high, quite glabrous; stems spreading from the base, covered with small ovoid fleshy leaves, these crowded on the short flowerless branches, scattered or opposite on the flowering branches; flowers (A, $\times 2$) few at the ends of the shoots; sepals (B, $\times 2$) ovate, fleshy, green; petals (C, $\times 2$) white or whitish-rose, more than twice as long as the sepals, broadly lanceolate, very acute; stamens 10, filaments slender, anthers small and rounded, nearly black; carpels (D, $\times 4$) 5, free, at first crimson-red, then pinkish; ovules few (family *Crassulaceae*).

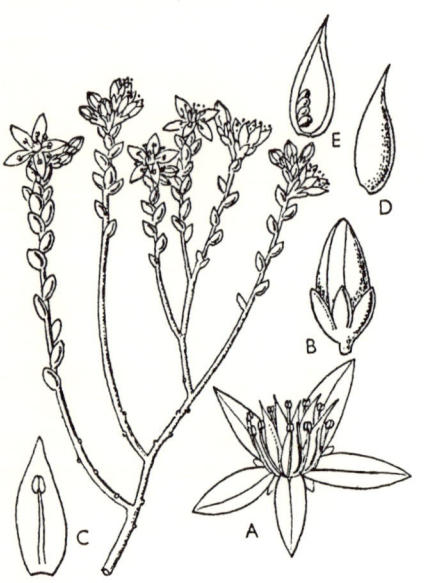

In rocky and stony places and on mountains, chiefly in maritime counties in southern and western England, Wales, west Scotland, and Eire; widely distributed in western Europe; flowers in early summer; nectar half-concealed and secreted at the base of the flower between the petals and stamens.

Grows in tufts on walls and rocks and in sandy places, forming
bright green and yellow patches when in flower; perennial and
procumbent, consisting of numerous short barren leafy stems and
erect leafy flowering branches, the whole very succulent and bitter
to the taste (sometimes called Wall-pepper); leaves alternate or
rarely a few opposite, sessile and very fleshy, ovoid or nearly
globose, those on the barren shoots especially arranged in
several rows and densely crowded, on the flowering shoots more
scattered; flowers (A, $\times 1$) crowded at the top of the shoots,
eventually spreading out in fruit into short cymes; sepals 5, short

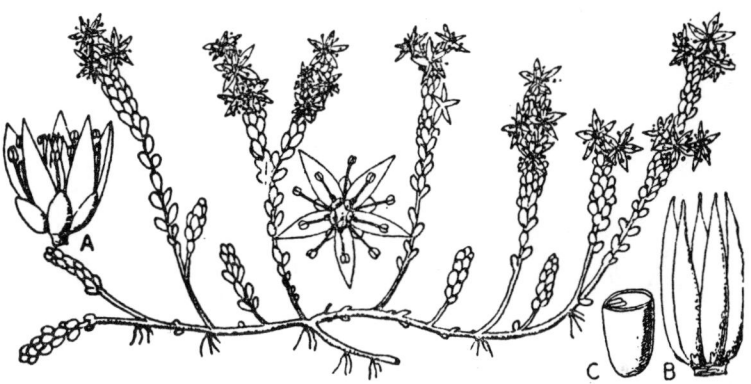

and fleshy like the leaves; petals free, bright yellow, ovate-lanceolate, acute; stamens 10, in 2 rows, the outer row opposite the
sepals, the inner row opposite the petals; carpels (B, $\times 4$) 5, free
from one another, each with a nectariferous notched scale outside
between their bases and the stamens; fruits splitting along the
inner side, and containing numerous very small seeds attached to
the inner angle (C, $\times 6$) (family *Crassulaceae*).

The five outer stamens are the first to mature and when they
have shed their pollen bend back towards the sepals; then the
other five anthers open, after which the very small terminal stigmas of the five carpels mature and are cross-pollinated by insects.

The succulent leaves are very characteristic of this family, to
which also the Penny-wort (fig. 424) belongs. Numerous species
occur in dry rocky regions, especially in the Karoo of southern
Africa, and in rocky districts of Europe and central Asia.

Perennial and almost woody at the base, the basal part of the stem curved; basal leaves on long stalks which gradually decrease in

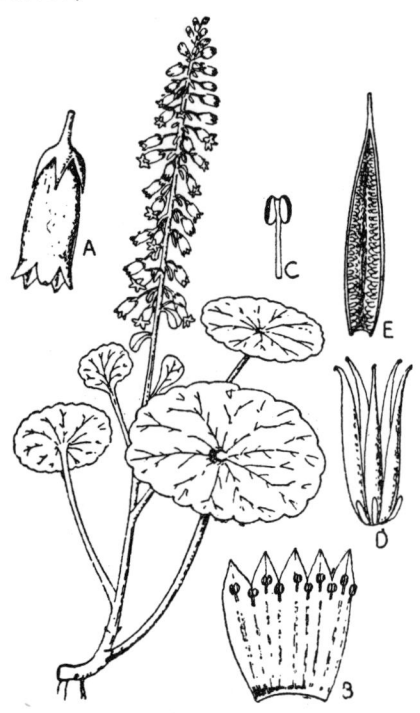

length upwards, the blade fleshy, orbicular, attached in the middle, crenate on the margin, the upper leaves gradually merging into bracts, the stalk becoming basal; flowers (A, ×2) usually solitary in the axils of the bracts, pendulous except when quite young; calyx divided into 5 narrow lobes; corolla (B, ×2) tubular, about $\frac{1}{3}$ in. long, with 5 short ovate-triangular acute lobes; stamens 10, adnate to the top of the corolla-tube, in 2 rows, the upper row opposite the corolla-lobes, the lower alternate with them; anther-lobes separate (C, ×8); carpels (D, ×3) 5, free from one another, each with a scale at the base, and gradually narrowed into the style; fruiting carpels (E, ×5) splitting up the inner side and releasing the very numerous minute brown seeds (family *Crassulaceae*). (Recorded in most botanical works as *Cotyledon umbilicus* L. or *C. umbilicus-veneris* L. and *Umbilicus pendulinus* DC.)

This grows often in great abundance in some districts, particularly near the coast from the south-west of England to south-west of Scotland, mostly on rocks, walls, and old buildings; in damp and shady hedge bottoms, sometimes 2–3 ft. high. It is an interesting plant from the evolutionary point of view, showing the rare combination of free carpels (a primitive feature) and the petals united into a tube (a comparatively advanced feature).

Saxifraga caespitosa L. ($\times\frac{1}{2}$)

Tufted herb, forming dense cushions; stems thickly covered with leaves, the latter deeply 3-lobed, rarely 5-lobed, rather fleshy, glabrous, up to $\frac{3}{4}$ in. long; flowering stem terminating each rosette of leaves, up to about 6 in. long, with very few scattered leaves towards the base, shortly hairy; flowers (A, $\times 1\frac{1}{2}$) few in a small cyme, the oldest in the middle; sepals 5, triangular, shortly hairy outside; petals (B, $\times 1\frac{1}{2}$) white, obovate, 3-nerved, glabrous; stamens shorter than the petals; ovary nearly completely inferior, 2-locular; styles 2, free; ovules numerous on a thick axile placenta (C, $\times 3$); capsule about $\frac{1}{4}$ superior (partly above the calyx), the free part glabrous, with divergent stigmas (family *Saxifragaceae*).

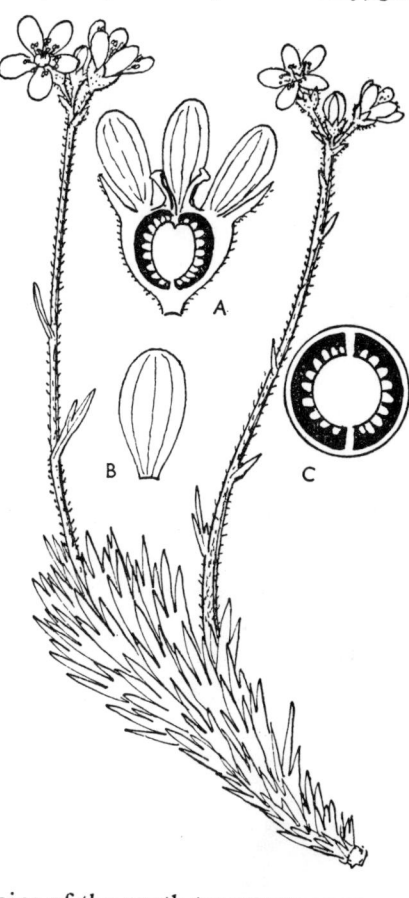

Found in Britain only in some Welsh and Scottish mountains flowering during summer; a very variable species widely distributed around the Arctic Circle and mountains of the north temperate zone.

Perennial herb with a short creeping rootstock; stems bearing at the base a number of barren shoots besides the flowering stem, the latter up to 6 in. high; leaves crowded, entire and linear or 3–5-lobed and rather moss-like, fringed with long hairs when young, soon glabrous or nearly so, the lobes acute; flowering stems slender, bearing very few entire leaves and a small number of flowers on slender glandular stalks each with a narrow bract at the base; sepals (A, ×4) 5, united towards the base, ovate-triangular, margined with short gland-tipped hairs (B, ×10); petals (C, ×2½) 5, free, white, $\frac{1}{3}$–$\frac{1}{2}$ in. long, 3-nerved; stamens (D, ×4) 10; ovary 2-locular, almost inferior, styles 2, separate; ovules numerous on 2 axile placentas (E, ×6); fruit a capsule opening at the top (family *Saxifragaceae*).

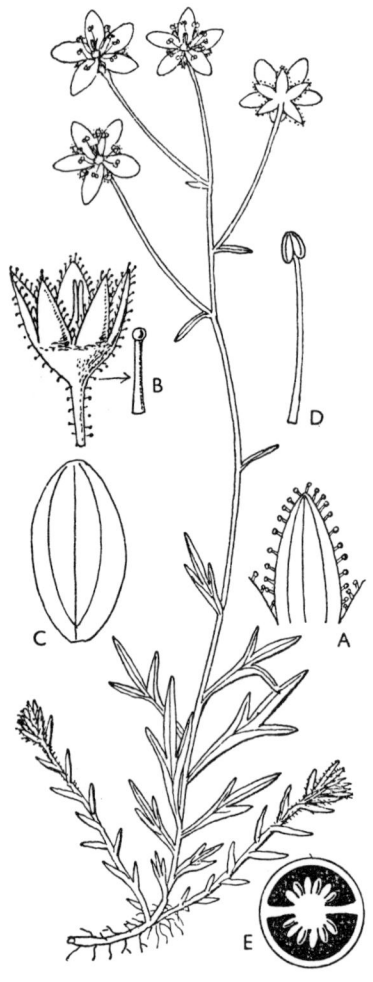

Grows on rocks and in grassy alpine places up to a high altitude on some mountains; confined to western Europe and Iceland.

This species is locally common in some hilly districts up to about 4000 ft. altitude. It is distributed from Somerset through Wales, Derby, and Lancashire as far north as Caithness.

The sterile shoots are more or less procumbent and usually bear leafy bulbils in the axils of the leaves.

Perennial herb with a stout upright rootstock crowned by a tuft
of spreading ovate-cuneate coarsely dentate leaves (A, ×1), these
rather thick and leath-
ery, tapered into a hairy
stalk, otherwise gla-
brous, up to 1 in. long
and $\frac{3}{4}$ in. broad; flowering stem simple, with a
single cymule at the top
or rarely a secondary
cymule just below,
sometimes one or two
bracts towards the top,
but mainly only sub-
tending the flowers, the
latter white; sepals 5,
united below and to
the ovary, oblong, thin-
ly hairy outside; petals
(B, ×5) 5, rounded-
obovate, shortly and
broadly clawed; sta-
mens 10; carpels (C,
×6) 2, tips recurved,
free nearly to the base;
ovules numerous on ad-
axial placentas (D, ×6);
fruiting carpels recurved
like a parrot's beak,
about $\frac{1}{3}$ in. long, becoming red (family
Saxifragaceae).

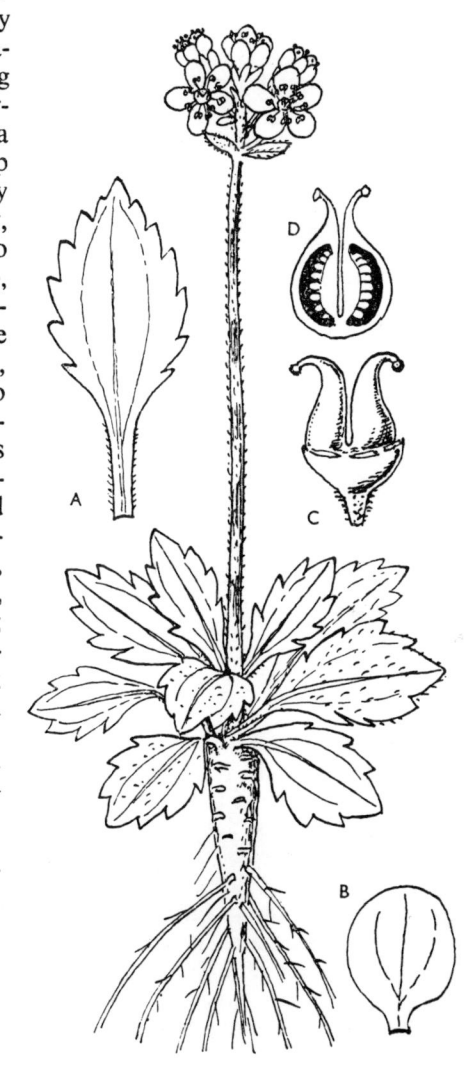

Confined in Britain
to the mountains of
Wales, northern Eng-
land, and Scotland, and
in Eire; widely distri-
buted in the mountains
of northern Europe
and Asia and in the
Arctic.

STAR SAXIFRAGE
Saxifraga stellaris L. ($\times\frac{1}{2}$)

Perennial herb growing on wet rocks and by water; rootstock small, crowned by one or more tufts of spoon-shaped oblanceolate leaves, these with a few teeth and sprinkled with hairs on the upper surface; flowering stems up to 5 in. high, bearing a few leaves near the base; flowers rather few, the first opened soon developing into fruit, each stalk with a leafy bract at the base; sepals (A, $\times 3\frac{1}{2}$) 5, soon becoming reflexed, oblong-lanceolate; petals (B, $\times 5$) spreading and star-like, white, with 2 yellow spots at the base of

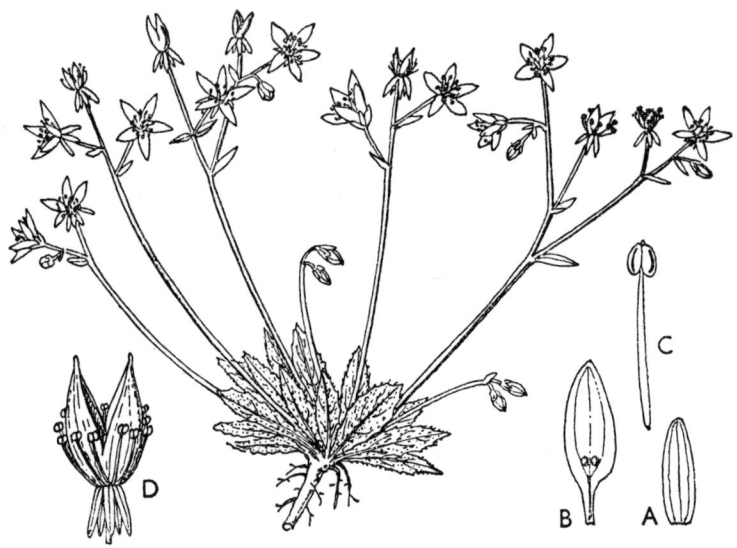

the lamina; stamens (C, $\times 6$) 10, anthers white to pale violet and purple; ovary 2-locular, with 2 divergent styles; ovules numerous on 2 axile placentas; fruit (D, $\times 2$) a capsule opening at the top (family *Saxifragaceae*).

Found only in Wales, northern counties of England, the Scottish Highlands, and in Eire, but widely distributed elsewhere in the northern hemisphere, in high latitudes; a var. *comosa* is propagated by rosettes of leaves which fall off and take root.

The flowers are star-like with half-concealed nectar, the terminal flower sometimes being female; normal flowers have white, clawed petals with 2 yellow spots at the base of the upper half; the pollen is vermilion.

Small perennial herb with small rootstock and a tuft of slender roots; basal leaves with long slender stalks, palmately 5–3-lobed, up to ½ in. broad, lobes ovate to obovate, glabrous; flowering stems very slender, up to 5 in. long, bearing a few stalked to sessile 3-lobed to entire leaves towards the two or three flowers (A, ×2) at the top; pedicels slightly hairy; sepals 5, oblong; petals 5, obovate-oblong, longer than the sepals, white; stamens 10; carpels (B, ×3) 2, united to the top, with

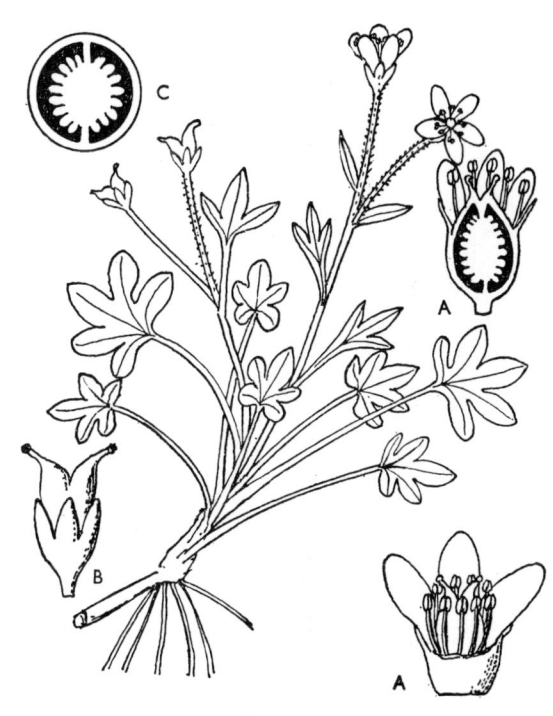

2 short divergent styles and axile placenta (C, ×5); fruit with two recurved beaks, well exserted from the calyx (family *Saxifragaceae*).

Found in Britain only on certain Scottish mountains; a high alpine species and circumpolar in distribution.

The character of whether an ovary is superior or inferior in relation to the calyx is in some families or genera not of much importance, though either the one or the other is constant in many, for example in *Rubiaceae*, always inferior.

In *Saxifraga*, however, the ovary varies from quite superior to completely inferior.

Perennial herb up to about 6 in. high, with a small rootstock bearing fine fibrous roots; lower leaves long-petiolate, palmately 5–3-lobed $\frac{1}{2}$–$\frac{3}{4}$ in. broad, lobes ovate to obovate, glabrous; stem bearing gradually smaller leaves up to the one to three nodding flowers (B, $\times4$) on rather slender pedicels, the latter slightly pubescent; upper smaller leaves often with little bulbils in their axils (A, $\times4$); sepals 5, oblong-elliptic, slightly hairy outside; petals (C, $\times1\frac{1}{2}$) 5, narrowly obovate, 3-nerved, white; stamens 10; carpels (D, $\times1\frac{1}{2}$) 2, united to the top but with 2 free

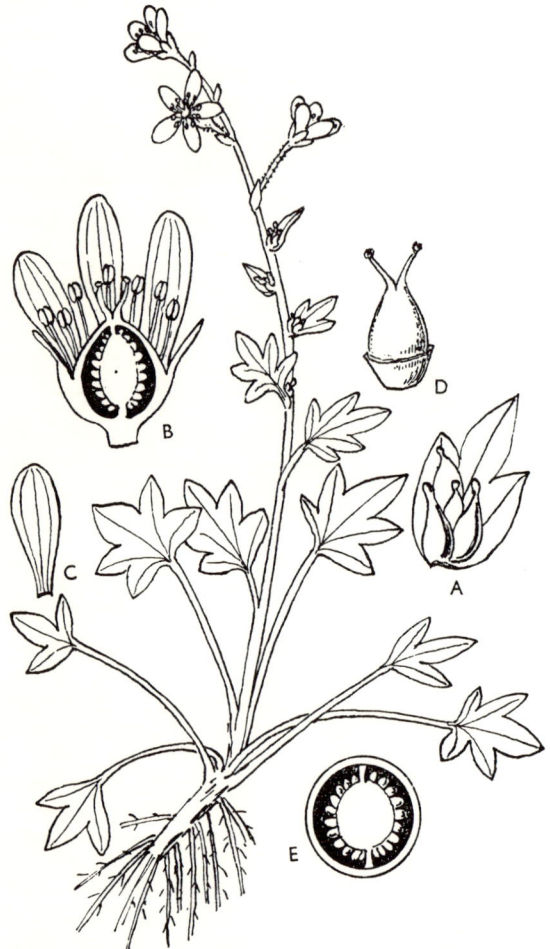

styles and half united with the calyx-tube; ovules numerous on axile placentas (family *Saxifragaceae*).

In Britain found only at the top of one or two Scottish mountains, but distributed in the mountains of Europe and Asia and all around the Arctic Circle.

Perennial herb with a slender erect or ascending rootstock with slender spreading leafy stolons; leaves narrowly oblanceolate to almost linear, entire, the lowermost narrowed into a short petiole, the uppermost sessile and clothing the stem up to the one or two flowers at the top; stem with woolly crispate hairs towards the top; flowers (A, $\times1\frac{1}{2}$) yellow; sepals 5, free nearly to the base, about $\frac{1}{3}$ in. long, fringed with hairs; petals (B, $\times1\frac{1}{2}$) 5, oblong-oblanceolate, nearly $\frac{3}{4}$ in. long, lined with 3 main nerves reaching almost to the tip, with intermediate nerves falling short of the top; stamens 10; ovary (C, $\times5$)

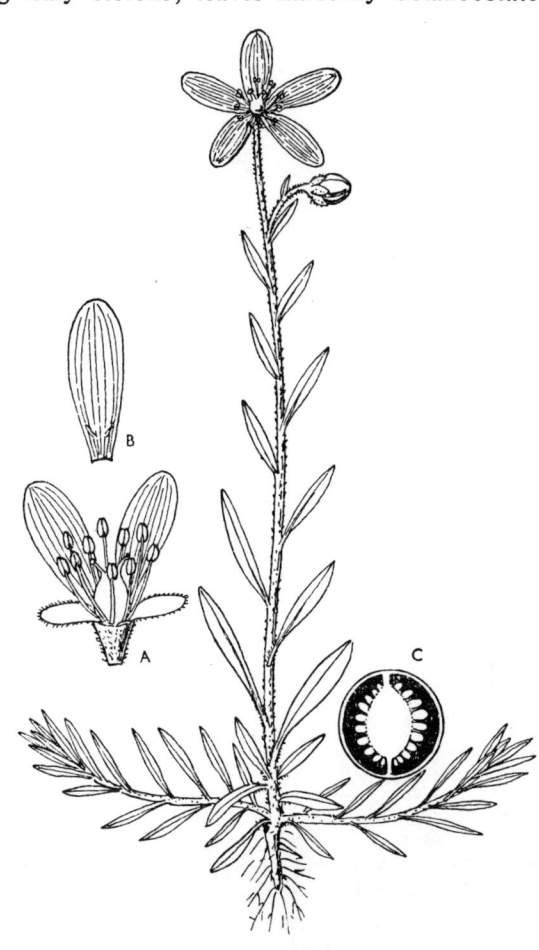

of 2 connate carpels with free divergent styles; ovules numerous on axile placentas; fruit about $\frac{1}{2}$ in. long, topped by two divergent beaks (family *Saxifragaceae*).

On wet moors in northern England, Scotland, and Eire, flowering during August; distribution circumpolar in the northern hemisphere.

Perennial herb with short rootstock, with one or more ascending flowering stems and several shorter leafy shoots; lower leaves becoming reflexed, remainder (A, $\times1\frac{1}{2}$) spreading or ascending, alternate, sessile, oblong-linear, acute, about $\frac{3}{4}$ in. long, thick and shining, entire or with a few sharp teeth on the margins; flowering stems up to about 6 in. high; flowers in a loose raceme-like cyme with the oldest flower at the top and soon turning into fruit; calyx-lobes (B, $\times3$) 5, spreading, triangular, 3-nerved, with a thin margin, yellowish; petals (C, $\times3$) 5, yellow with orange spots, oblong-oblanceolate, 3-nerved; stamens (D, $\times3$) 10; ovary (E, $\times3$) united for $\frac{1}{2}$ its length with the calyx-tube, 2-locular (F, $\times6$); capsule semi-inferior, with 2 suberect styles (family *Saxifragaceae*).

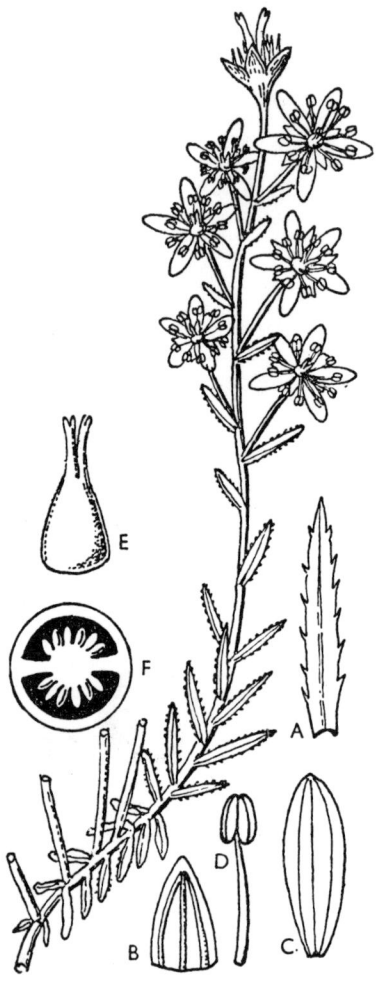

Found on wet rocks and gravelly places near rills and springs in the hills and mountains of northern Britain and parts of Eire; flowers in summer and autumn; circumpolar in distribution. The stamens and stigmas develop in succession and thus cross-pollination is secured, though self-pollination is not impossible. The nectar is exposed and is secreted by the outer wall of the ovary, pollination being brought about mainly by flies.

Saxifraga tridactylites L. ($\times\frac{1}{2}$)

Erect annual, covered all over with short gland-tipped hairs; leaves alternate or very rarely opposite here and there, broadly stalked, spoon-shaped in outline, deeply 3–5-lobed, lobes obovate to oblanceolate, rather blunt, entire; upper leaves becoming entire and gradually diminishing into bracts; pedicel opposite the leaf or terminal, very slender, glandular; calyx-tube (A, ×3) united high up with the ovary, lobes 5, erect, ovate; petals (B, ×4) 5, white, small, obovate, 3-nerved; stamens (C, ×5) 10; anthers rounded; ovary inferior, 2-locular; styles 2; ovules numerous on the axis; fruit (D, ×3) a capsule, with 2 short spreading beaks; seeds (E, ×15) minute, brown, obovoid, slightly tubercled (family *Saxifragaceae*).

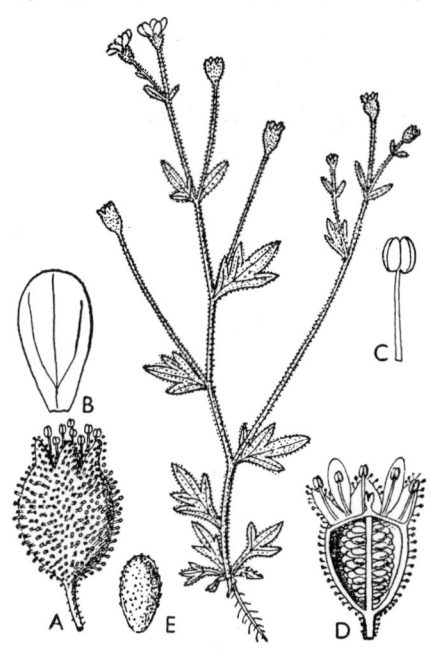

Distinguished among the British species in being an annual, growing on walls and rocks, and flowering during spring and early summer. It is widely distributed from the Arctic Circle to north Africa.

The flowers close in dull weather, but in the sunshine during the midday hours the nectary surrounding the style in the form of a yellow fleshy ring produces glistening drops. Besides the normally bisexual flowers there are often some of indeterminate sex, half male or half female. When the flowers open the stigmas are already mature, and the anthers then open one after another, first those of the outer whorl, then of the inner. Self-pollination is effective.

Perennial with small globose bulb-like structures (A, $\times 1\frac{1}{4}$) covered with whitish or brown scales; stems erect, up to about 1 ft.

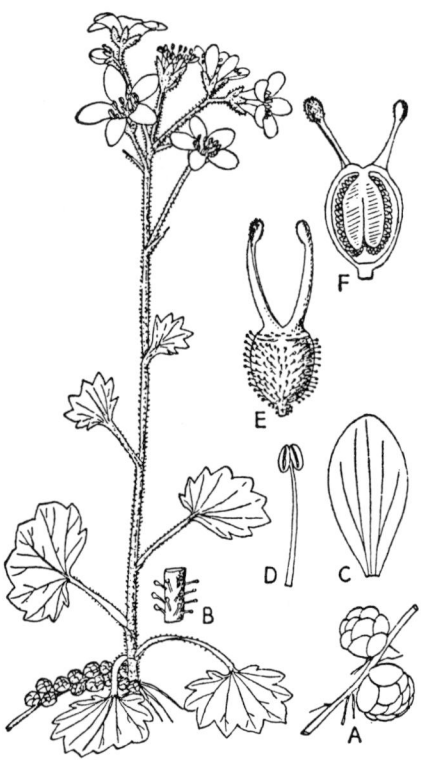

high, hairy, the hairs in the lower part long and without gland-tips, those higher up shorter and tipped by a gland (B, $\times 1\frac{1}{2}$); lower leaves kidney-shaped, coarsely toothed and sometimes almost lobed, very few on the stem and these becoming sessile, stalks and margins fringed with longish white hairs; flowers few in small terminal cymes (see below); bracts linear, like the deeply 5-lobed calyx (which is above the ovary) covered with gland-tipped hairs; tips of calyx-lobes sometimes tinged with dull crimson; petals (C, $\times 1\frac{1}{2}$) 5, free, white, lined with green in the lower half, about $\frac{1}{2}$ in. long; stamens (D, $\times 1\frac{1}{2}$) 10 (see below); ovary (E, $\times 2$) partly below the calyx (semi-inferior), 1-locular, with a large thick placenta hanging from the apex, split in two at the bottom and bearing very numerous ovules (F, $\times 2\frac{1}{2}$); seeds numerous in the capsule (family *Saxifragaceae*).

The stamens mature before the stigmas, and the central flower of the cluster opens first and differs markedly from the others in having the large fat papillous stigmas borne on long styles which become very conspicuous after the stamens have shed their pollen. Sometimes this central flower has the alternate stamens less polleniferous or almost sterile, whilst all the stamens of the lateral flowers are equally fertile.

Perennial creeping herb and very much branched, often forming low dense straggling carpets up to a foot or so in diam.; leaves on very short shoots up to about 1 in. high, densely crowded, oppo-site, sessile, obovate, clothed with bristly hairs on the margins and with a blunt thickened top with a pore in the middle (A, ×3); flowers (B, ×1¼) solitary but often so numerous as to almost con-ceal the foliage; calyx-tube united to the ovary and fruit for about half its length; lobes (C, ×2) 5, ovate, 3-nerved, fringed with hairs; petals (D, ×1½) 5, bluish-purple, obovate-elliptic, shortly clawed, 5-nerved from above the base; stamens (E, ×3) 10; ovary semi-

inferior, the two carpels (F, ×3) almost free down to the calyx (family *Saxifragaceae*).

A lovely dwarf alpine species and a great favourite in rock gardens; confined to the mountains of northern Britain and most common in Scotland, flowering in spring and early summer; widely distributed in the mountains of the northern hemisphere.

The flowers are pollinated by Lepidoptera which visit them for their concealed nectar. This is so deeply situated that short-tongued insects can reach it only with great difficulty. Failing insect visits, self-pollination frequently takes place and appears to be effective. The plant grows in such arctic places as Greenland and Spitzbergen, flowering from June until September.

Parnassia palustris L. (×⅗)

Perennial herb; leaves from the rootstock, long-stalked, rounded or ovate-rounded, cordate at the base, averaging 1–1½ in. long and broad, entire, 5–7-nerved from the base, sometimes marked with little brown streaks; flowers about 1 in. diam. (much smaller in the Alps), several to each plant, on long stalks which bear a large leaf-like bract about or below the middle; sepals (A, ×3) 5, ovate-elliptic, nerved lengthwise; petals (B, × 1½) 5, white, conspicuously nerved; stamens (C, ×3) 5, alternate with the petals; staminodes (D, ×3) 5, opposite the petals, yellow-green, deeply divided into thread-like parts each tipped with a glistening gland; ovary superior, 1-locular, with 4 or rarely 3 sessile stigmas; ovules numerous on as many placentas as stigmas (E, ×4) and spreading inwards from the walls (parietal placentation); fruit (F, ×1) a capsule opening by 4 (or 3) valves, surrounded by the persistent staminodes; seeds (G, ×12) reticulate (family *Saxifragaceae*).

Widely distributed through Europe, northern Asia, and North America, growing in bogs and flowering at the end of summer and in early autumn.

The flowers are fragrant with a honey smell, and are very interesting, not only for their structure, but for their pollination mechanism. Five of the original stamens are transformed into staminodes which are split into narrow gland-tipped segments. These glands attract insects. The 5 fertile stamens alternate with the petals and mature before the stigmas, but in a very remarkable way. The anthers face outwards and *ripen in succession*, each in turn lying on top of the ovary with the pollen side facing upwards (see fig. H, ×3). At the end of 4 or 5 days, when the anthers are all empty of their pollen, the apical stigmas become receptive and occupy the former position of the anthers.

Knuth (*Handbook of Flower Pollination*) says that the stalked glands of the staminodes attract insects by their glistening appearance, suggesting abundant nectar. The more intelligent insects, however, do not allow themselves to be deceived by this but the 'stupider ones' (flies and beetles) are repeatedly attracted and effect cross-pollination as they seek out the scanty nectar secreted at the base on the staminodes. Smaller flies hover round and round the flower licking the nectar but not touching the pollen or stigmas, and they render no service to the flower; but larger insects settle mostly in the middle of the flower to suck the nectar and thus transfer pollen to older flowers in which the anthers have all opened and the stigmas are exposed and receptive.

523

A delicate perennial herb in wet shady places and rill-sides, growing up to an altitude of more than 3,000 ft. in the Scottish and

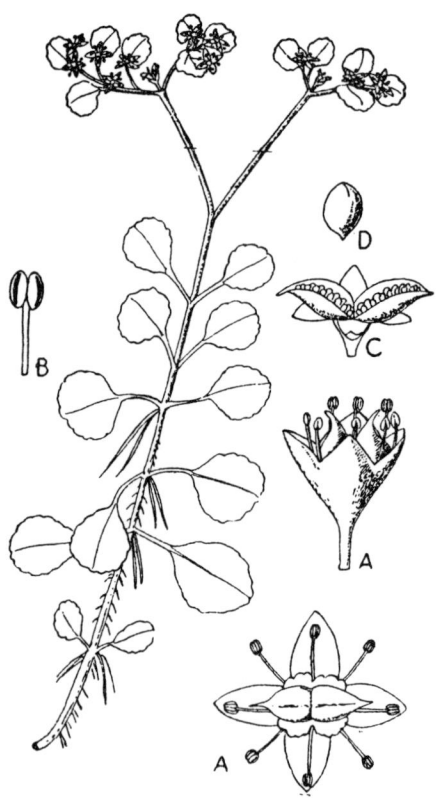

Welsh mountains; usually found in considerable patches; stems a few inches high, rooting at the lower nodes; leaves opposite, stalked, orbicular to obovate, undulate-crenate on the margin, without visible nerves and no stipules, sometimes with a few stiffish hairs on the upper surface and minutely speckled with brown, those around the flowers often streaked with golden yellow like the flowers; stem divided into two at the top and forming 2 small cymes of a few golden-yellow or greenish flowers (A, ×3), each flower subtended by a small leaf; middle flower sessile or nearly so, lateral flowers shortly stalked; calyx-tube joined to the lower half of the ovary, 4-lobed, lobes ovate; petals absent; stamens (B, ×8) 8, 4 alternate with and 4 opposite the sepals; anthers very small and rounded; between the stamens and ovary a broad crenate spreading disk; ovary half-inferior, consisting of two united pointed divergent carpels, 1-locular, with numerous ovules attached to the walls; fruit (C, ×6) a capsule splitting along the top, with numerous small reddish brown seeds (D, ×8) (family *Saxifragaceae*).

The large, prominent disk surrounding the base of the upper half of the ovary secretes nectar, which forms in drops and spreads out in a thin layer, and attracts numerous short-tongued insects.

Adoxa moschatellina L. ($\times\frac{1}{2}$)

A small weak pale-green perennial herb growing in moist shady places; rootstock short, covered with the remains of the old leaf-stalks and with half-underground runners; basal leaves on long stalks, divided into 3 separate parts, each part long-stalked and again divided into 3, with the terminal portion 3-parted to below the middle, each lobe rounded at the top, but with a little tip (mucronate); stem bearing a pair of opposite smaller stalked leaves and of similar pattern to the basal leaves, all glabrous; flowers (C,

vertical section, $\times 2\frac{1}{2}$) in a small globose stalked cluster at the top of the stem, usually 5 together, 1 terminal, the others facing outwards in 4 directions; calyx 2-3-lobed; corolla spreading, 4–6-lobed; no disk; stamens (A, $\times 8$) double the number of the corolla-lobes (due to splitting of the filaments) with 1-locular anthers; ovary (D, cross-section, $\times 6$) semi-inferior, 3–5-locular; style (B, $\times 4$) 3–5-lobed; fruits (E, $\times\frac{1}{2}$) pendulous on the bent stalk, rimmed by the persistent calyx (family *Adoxaceae*).

This interesting little plant was formerly included in the Honey-suckle family, *Caprifoliaceae*, but it is here as a separate family, more closely related to the *Saxifragaceae*. The arrangement of the flowers has been aptly compared with a town-hall clock, four of the flowers facing in different directions.

Herb growing in boggy acid soil often amongst Sphagnum moss; leaves in a rosette, on long stalks, spoon-shaped or orbicular, the

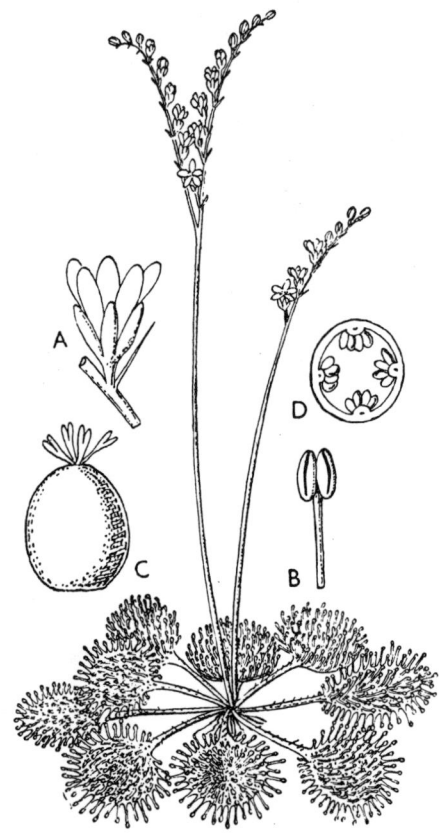

stalks clothed with a few fine hairs, the upper surface of the blade, and especially the margin, covered with viscid - tipped reddish processes which entrap small insects; flowering stems 1–3 from the rosette, leafless, slender, simple or divided into 2 branches, the flowers to one side of the axis, the lowest opening first; each flower (A, ×3) subtended by a thread-like bract; calyx deeply 5-lobed, glabrous; petals 5, free, white; stamens (B, ×6) 5, free anthers broadly ellipsoid, 2-locular; ovary (C, ×7) free from the calyx, 1-locular, with usually 4 divided styles, and with the numerous ovules borne on 4 marginal (parietal) placentas (D, ×7); fruit a capsule; seeds spindle-shaped, pointed at both ends (family *Droseraceae*).

This is Britain's best example of an insectivorous plant, the sticky hairs on the rounded leaves attracting and imprisoning small flies. The juices secreted in the hollow of the leaf are capable of digesting the flies, just as food in the stomach is digested by gastric juices. It is such plants as these that give rise to the belief in the lay mind that there are 'man-eating plants'.

Herb with radical leaves on slender stalks; leaf-blade narrowly oblanceolate, rounded at the top, gradually narrowed to the base,

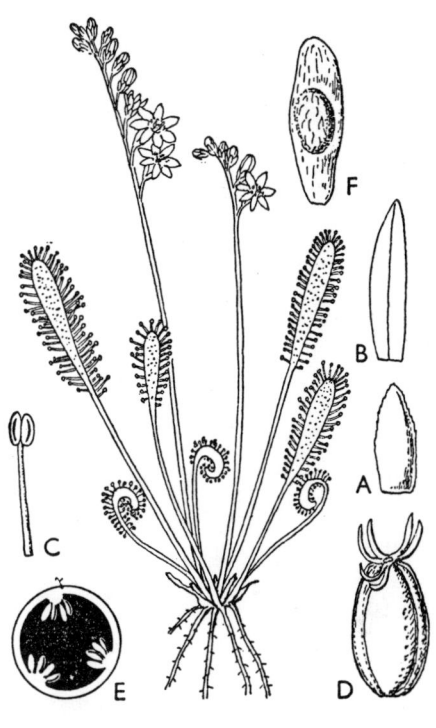

about 1 in. long, circinnate in bud, covered on the upper surface and margin with long gland-tipped sticky processes; flowers in one-sided (secund) racemes up to about 6 in. long (including the common stalk); pedicels about $\frac{1}{8}$ in. long; sepals (A, $\times6$) united at the base, oblong-elliptic, unequal-sized, slightly toothed on the margin; petals (B, $\times6$) white, free, narrowly oblong, 1-nerved; stamens (C, $\times6$) as many as the petals; ovary (D, $\times8$) ovoid, with 3 deeply divided styles divergent from the base, 1-locular, with numerous ovules on 3 parietal placentas (E, $\times9$); capsule longer than the sepals; seeds (F, $\times10$) winged at each end (family *Droseraceae*).

Found in bogs, flowering in summer and early autumn, mainly in Scotland and Eire.

Self-pollination is effective in this genus, each flower opening for only a short period about midday. The stigmas and anthers mature together before the flower opens. The pollen grains are golden-yellow and densely covered with spinous tubercles and are aggregated into 3–4-celled pollinia.

Herb growing in boggy acid soil often among Sphagnum moss; leaves erect or ascending in a basal cluster, on long stalks, spoon-

shaped or oblong, the stalks glabrous, the blades clothed, especially on the margin, with numerous viscid-tipped processes (A, ×5) which entrap small insects; flowering stems 2 or 3 from each rosette, scarcely twice as long as the leaves, flowering part curved and usually not branched; bracts linear, opposite to the short stalks; calyx deeply 5-lobed, glabrous; petals 5, white, oblong; stamens (B, ×10) 5, free; anthers oblong-ellipsoid, 2-locular; ovary (C, ×10) free from the calyx, 1-locular, with usually 3 divided styles, and the numerous ovules borne on 3 marginal (parietal) placentas (D, × 12); fruit a capsule (synonym *Drosera longifolia* L.) (family *Droseraceae*).

Very similar to the common Sundew (fig. 439), but the leaves with narrower blades 3 or 4 times as long as broad; the bracts are on the side of the axis opposite to the flower-stalk. Mainly in western Britain.

The anthers discharge their pollen as soon as the flower opens. They are at the same level as the stigmas which mature at the same time, so that automatic pollination takes place when the flower closes in the afternoon, if cross-pollination has not been effected.

Glabrous annual herb with zigzag stems and branches; leaves sessile, the lower clasping the stem at the base, elliptic, upwards gradually becoming perfoliate (see drawing) and more or less rounded, with a distinct tip, up to 2½ in. long, and 2 in. broad, with numerous fine nerves radiating from the base; flowers (B, ×4) small, in umbels, the primary umbels without bracts, the small umbels (A, ×⅔) surrounded by 4–6 large broad yellowish leafy bracts with sharp tips; petals yellow incurved; stamens 5; ovary inferior, of 2 carpels flat and rounded at the top, with 2 short stigmas on the inner side be-

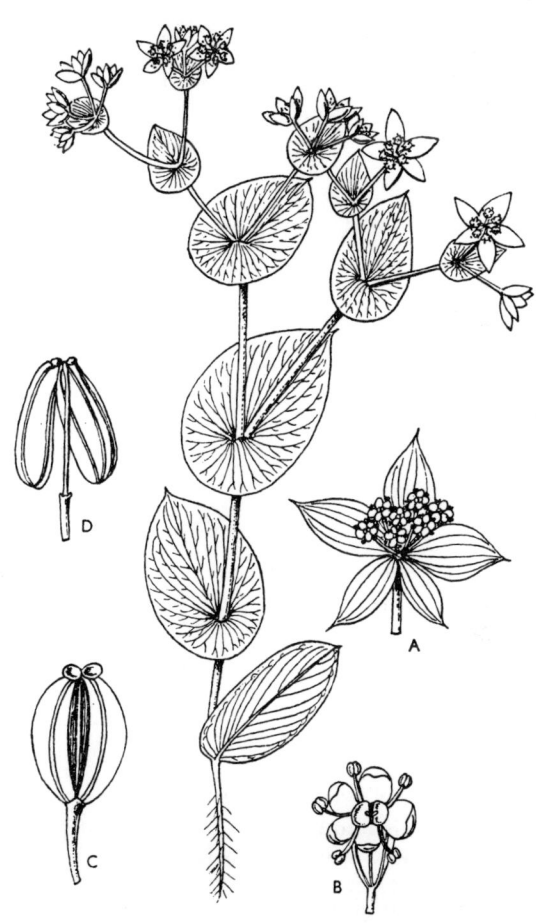

tween them; fruits (C, ×3) separating and hanging for a time from the slender axis (D, ×3), slightly 3-ribbed but with no vittae (family *Umbelliferae*).

In cornfields and waste places especially in chalky soils as far north as the south of Scotland; easily mistaken for a species of *Euphorbia*, but floral structure very different.

Crithmum maritimum L. ($\times\frac{1}{2}$)

Perennial herb with underground rootstock; stems fleshy, ribbed, bent at the nodes; leaves alternate, ternately compound, with thick narrow fleshy segments, glabrous, narrowed at the base into a broad ribbed sheath completely encircling the stem and with ·thin margins; flowers (B, $\times4$) greenish yellow to nearly white, in terminal compound umbels; primary and secondary umbels with

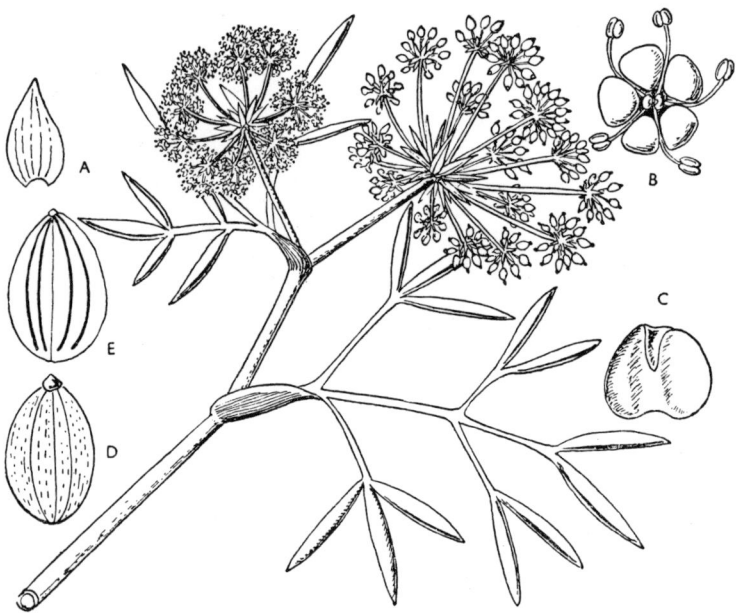

an involucre of several ovate-lanceolate bracts (A, $\times4$); petals (C, $\times7$) 5, rounded and with sharp inflexed tips; stamens 5, exserted; ovary inferior; stigmas sessile; fruit composed of 2 carpels flat on the inside (E, $\times3$) and with 3–4 resin canals, convex on the back (D, $\times3$) and with a narrow keel (family *Umbelliferae*).

On cliffs and rocks by the sea or more rarely on shingly or sandy beaches of our south and western coasts, flowering in late summer and in autumn; distributed on the coasts of Europe generally, and in north Africa and the Canary Islands.

Petroselinum segetum (L.) Koch (×⅓)

Annual or biennial herb producing at first a rosette of pinnate leaves spreading in a circle; leaflets opposite, sessile, ovate to ovate-lanceo-late, lobulate on one side near the base, rather coarsely doubly serrate, up to about 1 in. long, thin and finely veined, gla-brous; petiole widely sheath-ing at the base, nerved length-wise; stem-leaves similar to the basal ones but gradually re-duced to a few segments from a sheathing base; primary in-volucre com-posed of about 3 linear entire or slightly pinnate bracts; ultimate involucres of a few short subu-late bracts; rays unequal in length, on slen-

der peduncles; pedicels also unequal, up to ½ in. long; flowers (A, ×3) white; petals suborbicular, with an inflexed tip; fruit (B, ×3) ovoid, nearly ⅙ in. long, each half with 3 green elevated ridges (family *Umbelliferae*). – Synonym *Carum segetum* (L.) Hook. f.

Flowers in late summer by roadsides and in waste places and in cornfields in England as far north as Yorkshire; distributed from central Europe to western Asia.

Carum carvi L. ($\times\frac{1}{3}$)

A biennial herb with a slender carrot-like taproot several inches long; stem erect, up to 2 ft. high; radical leaves long-stalked, twice to thrice pinnate with linear to lanceolate 1-nerved lobes, glabrous; stem leaves similarly cut up into fine segments, but sessile with a broad sheathing base up to $1\frac{1}{2}$ in. long; umbels of about 8–10 main rays with an involucre of linear entire bracts at the base; smaller umbels without an involucre or rarely with one or two small bracts; flowers (A, $\times$3) white, the petals with sharply inflexed tips; fruits (B, $\times$3) oblong-elliptic, with 5 prominent ribs and single

vittas under the furrows; axis of fruit (C, $\times$3) splitting to the base when ripe, the carpels pendant (family *Umbelliferae*). – D, cross-section of fruit, $\times$4.

Widely distributed in temperate Europe and Asia, and naturalized in many parts of Britain, flowering in spring and early summer; the fruits are the Caraway 'seeds' used in cooking.

Rootstock tuberous and bulb-like, globose, about $\frac{3}{4}$ in. diam.; stem with a cluster of broad scales at the base, slender, glabrous; basal leaves soon disappearing, long-stalked, bi-pinnate, with narrow acute 1-nerved segments, glabrous; stem-leaves much smaller, with narrower segments, the blade sessile on the basal sheath, the latter $\frac{1}{2}$–$\frac{3}{4}$ in. long; all the involucres with a few narrow linear bracts; flowers (A, $\times 3$) white; petals equal, obovate, deeply bilobed, with an inflexed tip; stamens as long as the petals; styles fairly long; fruit (B, $\times 3$) nearly $\frac{1}{5}$ in. long, oblong, each half strongly 5-

ribbed, with a broad brown vitta between each rib (family *Umbelliferae*). – Synonym *Carum bulbocastanum* (L.) Koch.

Flowers in June and July, and confined to the south-eastern counties of England, especially in limestone districts; otherwise confined to western Europe. The bulb-like tubers are edible.

COMMON FALCARIA

Falcaria vulgaris Bernh. ($\times\frac{1}{3}$)

Annual to perennial herb, glabrous or minutely puberulous; stem full of pith, closely and finely ribbed; basal leaves long-petiolate,

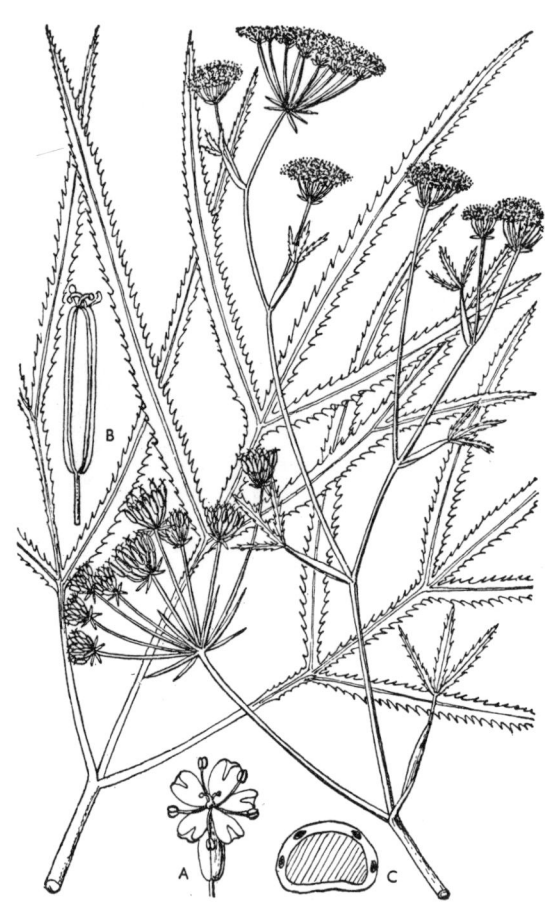

sheathing at the base of the stalk, bipinnate, the ends divided into 3 linear sharply toothed segments decurrent on the common petiole; midrib very broad; stem-leaves with large sheaths and the divided portion sessile at the apex of the sheath; umbels all with a few linear very acute bracts; rays about 10–15, with very slender peduncles; pedicels slender, longer than the bracts; flowers (A, $\times 3$) very small; petals white, with incurved apex; styles divergent, with rounded stigmas; fruit (B, $\times 2\frac{1}{2}$) narrowly oblong, nearly $\frac{1}{3}$ in. long, with reddish oilducts, the 2 carpels at length hanging from slender threads (family *Umbelliferae*). – Synonyms *Falcaria rivinii* Host. *F. sioides* (Wib.) Aschers. – C, cross-section of fruit, $\times 6$.

Introduced into some southern and eastern counties of England.

Annual or biennial herb with slender divided roots, up to about
$2\frac{1}{2}$ ft. high; stem closely ribbed, filled with pith; lower leaves

(A, $\times\frac{1}{3}$) long-
stalked, once
pinnate, leaflets
opposite, ses-
sile, ovate-
lanceolate in
outline, often
more or less tri-
lobed, lobes cre-
nate, very thin,
glabrous; upper
leaves becoming
small with very
narrow seg-
ments; umbels
of 3–5 rays with
very few small
white flowers
(B, $\times3$); pri-
mary and secon-
dary umbels
with only 2–3
bracts; petals
bilobed with in-
flexed tips; fruit
(C, $\times3$) com-
pressed, round-
ed, each half
with 5 equal fili-
form ridges, with
a short club-
shaped pendu-
lous vitta between each (family *Umbelliferae*).

On hedgebanks and by roadsides from Yorkshire southwards,
and widely spread through Europe to Asia Minor and Algeria.
Distinctive are the lower leaves (see drawing A), the tiny umbels
of white flowers, each umbel with a whorl of bracts, and especially
the striking fruits with their tear-drop like vittae 'hanging' from
the apex of the carpels.

Sium erectum Huds. ($\times\frac{1}{2}$)

Perennial; stems bent and ascending, up to 3 ft. high, leafy; lower leaves up to about 1 ft. or more, pinnate with about 10 pairs of sessile leaflets, these ovate to oblong-lanceolate, rounded at the base, very sharply and irregularly coarsely toothed and lobulate, glabrous; stem leaves smaller, but much in the same pattern, with broad sheathing base encircling the stem; umbels compound, terminal, and opposite the leaves (leaf-opposed); primary and secondary umbels with an involucre of several divided or toothed leafy

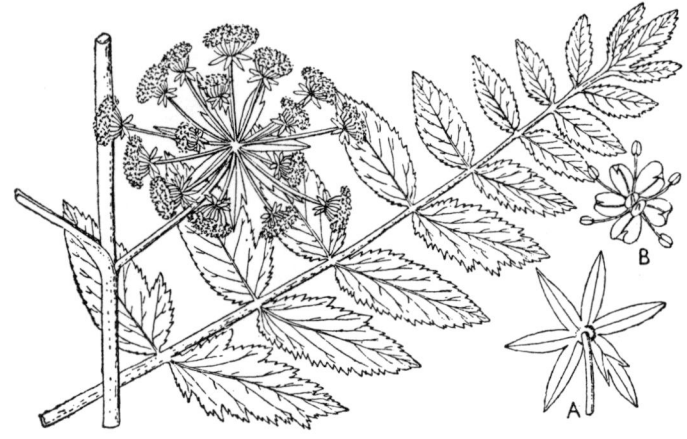

bracts (A, $\times 1$); flowers (B, $\times 2$) white, the secondary umbels about $\frac{3}{4}$ in. diam.; petals 5, obovate, with an oblique inflexed apex; stamens 5, alternate with the petals; ovary of 2 disk-like carpels, each with a short stigma; fruits on slender pedicels, more or less orbicular, subdidymous with the lateral ridges within the margin (synonym *Sium angustifolium* L.) (family *Umbelliferae*).

Grows in ditches, canals, ponds, etc., throughout Britain, but less commonly in Scotland and Eire, flowering in summer.

By some botanists this species is referred to a separate genus, *Berula* Koch, when it is called *Berula erecta* (Huds.) Coville. The fruits are very like those of Sium proper, but the lateral ridges are not marginal and the vittae are more deeply sunk. Some genera in this very natural family are of necessity separated by slight differences, just as they are in the very natural group *Compositae*.

Perennial herb with a slender carrot-like taproot; stem usually about 1 ft. high, hollow, glabrous; lower leaves on long stalks, ternately compound, each division with 3 broadly obovate segments coarsely toothed and more or less lobulate, several-nerved from the base; all the umbels with a few linear bracts; flowers (A, ×3) white or tinged with pink; petals equal-sized, each with a sharp inflexed point; stamens as long as the petals; styles very short; fruit (B, ×1¼) ellipsoid, nearly ½ in. long, each carpel with 5 prominent acute ribs and almost wing-like, with several vittas under each furrow; fruit axis

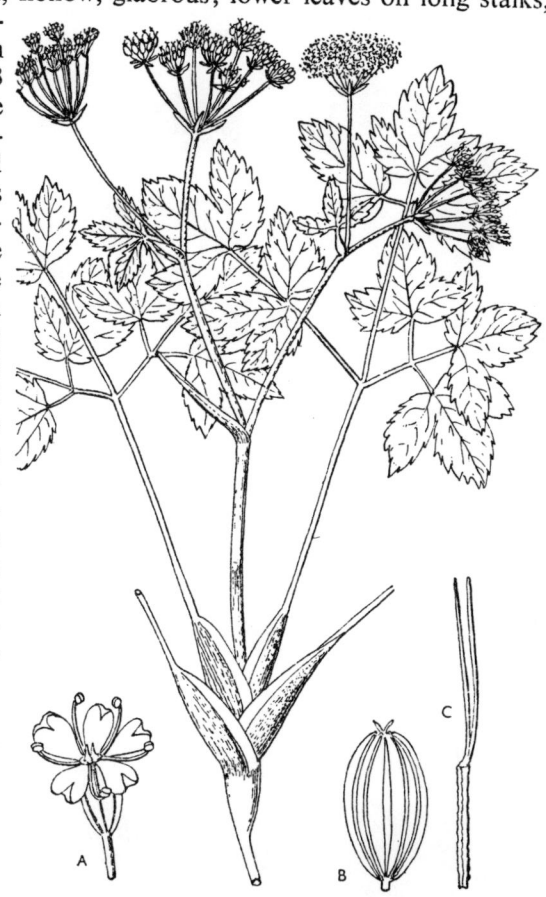

(C, ×4) splitting deeply into two arms (family *Umbelliferae*).

Grows all around the Arctic Circle and is common on the rocky coasts of Scotland and north-east England and of Northern Ireland. In the Hebrides it is gathered for use as a vegetable under the name of *Shunis*, its flavour being like that of celery.

Perennial dark green herb with a slender vertical taproot; stem up to 4 ft. high, closely ribbed; basal leaves on long finely granular stalks, twice or thrice ternate, the segments cuneate and deeply lobed, very minutely hairy only on the nerves and margin; upper stem-leaves becoming entire and narrow; primary umbels of 8–12 rays, with fairly large white flowers and several narrow bracts at the base; ultimate umbels with a few linear bracts and about a dozen flowers (A, ×3) on thread-like pedicels; petals with a hooked incurved apex; fruits (B, ×3) ovoid-globose, chestnut-brown, each half with 4

obscure vittae; styles persistent, recurved (family *Umbelliferae*). – Synonym *Danaa cornubiensis* Burmat – C, cross-section of fruit ×3.

Found only in some southern counties of England, flowering in late summer; also in western Europe and in the Mediterranean as far east as the Caucasus mountains.

Annual or biennial herb up to 5 ft. high; stems erect, branching, with an unpleasant odour when bruised, hollow and closely ribbed, glabrous; leaves bipinnate, leaflets (C, ×1) deeply pinnately lobed or coarsely serrate, glabrous; flowers (A, ×3) white; primary umbel with an involucre of reflexed bracts about ½ in. long; bracts of secondary umbels smaller and more or less all to one side; ovary ribbed; petals obovate, with inflexed acuminate tip; styles 2, clavate; fruit (B, ×5) ovoid, without vittae, but each half with 5 wavy ribs (family *Umbelliferae*).

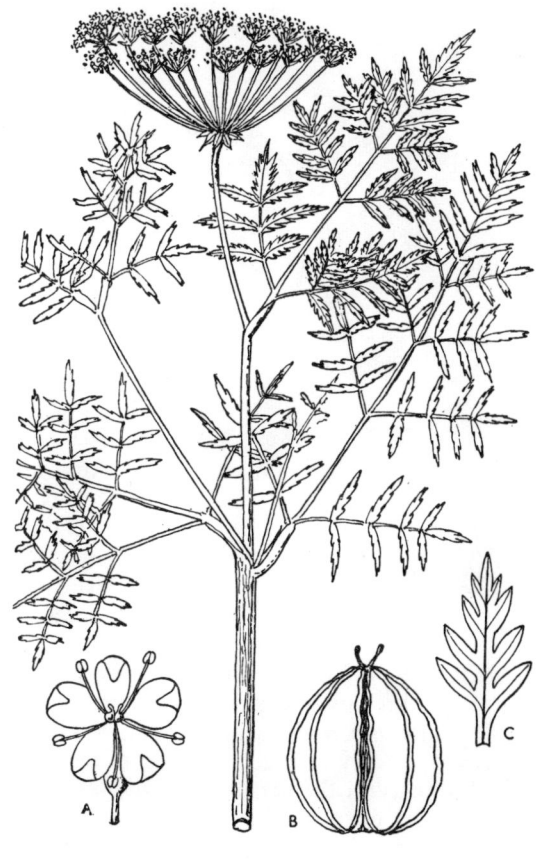

A widely distributed species in damp places along hedges and roadsides, open woods, and near water, flowering during summer.

Hemlock is a very poisonous plant to grazing animals; the seeds have been mistaken for anise, the leaves for parsely, and the roots for parsnips.

Oenanthe lachenalii, Gmel. (×⅓)

Perennial herb with nearly solid ribbed stems often tinged with purple; leaves twice pinnate, with narrow linear entire segments,

glabrous; stalks sheathing; flowers (A, ×½) in compound umbels on leaf-opposed peduncles, the primary umbel with a few narrow bracts, the secondary umbels with a definite involucre of narrow bracts; calyx teeth acute; petals white, tip inflexed; fruit (B, ×3) oblong, each carpel 3-ribbed and with 4 vittae (family *Umbelliferae*).

Grows in wet marshes, usually brackish, especially in maritime districts, flowering in summer and autumn; generally distributed as far north as Argyllshire; sometimes regarded as a variety or subspecies of *O. pimpinelloides*, but with very narrowly linear leaf-segments.

In the latest British *Flora* there are seven native species described out of the thirty-five comprising the genus, which is found in the north temperate regions of the Old World. The leaves of this species are nearly as much divided as those of *Silaum silaus* (fig. 463), but without the nervation of the leaflets of that species, and separated at once by the primary umbel having a few narrow bracts, and prominent calyx-teeth. The vittae of the fruits are very clearly marked.

Perennial herb; stems 2–3 ft. high, with whorls of slender roots at the lower nodes, often tinged with crimson, hollow, closely ribbed, with rather grass-like nodes; basal leaves (A, ×⅓) bipinnate, long-stalked, with narrow acute segments, glabrous; stem-leaves consisting mainly of a dilated hollow stalk and a few small lobes; flowers in head-like compound umbels, central main umbel usually 3-rayed, each ray with numerous very crowded flowers, surrounded by ovate bracts (B, ×1); outer flowers male, longer-stalked and quite 'irregular', i.e. 2 of the outer petals (C, ×2) much larger than the others; stamens with long filaments; remainder of flowers bisexual, 'regular' (D, ×2), with equal-sized petals; lateral umbels mostly 5-rayed with flowers which do not produce fruit; all

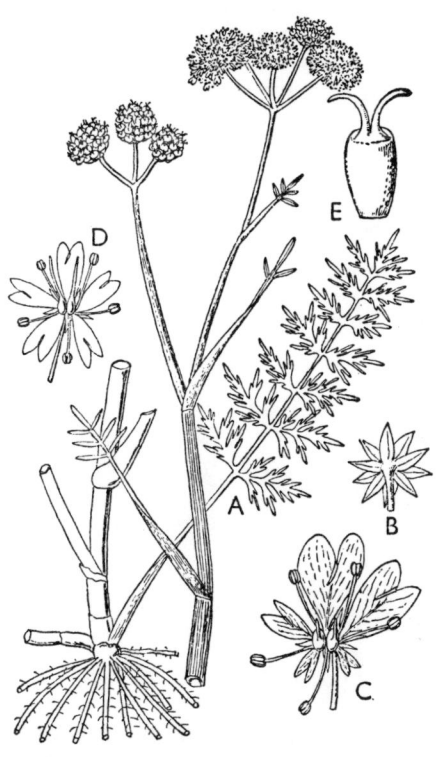

the petals white and deeply notched; styles (D, ×2) much longer in the middle flowers, and these developing into fruit, the latter (E, ×2½) rather corky, sessile and crowded, each with a pair of persistent long spine-like styles (family *Umbelliferae*).

Related to the Water Drop-wort (*Oenanthe crocata* L., fig. 455), but reputed to be less poisonous than that species; grows in wet meadows and marshes, but in Scotland only in the southern counties, flowering in summer and autumn; extends to western Asia.

Perennial up to about 5 ft. high; roots tuberous, like a bunch of small narrow carrots, and with numerous fine fibrous roots (A, $\times\frac{1}{4}$); stems thickened at the nodes, juice becoming yellow when exposed to the air; leaves bipinnate, the segments broadly cuneate and coarsely toothed or pinnately lobed, glabrous or nearly so; umbels numerous on long terminal peduncles; primary umbel usually without bracts, but sometimes with modified leaves,

smaller umbels with a few bracts, and these sometimes quite leafy (foliaceous); outer flowers in each umbel stalked and mostly infertile (male), the middle ones sessile or nearly so and fertile; petals white; ovary inferior, with 2 distinct styles; fruit (B, $\times 5$) narrow, oblong-cylindric, with a solitary vitta (resin channel) between each pair of ribs (family *Umbelliferae*).

This species is very poisonous in all its parts, and may be mistaken for celery and the rootstock for parsnips. It is liable to be collected amongst other herbs for rabbit food. The root is the most toxic, and drying does not destroy the poisonous property. In cases of poisoning the symptoms usually appear very quickly, and death may take place within an hour or two. It grows in marshes and ditches and along the banks of tidal rivers such as the Thames, flowering in summer.

Erect annual about 2 ft. high; stem ribbed, hollow, loosely covered with downwardly directed bristly hairs; leaves once pin-nate, the upper gradually smal-ler and becom-ing deeply tri-lobed; leaflets 2–3 pairs, ses-sile, broadly oblanceolate, coarsely toothed and pinnately lobulate, thinly hairy on both surfaces, leaf-sheath small; umbels small and with few rays, all with a few longish linear hairy bracts; flowers (A, ×3) pink; petals unequal, the outer larger and without the inflexed tip as in the others; fruit (B, ×⅓, C, ×2½) compressed, or-bicular, with a very thick bor-der, shortly

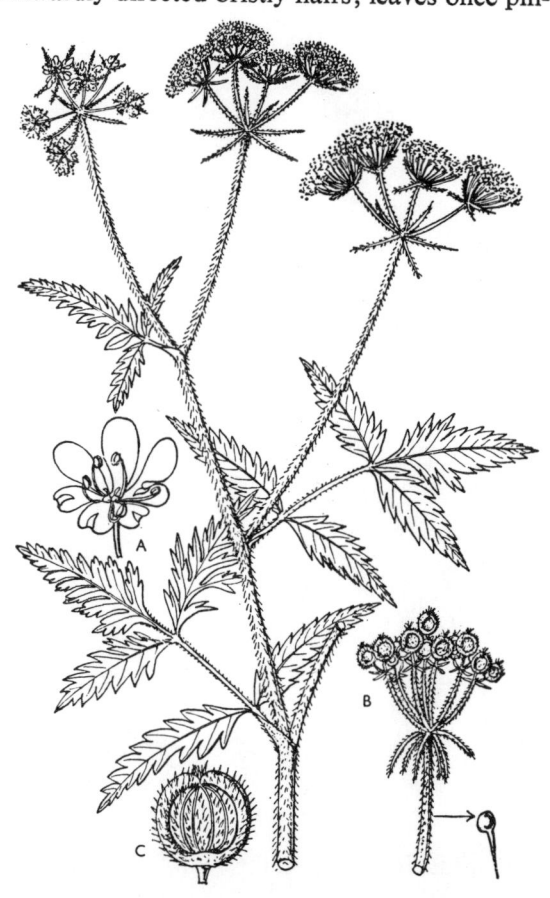

bristly all over, ¼ in. diam. (family *Umbelliferae*).

Flowers from July onwards and found only in some southern counties of England; doubtfully native; widely distributed from western Europe eastward to the Caucasus.

Recognized by the stems covered with stiff downwardly directed bristles, both primary and secondary umbels with an involucre of narrow sharp bracts, the unequal-sized petals, and the fruits with very thick whitish margins.

Astrantia major L. ($\times\frac{1}{3}$)

Perennial up to 2 ft. high or more, with underground rootstock; radical leaves long-stalked, digitately 5–7-lobed, up to about 6 or

8 in. diam., the lobes often lobulate, sharply toothed, glabrous; stem leaves smaller and becoming sessile with a broad sheathing base, gradually changing into bracts; flowers (A, B, ×3) white or pale pink, in compound umbels, the latter surrounded by an involucre of about 15–20 oblanceolate veiny bracts with sharp tips and sometimes one or two sharp teeth at the top; outer flowers (A, ×3) male, inner flowers (B, ×3) bisexual and producing fruit; stalks nearly as long as the bracts; sepals 5, narrow; petals (C, ×5) 5, their upper half bent inwards and downwards; stamens (D, ×5) 5; ovary of the bisexual flowers inferior, densely warted; styles 2, free; fruit (E, ×2) ellipsoid, densely warted between the 10 ribs (family *Umbelliferae*).

Found wild in south Europe from the Pyrenees to the Caucasus in south-east Asia; for a long time established in a wood in Shropshire and in other places, such as the banks of the Tay below Perth, as an escape from gardens.

Sanicula europaea L. (×⅔)

Rootstock short and rather woody; leaves nearly all radical, with purplish-based expanded stalks much longer than the blade, the latter rounded or pentagonal in outline and divided almost to the base into 5 obovate lobes, these again lobed and toothed, the teeth incurved to the margin and with very sharp points, the principal nerves even more prominent above than below; flowering stems up to about 1½ ft. high, leafless or bearing one or two smaller ones which gradually become reduced to bracts below the

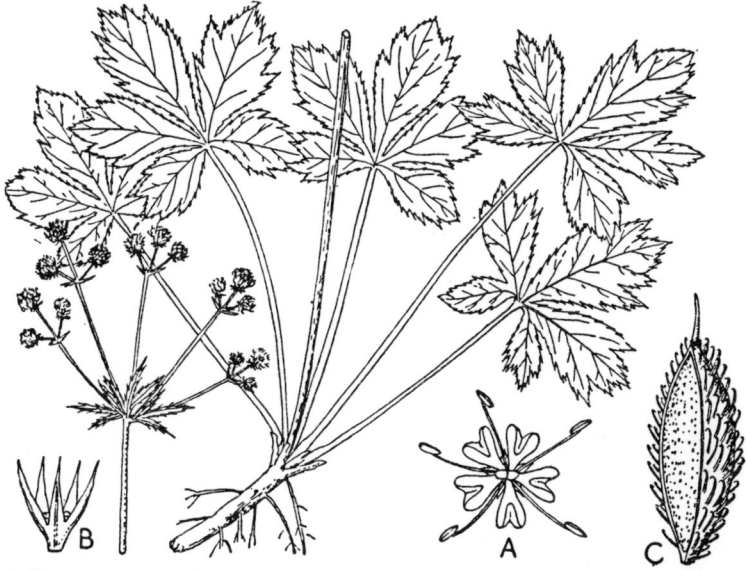

inflorescence and these sessile; flower-heads (really very small umbels) few in terminal panicles; all the umbels with an involucre of small bracts; flowers (A, ×8) unisexual, the males in 2 or 3 rows around the females; calyx (B, ×8) deeply 5-lobed; petals white, tinged with pink, obovate, with markedly inflexed tips; stamens much longer than the petals; fruit (C, ×6) about ⅓ in. long, narrowly ellipsoid, covered with hooked prickles (family *Umbelliferae*).

On account of the flowers being nearly sessile in small globose head-like clusters, the beginner will probably not at first recognize this as belonging to the Hemlock family, but may mistake it for the Rose family (*Rosaceae*), as the leaves resemble those of some members of that group.

Torilis nodosa (L.) Gaertn. ($\times\frac{1}{3}$)

Annual with stems lying on the ground or slightly ascending, up to about 1 ft. long, clothed with short backwardly directed hairs with thicker bulbous bases; leaves alternate, bipinnately and deeply divided into narrow hairy segments, the sheathing stalk with wide membranous margins; umbels head-like, sessile or shortly stalked and opposite to the leaves; no bracts; petals (A, ×3) outer flowers with one or both carpels furnished with hooked spines (B, ×4), inner (C, ×4) tuberculate only or sometimes with a few stiff hairs at the top (synonym *Caucalis nodosa* Sm.) (family *Umbelliferae*).

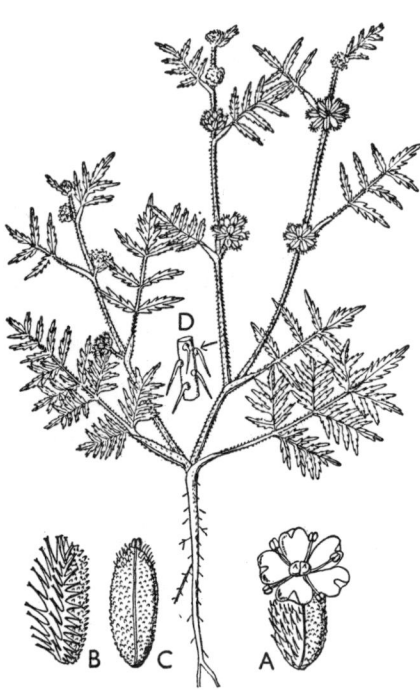

Grows on dry sunny banks by roadsides and in waste places, flowering in spring and summer; distributed from Europe to the Caucasus.

This is referred to the genus *Caucalis* in most *Floras*. *Torilis* differs from *Caucalis* in having many bristles between, as well as on, the primary ridges of the fruits, in *Caucalis* the bristles being confined to the primary ridges.

Two other species are found in Britain, *T. japonica* (Houtt.) DC., the Upright Hedge Parsley, with long-stalked umbels subtended by several bracts, very widely distributed in the northern hemisphere, and *T. arvensis* (Huds.) Link, the Spreading Hedge Parsley, also with long-stalked umbels, but with not more than one bract to the umbel, distributed from south Europe to the Near East.

Perennial herb up to 4 ft. high with an erect carrot-like rootstock clothed at the top with the fibre-like remains of the old leaf-sheaths (A, $\times\frac{1}{3}$); stems full of pith, often tinged with crimson; basal leaves up to 1 ft. or more long, thrice pinnate with numerous pinnately lobed curved sharp-pointed segments; peduncles slightly pubescent; all umbels with several narrow bracts with fine points; upper leaves gradually much smaller but similarly cut, with a large basal sheath with membranous margins; stalks of primary rays and of the flowers softly pubescent; flowers (B, $\times 3$)

white; petals equal-sized, obovate, with inflexed often bifid tips; stamens longer than the petals; styles long, clavate; fruit (C, $\times 3$) hairy, ellipsoid, each half with 5 prominent ribs (family *Umbelliferae*).

Found only in chalky districts in a few south-eastern counties of England; extends eastwards into Asia.

SEA HOLLY
Eryngium maritimum L. ($\times\frac{1}{3}$)

Perennial herb up to 2 ft. high and armed with sharp prickles on the leaves; stems solid, nearly white, slightly ribbed; leaves alternate, sessile and clasping the stem, the upper ones whorled, more or less elliptic-obovate, irregularly lobed, the lobes ending in very sharp points, glaucous with nearly white and very conspicuous nerves and veins, margins thickened; flowers crowded into terminal sessile heads surrounded by the whorled leaves, each flower subtended by a 3-forked spiny bract (A, $\times 2$); calyx-lobes (B, $\times 3$) 5, on top of the inferior ovary, subulate-lanceolate and very sharp-pointed, longer than the petals; petals (C, $\times 3$) 5, lavender-blue, deeply notched and with sharply inflexed tips; stamens (D, $\times 2\frac{1}{2}$) 5, longer than the petals; disk crenulate; ovary (E, $\times 4$) 2-locular, covered with papillae and spinules; styles (F, $\times 3$) 2, free to the base, blue; fruit ovoid (family *Umbelliferae*).

The beginner with a little knowledge of plant families might be excused for mistaking this plant for a member of the Daisy family, *Compositae*, the flowers being in heads surrounded by an involucre of bracts. In fact it rather resembles the genus *Echinops*, belonging to the *Compositae*. In the Sea Holly, however, the ovary is 2-locular, the two styles are free, the petals are separate and the anthers not united in a tube as they are in *Compositae*.

The species inhabits sandy maritime shores, flowering in July and August. It is distributed on the shores of the Atlantic, Mediterranean, and Black Seas.

In the densely packed flowers the stamens mature before the stigmas. The filaments are inflexed in bud, the anthers being at first enclosed by the petals which also have inflexed tips. These organs are also closely packed together making it impossible for any but the strongest insects to reach the nectar secreted by a disk on top of the inferior ovary. After releasing their pollen, the anthers drop off, after which the long stigmatic branches project far out of the flower, thus preventing self-pollination. The stiff, sharp, involucral bracts and sepals, in addition to the spiny-toothed foliage, serve as a protection against soft-skinned animals like snails and caterpillars.

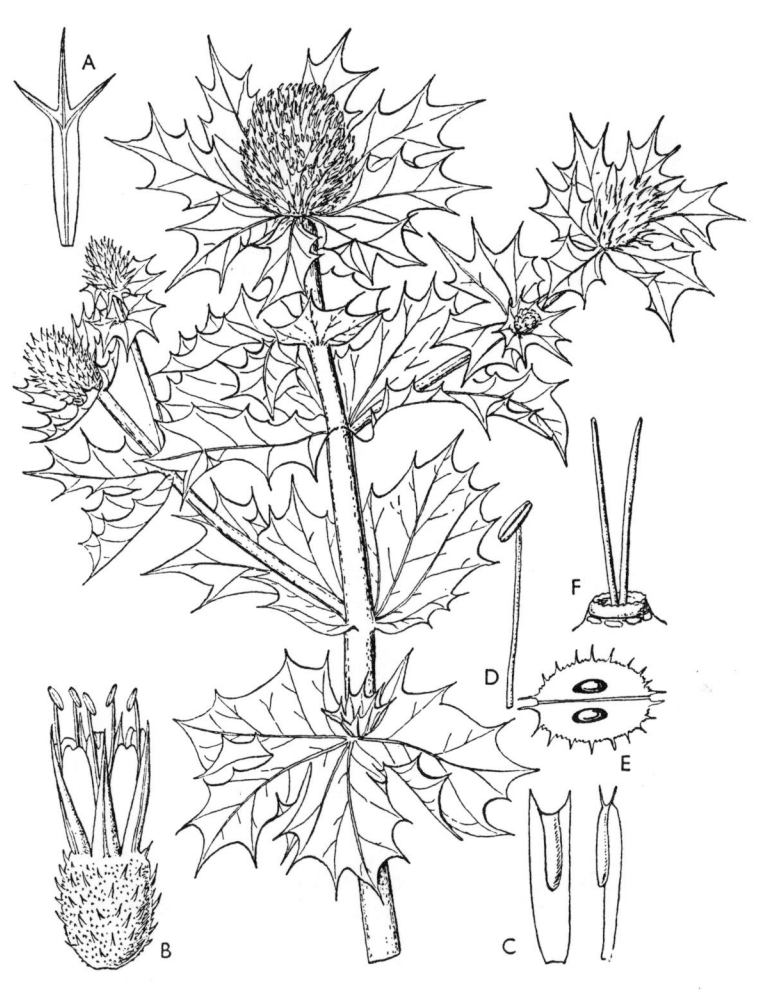

WILD CARROT
Daucus carota L. ($\times \frac{2}{3}$)

An erect annual or biennial with a branched stem up to 3 ft. high with a carrot-like taproot; stems closely ribbed and clothed, espe-

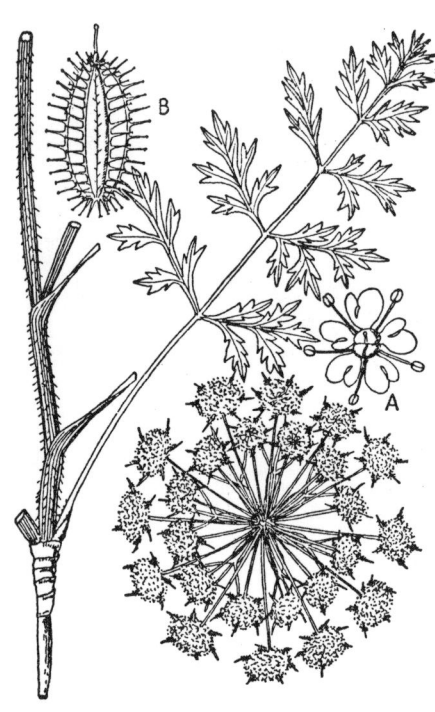

cially towards the base and at the nodes, with stiff bristle-like hairs; lower leaves bipinnate, long-stalked, the ultimate segments deeply cut into acute lanceolate lobes; basal sheath with a narrow membranous margin bristly at the base; upper leaves becoming much smaller and less cut up; umbels terminal and opposite to the leaves, on rather stout common stalks with bristly bulbous-based hairs; general umbel girt by narrow 3-forked bracts with broad membranous sheathing bases conspicuous in the bud stage; ultimate umbels numerous, surrounded by several narrow bracts with membranous margins and fringed with hairs; flowers (A, ×3) with minute calyx; petals white, broadly obovate, notched into 2 unequal lobes with sharply inflexed tips; stamens a little longer than the petals; ovary covered with shortly bristly hairs; ribs of the carpels (B, ×4) covered with sharp bristles like the teeth of a comb, the bristles with very minute reflexed tips (family *Umbelliferae*).

This is the wild form of the cultivated Carrot of our gardens, its original habitat being the sea-coasts of southern Europe, but now found in fields and waste places; it flowers during the summer and autumn. Near the sea the leaves are more fleshy, this form being distinguished as *D. maritimus*.

Silaum silaus (L.) Schinz and Thell. ($\times\frac{1}{3}$)

Erect-branched perennial herb up to 3 ft. high; stems solid, closely ribbed, glabrous; basal leaves repeatedly dissected, long-stalked, segments (A, $\times\frac{2}{3}$) nar-rowly lanceolate, with numerous distinct side-nerves, not hairy; stem-leaves very shortly stalk-ed, much divided, the uppermost reduced to the sheath and a narrow blade; flowers (B, $\times3$) yellowish, arranged in compound umbels, the main umbel without bracts at the base, the smaller umbels with an involucre of narrow bracts nearly as long as the flower-stalks; petals with inflexed tips; sta-mens nearly as long as the petals; styles 2, very short; fruiting carpels (C, $\times2\frac{1}{2}$) ellipsoid, $\frac{1}{5}$ in. long, with 3 prominent ridges on the back and very obscure vittas be-tween (synonym *Silaus pratensis* Besser) (family *Umbelliferae*).

This species flowers rather late in summer and grows in meadows and amongst bushes in pastures. It is widely distributed in Britain, becoming rare northwards.

There are about eight species of this genus distributed through the north temperate regions of the Old World. This is the only British example, recognized by its repeatedly divided leaves with very narrow segments with distinct looped side-nerves, yellow flowers, the main umbel without an involucre of bracts, and the fruits with three prominent ribs on the back of each carpel with obscure vittas between them.

Scandix pecten-veneris L. ($\times\frac{1}{2}$)

Annual up to about 1 ft. high, sometimes much branched and spreading from the base; stems with short stiff spreading hairs; leaves sheathing at the base, on slender stalks, twice to thrice pinnate and dissected into fine narrow acute segments, glabrous or with short stiff hairs; umbels usually 2 together, terminal and leaf-opposed, on short peduncles; bracts leafy, deeply divided into 2 acute lobes (A, $\times$3); flowers (C, $\times2\frac{1}{2}$) very shortly stalked, few (5–8) in each umbel (B, $\times1\frac{1}{2}$) small and white; petals (D, $\times$6) very unequal, white; styles (E, $\times$5) 2, very short; ovary soon elongating into the long awl-like long-beaked fruit about 2 in. long (F, $\times$1), the latter with short ascending teeth on the margins; fruit-body lined with dark vittas (family *Umbelliferae*).

Common in waste places and cornfields and flowering with the corn. The make-up (morphology) of this species is quite interesting; it is an annual (most British *Umbelliferae* are perennial), and the umbels are usually paired and terminal and opposite to the last leaf (leaf-opposed), one maturing in advance of the other.

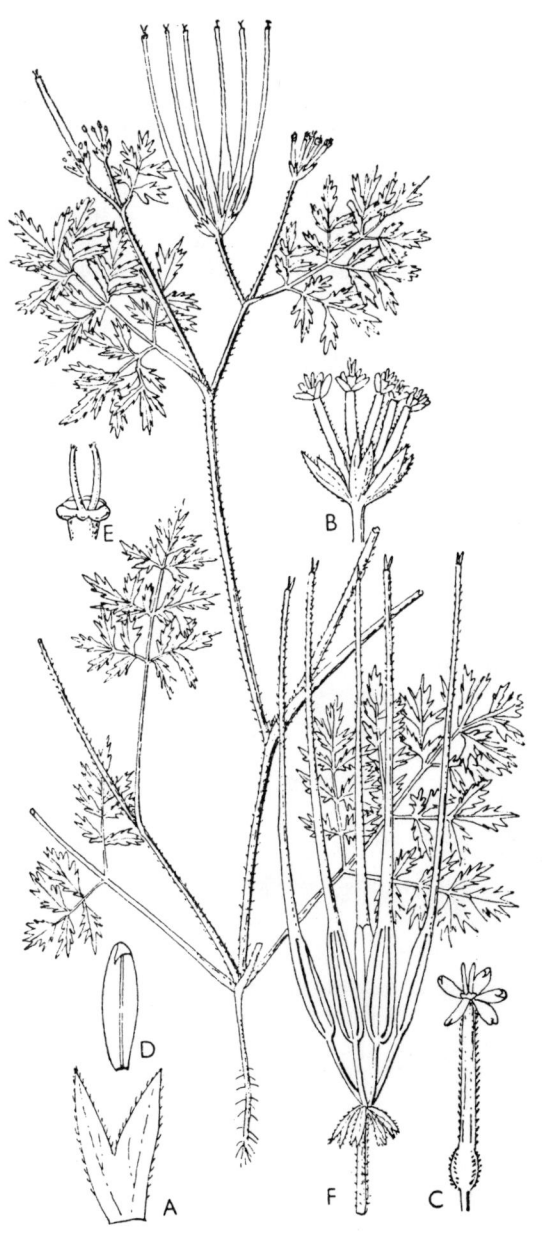

Aethusa cynapium L. ($\times\frac{1}{2}$)

An erect annual up to 2 ft. high, but sometimes very dwarf; stems ribbed, with a nauseous odour when rubbed; leaves glaucous-green, with long ribbed basal sheaths $\frac{1}{2}$–1 in. long and with a broad membranous margin produced beyond the tip; blade 2–3 times pinnate, with lanceolate acute lobes, glabrous; umbels on rather short common stalks opposite to the leaves; main umbel without an involucre of bracts; ultimate small umbels with about 3 linear

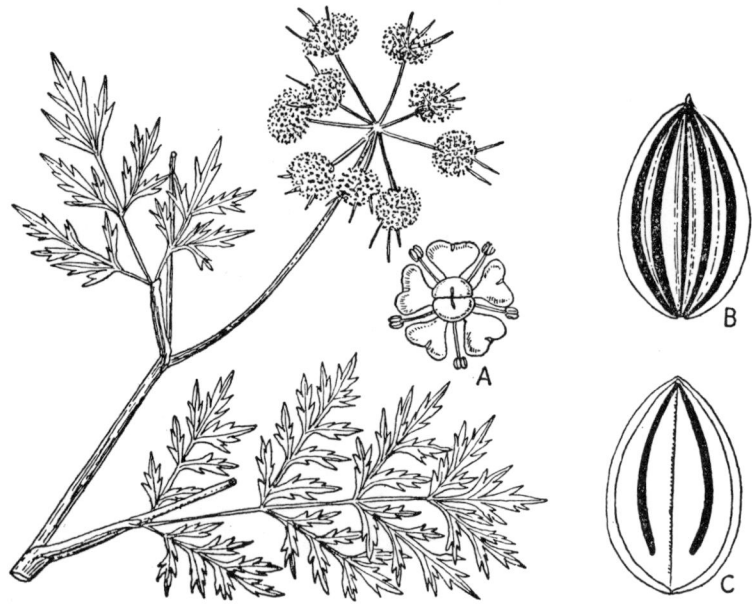

bracts all on the outer side of the cluster; rays about 9, up to $\frac{1}{2}$ in. diam.; flowers (A, $\times 3$) with minute calyx; petals white, broadly obovate, notched at the apex; fruit ovate, compressed, the carpels (B, $\times 3$) with 5 very thick prominent ribs and 5 narrow black vittas between the ribs, on the inside of the carpel (C, $\times 3$) only two vittas not extending to the base (family *Umbelliferae*).

This plant may be at once recognized amongst our native *Umbelliferae* by the bracts below the ultimate small clusters of flowers, these being few and arranged only on the *outer side* of the clusters. It is a common weed and regarded as poisonous.

Myrrhis odorata Scop. (×⅓)

Erect branched perennial up to 3 ft. high, very aromatic; stems hollow, closely and finely ribbed, very weakly hairy here and there; leaves twice pinnate, fern-like, the ultimate divisions deeply pinnately lobed and the lobes toothed, softly hairy all over; stalks sheathing at the base, the sheath forming a wing on the stalk, nerved lengthwise; flowers (A, ×2) in compound umbels; no bracts to the general involucre but the secondary umbels with large lanceolate pointed whitish bracts; petals white, wedge-shaped, with inflexed tips; filaments long; fruit (B, ×1) largest and

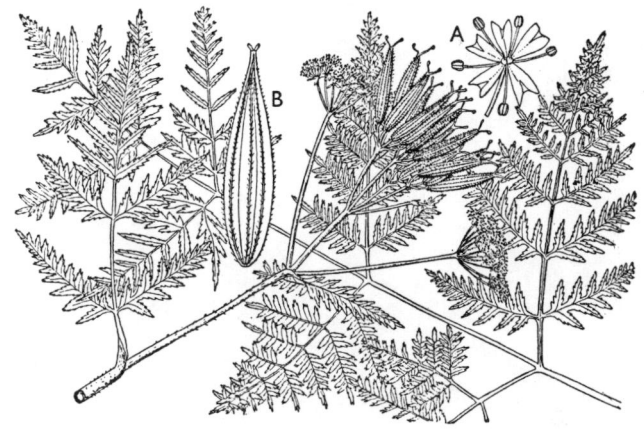

longest of all native species of *Umbelliferae*, oblong-lanceolate, 1–1¼ in. long, shining when ripe and at first setulose on the ribs; no vittas (family *Umbelliferae*).

Grows in pastures and often found near dwellings, probably a relic of cultivation, being formerly much grown as a potherb; flowers in spring and early summer. Some of the flowers are purely male, without ovary, styles, or stigmas; others are bisexual. The last flowers to appear are male, and these provide pollen for fertilizing the youngest of the bisexual flowers.

The genus embraces only this one species recognized by its very aromatic much cut-up fern-like leaves, its general umbel without bracts, the smaller umbels with large pointed whitish bracts, and the exceptionally long (for the family) fruits.

Anthriscus sylvestris Hoffm. (×$\frac{2}{5}$)

Perennial with a taproot; stems up to 3 or 4 ft. high, hollow, very shortly hairy, but becoming glabrous higher up except at the nodes which have a fringe of longer hairs; lower leaves with a long stalk between the sheathing base and the twice pinnate blade, the ultimate lobes deeply and pinnately lobulate with acute teeth; upper leaves gradually smaller and sessile on the broad fringed sheath, all slightly hairy especially on the nerves below; primary umbel (A, ×$\frac{2}{5}$) arising from the fork with a pair of small leaves,

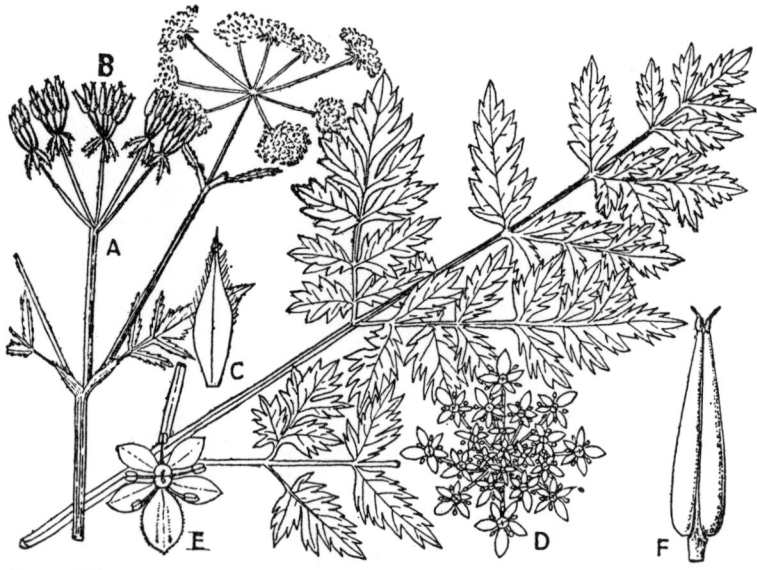

but without a general involucre; ultimate small umbels (B, ×$\frac{2}{5}$) with about 5 or 6 bracts resembling a calyx, these (C, ×2) fringed with hairs and reflexed in flower; rays of the first umbel (in the fork) usually 3–5, of the terminal umbels about 8 or 9; flowers white (D, ×1), about 15 in. each partial umbel, the outer flowers (E, ×2) with the outer petals larger than the others; styles very short in the middle of a pale fleshy disk; fruits (F, ×2) about $\frac{1}{3}$ in. long, narrow, smooth and shining, with 2 antennae-like styles at the top, but neither ribbed nor with resin canals (family *Umbelliferae*).

This is one of the most common of the hemlock family in Britain, and it grows in hedges, on the borders of fields, etc., being the first of the family to flower.

Cicuta virosa L. ($\times\frac{1}{3}$)

Perennial herb up to 4 ft. with thick hollow stems with transverse partitions within at the nodes and giving off whorls of slender roots; lower leaves 1–2 ft. long, thrice pinnate; leaflets opposite, sessile, linear-lanceolate, sharply toothed, glabrous, and bright green; upper leaves with a dilated sheathing base, becoming twice pinnate; umbels long-stalked, without a general involucre, the ultimate umbels with about 8 linear subacute 1-nerved bracts; flowers (A, $\times 3$) white; petals with a long inflexed point; anthers at first red, then violet pink; stigmas divaricate; fruit (B, $\times 3$) small, orbicular, ribbed,

with a solitary vitta between each rib (family *Umbelliferae*).

Grows in ditches and the margins of ponds and lakes, flowering in July and August. Like the Water Drop-wort, *Oenanthe crocata* L. (fig. 455), it is one of the most poisonous of our native plants, and numerous fatal cases of poisoning are on record of cattle after eating the leaves, and of human beings from eating the roots, which resemble parsnips.

Erect glabrous slender annual about 2 ft. high, with an unpleasant odour when rubbed; lower leaves once pinnate, the leaflets opposite, deeply pinnate, segments broad and cuneate, irregularly toothed, thin; upper leaves finely divided into narrow linear 1-nerved segments; basal sheaths about $\frac{1}{2}$ in. long, with membranous margins; all the umbels with a few linear bracts at the base; middle flowers not fertile, the outer flowers (A, $\times 3$) larger and fertile, the nerved petals of these unequal, the outer larger and without the inflexed tip of the others; stamens as long as the petals; fruits (B, $\times 2$) globular, with prominent ribs but no vittas visible outside (family *Umbelliferae*). – Note, the lower leaflets should have been drawn *toothed*.

Flowers in summer and autumn, cultivated and naturalized in some southern counties of England, usually in waste ground. The name is derived from the Greek word for bug, because of its bug-like smell when bruised. The fruit loses this odour when dry, and it is then used in curries and confectionery.

Meum athamanticum Jacq. ($\times\frac{1}{3}$)

Perennial herb with stems up to $1\frac{1}{2}$ ft. high from a rootstock densely covered at the top with the fibrous remains of the old leaves; radical leaves with broad ribbed basal sheaths and fairly long-stalked, much cut up into very fine thread-like segments rather resembling the *Asparagus* grown in pots as a decorative plant (*Asparagus plumosus*); flowers (A, $\times5$) in umbels of 10–15 rays, the primary with 2 or 3 narrow bracts, the ultimate ones with very few bracts; petals white or yellowish white, equal-sized, with short incurved tips; styles very short; fruit (B, $\times1\frac{1}{4}$) oblong-ellipsoid, $\frac{1}{2}$ in. long, each half

with 5 prominent ribs and 2 or 3 vittas between the ribs; styles persistent, recurved (family *Umbelliferae*).

Found only on the moors in the northern counties of England and Wales and in Scotland, flowering during summer. The rootstock was formerly used by the Highlanders as a vegetable.

ROUGH CHERVIL
Chaerophyllum temulentum L. ($\times \frac{2}{5}$)

Erect biennial up to about 3 ft. high, usually growing on shady banksides, often under trees; stems often purplish, loosely clothed

with rather bristly deflexed hairs; leaves alternate, stalked, the stalks sheathing at the base and with pale thinner margins, the blade twice pinnate (bipinnate), with the ultimate divisions deeply lobed or coarsely toothed and mucronate, bristly hairy on both surfaces; umbels compound, the primary one with about a dozen rays, but without any bracts at the base of the stalks, the ultimate umbels with about 20–25 flowers with an involucre of bracts at the base fringed with hairs (A, ×4); flower-stalks elongating as they develop into fruits; petals (B, ×5) white, obovate, bilobed with a hooked tip, the outer petals of the umbel rather larger; fruit (C, ×2) about $\frac{1}{3}$ in. long, narrow and turgid (family *Umbelliferae*). Synonym *C. temulum* L.

Though not so dangerous as *Oenanthe crocata* (fig. 455), this species is also poisonous, and is known to have caused the death of pigs and cows in Germany. The plant has a strong odour and acrid taste. It is widely distributed in Britain, but only locally common. Like so many other of our common species, it extends east to beyond the Caucasus mountains.

Perennial glaucous herb with dioecious white flowers; rootstock slender, densely covered towards the top with the filiform remains of the leaf-stalks; leaves glabrous, much divided into numerous linear 1-nerved segments; leaf-sheaths broad, with membranous margins, ribbed, the ribs remaining persistent and clothing the stock (as described above); male flowers (A, ×3) in panicles of umbels, each branch of the panicle with a small much divided leaf at the base; petals narrow, oblanceolate, with an inflexed apex; ovary rudimentary; sometimes a few female flowers developed on the male inflorescences; female flowers (B, ×3) without stamens; ovary globose;

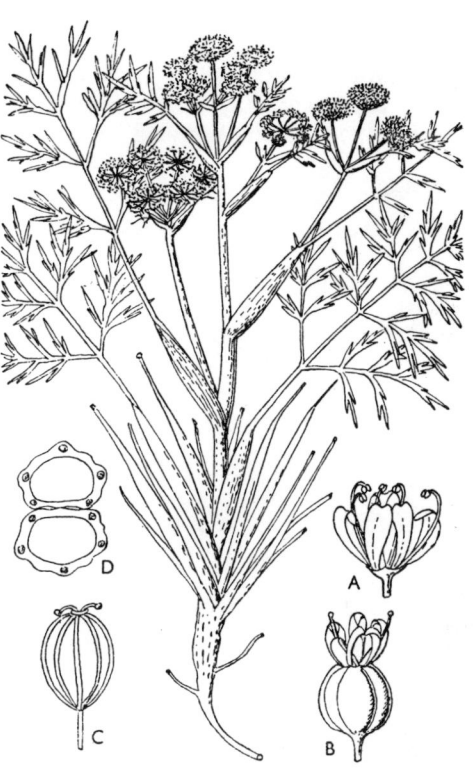

styles as long as the narrow petals; fruit (C, ×3) compressed, ellipsoid-globose, each half with 5 prominent ribs with a single vitta below each rib (family *Umbelliferae*). – Synonym *Trinia vulgaris* DC. *Pimpinella dioica* L. – D, cross-section of fruit, ×4.

Flowers in spring and early summer in southern England, chiefly in limestone districts; distributed from south-west Europe to the Balkans.

This is the only species of the genus in Britain and one of the few native *Umbelliferae* with unisexual (dioecious) flowers, and with the vittae underneath the ridges of the fruit and not in the spaces between them.

WILD ANGELICA
Angelica sylvestris L. (×⅔)

Perennial with a stout stem up to 4 or 5 ft. high, minutely hairy in the upper part; lower leaves large, twice pinnate, with rather large leaflets in threes, the terminal leaflet ovate to obovate and mostly equal-sided at the narrow base, the lateral leaflets more or less elliptic and unequal-sided at the base, all acutely triangular at the apex and coarsely toothed like a saw (serrate), paler and shortly hairy below especially on the nerves, the stem leaves gradually smaller upwards and reduced to the large sheathing base and a

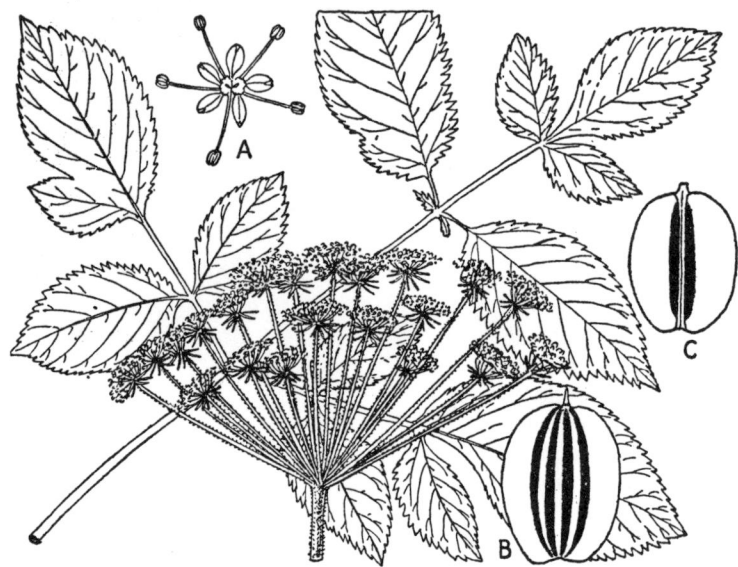

few small segments; umbels usually 3 together at the tops of the shoots, the middle flowering first and rather shorter than the two lateral, the primary umbels usually without bracts or of 2–3 linear bracts, the ultimate umbels with several narrow short bracts scarcely wider than the pedicels; rays 25–40, their stalks shortly hairy; flowers (A, × 2) with minute calyx; petals white, elliptic, with inflexed apex; stamens with long thread-like filaments; carpels (B, ×2) flattened, about ⅓ in. long, with 3 ribs on the back and 4 vittas between, broadly winged, on the reverse side (C, × 2) with only 2 vittas showing parallel against the middle (family *Umbelliferae*).

This species is easily distinguished in fruit by the double wing, the wing of each carpel becoming free before they separate.

A tall glabrous perennial herb; stems full of pith, angular and ribbed, glabrous or nearly so; leaves tripinnate, divided into narrowly lanceolate acute segments; main umbel without bracts or only one or two narrow ones, with many rays, secondary umbels with a few narrow bracts; peduncles scabrid towards the top; flowers (A, ×3) milky white; petals equalsized, obovate, deeply bilobed and with an inflexed tip; stamens longer than the petals; fruit (B, ×3) broadly elliptic, compressed, the edges of each carpel expanded into a broadish wing and with 3 wing-like keels on the back and

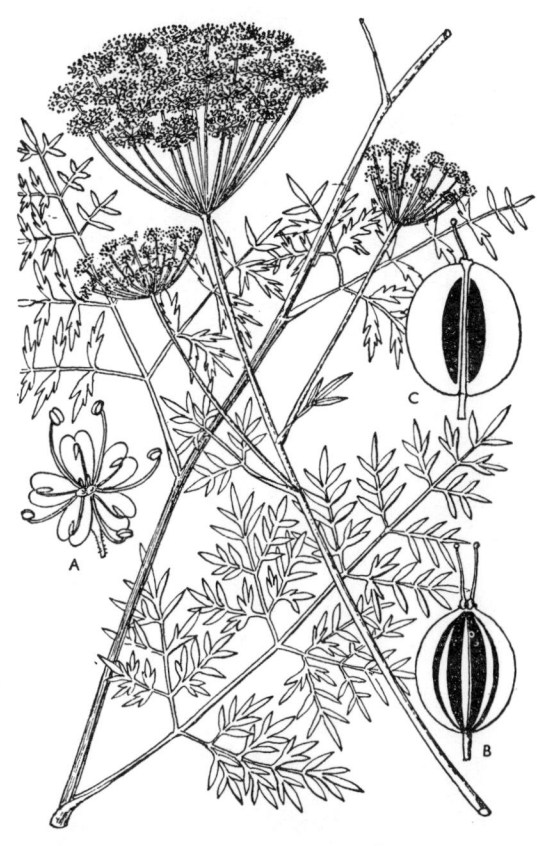

a broad resin vitta between each, only 2 of these visible on the inside (C, ×3); styles slender and more or less persistent in fruit (family *Umbelliferae*).

Found only in fens and damp meadows in a few eastern counties of southern England, but widely distributed in north and central Europe, east to central Asia, becoming rarer southwards.

Tall erect perennial with yellow milky juice; lower leaves large, long-stalked, twice or thrice pinnate, with linear or lanceolate

segments, glabrous; segments faintly pinnately nerved; upper leaves smaller but deeply divided and with a large basal sheath with membranous margins; primary and secondary umbels with several linear bracts with fine points; stalks of the rays and flowers markedly but minutely scabrid; primary rays up to about 25; flowers (A, $\times$3) white; petals bilobed with inflexed tips; stamens longer than the petals; styles long, spreading; fruit (B, $\times$3) broadly oval, each half with 3 prominent ribs on the back, the margins expanded into a wing; vittas single under each furrow (family *Umbelliferae*). – C, cross-section of carpel, $\times$5.

Flowers in late summer and found in marshes, especially in the eastern counties of England; widely distributed from western Europe eastwards to Siberia.

Pastinaca sativa L. ($\times\frac{1}{3}$)

Annual or biennial 2–3 ft. high, resembling *Heracleum sphondylium* but less coarse and smaller and with yellow flowers; taproot slender, with parsnip flavour; leaves widely sheathing at the base, irregularly pinnate, the divisions oblong-lanceolate, coarsely toothed and with 1 or 2 basal more deeply cut side-lobes, shortly pubescent below; upper leaves gradually reduced to stalked 3-lobed bracts; main umbel sometimes with a small bract at the base, producing fruit whilst the lateral umbels are still in flower; ultimate umbels without bracts or sometimes with 1 or 2 small ones; petals (A, ×3) yellow, inflexed; carpels with 5 slender ribs and 4 vittas on the outside (B, ×2½), the latter extending nearly to the base, only 2 visible on the reverse side (C, ×2½) (synonym *Peucedanum sativum* (L.) Hook. f.) (family *Umbelliferae*).

Found on roadsides and in waste places, often locally quite common in chalky districts; few British Umbellifers have yellow petals, but this is one of them, flowering in late summer; formerly much esteemed as food, and in the middle ages it formed an addition to the salt fish eaten during Lent; from it was raised the garden Parsnip.

Pastinaca is a genus of about fifteen species distributed through the north temperate regions of the Old World. The fruits of *P. sativa* are very distinctive, with slender ribs and four vittas on the outside, and two inside, some of them extending not quite to the base of the carpels.

MARSH PENNY-WORT
Hydrocotyle vulgaris L. ($\times \frac{2}{3}$)

Perennial with slender stems creeping along wet mud or floating in water, rooting and giving off a leaf or leaves and flower-stalks at every node; leaves (A, $\times \frac{2}{3}$) orbicular, attached in the middle to the long stalk, crenate and often very shortly lobed, with as many nerves as lobes radiating from the point of junction with the stalk; peduncles shorter than the leaf-stalks, with a single or more clusters of flowers towards the top; flowers (B, $\times 2$) minute, with a scarcely evident calyx and tiny free petals on top of the ovary;

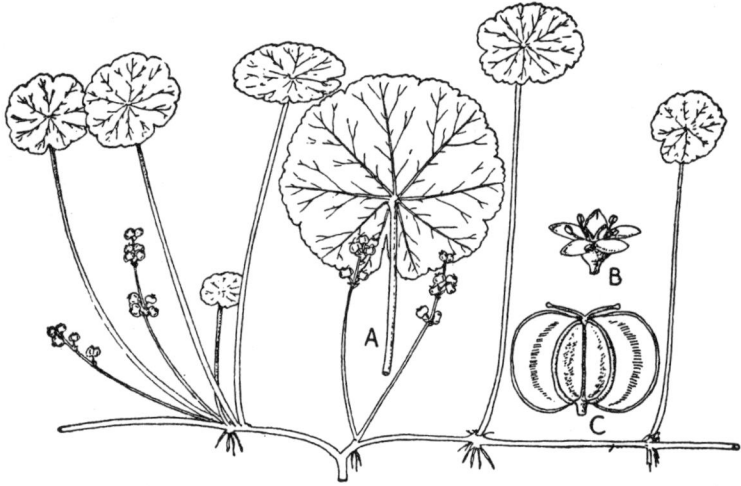

stamens as many as petals; ovary inferior, with 2 spreading styles, soon expanding into a rounded though very small compressed fruit (C, $\times 5$) widely notched at each end; flowers in summer and easily recognized amongst the family *Umbelliferae* by the orbicular leaves attached in the middle (peltate).

This is a striking little plant which the beginner at first sight may think has not much relationship with the hemlock family to which it belongs. The clusters of very small flowers form very imperfect umbels. Only one other fairly common British plant has very similar leaves, this being the ordinary Penny-wort, *Umbilicus rupestris*, shown in fig. 424.

Biennial, glossy herb up to 3 ft. high; stem filled with pith, ribbed; basal leaves 3 times divided (ternate), the leaflets unequally divided nearly to the base and together forming an ovate-rounded blade serrate in the upper part and about 2 in. diam., glabrous; stalks broadly sheathing at the base; stem leaves opposite with very broad sheaths hairy on the margin and forming a wing on the stalk; umbels compound, in flower forming a rounded mass;

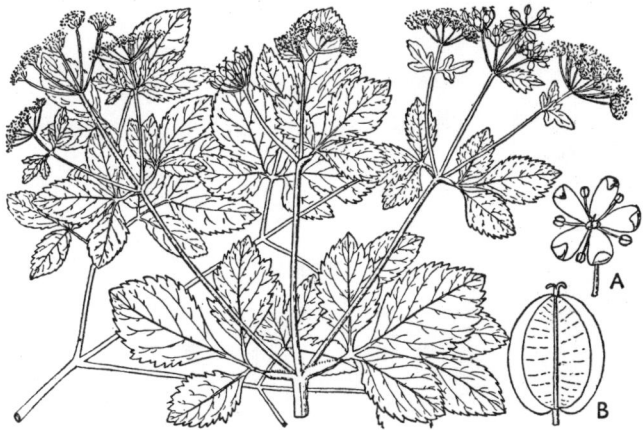

primary rays bractless or with one or two small ones, ultimate rays bractless; stalks glabrous; petals (A, $\times$3) yellowish-green, with inflexed tips; fruit (B, $\times$3) dark brown to black, 3-angular, about $\frac{1}{4}$ in. long, with several vittas between the ribs (family *Umbelliferae*).

Grows on cliffs, hedge-sides, and waste places near the sea, and round about old ruins; extends to the eastern Mediterranean and in the Atlantic Islands; formerly much cultivated as a potherb, the young shoots and leaf-stalks being eaten. The specific name refers to the black fruits.

Foeniculum vulgare Mill. ($\times\frac{1}{3}$)

Perennial herb sending up several stems yearly up to about 4 ft.
high, or taller in cultivation; stems very closely ribbed, glabrous,
full of soft pith; leaves with a long broad sheathing closely ribbed
petiole, 3–4 times pinnate with very fine long thread-like segments;
primary and secondary umbels without bracts, composed of many
rays; pedicels about $\frac{1}{5}$ in. long; flowers (A, $\times$4) numerous; calyx
reduced to a rim; petals yellow, inflexed, bifid at the apex; stamens longer than the petals; fruits (C, $\times$2) with 5 ribs on each

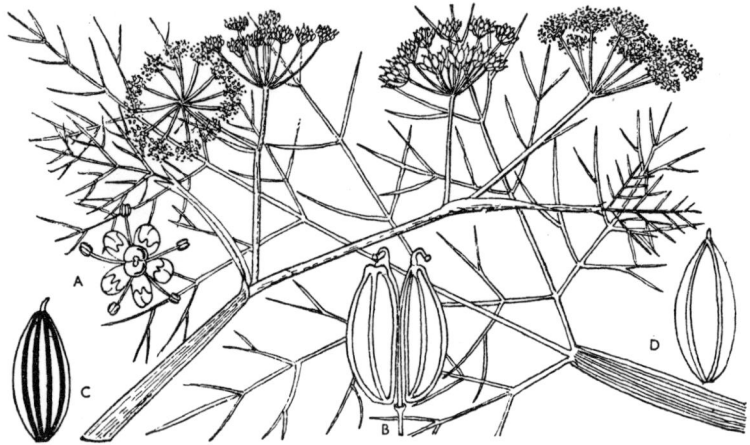

carpel with a single vitta under each furrow (family *Umbelliferae*).
– D, inner face of carpel, $\times$2.

Wild Fennel flowers late in summer and early autumn, and is
found in dry hilly places near the sea from Norfolk round to
north Wales; widely distributed in Europe and western Asia.

Nearly every garden of any size has a few Fennel plants growing in a corner to be used as a garnish for fish, and in other countries the leaves are employed to give a flavour to food and bever-
ages. Its supposed virtues have been much eulogized in old herbals
and in verse.

An aggressive perennial with a creeping rootstock; radical leaves on long stalks and often forming a complete carpet on the ground, twice ternate; lateral leaflets very unequal-sided at the base, oblong or oblong-elliptic, acutely pointed, terminal leaflet ovate or ovate-elliptic, those of the lateral divisions unequal-sided at the base, but of the terminal division mostly equal-sided, all rather coarsely toothed (crenate); stem leaves becoming sessile on the

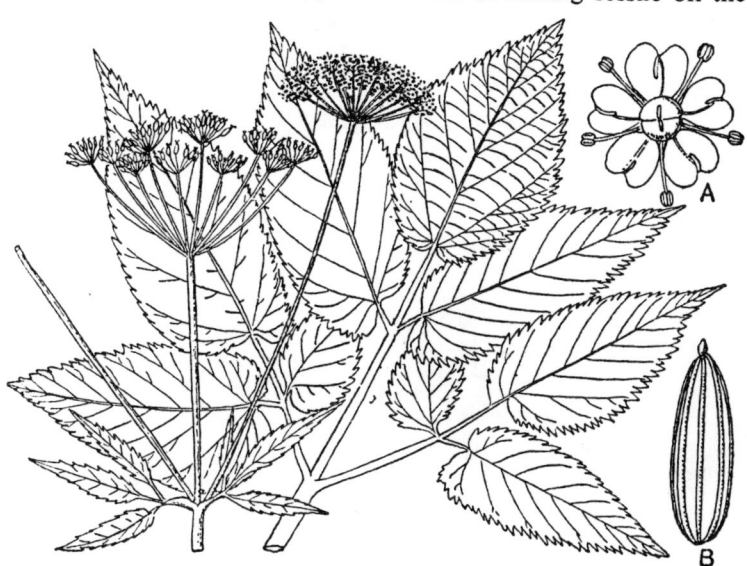

broad glabrous basal sheath with membranous margins and reduced to three leaflets; umbels usually 3 together terminating the main shoot, the middle one opening first and often overtopped by the others; general and ultimate umbels without an involucre of bracts; rays numerous; flowers (A, × 6) very small, white, on rather short stalks; calyx minute; petals rounded-obovate, deeply notched and with an inflexed point; stamens a little longer than the petals; carpels (B, × 4) with 5 slender ribs, but no resinous vittas (family *Umbelliferae*).

This is a notorious weed which is difficult to eradicate when once it has become established. It is supposed to have been introduced and cultivated in the Middle Ages, and is usually most plentiful near buildings. It flowers from June to August.

Perennial with a rather thick rootstock; stems erect, up to 2 ft. high, slender and wiry, very minutely hairy; radical leaves once pinnate, with rounded irregularly lobed and coarsely toothed leaflets slightly hairy on the nerves below; stem leaves (A, $\times \frac{2}{5}$), bipinnately lobed, with narrow acute segments, gradually reduced upwards to little more than a sheath about $\frac{3}{4}$ in. long, with paler margins and a sharp tip and streaked with nerves; umbels usually 2 together, the primary (first to flower) usually a little shorter than

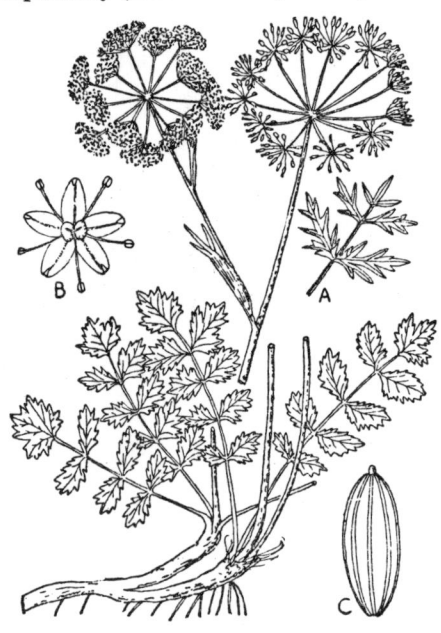

the other, all without bracts; rays 10–18, very slender; flowers (B, $\times$ 4) 15–20 in each cluster; petals white, narrowly elliptic, with an inflexed tip; stems longer than the petals; fruit (C, $\times$ 5) ovoid, scarcely compressed, the carpels with 5 slightly prominent ribs (family *Umbelliferae*).

Flowers all summer and is found in pastures, on banks, and by roadsides. The well-known Aniseed is the fruit of a related species, *Pimpinella anisum* L., a native of the Eastern Mediterranean and cultivated in many countries, especially in Spain, south Russia, and Bulgaria. It is most familiar as an ingredient of 'seed' cakes.

Apium nodiflorum (L.) Lag. ($\times \frac{1}{2}$)

Perennial with decumbent stems; annual flowering shoots more erect and sometimes several feet high; leaves with a long thin-margined sheath at the base, pinnate, with up to about 10 pairs of opposite elliptic or ovate-elliptic toothed sessile leaflets; terminal leaflet stalked and sometimes unequally lobed; umbels on a very short common stalk, appearing to be axillary, but really opposite the leaf (leaf-opposed); no common involucre, or rarely 1 or 2 bracts; partial involucres of a few leafy bracts (B, $\times 2\frac{1}{2}$) becoming reflexed; flowers (A, $\times 5$) very small, shortly stalked; petals (C, $\times 4$) white; ovary inferior; styles 2; stigmas capitate; fruit small, ovoid, each carpel with 5 slender ribs and a single vitta (resin canal) between each (family *Umbelliferae*).

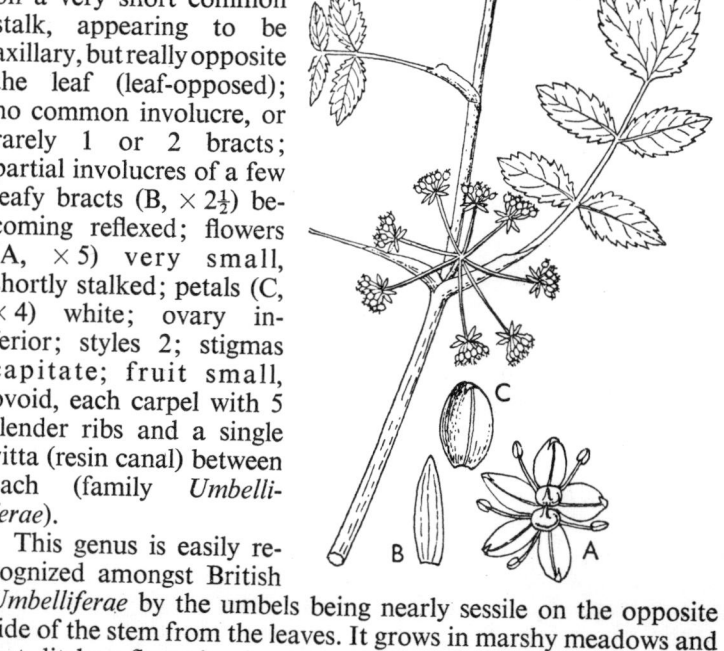

This genus is easily recognized amongst British *Umbelliferae* by the umbels being nearly sessile on the opposite side of the stem from the leaves. It grows in marshy meadows and wet ditches, flowering in summer. There is thus a danger of the plant being mistaken for Watercress, though it is not known to be poisonous, and is unpalatable. In consequence it is often called 'Fool's Watercress'. It is widely distributed as far east as Persia and into northern Africa.

Conpodium majus (Gouan) Lor. & Barr. ($\times \frac{2}{5}$)

Perennial with a rounded or 2-lobed tuberous roostock; stems annual, erect, slender, up to about 2 ft. high, simple or slightly branched, glabrous and closely ribbed; basal leaves few, soon disappearing, divided into 3 stalked segments, these deeply bipinnate into fine sharp narrow lobes; stem leaves sessile on the broad basal sheath, deeply and bipinnately divided into fine linear acute segments, the end lobe usually appreciably longer and a little broader than the others, all with minutely rough margins; main umbel which flowers first opposite the last leaf, with a younger lateral umbel, and usually one or two umbels, terminating

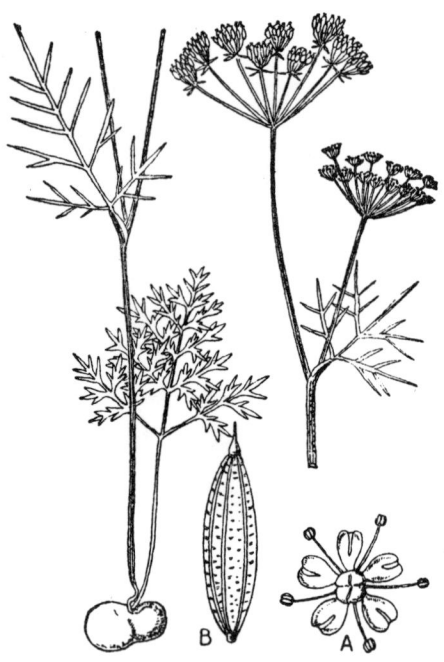

lateral axillary branches below; common stalks very slender, especially of the lateral umbels; main umbel without an involucre, only the ultimate small umbels with a few narrow bracts; rays of flowers about $\frac{1}{2}$ in. diam., the stalks thread-like; flowers (A, $\times$ 4) very small, white; calyx minute; petals obovate, with inflexed points; stamens longer than the petals; fruits (B, $\times$ 3) narrowly elliptic, about $\frac{1}{3}$ in. long, each carpel with 5 faint ribs and very slender vittas between (family *Umbelliferae*).

This plant flowers in summer and grows in woods and fields. It is generally distributed in the British Isles except on chalk and in the fen districts.

Heracleum sphondylium L. (×½)

A coarse plant up to about 6 ft. high, stem hollow, angular, and furrowed, hispid with stiff bristle-like hairs; leaves large, pinnate, with up to 9 leaflets, the latter broad and irregularly lobed and toothed, the lowermost stalked, the upper sessile and more or less decurrent on the common stalk, more markedly bristly at the joints, as well as shorter hairs all over the lower surface; stem leaves gradually becoming sessile on very large hispid sheathing

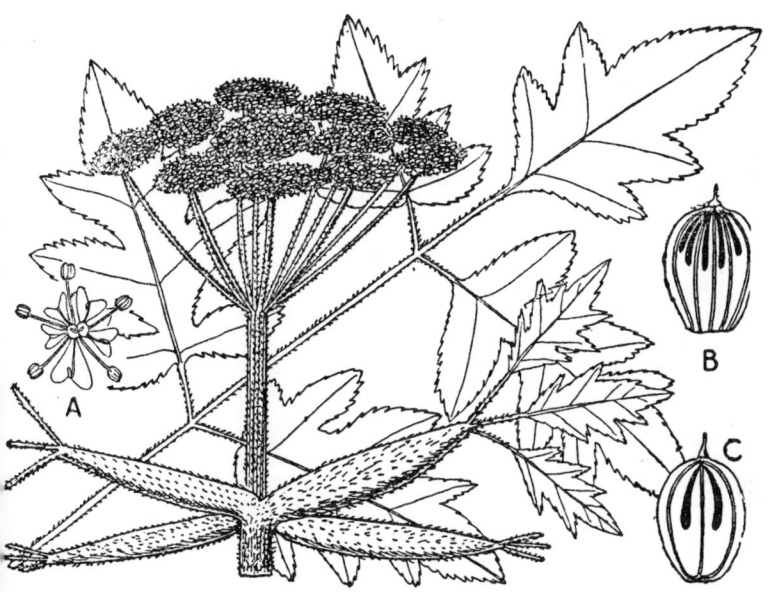

bases and composed of only three stalked leaflets; umbels of several to many rays, the primary umbel usually without bracts; ultimate umbels with an involucre of very narrow bracts; flowers (A, × 2) with a minute calyx; petals white, unequal-sized, wedge-shaped, widely notched and with inflexed points; stamens longer than the petals; ovary covered with woolly hairs; carpels (B, × 1½) with 5 slender ribs and a single vitta between each, these do not extend to the base; on the reverse side of the carpel (C, × 1½) only two vittas visible extending about half way down (family *Umbelliferae*).

This striking plant grows in hedges, open places in woods, and in moist meadows. It flowers in summer and autumn.

Ammi majus L. ($\times\frac{1}{3}$)

Herb divaricately branched; root whitish, woody, simple or branched; stems full of pith, obscurely ribbed, glabrous; basal

leaves simple to bipinnate, with obovate segments and small sharp cartilaginous teeth (A); stem-leaves cut into very narrow segments, sharply toothed, divided from the top of the broad basal sheath with very narrowly membranous margins; primary involucre with numerous rays and several deeply 3-lobed linear bracts; secondary umbels with a few very narrow undivided bracts longer than the pedicels; rays of primary umbels scabrid; flowers (B, ×3) white; petals equal-sized, obovate with deeply inflexed tips; fruit (C, ×3) ellipsoid, each half with 5 ribs (family *Umbelliferae*).

An alien from south Europe, in fields, on ballast heaps, and other waste places.

A strong-growing perennial herb up to 3½ ft. high and usually in masses; basal leaves (D, $\times\frac{1}{8}$) on very long stalks, widely ovate-cordate, the largest up to about 8 in. diam., coarsely but bluntly triangular-toothed, softly pubescent on both surfaces especially on the nerves below, several main nerves radiating from the base; stem-leaves opposite, shortly stalked, the uppermost becoming sessile and provided with a pair of smaller lateral leaflets near the base, connected across the stem and the rim with woolly margins; uppermost leaves becoming bract-like and deeply cut; flowers (A, ×1) numerous in a dense terminal corymb, becoming quite lax in fruit; bracteoles linear, woolly at the base; ovary inferior, crowned by a minute calyx whilst in flower but which in fruit expands into a pappus-like parachute; corolla pink; stamens (B, ×4) 3; fruit (C, ×2) like a ribbed achene of the family *Compositae* and with a pappus-like crown as described above (family *Valerianaceae*).

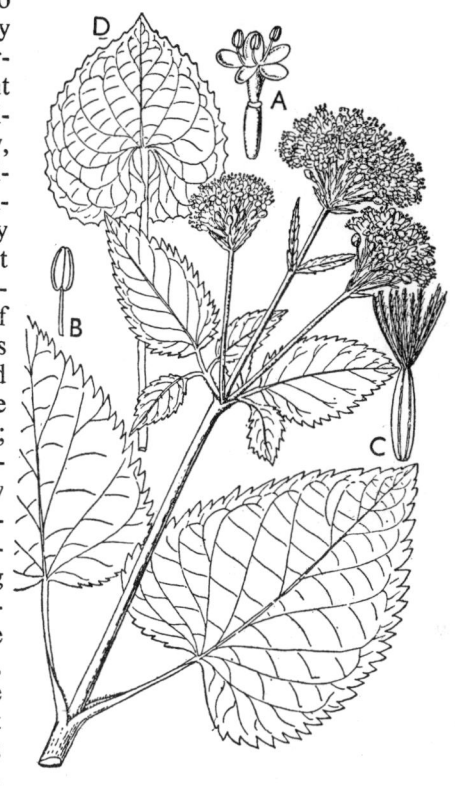

A native of the Pyrenees mountains which has become thoroughly naturalized in several localities, especially in southern and central Scotland.

VALERIAN
Valeriana officinalis L. ($\times \frac{1}{2}$)

Perennial with a short rootstock, giving off off-shoots (stolons); basal leaves soon withering, on long deeply grooved stalks, pinnate with about 5 pairs of leaflets and an end leaflet; middle pair of leaflets the largest, all sessile and more or less ovate-lanceolate, with coarse ascending blunt teeth, coarsely nerved below and slightly hairy on the nerves; stem-leaves without stalks, pinnate with about 4–6 pairs of narrow leaflets, gradually smaller upwards and becoming diminutive below the branches of the inflorescence (collection of flowers); bracts below the flowers very narrow; flowers (A, $\times$ 3) arranged in 3-forked loose clusters (cymes), the middle flower the oldest in each ultimate cluster; calyx above the ovary, very small in the flowering stage and inrolled like the fingers of a clenched fist, opening out in fruit like the rays of a parachute, the rays with slender side hairs (B, $\times$ 3); corolla pale pink or nearly white, of 5 united petals, the tube slightly saccate at the base; stamens 3, with rounded anthers raised above the corolla lobes; ovary below the calyx and corolla (inferior), bottle-shaped, 3-locular, but only 1 loculus with a single pendulous ovule, the others empty; fruit ribbed, topped with feather-like hairs, by means of which it floats in the wind (synonym *Valeriana sambucifolia* Mikan f.) (family *Valerianaceae*).

The small pouch nearly at the base of the corolla-tube conceals the nectar; the flowers are fragrant, and 5 purple lines serve as nectar-guides to insects. The anthers open before the stigmas are receptive, and project beyond them. Later the stigmas reach nearly the same level, and are pollinated by insects from younger flowers, the anthers of the same flower then curving outwards.

Besides the introduced species shown in fig. 486, there is another native species, *Valeriana dioica* L., with the lower leaves quite entire, the upper only being pinnatifid and with dioecious flowers.

Plants of this genus have mostly a very bitter taste and peculiar smell, especially when dry, and luring to cats.

577

A low often very much branched annual, repeatedly branched into two divisions; stems (A, $\times 1\frac{1}{4}$) slightly angular, minutely bristly

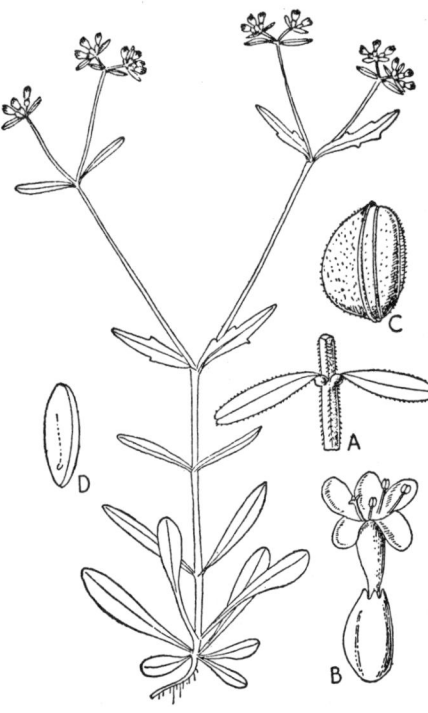

on the angles; leaves opposite, the lowermost rather spoon-shaped, the upper ones oblong-linear to linear, rounded at the apex, 1-nerved, shortly bristly on the margins, especially towards the base; flowers (B, $\times 12$) clustered at the ends of the ultimate branches, often a sessile middle flower already in fruit when the remainder are blooming; bracts similar in shape to the leaves but much smaller; calyx united to the ovary, divided into 5 very small teeth; corolla bluish white, very small, with a short slender tube and 5 equal spreading lobes; stamens 3, exserted from the corolla-tube; ovary inferior, grooved; style with a 3-lobed stigma exserted from the corolla-tube; fruit (C, $\times 5$) small and nut-like, ribbed lengthwise and with a groove on one side, minutely hairy, 1-seeded, with 2 empty loculi; seed (D, $\times 5$) flattened on one side (family *Valerianaceae*). Synonym *V. olitoria* Poll.

A very small plant compared with its tall relative, the Common Valerian, *Valeriana officinalis*, which is a perennial, and the calyx grows out into a feathery pappus-like structure. Tiny drops of nectar are secreted at the base of the expanded part of the corolla-tube. The three stamens mature at the same time as the stigmas and automatic self-pollination occurs if cross-pollination is not effected by insects. As the common name implies the plant is sometimes used as a salad.

Perennial strong-growing glaucous-green (covered with 'bloom') herb up to 2½ ft. high, glabrous; leaves opposite, in 2 ranks, the lower narrowed a little at the base and ovate-lanceolate, about 5 in. long and 2 in. broad, the others quite sessile and broadly ovate and pointed, entire or slightly toothed, with several nerves radiating from the base; lower bracts leaf-like, upper much reduced; flowers (A, ×2) very numerous in an oblong panicle of cymes, the oldest flowers in the forks of the branches and maturing first into fruit; bud club-shaped (B, ×2); calyx a disk-like ribbed structure; corolla usually deep pink or crimson-red, less commonly white, slender, with a long spur at the base; lobes 5, 1 forming the upper lip and separate from the other 4 and enclosing them in bud; stamen (C, ×4) 1, exserted; style slender; ovary (D, E, ×3) inferior (below the calyx), with a single pendulous ovule; fruiting calyx unrolling and becoming 'a little elegant bell-shaped feathery pappus' (family *Valerianaceae*).

This is a lovely plant commonly met with on old walls, especially in maritime counties; very familiar in Cornwall; naturalized in Britain, and a native of the Mediterranean region. The stamens mature first, the nectar being secreted in the spur at the base of the corolla-tube.

DEVIL'S BIT
Succisa pratensis Moench. ($\times \frac{1}{2}$)

Perennial with a short thick rootstock; stems and leaves thinly clothed with long rather stiff hairs; basal leaves oblanceolate, tapered into long stalks, entire, gradually narrowed to the apex but scarcely acute, up to about 8 in. long and $1\frac{1}{2}$ in. wide, thin, with a faint very loose network of veins; stem leaves opposite, gradually narrowing upwards and becoming linear, the lateral flower-head stalks sometimes with a pair of small bract-like leaves an inch or so below the head; flowers (B, $\times 2\frac{1}{2}$) collected into globose heads surrounded by an involucre of about 2 rows of narrow green bracts; each flower in the head subtended by a narrow bract and a little cup (involucel) with 5 teeth; calyx (E, $\times 5$) on top of the smooth, inferior ovary, deeply 4–5-lobed with sharp black lobes; corolla blue, tubular, the tube hairy, with either 4 or 5 rather unequal-sized lobes; stamens 4, inserted between the lobes, their stalks inflexed in bud, filament attached at the back of the anthers (D, $\times 5$); style slender; fruit girt by the little hairy cup and crowned by the calyx, with a single pendulous seed (family *Dipsacaceae*).

This plant is usually called *Scabiosa succisa* L. in British *Floras* and text books, and may easily be mistaken by the beginner for one of the daisy family, *Compositae*. Its floral structure, however, is very different from that family. Each flower is enclosed at the base by a small calyx-like *involucel*, a like structure never found in *Compositae*, and the anthers are not joined into a tube around the style as they are in the latter family. In addition the ovule, and consequently the seed, hangs from the top of the ovary, whereas in *Compositae*, it is erect from the base. *Succisa pratensis* differs from the other less common members of its genus in having entire leaves and the outer flowers of the head not markedly larger than the others. Nectar is secreted in the smooth narrow base of the corolla-tube, which is lined just above by stiff hairs. The stamens are curved downwards in bud (A, $\times 3$), and when the flower opens straighten up in succession, and their anthers release the pollen and fall off (B and C). After this the style lengthens, and the stigma becomes receptive and cross-pollination is effected by insects.

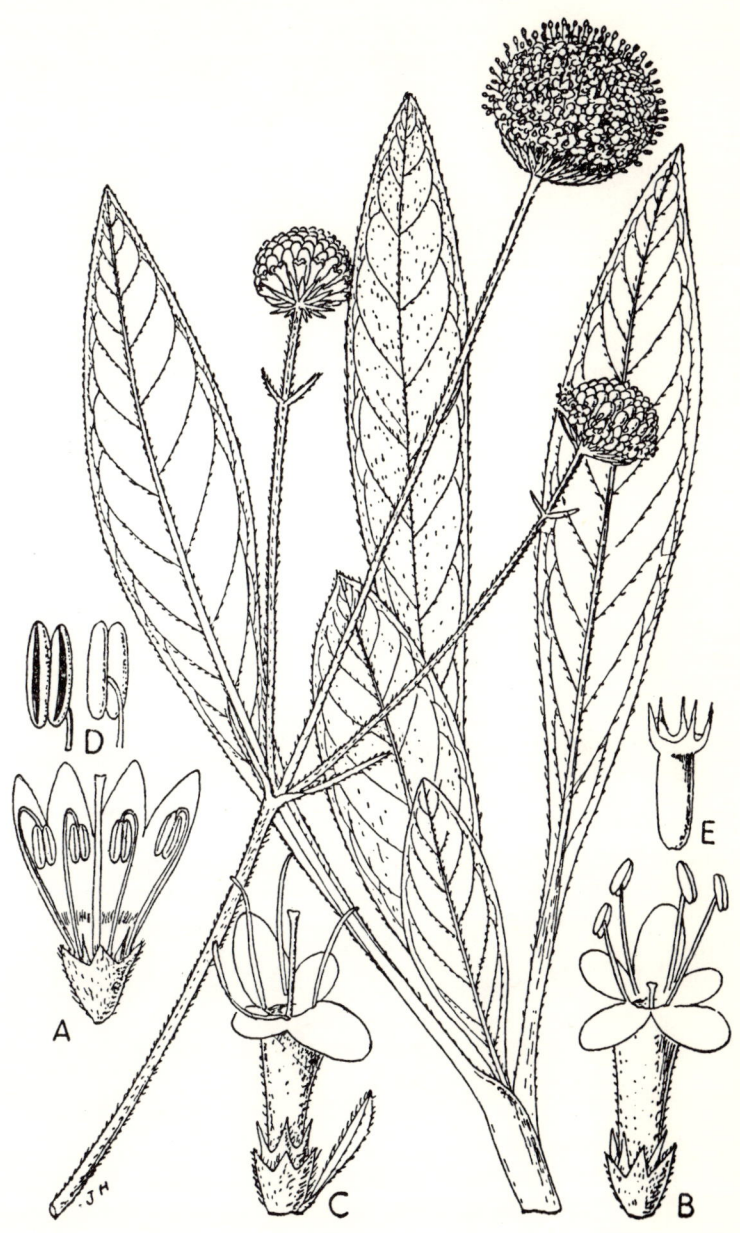

581

FIELD SCABIOUS
Knautia arvensis (L.) Coult. ($\times \frac{2}{3}$)

Perennial, often flowering the first year; stems up to 5 ft. high, clothed with stiff downwardly directed bulbous-based hairs; leaves opposite, connate at the base around the stem, the lower narrowly oblanceolate and usually not lobed, becoming deeply pinnately lobed upwards, gradually forming a pair of lanceolate bracts, all clothed with bristly bulbous-based hairs; flower-heads mostly 3 together on long stalks, the middle stalk the longest and opening first; bracts of the involucre in 2–3 rows, ovate to lanceolate, green, margined with long hairs; flowers (A, × 2) numerous; ovary inferior, 1-locular, with a ciliate rim, above a narrow neck below the short green calyx crowned by about 8 slender bristles (D, × 3); corolla (B, × 3) tubular, pale lilac or blue, that of the outer flowers with larger spreading lobes and more irregular than those towards the middle; stamens 4, long-exserted; anther (C, × 3) attached in the middle, with large reddish pollen grains; ovule (E, × 3) solitary, pendulous (family *Dipsacaceae*).

This is a lovely plant, often still flowering after the corn has been cut. The anthers are a paler blue until they open, when they assume a pale reddish colour on account of the colour of the large pollen grains. The heads are composed of about 50 flowers, the outer ones being larger. Nectar is secreted on the upper part of the ovary, and is protected from rain by the hairs lining the corolla-tube. The stamens mature in turn, after which the anthers drop off and the filaments shrivel. Meanwhile the style has been retained in the mouth of the corolla, and now grows out with the stigma into the position formerly occupied by the anthers. It is of great interest that in order to ensure cross-pollination the stamens of all the flowers in the same head are withered before the styles elongate and the stigmas are receptive. The entire inflorescence is therefore at first in a purely *male* state and then purely *female*.

Field Scabious has several other local names, such as 'Bachelor's Buttons', 'Black-soap', 'Blue-buttons', 'Lady's Cushion', 'Scabridge', and others.

SMALL SCABIOUS
Scabiosa columbaria L. ($\times\frac{1}{3}$)

Erect perennial herb up to about 2 ft. high; rootstock rather woody; stems rounded in section, tough, slightly hairy or glab-

rous; lowermost leaves crowded, spreading, more or less spoon-shaped on long stalks and at most crenately toothed, the re-mainder opposite and becoming bipinnately di-vided into linear segments, all shortly pubescent, the uppermost becoming smaller, entire, and bract-like; shoots usually end-ing in 3 long-stalked flow-er-heads; involucre com-posed of a single row of narrow green bracts usu-ally shorter than the flowers; scales on the receptacle (A, $\times\frac{2}{3}$) linear, hairy; outer flowers fe-male, pale purplish-blue; corolla 5-lobed, larger and more oblique than those of the inner bisexual flowers (B $\times\frac{2}{3}$); ovary (C, $\times 1\frac{1}{2}$) inferior, surrounded by the involucel, the latter expanded into a dry cup-shaped structure, within which are 5 bristle-like calyx-lobes; involucel (D, $\times 2\frac{1}{4}$) enclosing the fruit strongly ribbed (family *Dipsacaceae*).

In dry, mostly chalky pastures, downs, and waste places, flower-ing in summer and early autumn.

Nectar is secreted by the upper surface of the ovary and is stored in the base of the corolla-tube. In the bisexual flowers the stamens mature before the stigmas. The female flowers are most numerous at the beginning of the season.

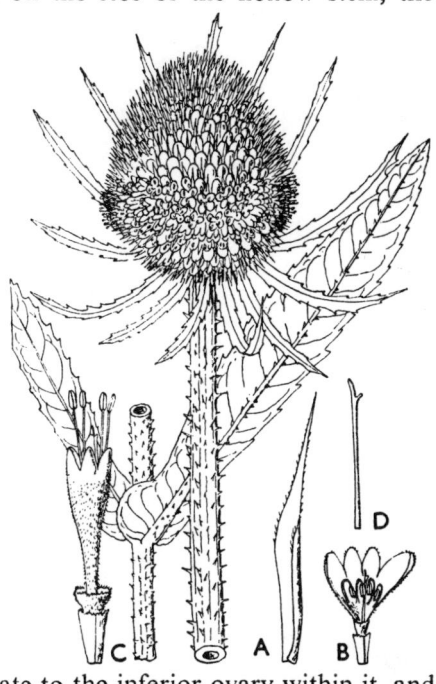

FULLER'S TEASEL

Dipsacus fullonum L. ($\times \frac{1}{3}$)

A strong-growing biennial up to about 5 ft. high, armed with short triangular-shaped prickles on the ribs of the hollow stem, the midrib on the under surface of the leaves and the bracts around the flower-head; leaves opposite, sessile, lanceolate, the lower toothed like a saw (serrate), the bases clasping and meeting around the stem, upper leaves entire; flowers arranged in a very dense oblong-ovoid head bristly all over with very sharply pointed bracts (A, $\times 1$), and surrounded by green narrow prickly toothed bracts, some of these as long as the head itself; bracts spirally arranged and longer than the flowers; each flower girt by a little secondary involucre (involucel) (see fig. C, $\times 10$), which is adnate to the inferior ovary within it, and above this the small cupular calyx on top of the ovary; corolla hairy, 4-lobed, lobes nearly equal; stamens 4, inflexed in bud (B, $\times 1$); style (D, $\times 1$) shortly divided into 2 unequal lobes; fruitlet enclosed by the involucel (synonym *Dipsacus sylvestris* L.) (family *Dipsacaceae*).

This is called 'Fuller's Teasel', the fruiting heads, which bear stiff hooked bracts, being used by woollen cloth-manufacturers to give a 'nap' to their fabrics by raising to the surface some of the finer fibres of the material. So far no mechanical contrivance has been invented to equal the efficiency of this common wild plant, and one may often find fragments of the bracts adhering to certain kinds of cloth. Teasels are grown for the purpose in Yorkshire, but most of the supply comes from France.

Wahlenbergia hederacea (L.) Reichb. ($\times\frac{1}{2}$)

Perennial herb with a small creeping rootstock; stems very weak and thread-like, creeping, glabrous; leaves alternate on slightly winged stalks, rounded, cordate at the base, at most $\frac{1}{2}$ in. diam., coarsely angular-toothed, not hairy, the nerves radiating from the base; flowers (A, $\times 2$) few, axillary and terminal, erect on thread-like stalks up to 2 in. long; calyx-lobes 5, subulate, glabrous; corolla pale blue, bell-shaped, about $\frac{1}{2}$ in. long, glabrous; lobes 5, ovate, spreading; stamens (B, $\times 7$) 5, free from and included in the tube; filaments minutely hairy; ovary inferior, 3-locular; style (C, $\times 3\frac{1}{2}$) 3-lobed, hairy; ovules several on axile placentas; capsule (D,

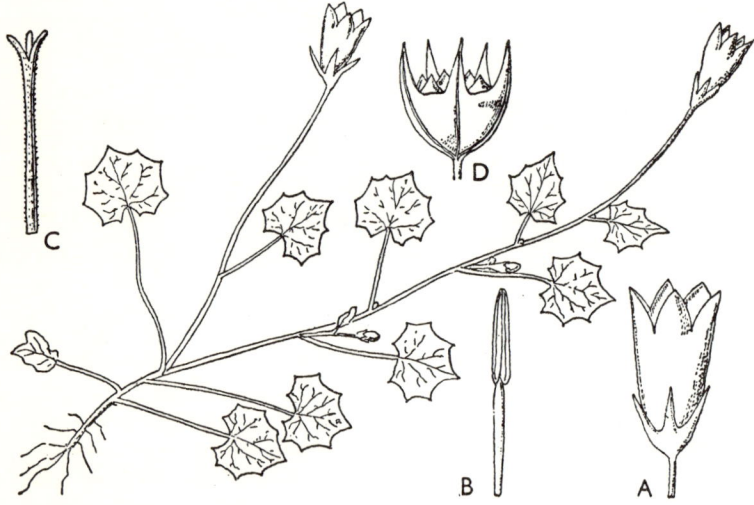

$\times 2\frac{1}{2}$) opening by 3 valves at the top between the calyx-lobes (family *Campanulaceae*).

Grows in moist shady fields and woods, chiefly along rills and banks; flowers in summer and autumn.

The flowers are odourless, pale blue, and marked by darker veins. Nectar is secreted in a fleshy disk on the ovary and surrounding the base of the style, which is hairy. From the inner side the pollen is swept out by the hairs of the style. The anthers wither after the pollen has been shed, but the filaments persist as nectar covers. If cross-pollination fails, self-pollination is possible by the stigmas bending so far back that they touch the pollen clinging to their own style.

A perennial with a slender creeping rootstock; basal stems erect or ascending, but rather weak, up to 1½ ft. or rarely 2 ft. high;

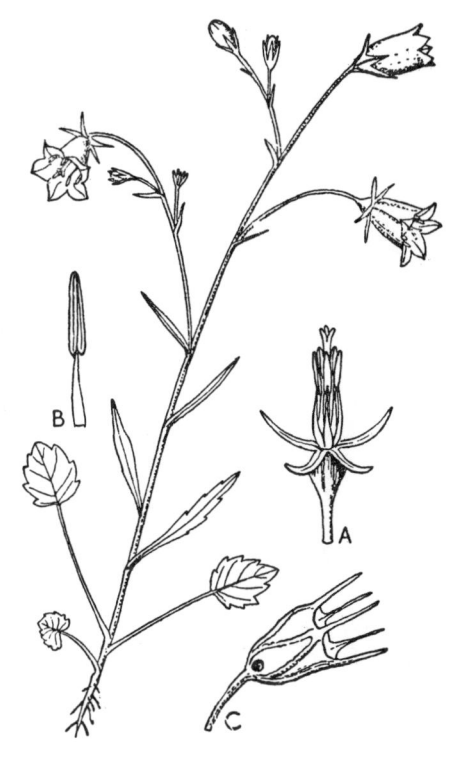

leaves rounded, heart-shaped at the base, often withering and disappearing by flowering time, undulately toothed on the margin; stem-leaves alternate, narrowly lanceolate to linear, only the lowermost a little broader, entire or rarely with a few obscure teeth, glabrous; flowers blue, few, nodding, in a loose terminal raceme or panicle or sometimes solitary; calyx-lobes 5, on top of the ovary, linear, not as long as the corolla-tube, the latter bell-shaped and about ½ in. long, with 5 broad short lobes; stamens (B, × 2) 5, inserted within the base of the corolla; anthers included in the tube, free from each other; ovary inferior; style nearly as long as the corolla, divided into 3 short stigmas; capsule (C, × ½) ovoid or globose, pendulous, opening by pores near the base (A, flower with corolla removed, × 1½) (family *Campanulaceae*).

The Harebell, or the Bluebell of Scotland and northern England is very widely distributed in north temperate regions, right from the Mediterranean to the Arctic Circle, sometimes at great elevations, and it is common in the northern United States of America and in Canada. Young botanists are often puzzled by the specific name, as the rounded basal leaves to which it applies have often quite disappeared at flowering time.

Campanula patula L. ($\times\frac{1}{3}$)

Erect slender annual or biennial herb up to 2 ft. high; stems (A, $\times\frac{1}{3}$) sparingly clothed with longish spreading hairs on the distinct

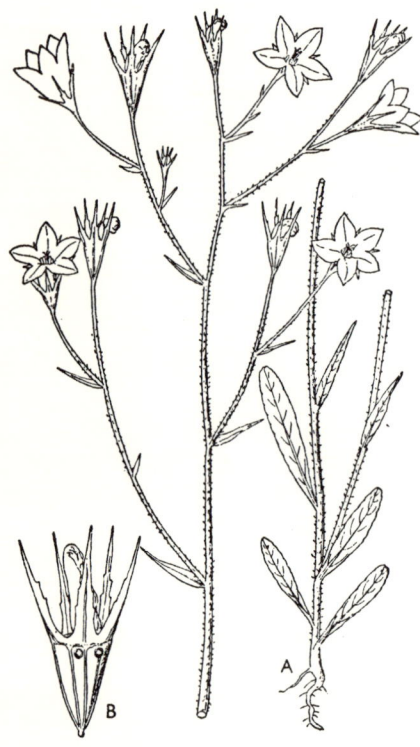

ribs; lower leaves narrowed to the base but not stalked, oblanceolate, up to about 2 in. long, distantly crenulate on the margin, clothed with a few spreading hairs; flowers in a loose panicle, i.e. the branchlets of the inflorescence bear 2–3 flowers, one of which quickly develops into fruit; calyx-lobes 5, linear, with 1 or 2 teeth on each side; corolla bell-shaped, purplish-blue, very open, nearly 1 in. long, with 5 spreading lobes; stamens 5, anthers linear; style hairy, 3-lobed; ovary inferior (below the calyx), prominently 10-ribbed; capsule (B, $\times1\frac{1}{2}$) remaining erect and opening by holes near the top below the calyx (family *Campanulaceae*).

Grows under hedges, on banksides, and among bushes; Europe, generally and widely spread into Asia; flowers in summer and autumn.

In this book we have illustrated as many as seven out of the nine native species of *Campanula*, so their identification should not present much difficulty. The two not shown are *C. persicifolia* L., an introduced species well established on some commons and in open woods, with narrow radical leaves and few suberect very widely bell-shaped flowers; and *C. medium* L., another casual species, very hispid, the calyx with broad cordate reflexed appendages between the teeth, and five instead of the usually three stigmas.

Campanula rapunculus L. ($\times\frac{1}{3}$)

Erect, stiff-growing perennial, with a thick upright tuber-like root (A, $\times\frac{1}{3}$); stems more or less clothed on the ribs with spreading hairs; basal leaves stalked, oblong-oblanceolate, crenate, about $2\frac{1}{2}$ in. long and $\frac{1}{2}$ in. broad, thinly hairy; stem-leaves sessile, oblanceolate, more or less rounded at the apex, up to 3 in. long and $\frac{3}{4}$ in. broad, entire or slightly toothed, glabrous or slightly hairy; flowers numerous in long racemes arising from the upper leaf-axils, each individual stalk with a narrow leafy bract at the base; corolla blue, bell-shaped, about $\frac{3}{4}$ in. long, with 5 ovate-lanceolate lobes; stamens 5, anthers linear; style hairy, 3-lobed; ovary inferior (below the calyx), 10-ribbed; capsule (B, $\times1\frac{1}{4}$) erect, opening by holes well below the top under the calyx (family *Campanulaceae*).

Found on banksides, roadsides, and in open fields, sometimes an escape from cultivation and an occasional weed in gardens; the tuber was formerly blanched like celery and eaten raw in salads or boiled like *Asparagus*; flowers in summer.

Towards the end of flowering, the style-branches roll back spirally and come in contact with the pollen brushed out by the hairs, and automatic self-pollination may then take place.

Campanula latifolia L. ($\times\frac{1}{3}$)

Perennial herb with woody rootstock; stems up to 4 ft. high, erect, unbranched, glabrous or slightly hairy; basal leaves on long stalks,

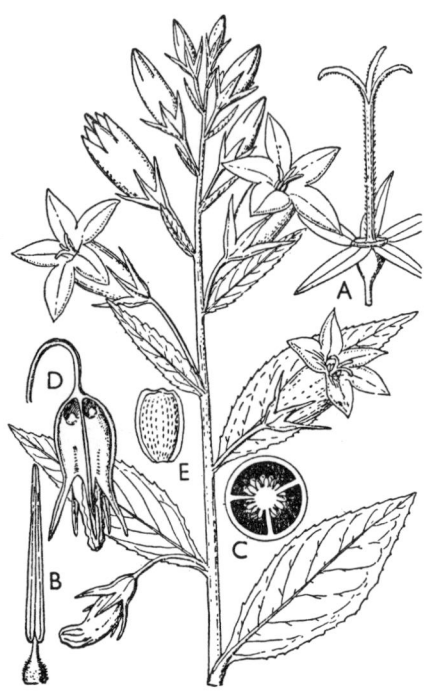

ovate-triangular, cordate at the base; stem-leaves alternate, lower narrowed into a stalk-like base, becoming sessile upwards, ovate-lanceolate, pointed, 3–5 in. long and 1–1½ in. broad, iregularly toothed, minutely hairy above, mostly hairy on the nerves below; lateral nerves about 5–6 pairs; flowers solitary in the upper leaf-axils, their stalks up to 1 in. long and with a pair of narrow bracteoles near the middle; calyx-lobes (A, $\times\frac{2}{3}$) 5, lanceolate, very acute, about ¾ in. long, slightly toothed on the margin; corolla bell-shaped, 1½–2 in. long; lobes 5; ovate-lanceolate, acute; stamens (B, $\times 1$) 5, free from but included in the corolla-tube; filaments swollen and hairy at the base, anthers ⅔ in. long, facing inwards; ovary inferior, 3-locular, with numerous ovules on axile placentas (C, $\times 2$); fruit (D, $\times\frac{2}{5}$) pendulous, opening by holes at the (actual) base; seeds (E, $\times 3$) flattened, with thin margins (family *Campanulaceae*).

Fairly common in central and southern Scotland and northern England; but rare in the south; widely distributed in Europe and Asia; flowers in summer; referred to by Sir Walter Scott as the 'throat-wort with its azure bell, adorning the banks of the Greta river'.

Perennial herb up to about 3 ft. high; stems erect, ribbed, with stiff hairs here and there on the ribs; lower leaves on very long stalks, the other leaves gradually becoming nearly sessile; blade of lower leaves (A, ×⅓) ovate-triangular, deeply cordate at the base, lobulate or very coarsely toothed on the margin, up to about 5 in. long and 2½ in. broad, thin, sparingly bristly-hairy mainly on the nerves on both surfaces; flowers in the axils of the upper leaves, 2 or 3 together, becoming solitary at the top; ovary inferior, 3-locular, bristly-hairy; calyx-lobes (B, ×1) 5, bristly-hairy; corolla 1–1½ in. long, blue-purple or rarely white, the triangular-ovate lobes with a few bristles on the midrib outside; stamens (C, ×1½) 5, free from the corolla but included; ovary (D, ×2)

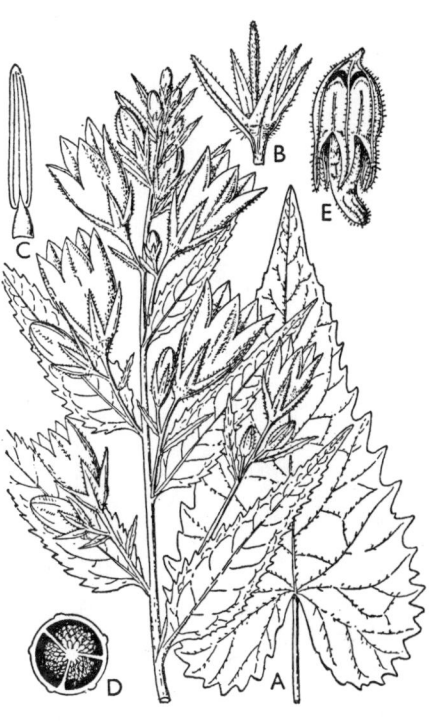

3-locular; style densely hairy outside divided into 3 lobes; capsule pendulous (E, ×⅓) opening by 3 large holes near the base (family *Campanulaceae*).

Grows in woods, flowering from July to September. The style is at first columnar and pushes through the cylinder of anthers, brushing out the pollen before the 3 stigmas open out and become receptive. If cross-pollination fails, self-pollination may take place by the style-branches recurving, when the stigmas may touch the pollen still held by the hairs. Nectar is secreted in a yellow fleshy disk on top of the ovary and is protected by the broad short filaments. The pollen grains are yellow, spheroidal, and beset with spine-like tubercles.

Rootstock creeping, with underground stolons; stems usually unbranched, up to 2½ ft. high, slightly ribbed and with very short 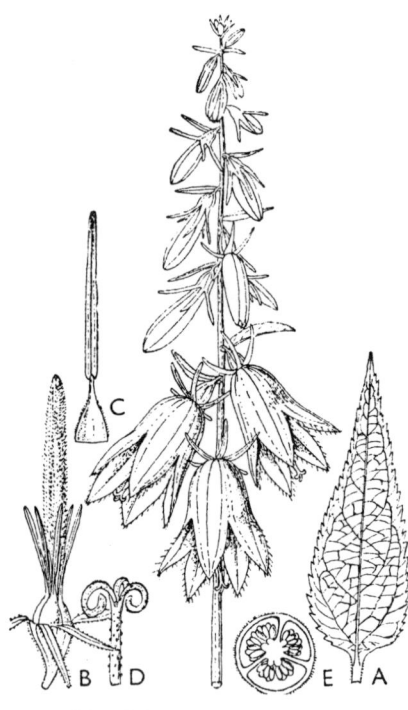 deflexed hairs; leaves (A, × ½) alternate, broadly lanceolate, apex acute, base rounded into the broad petiole, irregularly serrate, nearly glabrous, the lower on long petioles, gradually becoming sessile upwards and merging into bracts; flowers pendulous in a slender leafy raceme, very shortly stalked, spreading or pendulous; bracts gradually decreasing upwards, becoming linear; calyxlobes (B, × 3) linear, recurved, ½ in. long; corolla bright blue, 1 in. long, lobes margined with long white hairs; stamens (C, × 6) 5, anthers opening before the stigmas are receptive; style (B, × 3) very hairy outside, and covered with pollen, with 3 recurved stigmas (D, × 3); ovary inferior (below the calyx-lobes), 3-locular, with numerous ovules in each chamber (E, ×4); fruit opening by pores at the base (family *Campanulaceae*).

This species is doubtfully native, as it is usually found in cultivated fields, on railway banks, and in waste land. It is widely distributed as far east as the Caucasus.

The densely hairy style of the pendulous flowers pushes out the pollen from the anther 'cylinder', after which the stamens shrivel and the stigmas spread out and become recurved. The little drops of nectar on top of the inferior ovary are covered by the expanded bases of the filaments, which are fringed with hairs.

Campanula glomerata L. ($\times \frac{2}{5}$)

Perennial with short creeping rootstock; stems erect, up to 15 in.
high, flushed with crimson, very slightly hairy; leaves alternate,
lower (A, $\times \frac{2}{5}$) long-
stalked, and cordate at
the base, upper sessile,
ovate-lanceolate, rounded
at the base, acute at apex,
doubly crenulate, softly
hairy on both surfaces;
flowers (C, $\times \frac{4}{5}$) solitary
or paired in the upper
leaf-axils and also in a
terminal bunch, remain-
ing vertical or spreading
horizontally; bracts 3 or
4 to each flower, very
similar to the linear erect
calyx-lobes; corolla blue,
5-lobed, about 1 in. long;
lobes not hairy on the
margins; stamens (D,
$\times$ 3) 5, opening before the
stigmas; style (B, $\times$ 0)
covered with short hairs,
which soon fall off, the
3 stigmas at length re-
curved; ovary (E, $\times$ 5) 3-

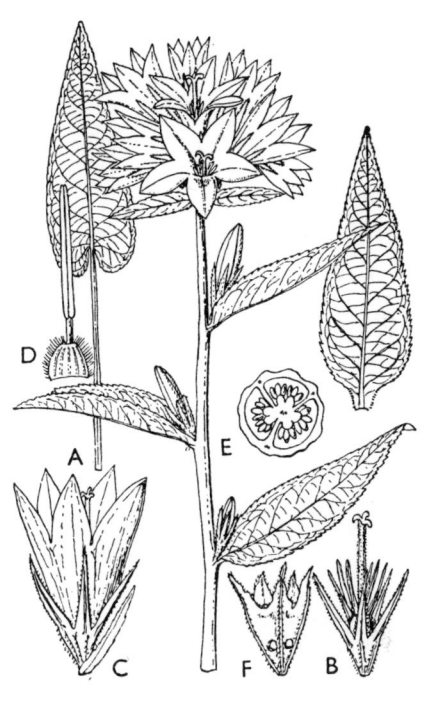

locular, with numerous ovules on axile placentas; fruit (F, $\times$ 3)
opening by pores near the base (family *Campanulaceae*).

In the young flower the very hairy style is closely embraced by
the long anthers, which open on the inside (introrse). When the
flower opens the pollen is carried upwards by the hairs as the style
elongates. Eventually the hairs fall away from the style, leaving it
quite smooth, and the stigmas become receptive to pollen carried
by insects from younger flowers.

This species shows in a striking manner how readily a head of
flowers may be evolved by the crowding together of the upper
leaves. In a similar way the dense head of flowers surrounded by
crowded bracts has, no doubt, been brought about in the related
and more advanced Daisy family, *Compositae*.

Erect or decumbent annual clothed all over with very short setulose hairs; leaves alternate, sessile, oblong, about ½ in. long, with
wavy or slightly toothed
margins; no stipules; flowers (A, ×1¼) sessile in the
axils of the upper leaves
and very soon developing
into fruit; calyx at the top
of the long triangular
ovary, lobes 5, linear to
lanceolate, setulose; co-
rolla blue, as long as the
calyx-lobes or shorter,
tube very short, the 5
lobes spreading widely
and tipped with short
hairs; stamens (B, ×3) 5,
erect, free, anthers acute;
ovary inferior, elongated,
3-locular, 3-angled; style
(C, ×3) erect, 3-fid at the
apex; ovules numerous
on axile placentas; fruit
(D, ×1¼) an elongated
ribbed and 3-sided cap-
sule opening by 3 holes
(F, ×3) below the calyx;
seeds (E, ×3) ellipsoid,
brown, shining brightly
(family *Campanulaceae*). –
Synonym *Specularia hy-
brida* (L.) A. DC.

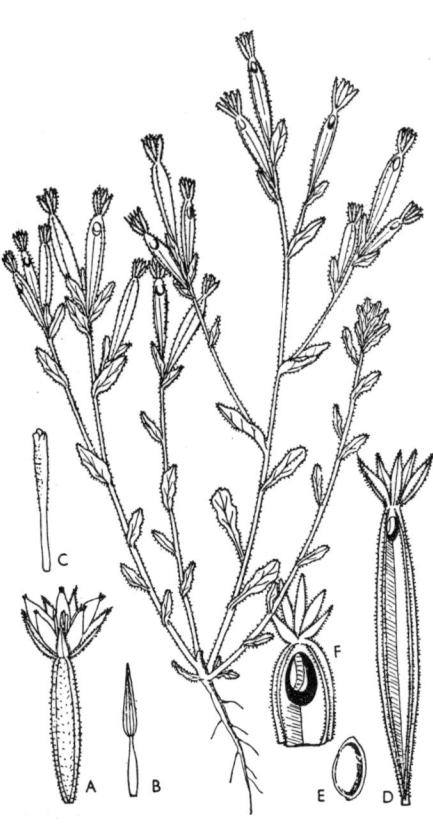

A weed mostly in cornfields; native of Europe, north Africa,
and western Asia. The specimen drawn is in fruit which develops
very quickly and by which it may be readily recognized, the holes
at the top from which the bright shining seeds escape being very
conspicuous.

The flowers open each morning and close again in the evening.

Phyteuma tenerum R. Schulz (× ½)

Perennial with slender creeping rootstock; stems erect or arching, undivided, slightly ribbed, glabrous; basal leaves on long slender stalks, lanceolate, rounded to slightly cordate at the base, about 1½ in. long and ⅔ in. broad, finely crenate, glabrous; stem leaves becoming sessile upwards and narrower to linear and bractlike, the uppermost few forming a leafy involucre below the globose bunch of 15–30 deep blue flowers (B, ×3), these bracts fringed with white hairs; bract (A, ×5) below each flower ovate-lanceolate, pilose; calyx-lobes 5, triangular, shortly hairy; corolla deeply split into 5 long linear segments, cylindric and curved in bud whilst the segments are clinging together; stamens (C, ×5) 5, free from each other, filaments slender, anthers very narrow and long; ovary inferior, usually 3-locular; style hairy, 3-lobed at the apex; ovules numerous on axile placentas; fruit a capsule crowned by the calyx, bursting at the sides (family *Campanulaceae*). Synonym *P. orbiculare* L.

Found only in the chalk downs in southern England, flowering during the summer; extends to central and southern Europe. A second species, *Phyteuma spicatum* L., occurs in Britain, distinguished by its oblong yellowish-white flower-heads and broader leaves.

Jasione montana L. (×$\frac{1}{2}$)

Annual or biennial, up to about 1 ft. high; stems branched from the base, loosely clothed with white bristly hairs; leaves alternate,

sessile, narrowly oblong-lanceolate, with wavy margins, loosely covered with long bristly hairs on both surfaces; flowers (B, × 4) on short stalks and collected into a small rounded head on a long peduncle, surrounded by 2 or 3 rows of broadly ovate-triangular bracts (A, × 2), toothed on the margin and clothed with a few bristly hairs; calyx-tube united with the ovary, divided into 5 narrow lobes; corolla pale blue, deeply divided into 5 very narrow segments; stamens (C, × 4) 5; anthers united at the base into a ring, with very broad filaments fringed with hairs; ovary below the calyx (inferior); style slender; fruit a capsule opening at the top by 2 valves; seeds very small, shining (family *Campanulaceae*).

In heathy pastures mainly in light soils, flowering from June to September; widely distributed in Europe and as far east as the Caucasus.

In well-grown specimens a head contains 100–200 blue flowers, the corollas of which are divided nearly to their base into 5 narrow lobes, so that the nectar secreted on the top of the ovary is accessible to insects of the most varied kind. In a young stage the end of the style is covered with closely set erect hairs as in *Campanula*, and these receive the pollen, which is released in the bud-stage and pushed out by the growing style. After that the stigmas open out and become receptive to pollen.

Perennial herb with simple or little-branched stems up to $1\frac{1}{2}$ ft. high, and with a short creeping rootstock; stems glabrous, bearing in the lower part almost sessile oblong or oblong-lanceolate thin leaves rather irregularly toothed on the margin and 2–3 in. long; flowers in a terminal raceme with leafy narrow bracts becoming even narrower upwards; flowerstalks about as long as the ovary and calyxlobes combined, the latter (A, $\times 2$) 5, narrow, shortly hairy; corolla purplish-blue, 2-lipped, the upper lip 2-lobed, the lower 3-lobed, about $\frac{1}{2}$ in. long; stamens (B, $\times 2$) 5, inserted on the receptacle, united into a column, the anthers (C, $\times 5$) with hairy tips and closely surrounding the head-like stigma; ovary below the calyx (inferior); fruit a capsule, erect (family *Lobeliaceae*).

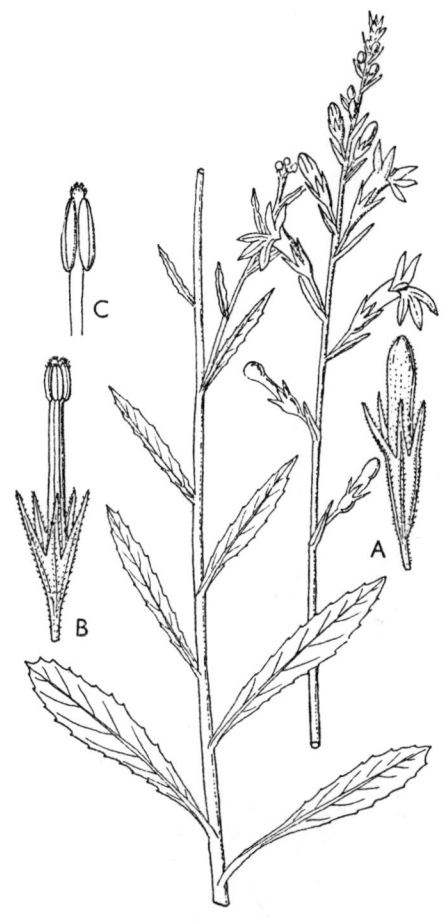

A very rare species on moist heaths and found only in a few southwest counties, flowering in late summer and autumn; confined to western Europe.

WATER LOBELIA
Lobelia dortmanna L. ($\times\frac{1}{2}$)

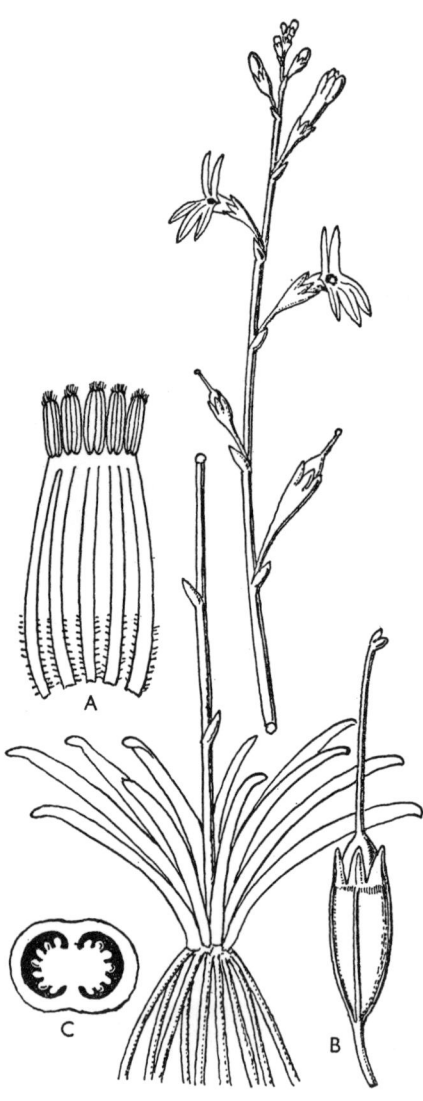

An aquatic perennial herb with a dense bunch of pale yellow, rather thick roots; leaves in a dense basal tuft at the bottom of the water, cylindric and hollow with curved tips, up to 3 in. long; flowering stems erect and unbranched, bearing 2 or 3 small bracts and a small number of flowers in the upper part raised above the water level; calyx of 5 narrow lobes on top of the ovary; corolla pale-blue or whitish, of 5 united petals, about $\frac{3}{4}$ in. long, 2-lipped, the upper lip deeply 2-lobed, the lower 3-lobed; stamens (A, ×5) 5, united at the base and apex, the anthers with a short tuft of hairs at the top; ovary (B, ×5) inferior, 2-locular, with numerous ovules on axile placentas (C, ×8); fruit a capsule (family *Lobeliaceae*).

A very interesting species growing in the shallow parts of lakes in Scotland and Eire, and in the western parts of Britain south to south Wales; flowers during the summer; confined to western Europe.

Annual with purplish-green stems up to 2 ft. high, covered with a few short, slightly hooked hairs; leaves opposite, touching each other at the base, not divided, narrowly lanceo-
late, rather distantly and
sharply toothed, glabrous;
upper leaves alternate;
flower-heads nodding,
surrounded by a whorl of
about 3–6 leaf-like bracts
(A, $\times \frac{2}{3}$) with short stiff
hairs on the margins;
smaller involucral bracts
(B, $\times 1$) in two rows, overlapping, green, closely
streaked with dull brown,
the outer oblong-ovate;
flowers (C, $\times 2$) all tubular or rarely a few short
broad rays, each sub-
tended by a narrow bract-
scale (C, $\times 2$); corolla dull
yellow, 5-lobed; anthers
(D, $\times 4$) with barren tips
and rounded bases; stig-
mas (E, $\times 4$) blunt, with
cone-like tips; achene (C,
$\times 2$) often with 3–4 bristles

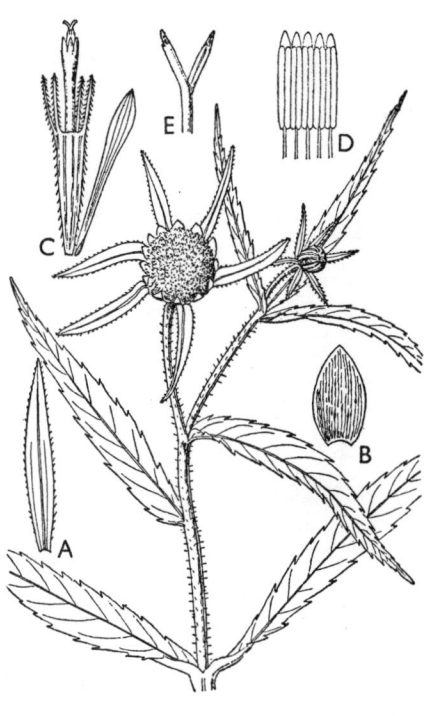

at the top with reflexed barbs (family *Compositae*).

Easily distinguished from *B. tripartita* (fig. 508) by the unlobed leaves with more numerous teeth; in wet ditches and marshes, flowering in late summer and autumn.

There are three forms, (a) *discoidea*, without ray flowers, (b) *radiata*, with large ray-flowers, and (c) *minima*, a low plant with usually only 1 small flower-head.

Bidens tripartita L. ($\times \frac{1}{2}$)

Annual with purplish nearly glabrous stems; leaves opposite, with a broad sheathing base, divided into 3 main segments, these lanceolate and lobulate or with a few sharp teeth; broadened base ciliate, otherwise glabrous; heads more or less erect (not nodding), surrounded by a whorl of unequal-sized bracts similar to the foliage leaves, but much smaller; smaller involucral bracts in 2 rows, closely overlapping the outer (A, $\times$ 2), broader and nearly black,

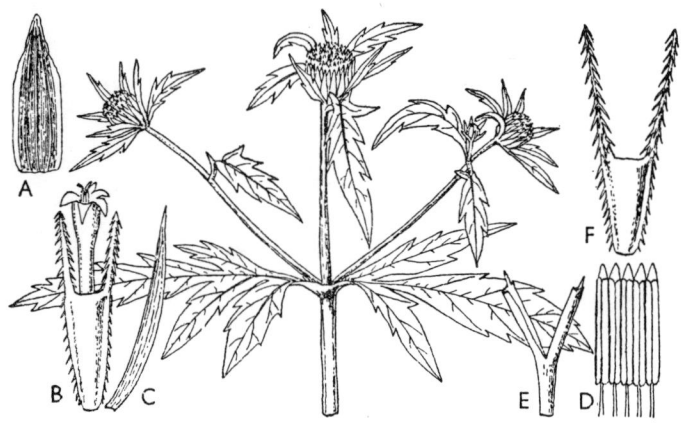

shining; flowers (B, $\times$ 4) all tubular, or sometimes a few radiate, each subtended by a long membranous bract-scale (C, $\times$ 4) corolla dull yellow-brown, 5-lobed; anthers (D, $\times$ 6) with barren tips and rounded bases; stigmas (E, $\times$ 6) blunt and with a short sharp appendage; achene (F, $\times$4) flattened, margined with reflexed barbs and with 2 bristles at the top also with reflexed barbs (family *Compositae*).

There are 2 species of Bidens in Britain, the one shown in the drawing and *B. cernua* L. (fig. 507). In the latter the leaves are lanceolate and toothed, but not divided as they are in *B. tripartita*. Both species grow in wet ditches and marshy places and flower during summer and autumn. The achenes attach themselves to animals by means of the barbed bristles which represent the calyx.

Galinsoga parviflora Cav. ($\times \frac{2}{5}$)

A rather strong-growing annual, an escape from cultivation and now naturalized in many places; stems smooth, branched; leaves opposite, the lower stalked, ovate, acute, 3-nerved from the base, not hairy, bluntly toothed (crenate-dentate); upper leaves becoming sessile and much narrower; flower-heads (A, $\times 1\frac{3}{4}$) few, small, with a small green involucre or bracts, the larger bracts opposite the white shortly tubular 3-lobed ray-flowers (B, $\times 3$); disk-flowers (C, $\times 3$) yellow; ovary of ray (female) flowers slightly pubescent, becoming black when ripe; corolla of the disk-flowers (D, $\times 4$) 5-lobed, hairy; style branches (E, $\times 12$) of these blunt at the ends; ripe achenes (F, $\times 3$) topped by

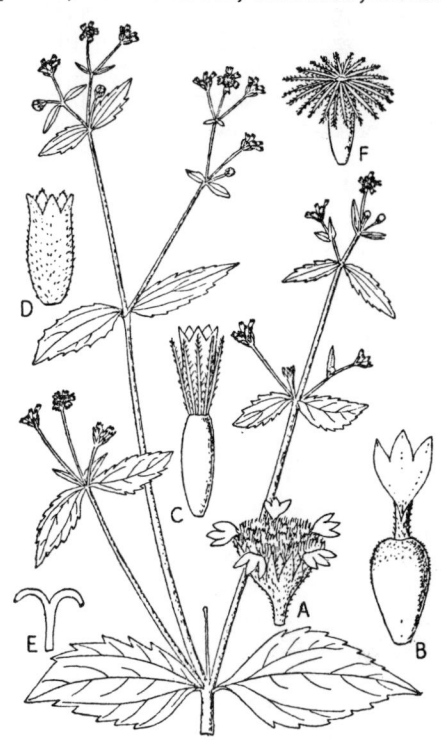

a spreading series of flat hairy bristles (family *Compositae*).

This is a very interesting alien plant. It was introduced from Peru into the Royal Gardens at Kew in 1796, and was first recorded as having escaped and become naturalized between Kew and East Sheen in 1863, hence 'Kew Weed', and it soon grew in the neighbourhood as common as groundsel and spread rapidly. Local people were naturally curious as to the name, and converted it into 'Gallant Soldiers', and it even became 'Soldiers of the Queen'. The plant was also introduced into the Paris Botanic Garden in 1785, and from these two sources it has spread all over Europe. The number of ray flowers is reduced to five, which causes the head to look like a single flower with five petals (see also notes under fig. 532).

Petasites hybridus (L.) Gaertn. (A, male plant, × ½; B, part of female inflorescence in fruit, × ½)

Perennial with thick creeping rootstock and thickish roots; leaves appearing with or just after flowering time, more or less orbicular, becoming large and resembling those of rhubarb, widely cordate at the base, lobulate and toothed (dentate) on the margin, coated with whitish cobwebby hairs especially below, and easily rubbed off; nerves radiating from the base; flower-heads pink to purple, unisexual, the male and female on separate plants (dioecious), arranged in a large spike-like raceme up to 1 ft. long; stalks of the male up to ¾ in. long, with a narrow bract nearly as long as the base; bracts of the involucre in 2 rows, fairly broad, with 3–5 nerves on the back; male flowers (C, × 3) all tubular, with fertile anthers (D, × 6) rounded at both ends; ovary sterile, and pappus very small; female heads (B, × ½) more widely bell-shaped than the male, and with the stalks in fruit becoming longer than those of the male; bracts nearly in a single row, linear-oblong, rounded at the apex, conspicuously 3-nerved; flowers (E, × 2) very narrowly tubular, 4-toothed at the apex; style (F, × 5) shortly 2-lobed at the apex; fruits (achenes) slightly angular, smooth, crowned by a white almost smooth pappus nearly twice as long as the corolla (family *Compositae*).

This plant grows in damp sandy places and on clay, usually near streams, and when in leaf very much resembles rhubarb. It has sometimes been placed in the same genus as the Coltsfoot (fig. 511) but is quite distinct by its flower-heads, being usually quite unisexual and arranged in large spike-like racemes on different plants. Sometimes the male flower-heads have a few thread-like female flowers around the outside, and occasionally the females have a few males in the middle, which tends to show that this plant has descended from a stock in which the flowers were bisexual. The large leaves of the Butterbur cause a dense shade all through the summer, and for this reason few plants are able to grow amongst it. It is rare north of the Forth and Clyde. A closely related cultivated and sometimes naturalized species is the Winter Heliotrope, *Petasites fragrans* L., but with much smaller leaves and fragrant flowers. This flowers earlier than the Butterbur, sometimes in favourable seasons just after Christmas.

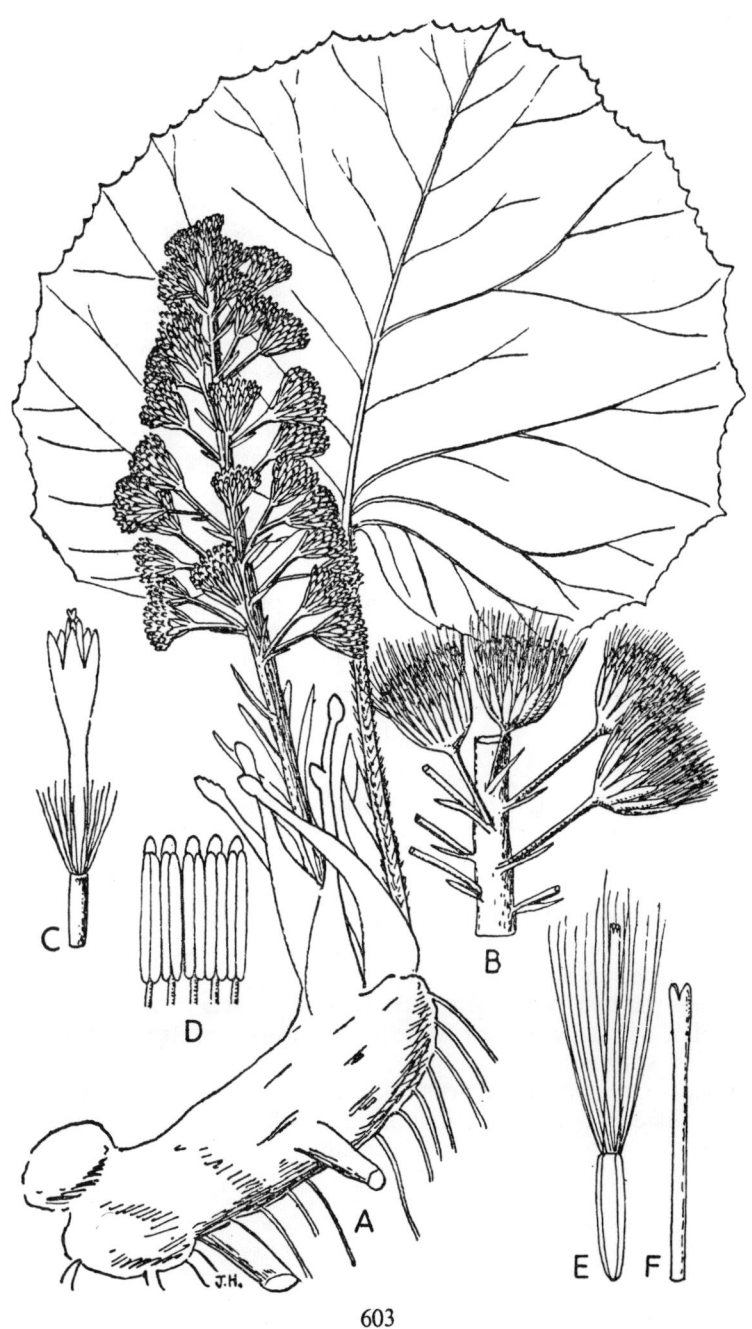

Perennial with creeping rootstock; leaves appearing on separate shoots after the flowers, long-stalked, orbicular in outline, deeply

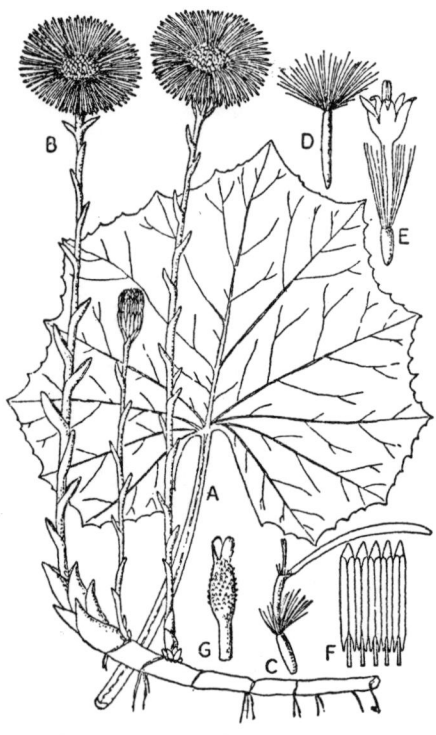

cordate at the base, and with radiating nerves which are forked and branched towards the short toothed (dentate) lobes, leathery, covered below with white cobwebby hairs; flowering stems with short bract-like leaves clasping them; bracts about 20 in one or two rows, minutely hairy outside; ray-flowers (C, × 1½) female, golden yellow, in three or four rows and developing into the achenes ('seeds') surmounted by a light pappus; achenes (D, × 3) smooth; flowers in the middle (E, × 3) with both stamens and style, but not producing seeds (F, stamens, × 6; G, top of style of male flowers, ×12) (family *Compositae*).

Coltsfoot was formerly used as a remedy for coughs, and the leaves used in smoking mixtures. They have been so employed during the two World Wars. *Farfara* is the ancient name of white poplar, whose leaves resemble those of *Tussilago*. It is one of the earliest spring flowers and bees effect cross-pollination, the disk (male) flowers secreting nectar at the base of the style, the female being nectarless. Self-pollination is possible owing to closing of heads at night or during cold weather.

Perennial with a short thick rootstock; stems up to about 4 ft. high or even a little higher in suitable soil, branched only in the upper part, the numerous flowering heads sometimes forming a wide corymb; basal leaves of the first year (A, $\times \frac{2}{5}$) deeply and irregularly pinnately lobed with the end lobe the largest and less divided, all coarsely lobulate and toothed, minutely scurfy pubescent on both surfaces, especially on the nervés; stem leaves sessile and much divided; flower-heads usually very many, on slender, somewhat woolly stalks, $\frac{1}{2}-\frac{3}{4}$ in. diam.; involucral bracts (B, $\times 3$) in one main series with a few extra smaller ones at the base, with rather thin edges

and often darker coloured tops; ray-flowers (C, $\times 2\frac{1}{2}$) yellow, about 15–20, spreading, with glabrous achenes; disk-flowers (D, $\times 2\frac{1}{2}$) numerous, with shortly pubescent achenes and a longer more copious pappus; anthers (E, $\times 8$) slightly ear-shaped at the base; style-arms (F, $\times 8$) very blunt, with a brush of thick short hairs at the apex (family *Compositae*).

A common and quite handsome species in pastures and on roadsides; usually avoided by stock but has been eaten by sheep in this country without any harmful effects; in other countries, however, regarded as dangerous. This species may be at once distinguished from amongst others closely resembling it, such as *S. aquaticus* Huds., and *S. erucifolius* L., in having two kinds of achenes, those of the ray-flowers being glabrous and of the disk hairy.

Erect perennial or biennial up to about 2 ft. high; basal leaves lobulate, soon withering; lower stem-leaves (A, × ⅓) lyrate-

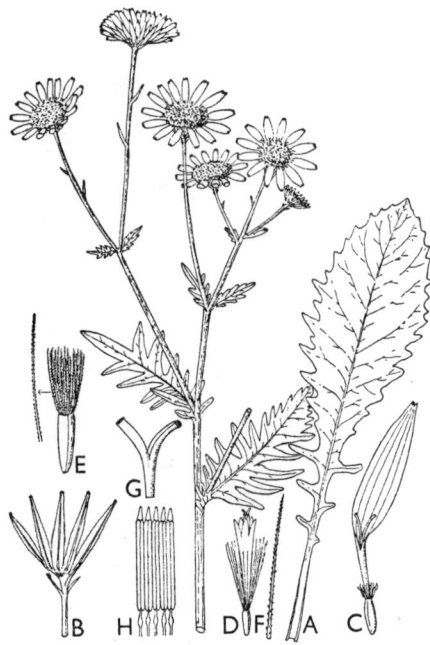

pinnatisect or lobed, the upper part of the blade sharply and coarsely toothed; upper leaves gradually becoming smaller and sessile, deeply cut, thinly woolly to nearly glabrous below; heads few in a loose corymb, about 1 in. diam.; outer bracts (B, × 1⅔) few, awl-shaped (subulate), inner narrowly lanceolate, frilled on the margin and with hairy tips; ray-flowers (C, × 1⅔) yellow, about 12–15; disk-flowers (D, × 1⅔) numerous, yellow; achenes (E, × 4) of both kinds of flowers ribbed, smooth and not hairy; pappus-hairs (F, × 5) white, rough; style-arms (G, × 5) truncate and papillous at the tip; anthers (H, × 7) with barren tips and rounded bases without tails, the filaments swollen towards the top (family *Compositae*).

Very like the common Ragwort (fig. 512), but the lower leaves less cut up, and the achenes of the disk-flowers not hairy (glabrous); it grows in wetter places than the Ragwort, by the sides of rivers, ditches, and rills in meadows, especially in peaty soil.

Senecio squalidus L. ($\times \frac{2}{3}$)

Annual or biennial much resembling the common Groundsel (fig.
516), but with conspicuous ray-flowers; leaves all on the stem,
with the base half-clasping it and ear-shaped, pinnately and deeply lobed, the lobes narrow and acutely toothed (denticulate), quite glabrous; flower-heads few to numerous, more or less elevated to the same level, about $\frac{3}{4}$ in. diam., the stalks with a few scattered small bracts; involucre (A, $\times \frac{4}{5}$) of two rows of bracts, the outer ones quite small and usually black, the inner about $\frac{1}{4}$ in. long, and mostly with black tips (B, $\times 1\frac{3}{4}$); ray-flowers (C, $\times 2$) 15–20, bright yellow, the blade about $\frac{1}{3}$ in. long; achenes minutely hairy, with a white slightly rough pappus; disk-flowers (D, $\times 2$) numer-

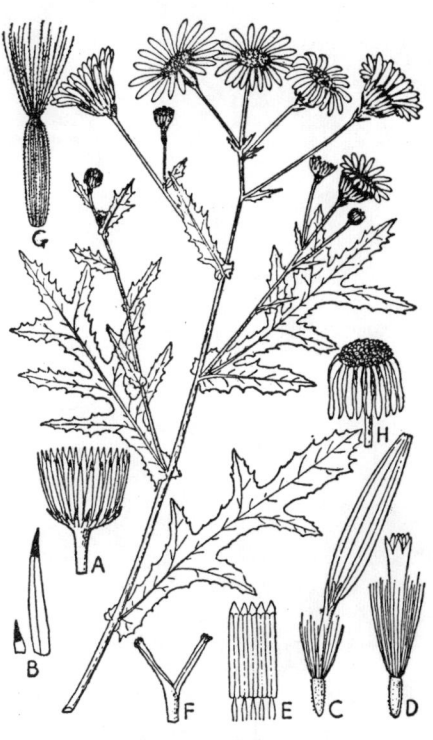

ous, yellow; anthers (E, $\times 10$) rounded at both ends, with a triangular membranous tip; style-arms (F, $\times 10$) very blunt, with a
tuft of short hairs at the tip; ripe achenes (G, $\times 2$) closely ribbed
and minutely hairy, crowned with the white pappus; receptacle
(H, $\times 2\frac{1}{2}$) honey-combed, the bracts abruptly reflexed after fruiting (family *Compositae*).

When out of flower this species, an alien from south Europe,
might be mistaken for the common Groundsel. It is well established in many districts, especially on walls and embankments in
the vicinity of railway stations. It was first established at Oxford
and Bideford. Striking features are the black tips to the bracts of
the involucre, and the large ray-flowers. In the Groundsel (fig.
516) there are normally no ray-flowers.

WOOD SENECIO
Senecio sylvaticus L. (×½)

Annual much like the common Groundsel, but taller and more slender, the stems very minutely pubescent, and lined with several

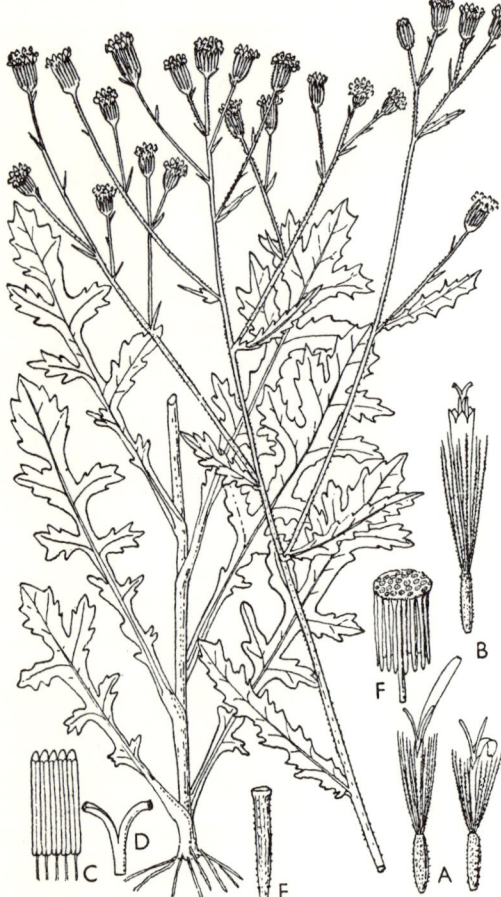

ribs; leaves deeply pinnate, divided into irregularly cut sharply angular lobes as shown in the drawing; flower - heads usually very numerous and forming a wide loose corymb, weaker specimens with fewer heads, as in the drawing; stalks slender and bearing 2 or 3 thread-like bracts; involucres bell-shaped, with about 12–15 narrow very shortly pubescent bracts in a single row and with darker tips; outer flowers (A, × 2½) very small and inconspicuous, the corolla limb being rolled up in dry weather; achenes (E, × 4) nearly black, ribbed when dry, and shortly and softly hairy, crowned with a pappus of soft white hair-like bristles; fruiting heads with sharply deflexed involucral bracts (F, × 1¼) (family *Compositae*) (B, disk-flower, × 3; C, anthers; D, style-arms of disk-flowers).

Rather like Groundsel (fig. 516), but usually much taller and with more numerous flower-heads.

Senecio vulgaris L. ($\times \frac{2}{3}$)

Annual herb up to about a foot high, with a finely fibrous root; stems succulent, glabrous or thinly clothed with rather long cottony hairs; leaves alter-nate, sessile and half clasping the stem, pin-nately lobed and irre-gularly dentate, succu-lent, not hairy or only slightly so when young; flower-heads (A, $\times 1\frac{1}{2}$) few, in close terminal and axillary corymbs; involucre narrowly bell-shaped, with one principal row of bracts and several very small black-tipped bracts at the base; longer row of bracts forming a tube; flow-ers (florets) (B, $\times 1\frac{1}{2}$) all of one kind, yellow, no ray-flowers (or very rarely a few small ones present); pappus of many slender white toothed (barbellate)

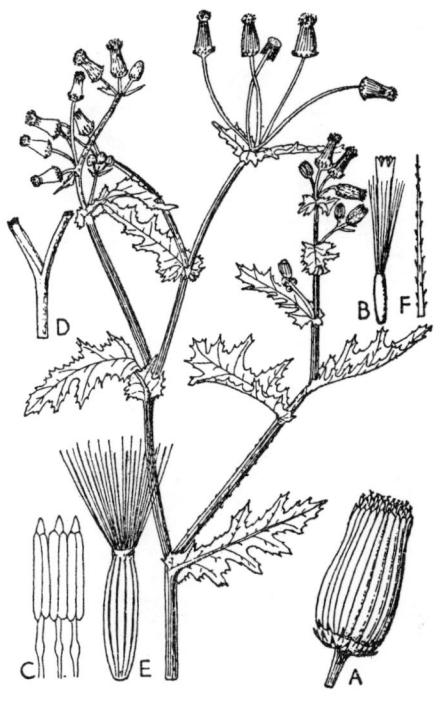

bristles (F, $\times 6$); corolla tubular, 5-lobed; ovary minutely hairy; anthers (C, $\times 5$) rounded at the base and with produced barren tips; style-branches (D, $\times 5$) very blunt, with short club-shaped hairs (papillae) at the tips; achene (fruit) (E, $\times 5$) with longitudinal ribs, not hairy (family *Compositae*).

Groundsel needs no introduction, being a 'noxious' weed of cultivation in temperate regions. It has its uses, however, being a good rabbit and cage-bird food-plant. The flowers contain nec-tar which ascends into the upper bell-shaped part of the corolla. But insect visitors are few, and automatic self-pollination regular-ly takes place. It has been shown, however, that cross-fertilized seeds produce larger and more fertile plants.

Perennial with erect stems up to 4 ft. high; stems ribbed, woolly-hairy especially in the upper parts; leaves alternate, sessile, pin-

nately divided from the base into several narrow coarsely-toothed lobes, more or less woolly-hairy; heads numerous in a dense terminal corymb; bracte-oles several, narrow; in-volucral bracts (A, ×2) with a thick midrib and broad thinner margins; ray-flowers (B, ×2) 12–15, yellow; disk-flowers (C, ×2) yellow; achenes of both types of flower hairy; pappus white; an-thers (D, ×6) with barren tips and rounded bases; style-arms (E, ×6) very blunt (family *Compositae*).

Very similar to the Ragwort (*Senecio jaco-baea*) (fig. 512), but the terminal lobes of the leaf very narrow and the achenes of both ray- and disk-flowers hairy; flowers in summer and autumn.

Widely distributed as far east as Siberia; in Britain only as far north as southern Scotland.

Of the remaining seven species of *Senecio* not shown in this book, the most striking are *S. cineraria* DC., with pinnately lobed leaves densely white-felted beneath, naturalized on maritime cliffs in southern districts; *S. paludosus* L., the Great Fen Ragwort, from the fens of East Anglia, but now extinct, with lanceolate sharply toothed cottony-hairy leaves and few large heads of yel-low flowers; *S. congestus* (R. Br.), DC. (*S. palustris*) the Marsh Fleawort, also in the fens but probably also extinct, with sessile lanceolate toothed stem-leaves and corymbs of large heads with short rays.

Annual weed very much like the common Groundsel (fig. 516), but
very sticky all over with short gland-tipped hairs (A, ×8); stem up
to 2 ft. high, ribbed; leaves alternate, sessile, very deeply and pinnately divided, the segments rather jagged or irregularly toothed;
flower-heads usually numerous and forming a loose leafy corymb;
main involucre with a few bracteoles at the base; bracts about 20,
glandular except for the overlapped margins; ray-flowers (B, ×5)
yellow, at first spreading but soon withering and curling up; disk-
flowers (C, ×5) dull yellow; anthers (D, ×10) rounded at the

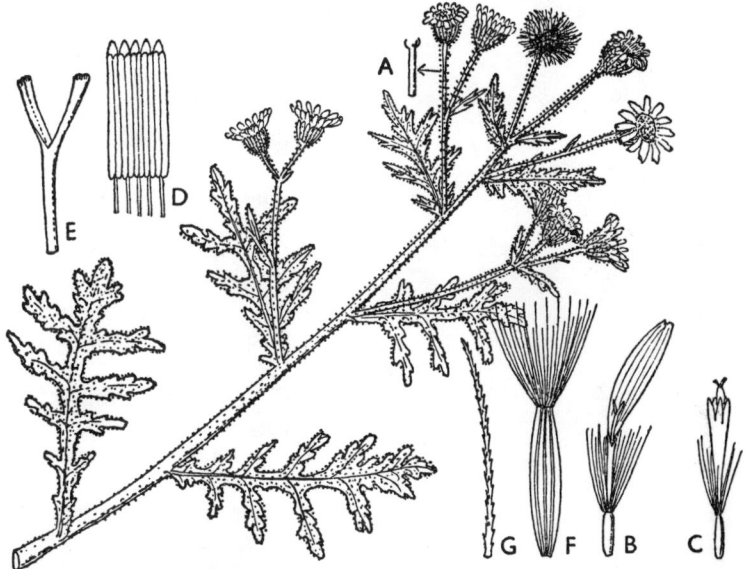

base; achenes (F) strongly ribbed, not hairy; pappus (G, ×10)
white, very minutely barbellate (family *Compositae*).

Not so common as the Groundsel and found mostly in waste,
rather dry places; very sticky to the touch.

Distributed in Europe and Asia Minor and naturalized in the
eastern states of North America; flowers in summer and autumn.

The stylar branches (E, ×10) in this species at length roll back
in a semicircle so far that their stigmatic papillae touch the pollen
which remains clinging to the elongated pappus-hairs of the same
floret, thus effecting automatic self-pollination if cross-pollination
has not taken place.

Senecio fluviatilis Wallr. (× ⅓)

Perennial with creeping rootstock; stems erect, up to 5 ft. high, ribbed, nearly glabrous; leaves alternate, sessile, oblanceolate, acute at the apex, narrowed to the base, averaging about 6 in. long and 1½ in. broad, sharply and rather closely toothed (serrate), glabrous, with numerous much-branched lateral nerves and fine venation; flower-heads numerous in a wide terminal corymb with leaf-like toothed bracts (reduced leaves); flower-head stalks thinly hairy; involucre with a few outer free bracts, the inner row thinly pubescent and with darker tips; ray-flowers (A, ×2) yellow, about 6–8, spreading; disk-flowers (B, ×2) yellow; anthers (C, ×4) with swollen filaments; style-arms (D, ×6) blunt; achenes glabrous; pappus (E, ×10) white, very minutely bar-

bellate (family *Compositae*). Synonym *S. sarracenicus* L.

A naturalized species but very local growing by riversides and in moist meadows or woods, flowering in late summer; a native of southern Europe and north-west Africa; related to *S. paludosus* L., which, however, has cottony-hairy leaves and more numerous ray-flowers.

Perennial herb with thick fleshy rootstock transversely scarred with the marks of scales; stems up to $1\frac{1}{2}$ ft. high, erect, almost villous with longish hairs; basal leaves on long hairy stalks, ovate, deeply cordate at the base, not pointed, 3–4 in. long and up to 3 in. broad, slightly repand-dentate, thinly hairy on both surfaces; stem-leaves shortly stalked, with a broad ear-like base clasping the stem; flower-heads about 2 in. diam., usually 2 or 3 to each stem, on slender stalks, with an ovate bract at the base of each stalk; involucral bracts in 1–2 rows, linear-lanceolate, nearly as long as the ray-flowers, the latter (A, $\times 1$) spreading, numerous, yellow; no pappus in the ray-flowers; disk-flowers (B, $\times 2$) with a dense nearly smooth pappus; anthers (C, $\times 6$) rounded at both ends; style-arms (D, $\times 6$) very short and blunt, papillous; achenes (E, $\times 2\frac{1}{2}$) ribbed, hairy (family *Compositae*).

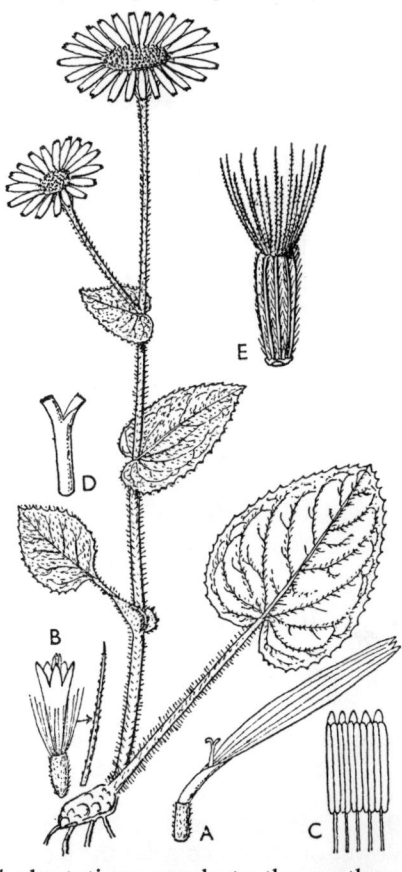

An introduced species native of central and southern Europe; found in woods and plantations nearly to the northern end of Scotland.

The ray-flowers of the family *Compositae* were probably evolved from the more regular disk-flowers which occupy the middle of the head, and in which there are 5 stamens as well as style and stigmas. A very interesting feature of this species is that the ray-flowers have retained vestiges of the 5 stamens with which their ancestors were probably provided. Their nectaries are also as well developed as in the disk-flowers.

SCENTLESS MATRICARY
Matricaria inodora L. ($\times \frac{2}{5}$)

Erect or spreading branched annual with numerous barren shoots; branches long and forming a loose corymb; leaves 2–3

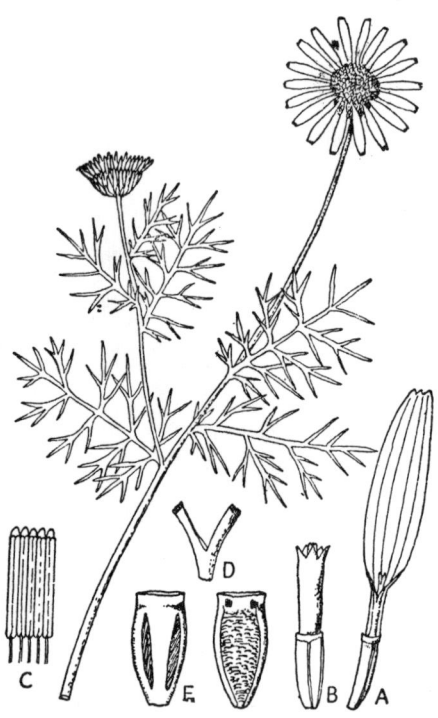

times pinnate, cut up into very narrow or thread-like segments right to the base of the common axis, glabrous; flower-heads large, on terminal peduncles; bracts of the involucre in several rows, nearly of equal length and with brown jagged margins; ray-flowers (A, $\times$ 3) numerous, white, $\frac{1}{2}$–$\frac{3}{4}$ in. long, 4–5-nerved; disk-flowers (B, $\times$ 3) very numerous, yellow, arranged on a convex or ovoid receptacle (axis) which does not elongate or enlarge as in the nearly related *M. chamomilla* L.; style (D, $\times$ 4) arms truncate; achenes (E, $\times$ 4) thickly ribbed on one side and with two glandular spots like little eyes at the top; pappus a narrow almost entire rim (family *Compositae*).

This plant is easily mistaken for *Anthemis cotula* L., in the flower-heads of which, however, there is a bract below each flower on the receptacle; the pair of glands on one side at the top of the achene (see fig. E) is a good spotting feature. A seaside form of the plant with thicker more fleshy leaves is sometimes called var. *maritima*.

A third species which is introduced is a common weed on roadsides and on pathways which it sometimes covers completely. This is *Matricaria matricarioides* (Less.) Porter (fig. 522), a very dwarf plant with no ray-flowers, and yellowish-green disk-flowers.

Annual, from very dwarf to about 9 in. high; stems green, often crimson towards the base, without hairs (glabrous), not hollow; leaves alternate, with a broad flat base (A, ×1), divided to the middle into very fine much-divided lobes, each leaf bearing in its axil a flowering branch, the oldest flower-head at the top; flower-heads (B, ×1) about 3 on each branch, shortly stalked; bracts of the involucre in 3–4 rows, pale green but with membranous tips and margins; no ray-flowers; disk-flowers (D, ×6) numerous, spirally arranged on a cone-like axis (C, ×1); corolla 4-lobed; stamens 4; anthers with barren tips and rounded base (E, ×12); ovary smooth, crowned by a slightly toothed rim at the top; style-arms very blunt (F, ×12); achenes (G, ×4) marked with two

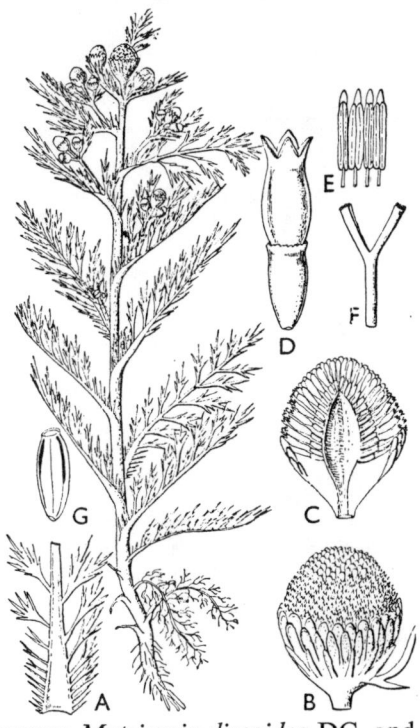

or three resin-like lines (synonyms *Matricaria discoidea* DC. and *Matricaria suaveolens* (Pursh) Buchen. non L. (family *Compositae*).

This species is an introduced weed and common on roadside and along pathways, often among cobbles in farmyards. The more it is trodden on the better it seems to thrive. It spreads rapidly because of the great number of fertile flowers, none of which is radiate, as in most other species of the genus. The tiny achenes are pretty microscopic objects. When ripe they will be seen to have two or three resin-like streaks running lengthwise, and recalling those so characteristic of the Hemlock family, *Umbelliferae*.

523   WILD CHAMOMILE
Matricaria recutita L. (× ½)

The description for *Matricaria inodora* L. given in fig. 521, would do equally well for the plant shown here, except that the bracts of

the involucre have pale (not brown) margins, and the floral axis (receptacle) (A, ×1) is more or less cone-shaped from an early stage, very much more so later on, and it is hollow; in *M. chamomilla*, too, the achenes (E, ×5) are different; they have not the two eye-like spots at the top, and one of the faces (D, ×5) has 5 ribs lengthwise. Instead of a full description, therefore, I give below a key to the white ray-flowered species of *Matricaria* and *Anthemis* which are so difficult for the beginner to distinguish:

Floral axis (receptacle) bearing a bract below all or some of the disk-flowers:
Floral axis (receptacle) with a bract below only the uppermost disk-flowers; ray-flowers barren (without a style); annuals; (fig. 530) . . . . *Anthemis cotula*
Floral axis (receptacle) with a bract below all the disk-flowers; ray-flowers fertile (with a style):
Bracts below the disk-flowers oblong, rounded at the top; perennials; (fig. 528) . . . . . . *Anthemis nobilis*
Bracts below the disk-flowers narrow and sharply pointed; annuals; see fig. 531 . . . . . . *Anthemis arvensis*
Floral axis (receptacle) not bearing bracts below the disk-flowers:
Floral axis at most convex or at length ovoid; bracts of the involucre with brownish jagged margins; ripe achenes with two gland-like 'eyes' near the top; (fig. 521) *Matricaria inodora*
(continued at foot of next page)

Artemisia absinthium L. ($\times\frac{1}{3}$)

Perennial, strongly aromatic herb with woody rootstock and annual ribbed stems up to 3 ft. or more high; whole plant densely covered with short grey-ish-white silky hairs; lower leaves long-stalked, rounded in outline but much divided into narrow rather blunt segments; flower-heads yellow, numerous, drooping, arranged in large leafy terminal panicles, nearly sessile on the branchlets; outer bracts (A, ×6) linear-spoon-shaped, inner broad and with thin margins; outer flowers (florets) (B, ×6) slender, female or barren, the inner (C, ×6) bisexual with a broader corolla and mostly fertile; anthers (D, ×10) with narrow tips and rounded bases; style-arms (E, ×10) very blunt; achenes obovoid, without a pappus (family *Compositae*).

Grows near the sea and inland near cultivated ground and in waste places.

In the genus *Artemisia* the flowers are usually pollinated by the wind (anemophilous), a very rare feature in the family *Compositae*. In this species, however, this may also be brought about by alighting insects attracted by the yellow colour of the tiny flowers, of which about 50 are crowded into each head; but there is no nectary.

Floral axis cone-shaped almost from beginning, hollow (when cut across); bracts of the involucre with pale margins; achenes without 'eyes' (fig. 523) . . . *Matricaria chamomilla*

Perennial on roadsides and waste places, rank growing to about 3 ft. and flowering in late summer and autumn; stems ribbed,

pubescent; leaves (A, ×⅖) alternate, twice pinnately lobed, green above, white with a coat of woolly hairs beneath; flower-heads very numerous in a terminal leafy panicle, the leaves gradually reduced to bracts; involucral bracts few, cottonywhite; flowers in each head of two kinds, the outer female (B, ×6) with a narrow corolla, a bilobed smooth style and a smooth ovary with rim-like pappus (calyx); the inner (C, ×6) bisexual with the corolla bell-shaped at the top, anthers (D, ×10) with sharp barren tips and sagittate bases, and style branches (E, ×10) very blunt (truncate) and papillous at the tip (family *Compositae*).

The group or tribe of the family to which *Artemisia* belongs is very interesting because the flowers are *anemophilous*, i.e. their pollen is carried by the wind from flower-head to flower-head or from one plant to another. The individual flowers are very small and inconspicuous, and the flower-heads are often pendulous and therefore do not provide a suitable landing-place for insects; and they secrete no nectar. Where the plant is common it may be the cause of hay fever to those who suffer from this complaint. A closely related genus *Ambrosia* (fig. 527) is the cause of much hayfever in the eastern United States of America.

Artemisia norvegica Fries ($\times\frac{1}{2}$)

Perennial herb, in its Norwegian habitat up to about 1 ft. high, but in Scotland only a few inches; basal leaves in a rosette, several,

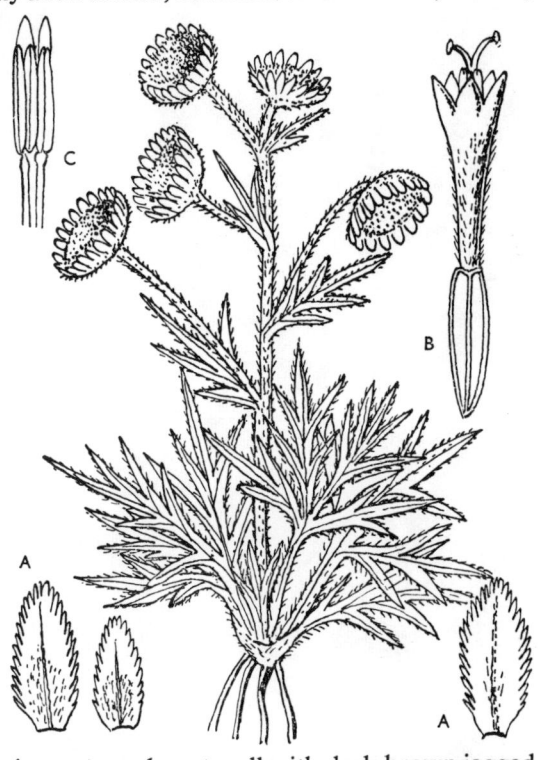

spreading or ascending, deeply bipinnate into narrow acute segments softly pilose all over or only below, the longish stalks sheathing at the base; stem softly pilose, bearing a few smaller simply pinnately divided leaves, the upper leaves with a long-pedunculate-nodding head in the axil of each; peduncles very hairy; flower-heads about $\frac{1}{2}$–$\frac{3}{4}$ in. diam.; involucral bracts (A, $\times 2\frac{1}{2}$) in 3–4 rows, the outer broadly ovate, the innermost obovate, all with dark brown jagged margins and more or less pilose in the middle; flowers (B, $\times 6$) numerous, yellow; corolla pilose outside; stamens (C, $\times 8$) with rounded-based anthers; achenes prominently ribbed, glabrous (family *Compositae*).

This interesting plant was first found in Britain by Sir Christopher Cox, K.C.M.G., in August 1950, growing on the spur of a mountain between 2,350 and 2,459 ft. altitude in the north-west of Scotland. Outside Britain it is confined to the Dovrefjeld district and adjacent mountains in Norway and to the northern Urals. A full account of this addition to the British flora is given by Blakelock in *Kew Bulletin* 1953: 173. (The specimen drawn is one from the Dovrefjeld area.)

A much-branched annual herb about 2 ft. high or more with the habit of an *Artemisia* and more or less clothed with long whitish

hairs; leaves twice pinnate and finely cut up, the lower mostly opposite, the upper alternate, shortly hairy on both surfaces, with longer hairs on the nerves below, gradually becoming smaller upwards and bracteate; flower-heads in leafy bracteate panicles with slender branches, the males in terminal racemes with the females below in the axils of leafy bracts; male involucre (A, ×2) deep green, orbicular, shortly stalked, nodding, ciliate, bearing several male flowers; male flowers (B, F, ×3) with a greenish 5-lobed corolla, 5 free pale yellow stamens with apiculate anthers (C, ×3), and rudimentary style; female flowers (E, ×1¼) few in 2 leafy bracts (D, ×2) in the axil of a reduced leaf; involucre 5-toothed; calyx, corolla, and stamens absent; style-branches 2, filiform, pale whitish yellow; achenes shortly beaked, with short spines near the top (family *Compositae*).

An introduced American plant often found in waste ground. In North America this species is the worst cause of hay fever and is called, beside Ragweed, Roman Wormwood, Hogweed, Bitter-weed, and by the French-speaking Canadians Herbe à Poux and Sarriette. It is rather a variable species, the form here shown being the var. *elatior* (*A. elatior* L.).

A spreading procumbent perennial herb with slender stems up to 2 ft. long, slightly hairy all over; leaves alternate, sessile, pinnately or twice pinnately divided into fine acute segments; flower-heads solitary on long slender stalks, about $1\frac{1}{2}$ in. diam.; rays white, disk yellow; involucral bracts in about 3 rows, broad and with membranous margins, hairy outside; ray-flowers (A, $\times 3\frac{1}{2}$) numerous, spreading; disk-flowers (B, $\times 3\frac{1}{2}$) numerous, each subtended by a broad, obtuse scale hairy on the margin; anthers (C, $\times 10$) rounded at both ends; style-arms (D, $\times 10$) very blunt and papillous at the tip; achenes without a pappus, smooth (family *Compositae*).

Flowers in summer and autumn, long cultivated but probably native in southern England and in Eire; generally distributed in western Europe.

The genus *Anthemis* resembles *Chrysanthemum* and *Matricaria*, but is distinguished from them especially by the receptacle on which the tiny flowers are inserted, having a *bract below all or at least the central flowers*, a character it shares with *Achillea* and *Otanthus* (*Diotis*).

YELLOW CHAMOMILE
Anthemis tinctoria L. ($\times \frac{1}{2}$)

Biennial or perennial herb up to $2\frac{1}{2}$ ft. high, usually with several erect or ascending branches, whole plant thinly pubescent all over;

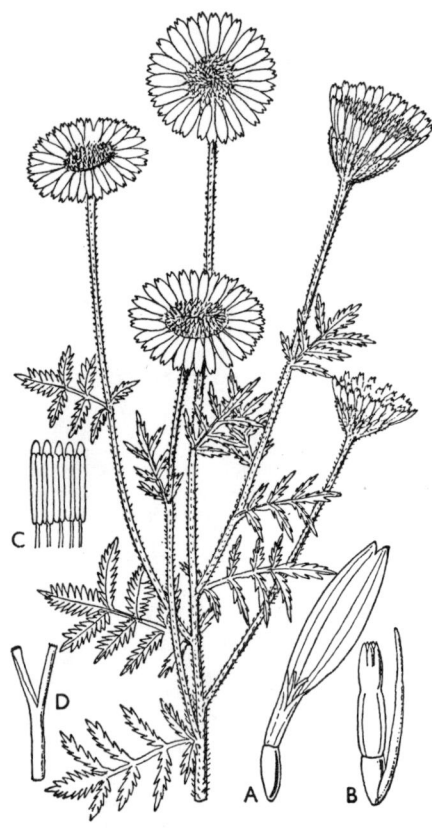

leaves alternate, small in proportion to the size of the plant, sessile, deeply twice-pinnately lobed, lobes acute; flower-heads handsome, bright yellow, about $1\frac{1}{2}$ in. diam., on long stalks; involucral bracts in 2–3 rows, hairy; ray-flowers (A, $\times 3$) 2-toothed at the tips; corolla-tube slightly winged; disk-flowers (B, $\times 5$) 5-lobed; anthers (C, $\times 8$) rounded at each end; style-arms (D, $\times 8$) truncate; achenes glabrous, without a pappus; receptacle with a narrowly pointed bristle (B, $\times 5$) outside each of the flowers (family *Compositae*).

This species flowers towards the end of summer and is easily recognized by the yellow flower-heads, the individual flowers each having a narrow pointed scale below; these are clearly visible amongst the flowers; grows mostly in cultivated and waste places; variety *discoidea* has no ray-flowers.

Regarded as an introduced plant, but completely established on banksides and waste places; widely distributed from Europe to eastern Asia.

Anthemis cotula L. ($\times\frac{1}{2}$)

A much-branched annual and very like *A. arvensis* (fig. 531), but the receptacle is furnished with bristly scales only in the upper half

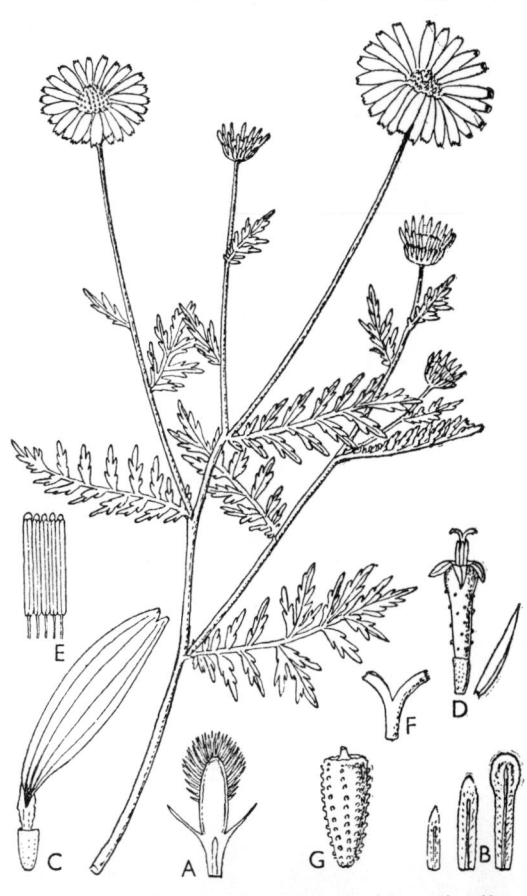

(fig. A) whereas in *A. arvensis* it is scaly-bracteate all over (i.e. one bract below every flower), the ray-flowers are barren and have no style, and the achenes (G, $\times 8$) are prominently warted. For the difference between *Matricaria* and *Anthemis* see notes under fig. 523.

The tribe to which *Anthemis* belongs, tribe *Anthemideae*, is characterized by having no pappus (modified calyx), or merely a rim in its place. In spite of this 'handicap' – for a pappus is usually an aid to distribution – several species are very widely spread, and some are even weeds of cultivation. A very common example is the Milfoil, shown in fig. 532, which is troublesome on lawns and in pastures. – B, $\times 2$, bracts of involucre; C, $\times 2$, ray-flower; D, $\times 2$, disk-flower and subtending scale; E, $\times 6$, anthers; F, $\times 6$, style-arms of disk-flower; G, $\times 8$, achene of disk-flower.

Anthemis arvensis L. ($\times\frac{1}{2}$)

Erect or spreading much-branched annual, pubescent all over; leaves deeply pinnately divided into narrow acute segments; bracts of the involucre (B, $\times 2\frac{1}{2}$) in about 3 rows, gradually longer, the inner with membranous margins, hairy outside; ray-flowers (C, $\times 2$) white, numerous, about $\frac{1}{2}$ in. long, provided with a bilobed style; tip 3-toothed; disk-flowers (D, $\times 2$) yellow, numerous, each flower with a very narrow pointed scale at the base (A); anthers (E, $\times 10$) rounded at the base; style-arms (F, $\times 10$) truncate; achenes (G, $\times 6$) narrowed to the base, with rounded smooth ribs; no pappus

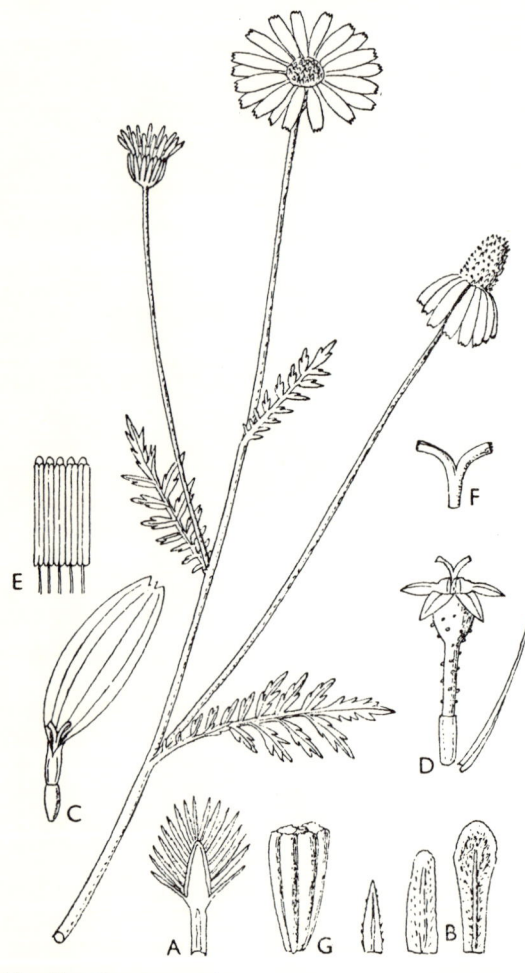

(family *Compositae*).

The genus *Anthemis* differs from *Matricaria* in that each of the upper disk-flowers, at any rate, is subtended by a narrow bract. In *A. arvensis* there is a style in the ray-flowers.

Perennial, in pastures, meadows, and waste places, with creeping underground rootstock and numerous short leafy flowerless

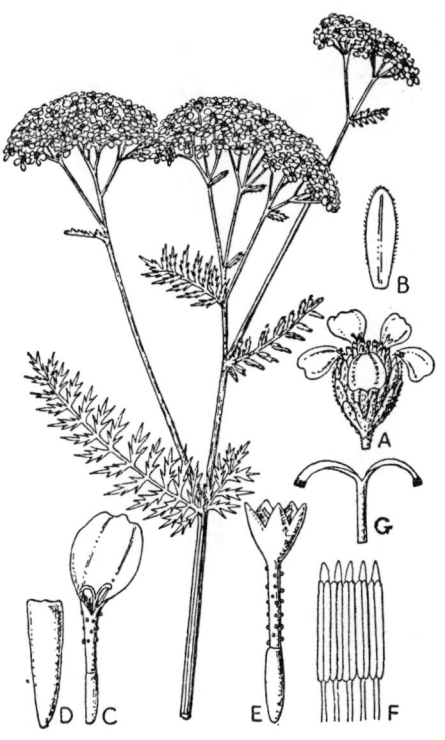

shoots; flowering stems about 1 ft. high, erect, ribbed; basal leaves pinnately and finely cut into narrow segments which are also deeply divided, lobes ending in a fine point; stem-leaves gradually decreasing upwards; flower-heads (A, $\times$ 3) white or pink, numerous, small, densely arranged in flat corymbs, the side branches often longest; involucral bracts (B, $\times$ 5) in 3–4 series, green up the middle and with brown hairy margins; ray-flowers (C, $\times$ 5) usually 5 (thus resembling a simple flower), female, the corolla with a broad blade 3-toothed at the apex; tube glandular; achene ('seed') (D, $\times$ 4) with a mere rim at the top, smooth; disk-flowers (E, $\times$ 6) tubular, bisexual, upper part bell-shaped, tube glandular; anthers (F, $\times$ 10) with a barren tip and rounded base; style-branches (G, $\times$ 10) papillous at the tip; flowers all summer (family *Compositae*).

The ray-flowers of the individual heads are usually not more than five, each head, therefore, mimicking a single flower with five petals, a very interesting biological feature, as pointed out in the description of *Galinsoga* (fig. 509), in which the same reduction in number has taken place. But plants, like proprietors of fêtes, often gain on the swings what they lose on the roundabouts, and in this case the smallness of the heads is compensated for by their crowding together into a conspicuous flat corymb.

SNEEZEWORT YARROW
Achillea ptarmica L. ($\times \frac{2}{3}$)

Perennial with slender rootstock and erect stems up to 2 ft.; leaves linear, acute, margined with very small close sharp teeth like a fine

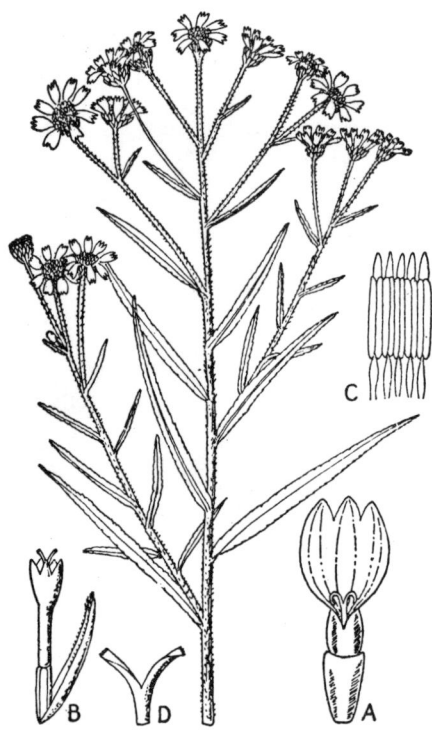

saw; flower-heads several in a loose terminal cluster and at the ends of the branches, about $\frac{3}{4}$ in. diam.; involucral bracts about 3-seriate, woolly-pubescent, with thinner brown margins; axis of the head furnished with a bract below each flower; ray-flowers (A, × 2) usually about 8, white, with a very broad 3-toothed blade; disk-flowers (B, × 4) greenish-white; anthers (C, × 10) rounded at the base, and with large barren oblong tips; style-branches (D, × 8) very blunt, papillous at the ends; achenes flattened and short, without a pappus (family *Compositae*).

This species has larger heads than *A. millefolium* (fig. 532) and there are more ray-flowers. But not so many of the heads are grouped together, so the two species are about equally conspicuous when in flower. Wherever the two grow in abundance they are almost equally common, flower at the same time, and are visited by the same insects. The plant was formerly used in some localities for making tea, and a double form, known as Bachelor's Buttons, is a familiar plant in gardens.

Otanthus maritimus (L.) Hoffmgg. & Link (×½)

Perennial maritime herb with creeping rootstock; stems up to about 1 ft. high, erect, simple or slightly branched, densely covered like the leaves with soft woolly hairs; leaves crowded along the stems, sessile, narrowly oblong, crenate, ½–¾ in. long, covered with woolly hairs, often with short shoots in their axils; flower-heads (A, ×1) globose, discoid, corymbose; peduncles short; involucre of 2–3 series of woolly bracts; flowers all tubular, yellow, slightly exserted from the bracts, each flower subtended by a large dry scale (C, ×5); corolla widened at the base and produced into two large auricles embracing the upper part of the ovary; anthers (B, ×10) rounded at the base; style-arms (D, ×10) truncate and penicellate at the apex; achenes partly hidden by the persistent hardened auricles of the corolla base; no pappus (family *Compositae*). – Synonym *Diotis maritima* (L.) Coss.

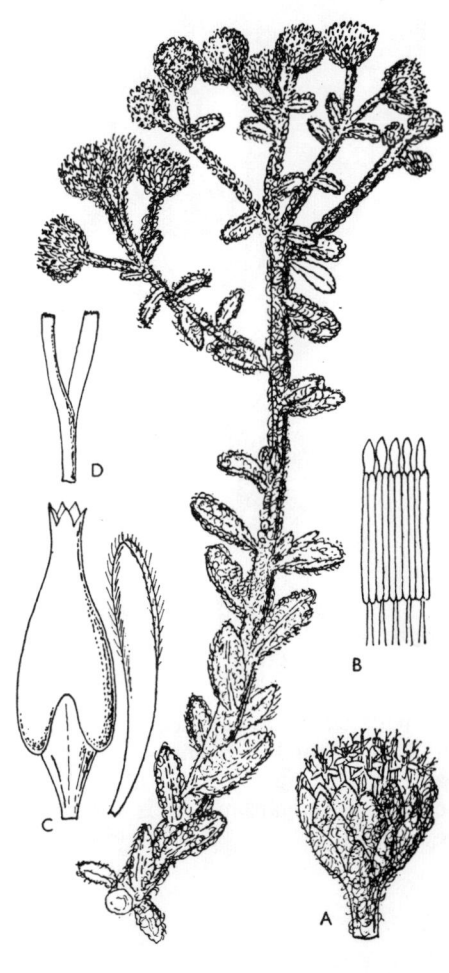

Maritime sands on the Mediterranean and Atlantic coasts of Europe, extending in Britain as far north as Anglesey and Suffolk, but now extinct in some parts; also in south-west Eire; flowers in late summer and autumn.

535   FEVERFEW

Chrysanthemum parthenium (L.) Bernh. ($\times \frac{2}{3}$)

Perennial, stems branched up to about $1\frac{1}{2}$ ft. high, leafy from the base, ribbed; leaves (A, $\times \frac{2}{3}$) deeply pinnately lobed, the lobes very

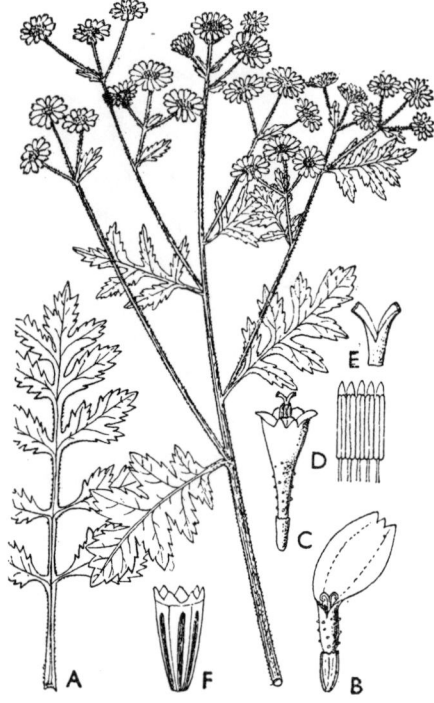

coarsely toothed or lobulate, at most slightly hairy; flower-heads $\frac{1}{2}$–$\frac{3}{4}$ in. diam., about 3 or 4 at the end of each branch and forming a wide corymb; peduncles slender; bracts of the involucre in about 3 rows, each with a keeled midrib, slightly hairy; no scaly bracts below the disk-flowers; ray-flowers (B, $\times$ 3) about 15, white, spreading, broadly elliptic, 3-toothed at the apex; disk-flowers (C, $\times$ 3) numerous, yellow; corolla-tubes with a few scattered glands; anthers (D, $\times$ 6) rounded at the base; style-arms (E, $\times$ 6) of the disk-flowers very short and blunt; achenes (F, $\times$ 6) crowned with a dentate pappus, with dark ribs (family *Compositae*).

This rather handsome species grows by roadsides, near walls, and in waste places, and is doubtfully native, being usually an escape from gardens. It is distributed eastwards as far as the Caucasus.

Perennial in pastures, meadows, cultivated fields, roadsides, etc.; radical leaves spoon-shaped (spathulate), bluntly toothed, 3-nerved; stem leaves narrowly oblong to linear, sessile, eared at the base, coarsely toothed; flowerheads on long stalks, about 1½–2 in. diam.; bracts (A, × 2) in 4–5 series, with membranous jagged margins; rayflowers (B, × 1½) white; disk-flowers (C, × 2) creamy yellow, with a few glands near the middle of the tube; anthers (D, × 6) rounded at the base, with triangular barren tips; style-branches (E, × 8) very blunt and papillous at the tips; achenes blackish, with several lighter coloured ribs, without pappus (family *Compositae*).

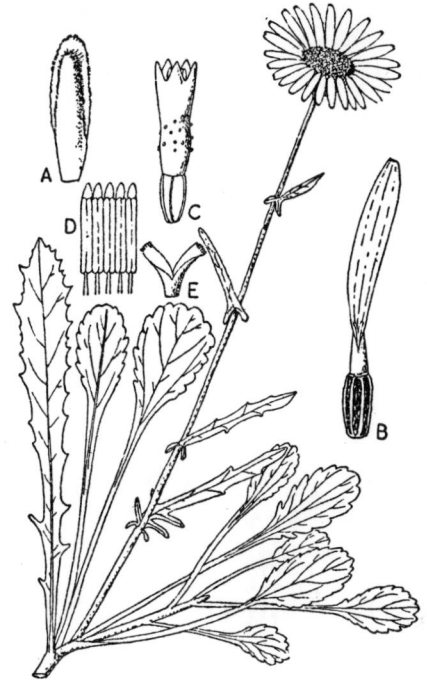

This is one of the most handsome members of the Composite family in the British flora, and is to be found in pastures and hayfields. The size of the plant and flower-heads varies much according to soil and situation. For example, at the Lizard, where it is exposed to the winds off the sea, the plant is reduced almost to the size of the common Daisy. Nectar rises into the bell of the disk-flowers, and in the first stage of flowering pollen is pushed up from the anther-tube by the brush on the ends of the style-arms. Visiting insects then transfer it to the stigmas of other flowers which are in the second stage of development.

Chrysanthemum segetum L. ($\times\frac{1}{3}$)

Annual with a taproot and very numerous fibrous rootlets; stem erect, glabrous, leafy; leaves alternate, sessile, oblong-oblanceolate in outline, coarsely toothed or pinnately lobed, lobes acute, glabrous and rather glaucous; flowerheads up to 2 in. diam., on long leafy peduncles; bracts (A, B, C, $\times 1$) in 3–4 rows, with broad membranous margins and tops, glabrous; ray-flowers (D, $\times 1\frac{1}{3}$) numerous, spreading, golden-yellow; corolla obovate-elliptic, 2-lobed at the top; disk-flowers (E, $\times 1\frac{1}{3}$) tubular; anthers (F, $\times 4$) with triangular tips and rounded bases; style of the disk-flower (G, $\times 6$) with truncate papillous tips; achenes of the ray-flowers narrowly 2-winged, of the disk not winged; no pappus; receptacle nearly flat, without scales amongst the flowers (family *Compositae*).

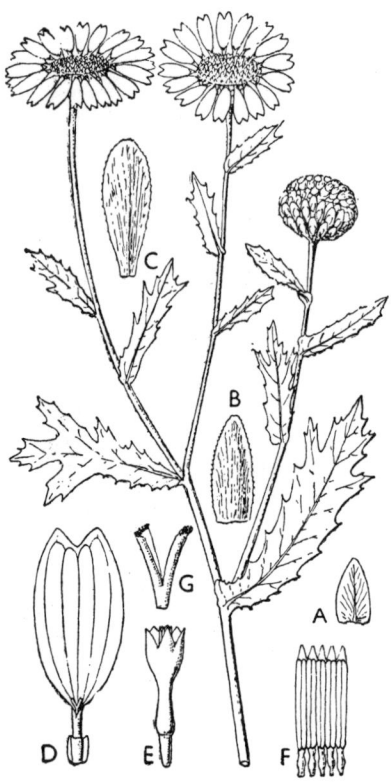

Widely distributed in Europe, north Africa, and western Asia, and elsewhere as a weed of cultivation, often in cornfields. It is worth growing in a garden for its handsome flower-heads and glaucous foliage, though the farmer with a glut of it in his fields will scarcely appreciate its beauty, for it is a very troublesome weed. Its seeds have the power of lying dormant in the soil for several years, and coming to life again when turned up by the plough. Yellow Gowans, Gowlans, Gools, and Yellow Bottle are names for it in different parts of the country. This and *Chrysanthemum parthenium* (fig. 535), together with *C. leucanthemum* (fig. 536), show all the species of this genus found in Britain.

Herb in wet ditches and sandy or muddy places; stems decumbent, rooting at the nodes, glabrous; leaves alternate, forming a tubular sheath at the base, broadly linear, entire or more often variously pinnately lobed or lobulate, sometimes more deeply cut, finely nerved; flowers in disk-like heads on slender peduncles with or without one or two leafy bracts; involucral bracts in 2 rows, thin with rounded tips; flowers of two kinds, the outer female, the inner (A, $\times 6$) bisexual; corolla winged; anthers (B, $\times 6$) rounded at each end; style-arms of bisexual flowers (D, $\times 6$) truncate; achenes of female flowers stalked and winged, the inner surface (C, $\times 6$) covered with short processes, smooth outside (E, $\times 6$); receptacle studded with the remains of the stalks of the flowers (family *Compositae*).

An alien found in wet places often not far from the coast; native of southern Africa.

Tanacetum vulgare L. ($\times \frac{2}{3}$)

Perennial; stems leafy, purplish, closely ribbed; leaves alternate, pinnate, the lobes again deeply cut and often toothed, finely gland-

dotted all over; common stalk clasping the stem, ribbed on the back; upper leaves gradually reduced to bracts at the base of the branches of the more or less flat corymb; flower-heads (A, $\times 1\frac{1}{4}$) usually numerous, scented, with 3–4 rows of hairy bracts (B, $\times 4$) with rather jagged edges; flowers (C, $\times 15$) all of one kind, dull yellow, tubular, between 200 and 300 in each head; pappus (calyx) a mere rim on top of the ribbed ovary; corolla with 5 small bladder-like lobes; anthers with barren tops and rounded bases; style branches (D, $\times 25$) very blunt (truncate) and papillous at the apex (family *Compositae*).

The flower-heads of this species are arranged more or less in one plane so that insect visitors can creep over all of them without using their wings. A large number of flowers may, therefore, be pollinated at the same time by a single insect. This crowding together of the head renders them very conspicuous, which would not be the case were they borne singly, for there are no ray-flowers, as in many other members of the family. The style-arms are covered at the tips with a dense bunch of short hairs which brush out the pollen from the anther-tube; they then spread out over the top of the corolla and become receptive for pollen from other flowers or flower-heads. All parts of the plant are bitter and acrid and avoided by stock as a rule. Cattle have been poisoned by it.

A coarse growing spiny annual herb; stem and branches thinly setulose-hairy; leaves alternate, stalked, lanceolate in outline but deeply pinnately lobed, densely covered with white hairs on the lower surface and on the nerves above, in the axil of each leaf a pair of straw - coloured 3-pronged spines about 1 in. long; flowers unisexual, the males in a terminal raceme of heads, the female axillary and solitary; male flowers in a depressed globose head surrounded by a few narrow involucral bracts and each subtended by a bract; corolla (A, $\times$4) funnel-shaped, 5-toothed, glandular outside; stamens (B, $\times$3) united in column from the base of the corolla, anthers (C, $\times$7) 5, free from each other, apiculate; female flowers 2 in a tubular closed involucre, without a corolla, the involucre becoming a 'bur' (D, $\times$1) which in fruit is covered with hooked prickles (family *Compositae*).

In waste ground, especially near ports and mills, introduced with sheep's wool in which it becomes entangled at the source.

SEA ASTER
Aster tripolium L. ($\times \frac{2}{3}$)

Perennial only found in low salt marshes, often lining the gulleys or forming pure stands; stems from 1–3 ft. high, from little- to much-branched, fleshy, glabrous, with 3 grooves below each leaf, 1 representing the midrib, the other 2 the lateral nerves, these lines continued down to the next leaf; leaves (A, $\times \frac{2}{3}$) half clasping the stem, broadly linear, with a wide midrib and 2 fainter parallel nerves, fleshy and glabrous; flower-heads either radiate (B, $\times \frac{2}{3}$) or discoid (C, $\times \frac{2}{3}$) or with very few rays, the latter (D, $\times 2\frac{1}{2}$) mauve-blue (rarely white), the disk-flowers (E, $\times 2\frac{1}{2}$) bright cream-yellow; bracts of the involucre in about 3 series, green and fleshy; ray-flowers (D, $\times 2\frac{1}{2}$) varying in number, up to about 25, or completely absent; anthers (G, $\times 10$) rounded at the base, with narrow barren tips; style-arms (H, $\times 10$) triangular; achenes pubescent; pappus-bristles (F, $\times 8$) white, barbellate (family *Compositae*).

This is a remarkable species, radiate and discoid heads sometimes being found on plants growing side by side. When the rays are numerous on a large much-branched specimen up to 3 ft. high, it vies in beauty with some of our cultivated Michaelmas daisies. There are large quantities of this species on the salt marshes south of Aldeburgh, in Suffolk, and it is widely distributed in similar situations in Britain generally, and in Europe and Asia.

This plant is rendered very conspicuous by the contrast in the ray- and disk-flowers when the former are present, and by the crowding together of the heads. The ray-flowers are female and the disk-flowers bisexual. The pollen is swept out of the latter by the rhombic tips of the style branches, which are provided with sweeping hairs directed obliquely upwards. The pollen is thus exposed to visiting insects and is carried to older flowers in which the stigmas have become receptive. After fertilization the disk-flowers fade to a discoloured orange, and at last become brown.

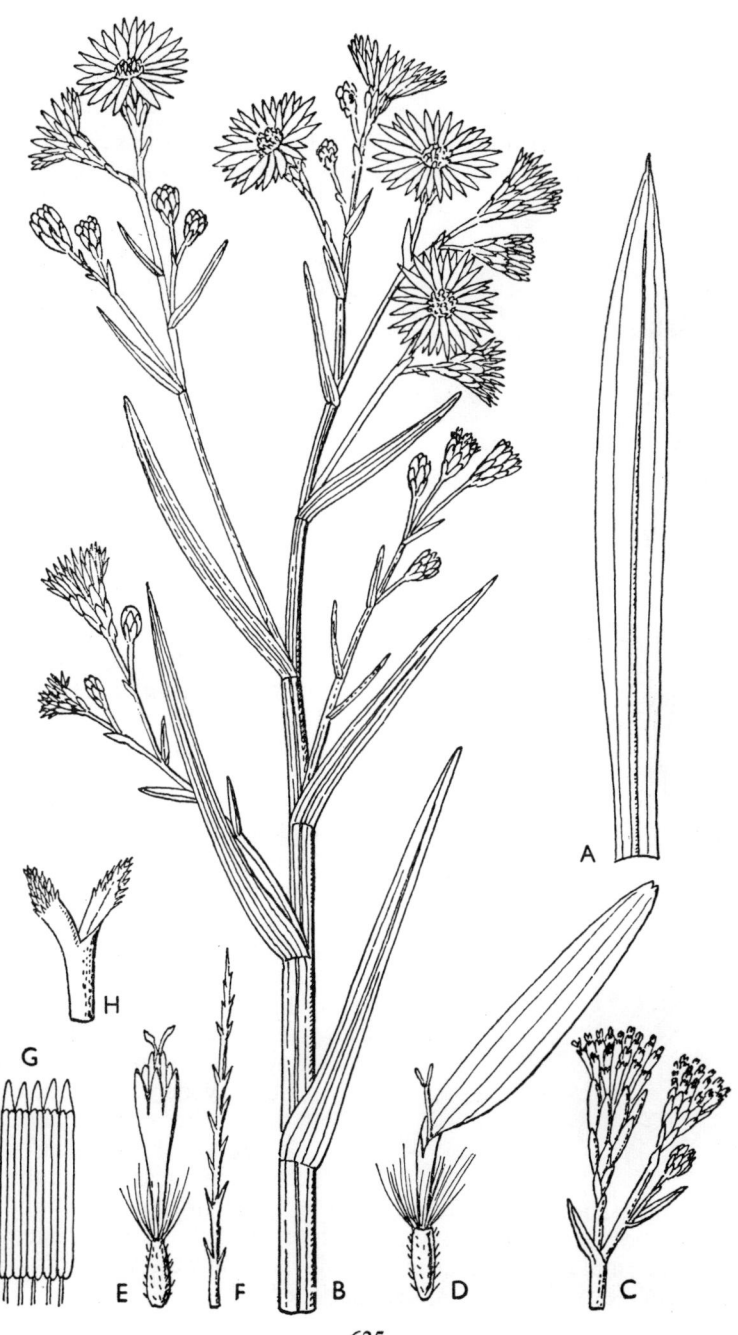

635

Erect annual or biennial; stem 1–2 ft. high, more or less crimson, thinly hairy and ribbed; basal leaves tapered to a long narrow base, narrowly spoon-shaped (spathulate), the stem leaves smaller, sessile, and more linear, all entire and 3-nerved from below the middle, hairy all over; flower-heads few, forming a loose corymb, the oldest head in the middle and soon producing fruits; involucral bracts in 3–4 rows, very narrow, crimson, hairy; outer flowers (A, $\times 3$) female and in 2–3 rows, slightly exceeding the bracts, the rays mauve; disk-flowers (B, $\times 3$) yellowish, but rather hidden by the brush-like pappus-hairs, the latter (F, $\times 10$) scabrid; anthers rounded at the base (C, $\times 8$); style-arms (D, $\times 8$) hairy on the outside, typical of the tribe *Asteroideae*, to which it belongs; achenes hairy; pappus dingy white, in fruit forming a ball nearly 1 in. diam. (family *Compositae*).

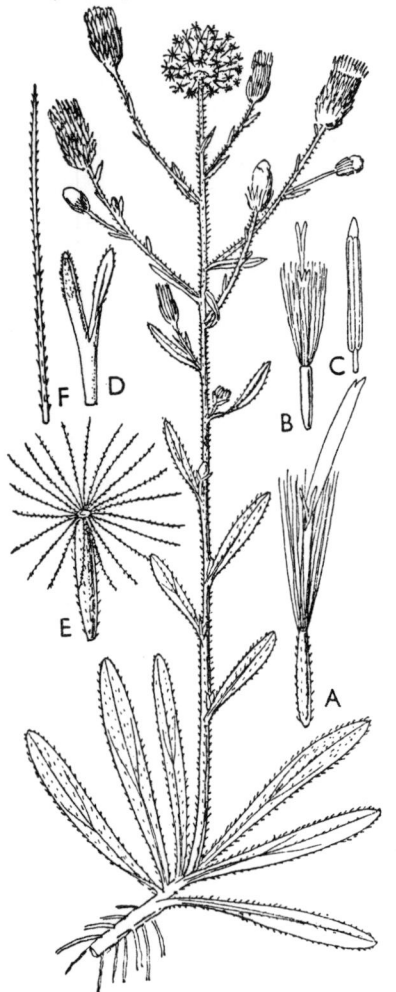

In gravel pits, waste places, and by roadsides, flowering in August and September; widely distributed in the northern hemisphere.

There are three kinds of flowers in each head, the outermost 30–40 being female with a slender tongue-like limb; within these are a great number of white female flowers without a 'tongue'; and in the middle are 6–12 bisexual flowers, which, after flowering is over, assume a dirty dark-red colour.

636

Annual 1–2 ft. high; stems slender, thinly clothed with rather stiff hairs, prominently ribbed; seedling leaves spoon-shaped or obo-vate, entire or slightly toothed; stem leaves linear-oblanceolate, acute, slightly toothed or entire, fringed with rather stiff hairs; flower-heads numerous, in a terminal leafy panicle, with slender stalks; in-volucral bracts in about 2 rows, slender, green, with pale thin margins; ray-flowers (A, × 3) small and inconspicu-ous, white or tinged with purple, with a slen-der and very small blade; disk-flowers (B, × 3) yellowish white, narrowly tubular; an-thers (C, × 3) rounded at the base, produced at the apex; style-bran-ches (D, × 4) hairy all over in the upper part; achenes (E, × 3) ('seeds') cylindric, not ribbed, 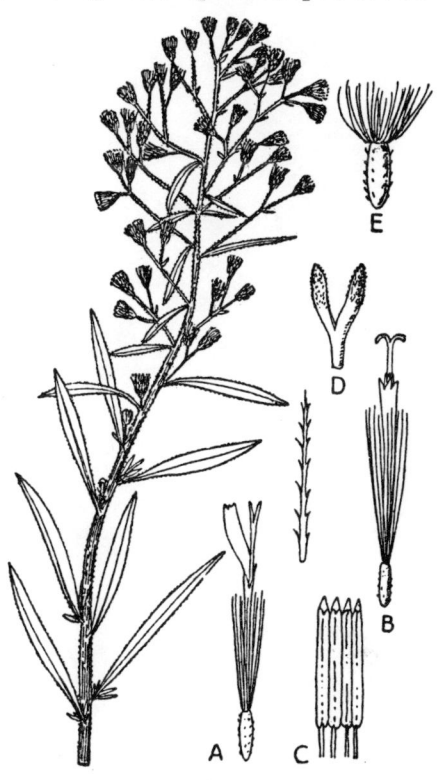 slightly hairy, topped with a spreading white pappus of minutely toothed (barbellate) bristles (family *Compositae*).

A native of North America, and now widely spread nearly all over the world as a weed in cultivated and waste places and by roadsides. It flowers during summer and autumn.

Perennial herb with annual slightly woody stems up to 2½ ft. high, prominently ribbed and softly hairy; radical leaves narrowly

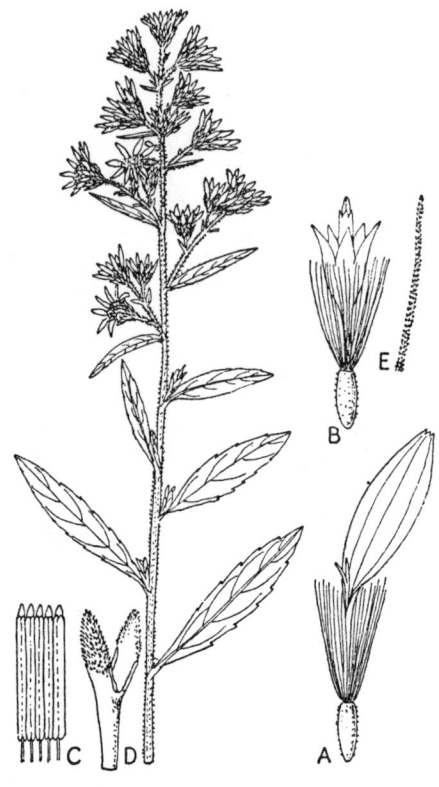

obovate, coarsely toothed (serrate), stalked, soon withering; stem leaves oblanceolate, acute at the apex, long-tapered to the base, gradually smaller upwards, minutely hairy on the margins and very obscurely and distantly toothed; flower-heads in a narrow oblong leafy panicle, the leaves gradually reduced upwards to small bracts; stalks very short; involucral bracts in about 5 rows, gradually increasing in size upwards, with a green midrib very shortly hairy; flowers bright yellow, the rays (A, × 3), 10–12, the limb toothed at the tip; disk-flowers (B, × 2¼) about twice as many; anthers rounded at the base (C, × 3); achenes hairy, with a white finely toothed pappus (E, × 5) nearly as long as the corolla-tube (D, style-arms, × 4) (family *Compositae*).

The chief interest in this species is that it is the only European and Asiatic representative of a large North American genus. It is very like many species of *Aster* in the latter region, but with yellow ray-flowers, which are produced in summer and autumn, like so many others of the *Aster* tribe to which it belongs.

Very dwarf perennial, with a short rootstock; leaves all from the base (radical), spoon-shaped to obovate, more or less toothed and pubescent; flower-head stalks (peduncles) one or more from each tuft of leaves, bearing a single head, variable in size but usually about $\frac{3}{4}$ in. diam.; bracts of the involucre (B, $\times 1\frac{3}{4}$) very dark green, more or less in two rows, narrowly oblong, with long scattered several-celled hairs outside; receptacle ovoid, hollow; ray-flowers (C, $\times 3$) numerous in 2–3 rows, white or the tips tinged with pink outside; corolla-tube clothed with a few long hairs; blade

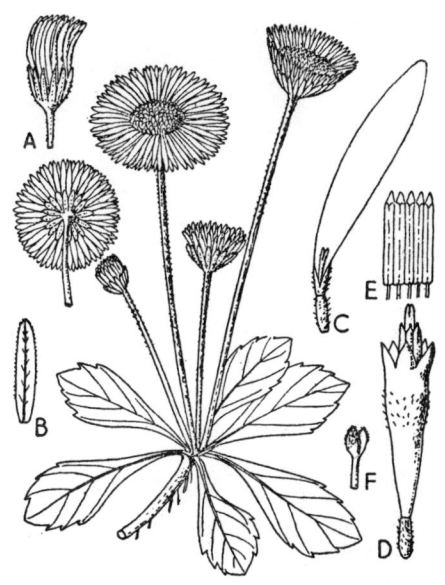

(limb) entire or slightly toothed at the apex; disk-flowers (D, $\times 6$) numerous, rich cream-yellow; corolla-tube slightly hairy above the middle; anthers (E, $\times 6$) with narrowly triangular tops, rounded at the base; style-branches (F, $\times 6$) very short and broad, hairy on the outside; achenes slightly hairy, without a pappus (family *Compositae*).

This neat and much beloved little plant is, of course, known to almost everyone from early childhood. It is only found from Europe to as far east as the Caucasus, though the genus, a small one, is distributed over the temperate regions of the whole of the northern hemisphere. In Britain it flowers nearly all the year round and is among the first to bloom in very early spring. Though the Daisy is capable of spreading rapidly, as owners of lawns know to their cost, it possesses no pappus to assist its distribution by the wind like so many other members of the family *Compositae*. A notable feature is the closing of the heads at night and during dull weather (A, $\times \frac{3}{5}$).

Perennial in damp places by river and roadsides and on moors,
flowering late summer and autumn; stems with purplish jointed

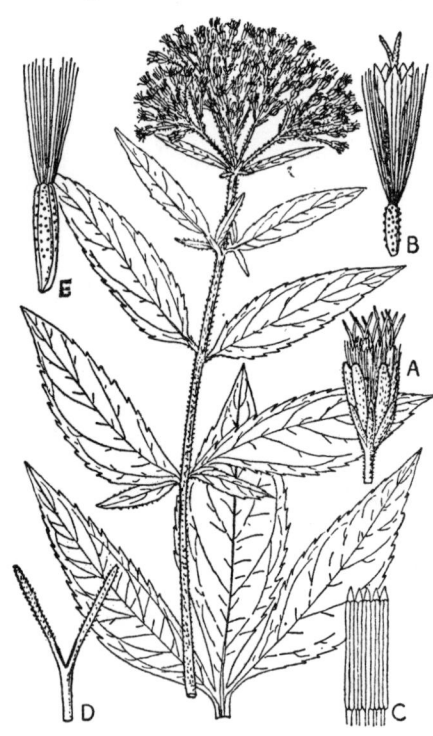

hairs; stem-leaves op-
posite, gland - dotted
below, mostly divided
into 3 lanceolate acu-
minate toothed leaflets,
those of the smaller
branches often un-
divided; flower-heads
(A, $\times 2$) crowded into
compound clusters,
pink, reddish, or nearly
white; flower - head
bracts few and loose;
flowers (B, $\times 3$) about
5 in each head, tubular
and bisexual; corolla
5-lobed; pappus-hairs
white; achene glandu-
lar; anthers (C, $\times 6$)
with barren tips and
rounded bases; style
(D, $\times 4$) with 2 spreading branches shortly
hairy in the upper part,
stigmatic in the lower-
most fourth; ripe ach-

enes ('seeds') (E, $\times 6$) ribbed (family *Compositae*).

The common name of this plant is due to the leaves resembling
those of hemp. It usually grows in clumps on banks near water,
and is widely distributed in Europe and Asia. The heads are much
reduced in size, and are individually not very conspicuous, but
this is compensated for by their aggregation into a dense corymb.
These are conspicuous because the margins of the involucral
bracts are reddish, and the protruding stylar branches are white.
The latter are very hairy all around, and these hairs serve to sweep
out the pollen from the anther-cylinder, retaining them so that insects visiting the flowers brush against them and carry them to
another flower.

Perennial with clumps of erect stems 1–1½ ft. high, glabrous and succulent, shining; leaves alternate, shortly linear, entire or with
one or two small teeth near the apex, thick and fleshy, faintly 3-nerved towards the base, minutely pustulate (under a strong lens); flower-heads on rather long leafy erect peduncles and forming a corymb, the oldest head in the middle and with the shortest stalk; bracts of the involucre. green, slightly keeled, in about 4 rows; ray-flowers (A, ×3) rich cream-yellow, about 40–50, soon becoming recurved; disk-flowers (B, ×4) darker yellow; style of disk-flowers (C, ×10) 2-lobed, lobes smooth, shaped like Indian clubs; anthers (D, ×10) tailed at the base; pappus hairs (E, ×6) white, slightly roughened (barbellate) (family *Compositae*).

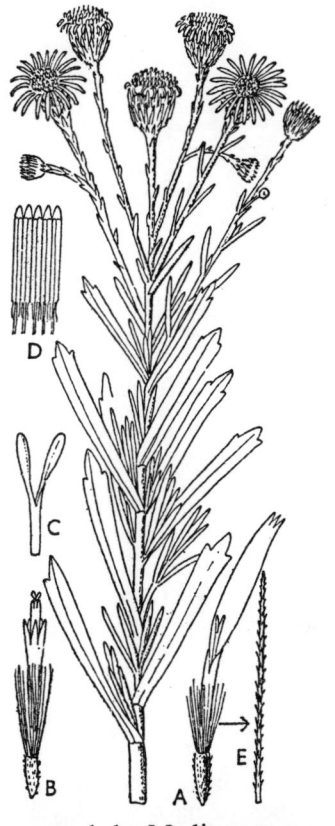

A lovely species in salt marshes and amongst maritime rocks, in Britain mainly in the south and west as far north as south-west Scotland, and also in south-east Eire; very distinct, and recognized at once by the narrow thick succulent leaves and conspicuous bright yellow ray-flowers; distributed in
western Europe and in the countries around the Mediterranean.

We have illustrated three of the seven species of *Inula* found in Britain, most of the others being introduced and naturalized in some localities. The only other native species is *I. salicina* L., Willow-leaved Inula, with elliptic-lanceolate toothed leaves and ligulate flower-heads, is found only in Eire.

A stout erect perennial herb up to nearly 6 ft. high; basal leaves (A, $\times\frac{1}{5}$) large, long-stalked, elliptic-lanceolate, decurrent at the

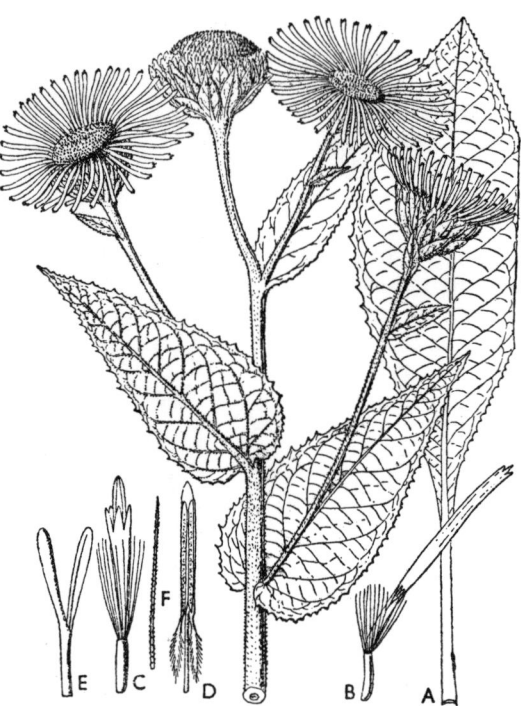

base, averaging about 1 ft. long and 4 in. broad, repand‑dentate, slightly pubescent above, woolly-hairy below; lateral nerves numerous and much branched; stem-leaves sessile and rounded or cordate at the base, ovate, pointed, doubly dentate, softly hairy below; flower‑heads forming a loose corymb, each head about $3\frac{1}{2}$ in. diam.; involucral bracts leafy, green, lanceolate, pointed, softly pubescent, the innermost much narrower and almost linear; receptacle slightly concave; ray-flowers (B, $\times\frac{2}{3}$) numerous, narrow, rich yellow, 3-toothed at the apex; disk-flowers very numerous (C, $\times1\frac{1}{3}$); pappus (F, $\times3$) dingy white, minutely barbellate; anthers (D, $\times5$) with long feathery tails at the base; style-arms (E, $\times6$) club-shaped; achenes ribbed when dry (family *Compositae*).

Probably a relic of cultivation but naturalized in fields, copses, and waste places; candied root used as sweetmeat; one of the most spectacular of our herbaceous plants; found wild in central and southern Europe as far east as the western Himalayas and northern Asia; naturalized in North America.

Inula conyza DC. (×⅓)

An erect biennial 2–3 ft. high; stems ribbed, pubescent; lower leaves (A, ×⅓) stalked, broadly lanceolate, mostly about 6 in. long, toothed, softly pubescent below; stem-leaves becoming sessile but narrowed to the base, becoming entire and reduced to leafy bracts in the heads (B, ×1) of the many-flowered corymb; involucral bracts in several rows, outer with spreading leafy tips, pubescent; ray-flowers (C, ×2) very small, with crimson styles; disk-flowers yellow; anthers (E, ×8) with long feathery tails; style-arms (F, ×8) club-shaped; achenes (G, ×12) ribbed, shortly pubescent; pappus-hairs (H, ×12) white, scabrid (family *Compositae*).

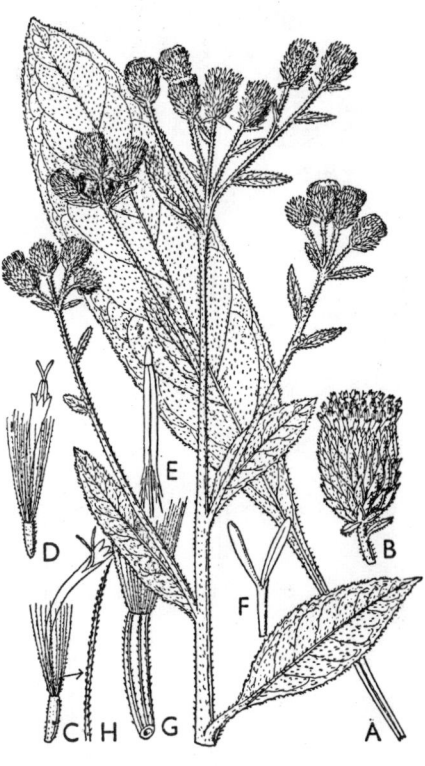

At first sight this appears to be a rayless Composite, but a close inspection shows there are very inconspicuous ray-flowers with a small toothed limb.

The plant is in some books called *Inula squarrosa* L., but that species is not found wild in Britain.

Found in hedges and open woods and by roadsides in England and Wales, but not in Scotland or in Eire; rather partial to chalky soils; flowers in summer and autumn.

Distributed through central and south-eastern Europe south to Algeria. The basal leaves are rather like those of the Foxglove, especially in the autumn of the first year.

LESSER FLEABANE
Pulicaria vulgaris (L.) Gaertn. ($\times\frac{1}{2}$)

Annual herb, much-branched, up to about 1 ft. high, softly pubescent all over, the young parts woolly; leaves alternate, sessile,

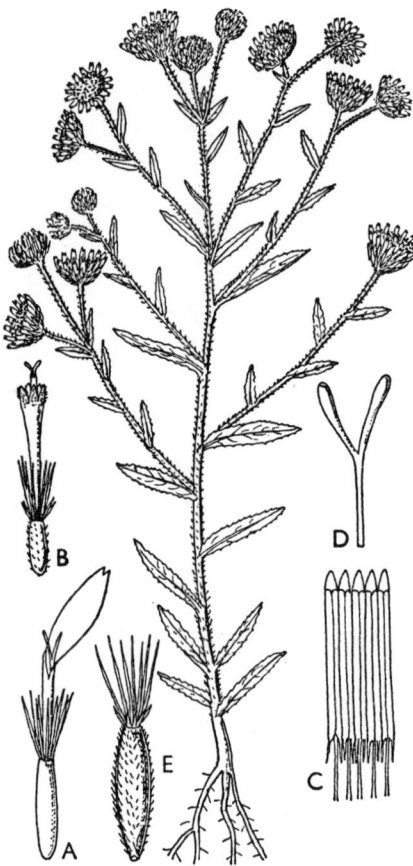

oblong-lanceolate, largest about 1 in. long, with wavy margins, shortly hairy; flower-heads solitary at the ends of all the leafy branchlets, shortly stalked, shortly and broadly bell-shaped; involucral bracts in 4–5 rows, narrow, hairy outside; receptacle without scales amongst the flowers; ray-flowers (A, ×6) numerous, yellow, small, and quite inconspicuous; disk-flowers (B, ×6) numerous; anthers (C, ×12) with barren tips and tailed at the base; style-arms (D, ×12) club-shaped, smooth; achenes (E, ×7) hairy; pappus composed of 2 rows, an outer row of very short bristles and an inner row of few longer bristles, these almost smooth (synonym *Inula pulicaria* L.) (family *Compositae*).

A very local plant, and confined to south-eastern and southern England; extends to eastern Asia; flowers in summer and autumn.

Readily distinguished from the only other British species *P. dysenterica* (L.) Gaertn. (see fig. 551), by the leaves which are not arrow-shaped at the base, and by the smaller flower-heads.

Greyish green perennial with creeping rootstock, by the banks of ditches, damp places by roadsides, and in damp pastures; stems erect, densely leafy, ribbed, white wooly-hairy like the under-surface of the leaves; leaves sessile, oblong-lanceolate, arrow-shaped at the base, rather thin and toothed (dentate); flower-heads usually 3 or more at the end of each stem or branch, about 1–1½ in. diam.; involucral bracts numerous, very narrow with thread-like tips; ray-flowers (A, $\times 2$) numerous, yellow, spreading, very narrow, with 3 teeth at the top; pappus-hairs few inside a short jagged cup; disk-flowers (B, $\times 3$) numerous, yellow; anthers (C, $\times 12$) with long slender tails at the

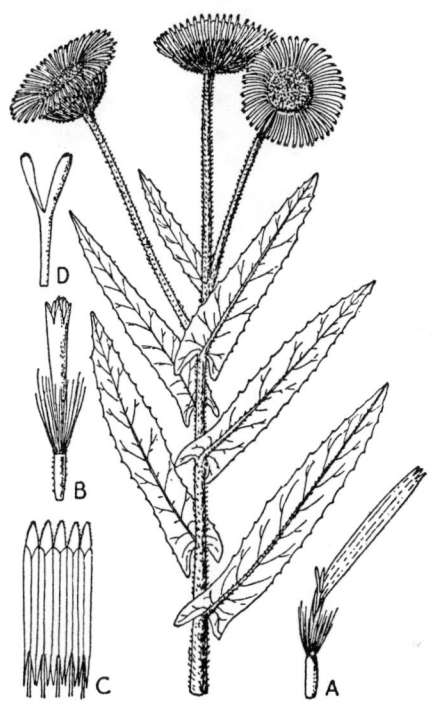

base, and rather long terminal sterile tips; style-branches (D, $\times 12$) club-shaped; achenes slightly pubescent; flowers in late summer and autumn (family *Compositae*).

The larger flower-heads of this species have sometimes as many as six hundred disk-flowers and up to a hundred ray-flowers; the ray-flowers are unisexual (female) and the disk-flowers bisexual; the latter bear the anthers and style-branches, these possessing hairs directed upwards on the outer side which brush out the pollen as they emerge from the anther-tube. They then spread out horizontally, become recurved and receptive, and receive pollen from other flowers or flower-heads by means of insect visitors. The pollen that is brushed out is largely held by a fringe of hairs on the upper triangular sterile portions of the anthers (see fig. C).

CUDWEED
Filago germanica L. ($\times\frac{2}{3}$)

Slender annual cottony herb, with fibrous roots; stems up to about 1½ ft. high, forking here and there into 2 divergent branches with

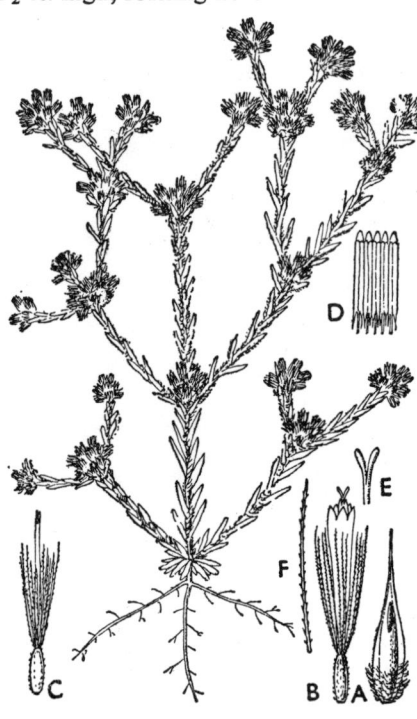

bunches of sessile flower - heads in the forks and at the ends; leaves shortly linear, with a hardened tip, covered with white cotton-wool-like hairs; bracts of the involucre (A, × 4) woolly in the lower part, glabrous upwards, membranous and shining, the outer one with a green spot towards the top; very sharply pointed; receptacle with a row of scales only within the outer flowers; flowers in the middle (B, × 3), bisexual, though sometimes infertile, those on the outside (C, × 3) female and with a narrow thread-like corolla; anthers (D, × 8) tailed at the base; style-arms (E, × 6) club-shaped; achenes slightly hairy; pappus (F, × 8) of white slightly rough bristles (family *Compositae*).

Grows in dry fields and stony and waste places, flowering in summer; widely distributed in Europe and western Asia, north Africa, and the Atlantic islands.

It has some curious local names, such as Clodweed, Downweed, Herb Impious, Old Owl, Quidwort, Son-before-the-Father, and several others.

Gnaphalium uliginosum L. ($\times \frac{1}{2}$)

Annual much branched from the base, covered all over with woolly hairs, the leaves at length becoming less hairy on the upper surface; leaves alternate, linear or slightly spoon-shaped, often bearing in their axils a short leafy shoot; flower-heads in terminal leafy clusters, sessile; involucral bracts brownish and shining; receptacle without scales between the flowers; outer flowers thread-

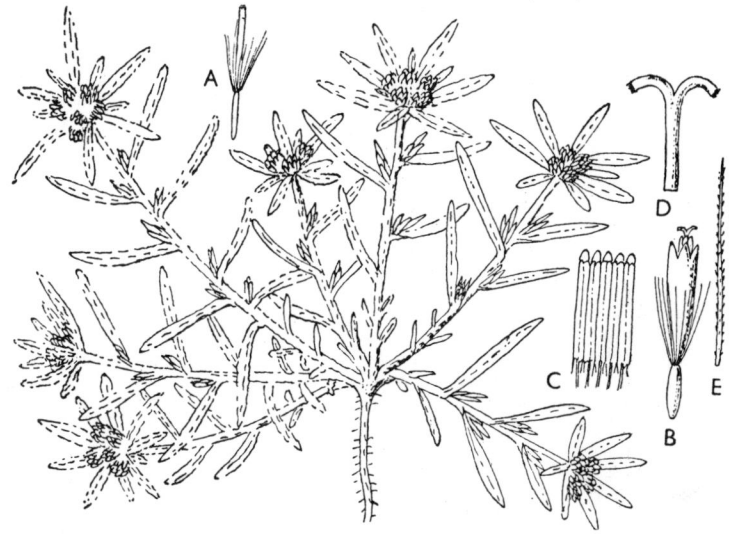

like and female (A, $\times$ 5), inner flowers tubular and bisexual (B, $\times$ 10); anthers tailed at the base and with barren tips (C, $\times$ 20); style-branches very blunt at the tip (D, $\times$ 30); achenes very small, glabrous, crowned with a pappus of shining white bristles (E, $\times$ 20) which soon fall off (family *Compositae*).

Grows in wet sandy places by roads, in waste land, and on heaths, flowering in summer and autumn. It is common throughout the British Isles, though shy of limestone soils.

A tufted perennial herb, up to about 1 ft. or 15 in. high; basal
leaves long and narrow, entire, green above and thinly hairy,

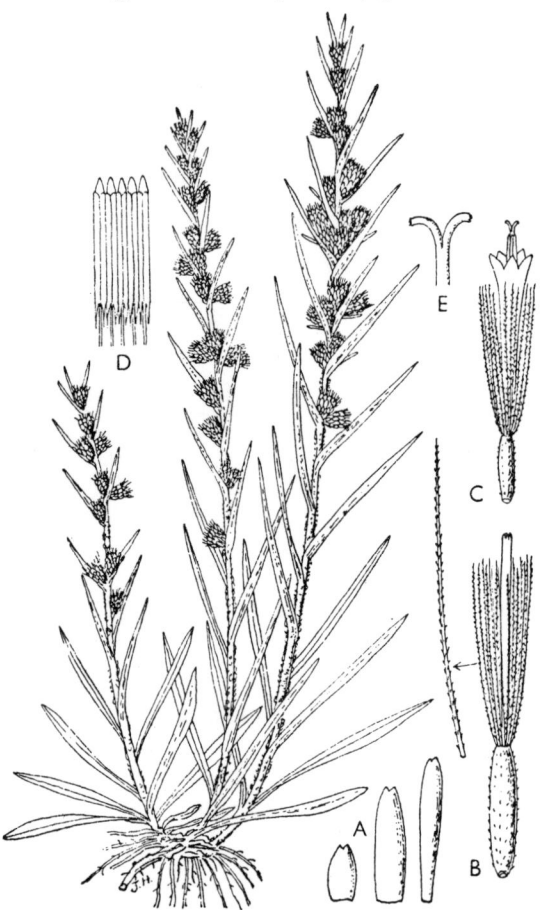

covered with woolly white hairs below; stems erect, leafy to the top, woolly; leaves linear, entirely covered on both surfaces but es- pecially below with woolly white hairs, sometimes more green on the upper surface; flower - heads sessile to shortly stalked in the axils of the leaves on the upper half or two-thirds of the stem; in- volucral bracts (A, $\times$ 3) in 3–4 rows, tinged with brown and shin- ing, glabrous outside; re- ceptacle without scales amongst the flowers;

outer flowers (B, $\times$ 8) thread-like and female, more numerous
than the bisexual inner tubular ones in the middle (C, $\times$ 8);
achenes slender, slightly pubescent; pappus nearly as long as
the corolla, white, barbellate; anthers (D, $\times$ 16) tailed at the
base; style-arms (E, $\times$ 16) very blunt (truncate) (family *Compositae*). This very distinctive species is found in dry pastures, in
open places in woods, and on heaths.

Perennial herb; stems about 2 ft. high, with dense woolly hairs; leaves alternate, sessile, narrowly lanceolate, 3–4 in. long, entire, rather obscurely 3-nerved lengthwise with woolly hairs; flower-heads numerous; involucre of numerous white pearly bracts about $\frac{1}{2}$ in. diam.; flowers dioecious; no rays; males (A, $\times 10$) with a very small abortive ovary, tailed anthers (B, $\times 15$), and a truncate

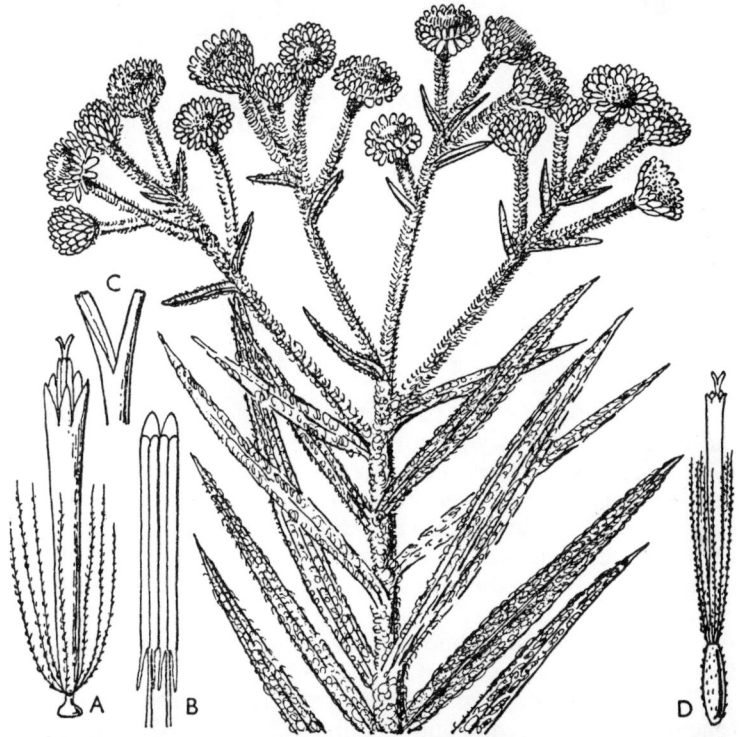

style (C, $\times 15$); females (D, $\times 10$) with a very slender tube, a hairy ovary, and no anthers; achenes hairy; pappus-hairs few, white, barbellate (family *Compositae*).

Widely spread in North America and eastern Asia and naturalized in Europe; in Britain found sometimes in railway cuttings. In North America it has numerous common names such as Silver-leaf, Life-everlasting, Moonshine, Cotton-weed, None-so-pretty, Lady-never-fade, Indian-posy, Ladies'-tobacco, Poverty-weed, and Silver-button.

Antennaria dioica (L.) Gaertn. (× ⅔)

Densely tufted perennial; stems up to 9 in. high; leaves crowded, spathulate to narrowly oblanceolate, glabrous above, densely cov-

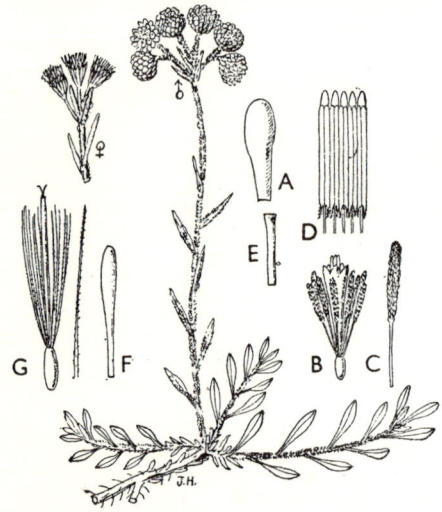

ered below with white woolly hairs; flowering-stems densely woolly with scattered linear leaves, bearing a cluster of shortly stalked heads at the top; flower-heads dioecious (unisexual and on different plants); male bracts (A, × 1½) shorter and broader than the female (F, × 1½), all white and glabrous except the woolly base; male flowers (B, × 4) with short infertile ovaries and pappus-hairs swollen towards the top and densely papillous (C, × 6); anthers with barren tips and tailed at the base (D, × 15); style undivided (E, × 8); female flowers (G, × 4) with longer ovaries and longer nearly smooth pappus, and a very slender (almost thread-like) corolla, no stamens, and a slender divided style (family *Compositae*).

The flower-heads are of one sex, the males on one plant, the females on another; the heads of the two sexes look rather different, because the bracts of the male are much shorter than those of the female, which are white or rose-coloured, and the pappus of the two sexes is quite distinct.

The filaments of the male flowers are irritable, and curve when touched. In this way the anther-cylinder is retracted, so that pollen protrudes from its upper end and is exposed to insect visitors.

Serratula tinctoria L. ($\times\frac{1}{3}$)

Erect perennial herb with stiff ascending branches each ending in a cluster (usually 3) of almost sessile or stalked heads; lower leaves (A, $\times\frac{1}{3}$) deeply pinnately lobed, the upper lobes tending to join up, the remainder lanceolate to almost linear, sharply toothed on the margin, not hairy or only very slightly so; stem-leaves becoming less lobed or only serrate upwards, lanceolate, bright green and closely net-veined; heads (B, $\times 1$) narrowly oblong-ovoid, about $\frac{3}{4}$ in. long; bracts in about 6–8 rows, spirally arranged, triangular-lanceolate, margined with short woolly hairs, the uppermost with coloured tips like the pale purple or white flowers; flowers subdioecious; receptacle bristly between the flowers; achenes (E, $\times 3$) smooth, with an oblique scar at the base; pappus (F, $\times 5$) bristly, slightly rough; corolla (C,

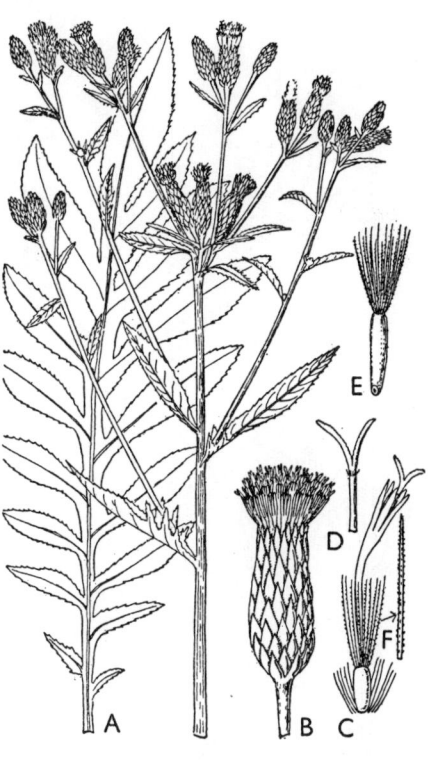

$\times 5$) bent, 5-lobed; style (D, $\times 10$) with a ring of very short hairs below the stigmas (family *Compositae*).

Found as far north as southern Scotland, and widely distributed in Europe and northern Asia; much resembles a *Centaurea*, but the bracts are not comb-like on the margins, and the receptacle is covered with bristles among the flowers. The flower-heads are gyno-dioecious, i.e. some are entirely female and some bisexual (male and female), but there are transition forms with both kinds in the same head.

MILK THISTLE
Silybum marianum (L.) Gaertn. ($\times \frac{1}{3}$)

Annual or biennial herb, up to 3 ft. high; stems closely ribbed, full of pith but hollow at the core; lower leaves over 1 ft. long, with broad flattened petioles prickly on the margin, deeply pinnately lobed with rather overlapping lobes, dentate, teeth ending in very sharp prickles, mostly variegated with white nerves and veins; upper leaves sessile and stem-clasping, auriculate at the base; flower-heads nodding at the ends of the branches, $1\frac{1}{2}$–2 in. diam.; bracts of involucre scale-like but terminated by a leafy appendage ending in a sharp prickle and margined with prickles; flowers purple to crimson; corolla (A, ×1)

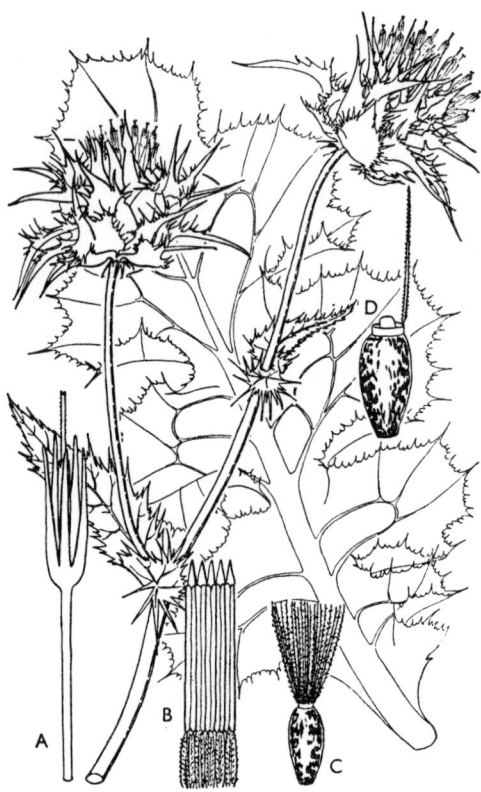

long and cylindric, 5-lobed, lobes linear; anthers (B, ×2) with long hairy tails; achenes (C, × 1¼) mottled with black; pappus (D, × 2) of barbellate bristles (family *Compositae*).

An introduced plant from southern Europe, flowering in summer, mostly in waste places; easily recognized by the prickly leaves mostly variegated by white nerves and veins, and the mottled achenes with finely barbellate pappus.

Other names are 'Blessed Thistle', 'Holy Thistle', and 'Our Lady's Milk Thistle'. It was formerly grown for its root which was boiled; the heads were treated like those of the Globe Artichoke and the leaves used as a spring salad. Drawn by Olive Tait.

Onopordon acanthium L. ($\times \frac{1}{2}$)

A vigorous biennial herb up to about 6 ft. high, very prickly and covered all over with loose woolly hairs; stem clothed by the decurrent leaf-bases from top to bottom; basal leaves (A, $\times \frac{1}{2}$) stalked, 1 ft. or more long, coarsely lobulate, the lobules with a few sharp prickle-like teeth; stem-leaves narrow and very prickly; flower-heads large and at the ends of the few branches; bracts of the involucre very numerous in several series, awl-shaped from a broader base, matted together with woolly hairs; receptacle (B, $\times 1\frac{1}{2}$) honeycombed into cavities with jagged margins; flowers (C, $\times 1\frac{1}{2}$) pale purple, all of one kind, tubular, 5-lobed; anthers (D, $\times 4$) with narrow barren tips and arrow-shaped at the base; style

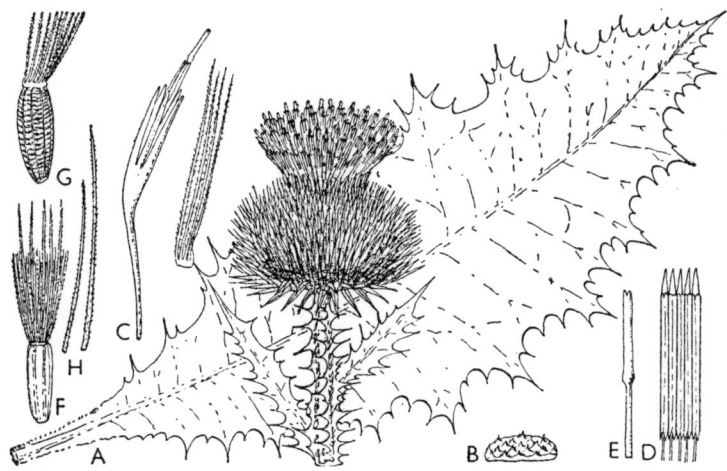

(E, $\times 4$) very shortly split at the tip; achenes (F, $\times 2$) slightly compressed, ribbed lengthwise and transversely rugose when ripe (G, $\times 2$); pappus-bristles (H, $\times 5$), rough, a few longer than the others (family *Compositae*).

A widely spread and handsome species, and representing the Scotch heraldic thistle; common in the Mediterranean region.

This is an imposing plant, and well worth a place in the garden. The stems are broadly winged and more or less function as leaves, the latter becoming reduced to very small proportions towards the top of the plant. It prefers rather dry sandy soil, and flowers in July and August. Besides the names given above it is also called 'Argentine', 'Oat', 'Queen Mary's', and 'Silver Thistle'.

A stiff annual or biennial herb to 3 or 4 ft. high; stems not or only slightly branched, winged with the decurrent blades of the leaves, the wings sharply bristly and toothed; leaves sessile, pinnately lobed, the lobes spine-tipped, scabrid above, woolly below; flower-heads few in a cluster, sessile, narrowly campanulate, about $\frac{3}{4}$ in. long; involucral bracts about 6 rows, sharply pointed; flowers (B, $\times 5$) all tubular, pink; achenes (E, $\times 3$) lined when ripe, glabrous; anthers (D, $\times 6$) tailed, filaments hairy; pappus-bristles (C, $\times 10$) white, scabrid; receptacle (A, $\times 3$) with numerous narrow bristles (family *Compositae*).

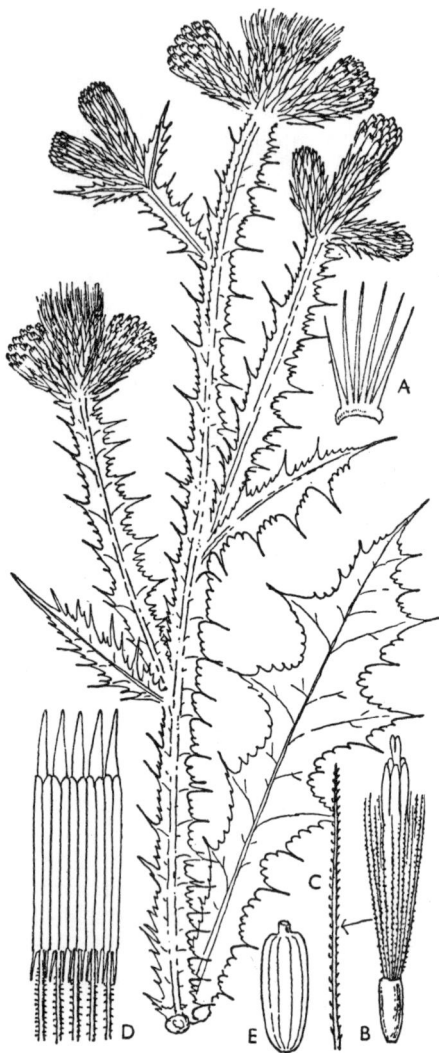

Hedgesides and sandy waste places, especially in coastal districts; widely distributed in southern and western Europe.

This is mostly regarded in various *Floras* as being the same as, or a variety of, *Carduus pycnocephalus* L., a rare alien which has only slightly winged, long branches, bearing 1–3 larger heads with more spreading involucral bracts, and with the leaves more densely cottony below.

Carduus nutans L. ($\times \frac{1}{2}$)

Biennial herb up to about 3 ft. high, usually covered very slightly with cottony hairs but not conspicuously so; stems winged with the very narrow prickly extensions of the leaf-bases; basal leaves pinnately lobed and with very prickly margins; stem-leaves narrow and sessile, very prickly on the lobulate margin and thinly hairy; flower-heads nodding, about $1\frac{1}{4}$–$1\frac{1}{2}$ in. diam., solitary on simple stems or these with a few branches at the top, each ending in a flower-head; bracts of the involucre in about 6 or 7 rows, narrowly lanceolate, with a long sharp point, interlaced with woolly hairs; receptacle with long smooth bristles (A, $\times 1$) between the flowers; flowers (B, $\times 2\frac{1}{2}$) all tubular, crimson; achene

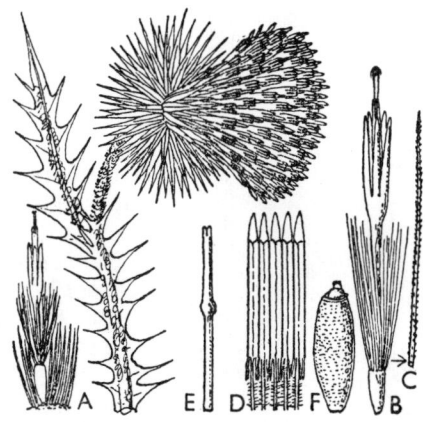

glabrous; pappus-bristles (C, $\times 3$) slightly rough; corolla slender, deeply 5-lobed; anthers (D, $\times 3$) with long tails at the base, and very hairy filaments; style (E, $\times 3$) smooth, slightly 2-lobed at the apex; ripe achenes (F, $\times 2\frac{1}{2}$) straw-coloured, very minutely wrinkled (family *Compositae*).

The Musk Thistle is often conspicuous on waste ground and rubbish-heaps, and seems to follow man wherever he goes, though it shows a definite preference for light and sandy soils, especially in chalky districts. The seeds are used for feeding cage-birds. Other commons names for the plant are Queen Ann's thrissel, and Bank, Buck, and Dog Thistle.

It is widely distributed to north Africa, and eastwards to the Himalayas and Siberia.

Saussurea alpina (L.) DC. ($\times \frac{1}{3}$)

Perennial herb with unbranched stems up to 1 ft. high, clothed here and there with white woolly hairs; rootstock covered with

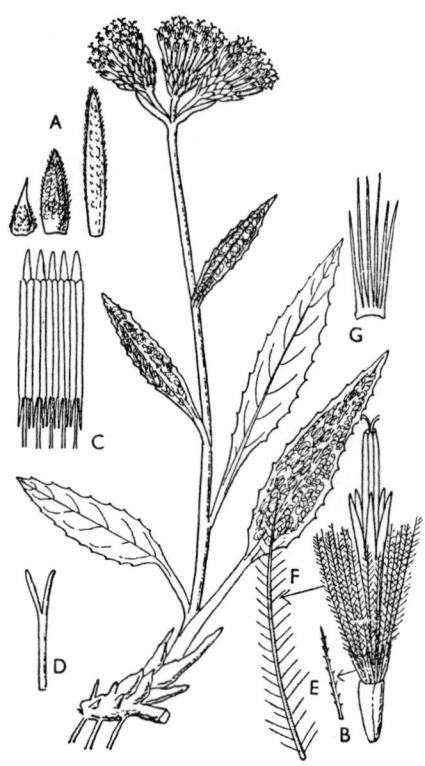

the persistent leaf-scales; leaves alternate, stalked, lanceolate, acute, narrowed to the base, about 3 in. long and nearly 1 in. broad, remotely repand-denticulate, woolly below but the wool soon falling off; flower-heads clustered at the tip of the stem, nearly sessile; involucral bracts (A, $\times 1\frac{1}{2}$) about 4 rows, the outer short and ovate, the innermost broadly linear, and with hairy upper part; flowers (B, $\times 8$) about 15, all of one kind, bisexual, tubular, violet-purple; anthers (C, $\times 12$) with long tails at the base and narrow, barren tops; style-arms smooth; achenes glabrous; pappus of 2 kinds of bristles, the outer (E, $\times 15$) short and scabrid, the inner (F, $\times 15$) long and feather-like (plumose); receptacle with numerous narrow bristles (G, $\times 10$) amongst the flowers (family *Compositae*).

A mountain species confined to northern Britain and Northern Ireland; otherwise widely distributed in mountainous regions in the northern hemisphere.

The flowers smell like violets or vanilla. The stamens mature before the style-arms are receptive. The outer surfaces of the latter are completely covered with long pointed hairs, which are longest below and which sweep out the pollen, the inner surface being covered with stigmatic papillae. After spreading out they roll back.

Cirsium acaule Scop. ($\times \frac{1}{2}$)

Perennial, stemless or the stem very short and unbranched; leaves all radical, spreading in a rosette, usually about 6 in. long, narrow, deeply pinnately lobed, the lobes increasing in size upwards and lobulate, the lobules ending in long sharp prickles, glabrous above, clothed on the midrib below with long rope-like many-celled hairs (A, ×5); flower-heads sessile or nearly so in the middle of the leaves, solitary or with one or two lateral heads, narrowly ovoid, with many rows of ovate-lanceolate pointed bracts slightly frilled on the margin, the uppermost bracts elongated and with deep mauve tips; outer flowers (B, ×1) spreading and longer than the inner (C, ×1), the latter forming a 'cone'; achenes (D, ×3)

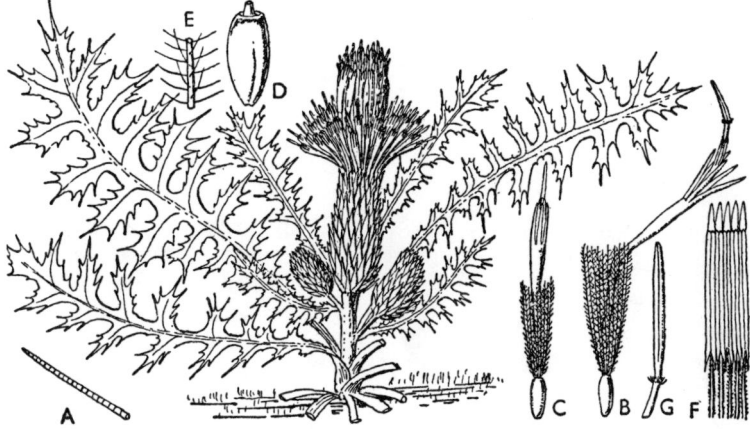

smooth, not beaked except by base of style; pappus (E, ×3) clothed with long slender hairs (plumose); corolla deeply 5-lobed, deep mauve or crimson; anthers tailed, their stalks hairy (F, ×5); style crimson, with a ring of short hairs below the stigmas (G, ×5) (family *Compositae*).

Grows in dry pastures and is sometimes a troublesome weed owing to its dwarf stature by which it escapes the scythe or mowing machine; nevertheless a very pretty plant. Hybrids occur between this and *C. arvense* (fig. 565).

The style-branches remain almost closed and are covered externally with small sweeping hairs, with a ring of longer hairs at their base, which sweep out the pollen from the anther cylinder. The margins are covered with stigmatic papillae and bend outwards to catch the pollen from the bodies of insects.

Biennial up to about 4 ft. high; stem continuously winged and armed with long pointed very sharp prickles, ribbed and rather

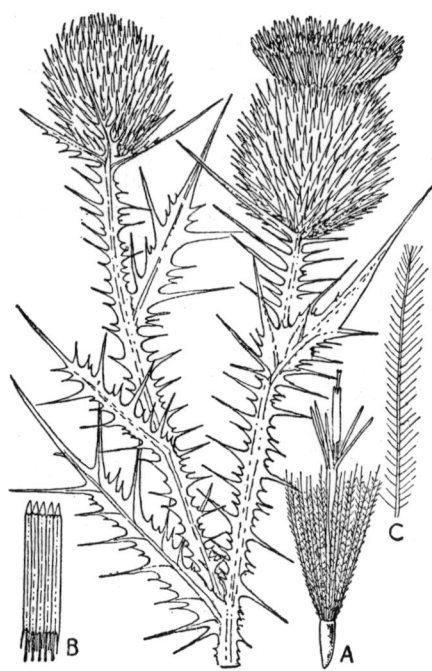

woolly hairy like the lower surface of the leaves; basal leaves elongated but less prickly than the stem leaves, the latter rather narrowly lanceolate, decurrent on the stem and forming the wing, deeply pinnately lobed, the lobes ending in a very long and very sharp prickle with much smaller prickles between them; upper surface loosely clothed with very short bristly hairs, woolly below with whitish hairs; flower - heads rather large, few, stalked or sometimes subsessile and about 3 in a cluster, about 1¾ in. long when in flower; involucre broadly campanulate, composed of very numerous bracts in about 10–15 rows, all narrow and ending in a long sharp hard prickle, and with a hard nearly glabrous basal portion; flowers all alike (A, $\times 1\frac{1}{4}$), very numerous, bright purple, bisexual; corolla-tube long and slender, with narrow lobes; anthers (B, $\times 2$) with tails at the base; achenes glabrous; pappus (C, $\times 2\frac{1}{2}$) very copious, feathery (family *Compositae*).

This species is common in fields, pastures, and waste places and is a nuisance to the farmer when once it gets established, as the heads mature rapidly and the achenes ('seeds') are blown about by the wind. Being a biennial it is more easily eradicated, however, than the Creeping Thistle, especially if cut before flowering. Long-tongued bees visit the flowers for the nectar concealed at the base of the very long corolla-tube.

Cirsium arvense (L.) Scop. ($\times \frac{2}{5}$)

Perennial with creeping rootstock; stems annual, erect, leafy, ribbed and prickly with the decurrent bases of the leaves; leaves oblanceolate in outline but deeply and undulately lobed, woolly when young, embracing the stem at the base, the very prickly margins often continued down the latter for some distance, glabrous or nearly so below when mature; flower-heads rather small, few in a lax terminal corymb, unisexual, the males (A) on

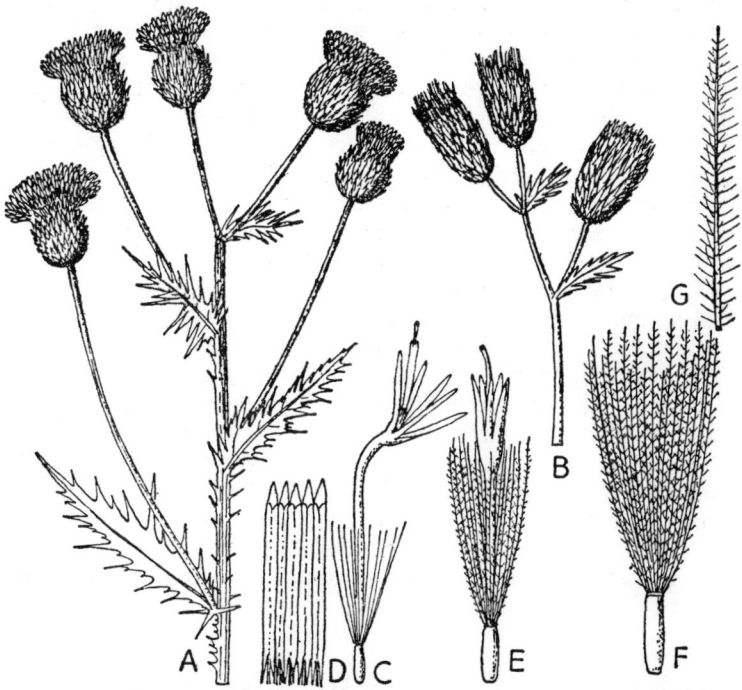

one plant, the females (B) on another, the males nearly globose with very projecting rose-purple or rarely white flowers (C, $\times 2\frac{1}{2}$) and conspicuous anthers (D), the females narrower and with longer bracts but shorter flowers (E, $\times 2\frac{1}{2}$) with conspicuous stigmas, and the pappus soon a prominent feature, both kinds of heads with numerous rows of narrow bracts with short spiny tips; pappus feathery (i.e. with long side hairs); achenes ('seeds') (F, $\times 2\frac{1}{2}$) quite smooth (family *Compositae*).

A very common Thistle in cultivated and waste places.

MARSH THISTLE

Cirsium palustre (L.) Scop. ($\times \frac{1}{2}$)

A stiff-growing annual or biennial, variable in height up to about $4\frac{1}{2}$ ft.; stems mostly unbranched except at the top, closely ribbed and beset with prickles; leaves narrowly lanceolate in outline to linear, pinnately lobed, the lobes ending in very sharp prickles, thinly cobwebby below; flower-heads usually 3 or more in the axils of the leaves and crowded towards the top and making the plant appear top-heavy; heads almost sessile on the common short stalk, about 1 in. long and as much in diam.; bracts of the involucre very numerous narrow, with sharp tips and woolly margins; flowers purple, all tubular; corolla (A, $\times$ 4) slender, 5-lobed; anthers (B, $\times$ 3) connate, with hairy filaments and with tails; stigma (C, $\times$ 10) with a ring of hairs around the base; achene (D, $\times$ 5) glabrous, crowned by several circles of feather-like (plumose) bristles (E, $\times$ 6) (family *Compositae*).

Grows in marshy fields and meadows, often at a spot where a spring of water occurs, flowering in summer; widely distributed in the northern hemisphere as far as Asiatic Russia.

Thistles belong to the Daisy family, *Compositae*, but, unlike the Daisy, there are no ray-flowers in the flower-heads, all being tubular, as shown in the drawing. In the dim past, perhaps millions of years ago, when the ancestors of the *Compositae* were beginning to change their inflorescence (collection of flowers) into their flower-head as we know it to-day, the flowers were probably arranged in a loose elongated spike, each with a bract below, and the calyx was not much modified, certainly not into the bristly, feathery thing shown in the drawing. As more crowding took place on the shortening of the axis, the outer flowers became modified into strap-shaped bodies in order to continue to attract insects.

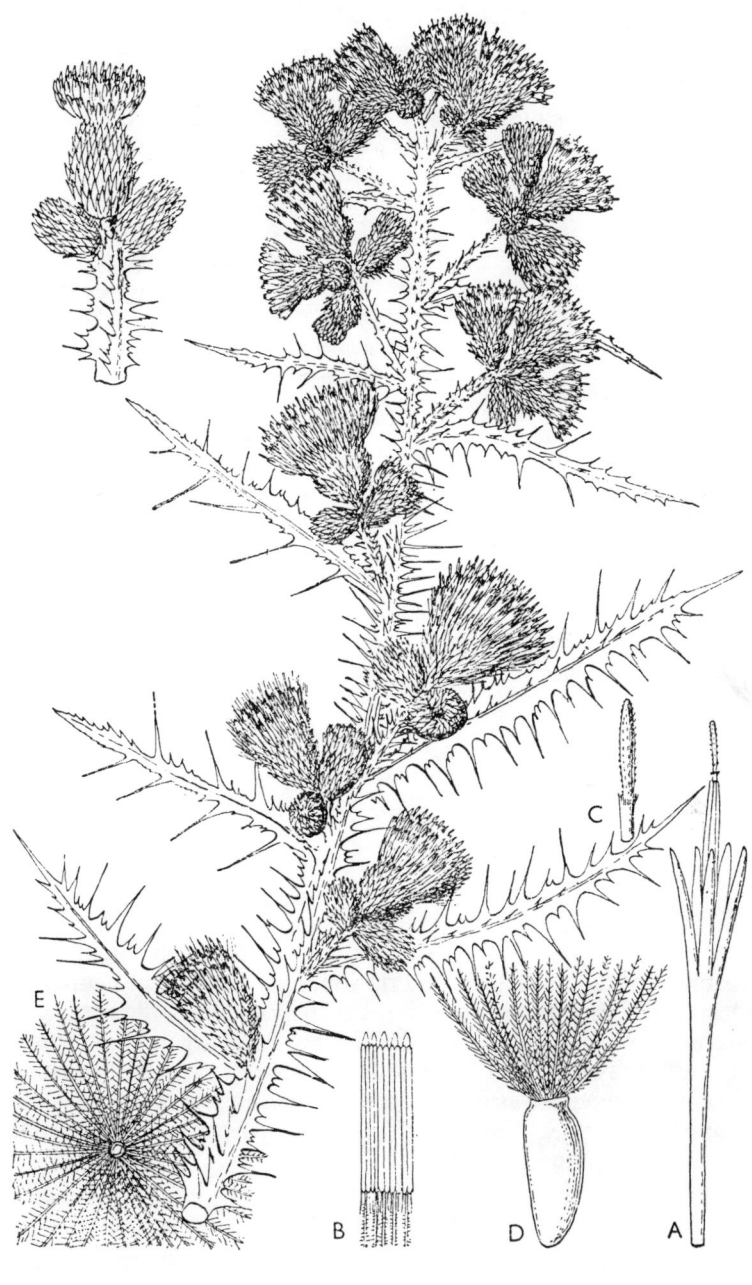

Cirsium heterophyllum (L.) Hill (× ⅓)

Perennial with stoloniferous rootstock and slender roots; basal leaves long-stalked, broadly lanceolate, see text-figure A, the

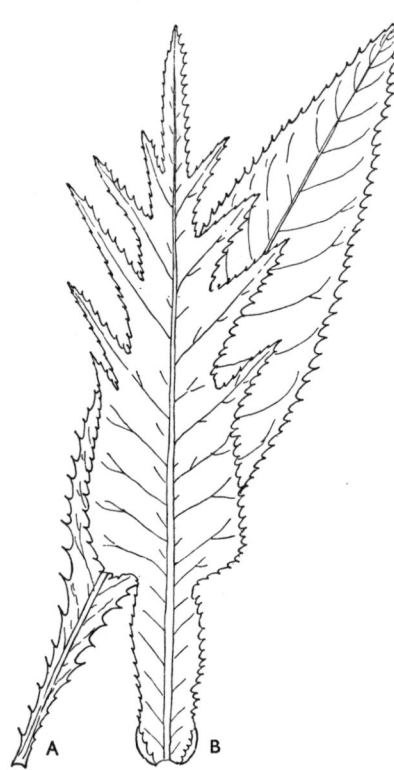

blade up to a foot long or more and 6 in. broad; lower stem-leaves lanceolate and sessile, finely toothed or more rarely deeply divided in the upper half into narrow lobes (see text-figure B, alongside), tapered to a sharp point, all the leaves covered below with white soft woolly hairs; heads single or paired on longish stalks, the involucre of numerous narrow entire green and purple bracts about 1½ in. diam. and globose in bud (B, ×½); flowers all of one kind (C, ×1¼), mauve like the style; stamens (D, ×6) with hairy filaments and deeply sagittate bases; achenes (C, ×1¼) smooth, with a white feathery pappus (E, ×2½) (family *Compositae*) (synonym *Cirsium helenioides* L.

This lovely plant is so distinct that it needs little description, and the general figure and drawing of the lower leaves in the text should be sufficient for its recognition. It has been recorded from as far south as Glamorgan, in south Wales, but is otherwise found mainly in northern Britain where it favours wettish places in pastures and on grassy hill slopes. In Upper Teesdale, Yorkshire, where the sketch was made, it is quite common.

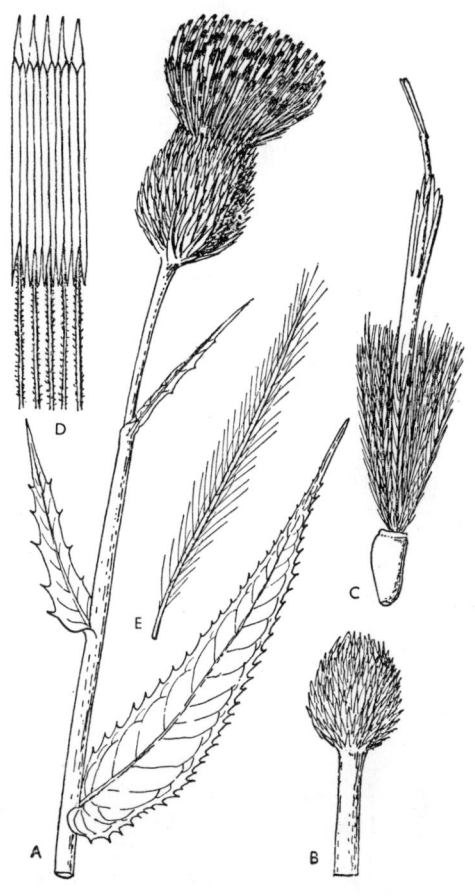

Cirsium dissectum (L.) Hill (×½)

Perennial herb; leaves few, basal oblong-lanceolate, narrowed to the base, tipped by a bristle, 4–5 in. by 1 in. broad, thinly covered

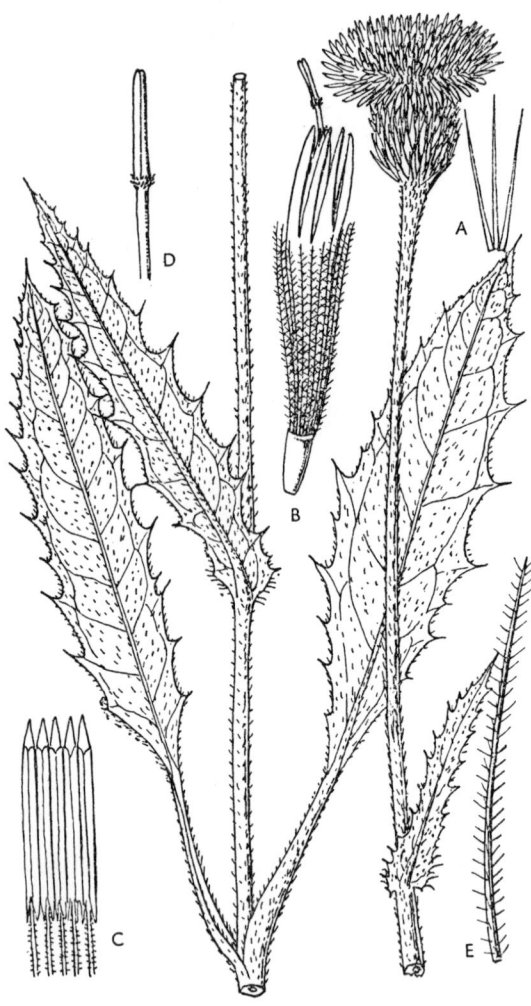

below with soft white hairs, coarsely toothed or shortly pinnately lobed, teeth bristly; stem-leaves sessile, auriculate flower-heads solitary or rarely 2 or 3 on a common stalk, 1½ in. diam.; involucral bracts connected by long woolly hairs; receptacle with slender bristles (A, ×1¼); flowers (B, ×1) mauve-purple; achenes smooth; pappus of plumose bristles (E, ×2); anthers (C, ×2½) with shortly hairy filaments; stigmas (D, ×3) covered with white pollen (synonyms *Carduus pratensis* Huds., *Cnicus pratensis* (Huds.)

Willd., *Cirsium anglicum* (Lam.) DC.) (family *Compositae*).

A native species, flowering in June, in fens and bog marshes, northwards as far as Yorkshire, and in Europe generally. Also called 'Marsh Plume Thistle'.

Biennial up to about 9 in. high; root tapered, slender; leaves very prickly, the lowermost more or less straw-coloured, the others yellowish-green, narrow, armed with numerous slender, very sharp prickles on the margin; flower-heads solitary or 2 or 3 at the top of the stem, the leaves gradually merging into bracts, the middle bracts (A, ×1) very much cut up into sharp prickles and clothed with cobweb-like hairs; innermost bracts (A², ×1) spreading and resembling ray-flowers, about 30, pale straw-coloured and shining, not toothed; receptacle covered with much-divided scales (B, ×⅔) which show as bristles above the flowers; flowers (C, ×⅔) all tubular; corolla crimson, the lobes shrinking as

the anther-cylinder pushes upwards; anthers (D, ×1½) with hairy tails and sharp tips; style-arms (E, ×1½) united, hairy around the base; achenes silky hairy; pappus-bristles slender, connate at the base in threes, fringed with slender hairs (F, ×1½) (family *Compositae*).

The innermost bracts are straw-coloured and resemble ray-flowers. They function as such because they render the head visible at a considerable distance. In dull weather and at night the bracts bend inwards and upwards so as to perform a protective cover.

This is the only species of the genus in Britain and is locally common in chalk and limestone districts as far north as Ross; extends eastwards as far as Siberia. Note the characteristic pappus shown in the drawing (fig. F).

GREATER KNAPWEED
Centaurea scabiosa L. ($\times\frac{1}{2}$)

Perennial with a thick woody rootstock and with hard ribbed rather woolly-pubescent stems; all the leaves pinnately lobed, the basal more deeply so with a slender stalk, the stem leaves sessile, the side lobes coarsely toothed or shortly lobulate; flower-heads large and very showy, the outer flowers always larger and sterile; peduncles ribbed, thicker towards the involucre; bracts of the involucre (A, $\times 1\frac{1}{2}$) in about 8–10 rows, gradually larger from the base upwards, but more or less the same shape and narrowly triangular to lanceolate, with a black margin and fringed with bristles like a comb, green up the middle; flowers (B, $\times 2$) all tubular, purplish crimson; achenes pubescent; pappus of stiff, flat, white bristles bordered by short hairs; corolla rather deeply 5-lobed; anthers (C, $\times 4$) rather thick and forming a cone; filaments densely hairy; style shortly lobed, with a ring of hairs around the base of the lobes (family *Compositae*).

This handsome species is not nearly so common as *C. nigra* (fig. 572), and is well worth a place in a flower garden. It is generally distributed in England and Wales, being more common in chalky districts, but does not extend far into Scotland, and is local and rare in Eire.

The sterile outer flowers serve to render the head conspicuous. The filaments are irritable and when touched by an insect bend and pull down the anther cylinder, the ring of hairs at the base of the style-branches brushing out the pollen. The attractiveness of the flower-heads is very greatly enhanced by the neutral outer flowers, which in a way mimic the ray-flowers of other members of the family. That this is their function seems clear, because they have no bell for the storage of nectar, which is confined to the bisexual flowers.

The genus is readily recognized amongst British members of the family by the comb-like structure of the involucral bracts. It is very richly represented in species in the Mediterranean and Caucasus regions, and many handsome species are grown in our gardens.

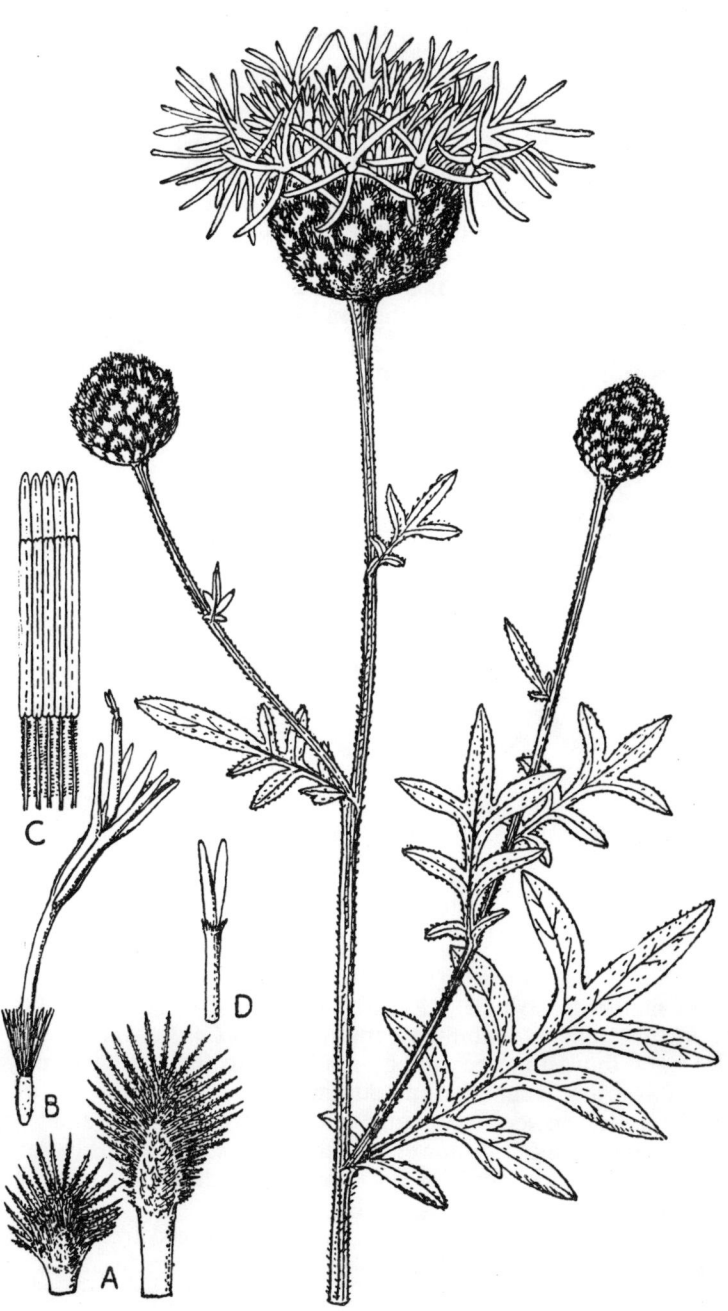

667

A much-branched spreading annual clothed with woolly hairs when young; basal leaves (F, $\times\frac{1}{2}$) up to 9 in. long, deeply pinnately lobed and finely toothed; stem leaves sessile and much smaller, varying from pinnately lobed to toothed or nearly entire, green and more or less woolly hairy; flower-heads shortly stalked or sessile on the branches near the forks and at the tips; involucral bracts (A, $\times1\frac{1}{2}$) rigid and ending in long sharp spines up to 1 in. long with 2 or 3 shorter spines on the margins near the base; flowers (C, $\times2$) purple; receptacle densely setose between the

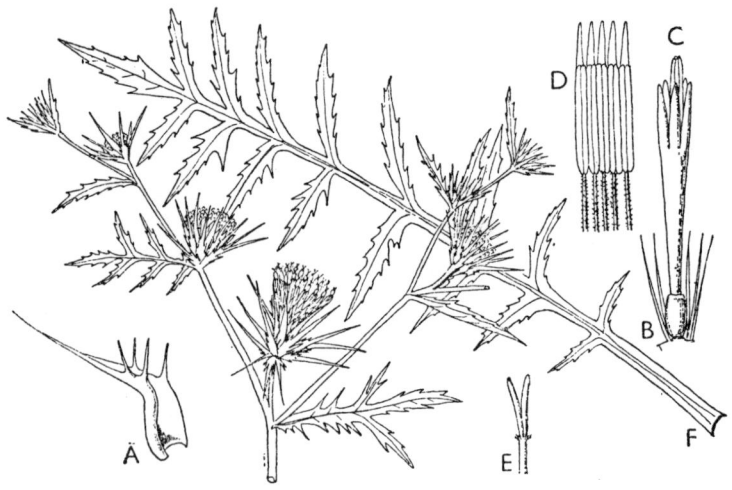

flowers (B, $\times2$); anthers (D, $\times3$) long, with long barren tips and hairy filaments; style (E, $\times2$) with a ring of hairs at the base of the branches; achenes without a pappus (family *Compositae*).

Found in waste places and by roadsides in the southern counties, flowering in summer and autumn.

The outer flowers are neuter and are tubular and radiating, taking the place of ray-flowers in other *Compositae*, thus increasing the conspicuousness of the head, the disk-flowers being bisexual and fertile.

Nowhere common in Britain, but widely spread from Europe into north Africa, the Atlantic islands, and western Asia. Recognized by the purplish flowers and the bracts with a terminal spine.

Perennial with tough hard stems and branches strongly ribbed and somewhat rough (scabrid); basal leaves larger, oblanceolate,

shortly lobed or with coarse teeth, the stem leaves oblanceolate to almost linear, sessile, narrowed to the base, entire, or slightly tooth-ed, rather rough (sca-brid) below; flower-heads globose, termi-nating the branches which become rather thicker below the heads; bracts (A, B, C, × 2) of the involucre numerous in about 6–8 rows, closely overlapping and showing only their up-per part or 'append-age', the latter dark brown or black and deeply cut like a comb, the innermost bracts al-most entire and shin-ing; flowers (D, × 1½)

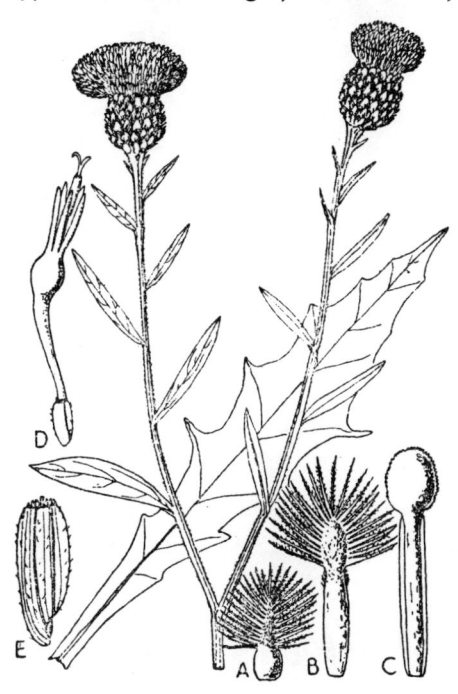

purple or bluish red, all of one kind and tubular, bisexual, or the outer row larger and sterile; achenes (E, × 4) with a large oblique scar at the base, longitudinally lined and slightly hairy; pappus consisting of a few very short teeth; receptacle between the flowers very densely bristly (family *Compositae*).

A common plant in fields, flowering all summer. This species is remarkable in that it sometimes has a row of larger sterile flowers around the outside of the head and sometimes these are absent. Many other species have these larger ray-flowers, which are an additional attraction to insects, so that *C. nigra* seems to represent an older stock of the genus which is in the process of acquiring this additional character, a stage of evolution before our eyes!

Centaurea cyanus L. (×⅘)

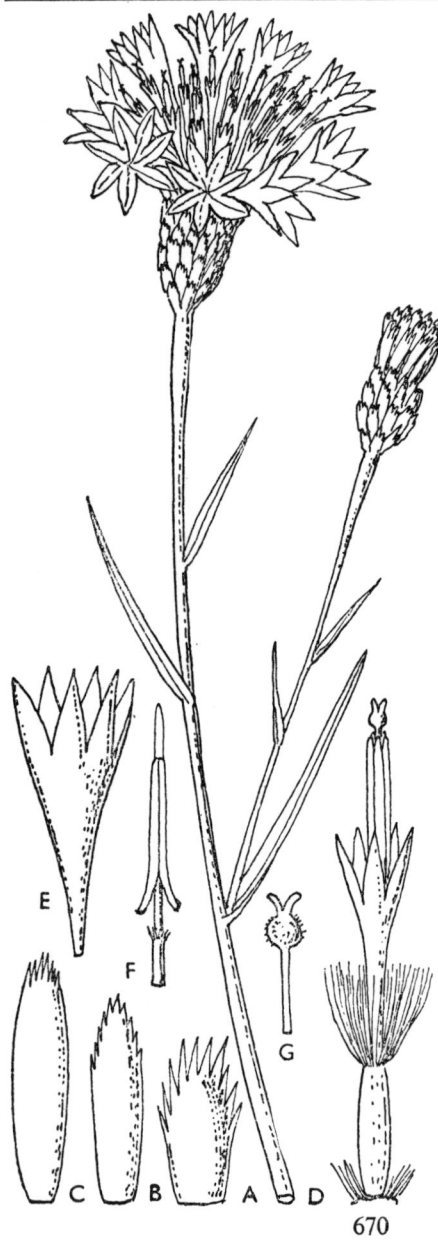

Annual about 2 ft. high; stems ribbed, clothed in the upper parts with woolly hairs; lower leaves toothed or pinnately lobed, the upper linear and entire, very acute, more or less woolly with white hairs; flower-heads on woolly stalks; bracts (A, B, C, × 2) of the involucre in 4–5 rows, chaffy, the outermost quite short, all cut around the top like a comb; flowers in the middle (D, × 1½) bluish-purple, smaller than the outer (E, × 1½) bright-blue ones; anthers (F, × 3) with blunt tails at the base; achene smooth, with a short pappus; receptacle bristly (family *Compositae*).

The outer flowers are tubular but not fertile. The disk-flowers are bisexual, and the filaments are highly irritable. When touched by an insect these are drawn downwards (retracted), and the pollen within the anther-cylinder is swept out by the ring of hairs below the style-branches.

670

Strong-growing biennial herb with rather large almost rhubarb-like leaves; lower leaves ovate, widely cordate at the base, triangular at the apex, up to 1 ft. or more long and little less broad, rather undulate-denticulate, thinly cottony below, but becoming glabrous or nearly so; upper leaves becoming much smaller and entire or almost entire, and not cordate at the base; heads ovoid, forming a leafy one-sided raceme, the lateral shortly stalked; involucral bracts numerous (A, $\times 1$), hooked at the apex, inner purple, not or only slightly connected with cottony hairs; receptacle covered with bristles of unequal length (B, $\times 1$); flowers (C,

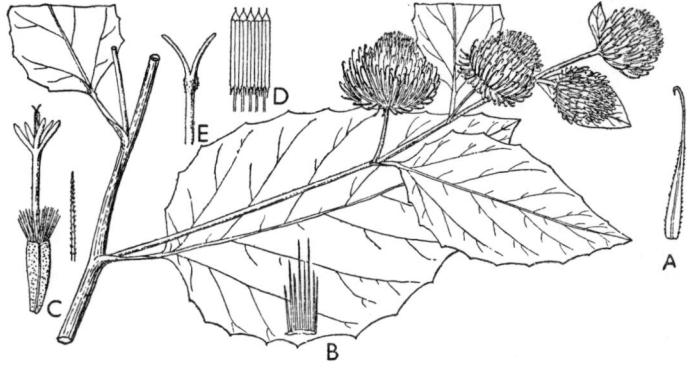

$\times 1\frac{1}{4}$) all tubular; corolla purple; anthers (D, $\times 2$) tailed; style (E, $\times 2$) swollen and hairy below the arms; achene (C, $\times 1\frac{1}{4}$) angular, closely warted between the ribs; pappus-bristles in several whorls, short, scabrid (family *Compositae*).

A weed of waste places, rubbish-dumps, and on roadsides, flowering from July to August.

The hooks of the involucral bracts surrounding the flower-head catch on the clothing and to the coats of animals, and assist in distributing the seed. It is little more than a small edition of the larger and less widely spread Greater Burdock, in which the size of the flower-heads varies considerably.

WILD LETTUCE
Lactuca virosa L. ($\times\frac{1}{2}$)

Biennial, with erect stems up to 6 or 7 ft. high or shorter, according to soil; juice milky and bitter; basal leaves obovate to oblong, with wavy toothed margins; stem leaves (A, $\times \frac{1}{2}$) sessile and clasping, with deflexed auricles at the base, oblong or slightly broader above the middle, bright green, with wavy irregularly toothed (dentate) margins; lateral nerves numerous and spreading, branched and looped; midrib often prickly below; flower-heads (B, $\times \frac{1}{2}$) in a lax panicle with slender spreading branches; bracts clasping and ear-like at the base; bracts of the involucre (C, $\times$ 0) about 10, with a few outer unequal sized, green, the whole head about $\frac{3}{4}$ in. long; flowers (D, $\times$ 2) all of one kind, about 15–20 in each head, with a yellow strap-shaped corolla; anthers (E, $\times$ 8) tailed at the base; ovary at first yellow, but becoming nearly black in fruit (H, $\times$ 3) and flattened, with about 7 ribs on each face, at length narrowed into a slender beak, bearing the white spreading slightly roughened pappus-hairs (J, $\times$ 8); style (F, $\times$ 6) hairy all over; bracts (G, $\times$ 0) spreading in fruit (family *Compositae*).

Nowhere common, but generally distributed, and found mostly on hedgebanks and waste places, and on cliffs, flowering from about the first week in July; easily recognized by its ribbed almost black fruits and long-stalked pappus of spreading hairs. The flower-heads open at Kew on a fine day about 9 and close again about 1 o'clock (Greenwich time), and only a few heads are open each day. The fruits mature rapidly, when the bracts surrounding them become reflexed and the pappus-hairs spread out horizontally, by means of which the fruits ('seeds') float away in the wind; a few flowers remain sterile. In a related species, *Lactuca sativa* L., observations have shown that there is quite a considerable difference in the time of the opening of the flower-heads at different latitudes. For example, at Upsala, in Sweden, the flower-heads opened at 7 a.m. (Greenwich time) and closed at 10 a.m., whilst at Innsbruck, in Austria, they opened between 8 and 9 a.m., and closed between 1 and 2 p.m. This is probably due to the fact that during the flowering time of the species the sun rises about an hour and a half earlier at Upsala than at Innsbruck.

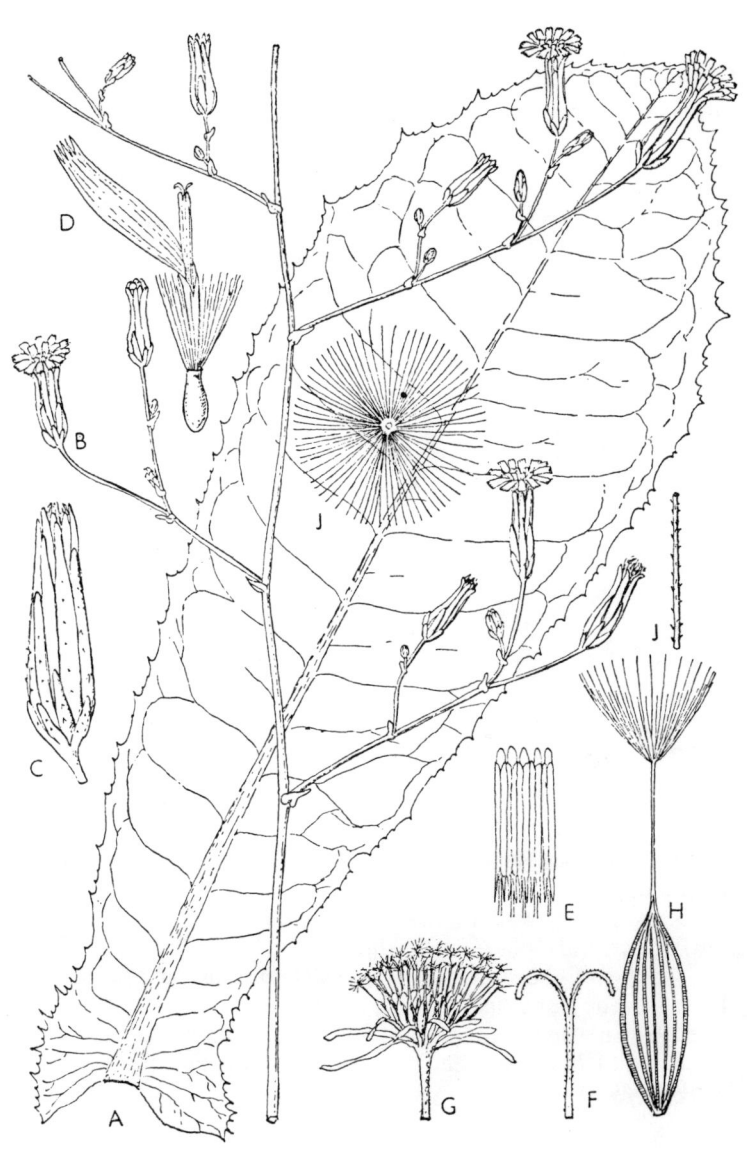

WALL LETTUCE
Lactuca muralis (L.) Fresen. ($\times \frac{1}{2}$)

An annual or biennial up to about 2 ft. high, or taller in shady places; stems slender, branched at the top into a loose slender

panicle, glabrous and sometimes covered with 'bloom'; leaves, especially those up the stem, auriculate at the base, then narrowed into a winged part like a stalk, and in the upper half irregularly pinnately lobed, the lobes remotely denticulate, green or tinged with crimson and glaucous below; flower-heads (A, $\times \frac{2}{3}$) very narrow, about $\frac{1}{2}$ in. long, with a few short bracts at the base of the main involucre consisting of a few narrow bracts with broad thin margins; flowers (B, $\times 2$) few, all of one kind (ligulate), yellow; achenes glabrous, ellipsoid in flower; pappus-hairs (D, $\times 5$) white, barbellate; anthers (E, $\times 5$) short-tailed at the base; achenes in fruit (C, $\times 2\frac{1}{2}$) with a short slender beak, closely ribbed lengthwise (family *Compositae*).

This is a very well marked species, which is usually found growing in shady places, and should not be difficult to identify with the aid of the drawing. It is distributed as far east as Asia Minor and the Caucasus, and it is also found in Algeria. The stem-leaves are markedly auricled at the base, and more deeply cut than those of *L. virosa* (see fig. 575), whilst the achenes are more shortly beaked.

A stiff erect annual or biennial up to 4 ft. high; stems slender, smooth, or often armed with sharp spreading prickles; stem-leaves sessile, eared (auriculate) at the base, usually deeply pinnately lobed with the lobes spreading or slightly recurved, the margin sharply dentate, often clothed on the midrib below with sharp prickles, otherwise not hairy; flower-heads forming a narrow oblong leafy panicle; involucral bracts in about 3 rows, narrow, glabrous; flowers (A, $\times1\frac{1}{2}$) few in each head, all of one kind, strap-shaped, pale yellow; anthers tailed (C, $\times8$); style-arms (D, $\times8$) hairy; ovary smooth, and not beaked until formed into fruit (E, $\times2$) when it becomes flattened and finely ribbed lengthwise and elongated at the top into a very slender beak as long or longer than the achene itself; pappus (B, $\times5$) rough (synonym *Lactuca scariola* L.) (family *Compositae*).

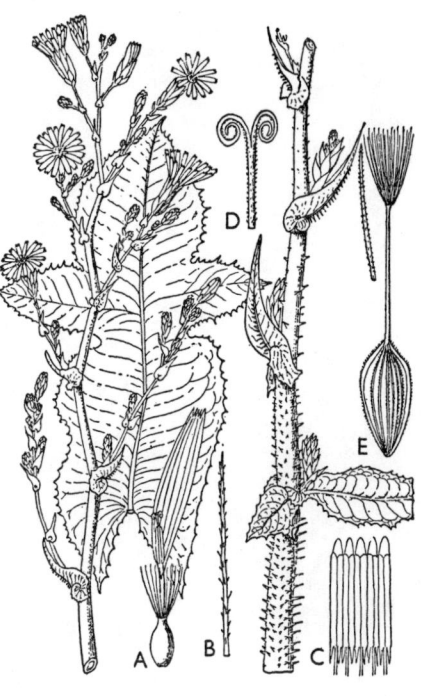

Found in dry, stony places on banks and roadsides, flowering in summer; widely distributed into Asia.

Lactuca serriola (1756) is an older name than *Lactuca scariola* (1762–3), and should be used instead of the latter, which will be found in many botanical books. According to International Botanical Rules the oldest specific names are to be used.

A perennial herb and troublesome weed in fields, lawns, and waste places, with a thick taproot, full of milky juice; leaves all

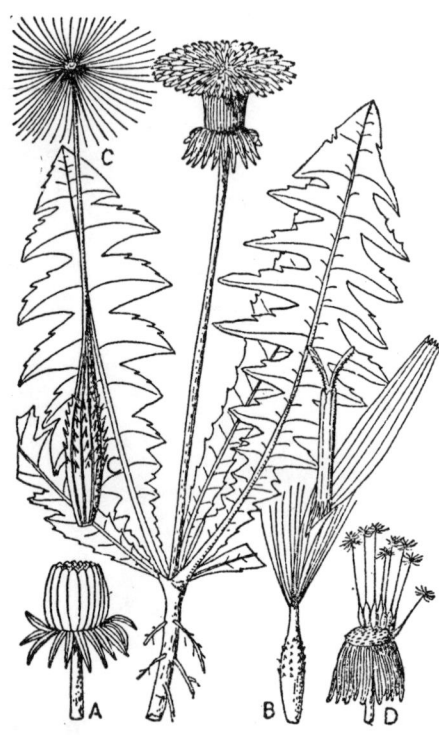

from the root (radical) very variable, from entire or nearly so to deeply pinnate-lobed, the lobes triangular or lanceolate and usually more or less recurved, the terminal one often the largest; flower-head stalks (peduncles) up to about a foot high according to soil and exposure, without small subsidiary bracts, hollow; involucre (A, $\times \frac{2}{3}$) double, the outer bracts abruptly reflexed, the inner erect, glabrous; flowers (B, $\times 2$) numerous in the head, bright golden yellow, all bisexual and fertile; achenes at first shortly beaked, at length with a very long beak (C, $\times 2\frac{1}{2}$) topped by a spreading pappus of smooth silky white hairs; body of achene with short sharp points; corolla-tube not hairy, the limb (blade) with 5 teeth at the top; all the achenes at length fall from the receptacle, with the bracts reflexed (D, $\times \frac{2}{3}$) (family *Compositae*).

Like the Daisy, the Dandelion is known to everybody. It is a very variable plant according to soil and situation, and some botanists prefer to regard the various forms, few of which are constant, as distinct species, and a great number have been described in consequence. This genus, like the Brambles (*Rubus*), and Roses (*Rosa*), is still evolving rapidly.

An annual with a rosette of radical leaves, usually a foot or two high; stems hollow and succulent, with white milk-like juice, often

tinged with crimson, glabrous but often covered with a fine bloom; basal leaves more or less spoon-shaped, with an obovate upper portion and a long tapered lower part, closely and very sharply toothed, the teeth unequal-sized and spreading at a right angle, often tinged with crimson; stem leaves sessile, oblong-lanceolate, markedly earshaped at the base and embracing the stem, with sharp prickly spreading teeth, dark green above, often with a purplish midrib; flower-heads in an irregular corymb, the end clusters subumbellate, becoming conical and pointed after flowering; bracts in about 3

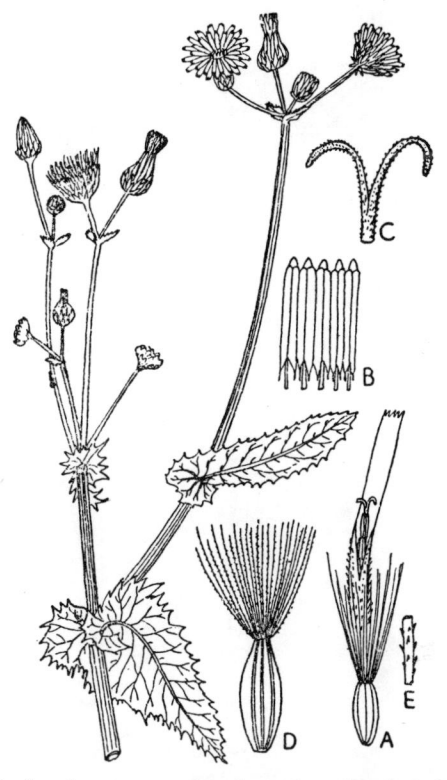

rows, the outermost much the shortest, rather broad and pointed; flowers (A, × 1¾) pale yellow, strap-shaped, all of one kind, with a narrow tubular base hairy in the upper part, with 5 sharp teeth at the apex of the limb; anthers (B, × 6) united into a tube with tails at the base, and with black tops; achene (seed) (D, × 4) flattened, brown, with parallel ribs; pappus of many slender white slightly roughened hairs (E, × 10); style-branches hairy (C, × 6) (family *Compositae*).

This is a common weed and is closely related to *Sonchus oleraceus* L., the Smooth Sowthistle, which is much less prickly with the basal lobes of the stem-leaves spreading in the same plane as the rest of the blade. The achenes of *S. oleraceus* are covered with short prickles.

Sonchus oleraceus L. (×⅔)

An annual with a rather thick hollow stem, up to about 4 ft. high, glabrous all over except a few scattered stalked glands towards the top of the main flower-head stalk; basal leaves (A, × ⅔) rather

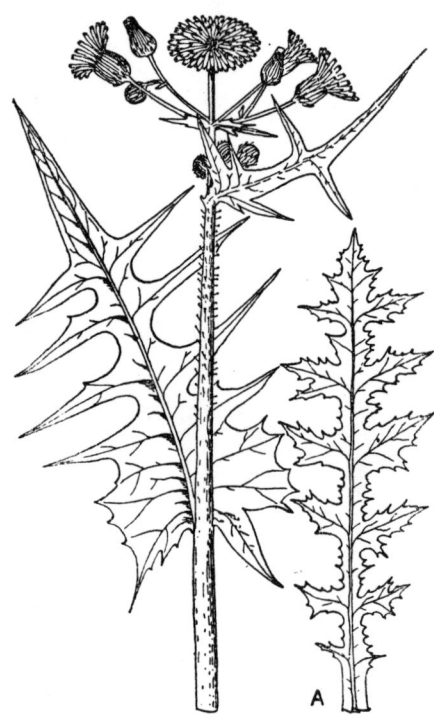

irregularly pinnately divided almost to the middle, lobes narrowly triangular and sharply and irregularly toothed; stem leaves sessile, clasping the stem with long often very acute ear-like base (auricles), deeply pinnately lobed like the basal leaves or less lobed and with a large terminal triangular lobe, or the uppermost ovate-lanceolate and at most coarsely dentate; flower-heads subumbellate above the last leafy bract, in the axils of the stalks often little balls of woolly hairs; involucral bracts in about 3 rows, the outermost much shorter, glabrous or with a few stiff hairs outside; flowers all of one kind, ligulate, the blade toothed at the top; achenes with slender ribs when ripe, glabrous; pappus white, smooth (family *Compositae*).

As mentioned under *Sonchus asper* (fig. 579), this species is not at all prickly, the leaf-teeth being sharp but not pungent. It is the more common species, being also a weed of cultivation, and widely distributed over the world. Frequently the two species are found growing together.

Sonchus palustris L. (×⅓)

Tall strong-growing perennial with underground rootstock; stems up to 1 in. or more diam.; basal leaves about 18 in. long, pinnately lobed, the lobes 2–3 on each side and spreading at a right angle, glabrous; stem-leaves sessile and clasping the stem, eared (auriculate) at the base, varying from deeply pinnately lobed to unlobed, or sometimes with a single lobe on one side only (as shown in the drawing), rather glaucous below, the margin closely and finely toothed; inflorescence forked like a catapult, with the oldest flower soon turning into fruit in the middle of the Y; stalks of flower-heads clothed with numerous gland-tipped hairs (A, ×4); bracts of involucre (B, ×1⅓) linear, glandular-hairy; flowers (C, ×2) all of one kind, strap-shaped, yellow; anthers (D, ×3) 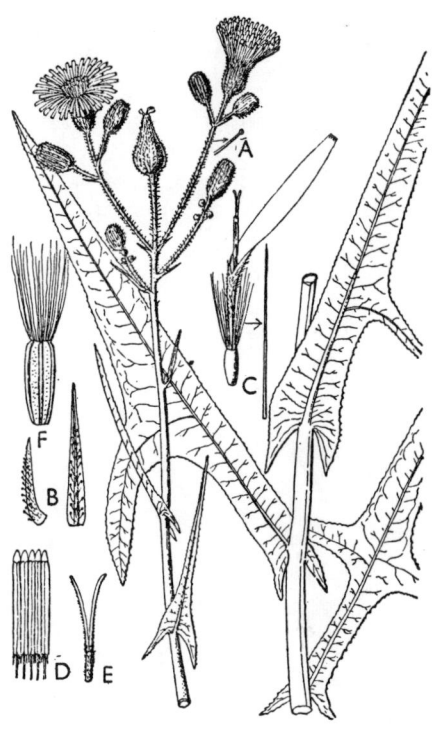 and style-arms (E, ×3) as shown in the drawing; pappus (C, ×3) white, silky and smooth; achenes (F, ×2) straw-coloured, strongly ribbed (family *Compositae*).

A very rare plant found only in marshy places in a few eastern counties; distributed east to the Caucasus.

It is a very handsome erect plant sometimes as much as 7 ft. high, distinguished from *S. arvensis* L. (see fig. 582) by the erect rootstock, and especially by the hastate base of the stem leaves, which in *S. arvensis* are rounded at the base, and by the smooth pappus.

Sonchus arvensis L. ($\times \frac{1}{2}$)

Perennial herb with a creeping rootstock; stem up to about 3 ft. high, succulent, glabrous; lower leaves (A, $\times \frac{1}{2}$) oblong in outline,

but pinnately lobed to about the middle of the blade or less, lobes often rather recurved, margins sharply prickly-toothed, eared (auriculate) at the base, rather glaucous below; flower-heads in a loose terminal panicle, sometimes the branches somewhat umbellate and mostly clothed with slender gland-tipped hairs (B, $\times 6$) bracts of the involucre in about 3 rows, with long hairs up the middle outside; flowers bright yellow, all of one kind and strap-shaped (C, $\times \frac{3}{4}$), the tube hairy, the blade toothed at the apex; anthers (D, $\times 1\frac{1}{2}$) tailed at the base; style (E, $\times 1\frac{1}{2}$) hairy; achene in fruit (F, $\times 3$) closely ribbed lengthwise, crowned by slightly rough white pappus-bristles (family *Compositae*).

This Sowthistle is a frequent cornfield plant, and is also common on waste ground. Like that of the Dandelion, the root is perennial and difficult to eradicate. Slender gland-tipped hairs are characteristic of the branches of the inflorescence, though they vary much in density. The flowers are to be seen in July and August. In common with other cornfield weeds, it has a great variety of vernacular names, according to different districts. Among these are 'Dindle', 'Gutweed', 'Hogweed', 'Rosemary', 'Swine-thistle', and 'Tree Sowthistle'. It is called 'Gutweed' because of its long creeping roots, and is a favourite food of rabbits and hares.

Mulgedium alpinum (L.) Less. (×½)

Perennial herb with erect ribbed stems up to 3 ft. high, often clothed with stiff gland-tipped hairs; lower leaves pinnately lobed, auriculate at the base, broadly winged in the lower portion and with a large triangular sharply dentate top, sometimes with spreading stiff hairs on the midrib and lateral nerves, very thin upper leaves sessile and auriculate, more or less fiddle-shaped, dentate; flower-heads in a terminal raceme, each glandular stalk (peduncle) subtended by a long narrow leafy bract fringed with hairs; involucral bracts in a single row, narrow, slightly setose on the midrib; flowers (A, ×2) about 20 in each head, all of one kind, deep blue; corolla-limb deeply 5-toothed; anthers (B, ×8) with tails at the base; style (C, ×8) slender, 2-armed, hairy; achenes (D, ×3) contracted at the top, ribbed, glabrous; pappus dingy white, bristles (E, ×6) finely barbellate (synonyms *Sonchus alpinus* L., *Lactuca alpina* (L.) Hook. f.) (family *Compositae*).

As indicated by the species name, this is an alpine plant, and a very rare one, which grows in sheltered or shady places on moist mountain cliffs in Scotland. Thence it extends eastwards as far as western Siberia and south to Spain and the Balkans.

MARSH CREPIS

Crepis paludosa (L.) Moench. ($\times \frac{1}{3}$)

Erect perennial herb up to 2–3 ft. high, growing in moist shady places; basal leaves few, oblanceolate, narrowed to a more or less

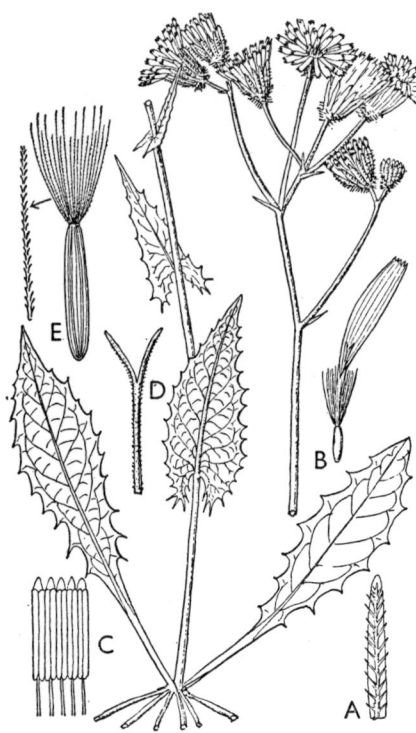

winged stalk, acutely toothed with spreading triangular teeth, not hairy; stem-leaves sessile, deeply cordate-auriculate at the base, oblong-ovate, acutely pointed; flower-heads few in a lax corymb; involucral bracts in 2 rows, an outer of few short ones, an inner of longer bracts (A, ×2), all clothed outside with black spreading hairs, the latter continued a short way down the stalk; flowers (B, ×2) all of one kind, strap-shaped, 5-toothed at the apex; anthers (C, ×5) without tails; style (D, ×5) hairy; achenes (E, ×8) contracted but not beaked at the top, ribbed, not hairy; pappus dirty white (family *Compositae*).

In general appearance this is like some species of Hawkweed (*Hieracium*).

Grows in wet meadows and by streamsides, mostly in northern Britain; distributed from Europe east to western Siberia.

Species of this large genus, of which there are about seven in Britain, are not easy to identify. *C. paludosa* is characterized especially by its glabrous 10-ribbed non-beaked achenes tipped by a rather dirty white barbellate pappus, the stem-leaves being sessile and deeply cordate-auriculate at the base as shown in the drawing. The involucral bracts are clothed outside with black spreading hairs.

Erect biennial herb up to 2 ft. high; stem ribbed, scabrid with very short hairs; leaves mostly at the base of the stem, 6–8 in. long, irregularly pinnately lobed with a large terminal toothed lobe, hispid mostly on the nerves, shortly setulose above; lower stem-leaves like the basal leaves but the upper becoming sessile and very jagged, eared at the base; flower-heads numerous in a terminal corymb; stalks clothed with gland - tipped hairs; involucral bracts in 2 rows, the outer (A, $\times 1\frac{1}{3}$) ovate and pointed, woolly-hairy, the inner (B, $\times 1\frac{1}{3}$) broadly linear and clothed outside with gland-tipped hairs as well

as short woolly hairs; flowers (C, $\times 1\frac{1}{3}$) all of one kind, ligulate, yellow, the outer ones striped with brown below; all the achenes (D, $\times 3$) with long beaks, very shortly setulose on the ribs; pappus white, barbellate (family *Compositae*).

Found mainly in limestone districts, flowering in summer; recognized amongst the British species by all the achenes being long-beaked; distributed in west and south Europe and north Africa.

683

Crepis capillaris (L.) Wallr. (×⅔)

An erect branched annual or biennial, up to 3 ft. high; stem with few scattered leaves, green or purplish, glabrous or hairy towards

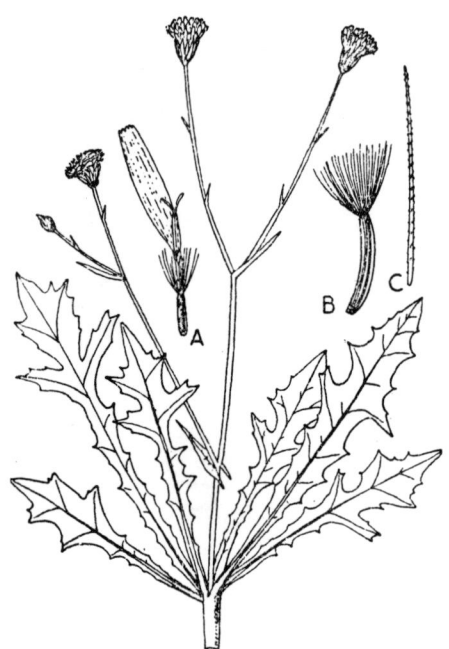

the base; basal leaves long and narrow, up to about 9 in. long, rather irregularly and pinnately lobed and toothed, tapered to and sheathing at the base of the stalk; stem leaves (when present) sessile, linear, markedly arrow-shaped (sagittate) at the base, sometimes with rather long narrow spreading or slightly recurved side-lobes; flower-heads rather small for a kind of hawkweed or dandelion, erect in bud, few together in irregular corymbs or rarely solitary according to vigour of growth; peduncles with a rather small linear bract at the base; bracts of the involucre in 2 distinct rows, an outer row of few very narrow short bracts, and an inner row of linear erect bracts slightly glandular-hairy on the outside, closing up and becoming conical in fruit; flowers (A, × 2) yellow, all of one kind, with both stamens and style; achenes (B, × 3) closely rubbed when ripe, not contracted into a beak; pappus pure white, soft and silky, though minutely roughened (barbellate) (C, × 10) (family *Compositae*).

Except for *Lapsana* (fig. 599) in which there is no pappus, and for species of *Lactuca* (which have beaked achenes) this species has the smallest flower-heads of any British plant of the Hawkweed or Dandelion type, and with the aid of the figure and description will probably be recognized. It is common in fields, dry banks, roadsides, and waste places, and it flowers the whole summer and well into the autumn.

Perennial herb with mostly basal leaves; stems up to 2 ft. high, bearing a few-headed corymb at the top, loosely clothed with dark-coloured bristles, these in the upper parts interspersed with gland-tipped hairs (A, C, ×5) and minute short stellate hairs (B, ×5); basal leaves oblanceolate, up to 9 in. long and 1 in. broad, not, or only very slightly, toothed, gradually narrowed into a longish stalk, loosely clothed above with long slender bristly hairs; one or two smaller lanceolate stem leaves; flower-heads 1 in. diam., few, the middle one the oldest; involucre ovoid, $\frac{1}{3}$ in. long, bracts densely covered with long black hairs; florets (D, ×2) all of one kind, rich dark orange, their tips 5-lobed; anthers (E, ×8) exserted, with long tails at the base; style-arms (F, ×5) recurved after pushing through the an-

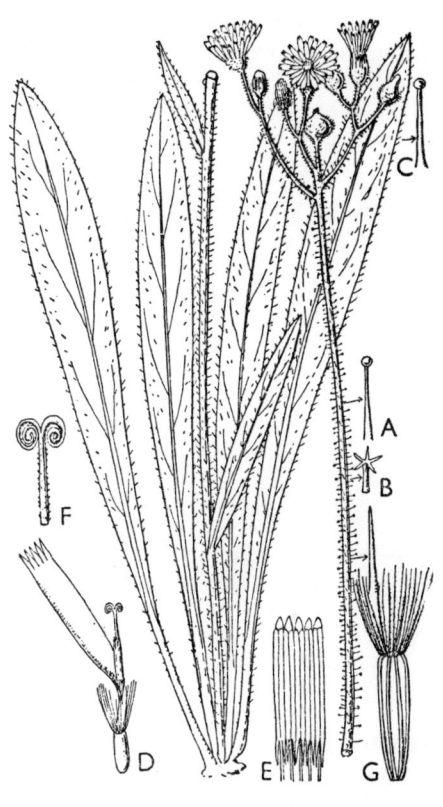

ther-cylinder; achene (G, ×6) rich crimson, 8–10-ribbed; pappus pale, barbellate (family *Compositae*).

An introduced species naturalized on railway banks and in open woods, native of north and central Europe. Also introduced into the north-eastern United States of America, where it enjoys the remarkable common names of Grim-the-Collier, Devil's or Flora's Paint-brush, Red Daisy, and Missionary Weed.

Hieracium pilosella L. ($\times\frac{1}{2}$)

Rootstock perennial with spreading tufts of radical leaves, with creeping offshoots bearing smaller narrow spoon-shaped leaves, rather densely clothed with long slender and very short white hairs; leaves oblanceolate, tapered to the base, not toothed, green above and loosely covered with long stiff bulbous-based hairs (A, × 7), woolly tomentose below with white star-shaped hairs (B, × 7); flower-head stalks arising from among the leaves, usually up

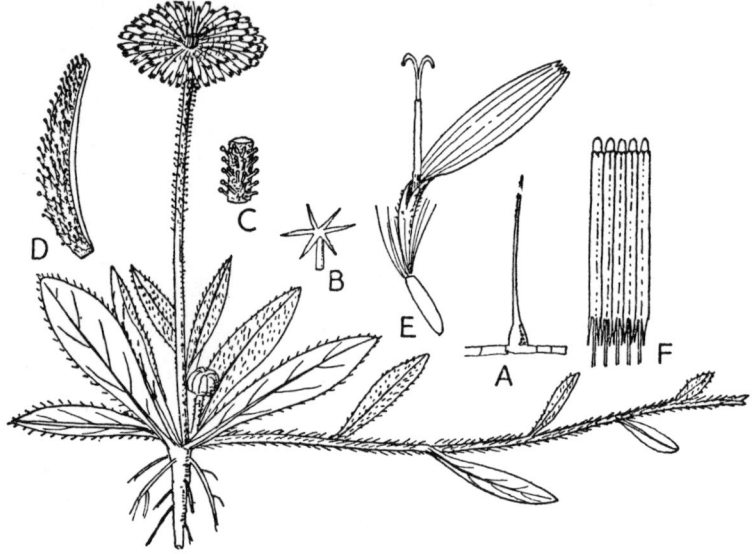

to about 6 in. high, clothed with very short star-shaped hairs and longer gland-tipped hairs (C, × 2); involucral bracts (D, × 2½) in 2–3 rows, broadly linear, with a thin membranous margin, covered outside with short stiff blackish often gland-tipped hairs and an under layer of minute star-shaped hairs; flowers (E, × 2) all of one kind, ligulate, lemon yellow above, often tinged with dull crimson below, 5-toothed at the apex; anthers with long tails at the base (F, × 5); pappus white, slightly rough; achenes smooth, rather short (family *Compositae*).

This is a very distinctive plant and the most easily recognized of this large and puzzling genus. Perhaps in no other is there so little unanimity of opinion amongst botanists with regard to the number of species.

A coarse annual or biennial up to about 3 ft. high, covered with numerous stiff bristly hairs with anchor-like tips (glochidiate hairs) (A) as well as bristles (B) with bulb-like bases; basal leaves lying flat on the ground in a rosette, sprinkled with bulbous-based bristles; stem irregularly branched; stem-leaves sessile, eared (auriculate) at the base, lanceolate, bristly and with very sharp tips; flower-heads shortly stalked, with a double involucre of bracts, the outer leafy and calyx-like and composed of 5 ovate parts cordate at the base, spreading, the inner erect and about 10, with a long bristle-like appendage below the apex; flowers (C, ×1⅓) all strap-shaped and bisexual, yellow; anthers (D, ×2) shortly tailed at the base; achenes (E, ×2) orange-brown, transversely ribbed, narrowed into a very long slender

beak crowned by a spreading plumose pappus (family *Compositae*).

Grows on hedgebanks, margins of fields, and on waste places; very easily recognized by the remarkable bristles on the stems and leaves with sharp anchor-like hooked tips which cling to passersby; the long-beaked achenes with a feathery (plumose) pappus and the double involucre are other distinctive features.

It is mainly distinguished by its remarkable double involucre, the outer bracts of which are leafy and calyx-like and cordate at the base. Note the very long slender stalk to the pappus. Synonym *Helminthia echioides* Gaertn.

687

Hypochaeris radicata L. ($\times \frac{2}{5}$)

Strong growing perennial with a Dandelion-like rootstock; stems erect, leafless, up to 2 ft. high, simple or branched into 2 or 3 peduncles; leaves all from the rootstock, spreading, oblanceolate in outline, pinnately lobulate with spreading or slightly recurved lobules, clothed on both surfaces with rather stiff hairs (hispid); midrib broad; lateral nerves slender and inconspicuous; peduncles smooth, with here and there a small bract; flower-head pale yellow, about $1\frac{1}{3}$ in. diam.; bracts of the involucre in about 3 rows, the outer (A, $\times 1\frac{1}{4}$) short and lanceolate with a row of bristles up the middle, the innermost (B, $\times 1\frac{1}{4}$) as long as the flowers and smooth on the back, long-pointed; flowers (C, $\times 2$) all of one kind, as in the Dandelion; achene smooth; pappus consisting of slender bristles with long side hairs (plumose); corolla-tube slender spreading out into a 5-toothed blade; anther cone erect, slender, with the stigmas at length protruding, the base of the anthers with long tails (D, $\times 5$); ripe achenes (E, $\times 3$) closely tuberculate and all narrowed into a long slender beak with the spreading plumose pappus at the top (family *Compositae*).

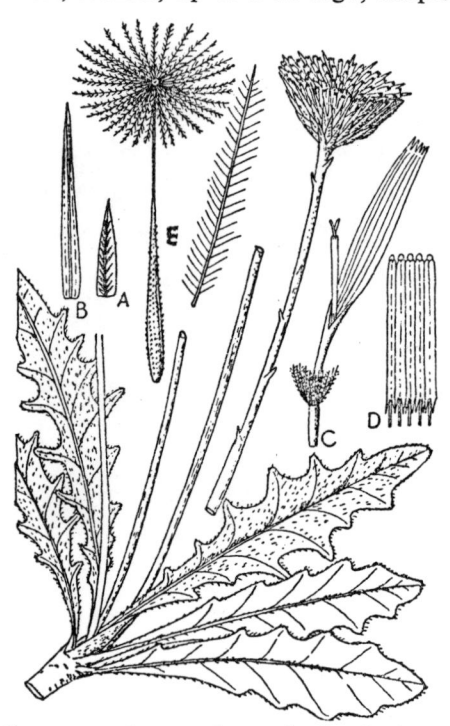

This rather rank growing Dandelion-like plant occurs in meadows, pastures, roadsides, and waste places, and flowers in summer and autumn. It is easily distinguished from the Dandelion (fig. 578) by the long lateral hairs on the pappus-bristles. In the closely related but less common *Hypochaeris glabra* L., the outer achenes have no beak, and the leaves are glabrous.

A Dandelion-like annual herb with a rosette of basal leaves more or less deeply pinnately lobed or toothed, the lobes mostly some-what recurved, glabrous or nearly so; flower-heads numerous, the peduncles branched; in-volucral bracts in 2 rows, the outer about ⅓ as long as the inner which are thin and shining; in addition there are long shining membranous scales amongst the flow-ers, the latter all of one kind, strap-shaped, yel-low; outer achenes (A, ×4) hardly beaked, re-mainder (C, ×4) tapered into a slender beak, all ribbed lengthwise and acutely tuberculate on the ribs; pappus (B, ×6) of two kinds, an outer row of short barbellate bristles and an inner row of longer bristles clothed with long slender hairs (plumose) (family *Com-positae*).

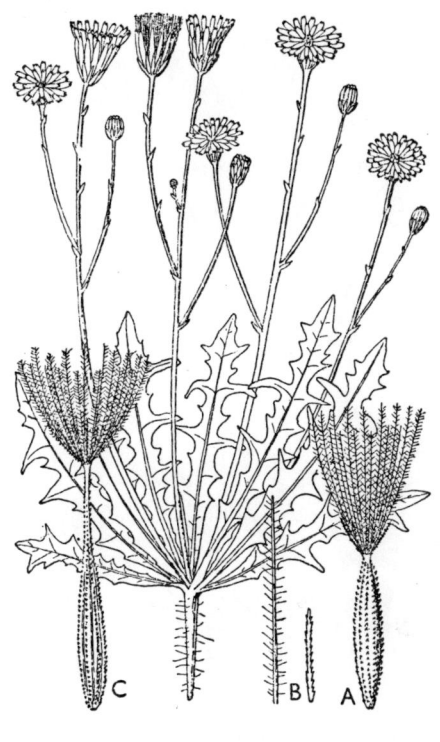

Grows in gravelly and sandy soil on heathy places and fixed dunes, widely distributed to Asia Minor and north Africa.

The genus is recognized amongst plants of the Hawkweed type by the chaffy scales on the receptacles between the flowers.

A third species not shown in our book is *H. maculata* L., the Spotted Cat's-ear, which has hairy leaves like *H. radicata*, and in which the leaves are usually spotted with dark purple, the pe-duncles are more or less unthickened below the flower-head and the pappus-bristles are in a single row.

HAWKWEED PICRIS
Picris hieracioides L. ($\times\frac{1}{3}$)

Biennial herb up to 3 ft. high, hispid with anchor-like hairs (A, $\times$5); leaves alternate, rather few, oblanceolate, the lower up to 9

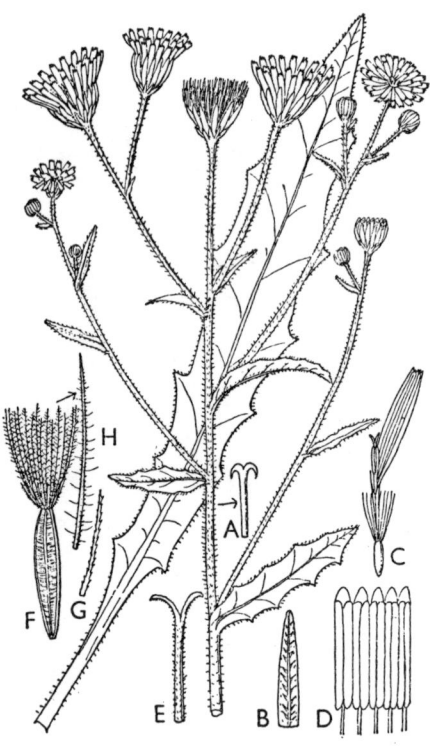

in. long, all more or less repand-dantate or pinnately lobed; flower-heads in a loose corymb; outer involucral bracts few, shorter than the inner (B, $\times$1) which are setulose up the middle; flowers (C, $\times$1) yellow, all of one kind, strap-shaped, toothed at the apex; anthers (D, $\times$8) not tailed at the base; style (E, $\times$8) hairy; achenes (F, $\times$3) ribbed and finely lined transversely; pappus dirty white, composed of outer (G) shorter scabrid bristles and longer inner (H) bristles both scabrid and plumose (feather-like) (family *Compositae*).

Interesting characters of this species are the hooked (anchor-like) hairs on the stem and branches, which enable the plant to cling to others, and the two kinds of pappus-bristles shown in the drawing; flowers in summer and grows on roadsides and borders of fields and in waste places.

As numerous heads are borne on a stem about 3 ft. high, the plant is rendered very conspicuous, for in sunny weather each head spreads out into a golden yellow disk an inch or more in diameter. In dull weather, however, it contracts to about a quarter this size.

Leontodon hispidus L. ($\times \frac{2}{5}$)

Perennial clothed with rather long hairs forked into 2 or 3 rays at the top (A); leaves up to about half as long as the peduncles, coarsely toothed or lobulate, with reflexed teeth or lobes, gradually narrowed to the base into winged stalks; flower-head stalks (peduncles) up to 1 ft. long, hispid with 2–3-forked hairs; bracts of the involucre in 2–3 rows, the outer much shorter than the others (B, $\times \frac{4}{5}$), hispid with rather long unbranched hairs, reflexed in fruit (C, $\times 0$); flowers (D, $\times 0$) all of one kind (bisexual) and ligulate, having both stamens and style with fertile ovary; corolla rather deeply 5-toothed at the apex; tube hairy at the top; anthers (E, $\times 2\frac{1}{2}$) tailed at the base; style-arms (F, $\times 2\frac{1}{2}$) hairy outside; achene (G, $\times 1\frac{1}{2}$) scarcely narrowed to the top, slightly rough; pappus of 2 sets of bristles, the outer few much shorter and nearly smooth, the inner longer than the achene and feathery (family *Compositae*).

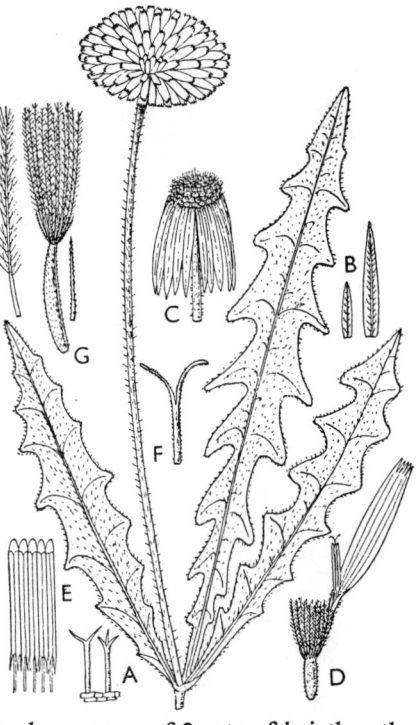

This species is common and widely spread, especially in chalky soils. It extends into south-west Asia.

The genus *Leontodon* is closely related to the Dandelion, *Taraxacum*, but differs in the pappus, which in the former is feathery. In *L. hispidus* the pappus consists of 2 distinct rows, an outer of very short bristles which are slightly rough (see fig. G), and an inner row of longer feathery (plumose) bristles.

Perennial and very like a small dandelion in general appearance; leaves all from the root, spreading, rather deeply pinnately lobed,

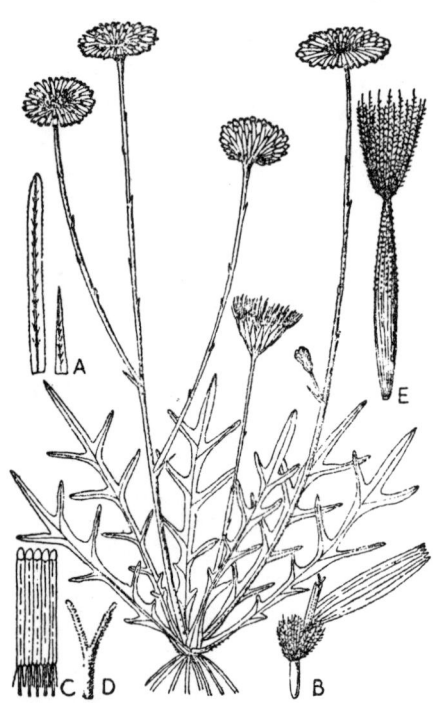

having a narrow blade and spreading linear side-lobes, glabrous or with a few long stiff hairs on the midrib below; flowering stems leafless or nearly so, simple or with a few branches in the upper part, the branches with a small bract at the base, and bearing here and there a few, short subulate-lanceolate bracts; heads about $\frac{3}{4}$–1 in. diam., golden-yellow; involucre tapered at the base into the stalk, with one main whorl of long narrow bracts setose along the middle, and a much shorter outer series more or less subulate (A, $\times 2$); flowers (B, $\times 1\frac{3}{4}$) all of one kind (bisexual) and ligulate, having both stamens and style with fertile ovary; corolla minutely 5-toothed at the apex; anthers (C, $\times 4$) tailed at the base; style-arms hairy outside (D, $\times 4$); achene (E, $\times 4$) narrowed to the top but not beaked, minutely tuberculate in the upper half and microscopically reticulate all over, brown when ripe; pappus feathery (family *Compositae*).

Grows in meadows, pastures, and waste ground, flowering in summer and autumn; the heads expand in the sunshine and form a golden-yellow disk up to an inch in diameter, but contract to very small dimensions during rainy weather; either cross-pollination by insects or self-pollination occurs. The floral structure is very similar to that of Cat's-ear, *Hypochaeris radicata* L. (fig. 590), but the heads are more dainty and the achenes lack the long beak of that species.

Leontodon taraxacoides (Vill.) Mérat ($\frac{1}{3}$)

Perennial herb with a rosette of leaves, these narrowly oblanceolate, tapered to the base, rather blunt at the apex, up to about 6 or
7 in. long, from almost entire to deeply and irregularly pinnately
lobed, pilose with rather stiff, mostly forked hairs below; flower-
heads several on peduncles up to a foot or so long ($1\frac{1}{2}$ ft. in fruit);
involucral bracts in 3–4 series, the innermost the longest and with
thinner margins, glabrous or nearly so; flowers (A, ×$1\frac{1}{2}$) yellow,
all strap-shaped (like those of a Dandelion); style (B, ×3) hairy;

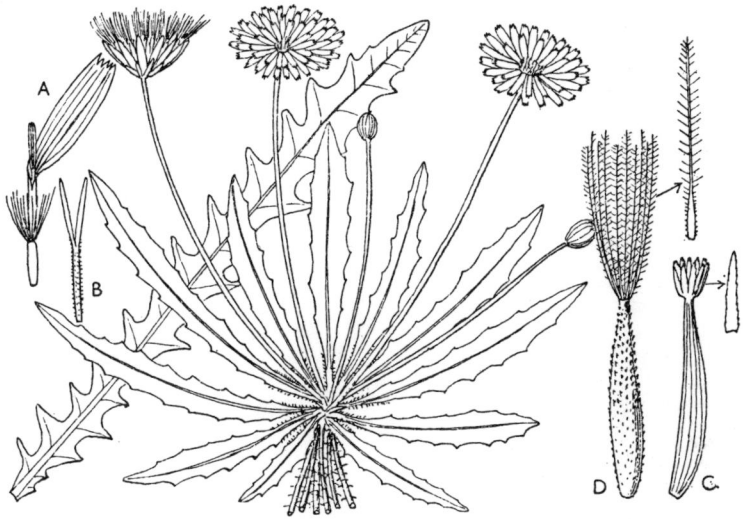

outer achenes (C, ×6) nearly smooth and with a short scaly
pappus, the remainder (D, ×6) more or less beaked, tuberculate
and with a long feathery pappus (synonym *Leontodon hirtus* of
authors, not L. and *L. leysseri* (Wallr.) Beck *Thrincia hirta* Roth)
(family *Compositae*).

In gravelly pastures and sandy waste places, flowering during
summer and early autumn; generally distributed over Europe.

At once recognized by the pappus of the outermost achenes
being short and scaly, the achene itself being less tuberculate than
those of the remainder of the inner flowers, which have a feathery
pappus only.

Scorzonera humilis L. ($\times\frac{1}{3}$)

Perennial herb up to 15 in. high with a carrot-like rootstock; basal leaves linear-lanceolate, very acute, tapered to the broadly sheathing petiole, up to 10 in. long, $\frac{1}{2}$–$\frac{3}{4}$ in. broad, entire, with 3 prominent parallel nerves and a less prominent marginal nerve, glabrous; flowering stem solitary, bearing 2 or 3 linear leaves; heads solitary; involucral bracts in about 5 rows, triangular-lanceolate; flowers (florets) (A, ×2) strap-shaped; achenes (D, ×1$\frac{1}{4}$) oblong; corolla-limb 5-nerved, 5-toothed; stamens (B, ×3) with sagittate bases; outer pappus-bristles (A, ×2) shorter and plumose (feathery), the inner fewer, longer and barbellate; style-arms (C, ×2$\frac{1}{2}$)

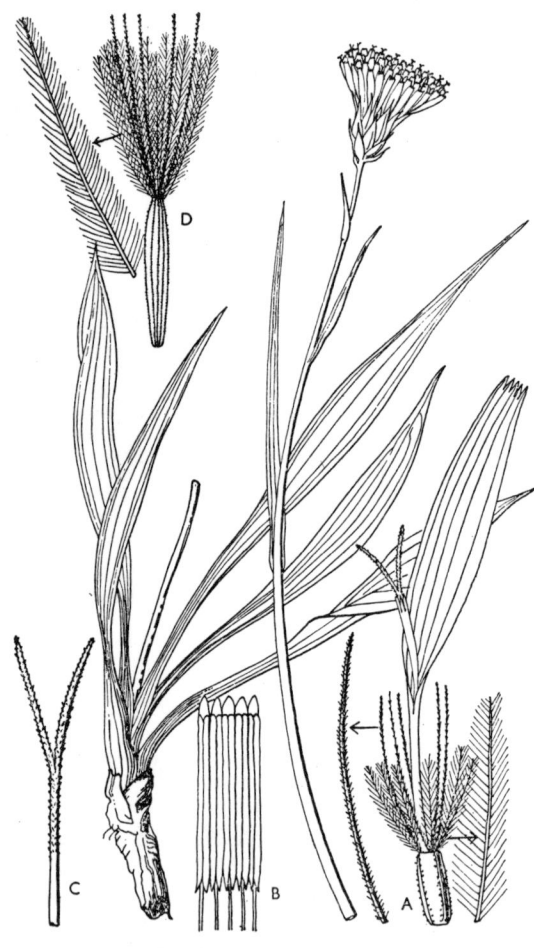

hairy to below the junction with the style (family *Compositae*).

Found in damp meadows at one locality in Dorset flowering from June to July. Widely distributed in Europe, where a broader leaved variety (var. *plantaginea*) occurs. – Drawn by Olive Tait.

694

Perennial herb up to about 3 ft. high; radical leaves spreading horizontally, pinnately lobed, the lobes spreading or slightly re-curved and toothed on the upper side, sparingly hairy (hispid); stem-leaves ses-sile, gradually becoming smaller and bract-like up-wards, setose-hairy on the margin; flower-heads single or 2–3 together and stalkless along the shoots, usually few in bloom at any one time; involucral bracts in 2–3 rows, the outer shorter, the inner fringed with a few stalked glands (A, ×2); flowers (B, ×2) bright blue, rarely pink or white, all of one kind, bisexual, strap-shaped; limb about $\frac{3}{4}$ in. long, 5-toothed; achenes crowned by a ring of minute scales; tube hairy; anthers (C, ×8) blue, rounded at both ends; style-arms (D, ×8) blue, hairy outside; ripe achenes

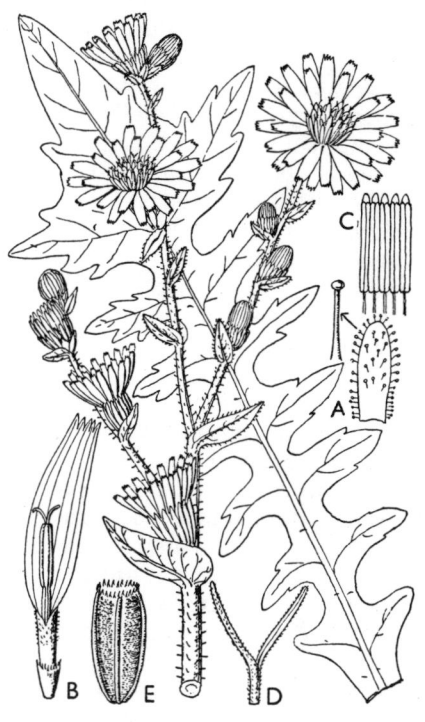

(E, ×3) ribbed and marked with small transverse lines (family *Compositae*).

The dried roots are roasted and ground and added to ground coffee. The style is covered externally with strong sweeping-hairs directed obliquely upwards and extending for some distance below the cleft, whilst the inner surfaces of the branches are beset with stigmatic papillae. After the pollen is swept out, the style-arms are twisted into a spiral, so that the inner stigmatic surfaces come into contact with the pollen grains that remain among the sweeping-hairs, and automatic self-pollination is thus effected in the absence of insect visitors. The pollen grains are white, polyhedral, and with spine-like tubercles on their edges.

Tragopogon pratensis L. ($\times \frac{1}{3}$)

Perennial up to 2 ft. high, with a taproot; juice milky; leaves alternate, grass-like, entire, linear and gradually broadened to the half-clasping base, with a few nerves parallel with the midrib, the tips curled, quite glabrous; peduncles elongated above the leaves, gradually thickened upwards; involucral bracts in 2–3 rows, about 20, tapered to a point, a little longer than the flowers, the latter numerous, yellow, and all ligulate (A, $\times$ 2); achenes in the flowering stage smooth, short, and ovoid, contracted towards and top; pappus of about 3 longer, and numerous shorter plumose bristles; corolla about 6-nerved, 5-toothed at the apex; anthers (B, $\times$ 3) with slender tails at the base; style-arms (C, $\times$ 6) finely hairy; achenes in fruit (D, $\times$ 4) very long (about $\frac{3}{4}$ in.), gradually narrowed into a slender beak about as long, the body of the achene with several rows of tubercles; pappus (E, $\times$ 8) spreading like a parachute, composed of about 25 slender bristles clothed with soft spreading hairs (family *Compositae*).

The golden-yellow flowers in sunny weather spread out in the early morning, but in the afternoon and during dull weather they close up together in the head. The pollen-grains are also golden yellow, polyhedral, and covered with spinose tubercles. In the flowering stage the achenes, except for a contraction at the top, show no signs of the long beak which develops in the fruit. About 3 of the pappus-bristles are longer than the rest and somewhat thicker, this character showing more in the flowering stage.

Goat's Beard grows in fields and meadows, especially in hilly pastures. It also flourishes by the side of pathways, and is often common on railway-embankments, where so many British wild flowers find sanctuary from man's operations and browsing animals. Its numerous native names nearly all refer to the habit of closing its flowers in the afternoon: 'Shepherd's Clock', 'Go-to-bed-at-noon', 'Nap-at-noon', 'Noontide', 'Sleep-at-noon'. Others refer to the bearded fruiting head.

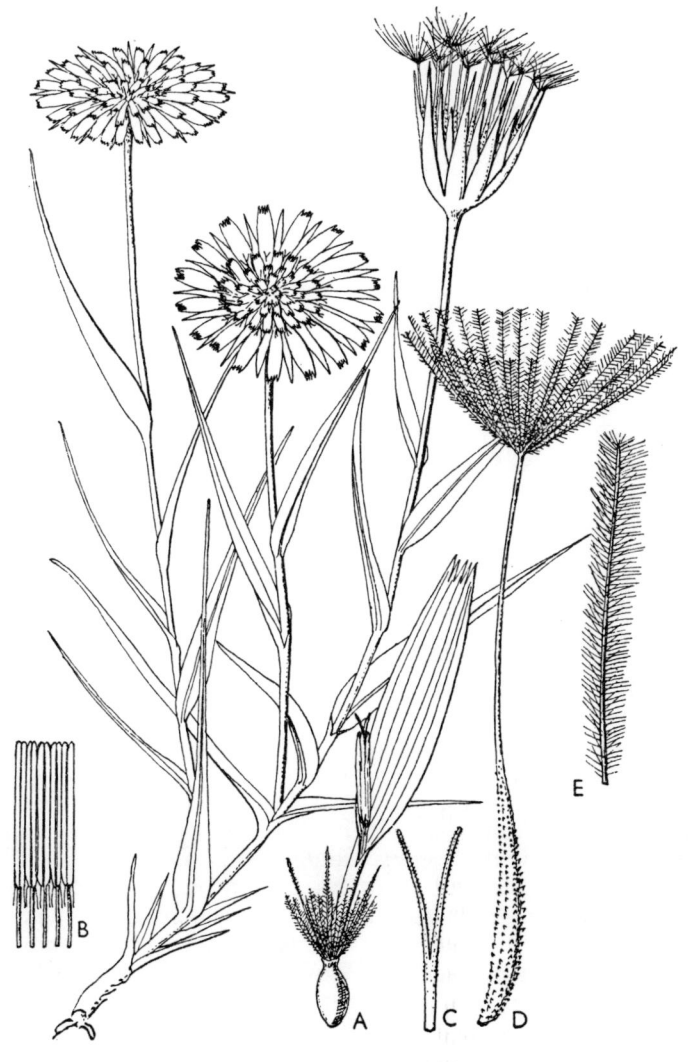

697

Lapsana communis L. ($\times \frac{2}{5}$)

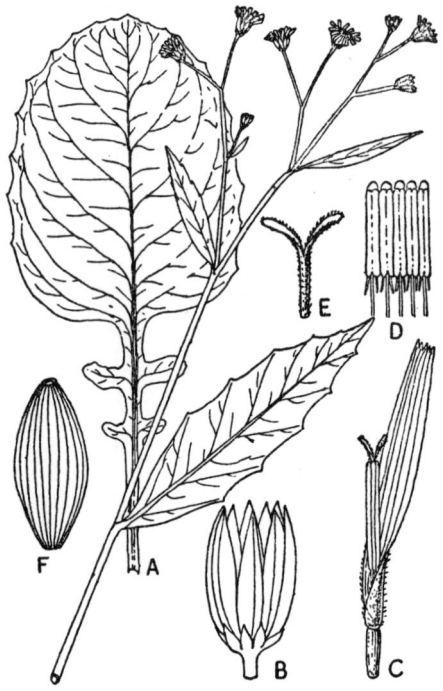

Annual; lower leaves (A, $\times \frac{2}{5}$) with a large end lobe and one or two pairs of side-lobes; upper leaves lanceolate, not stalked, and with a few teeth; stems hollow; outer bractlets of flower-head (B, $\times 2\frac{1}{4}$) about 6, inner bracts about 8, green, exuding a milky juice when bruised; flowers (C, $\times 4$) all alike, lemon yellow, with 5 stamens (D, $\times 8$) united in a tube around the hairy style (E, $\times 8$); anthers tailed; fruits ('seeds') (F, $\times 3$) closely lined with greenish nerves, but without a pappus (family *Compositae*).

A common weed by roadsides and in waste and cultivated places, flowering from late summer until late autumn. The common name refers to its former reputed use in curing sore nipples. The flowers in the heads are all of one kind, i.e. with male and female organs in the same flower. In each head there are up to about 18 flowers which open between 6 and 7 a.m., closing again at 10 or 11 a.m. (normal time). In bad weather they remain closed, when self-pollination may take place.

Annual herb with a basal rosette of leaves; leafless flowering stems up to 1 ft. high; leaves shaped, about 2–3 in. long, coarsely and distantly toothed, scabrid on the nerves and margin; flowering stems each bearing 2 stalked flower-heads, one stalk thickened upwards in advance of the other, becoming hollow and soon developing fruits; outer bracts few and much smaller, awl-shaped, the inner (A, $\times$3) with sharp tips and a wing down the middle

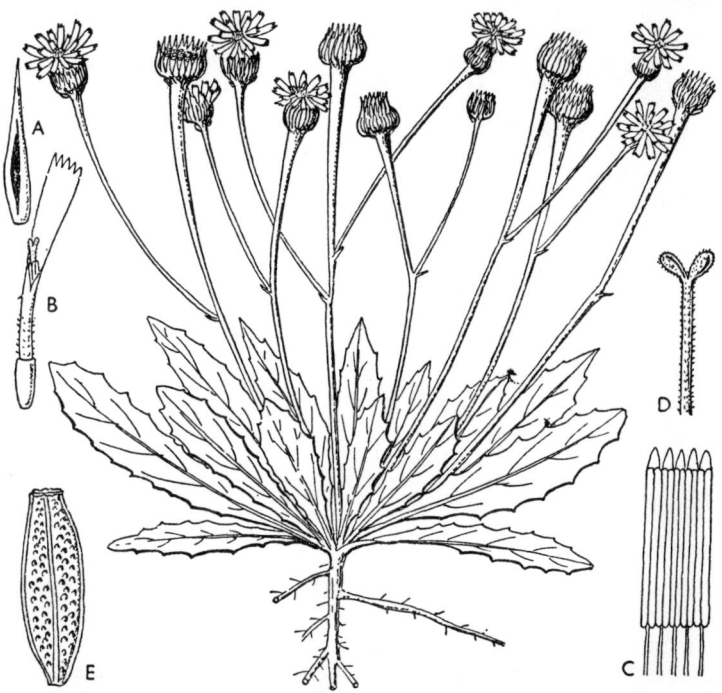

outside; flowers (B, $\times$3) all of one kind (ligulate), yellow, tube hairy in the lower part, blade 5-toothed at the apex; anthers (C, $\times$15) rounded at the base; style (D, $\times$15) hairy, with 2 short rounded lobes; achenes (E, $\times$10) strongly ribbed, warted; no pappus (synonym *Arnoseris pusilla* Gaertn.) (family *Compositae*).

The style below its branches is covered with short hairs which spread horizontally. These sweep out the pollen from the anther-cylinder, after which the short arms diverge in a crescentic manner and are receptive to pollen from another flower.

Annual herb with an unpleasant odour, more or less hairy and viscid all over; radical leaves large, with short stalks, coarsely and

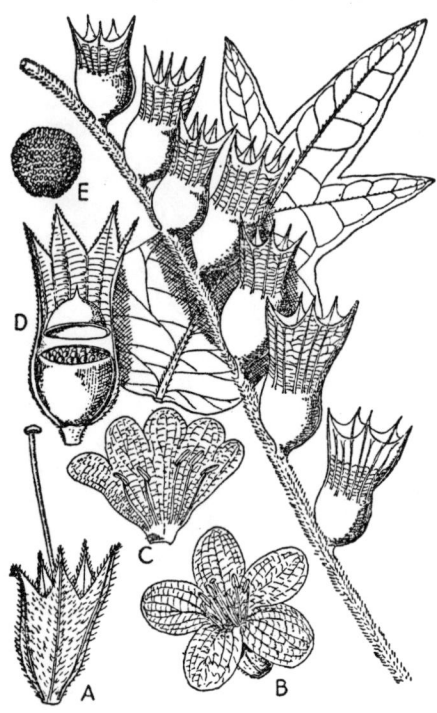

pinnately lobed; stem-leaves alternate, smaller, not stalked, narrowly ovate in outline, with 2 or 3 coarse teeth or short pointed lobes on each margin, hairy especially on the nerves below; flowers numerous, at first crowded amongst the upper leaves and sessile, but spreading out in fruit on one side of the shoot like that of a Borage; calyx (A, $\times \frac{3}{4}$) with a broadly bell-shaped very hairy tube and 5 broad short lobes each ending in a sharp point which hardens and is spine-like in fruit, tube strongly ribbed; corolla (B, $\times \frac{1}{2}$) yellowish white, closely veined with dark purple, and with a purple 'eye', lobes rounded and slightly unequal; stamens (C, $\times 1\frac{1}{4}$) 5, with purple anthers; ovary 2-locular, with numerous ovules; fruit (D, $\times \frac{2}{3}$) enclosed in the enlarged markedly ribbed calyx, the upper part of the fruit splitting off like a helmet and thicker and harder than the lower portion; seeds (E, $\times$ 5) very numerous (family *Solanaceae*).

Not a common plant, but included here because of its medicinal importance; grows chiefly on rubbish-heaps and waste places near habitations, and flowers in summer. The seeds are poisonous, and animals may be affected by them if mixed with fodder.

Glabrous or slightly hairy strong-growing annual herb up to 5 ft. high, with divergent forked branches; leaves alternate, stalked, more or less ovate in outline but coarsely divided into sharp pointed lobes, up to about 6 in. long and 4 in. wide, very strongly nerved, glabrous or slightly hairy; flowers in the middle of the forks, shortly stalked; calyx green, 2 in. long, tubular, with 5 triangular acute lobes; corolla white or violet, tubular and funnelshaped, nearly twice as long as the calyx, with 5 very narrow sharply pointed lobes from the spreading limb about $1\frac{1}{2}$–2 in. diam.; stamens (A, ×2) 5, included in the corolla-tube; ovary (B, ×2) 2-locular; style slender, stigma shortly 2-lobed; fruit (C, ×$\frac{2}{3}$) erect, ovoid, 4-valved

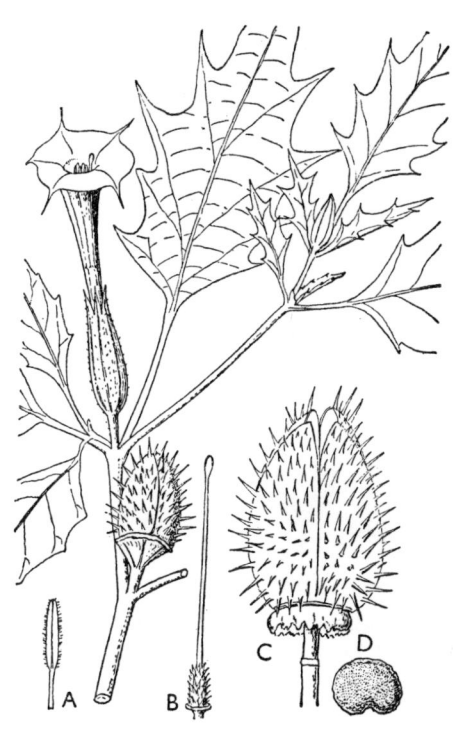

from the top, about 2 in. long, very prickly, girt by the short basal part of the calyx; seeds (D, ×2) kidney-shaped, dark coloured, closely pitted (family *Solanaceae*).

A native of tropical and sub-tropical regions, in Britain an escape from cultivation into waste places.

All parts are poisonous, especially the seeds; common in North America, where cattle have been poisoned by eating leaves of young plants in hay.

Plants of this species flower nearly all summer and have a very foetid disagreeable odour when bruised. In America it is called the 'Devil's Apple' because of its dangerous qualities.

Annual, densely and finely glandular-pubescent; stem stout, much branched, up to 8 ft. high; leaves alternate, stalked, broadly ovate

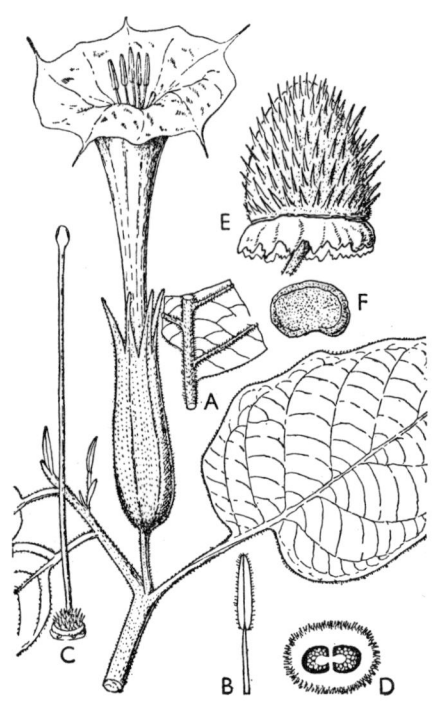

and rather unequal-sided, rounded or somewhat cordate at the base, 4–8 in. long, entire or with wavy margins; flowers in the forks, shortly stalked; calyx tubular, about 3 in. long, shortly 5-lobed; corolla white, twice as long as the calyx, with a funnel-shaped limb 3–4 in. across and with 5 very short lobes; stamens 5, exserted from the corolla-tube; ovary 2-locular; fruit (E, $\times \frac{2}{3}$) nodding, globose or ovoid-globose, very closely prickly and hairy, 1–$1\frac{1}{2}$ in. diam., girt by the large persistent basal part of the calyx; seeds (F, $\times 2$) kidney-shaped, brownish, closely pitted (family *Solanaceae*).

Grows in waste places, escaped from gardens; native of tropical America; the leaves and seeds are poisonous.

Datura leaf, the 'Daturae Folium' of British pharmacists, consists of the dried leaves and flowering tops of *D. metel* L., and another species *D. innoxia* Miller, a Mexican species cultivated in India and England.

Rootstock thick and fleshy; stem branched, often dividing into 3, the whole plant minutely hairy; leaves in pairs on one side of the stem, very unequal-sized in each pair, often one hardly half the size of the other, ovate or ovate-elliptic, triangular at the apex, wedge-shaped at the base and continued down the stalk, with about 5–8 pairs of widely spreading arched lateral nerves; no stipules; flowers drooping, solitary, and placed between the stalks of the two leaves or in the forks of the stem; stalks about as long as or longer than the flower; calyx bell-shaped, 5-lobed to about the middle, lobes triangular-ovate, acute;

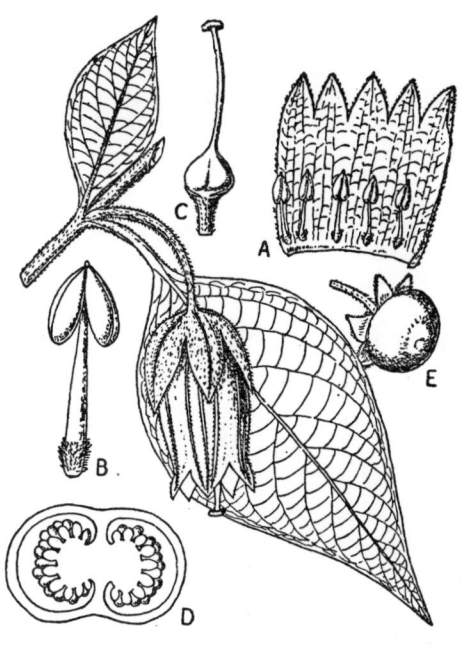

corolla dull-purple tinged with green, especially near the base, tube bell-shaped, with 5 recurved rather acute broad lobes; stamens included in the tube and inserted near the base; style as long as the corolla, with a rounded head-like green stigma; fruit a purplish black berry about $\frac{1}{2}$ in. diam., depressed-globose, girt by the persistent spreading calyx (family *Solanaceae*).

Not a common plant, but included here because of its medicinal and poisonous properties. All parts are poisonous, especially the berries. It is usually found in waste places especially amongst ruins and by roadsides, and flower in summer. Nectar is secreted at the base of the ovary and cross-pollination is effected chiefly by humble-bees. The style usually falls off and the corolla withers about an hour after pollination, so that fertilization is very rapid.

Lycium chinense Mill. ($\times\frac{1}{2}$)

A slender shrub often growing on old walls, with long whip-like pendulous branches; bark greyish, angular; leaves alternate, oblanceolate, tapered to each end, pale gluacous-green, entire, glabrous, very obscurely nerved; flowers (A, × 10) 1–3 in the leaf axils; pedicels about $\frac{1}{2}$ in. long; calyx irregularly divided into 2 or 3 lobes; corolla deep lilac, tubular, with 5 spreading lobes with dark honey-guide markings at the base, minutely fringed with hairs;

stamens (B, × 1$\frac{1}{2}$) 5, inserted inside the corolla-tube; filaments with a tuft of hairs towards the base; anthers attached in the middle, sagittate at the base, opening by slits; ovary (C, × 1$\frac{1}{2}$) 2-locular, with numerous ovules on axile placentas; fruit (D, × 1) an oblong berry (family *Solanaceae*).

Naturalized on walls and in hedges around dwellings; in many British botanical books it is called *Lycium barbarum*.

Nectar is secreted by the ovary and stored in the base of the corolla-tube. The inside of the throat of the corolla is lined with thick woolly hairs, which protect the nectar from rain and unwelcome guests. The stigma and anthers mature at the same time, and the filaments and the style are about the same length, but the latter may be bent away from the anthers. Insect visitors may therefore bring about self- or cross-pollination.

Annual or biennial up to a foot or so in height, stem much branched, glabrous or minutely hairy; leaves alternate, more or less ovate or rhomboid-ovate, narrowed at the base into the winged stalk, with a few coarse blunt teeth or short lobes; flowers small, drooping, in an umbel-like stalked cluster remote from the axils of the leaves, usually from the upper part of the internode; no bracts; calyx (A, $\times \frac{4}{5}$) 5-lobed to about the middle; corolla (B, $\times \frac{4}{5}$) white, with a short tube and 5 triangular lobes at length reflexed and shortly hairy on the margin; stamens (C, $\times 2\frac{1}{2}$) 5, inserted in the throat of the corolla, and alternate with the lobes, the anthers connivent and forming a little cone covering the

mouth of the corolla-tube, each opening by two terminal holes (pores); ovary (D, $\times 2\frac{1}{2}$) 2-locular; style short; berries fleshy, drooping, small, globose, usually black or green, rarely pale yellow or red, containing numerous flattened almost orbicular minutely pitted seeds (family *Solanaceae*).

This is a weed widely spread nearly all over the world, and flowers and fruits all summer and autumn. The flowers do not secrete nectar, but provide pollen for insect visitors. They hang downwards and close at night. Considering the small size of the flower the anthers are large and connivent in a cone with the stigma protruding a little beyond, so that self-pollination is easy, the pollen falling out through the terminal pores of the anthers. The plant is poisonous, but varies in toxicity according to soil.

BITTERSWEET

Solanum dulcamara L. (×$\frac{2}{5}$)

Perennial, woody at the base, with straggling branches several feet long and clinging to hedges; branches very softly and shortly hairy or sometimes with only a few stiffer hairs; leaves alternate, the lower often deeply 3-lobed, with a large ovate middle and two small side lobes; upper leaves ovate, cordate at the base, pointed at the apex, softly to thinly hairy below when mature, rather densely so when young, margins entire; flowers (A, × 1$\frac{3}{4}$) in small

panicles, the common stalk placed opposite to the leaf (leaf-opposed); stalks hairy; calyx with 5 short broad lobes; corolla (C, × 1$\frac{3}{4}$) blue, marked with violet veins, with a short tube and 5 spreading lobes which do not overlap in bud (B, × 1$\frac{3}{4}$), the latter shortly hairy outside; stamens (D, × 4) 5, alternating with the lobes, the anthers standing up in a cone around the style, large and opening by a pore at the top; ovary (E, × 3) above the corolla, 2-locular (F, × 6), style slender, unbranched, exceeding the anthers; fruit (G, × 1$\frac{1}{4}$) a small globular or ovoid red berry (family *Solanaceae*).

Bittersweet is included in the British Pharmaceutical Codex, but is now rarely used in medicine. The drug is prepared from the dried stems and branches. The berries are poisonous, though stock rarely touch the green parts of the plant.

Perennial with a slender creeping rootstock; stems prostrate or twining up supports to about 2 ft. high, often strangling other plants, twisting spirally, glabrous; leaves alternate, stalked, ovate or oblong-ovate, rounded to a small point at the apex, with spreading lobes at the base (hastate), otherwise with entire margins, glabrous and the nerves rather radiating from the base; flowers usually paired on axillary peduncles, only one of a pair

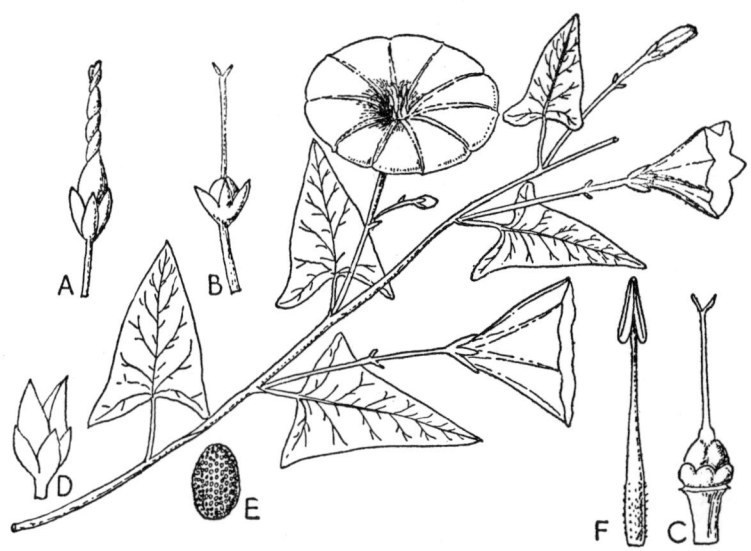

open at the same time, with a small narrow bract at the base of each ultimate stalk (pedicel) and often a pair of small bracts below only one of the flowers; calyx (B, $\times \frac{4}{5}$) of 5 rounded free sepals about $\frac{1}{6}$ in. long; corolla pink or nearly white, funnel-shaped, about 1 in. diam., very shallowly 5-lobed, the lobes forming little more than a wavy margin and spreading or slightly recurved; stamens 5, inserted at the base of the corolla; anthers facing outwards; ovary (C, $\times \frac{4}{5}$) 2-locular, each with 2 ovules; fruit (D, $\times \frac{3}{4}$) a small capsule divided into 2 compartments by a thin partition; seeds (E, $\times$ 3) minutely pitted (family *Convolvulaceae*).

Though a very beautiful little plant, this is a troublesome weed in cultivation and difficult to eradicate. This is because of its extensive root-system, which may penetrate the soil to a great depth.

WHITE BINDWEED
Calystegia sepium (L.) R. Br. ($\times \frac{1}{2}$)

Perennial with a creeping rootstock; stems twining and twisting spirally over hedges and bushes; leaves alternate, broadly ovate or ovate-triangular, acutely pointed at the apex, deeply heart-shaped (cordate) and often with angular lobes at the base, not hairy, with several main nerves radiating from the base; flowers axillary, rather long-stalked; calyx enclosed by two large overlapping green bracts, bell-shaped, 5-lobed; corolla (B, $\times \frac{1}{2}$) large and pure white or with a pink band up the middle of each lobe, bell-shaped, with short spreading-recurved lobes; lobes twisted and plaited in bud (opening out like a fan) (A, $\times \frac{3}{4}$); stamens (C, $\times 2$) 5, alternate with the corolla-lobes, the stalks arising from the base of the corolla-tube, expanded and coarsely hairy (papillous) in the lower part; anthers large, facing outwards; ovary (D, $\times 2$) girt at the base by a thick fleshy ring-like disk; style slender, divided into 2 corrugated stigmas (E, $\times 7$); fruit a globose capsule, almost membranous, containing 4 seeds, enclosed by the persistent bracts and calyx which become thin and brown; seeds (F, $\times 2$) with a horse-shoe-shaped portion (caruncle) at the base (G, $\times 2$) (family *Convolvulaceae*).

Unlike its relative, *Convolvulus arvensis* L. (fig. 608) the flowers of this species have no scent and remain open on moonlight nights though they close during wet weather. Nectar is secreted by the base of the ovary, and diurnal hawk-moths visit the flowers. Although very conspicuous they are not much visited by other insects. The broad bases of the filaments surround the nectar and leave only five narrow passages, and when an insect visits the flower it becomes dusted with pollen from the anthers which in this case face outwards.

In many botanical works this plant is referred to *Convolvulus*, but the famous British botanist, Robert Brown, who flourished at the beginning of last century, considered it to be distinct and there are good reasons for upholding this view. It differs from *Convolvulus* by the presence of large leafy bracts which enclose the real calyx.

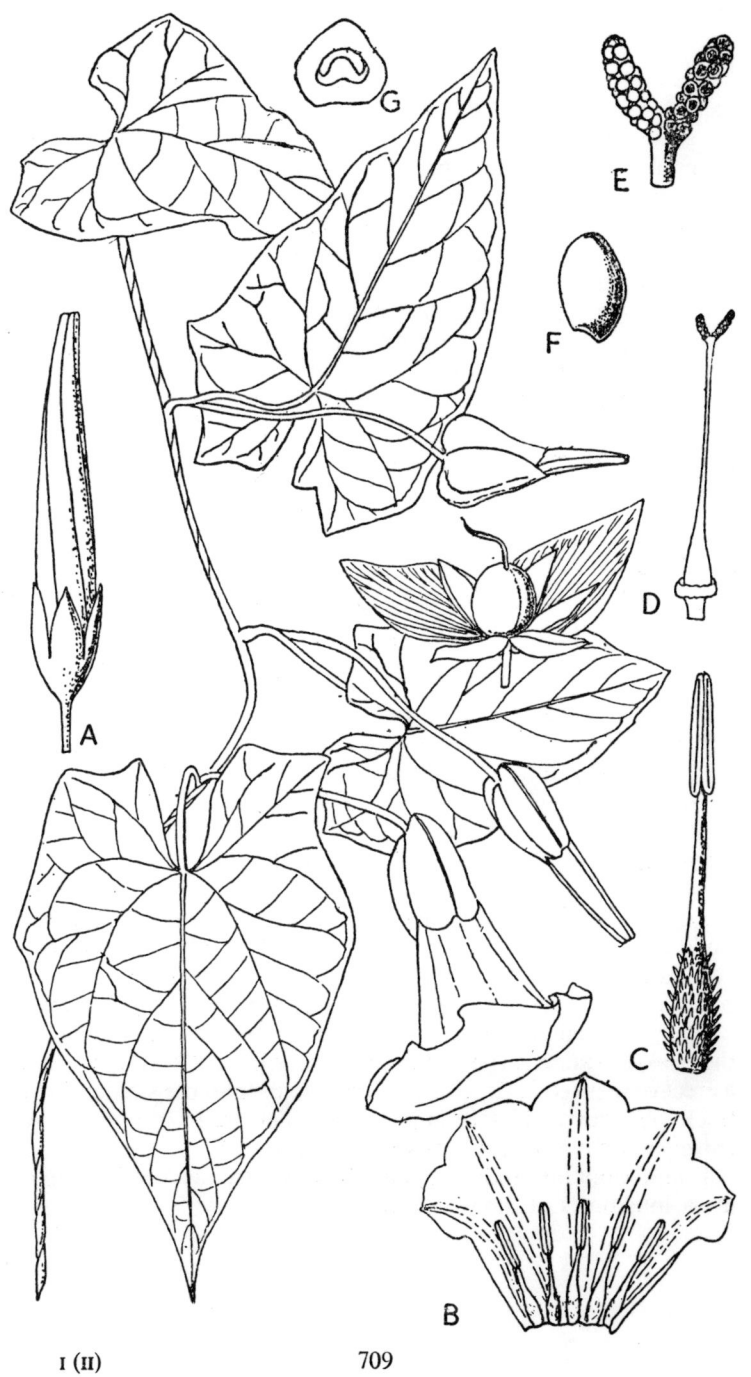

Calystegia soldanella (L.) R. Br. ($\times\frac{1}{2}$)

Perennial with slender spreading rootstock; stems procumbent and often half buried in sand, angular; leaves alternate, long-stalked, rounded-ovate or kidney-shaped, widely cordate at the base, úsually about 1 in. broad, slightly 3-lobed, pale green and minutely pustulate on both surfaces, 5-nerved from the base, fairly thick; flowers axillary, solitary on long stalks, the stalks 4-angled; bracts (A, ×1) 2, $\frac{2}{3}$ in. long, enclosing the calyx, sharply keeled; sepals (C, ×1$\frac{1}{2}$) 5, unequal-sized, rounded to a short crimson tip, about as long as the bracts; corolla funnel-shaped, 1$\frac{1}{2}$ in. long,

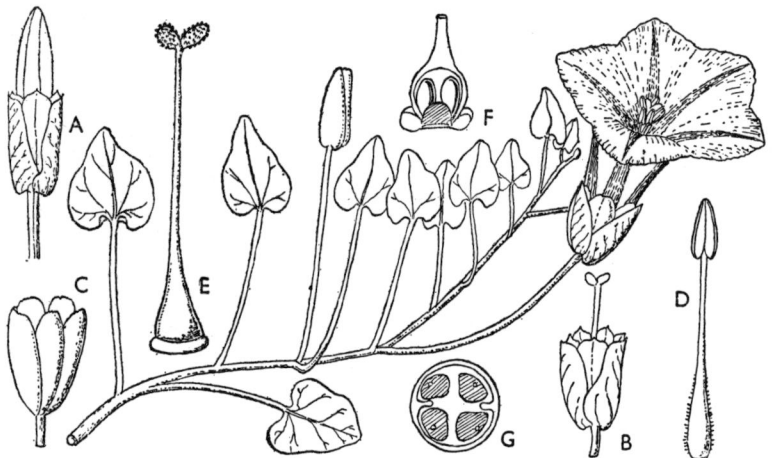

nearly 2 in. diam., pale mauve or pink with paler bands down the middle of the 5 lobes; stamens (D, ×1$\frac{1}{2}$) 5, alternate with the corolla-lobes, inserted towards the base of the tube; filaments broadened and hairy towards the base; anthers facing outwards, white, $\frac{1}{4}$ in. long, opening by slits; nectary embracing the base of the ovary, orange, large and fleshy; ovary (F, G, ×2$\frac{1}{2}$) containing 4 erect ovules; style (B, ×1$\frac{1}{2}$) a little longer than the stamens, with thick lobes covered by the large white pollen grains (synonym *Convolvulus soldanella* L.) (family *Convolvulaceae*).

Found only on sandy and shingly seashores, widely distributed in various parts of the world; a very lovely wild flower.

A stout erect biennial up to about 4 ft. high, densely covered with star-shaped (stellate) hairs (A, $\times 10$); leaves forming a rosette the first year, oblong-lanceolate; stem leaves decurrent, the lower more or less stalked, the upper sessile, pointed, shortly toothed on the margin; flowers numerous and crowded in a long dense spike-like raceme and densely hairy; bracts lanceolate, as long as the flowers; calyx deeply 5-lobed, lobes narrowly lanceolate; corolla (B, $\times \frac{2}{3}$) yellow, with a short tube, and 5 broad spreading lobes; stamens 5, three of their stalks covered with yellowish woolly hairs, the other two glabrous or nearly so; ovary (C, $\times 1\frac{1}{2}$)

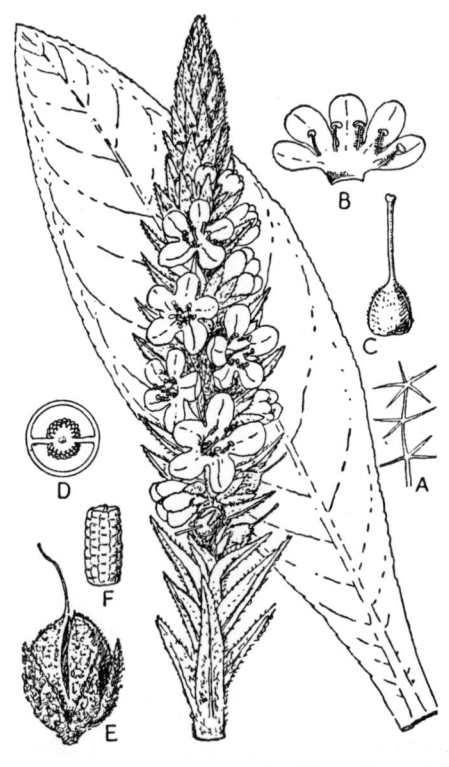

2-locular, style with a club-shaped stigma; capsule (E, $\times \frac{4}{5}$) ovoid, opening by 2 valves, with numerous small rugose seeds (F, $\times 8$) (family *Scrophulariaceae*).

Whilst nearly all this family have only 4 stamens, the Mullein genus, *Verbascum*, has retained 5, showing it to be a rather primitive member of the group. In addition the corolla is quite 'regular' and not 2-lipped as in many of the more advanced types such as the Snapdragon.

When out of flower the Mullein is sometimes mistaken for the Foxglove, and the leaves are occasionally found mixed with the latter when gathered for medicinal purposes; they are densely covered with several-rayed star-shaped hairs.

BLACK MULLEIN
Verbascum nigrum L. ($\times \frac{1}{2}$)

Biennial; stems simple or branched (see A), up to 3 or 4 ft. high; basal leaves on lòng stalks loosely clothed with branched (dendriform) hairs; blade (B, $\times \frac{1}{2}$) up to 1 ft. long and 6 in. broad, oblong-elliptic, broadly pointed at the apex, rounded-heart-shaped at the base, bright green above and with a few minute star-shaped hairs, paler below and loosely clothed with soft hairs, the hairs on the midrib and nerves mainly tree-like (dendriform) (C, $\times$ 2), those between the nerves star-shaped (C, $\times$ 2); nerves very prominent below; stem leaves becoming stalkless upwards, ovate to almost rounded, sharply and abruptly pointed, gradually merging into narrow sharp-pointed bracts; flowers numerous in clusters on the angular axis; stalks up to $\frac{1}{3}$ in. long, hairy like the narrow 5 calyx-lobes and ovary; corolla (E, $\times$ 1) yellow with small anchor- or spade-shaped crimson or chestnut-brown spots at the base of each of the 5 lobes, these markedly overlapping in bud (D, $\times 2\frac{1}{2}$); stamens (F, $\times$ 3) 5, alternate with the lobes, their stalks densely covered with long crimson gland-tipped hairs; antherloculi merging into one when open, orange-red; ovary (G, $\times$ 6) 2-locular; style (H, $\times 2\frac{1}{2}$) slender, with an orange head-like stigma; fruit a capsule opening by two valves, with numerous small seeds (family *Scrophulariaceae*).

This species flowers in summer and autumn and the colour of the yellow corolla is enhanced by the gland-tipped crimson hairs on the filaments of the stamens, and the orange-red anthers. The five stamens project from the corolla almost horizontally, and are only slightly bent upwards. The uppermost is short, and the lower 2 the longest. The style is a little shorter than the longer stamens, and is usually bent downwards, so that an insect alighting on the lowest corolla-lobe will generally touch the stigma first, bringing about cross-pollination.

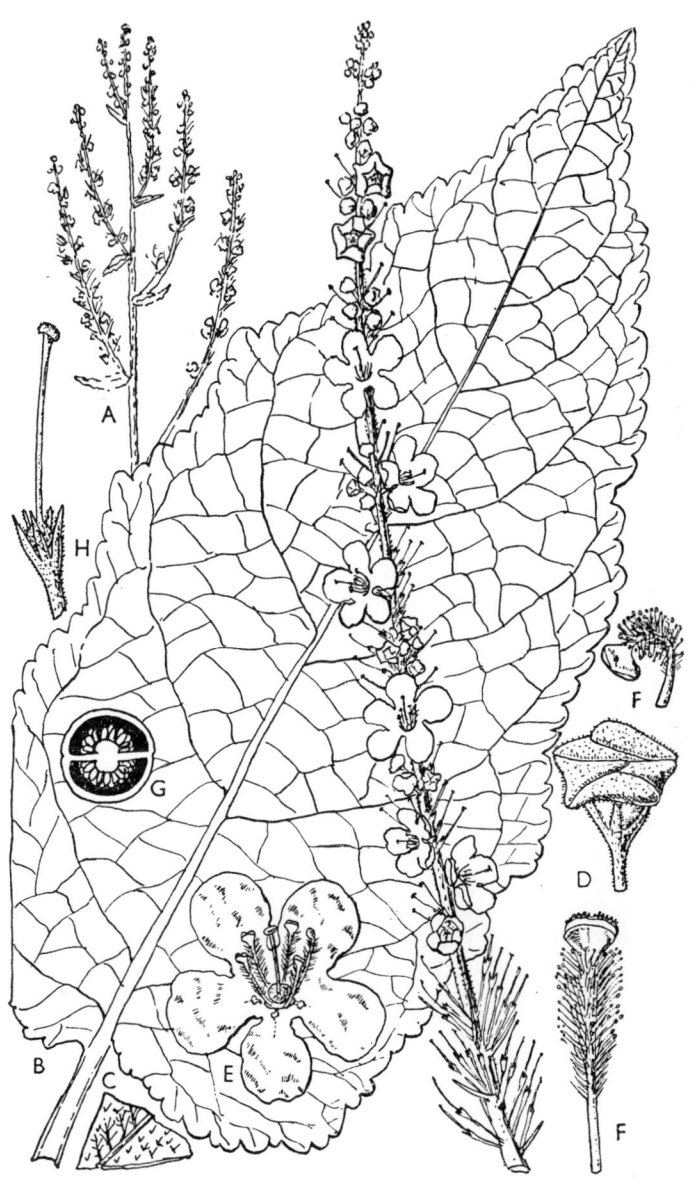

713

FIGWORT

Scrophularia nodosa L. ($\times\frac{1}{2}$)

Perennial with a tuberous rootstock; stems up to 3–4 ft. high erect, square in section with sharp angles, dull green finely speckled with purple, glabrous; leaves (A, $\times\frac{1}{2}$) opposite, stalked, triangular-ovate, acute at the apex, doubly dentate with larger teeth towards the base, paler green below, not hairy (glabrous); an oblique glandular line across the stem between the base of the leaf-stalks; flowers (B, $\times$ 2) arranged in a loose terminal panicle made up of little opposite to alternate cymes, the oldest flowers in the middle of each; branches of the inflorescence covered with short gland-tipped hairs; calyx (C, $\times$ 2$\frac{1}{2}$) saucer-shaped, 5-lobed, lobes ovate, with short teeth on the margin; corolla (D, $\times$ 2) sub-globose in bud, irregular (zygomorphic), 2-lipped, nearly $\frac{1}{2}$ in. long, green, the back of the tube and two back lobes dull purple; stamens 4, at first curled downwards away from the style, which matures first and occupies the mouth of the corolla; 5th stamen changed to a staminode (E, $\times$ 6) closely adnate to the back of the corolla-tube, slightly 2-lobed, on the inside covered with gland-like, knob-like hairs (papillae); ovary (F, $\times$ 5) seated on a large fleshy nectar-secreting disk, 2-locular, with numerous ovules on the two fleshy axile placentas (G, $\times$ 5); fruit a broadly ovoid pointed capsule; seeds rugose, brown (family *Scrophulariaceae*).

To be found in shady moist places, flowering most of the summer; widely distributed across the northern hemisphere. The flowers are cross-pollinated, mainly by wasps. The stigmas are receptive before the anthers open (protogynous), and they remain so for 2 days. Then the filaments of the stamens straighten, the pollinated stigmas wither and the style bends down over the lower lip, its place being taken by the discharging anthers. Visitors first alight on the upper younger flowers (in the first female stage) and work downwards to the older flowers (in the male stage), thus bringing about pollination from different plants.

A closely related species is *Scrophularia aquatica* L., a taller plant by the sides of ditches and streams and rather less branched, the angles of the stem narrowly winged, and the rootstock without tubers.

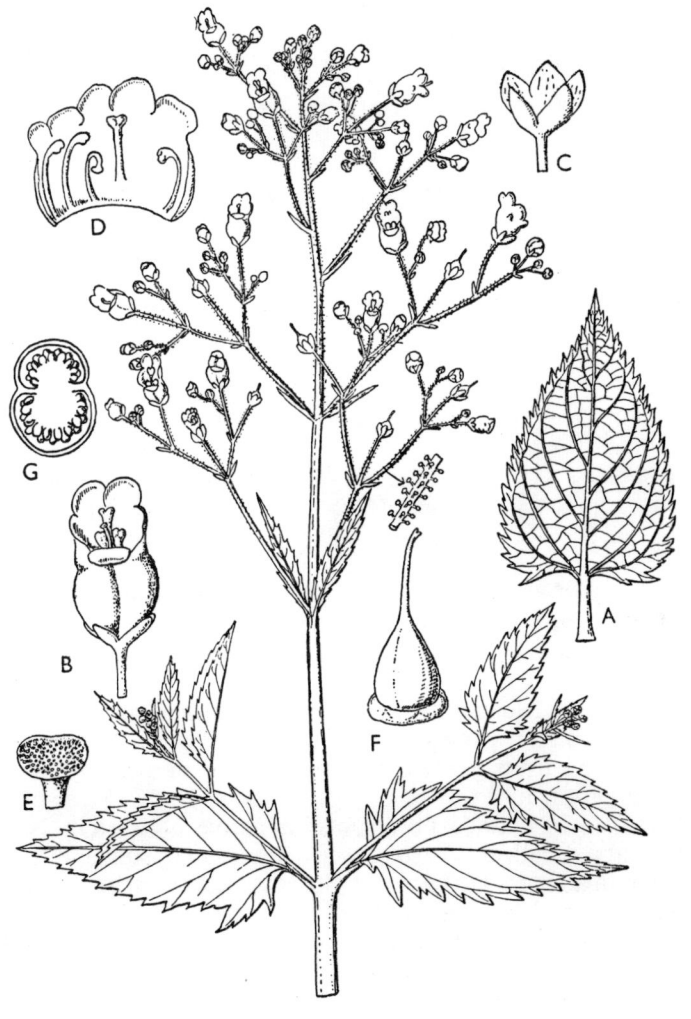

715

MUSK
Mimulus moschatus Dougl. ($\times\frac{1}{2}$)

Perennial herb, often growing in a dense clump in swampy places by streams; stems procumbent to semi-erect, clothed with soft

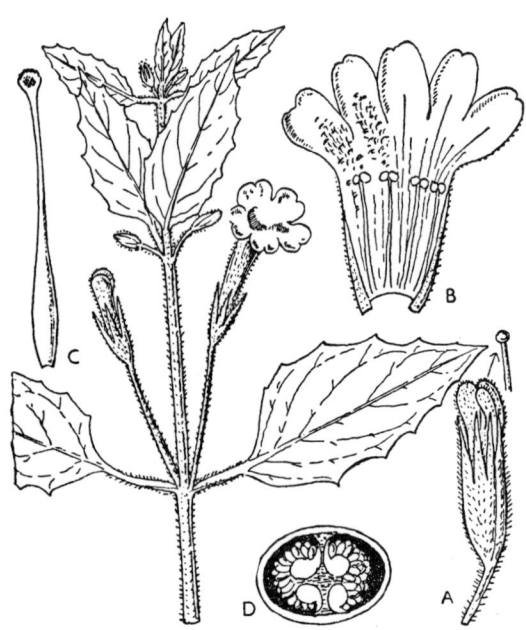

white hairs; leaves opposite, very shortly stalked, ovate-elliptic, entire or distantly tooth-ed, up to 2 in. long and $1\frac{1}{4}$ in. broad, clothed with soft whitish hairs; flowers solitary or in pairs in the axils of the leaves, on slender stalks; calyx (A, $\times 1\frac{1}{2}$) tubular, with 5 narrow lobes about $\frac{1}{3}$ as long as the tube; corolla (B, $\times 1$) tubular, yellow, the throat usu-

ally striped with red and with two densely bearded lines below the lower lip; lobes 5, rounded, notched, subequal; stamens 4, in-cluded in the tube; anthers hairy; style with a disk-like stigma; ovary (C, $\times 2$) 2-locular, with numerous ovules on axile placentas (D, $\times 5$); fruit a capsule, pointed (family *Scrophulariaceae*).

An escape from gardens and naturalized in swampy places, flowering from June to late August. The well-known Musk plant, a favourite in cottage flowerpots; a native of western North America; a decade or so ago caused a sensation by suddenly losing its scent in all parts of the world. Scent is a characteristic of many flowers and mainly of use to the plant for attracting insects which bring about cross-pollination; probably, therefore, an evolu-tionary loss, just as the sepals, petals, etc., in other plants may be reduced or completely suppressed, being no longer needed to carry on the vital functions.

Herb up to about 1 ft. high, often found naturalized in or near brooks and by the side of streams; leaves (A, $\times \frac{1}{2}$) opposite, lower broadly petiolate and connected at the base, rounded-elliptic, denticulate, glabrous, with several nerves running lengthwise; no stipules; flowers solitary in the axils of the upper leaves; stalks up to $1\frac{1}{2}$ in. long; calyx (B, $\times \frac{1}{2}$) leafy and bell-shaped, with 5 short broad teeth; corolla 2-lipped, yellow, variously marked inside with small purple spots at the mouth of the tube and sometimes with a large purple-red or pink spot on each lobe; stamens 4;

ovary 2-locular, with numerous ovules; style slender, with a broad stigma; fruit a capsule, opening by two valves into the loculi (family *Scrophulariaceae*).

This plant is a native of North America. It is naturalized in wet places and is rather a puzzle to the young botanist, for it seems to be quite at home amongst the native vegetation in some parts of the country. To the same genus belongs the Musk plant, *Mimulus moschatus* Lindl., which mysteriously lost its scent not many years ago (see fig. 614).

The stigma of this beautiful flower is irritable. Bees first touch the lower lobe of the stigma, which covers the anthers, and they pollinate it if they have previously been dusted with pollen at another flower. The stigmatic lobe then turns upwards, exposing the pollen-covered anthers, by which the insect is dusted again. Nectar is secreted at the base of the ovary.

Antirrhinum orontium L. ($\times\frac{1}{2}$)

Annual erect herb up to about 1 ft. high; stems sticky with gland-tipped hairs; lower leaves opposite, remainder alternate, lanceolate to almost linear, narrowed to the base, glabrous to slightly hairy with short gland-tipped hairs, up to 2 in. long and $\frac{1}{2}$ in. broad, entire; flowers solitary in the axils of the upper leaves, shortly stalked, stalks with long gland-tipped hairs; calyx 5-lobed to the base, longer than the corolla and like narrow leaves, glandular-hairy; corolla (A, $\times\frac{1}{2}$) red or rarely white, tubular, 2-lipped, saccate at the base, mouth tightly closed, upper lip marked with darker red streaks, top of lower lip with a pale yellow nectar guide; stamens 4, in pairs, the anthers of each pair connivent; ovary (B, $\times 3$) 2-locular, setose; style glandular-hairy; ovules numerous on axile placentas; fruit (C, $\times 3$) an oblique capsule opening at the top by 2 or 3 pores; seeds (D, $\times 8$) bifacial, smooth and with a narrow keel on the back and a marginal rim, scooped out and lobulate inside, the lobules warted (family *Scrophulariaceae*).

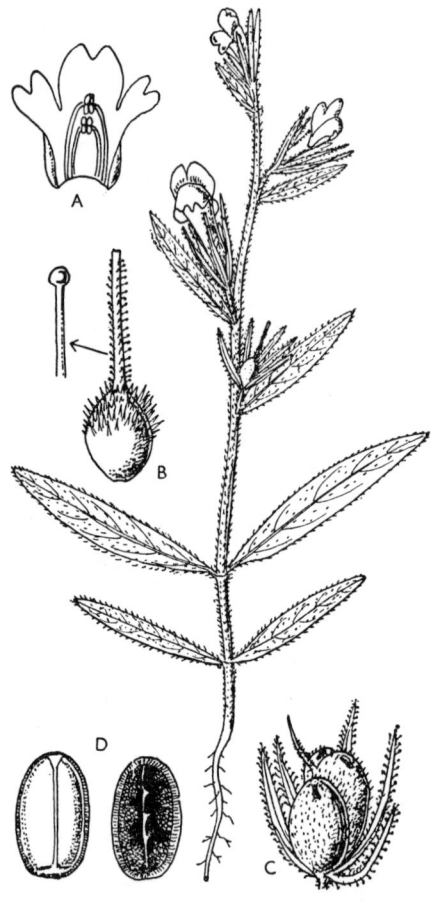

Found mostly in cornfields in England from Cumberland southwards and in southern Eire; widely spread as a weed of cultivation.

Nectar is secreted in a swelling at the base of the ovary, and only bees which can open the tightly closed corolla-tube are able to effect cross-pollination.

Perennial with a creeping rootstock; stems erect, rounded, shining, green, without hairs; leaves alternate, linear or linear-lanceolate, entire, 1-nerved or obscurely 3-nerved from the base, bright green, but rather glaucous below, often with a short leafy shoot in the axil; no stipules; flowers (A, × 1½) crowded into a leafy raceme with a bunch of young leaves at the top; stalks up to ⅓ in. long; sepals 5, very shortly united at the base, almost equal, oblong or lanceolate, often slightly tinged with dull crimson; corolla 2-lipped, pale yellow, but the bulging portion of the lower lip bright orange and densely hairy inside; tube prolonged into a sharp-pointed spur ½–¾ in. long; stamens (B, × 1½) 4, in unequal pairs and hidden below the upper lip; anthers 2-locular, the lobes divergent; ovary above the calyx (superior), 2-locular, containing numerous ovules on large

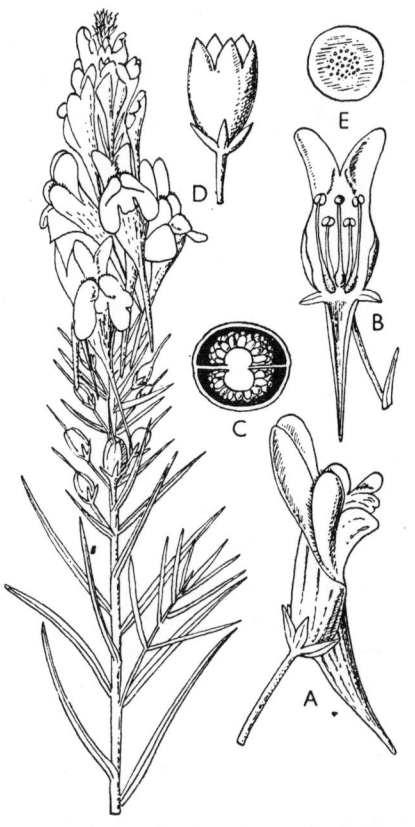

placentas (C, × 3); fruit (D, × 1½) a broadly ellipsoid capsule divided into 5 short lobes; seeds (E, × 5) orbicular, compressed, finely warted in the middle (family *Scrophulariaceae*).

Nectar is secreted at the base of the ovary, and it glides in a narrow groove down to the tip of the long spur, which it fills for a short space. Only long-tongued bees can suck the nectar and effect cross-pollination. They press down the lower lip, which is tightly closed, and creep into the flower, their backs becoming dusted with pollen, which they transfer to the stigma of another flower.

CREEPING TOAD FLAX
Linaria repens (L.) Mill. (×⅓)

Stems at first decumbent then erect and up to 2 ft. high, not hairy;
leaves in whorls at intervals on the stem, up to 5 in a whorl, shortly

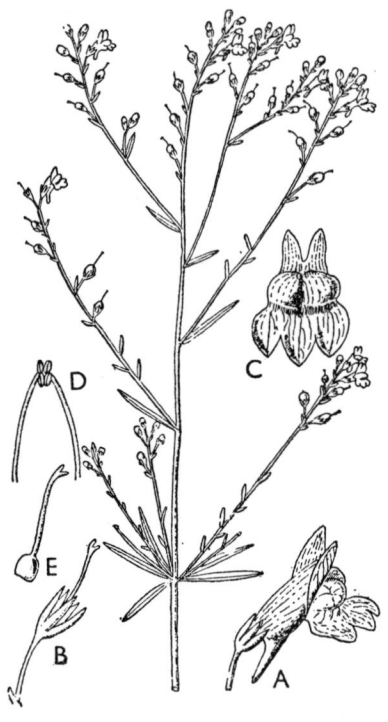

linear, acute, 1-nerved, not
hairy, margins entire; flowers
(A, ×2) in racemes in the axils
of the upper leaves and forming a loose panicle; leaves
gradually changing into smaller bracts; flower-stalks longer
than the bracts; calyx (B, ×2½)
deeply 5-lobed, lobes open in
bud; corolla pale mauve,
streaked with darker lines of
the same colour, 2-lipped,
upper lip erect and 2-lobed, the
lower 3-lobed (C, ×2), the
tube closed by a larger hump
tinged in the middle with yellow and hairy; spur at the base
longer than the calyx; stamens
(D, ×2) 4, the anthers of each
pair connivent; ovary (E, ×2)
above the calyx, rounded, with
a terminal style slightly 2-lobed
at the tip; capsule broad and
flattened; seeds angular,
wrinkled (family *Scrophulariaceae*).

Grows mostly in cultivated ground; not at all common; a very
pretty flower when seen under a hand-lens, with lovely deep mauve
markings. Nectar is secreted by the fleshy base of the ovary and
stored in the spur of the corolla.

Distributed from south and central Europe east to the Caucasus.

The genus *Linaria* is related to the Snapdragon, *Antirrhinum*,
but differs chiefly by the presence of a spur at the base of the
corolla-tube. There are six species, two of them introduced, *L.
purpurea* (L.) Mill, the Purple Toad Flax, and *L. arenaria* (Poir.)
DC.

Small succulent trailing perennial herb, with slender stems rooting at the lower nodes on rocks and old walls; leaves without stipules, long-stalked, reniform, shortly and very broadly 5-lobed, the lobes slightly pointed, glabrous, frequently tinged with purple below; flowers axillary, solitary; calyx 5-lobed nearly to the base, lobes narrow, glabrous; corolla (A, laid open × 2) lilac, the tube streaked with crimson-purple, the two humps on the lower side of the lip tinged with orange and closing the spurred tube; on the

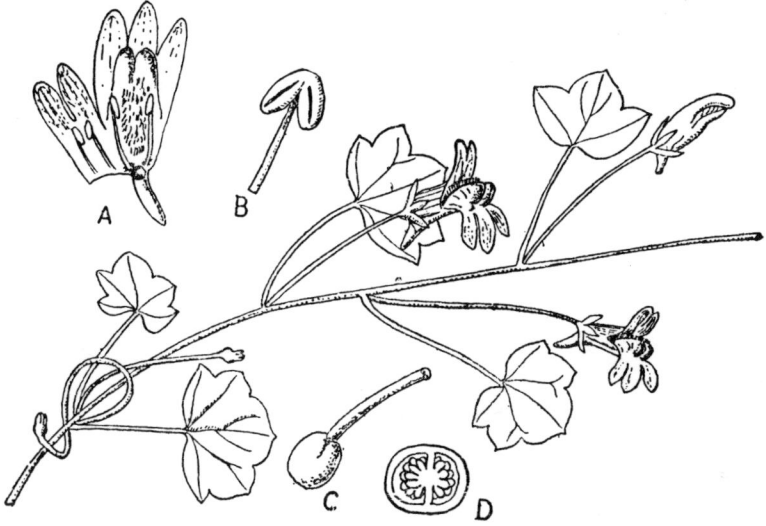

lower side of the tube a dense carpet of stiff inwardly directed hairs; stamens (B, × 3) 4, 2 longer and 2 shorter; stalks of longer stamens hairy at the base; ovary (C, × 3) deep crimson, 2-locular, with numerous ovules attached to the middle (D, × 6); style thick and undivided; fruit a globose capsule with several warted seeds (family *Scrophulariaceae*).

This pretty little plant flowers from the late spring until the autumn. Growing on old dry walls and rocks it is remarkably resistant to drought. The flowers are adapted to the visits of bees who are able to press down the lower lip and gain access to the nectar, which is secreted around the fleshy base of the ovary and stored in the spur at the bottom of the corolla. After fertilization takes place the flower stalks curve towards dark crevices in the wall where the seeds are deposited when the fruit ripens and bursts.

Sibthorpia europaea L. ($\times\frac{1}{3}$)

Small perennial herb with very slender prostrate stems (G, ×2) rooting at the nodes; leaves on long slender flattened hairy petioles up to nearly 4 in. long, orbicular or kidney-shaped in outline, primarily 5-lobed but the lobes often deeply bifid, setulose-pubescent on both surfaces; flowers (A, ×3) very small, usually 1 or 2, rarely 3 in the leaf-axils, shortly stalked; calyx 5-lobed lobes triangular, thinly pilose outside; corolla pale yellow with a purplish tinge in the upper three lobes, 2 of the 5 lobes smaller than the other 3; stamens (B, ×4) 5 or 4, alternate with the

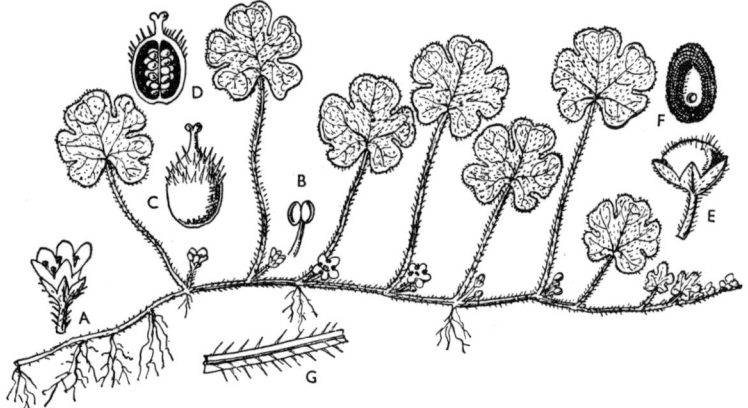

corolla-lobes; anthers didymous; ovary ovoid, hairy above, 2-locular, with numerous ovules on axile placentas; fruit (E, ×2) a capsule with several seeds (F, ×6) hollowed out on the side attached and finely pitted-reticulate (family *Scrophulariaceae*). – Synonym *Sibthorpia australis* Hutch.

Confined to the south-western counties of England from Sussex to Cornwall and in the Scilly Isles and south-west Eire; distributed in western Europe and the Mediterranean, and further south on the tropical African mountains which I considered at one time to be a distinct species, *S. australis*; intermediate forms have now been collected which link up the two extremes.

Limosella aquatica L. (×⅓)

A small annual herb forming little tufts about 2 in. diam, often with a few lateral very short stems repeating the tufts; leaves all radical, narrowly spoon-shaped on slender stalks, the blade about ½–¾ in. long, 3-nerved, glabrous; leaf-stalks broadened towards the base; flowers (A, ×⅔) pale-rose, axillary and radiating like the leaves; pedicels up to ½ in. long, at length decurved; calyx 5-lobed to the middle, persistent and becoming membranous in fruit; corolla shortly tubular, longer than the calyx, with 5 equal-sized spreading lobes; stamens 4, inserted at the mouth of the corolla and shortly exserted; anthers 1-locular; ovary (B, C, ×2)

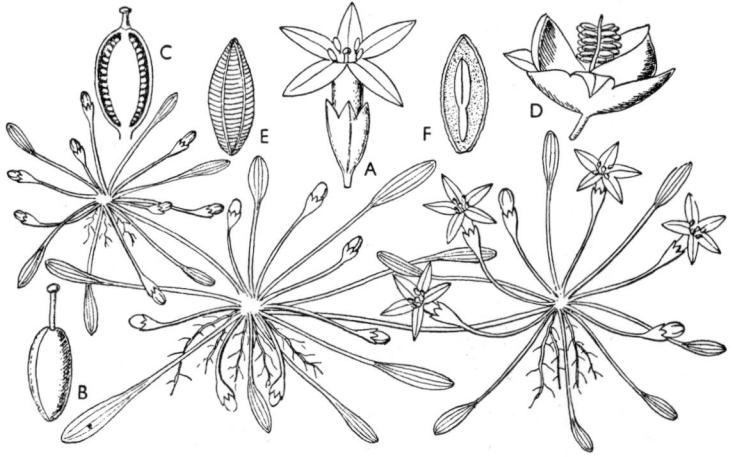

2-locular; style with a large capitate stigma; fruit (D, ×2) a capsule with a very thin coat; seeds (E, F, ×8) very small, ribbed (family *Scrophulariaceae*).

Widely distributed, in muddy swampy places or sometimes floating, in the north temperate zone, but mostly very local in Britain; flowers from June onwards.

A second very rare species of this genus occurs only in Wales and in eastern North America. This is *Limosella subulata* Ives, with all its leaves needle-shaped (subulate) and the calyx shorter than the corolla-tube. This points to a former connexion between the floras of these now widely separated areas and divided by the broad Atlantic Ocean.

Veronica chamaedrys L. ($\times \frac{3}{5}$)

Perennial, with several slender stems decumbent and rooting towards the base, then erect or ascending; stems glabrous except for

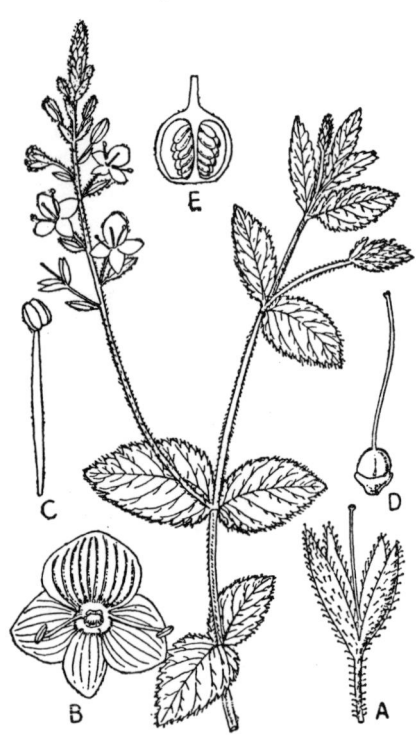

two opposite lines of rather long whitish hairs in line with the leaves; leaves opposite, nearly sessile, ovate, (toothed (crenate), with a few bristly fine hairs on the nerves below; the very short stalks margined with long fine hairs; flowers in slender racemes from the upper leaf-axils, the axis or common stalk with fine hairs all around; each flower with a shortly stalked green bract at the base; calyx (A, × 2) deeply 4-lobed, lobes broadly oblanceolate, hairy; corolla (B, × 1½) deep sky blue fading to mauve, marked with deeper blue lines and with a white 'eye', the mouth guarded with erect bristly hairs on the lower side, 4-lobed; stamens (C, × 4) 2, between the back and side lobes of the corolla, long-exserted; filaments and anthers blue; ovary (D, × 5) rounded, minutely hairy, 2-locular, with a nectariferous ring around the base; style slender, blue; fruit flat, notched at the top (family *Scrophulariaceae*).

The flowers of this plant are very beautiful when seen through a hand-lens. Nectar is secreted in a fleshy disk around the base of the ovary and protected by hairs partly across the mouth of the corolla. The two stamens are lateral and divergent and are seized by an insect alighting on the flower and drawn against its body, on which pollen is deposited and carried to the stigma of another flower.

724

Veronica scutellata L. ($\times\frac{1}{3}$)

Perennial herb with decumbent slender glabrous stems rooting at the lower nodes, growing in marshes and ditches; leaves opposite, sessile (not ˙ stalked), lanceolate to almost linear, appearing almost entire, but really with very minute and distant teeth, glabrous, with the nerves ascending from the base; flowers in slender racemes, each raceme from alternating leaf-axils (i.e. only one raceme at each node); bracts much shorter than the slender thread-like flower-stalks; sepals (A, $\times 1\frac{1}{2}$) 4, ovate, 3-nerved; corolla (B, $\times 1\frac{1}{2}$) pale pinkish-blue or white, deeply 4-lobed; stamens 2, inserted near the base of the corolla; anthers broadly ovoid; ovary rounded, style slender, with a capitate stigma; capsule (C, $\times 1\frac{1}{2}$) rounded, deeply notched,

reticulate, glabrous; seeds (D, $\times$ 3) quite flat and thin, rounded, pale brown (family *Scrophularicaeae*).

A very striking and characteristic feature of this species is the arrangement of the racemes, only one of which occurs at each node, first on one side of the stem and then on the other. The nearly entire leaves provide another good spotting character. The species enjoys a very wide distribution, being found almost all over Britain and right across the northern hemisphere, including North America. It grows in marshes and ditches and flowers during the summer.

Perennial herb usually much branched from the base and rooting at the lower nodes; stems thinly pubescent with rather long hairs

all around; leaves (A, ×1) opposite, very shortly stalked, ovate, wedge-shaped at the base, rounded or with a broad triangular top, very distinctly toothed (serrate), thinly hairy on both surfaces, with 3–4 pairs of lateral nerves; flowers (B, × 2) in terminal stalked spike-like racemes (i.e. they are nearly sessile on the axis), the axis softly and rather densely pubescent; bracts about as long as the calyx, pubescent; sepals lanceolate, hairy; corolla pale blue, marked by darker veins, 4-lobed; stamens (C, × 4) 2, inserted towards the base of the tube; anthers ovoid; ovary (D, × 4) rounded, smooth, with a terminal rather long style, and seated on a nectariferous disk; capsule (E, × 2½) rounded, notched, shortly pubescent; seeds (F, × 6) yellow, flattened, smooth (family *Scrophulariaceae*).

Insects touch the stigma and anthers with various parts of their bodies, effecting either self- or cross-pollination. Failing these the filaments twist inwards and downwards as the corolla withers until the anthers touch the stigma.

A very widely distributed species on banks, heaths, and in dry pastures, flowering during the whole summer.

Perennial herb with tufted ascending stems up to about 9 in. high and minutely hairy all around; leaves opposite, shortly stalked, ovate to very broadly elliptic, more or less rounded at each end and obscurely crenate, 3-nerved at the base, and with only 1 or 2 pairs of additional lateral nerves, glabrous or very nearly so; flowers rather numerous in terminal leafy racemes, the leaves gradually decreased in size upwards and becoming alternate, the lower flowers already in fruit before the upper have done blooming; flower-stalks shortly pubescent; sepals (A, × 2) oblong, slightly hairy; corolla (B, × 2) whitish, marked by blue veins, 4-lobed to below the middle; stamens 2, inserted near the base of the corolla; anthers ovoid; ovary rounded, smooth, with a slender terminal style and capitate stigma; fruit (C, × 2) a flat rounded notched capsule, slightly

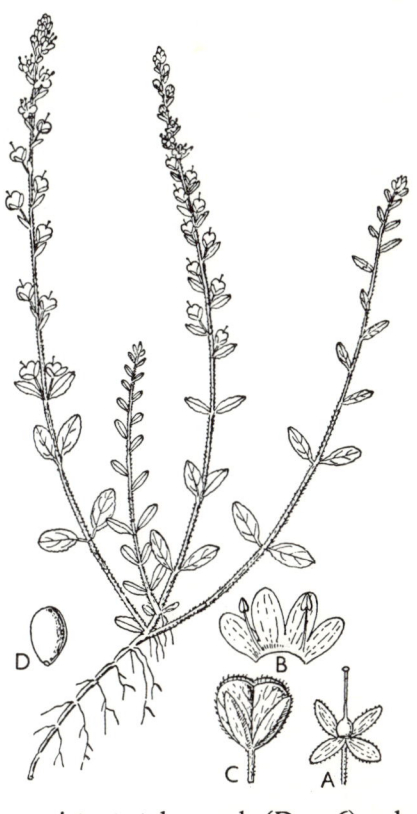

hairy, tipped by the slender persistent style; seeds (D, × 6) pale straw-coloured, obovoid (family *Scrophulariaceae*).

The anthers of this species lie close together on each side of the stigma, so that an insect visitor may effect self- or cross-pollination.

This is also a very widely spread species, found in fields and moist places, and flowering during spring and summer.

Veronica arvensis L. ($\times \frac{1}{2}$)

A small very spreading thinly hairy annual, usually much branched from the base; leaves (A, $\times 1$) opposite, sessile (not stalked),
ovate rounded at the base, with very few teeth, the upper bract-
like ones becoming entire or nearly so, thinly hairy on both surfaces, but mainly on the nerves below; flowers (B, $\times 1\frac{1}{2}$) axillary
and forming leafy racemes, though the flowers nearly sessile;
sepals (C, $\times 1\frac{1}{2}$) linear-lanceolate, fringed with short hairs and

glandular hairs; corolla (D, $\times 1\frac{1}{2}$) very much shorter than the
sepals, dark sky-blue marked by darker streaks and with a whitish
tube, 4-lobed; stamens 2, inserted towards the base of the tube;
anthers ovoid; ovary rounded, with a very short style; fruit (E,
$\times 2\frac{1}{2}$) rounded, notched, fringed with gland-tipped hairs; seeds
(F, $\times 6$) ellipsoid, slightly compressed, straw-coloured (family
Scrophulariaceae).

The anthers and stigma are at the same level, and so close together that self-pollination is easy, while insect visitors effect
cross-pollination equally well.

Common in cultivated ground and waste places and on banks
and old walls, where it flowers more or less during the whole of
the year.

Veronica agrestis L. ($\times\frac{1}{2}$)

A much-branched annual with procumbent or prostrate stems up to a foot or so long and slightly hairy all around; lower leaves (A, $\times$ 1) opposite, gradually becoming alternate upwards, ovate, abruptly narrowed into a broad short stalk, crenate-dentate, glabrous or very slightly hairy, with about 3 pairs of lateral nerves; flowers axillary, sometimes only 1 to each pair of leaves (when opposite), the rather long stalk recurving in fruit; sepals (B, $\times$ 3) leafy, longer than the corolla, pubescent; corolla (C, $\times$ 3)

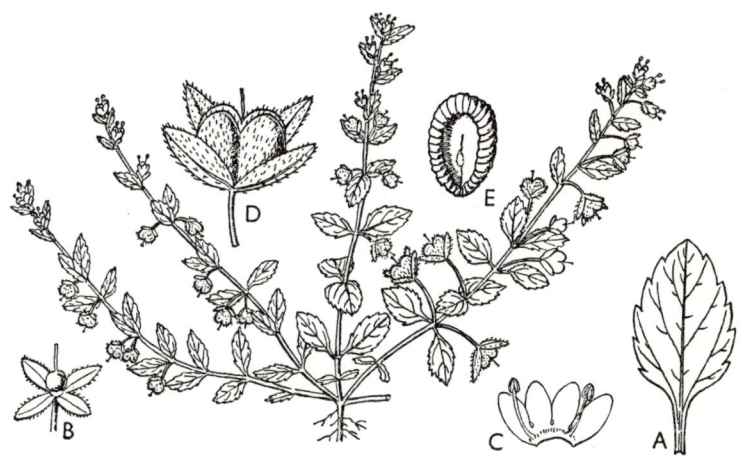

milky-white with a bluish tinge and marked with convergent lines serving as nectar-guides; stamens 2, inserted near the base of the tube; anthers ovoid; ovary minutely hairy, with a slender style and capitate stigma; capsule (D, $\times$ 1$\frac{1}{2}$) compressed, deeply notched, thinly pubescent; seeds (E, $\times$ 5) grub-like, i.e. with wrinkled beady margins and scooped out in the middle (family *Scrophulariaceae*).

Nectar is secreted in a fleshy disk below the ovary and covered by hairs lining the tube of the corolla. During dull weather the flowers open less widely, so that the anthers and stigma lie in contact, automatic pollination being effective.

This is a common weed in waste and cultivated places, and it flowers during the whole season. The seeds are very remarkable, and are shown in fig. E.

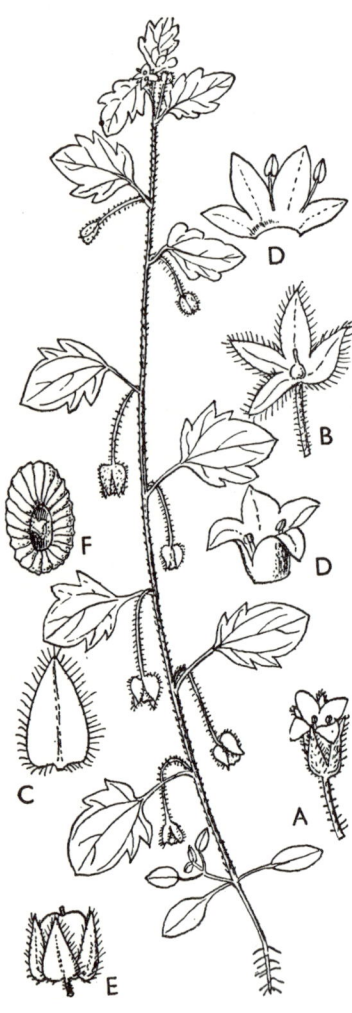

Slender annual, often with long side-branches spreading from the base; stems green, thinly pubescent; seed-leaves opposite, persistent for some time, entire, yellowish-green, 1-nerved; stem-leaves alternate, broadly spade-shaped, coarsely 2-toothed or lobulate on each side with a broadly ovate end lobe, rounded or truncate at the base, 3-nerved, $\frac{1}{2}-\frac{3}{4}$ in. long and broad, bright green, minutely sponge-like below, loosely clothed on the upper surface with short stiff white hairs; stalk a little shorter than the blade; flowers (A, $\times 2$) solitary, axillary, the stalks soon deflexed in fruit; sepals (B, C, $\times 2$) 4, ovate-triangular, fringed with stiff white hairs; corolla (D, $\times 3$) pale mauve-blue, shorter than the sepals, 4-lobed to the middle, lobes recurved; stamens 2; ovary 2-locular, with 2 ovules in each, sometimes only 1, 2, or 3 becoming seeds; style very short; fruit (E, $\times 3$) slightly 2-lobed, enclosed by the persistent sepals; seeds (F, $\times 6$) grub-like, i.e. ellipsoid and wavy, attached by a deep cavity to the central axis (family *Scrophulariaceae*).

A widely distributed weed of cultivation and in waste places, flowering most of the summer.

Veronica beccabunga L. ($\times \frac{2}{5}$)

Perennial by the sides of brooks and ditches, the stems sometimes floating in the water, rooting at the nodes, thick, succulent, and hollow, quite glabrous; leaves opposite, stalked, rounded-elliptic or obovate, rounded at the top, slightly toothed, glabrous and rather fleshy, with about 3 pairs of lateral nerves; a short rim across the stem between the leaf-stalks; flowers in slender-stalked axillary racemes about twice as long as the leaves and with very small bracts; flower-stalks longer than the calyx, the latter (A, $\times 2\frac{1}{2}$) 4-lobed to the base, lobes ovate; corolla (B, $\times 2\frac{1}{2}$) dark sky-blue, 4-lobed; stamens 2, exserted, attached near the base of the corolla-tube; anthers ovoid; ovary 2-locular, with a slender style and capitate stigma; capsule (C, $\times 2$), rounded, shortly notched, glabrous, tipped by the persistent style; seeds (D, $\times 8$) rounded, straw-coloured, smooth (family *Scrophulariaceae*).

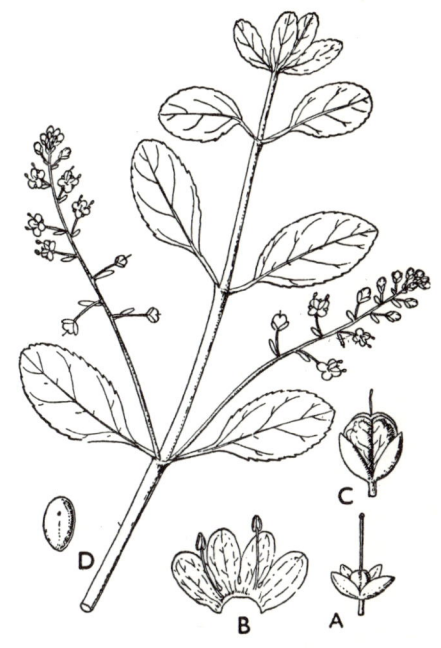

The dark sky-blue flowers expand in the sun to form a flat surface, from which the stigmas spread, the anthers being at a distance from the stigma when they open. In bad weather the flowers are half-closed, and automatic self-pollination takes place.

This species is like *Veronica scutellata* (see fig. 623), and is also spread across the northern hemisphere, but not in North America. It is also found in the same wet environment, but differs by the broader rounded leaves and by the racemes being in pairs at each node, i.e. one in the axil of each leaf. It flowers during the whole of the summer months.

Usually a biennial but sometimes persisting a year or two longer; basal leaves on long stalks which are winged with the continued base of the leaf blade, broadly lanceolate, up to a foot or more in length, rather abruptly narrowed into the stalk at the base, toothed on the margin, rather coarsely reticulate-veined, covered with soft white downy hairs below; flowering stems up to about 4 ft. high or higher bearing a few lanceolate leaves which gradually pass into bracts, the latter lanceolate, sessile, entire; flowers numerous in the raceme, drooping, light purple and usually beautifully spotted with crimson, rarely white; calyx large, 5-lobed to the base, 4 of the lobes ovate, the fifth (upper) smaller and more pointed; corolla up to 2 in. long, shortly 4-lobed; stamens 4, included; anther-cells (A, $\times 1\frac{1}{2}$) divergent; ovary 2-locular, with very numerous ovules; style shortly 2-lobed; capsule (B, $\times \frac{2}{5}$) with numerous very small minutely honey-combed seeds (C, $\times 5$) (family *Scrophulariaceae*).

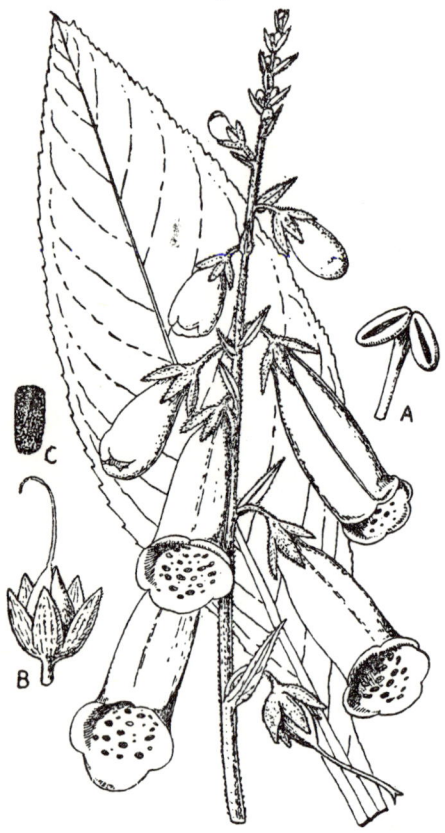

Everyone knows this beautiful plant which is well worth a place in the garden. It is official in the British Pharmacopoeia, the dried leaves being used in medicine for heart trouble. It has been recognized as poisonous for centuries, one of its common names being Dead Man's Bells! All parts of the plant are poisonous, especially the seeds.

Erect annual with simple stems or much-branched from the base; stems covered with downwardly directed hairs; leaves opposite, small, sessile, ovate in outline but deeply toothed, teeth ending in a fine point; flowers in the axils of the upper leaves, some crowded at the top and forming a rather dense bracteate spike; bracts (H, $\times 2\frac{1}{4}$) rounded, deeply toothed; calyx (A, $\times 2\frac{1}{2}$) 5-lobed to about the middle, lobes acute, hairy; corolla (B, $\times 1\frac{1}{4}$) very variable in colour, white or reddish and streaked with purple, with a yellow spot in the throat; upper lip forming a hood over the anthers and shortly 2-lobed; lower lip 3-lobed, each lobe deeply and widely notched; tube hairy outside; stamens (D, $\times 2\frac{1}{2}$) 4, on the co-

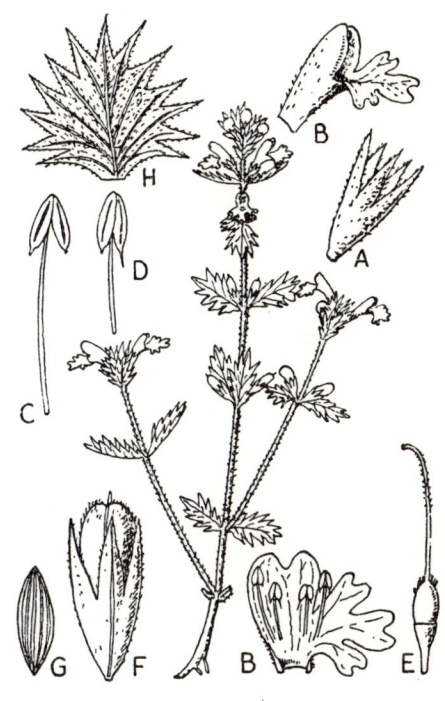

rolla, not protruded, one pair longer than the other, one of the anther-lobes of each of the shorter stamens with a long point at the base, the other bases with short points; ovary (E, $\times 3$) girt by a cupular disk; hairy at the top; style undivided, slender, hairy in the upper part; fruit (F, $\times 3$) clasped by the calyx; seeds (G, $\times 8$) few, pointed at each end, and marked by ridges (family *Scrophulariaceae*).

Odontites verna (Bellardi) Dumont (× ½)

Semi-parasitical erect annual up to about 1 ft. high or more; stems bluntly 4-angled, hispid with short downwardly directed hairs; leaves opposite, sessile, lanceolate, rather remotely toothed, hispid on both surfaces with short bulbous-based hairs, 3-nerved from the base; no stipules; flowers (A, × 1½) in one-sided spike-like racemes with leafy bracts; calyx 4-lobed to the middle, covered outside with bulbous-based hairs, persisting around the fruit; corolla purplish-red, 2-lipped, the upper lip hood-like and glandular outside as well as slightly hairy; stamens (B, × 2) 4, the anthers peeping out from under the hood, and with divergent loculi; ovary (C, × 1½) entire, abruptly ending in a slender hairy style; capsule (D, × 1½) opening by 2 valves into the middle of the loculi (loculicidal); seeds (E, × 4) numerous, brown, closely ribbed lengthwise (family *Scrophulariaceae*).

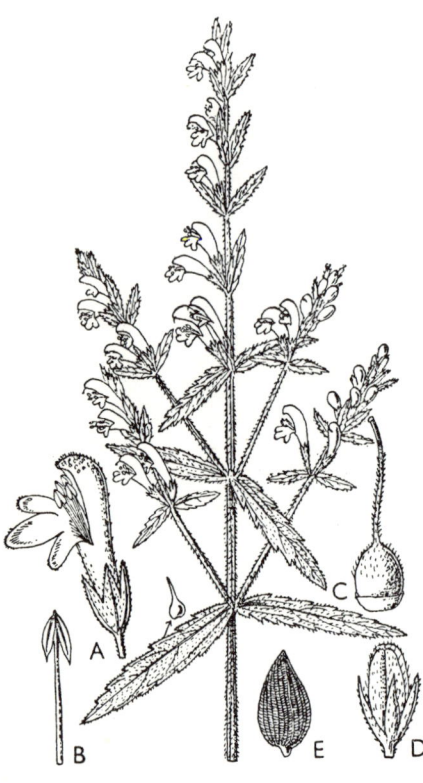

The beginner may mistake this plant for two other families than the one it belongs to; with its quadrangular stems, opposite leaves, and 2-lipped corolla it resembles *Labiatae*, whilst in its hairy covering of rough bulbous-based hairs it recalls some *Boraginaceae*. The entire ovary with a terminal style distinguishes it easily from both these families. Synonym *Bartsia odontites* Huds.

A much-branched annual up to $1\frac{1}{2}$ ft. high, leafy all over; stems slightly hairy below the nodes; leaves opposite or alternate, deeply pinnately divided into deeply cut or cristate segments, slightly hairy; flowers (A, $\times 1\frac{1}{2}$) nearly sessile in the axils of the upper leaves, but forming especially in fruit a dense spike; calyx large, with 2 broad irregularly toothed lobes thinly hairy outside; corolla deep purple-red, 2-lipped, upper lip hood-like and with 2 very

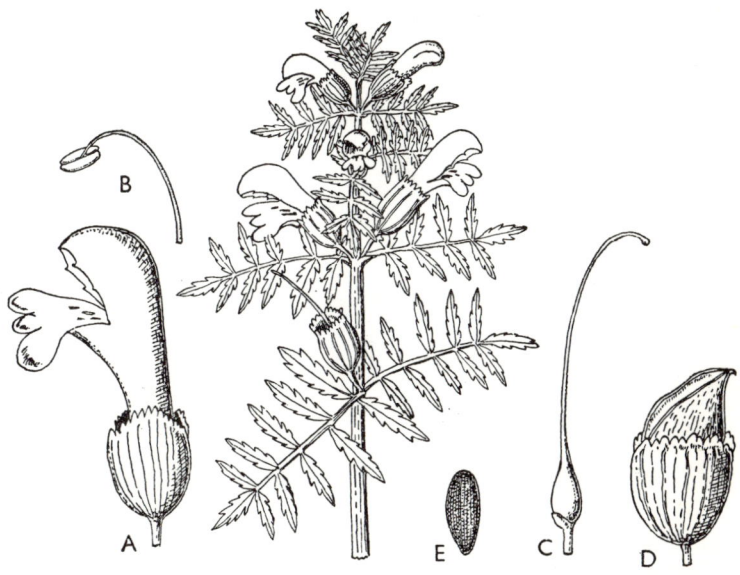

small teeth on each side, lower lip with 2 large side lobes and a smaller middle lobe; stamens (B, $\times 1\frac{1}{2}$) 4, inserted near the base of the corolla-tube; anthers attached in the middle, glabrous; ovary (C, $\times 1\frac{1}{2}$) gradually narrowed into the very slender style with a club-like stigma; capsule (D, $\times 1\frac{1}{4}$) ovoid, with a hooked lateral tip, splitting obliquely at the top, longer than the calyx; seeds (E, $\times 3$) narrowly obovoid, brown, minutely and closely striate (family *Scrophulariaceae*).

Nectar is secreted by the fleshy base of the ovary, and is col-lected in the bottom of the corolla-tube. The hooded upper lip of the corolla encloses the stamens, and the stigma protrudes obliquely downwards from between the anthers. Bees visiting a flower dust the stgima with pollen from one previously entered.

Melampyrum arvense L. (×⅓)

Erect semi-parasitical herb up to about 1½ ft. high; branches spreading, opposite; stems very shortly hairy; leaves opposite,

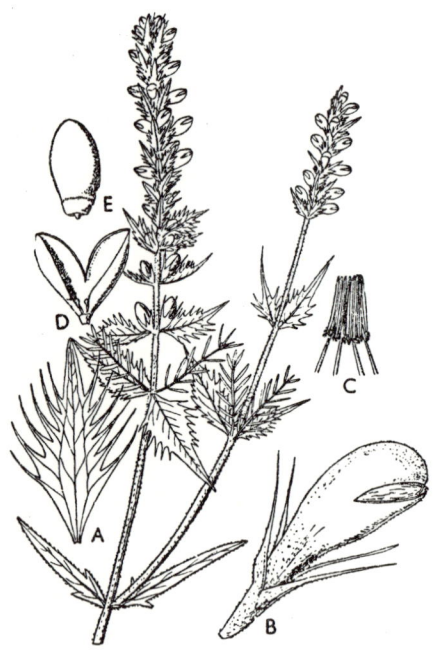

sessile or nearly so, lanceolate to almost linear, with a few long narrow lobes on each side towards the base, up to 2½ in. long, slightly hairy, the upper gradually passing into bracts pinnately lobed and all forming a dense terminal spike up to 5 in. long; bracts (A, ×1) at first pink to purple-red, turning green; calyx (B ×2) purplish-green, with long narrow lobes; corolla about ¾ in. long, with a pink tube, a bright yellow throat, and purple-red lips; stamens (C, ×2) 4, the anthers included and massed together; capsule (D, ×2) splitting into 2 valves; seed (E, ×2) ellipsoid, with a membranous caruncle (family *Scrophulariaceae*).

Grows in cornfields in south and east England. The inflorescence is very conspicuous to insects and is provided with nectar-secreting hairs (extra-floral nectaries) which attract ants. The upper lip of the corolla serves as a roof to protect the anthers from rain. Nectar is secreted in a lobe projecting downwards from the base of the ovary.

Widely distributed from Spain into western Asia. Besides the two species shown in this volume, there are two others in Britain; *M. cristatum* L., the Crested Cow-wheat, with 4-sided very dense spikes of flowers with cordate recurved bracts, and *M. sylvaticum* L., the Wood Cow-wheat, its flowers in a loose one-sided raceme with the lower lip of the corolla deflexed.

Annual herb chiefly in woods and parasitic on roots; stems branched from well above the base, glabrous or minutely hairy; leaves opposite, sessile or nearly so, linear-lanceolate to lanceolate, narrowed to the base, tapered to the apex, but rather blunt, most of them entire, but the uppermost among the flowers often pinnately lobulate or toothed towards the base; no stipules; flowers (A, $\times 2$) mostly all turned one way, axillary, solitary,

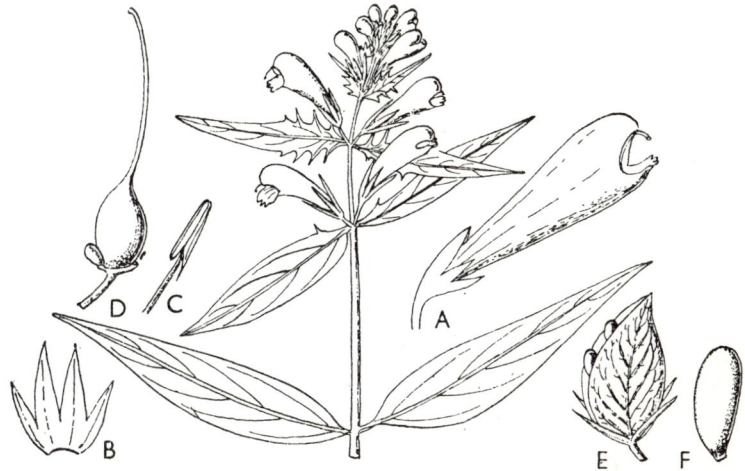

shortly stalked; calyx (B, $\times 1\frac{1}{2}$) deeply 4-lobed, lobes linear, longer than the tube; corolla pale pure yellow, about twice as long as the calyx, 2-lipped, the upper lip hood-like, the lower flat with 3 short lobes, the mouth of the tube nearly closed; stamens (C, $\times 5$) 4, hidden in the corolla; ovary (D, $\times 5$) not lobed, with 2 loculi and 2 ovules in each attached near the base; capsule (E, $\times 1\frac{1}{2}$) obliquely ovate, compressed, splitting on one side; seeds (F, $\times 2$) 4, oblong-obovoid, contracted at the base, blackish and smooth (family *Scrophulariaceae*).

The upper lip of the corolla acts as a hood and protects the anthers from rain. Nectar is secreted by a lobe projecting downwards from the base of the ovary, and is stored at the base of the corolla. It is protected from rain by a circle of converging hairs. In addition to the floral nectary the bracts are provided with nectar-secreting hairs (extra floral nectaries).

An annual with simple or branched stems up to about 1 ft. high, slightly hairy on the flattened part below the nodes; roots semi-parasitic on those of grasses and other herbs; leaves opposite, sessile, narrowly lanceolate, very coarsely toothed (serrate), clothed with very short stiff hairs like some of the Borage family; flowers in a rather dense spike-like raceme, with spreading leafy

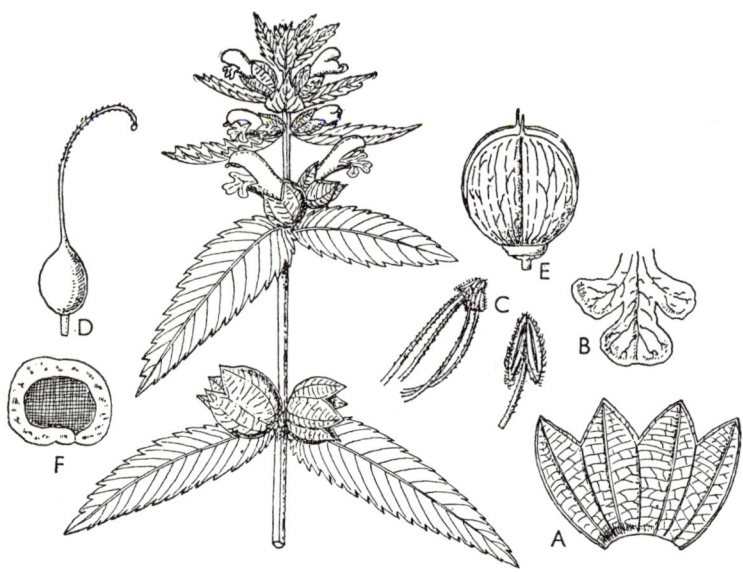

bracts; calyx (A, $\times$ 2) inflated and nearly orbicular, contracted into 4 small short teeth and covered with a close network of veins; corolla 2-lipped, yellow, sometimes with a purple spot on the upper or both lips, upper lip hooded, hiding the stamens and style, lower lip (B, $\times 1\frac{1}{2}$) 3-lobed; stamens (C, $\times$ 2) 4, in pairs; anthers held together by woolly hairs; ovary ellipsoid (D, $\times 1\frac{1}{2}$); style arched inside the hood, slightly hairy, stigma capitate; capsule (E, $\times 1\frac{1}{4}$) enclosed in the persistent inflated membranous calyx, compressed, splitting into 2 halves; seeds (F, $\times$ 2) compressed, kidney-shaped, broadly winged (family *Scrophulariaceae*)

In pastures, and widely distributed in the northern hemisphere.

Parasitic herb growing on the roots of various plants such as Gorse, Broom, *Centaurea scabiosa*, etc.; stem unbranched, up to 2 ft. high but often about 15 in., ribbed, covered by gland-tipped hairs; leaves scale-like, densely overlapping at the base of the stem, becoming scattered upwards, the lower ovate-lanceolate, all more or less glandular-pubescent; flowers densely crowded into a dense spike, $\frac{1}{3}-\frac{1}{2}$ as long as the whole plant; bract solitary to each flower, lanceolate, pointed, about 1 in. long, densely glandular; calyx (A, $\times 2$) deeply divided into 4 lobes, with gland-tipped hairs on the margin; corolla (B, $\times 1$) about 1 in. long, curved with an oblique limb, the upper lip shortly 2-lobed, the lower 3-lobed, the lobes toothed and wavy; stamens (C, $\times 2$) 4, in 2 pairs, anthers with a bristle at the base of each lobe; ovary (D, $\times 3$) with 4 parietal placentas (E, $\times 6$) and numerous ovules; style sometimes glandular above; capsule opening by 2 valves; seeds (F, $\times 10$) numerous, very small, coarsely pitted-reticulate (family *Orobanchaceae*). Synonym *O. major* L.

Widely distributed into western Asia.

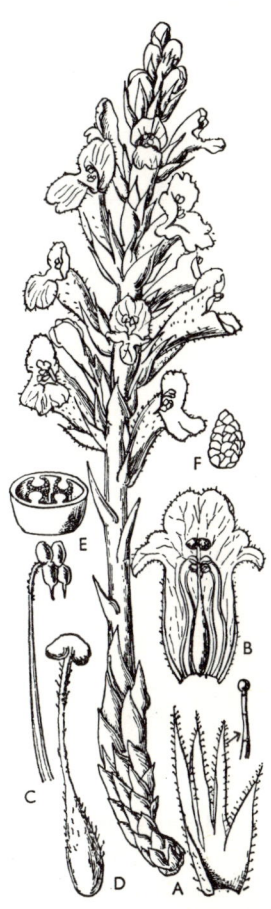

Lathraea squamaria L. ($\times\frac{1}{3}$)

Perennial growing on roots chiefly of hazel and poplar; stems thick and fleshy, creamy-white or purplish, becoming black when dry, glabrous or thinly pubescent; rootstock densely covered with broad overlapping cream-coloured scales; buds rounded, densely scaly; flowers in a dense bracteate raceme; bracts oblong-ovate; flower-stalks stout, shorter than the bracts; calyx (A, × 1) cream-pink, 4-lobed, the tube furnished with a few long several-celled

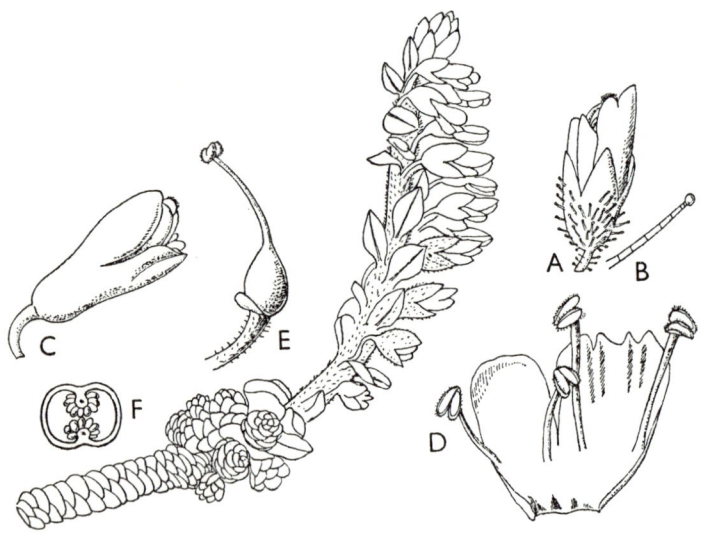

gland-tipped hairs (B, × 4); corolla (C, × 1) pink in bud, turning dark brown with age, irregularly lobed and 2-lipped; stamens (D, × 2) 4, inserted on the corolla; anthers at first connivent, hairy; ovary (E, × 3) ovoid, 1-locular, with 2 placentas nearly meeting in the middle and bearing numerous ovules (F, × 5); style with a large shortly 2-lobed hairy pale green stigma; capsule 2-valved, many-seeded (family *Orobanchaceae*).

This plant flowers in early spring, before the leaves of the trees on the roots of which it grows are produced; it is widely distri-buted to north and western Asia, and south to the Himalayas. Nectar is produced on the lower side of the ovary and secreted by a gland resembling a flattened bag. The flowers are at first insect pollinated, and later tend towards wind pollination.

A herb growing in mountain bogs or on wet rock; leaves forming a rosette, spreading, ovate to oblong and narrowed to the base, rather fleshy and covered with small crystalline points and clammy to the touch, margins entire; flowers 3 or 4 to each plant, on stalks up to about 6 in. long from the rosette of leaves; calyx (A, $\times 1\frac{1}{2}$) rather irregularly 5-lobed to about the middle; corolla (B, $\times 1$) bluish-purple, 2-lipped, the upper lip shorter than the lower and 2-lobed, the lower lip 3-lobed, the tube prolonged at the base into a slender spur; stamens 2, free from the corolla; ovary above the calyx

(superior), 1-locular, with numerous ovules attached to a free basal placenta (as in the Primula family); capsule opening by 2–4 valves; seeds oblong, rugose (family *Lentibulariaceae*).

Grows mainly in the hills and mountains of western Britain and in Eire, but is widely distributed across the cool northern zone, including North America. It is called 'Butterwort' from the greasy feel of the leaves, as if melted butter had been poured on them.

The downwardly curved spur of the corolla secretes and conceals nectar in its basal part, and the lower lip acts as a platform for insect visitors, mainly bees. These touch the stigma first, and dust it with pollen from a flower previously visited. On probing further into the corolla, the bee's head and back are dusted with fresh pollen, which is carried to another flower.

Utricularia vulgaris L. ($\times \frac{2}{3}$)

Aquatic floating herb rather like a fine green seaweed with long root-like capillary branches, all submerged; leaves (E, $\times 3$) much-

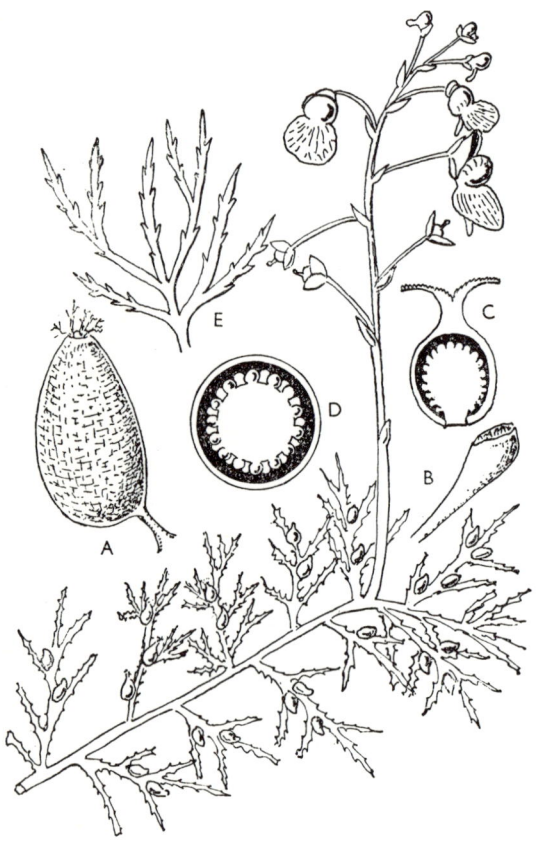

divided into fine distantly toothed segments bearing here and there small green bladders (A, $\times 5$) full of air; racemes up to about 9 in. long, bearing up to about 9 flowers exserted from the water, each subtended by a largish oblong bract; sepals 2, free; corolla 2-lipped and spurred, the mouth closed or nearly so by the convex palate, the lobes of the lip turned backwards; stamens (B, $\times 3$) 2; ovary (C, $\times 4$) superior, ovoid, 1-locular, with a deeply bilobed style; ovules (D, $\times 6$) numerous on a free basal placenta (as in the *Primula* family); capsule globose, 2-valved (family *Lentibulariaceae*).

In deep pools and canals, flowering during summer; widely distributed. The bladders borne on the leaves trap small aquatic animals whose decomposed bodies are sucked in by special absorption cells developed within the bladder. – These contrivances are well described by Kerner in his *Natural History of Plants* (English translation), a book obtainable at many large public libraries.

KEY TO THE BRITISH SPECIES OF GERANIUM

Below is given a key to the several species of *Geranium,* most of which are described and illustrated in this book of wild flowers; references to the figures are given. The key should assist the student to determine the species more readily. Those marked by an * are not considered to be native species.

Flowers *solitary* on long axillary stalks with a pair of bracts above the middle; leaves deeply divided into 5 main parts; sepals with a long tail-like point; seeds smooth or nearly so; perennial (FIG. 641) . . . . *sanguineum*

Flowers *in pairs* on a common stalk (peduncle):
Leaves once or twice pinnately and deeply divided into about three main parts (neither orbicular in outline nor palmately divided):
Carpels at most finely reticulate; petals pink or sometimes white; sepals with a very few glandular hairs (FIG. 642)
robertianum
Carpels strongly and transversely ridged (and grooved); petals purple or dark red; sepals glandular hairy; anthers yellow; southern maritime counties (FIG. 643) . . *purpureum*
Leaves more or less orbicular in outline and palmately divided into 5 (rarely 3) or more main parts:
Perennial plants with an underground rootstock (lasting more than two years); flowers usually very showy:
Sepals very shortly pointed at the apex:
Petals very dark (almost black) purple; upper leaves alternate with leaf-opposed peduncles . . . . . *phaeum* *
Petals pale purple; upper leaves opposite with axillary inflorescences (FIG. 644) . . . . . . *pyrenaicum*
Sepals with long tail-like points at the apex (as drawn in fig. 647);
Petals rather deeply notched or coarsely toothed at the top:
Stems and sepals clothed with rather long slender hairs:
Leaf-stalks at most thinly pilose towards the top (FIG. 645)
versicolor *
Leaf-stalks densely woolly towards the top . *endresii* *
Stems and sepals glabrous or with very minute hairs
nodosum *

Petals not notched or only very slightly so:
    Fruiting stalks spreading or reflexed; petals about double
        the length of the sepals (FIG. 646) . . . *pratense*
    Fruiting stalks remaining erect; petals not more than 1½
        times the length of the sepals (FIG. 647)   *sylvaticum*
Annuals or rarely biennials (according to season and locality):
  Petals not notched at the top or very slightly so:
    Seeds smooth (FIG. 648) . . . . *lucidum*
    Seeds reticulate (FIG. 649) . . . . *rotundifolium*
  Petals more or less distinctly notched at the top:
    Leaves divided nearly to the base into narrowly lobed seg-
      ments; seeds reticulate:
      Peduncles longer than the leaves (FIG. 650) . *columbinum*
      Peduncles shorter than the leaves (FIG. 651) . . *dissectum*
    Leaves at most divided to about or a little below the middle:
      All the stem-leaves opposite, with the flower-stalks in the
        axil of the shorter leaf-stalk; carpels falling from the
        axis; seeds smooth (FIG. 652) . . . . . *pusillum*
      Only the lowermost stem-leaves opposite, the rest alternate
        and the flower-stalk opposite the leaf (leaf-opposed);
        carpels in fruit remaining attached to the central axis,
        the beak curving upwards separately; body of carpel
        reticulate or (var. *aequale*) smooth; seeds smooth
        (FIG. 653) . . . . *molle*

Perennial with a blunt rootstock; stems covered at the base by overlapping scales, 1–2 ft. long, very slender, but thickened at the nodes, and with slender hairs spreading at right angles; leaves opposite, shortly stalked, each stalk with a pair of brown oblong stipules (A, × 2) at the base, which soon shrivel up; leaf-blade rounded in outline, deeply divided into 5 main parts, the lower divisions usually with 2 lanceolate lobes, the other 3 rather deeply 3-lobed, thinly clothed above with short bristle-like hairs, paler below and with a few hairs on the nerves; flowers axillary, in the alternate axils of the leaves, the end one flowering last; stalk with a pair of stipule-like bracts above the middle and fringed with hairs; sepals (B, × 2) 5, elliptic, green, and 3-nerved with pale thinner margins and ending in a long narrow point; petals (D, × 2) 5, crimson or pink with 5 deeper crimson nerves fringed with long soft hairs at the base; stamens (E, × 3) 10, their stalks close together; anthers attached in the middle, deep violet; nectaries 5, green, fleshy; ovary (F, × 2) 5-lobed, each lobe narrowed into a long reddish style; fruit (G, × $\frac{4}{5}$) dividing from the base into 5 parts which curl upwards and disperse the seeds (C, flower, petals removed) (family *Geraniaceae*).

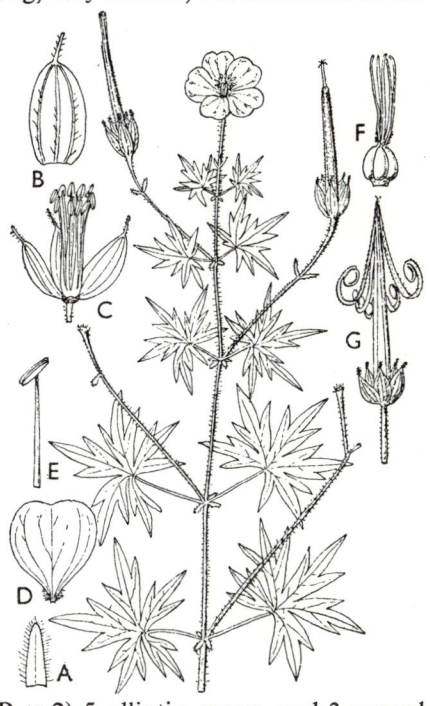

Grows in shady places on rocky cliffs and is partial to limestone; generally distributed, and in the greater part of Europe as far as the Caucasus; a decumbent variety (var. *lancastriense* Mill.), more hairy and sometimes with white or pale pink flowers, is found on an island near the Lancashire coast.

HERB ROBERT
Geranium robertianum L. ($\times \frac{2}{3}$)

Much branched annual; stems sprinkled with slender hairs, often turning bright red and with a disagreeable smell when rubbed;

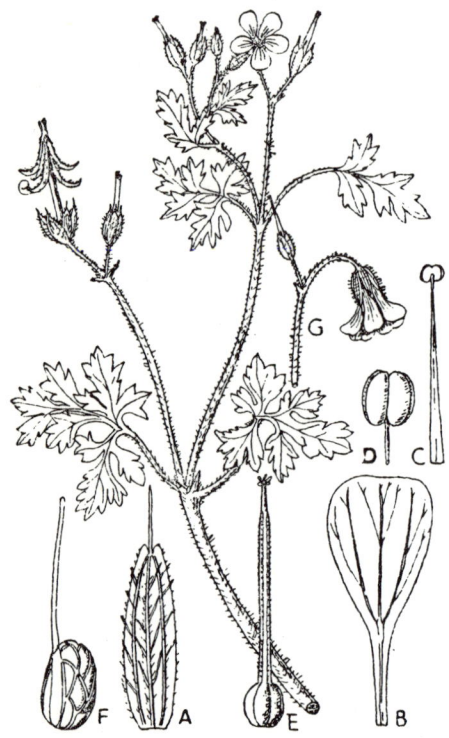

leaves opposite, pinnately divided into three main segments, these again deeply divided, sprinkled with a few weak setose hairs on both sides; petioles long; stipules ovate - lanceolate, hairy; flowers few on a long axillary peduncle; sepals (A, × 3) narrowly oblong, conspicuously 3-nerved, notched at the apex and with a long slender point; petals (B, × 2¼) broadly spoon-shaped, reddish-purple to white or pink; stamens 10 (C, × 3), anthers (D, × 5) suborbicular; ovary (E, × 4) deeply 5-grooved, with a stiff erect hairy style and 5 small stigmas; fruiting carpels (F, × 3) covered with a coarse network; easily recognized from the less common species by the deeply divided leaves (family *Geraniaceae*).

Nectar is secreted only outside the base of the five inner stamens, which are the first to open their anthers and shed their pollen. They are then in the middle of the flower with the stigmas above them, and insect visitors are dusted with the pollen which they transfer to the stigmas of another flower. The five outer stamens are at first curved widely outwards, but later they move towards the middle of the flower and likewise discharge their pollen. Self-pollination, however, is not impossible, owing to the flower, which is normally erect in daytime, being pendulous at night (fig. G) or during bad weather.

Geranium purpureum Vill. ($\times\frac{1}{3}$)

Weak straggly annual herb with crimson or purplish stems thinly pilose; leaves opposite, with slightly unequal-lengthed stalks, more

or less rounded-ovate in outline, divided to the midrib into 3 main parts, each part again deeply divided and toothed, about 2 in. wide, glabrous, except for a few weak hairs on the upper surface; flowers in pairs on a common stalk in the axil of the shorter leaf-stalk, the stalk usually longer than the leaf; stalks pilose with weak gland-tipped hairs; sepals (A, $\times2$) 5, elliptic, with a long tail-like point, 3-nerved and clothed with gland-tipped hairs; petals (B, $\times2$) 5, purple or dark red, with a long stalk, scarcely notched at the top, veiny; stamens 10, anthers yellow; carpels (C, $\times2$) 5, with 5 style-arms; fruits (D, $\times1$) soon becoming very strongly transversely ridged and grooved (E, $\times3$), otherwise glabrous or hairy; seed (F, $\times3$) ellipsoid, smooth (family *Geraniaceae*).

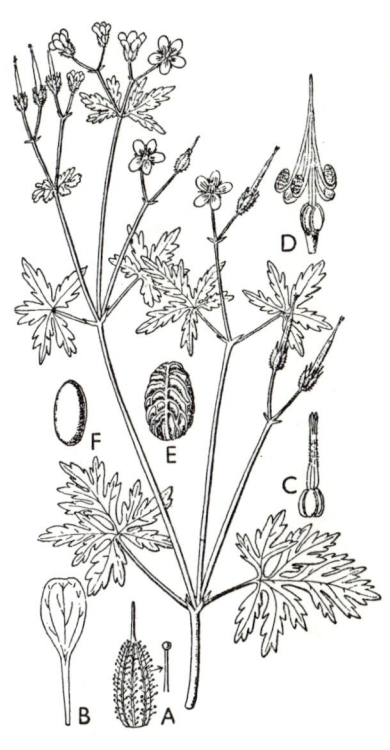

In most botanical books this is regarded as a variety or subspecies of the more common 'Herb Robert' (*Geranium robertianum*) described in fig. 642. The best way to distinguish them is by the ripe carpels, which in 'Herb Robert' are merely reticulate, whilst in *G. purpureum* they are very strongly and transversely ridged; in addition the sepals of the latter are more glandular-hairy than in those of 'Herb Robert'; found only in the southern maritime counties and in other parts of Europe.

Geranium pyrenaicum L. ($\times\frac{1}{3}$)

Perennial with stout taproot pale pink when cut across; basal leaves on long stalks, kidney-shaped in outline, 5–7-lobed to the middle, the lobes again 3–5-lobed or very coarsely toothed, shortly hairy on the margins and nerves below; stalks, and also the stems, covered with short glands and thinly clothed with long fine hairs; stem-leaves opposite, shortly stalked, each leaf-stalk with a pair of narrow hairy stipules at the base; flowers in pairs on a common stalk in the axil of the shorter leaf-stalk, about $\frac{2}{3}$ in. diam., in bud with 5 small reddish apical knobs; sepals (A, $\times3$) 5, oblong-elliptic, 3-nerved, densely glandular all over, and with short hairs on the margin; petals (B, $\times1\frac{1}{4}$) 5, mauve-purple, broadly obovate, widely 2-lobed, with a short hairy claw; stamens (G, $\times2$) 10, erect around the 5 styles; carpels (D, $\times3$) 5, united, each with 1 ovule attached to the central axis (E, $\times2$); capsule (F, $\times1\frac{1}{4}$) separating into five 1-seeded hairy carpels (G, $\times2$); seeds dark brown, smooth (family *Geraniaceae*).

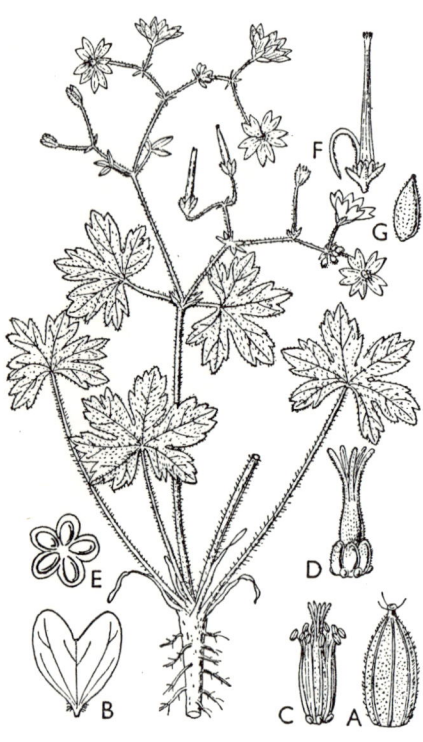

In meadows and by roadsides mostly in hilly districts; widely distributed in southern Europe and western Asia; flowers from June onwards.

Perennial with ascending rootstock, the latter densely clothed with the persistent sheathing bases of former leaves; stems weak and straggling, with long internodes, laxly clothed with long weak hairs; basal leaves on long slender stalks, these also clothed with weak slender hairs; blade deeply divided into 5 lobes, the lobes very coarsely toothed or lobulate, thinly hairy on the upper surface, also below, but mainly on the nerves; stem-leaves opposite, their stalks slightly unequal in length in each pair, the 5 lobes

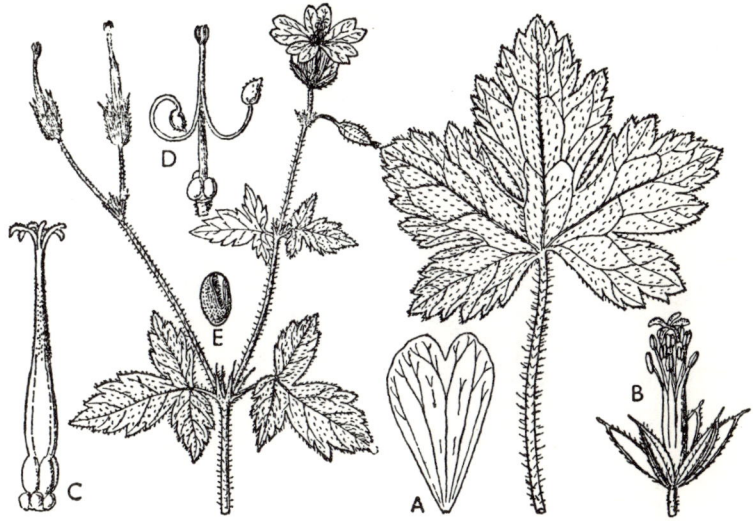

often reduced to 3, but otherwise similar to the basal leaves; stipules paired at the base of each stalk, about ½ in. long, long-pointed from a narrowly lanceolate base, fringed with slender hairs on the margin; flowers few, and only 1 or 2 out at a time, shortly stalked; sepals (B, ×1) 5, lanceolate, about ½ in. long, with long slender tips, slightly hairy on the 3 nerves and margin; petals (A, ×1) 5, spreading from the broadly clawed base, white or pale-lilac, rather deeply 2-lobed; stamens (B, ×1) 10, the filaments united around the ovary; ovary (C, × 2½) 5-locular, the 5 styles united in a column with 5 free stigmas; disk of 5 separate fleshy nectaries; fruit (D, × ¾) of 5 dehiscent 1-seeded carpels united together in a column, but separating elastically from the top; seeds (E, × 2) ellipsoid, dark brown (synonym *Geranium striatum* L.) (family *Geraniaceae*).

749

Perennial; basal leaves on long stalks, orbicular, deeply 5–9 lobed, the lobes deeply lobulate and coarsely toothed, strongly nerved below and hairy on the nerves, thinly downy above; leaf-stalks with very short downwardly directed hairs; stem-leaves opposite, shortly stalked to nearly sessile, with a pair of interpetiolar stipules to each; stipules narrowly triangular, 1-nerved, fringed with hairs;

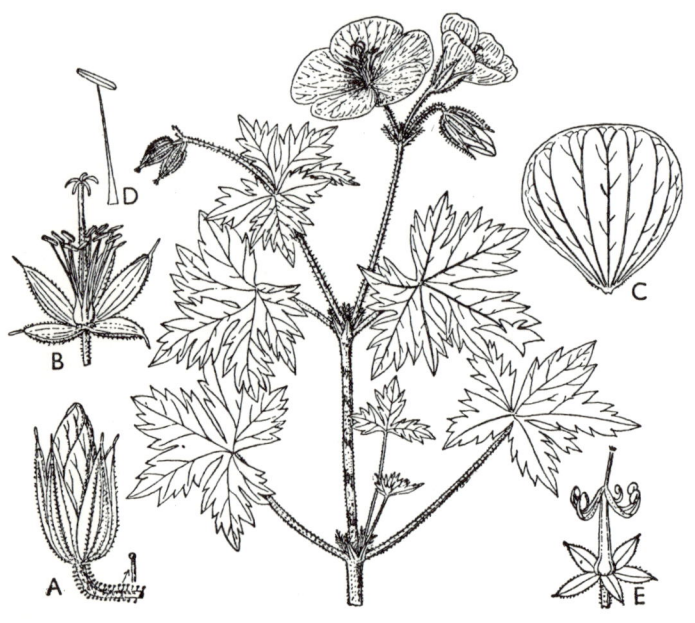

upper part of stem and flower-stalks covered with spreading gland-tipped hairs; flowers large, mostly in pairs on long peduncles; bracts crimson; buds (A, $\times 1\frac{1}{2}$) closely ribbed, covered with glandular hairs; sepals 5, beaked, 5-nerved, glandular-hairy; petals (C, $\times 2$) hairy on the margin near the base, deep violet-blue, with crimson nerves, nearly 1 in. long and broad; stamens (D, $\times 2\frac{1}{2}$) 10; anthers pale purple; carpels 5, united, the styles united in a column, hairy, with 5 recurved softly hairy stigmas; ovule solitary in each loculus; fruit (E, $\times 1\frac{1}{2}$) splitting into 5 carpels with long beaks, which open and release the seed (B, flower with petals removed, $\times 1\frac{1}{2}$) (family *Geraniaceae*).

Perennial with a short rootstock (A, $\times\frac{1}{3}$) covered with overlapping stipules from the previous year's leaves; basal leaves on long stalks, about 3–3½ in. diam., rounded-kidney-shaped in outline but divided nearly to the base into several segments like those of an Aconite, the segments lobulate and coarsely toothed, thinly hairy over the upper surface but mainly on the nerves below; lower stem-leaves shortly stalked, upper sessile, all divided after the pattern of the basal leaves; stipules ovate-triangular, ½ in. long, tailed-acuminate; flowers in a terminal leafy corymb, quite showy; stalks clothed with gland-tipped hairs (G, $\times5$); sepals (B, $\times1$) 5, ovate-elliptic, tailed at the top, 3-nerved, covered with long gland-tipped hairs; petals (C, $\times\frac{2}{3}$) 5, blue-

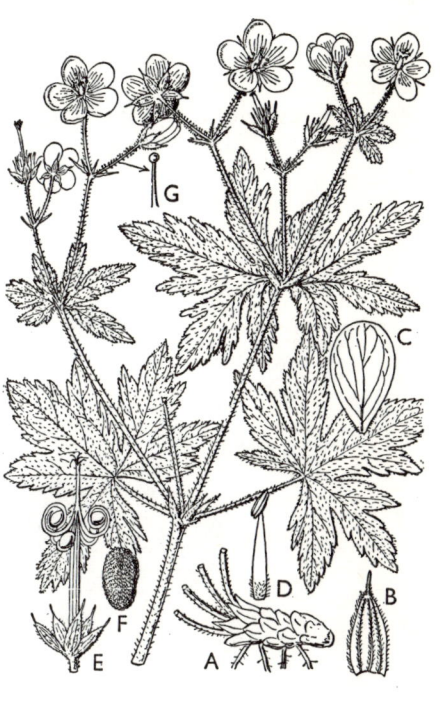

purple or rose-coloured, nearly twice as long as the sepals, veiny, hairy on the short broad claw; stamens (D, $\times1$) 10, filaments hairy at the base; carpels (E, $\times\frac{2}{3}$) 5, hairy, their beaks curling in fruit; seeds (F, $\times2$) ellipsoid, minutely reticulate (family *Geraniaceae*).

Grows in meadows and woody places in the hills and up to fairly high altitudes in Scotland, flowering in summer; not found in southern England; distributed in Europe and Asia.

Geranium lucidum L. ($\times\frac{1}{2}$)

Annual, with reddish glabrous stems and branches; leaves opposite, with stalks in each pair of unequal length, rounded in outline,
5-lobed to about the middle, averaging about 1 in. diam., lobes
with rounded teeth, glabrous or nearly so, shining; stipules ovate-
triangular; flowers in pairs on a common stalk in the axils of the
shorter petioles, the calyx forming a broad pyramid; sepals (A,
$\times$3) 5, unequal, not hairy, the larger strongly 3-nerved with a few
short cross nerves, apiculate; petals (B, $\times$2) 5, reddish-purple,

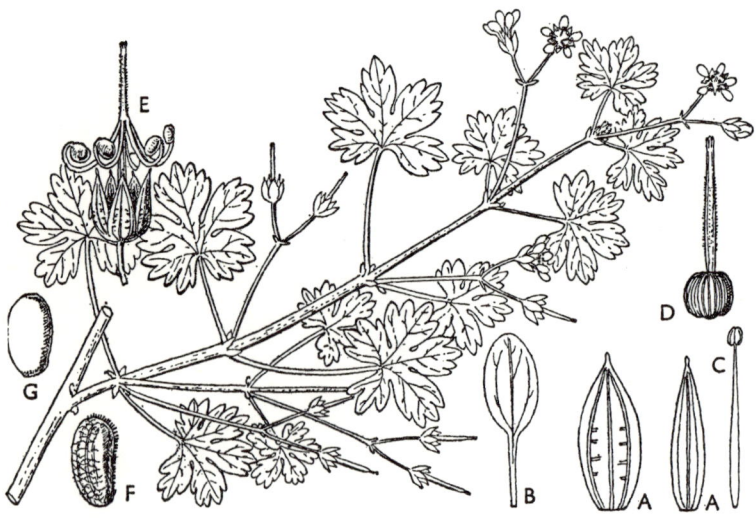

much longer than the sepals, claw nearly half as long as the entire
limb and glabrous; stamens (C, $\times$2) 10; filaments winged; carpels
strongly nerved lengthwise in the ovary stage (D, $\times2\frac{1}{2}$), becoming
wrinkled in fruit (E, $\times$2) and with short hairs on the inner margin
(F, $\times$5); seeds (G, $\times$5) brown, smooth (family *Geraniaceae*).

In stony and waste places and on old walls; distributed from
Europe to central Asia; flowers in spring and summer.

Besides the bisexual, protogynous flowers, which are capable of
self-pollination, there are flowers which are wholly female.

Geranium rotundifolium L. ($\times\frac{1}{3}$)

Annual or biennial herb, becoming much branched; stems and branches softly pubescent with gland-tipped hairs (A, $\times$4); leaves opposite, slightly unequal (anisophyllous), the stalk and blade of unequal length and size respectively, rounded or kidney-shaped, 1–2 in. diam., 5–7-lobed to about the middle, the lobes with rounded lobules, softly pubescent; stipules ovate-lanceolate; flowers in pairs on a common stalk in the axil of the smaller leaf with the shorter stalk; bracts like the stipules but smaller; sepals (B, $\times$3) 5, elliptic-lanceolate, 3-nerved, apiculate, hairy on the nerves and margin; petals (C, $\times$2) pink, only a little longer than the sepals, not hairy at the base and not notched at the top; stamens 10, ripening in two sets; carpels (D, $\times$4) 5, united, each with 2 ovules; style-arms 5; carpels (E, $\times 1\frac{1}{4}$) keeled, springing from the base in fruit and curving upwards, hairy; seeds (F, $\times$3) brown, finely reticulate (family *Geraniaceae*).

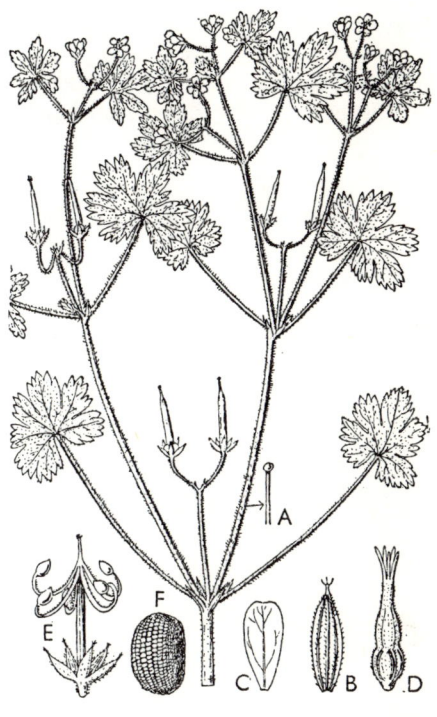

Grows on hedgebanks, by waysides, and in waste and cultivated places in south and central England, but not in Scotland; flowering during summer.

Owing to the small size of the flowers and the little amount of nectar secreted, there are few insect visitors. Failing these, automatic self-pollination takes place, the stigmas being at the same level as the anthers and maturing simultaneously.

Annual with slender straggling decumbent stems tinged with crimson and glabrous or nearly so; leaves opposite, with stalks of unequal length but sometimes not markedly so, orbicular in outline, divided to the base into very deeply cut segments, each segment 3–5-lobed, $1\frac{1}{2}$–2 in. diam., with a few appressed hairs on both surfaces; sepals (A, $\times 2\frac{1}{2}$) 5, subequal, ovate, with a long slender tail, 3-nerved, thinly appressed-hairy outside; petals (B, $\times 2\frac{1}{2}$) 5, a little longer than the sepals, rosy purple, slightly notched, shortly

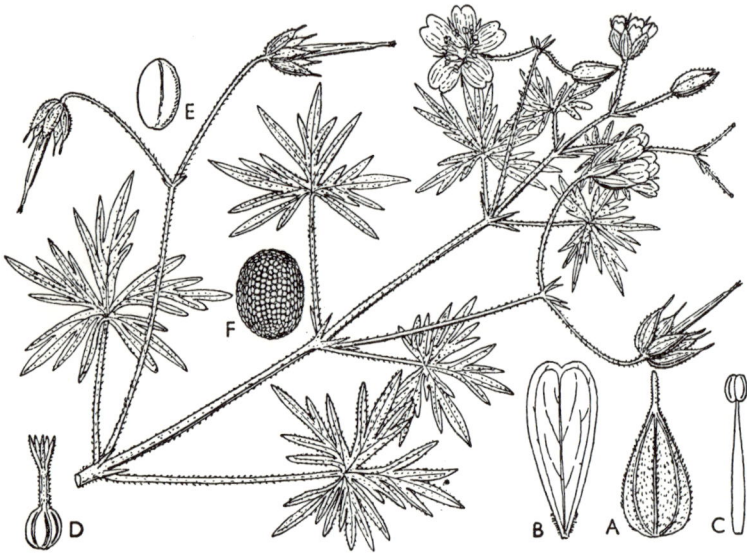

ciliate on the broad claw; stamens (C, $\times 2\frac{1}{2}$) 10, filaments narrow; carpels (D, $\times 5$) 5, slightly keeled in the fruiting stage (E, $\times 2$) but not reticulate; seeds (F, $\times 5$) rounded, finely reticulate (family *Geraniaceae*).

In addition to the normal bisexual flowers there are some entirely female. The rosy purple petals are marked with 3 dark veins that serve as nectar-guides to insect visitors.

Grows in dry pastures, on banks, and waste places, flowering in spring and summer; distributed in Europe and Asia.

Annual herb with pairs of branches; stems softly pubescent with reflexed hairs; leaves with stalks of unequal length, rounded in outline, up to 3 in. diam., divided nearly to the base into 5 main segments, each segment again deeply divided into narrow lobes, thinly clothed with short stiff hairs mainly on the nerves below; stipules in pairs, narrowly triangular and pointed, hairy; flowers in pairs on a common peduncle in the middle of each fork; bracts linear; sepals (A, ×2½) 5, ovate, tailed at the top, 3-nerved, clothed with gland-tipped hairs; petals (B, ×2) 5, reddish-purple, a little longer than the sepals, deeply notched at the top, shortly hairy on the claw; stamens (C, ×3) 10, filaments shortly ciliate; carpels (D, ×3) 5, splitting away in fruit from the central axis (E, ×1⅓) and hanging from the top by the beak which is clothed with gland-tipped hairs, body of carpel covered with bristly hairs; seeds (F, ×4) rounded, closely pitted-reticulate (family *Geraniaceae*).

The flowers of this species are protogynous, i.e. the stigmas are mature and their branches expanded when they open in the sunshine and while the anthers are still unripe. Later on the anthers open in turn, covering the stigma with pollen, when automatic self-pollination is effective if cross-pollination has not taken place.

Grows in dry pastures, waste and cultivated places, flowering in spring and summer; widely distributed in the northern hemisphere.

Geranium pusillum L. ($\times\frac{1}{3}$)

Annual with often crimson-tinged stems and branches, softly pubescent with very short hairs and scarcely glandular; leaves

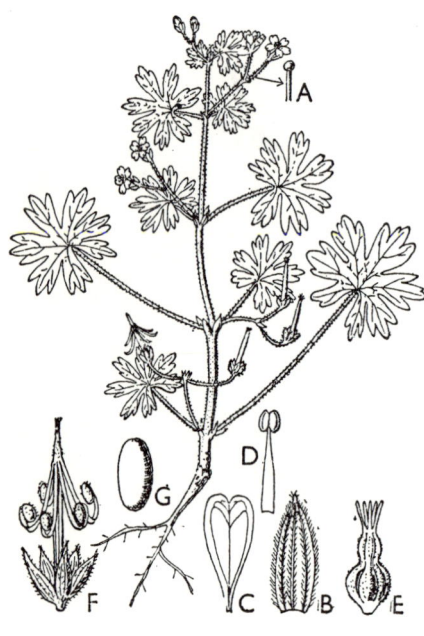

opposite, in unequal pairs, one with a shorter stalk than the other, rounded in outline, more or less 7-lobed to about or below the middle, usually about 1–1½ in. diam., but sometimes 2½ in., shortly and thinly pubescent on both surfaces; stipules ovate, often crimson; flowers in pairs on a slightly glandular stalk (A, ×3) in the axils of the shorter-stalked leaves; bracts awl-shaped, small; sepals (B, ×2) 5, ovate-elliptic, shortly horned at the apex, 3-nerved, pubescent; petals (C, ×2) 5, pale pink, only a little longer than the sepals, notched at the apex and with a few hairs on the claw; stamens (D, ×2) 10, only 5 with anthers, filaments broadened downwards; carpels (E, ×3) 5, shortly hairy, stigmas 5; fruiting carpels (F, ×2) curving upwards, hairy; seeds (G, ×4) brown, quite smooth (family *Geraniaceae*).

Grows in waste and cultivated places over most of Europe to western Asia; introduced into North America.

The flowers are very inconspicuous and insect visitors few. They are protogynous, with persistent stigmas. Only the 5 inner stamens those with nectaries at their base, bear anthers. When the flowers open, the stigmatic branches have already half spread out, while the anthers lying between them are still immature. When these open, the stigmatic branches diverge still more and the stamens bend towards the middle of the flower, and automatic self-pollination is effected by the falling pollen if insect visitors fail.

Geranium molle L. ($\times\frac{1}{2}$)

Annual with spreading stems, covered all over with soft hairs; lower leaves opposite, with stalks of unequal length, upper alternate, rounded in outline, usually about 1–1½ in. diam., divided to about the middle into several deeply lobed segments; stipules ovate, large (about ⅓ in.); flowers paired on a common peduncle opposite each leaf (leaf-opposed); bracts similar to the stipules but smaller; sepals (A, ×3) 5, ovate-elliptic, very shortly pointed, not visibly nerved outside except in fruit, pilose; petals (B, ×2½)

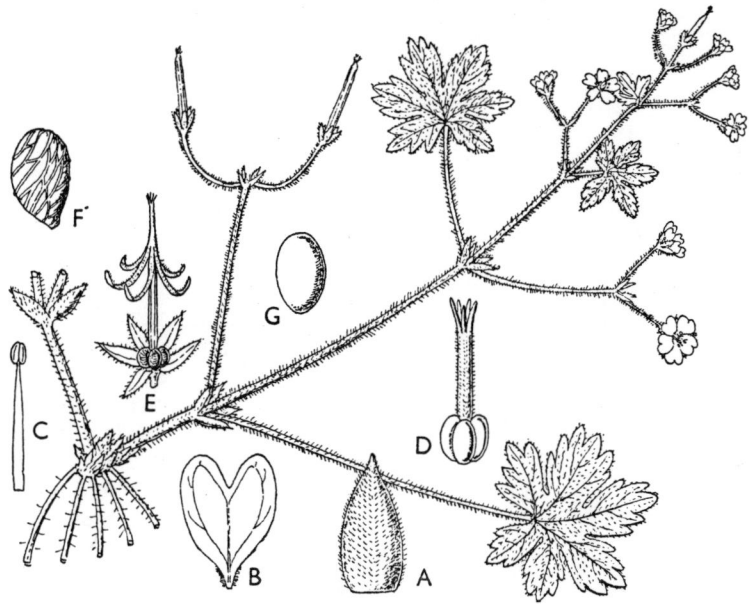

generally longer than the sepals, notched, pink to rosy purple (rarely white), ciliate on the claw; stamens (C, ×6) 10, filaments not hairy; carpels (D, ×6) 5, in fruit (F, ×6) strongly nerved and remaining attached to the axis, the beak falling away separately; seeds (G, ×6) smooth (family *Geraniaceae*).

In pastures and waste places and on neglected lawns; var. *aequale* Bab. has smooth carpels, but is not common.

Distributed in many parts of the world as a weed of cultivation; flowers the whole season.

STORK'S-BILL

Erodium cicutarium (L.) L'Hérit. ($\times \frac{2}{5}$)

Annual or biennial, covered with weak spreading hairs; radical leaves (A, $\times \frac{3}{5}$) on long stalks, pinnately divided with the seg-

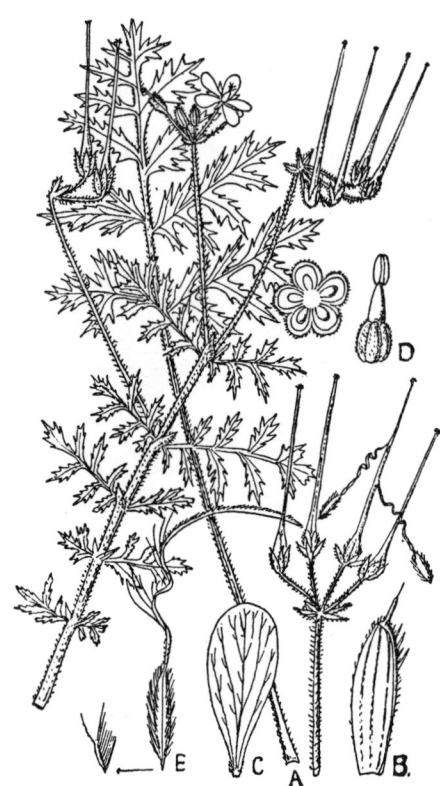

ments deeply cut; stem-leaves opposite, markedly unequal-sized in each pair (anisophyllous), much divided; peduncles long and slender, bearing an umbel of few small flowers from a whorl of small bracts; stalks very slender; sepals (B, $\times 3$) oblong, with short bristly hairs outside and a sharp horn at the tip; petals (C, $\times 4$) purple or pink, hairy at the base; stamens 5, with 5 rudimentary; ovary (D, $\times 4$) deeply lobed, hairy, topped by a columnar style and 5 connate stigmas; carpels (E, $\times \frac{4}{5}$) elongating into long beaks in fruit which separate from the central axis and become spirally twisted, falling and penetrating the soil (family *Geraniaceae*).

Only the five stamens opposite to the sepals bear anthers, those opposite the petals being broader and without anthers. Only those with anthers have nectaries at their bases. The character of the unequal-sized leaves is very rare among British plants, though much more common amongst other tropical species.

Pollination of this species has been much studied on the continent; two forms, that figured here which opens its flowers at about 7 a.m., is self-pollinated and sheds its petals by midday, and another (*pimpinellifolium*) cross-pollinated by insects and whose petals last until the second day.

Oxalis acetosella L. ($\times \frac{4}{5}$)

Perennial with a short creeping rootstock, knotted here and there with thickened hairy scales; leaves all radical, with long slender stalks, completely divided into 3 rounded-obovate leaflets notched at the apex and wedge-shaped at the base, very thin, sprinkled on both surfaces with long rather stiff hairs; nerves radiating from the base of the leaflet; flowers single on long slender stalks longer than the leaves; stalks bearing a pair of bracts about half-way up and these fringed with hairs; sepals 5, obovate, slightly pubescent; petals free, white, obovate, notched at the apex, about $\frac{1}{2}$ in. long; stamens (A, $\times$ 3) 10; ovary (B, $\times$ 3) 5-locular, with 5 almost separate styles, with several ovules in each loculus attached to the central axis; fruit an ovoid capsule, with 2 shining black seeds in each of the 5 compartments (family *Oxalidaceae*).

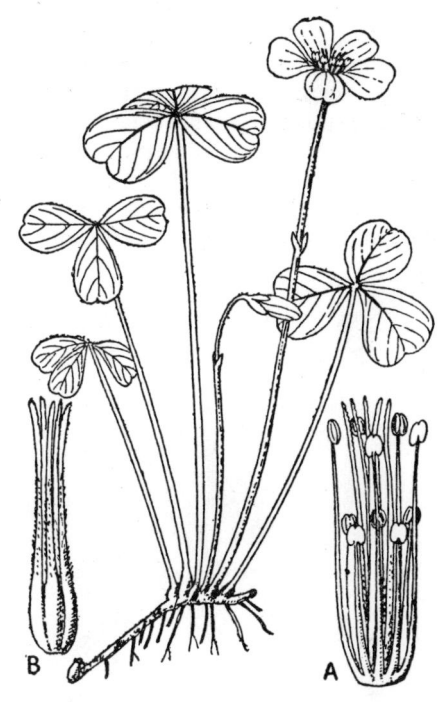

If cows eat this plant it may be the cause of serious illness and diarrhoea, and in the case of sheep even be fatal. It is recorded that the milk of cows after having eaten it is with difficulty converted into butter. They are only liable to encounter it, however, if turned out into woodlands where it grows. It flowers in early spring, and is believed to be the original of the Irish Shamrock, though that emblem is now transferred to a clover, *Trifolium repens* (fig. 89), which has rather similar leaves. The white petals are streaked with violet lines, which serve as nectar-guides, and there is a yellow spot above the nectaries which are borne on the claws of the petals.

A tall, sometimes very strong-growing herb up to 6 ft. or more; stems green or crimson, strongly ribbed, hollow and fleshy, glabrous; leaves alternate or subopposite, those below the flowers crowded, stalked, broadly lanceolate, pointed, usually about 4–6 in. long and up to 2½ in. broad, green with a crimson midrib, sharply serrate, with one or two teeth at the top of the stalk; a pair of large stalked glands at the base of the stalk; flowers in stalked short racemes clustered amongst the uppermost leaves; bracts in bud (A, ×1) ovate, pale crimson, soon falling off and leaving a scar; sepals 3, two obliquely ovate, with a prominent midrib prolonged into a free tip, pale crimson, the third forming a large wide

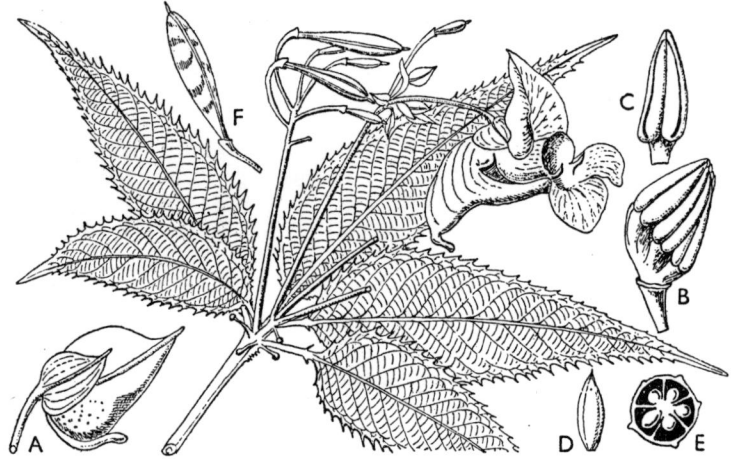

pouch with a spur at the base (A, ×1); petals 3, the upper like the standard of a Pea-flower, the other two of irregular shape and forming a lip in the front of the flower, all mauve or sometimes white; stamens (B, ×2) 5, the large anthers (C, ×2) crowded around the ovary; ovary (D, ×1) 5-locular (E, ×3), with several ovules in each chamber; fruit (F, ×1) a capsule which opens when ripe at the slightest touch, the valves curling up and scattering the dark mottled seeds (synonym *Impatiens roylei* Walp.) (family *Balsaminaceae*).

A favourite cottage-garden plant often naturalized and growing very rampant along river and canal banks; beloved of children because the fruits burst open and curl up when touched, a provision of nature to scatter the seeds.

Impatiens noli-tangere L. ($\times\frac{1}{2}$)

Erect glabrous annual up to 2 ft. high; stem zigzag, rather succulent and thicker at the nodes; leaves alternate, elliptic to oblong-elliptic, petiolate, up to 4 in. long and 2 in. broad, thin, coarsely toothed, the lowermost teeth (A, $\times\frac{3}{4}$) awl-shaped and glandular; lateral nerves numerous; peduncles axillary, bearing 2–3 flowers, these large and golden yellow, spotted with orange or red in the throat, dorsal sepal hooded and with a large spur at the base about 1 in. long, the end of the spur curved; stamens 5, filaments short and thick, the anthers coherent around the style; ovary 5-locular, with several ovules in each loculus; fruit (B, $\times 1$) bursting elastically into 5 valves which roll up when touched scattering the seeds (family *Balsaminaceae*).

Native and naturalized in other places; general Europe.

Nectar is secreted in the spur of the calyx. Some of the flowers are cleistogamous and produce fruits. When the normal showy flowers open the anthers have already dehisced so that a humble-bee after securing the nectar carries away the pollen on its back.

761

Annual up to about a foot high; stem unbranched, very succulent, slightly rimmed belôw the leaf-stalks, glabrous; lower leaves

opposite, upper alternate, long-stalked, elliptic or ovate-elliptic rather abruptly narrowed at the base, broadly and acutely acuminate at the apex, crenate with rather sharp teeth, the teeth at the base rod-like and gland-tipped, pale green and glabrous; leaf-stalks with a stipule-like rod-shaped gland (A, ×1⅓) on each side at the base; flowers (B, ×1⅓) axillary, few on a common peduncle scarcely exceeding the petiole; bracts small and ovate-lanceolate; 2 outer sepals small, ovate-triangular, greenish; 3rd sepal large and petaloid, spurred, pale yellow, the spur (about ¼ in. long) tipped with crimson; 4th sepal broad and broadly V-shaped; petals (C, ×1⅔) 2, forming a wide lower-lip, unequally 2-lobed, pale yellow, with small rich brown honey-guides on the inner side; stamens 5, with thick filaments, the anthers cohering in a mass around the pistil; ovary (D, ×2½) 5-locular, ovules several in each compartment; styles (E, ×2) 5, free, very short and spreading; capsule bursting elastically into 5 valves which roll up and scatter the seeds (family *Balsaminaceae*).

A garden escape and naturalized in some places in considerable quantity, often forming a carpet among bushes; easily completely destroyed if hoed before the fruits are formed; native of northern Asia.

Perennial, with a short creeping rootstock; stems up to 3 ft. high, with very fine gland-tipped hairs in the upper part; leaves alternate, pinnate, the last pair of leaflets united at the base and with the terminal one; sheathing base hairy on the margins; leaflets lanceolate, acute, glabrous; flowers in terminal and axillary cymes; bracts deeply divided; calyx 5-lobed to below the middle; corolla ¾–1 in. diam., pale blue, but white in bud or rarely remaining white; tube short; lobes 5, overlapping to the right in bud (A, ×2½), with 3 darker lines towards the base; stamens (C, ×7) 5, inserted in the throat of the corolla; filaments mauve, expanded and densely

covered with white hairs at the base; anthers (C, ×7) with the lobes pointed at the base, deep bright yellow; disk (D, ×2½) fleshy, saucer-shaped; ovary above the disk, 3-locular (E, ×8), ovules attached to the central axis; fruit a capsule opening by slits into the loculi (loculicidal) (family *Polemoniaceae*).

Nectar is secreted in the green saucer-shaped body below the ovary. The anthers are ripe before the stigmas separate, and they contract to about half their original size (C_1, ×7) when the orange yellow mass of pollen is released. Insects are guided to the nectar by 3 deeply coloured lines at the base of each corolla-lobe; cross-pollination is thus effected.

Asperugo procumbens L. ($\times\frac{1}{3}$)

A procumbent annual with long internodes armed with short recurved hook-like hairs (A, $\times 5$); leaves sessile, appearing to be
nearly opposite or sometimes 3 together, but really alternate, as
in all this family, obovate-oblanceolate, narrowed to the base,
$1\frac{1}{2}$–3 in. long and up to $1\frac{1}{2}$ in. broad, faintly nerved, entire, loosely
clothed on both surfaces by short bulbous-based hairs pointing
towards the apex; flowers (B, $\times 2$) 1–3 together in the axils of the
upper leaves, on very short recurved pedicels; calyx with 5 triangular lobes densely setose on the margins; corolla (C, $\times 3$)
blue, very small and with a short tube and 5 spreading lobes, each

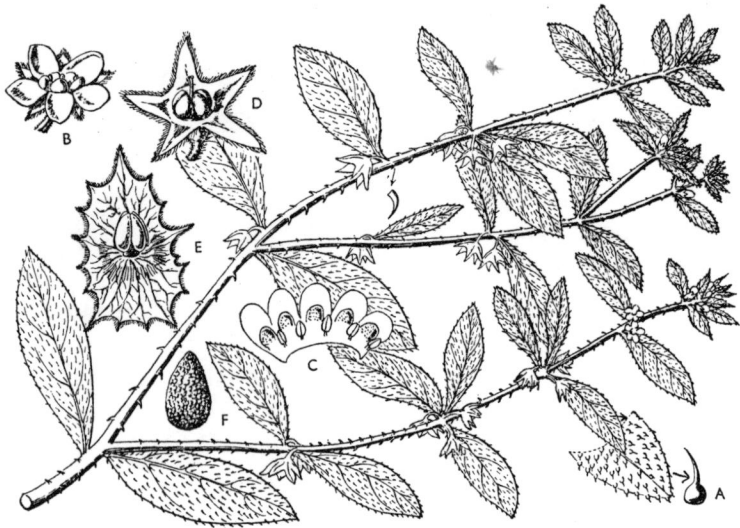

lobe with a large scale at the base; stamens 5, enclosed in the tube;
ovary (D, $\times 3$) of 4 ovoid lobes with a very short style between;
fruiting calyx (E, $\times 1$) enlarged and very nervose, lobed and
lobulate bearing the 4 compressed slightly warted nutlets (F,
$\times 2\frac{1}{2}$) in the middle (family *Boraginaceae*).

In cultivated and waste ground, found over nearly the whole of
Europe and Asia below the Arctic Circle; flowers during summer.

This genus is monotypic, i.e. there is only one species known.
It may be readily recognized by the procumbent habit, and by its
calyx, which becomes enlarged and toothed and forms a 2-lipped
envelope around the fruit.

Mertensia maritima (L.) S. F. Gray ($\times\frac{1}{3}$)

Maritime perennial fleshy herb with procumbent leafy stems 1–2 ft. long, covered all over with a glaucous 'bloom' like that of a grape; rootstock fleshy, stoloniferous; leaves alternate, obovate to spoon-shaped, curved, thick, very faintly nerved, up to $1\frac{1}{2}$ in. long and $\frac{3}{4}$ in. broad, distinctly dotted on the upper surface; flowers (A, ×2) arranged in a loose leafy cyme, the lower soon producing fruit whilst the upper still in bud; stalks elongating in fruit; calyx-lobes 5, valvate, triangular; corolla (B, ×2) at first pink, soon becoming a beautiful purple-blue, about $\frac{1}{3}$–$\frac{1}{2}$ in. long, tube constricted in the middle; lobes 5, imbricate, with slightly

jagged edges; 5 large fleshy orange-yellow scales between the lobes inside; stamens (C, ×4) 5, slightly exserted from the tube on which they are inserted between the corolla-lobes; ovary (D, ×2) on a fleshy disk, of 4 distinct lobes; nuts with jagged tips (family *Boraginaceae*). – Synonym *Pneumaria maritima* (L.) Hill.

A lovely maritime plant in spring and early summer on shingle from north Wales, Northern Ireland, and Norfolk northwards to the Shetlands; occurs also in northern Europe and Asia and North America, in high latitudes.

Exceptional in the family *Boraginaceae* in being quite smooth (glabrous) except for the base of the calyx, and not armed with rough often bulbous-based hairs.

VIPER'S BUGLOSS
Echium vulgare L. ($\times \frac{1}{2}$)

Erect, biennial herb up to about 3 ft. high, with a long stout tap-root; rosette-leaves stalked, narrowly oblanceolate, about 6 in. long, entire, covered with bristly bulbous-based hairs, usually withered away at the time of flowering; stem-leaves linear-oblanceolate, sessile, up to about 4 in. long, clothed with long white bulbous-based hairs; flowers (A, $\times 1\frac{1}{2}$) very numerous and arranged in a handsome oblong spike-like inflorescence sometimes more than 1 ft. long, each short branch of the inflorescence subtended by a narrow leaf-like bract; sepals 5, green, narrow; corolla at first of a reddish-purple changing to bright blue, limb oblique, 5-lobed; stamens (B, $\times 5$) 5, exserted from the corolla; style (C, $\times 3$) inserted between the 4 lobes of the ovary, 2-lobed; nutlets pointed, wrinkled (family *Boraginaceae*).

Locally common in some districts, especially near the sea and in limestone and chalky areas; one of our most spectacular wild plants, flowering most of the summer; widely distributed into western Asia.

The large blue flowers make this plant extremely conspicuous from a distance, so that it is visited by a very large number of insects, especially bees, hover-flies, butterflies, and moths. Nectar is secreted by the fleshy base of the ovary, and concealed in the contracted lower part of the funnel-shaped corolla-tube.

The anthers are exserted from the mouth of the corolla and release their pollen immediately the flower opens, and no bee can settle on the flower without getting its under-surface dusted with pollen. Thus pollen is carried to another flower in which the anthers have already dehisced and in which the style has elongated beyond them.

Besides stocks which bear only bisexual flowers (i.e. with stamens and pistil), some plants bear only female flowers. In these the corolla is much smaller and the style shorter, while the stamens are short and only produce abortive pollen grains. There are also transitional stages between these two types, and it may be said that the species is tending to produce unisexual flowers.

Perennial branched herb with stems becoming tough and up to 3 ft. high, like the leaves covered all over with short bulbous-based hairs (A); leaves alternate, lanceolate, sessile, entire, 2–3 in. long, with 2–3 pairs of ascending lateral nerves; no stipules; flowers (B, $\times2\frac{1}{2}$) solitary in the axils of leafy bracts and together forming a leafy panicle; stalks short; sepals (B, $\times2\frac{1}{2}$) 5, lanceolate, setose; corolla (C, $\times3$) yellowish-white, of united petals about twice as long as the sepals, lobes 5 (rarely 6), each with a rounded scale at the base; stamens (D, $\times10$) 5 (6), inserted half way down the tube; anthers apiculate; ovary (E, $\times6$) deeply 4-lobed, with a single short style between; fruit (F, $\times3$) of 4 pale shining smooth ovoid nutlets (G, $\times3\frac{1}{2}$) (family *Boraginaceae*).

Grows in waste places and on roadsides, flowering in spring and summer, distributed in Europe and Asia and introduced into North America.

Nectar is secreted by the ovary and hidden in the base of the corolla-tube.

This is a typical member of the family *Boraginaceae*, most members of which have sharp bulbous-based hairs on the stems and leaves, a corolla-tube with a regular 5-lobed limb, 5 stamens alternate with the lobes, and an ovary of 4 carpels with the style inserted between them.

A strong-growing annual becoming hard and almost woody at the base, up to 1½ ft. high, rough and hoary all over with rather short bulbous-based hairs (A, × 1); stems slightly angular; leaves lanceolate to almost linear, entire and without visible side-nerves, hairy on both surfaces; flowers small, in leafy terminal cymes which elongate in fruit and become zigzag; stalks very short; calyx 5-lobed nearly to the base, lobes linear, nearly as long as the corolla; corolla (B, × 2) white, 5-lobed, without scales in the throat, hairy half-way down inside the tube; stamens 5, inserted below the middle of the tube; ovary (C, × 3) on a fleshy disk, deeply 4-lobed, with the style inserted between the lobes (gynobasic); style about half as long as the tube; fruit (D, × 2) composed of 4 separate closely warted nuts (E, × 4) (family *Boraginaceae*).

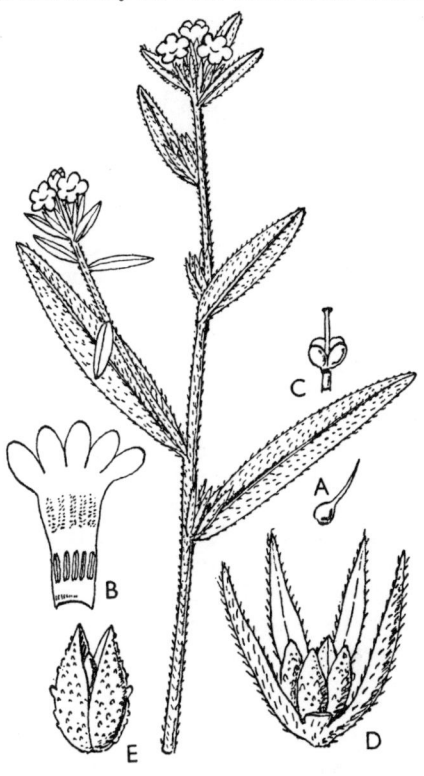

To be found mostly in cornfields and waste places, flowering during spring and summer.

The hairs above the anthers prevent rain from entering the corolla-tube. The anthers open before the corolla opens, but insect visitors are few. As the entrance to the nectar, which is secreted by the ovary and stored in the base of the corolla-tube, is completely closed, an insect visitor brings fresh pollen, and may effect cross-pollination. Eventually the anthers discharge such a quantity of pollen that the stigma becomes covered with it and self-pollination is effected.

Pulmonaria officinalis L. ($\times\frac{1}{2}$)

Perennial herb, hairy all over; basal leaves long-stalked, blade ovate, gradually acute at the apex, rounded to slightly cordate at the base, up to 6 in. long and $2\frac{1}{2}$ in. broad, setulose on both surfaces, entire, with faint lateral nerves and mostly with distinct large whitish spots here and there; petiole broadened at the base; flowers in a short scorpioid cyme, the oldest in the lower part and soon producing fruit; bracts leafy; pedicels about as long as the tubular calyx, the latter about $\frac{1}{2}$ in. long and 5-lobed, setulose; corolla (A, $\times 1$) at first pink then blue, a little exceeding the calyx, 5-lobed, glabrous outside; mouth of corolla with 5 rounded hairy scales; stamens 5, enclosed in the tube; anthers (B, $\times 5$) ellipsoid; ovary (C, $\times 2\frac{1}{2}$) of 4 almost separate lobes, with the style inserted between them; fruit composed of 4 spreading rugose nutlets (D, $\times 3$) (family *Boraginaceae*).

Introduced and naturalized in woods from gardens in several counties as far north as Edinburgh. The flowers are of two forms, some with long styles and some with shorter styles; in those with long styles the stigma reaches the mouth of the corolla and the anthers are halfway down in the tube; in the short styled kind the stigma reaches the middle of the tube and the anthers are near the mouth (as in the Primrose). Humble-bees effect pollination.

Plants with spotted leaves have been called var. *maculata*, those with unspotted leaves var. *immaculata*, but there is no other difference. A second very similar native species is *P. longifolia* Bor, with lanceolate basal leaves, a shorter corolla, and compressed crested nutlets.

Pulmonaria is a small genus of about 10 spp. distributed in Europe and western Asia, most of them in cultivation.

The name Lungwort was given because of the supposed resemblance of the spotted leaves to diseased lungs. Other names for it are 'Jerusalem Cowslip' and 'Spotted Dog'.

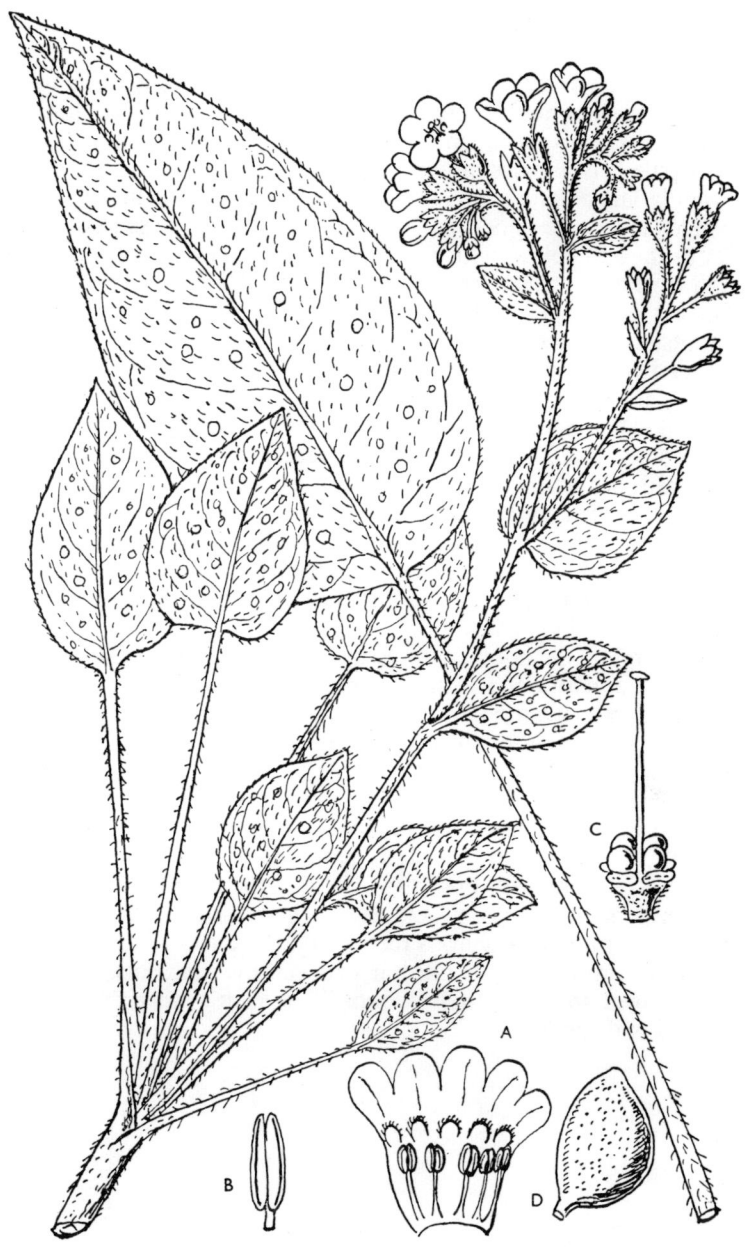

771

Symphytum officinale L. ($\times \frac{1}{2}$)

Perennial on river banks and wettish places, with a thick root-stock; stems annual, up to about 3 ft. high, growing very rapidly and flowering in spring and early summer, the whole plant clothed with pale bristly hairs rather rough to the touch; leaves alternate, broadly lanceolate, acutely tapered to the apex, the lower with a winged stalk, the upper sessile and decurrent on the stem often as far as the leaf below, with a few looped lateral nerves on each side and a very lax venation, bristly hairy especially on the nerves; flowers (A, $\times 1\frac{1}{4}$) in a 1-sided (scorpioid) cyme at the ends of the shoots, the cyme simple or sometimes 2-forked; calyx deeply divided into 5 narrow segments; corolla (B, $\times 1\frac{1}{4}$) pale yellow, white, or dingy purple, about $\frac{2}{3}$ in. long, tubular, the tube expanded and bell-shaped about the middle, very minutely hairy outside; lobes 5, very small and spreading; stamens 5, alternating with the corolla-lobes and inserted half-way down the tube; anthers not exserted; between the stamens large processes margined by sharp teeth; ovary (C, $\times 1\frac{1}{4}$) deeply 4-lobed, with the simple style, which is longer than the corolla, inserted between the lobes (gynobasic); fruit composed of 4 small smooth nutlets each containing a single seed (family *Boraginaceae*).

Comfrey is included in the British Pharmaceutical Codex, and the drug consists of the dried rootstock. It has been used as an application to wounds, sores, and ulcers of various kinds, a muci-laginous decoction of fresh root, peeled and bruised into a pulp, being applied.

Nectar is secreted by a ring-like ridge at the base of the ovary, and stored in the base of the corolla. Automatic self-pollination is inevitable because the flowers hang down, the stigma being brought into line with the pollen. Within the corolla and between the anthers are 5 large processes which are margined with sharp teeth (like miniature shark's teeth), and these teeth prevent insect visitors from probing for nectar between the filaments, and they are obliged to insert their proboscis in such a way that it gets dusted with pollen.

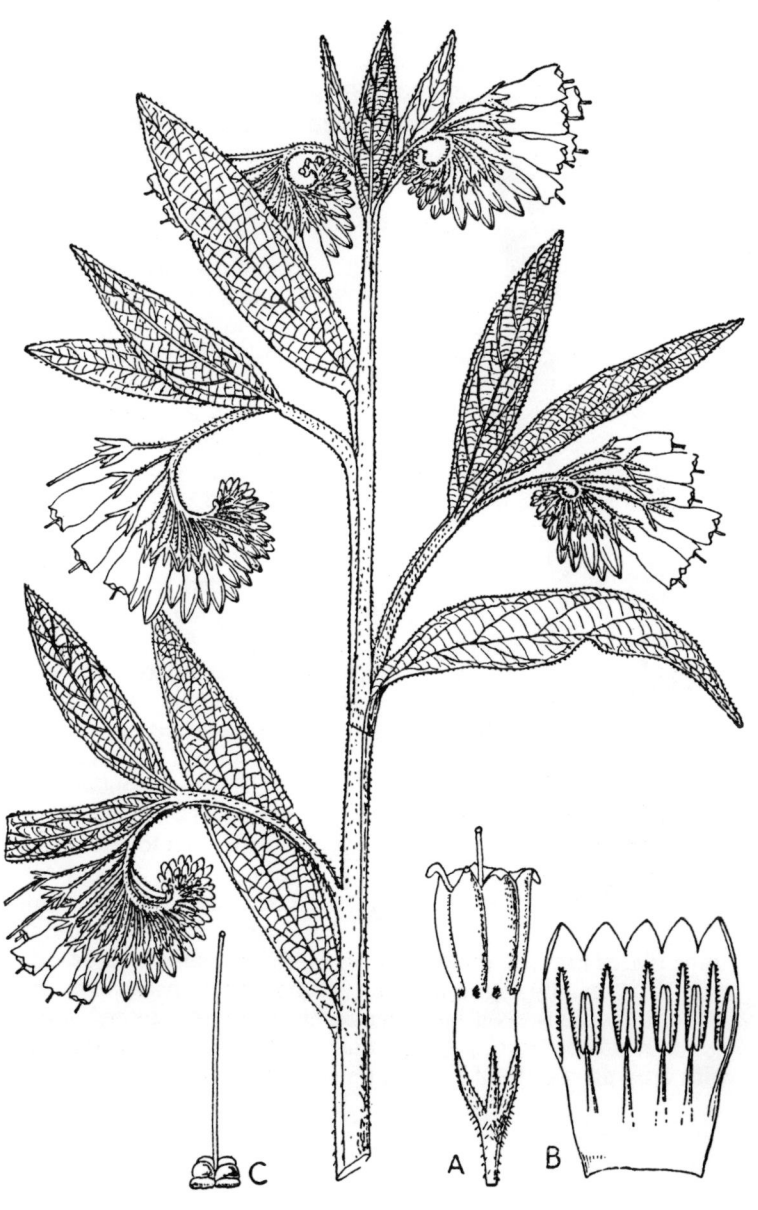

Anchusa sempervirens L. ($\times\frac{1}{4}$)

Perennial remaining leafy through the winter; leaves alternate, luscious green, broadly ovate, pointed at the apex, rounded at the base, covered like the rest of the plant with stiff hairs; flowers (A, $\times\frac{1}{2}$) small, arranged in one-sided clusters on short axillary branches; calyx (C, $\times\frac{1}{2}$) deeply 5-lobed, lobes fringed with hairs; corolla (B, $\times\frac{3}{4}$) a lovely deep sky-blue with a white 'eye'; stamens 5, included in the corolla-tube; ovary (C, $\times\frac{1}{2}$) deeply divided into 4 rounded lobes with the columnar style between them; fruitlets (D, $\times\frac{3}{4}$) 4, reticulate; grows in waste places (family *Boraginaceae*)

A very beautiful plant with Forget-me-not-like deep sky-blue flowers with a white 'eye'. Common in south-west Europe, and in south-west England, and in some places makes a delightful display in the hedgerows. In other parts it is usually found around villages and houses, sometimes invading gardens, as it has done recently in the Kew neighbourhood. It flowers during spring and the first half of the summer, with crop after crop of blooms on the same plant.

Perennial with creeping or suberect rootstock; stems ascending, rounded, with appressed hairs; leaves alternate, narrowly oblong or oblanceolate, blunt or rounded at the apex, narrowed to the base and sessile, faintly nerved, the nerves looped well within the margin, clothed on both surfaces with very short stiff bulbous-based hairs; flowers in a 2-forked 1-sided inflorescence (scorpioid cyme) the branches of which are coiled in the bud stage at the tip; no bracts; calyx (A, × 3) bell-shaped, shortly 5-toothed, loosely covered with very short stiff hairs; corolla (B, × $\frac{4}{5}$) bright clear blue with a yellow 'eye'; rather large (for the genus) and showy, with a small straight tube partly closed at its mouth by

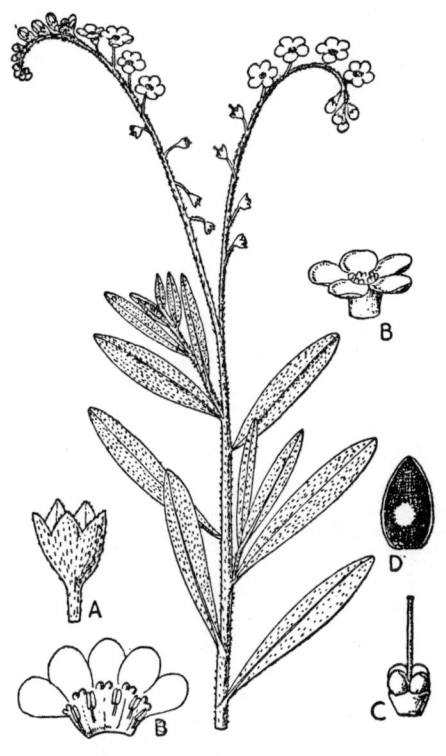

5 scales, and a spreading 5-lobed limb; stamens 5, hidden in the tube, alternate with the corolla-lobes; ovary (C, × 4) vertically divided into 4 lobes, with the unbranched style inserted between the lobes (gynobasic); nutlets (D, × 4) ovoid, slightly compressed, with a sharp margin, black, and highly polished (family *Boraginaceae*). Synonym *M. palustris* Hill

Grows in wet ditches and by the sides of streams and flowers all the summer; easily separated from nearly all the other British species, of which there are several, by the calyx which is only toothed, and not deeply lobed as in the others. *M. secunda* Murr. is very close, but has the calyx cut half-way down into narrow lobes, and *M. caespitosa* Schultz has a very small corolla.

Myosotis secunda A. Murr. (½)

Perennial herb with slightly creeping rootstock; stems more or less decumbent and then ascending, hairy, sometimes almost villous with spreading hairs; leaves (A, × ½) sessile, narrowly oblong-oblanceolate, rounded at the apex, up to 3 in. long and ¾ in. broad, the very few lateral nerves forming a continuous line well within the margin, hairy, with bulbous based hairs (B, × 2); flowers (D, × 1½) in a loose 1-sided raceme, the lower flowers often forming fruits whilst the upper are still in bud; stalks becoming more or less deflexed and about ½ in. long in fruit; calyx

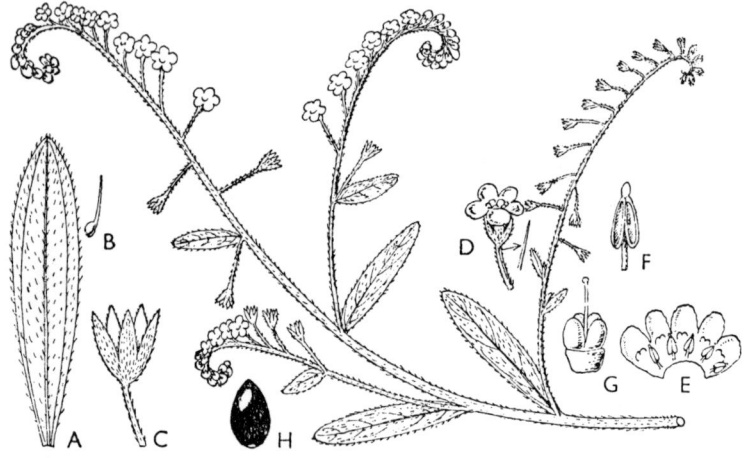

(C, × 2) 5-lobed to below the middle, the hairs on it very short and adpressed; corolla (E, × 2½) bright blue with a yellow 'eye', 5-lobed; stamens (F, × 5) 5, alternate with the lobes and hidden in the tube of the corolla; ovary (G, × 6) seated on a fleshy nectariferous disk, deeply 4-lobed, with the style between the lobes; nutlet (H, × 5) black and shining (family *Boraginaceae*).

Myosostis secunda is mentioned in the notes on the Water Forget-Me-Not, *Myosostis scorpioides* (see fig. 668). The drawings of the calyx should be compared, when it will be seen that in *M. secunda* it is much more deeply divided than in *M. scorpioides*.

Myosotis arvensis (L.) Hill ($\times \frac{2}{3}$)

Annual or biennial, mostly more or less branched from the base, occasionally very much branched; stems up to about 1 ft. high, clothed with rather long weak hairs, with a few scattered leaves; basal leaves spathulate-obovate narrowed into a short stalk, stem-leaves spathulate-oblanceolate, sessile, covered on both surfaces with bulbous-based hairs (A, × 6); flowers in scorpioid one-sided (secund) racemes, the lowermost developed into fruit whilst the uppermost are still in bud; stalks as long as or slightly longer than the calyx in fruit; calyx 5-lobed to below the middle, clothed with prominently hooked hairs (B, × 5); corolla (C, × 6) 5-lobed, very small, pale blue; stamens (D, × 8) 5, alternate with the corolla-lobes; anthers apiculate; ovary (E, × 6) deeply 4-lobed, with the style between the lobes (gynobasic); nutlets (F, × 5) obovoid, nearly jet black, shining (family *Boraginaceae*).

Hairs with a much swollen base (bulbous based hairs) are very characteristic of most of the Borage family. Another and more constant character is the ovary, which is vertically divided into 4 nearly separate lobes, with the single style inserted in the middle between them. A good spotting feature for *M. arvensis* is the nature of the hairs on the calyx, which are hooked at the top (see fig. B).

Myosotis ramosissima Rochel (½)

A small usually much-branched annual; stems and leaves clothed with slender simple hairs; lower leaves more or less spoon-shaped, about 1 in. long, entire; others more oblong-lanceolate and sessile; flowers in slender racemes, at first coiled and somewhat one-sided (secund); no bracts; flower-stalks shorter than the calyx; calyx (A, ×5) deeply divided into 5 lobes, these bristly hairy, the lower hairs hooked at the apex, the uppermost hairs not hooked; corolla (B, ×7) bright blue from the beginning, scarcely exceeding the calyx, lobes 5, spreading, with a yellow swelling at the base of each; stamens 5, inserted half-way down in the corolla-tube; ovary (C, ×10) deeply 4-lobed, with a short style and a knob-like stigma; fruit of 4 free smooth nutlets (D, ×6) rather compressed (family *Boraginaceae*).

Grows in dry open places on banks, walls, and heaths, to central and south Europe and north Africa, east to Himalayas; flowers in early summer.

The yellow pocket-like processes at the entrance to the corolla serve both as nectar-guides and nectar-covers. They compel insect visitors to insert their proboscis into the base of the flower in such a way as to touch the stigma and anthers. Thus pollen is carried from one flower to another. Synonym *M. collina* Hoffm.

Cynoglossum officinale L. (×⅓)

Biennial; stems simple or branched, up to 2 ft. high, thick and fleshy, pale green, with brownish-green ribs, softly but thinly villous; leaves spirally arranged, sessile, linear-lanceolate, gradually sub-acute, bright green above, paler below, covered with short soft hairs; flowers in nodding scorpioid cymes in the axils of most of the leaves; stalks pubescent; sepals 5, free, ovate-elliptic, densely pubescent; corolla (B, × 1¼) dull purplish-red, 5-lobed, nearly closed at the mouth by 5 humps, each opposite a lobe; anthers 5, alternate with the lobes; ovary (A, × 1) deeply divided into 4 lobes, with a stiff awl-shaped style between them; fruit (C, × 1) of 4 separate depressed nutlets covered with short hooked prickles (family *Boraginaceae*).

When bruised, the plant, and especially the flowers, have a disagreeable mouse-like smell; it grows on roadsides and waste places and on maritime chalky downs, flowering from early summer. In former times, among its many supposed virtues, it was recommended, curiously enough, for stuttering, and was also considered to be antiscorbutic.

Nectar is secreted by the fleshy receptacle below the ovary and concealed in the base of the corolla-tube. The 5 darker-coloured pocket-shaped hollow scales at the entrance to the corolla-tube serve as nectar-guides and their velvety covering of hairs as nectar-covers. The stigma of the short style is receptive at the same time as the anthers release their pollen, and self-pollination takes place if no insect has visited the flower.

Cynoglossum germanicum Jacq. ($\times\frac{1}{2}$)

Biennial herb up to about 2 ft. high; rosette-leaves of the first year stalked, elliptic-lanceolate, acute at each end, entire, about 5 in.

long and 2 in. broad, with long whitish hairs on the nerves below; flowering-stem leaves gradually becoming more oblong and sessile with a clasping base, entire, thinly hairy with bulbous-based hairs; racemes forming a terminal leafy panicle, the flowers at first coiled and crowded, much lengthening out in fruit; sepals (A, $\times 1\frac{1}{2}$) 5, oblong, persistent and longer than the fruiting carpels; corolla (B, $\times 1\frac{1}{2}$) dull blue-purple, with a short tube, closed at the mouth by prominent scales and with 5 spreading lobes; stamens 5; nuts (C, $\times 1$) flattened and burr-like, covered with short prickles (D, $\times 3$) crowned by several minute hooks at the top (synonym *Cynoglossum montanum* Lam., non Linn.) (family *Boraginaceae*).

Grows in woods, confined to the southern half of England; rare in Eire.

Nectar is secreted by the fleshy receptacle below the ovary and stored in the base of the corolla-tube.

Differs from the only other British species, *C. officinale* L., shown in fig. 672 by the fruits having no thickened border as they have in that species.

Lycopsis arvensis L. ($\times\frac{1}{2}$)

A rough, spreading annual up to about 2 ft. high, covered all over
with bristly bulbous-based hairs; leaves alternate, sessile, oblong-
lanceolate or oblanceolate, with wavy margins and rather obscure
lateral nerves, bristly on both surfaces and margins with longer
and shorter bulbous-based hairs; flowers (A, $\times 1\frac{1}{2}$) in simple or
branched bracteate clusters which lengthen and become one-sided
in fruit; calyx (C, $\times 1\frac{1}{2}$) 5-lobed to the base, lobes linear-lanceolate, nearly as long as the corolla, very bristly; corolla (B, $\times 4$)
pale-blue, 5-lobed, the tube curved in the middle, and hairy inside

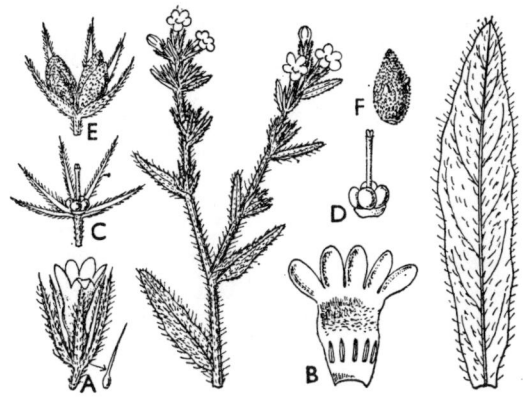

above the 5 anthers inserted towards the base of the tube; ovary
(D, $\times 3$) deeply 4-lobed, with the rather short style inserted between the lobes; lobes with 1 ascending ovule in each; fruit (E, F,
$\times 2$) composed of 4 separate ovoid densely warted nutlets (family
Boraginaceae).

Nectar is secreted by the base of the 4-lobed ovary and stored
in the lower part of the corolla-tube. The corolla-tube is bent in
the middle. Should insect visitors not effect cross-pollination,
automatic self-pollination is brought about by the dropping off
of the corolla, in the process of which the anthers, to which some
pollen still clings, are drawn over the stigma.

Borago officinalis L. ($\times\frac{1}{3}$)

Rough hairy annual or biennial herb covered with bristle-like bulbous-based hairs; leaves obovate to oblong, about 8 in. long and 3 in. broad, narrowed into a broad petiole, the upper ones becoming sessile; flowers (A, $\times 1$) hanging in loose forked terminal cymes; bracts leafy, lanceolate; sepals 5, narrowly lanceolate, densely hairy; corolla blue or white, rotate, mouth closed by short broad scales; lobes 5, spreading; stamens (B, $\times 2$) 5, forming an erect cone; filaments with a large erect appendage outside the apex; anthers nearly black, introrse, opening by slits lengthwise; ovary (C, $\times 2$) deeply 4-lobed,

with an erect style inserted between the lobes; fruit (D, $\times 8$) of 4 free reticulate nuts (family *Boraginaceae*).

Naturalized in many places and long cultivated in gardens, flowering most of the summer; native of the eastern Mediterranean. This species is the type of the genus *Borago*, which itself is the type genus from which the family name is derived. It is therefore the 'Borage of the Borages'.

Amsinckia intermedia Fisch. & Mey.* ($\times\frac{1}{2}$)

Herb up 1½ ft. high, hispid all over with stiff bristly hairs with a disk-like base (A, ×9); basal leaves linear-oblanceolate, entire, up to 6 in. long, 3-nerved, densely bristly; stem-leaves alternate sessile, lanceolate, 1–2 in. long, ½–¾ in. broad, bristly on both sides; flowers (B, ×5) yellow; calyx-lobes narrow; corolla (C, ×10) much longer than the calyx, shortly 5-lobed; ovary (D, ×7) deeply lobed into 4 parts; nutlets 4, closely warted (family *Boraginaceae*).

An alien from the European continent on waste ground and refuse heaps.

* As there is considerable difference of opinion as to the limits of species in this genus, I may say that the plant illustrated was collected by Mr V. S. Summerhayes, of Kew, at Pretty Corner, south of Sheringham, Norfolk, 15 Aug. 1951, no. 2446.

Omphalodes verna Moench. ($\times \frac{1}{2}$)

Perennial herb with decumbent scaly rootstock; leaves long-petiolate, ovate, more or less cordate at the base, shortly acumin-

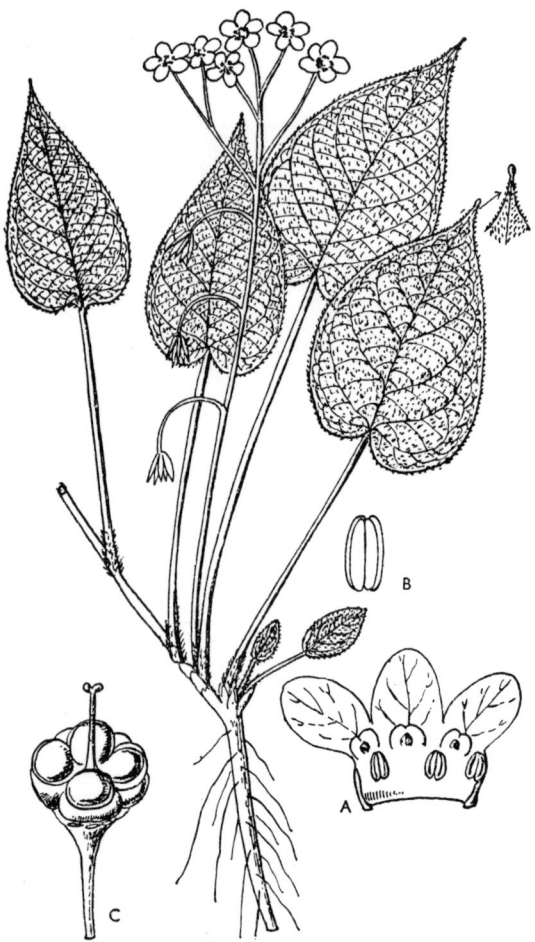

ate but with a blunt tip, averaging about 2–2½ in. long and 1–2 in. broad, thinly clothed below with short spreading hairs, closely setulose on the upper surface, with 5–6 pairs of lateral nerves; petioles with white hairs at the base; flowers few on a slender peduncle; pedicels slender, reaching nearly 1 in. in fruit; sepals 5, narrowly lanceolate, hairy; corolla-tube (A, ×2) very short, with a 5-lobed limb, bright blue with a white pentagonal 'eye'; scales large, opposite the lobes; stamens 5, anthers (B, ×4) inserted in the throat; ovary (C, ×4) of 4 rounded lobes; fruit composed of 4 nutlets (family *Boraginaceae*).

Naturalized here and there in dense shade in woods near gardens; native of western Europe; easily recognized by the ovate-cordate pointed leaves.

Perennial erect herb up to about 1½ ft. high; stems 4-angled, green or tinged with purple, glabrous or very slightly hairy; leaves spreading, all with short stalks, opposite, lanceolate, slightly irregularly dentate, with a broadish triangular apex, strongly nerved below, very minutely and sparingly hairy, also finely dotted below (punctate); flowers (A, ×3) in terminal cylindric somewhat interrupted spike-like inflorescences with small leaf-like bracts, the central 'spike' about 3 in. long and maturing first, the lateral ones a little shorter; calyx (B, ×3) purplish, shining, equally 5-lobed, lobes 10-ribbed, with prominent glands between the ribs and a few longish hairs on the margins of the lobes; corolla (C, ×2) mauve, 4-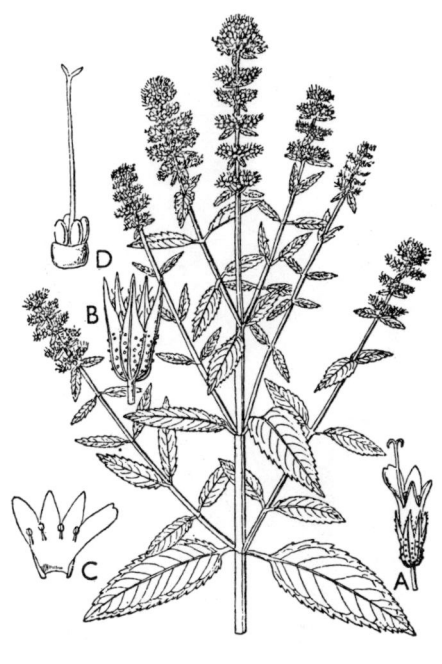lobed, one of the lobes bifid at the apex, not hairy outside; stamens 4, not exserted from the tube; ovary (D, ×6) deeply 4-lobed, the lobes glabrous; style exserted, inserted between the lobes of the ovary (gynobasic) (family *Labiatae*).

Flowers at the end of summer and with a fairly strong minty smell.

Peppermint grows in water places along stream banks and in waste ground throughout Europe. It is the source of Oil of Peppermint, used as a flavouring and therapeutic agent, for which it has long been cultivated, especially in districts to the south-west of London, for example around Mitcham, in Surrey.

Mentha spicata L. (⅓)

Perennial herb with slender creeping rootstock, smelling like garden mint when bruised; stems quadrangular, 1–2 ft. high, erect,

covered with short whitish downwardly directed soft hairs; leaves without stalks (sessile), at first spreading, soon decurved, opposite, oblong or oblong-lanceolate, rounded (almost cordate) at the base, triangular-pointed, rather unevenly toothed, minutely hairy and pale green above, covered with soft whitish woolly hairs below and with prominent nerves; flowers (A, ×3) in slender catkin-like spikes, the latter collected into a loose panicle and either continuous or slightly broken up (interrupted), with occasionally a small lateral spike at the base; bracts awl-shaped, prominent in bud; flowerstalks short; calyx (B, ×3) with 5 equal short lobes, hairy outside; corolla mauve, more deeply tinged inside the lobes, 4-lobed, hairy outside; stamens 4, exserted; ovary (C, ×3) deeply 4-lobed, the lobes slightly hairy; style inserted between the lobes (gynobasic) (family *Labiatae*).

Found in moist places, often in a ditch alongside a hedge, flowering in late July; rare in the north; a beautiful species easily distinguished by its oblong sessile leaves which are hoary all over, and by the slender catkin-like species collected into a leafy panicle. Synonym *M. sylvestris* L.

Mentha x smithiana R. A. Graham ($\frac{1}{3}$)

A branched perennial herb up to about 5 ft. high; stems 4-sided, crimson-purple, glabrous or slightly pubescent; leaves opposite, ovate or ovate-elliptic, tri-angular pointed, the largest about 2 in. long and 1 in. broad, with purple nerves, few-toothed, gland-dotted below, but scarcely hairy; stalks very short; flowers (A, ×2) in axillary whorls, each little bunch on a very short common stalk; flower-stalks crimson, not hairy; calyx (B, ×2) tubular, equally 5-lobed, 10-ribbed, lobes narrowly triangular, setulose; corolla light-crimson, 5-lobed, glabrous; stamens 4, exserted from the tube; style long-exserted, inserted between the 4 lobes of the ovary (C, ×8) (family *Labiatae*).

Flowers from July to September; considered to be a triple hybrid between the Water Mint, *M. aquatica* L.,

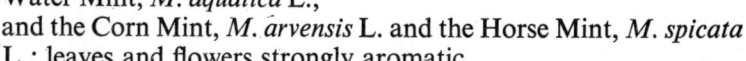

and the Corn Mint, *M. arvensis* L. and the Horse Mint, *M. spicata* L.; leaves and flowers strongly aromatic.

In this genus, as in many members of the family *Labiatae*, nectar is secreted by the base of the ovary.

In several species of *Mentha* the flowers are mixed, some being bisexual and protandrous, and are larger than others which are female. The latter are most numerous at the beginning of the flowering season.

WATER MINT
Mentha aquatica L. ($\times\frac{1}{2}$)

A rather rank growing perennial, in wet places; rootstock slender, creeping; stems usually up to about 1½ ft. high, or much higher, almost villous with rather soft long spreading or downwardly pointing white hairs; leaves opposite, shortly stalked, ovate, rounded at the base, obtusely and broadly triangular at the apex, the largest about 2 in. long, crenate-dentate on the margin with rather few teeth, softly hairy on both surfaces and minutely gland-

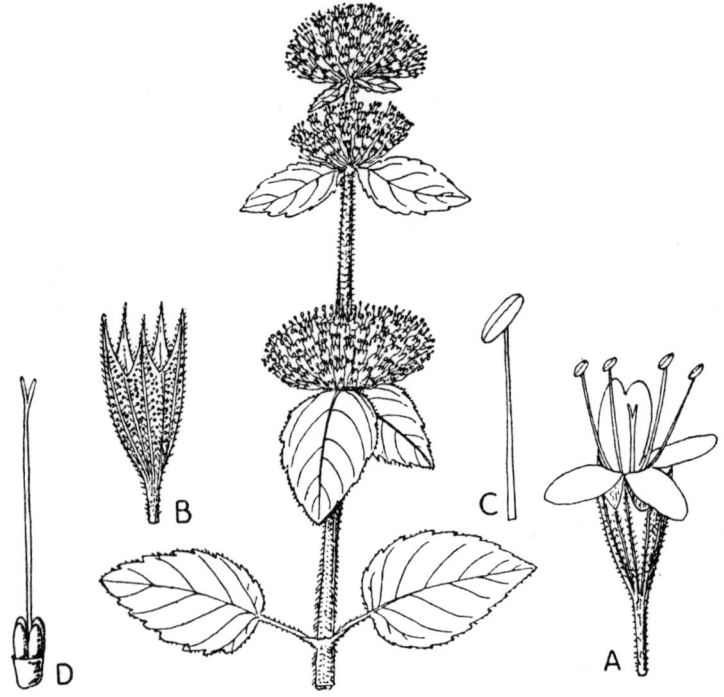

dotted below; flowers (A, $\times$ 3) in dense globose clusters at the top of the stem and in the axils of the last 2–3 pairs of leaves; calyx (B, $\times$ 5) tubular, ⅙ in. long, acutely 5-lobed, and with 10 prominent ribs, markedly glandular between the ribs; corolla pink, nearly regular, 4-lobed, one of the lobes notched at the apex (showing union of 2 lobes); stamens (C, $\times$ 10) 4, inserted half-way down the corolla-tube; anthers short, attached in the middle; ovary (D, $\times$ 7) deeply lobed, with the style between the lobes; style slender, shortly 2-lobed; nutlets smooth (family *Labiatae*).

Perennial, often forming a dense carpet to the exclusion of other plants, and covered by a mass of flowers; stems wiry, slender, with a line of short recurved hairs along each of the 4 angles; leaves (A, × 2) opposite, very shortly stalked, ovate, oblong or obovate, glabrous or with a few long marginal hairs towards the base, deeply pitted with large glands; flowers (B, × 3) in whorls in the axils of the upper smaller leaves and forming a dense spike-like inflorescence; bracts very small and crimson; calyx (C, × 3) half crimson-purple and half greenish, obliquely bell-shaped, 2-lipped, the upper lip broad and with 3 ovate teeth, the lower of 2 narrow

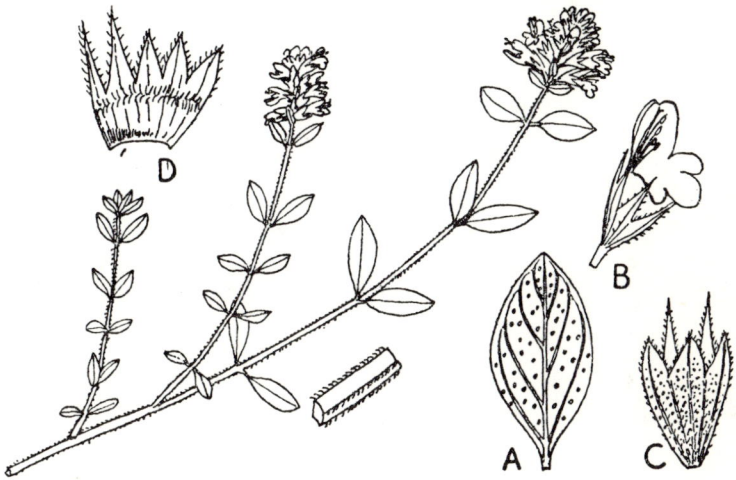

awl-shaped lobes, 10-ribbed, hairy and minutely glandular outside, with a ring of hairs inside which closes over the nutlets in fruit; corolla pink, short and broad, 2-lipped, the upper lip broad and notched, the lower 3-lobed; stamens 4, as long as the corolla; ovary deeply 4-lobed, with the bifid style between the lobes; nutlets dark brown; smooth (family *Labiatae*).

On dry grassy banks, flowering in summer. The flowers are much visited by insects. A general favourite, for most people 'Know a bank whereon the Wild Thyme blows'. After the corollas have dropped off a ring of hairs inside the top of the calyx-tube (D, × 3) spreads over the little nutlets.

Origanum vulgare L. ($\times\frac{1}{2}$)

Strongly aromatic harbaceous perennial with creeping rootstock and annual stems up to 2 ft. high, these softly hairy and more or less crimson; leaves opposite, ovate, rounded to shortly wedge-shaped at the base, not pointed at the apex, slightly dentate, thinly hairy on both surfaces, markedly punctate-glandular especially below (A, $\times 1$); stalks nearly quarter as long as the blade, bristly hairy; no stipules; very short leafy branchlets in the lower leaf-axils; flowers (B, $\times 2\frac{1}{2}$) in terminal clusters, these forming a leafy panicle; bracts ovate, longer than the calyx and often tinged with crimson or purple; calyx (C, $\times 1\frac{1}{2}$) very small, equally 5-toothed,

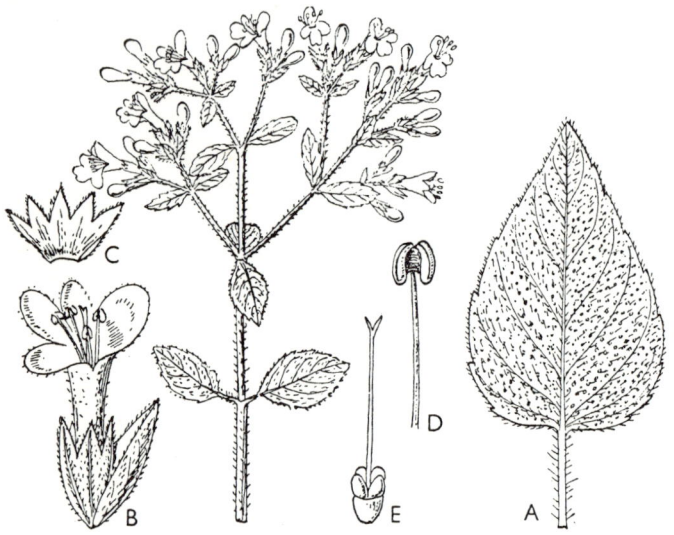

shortly hairy; corolla dull-purple, twice as long as the calyx, nearly equally 4-lobed, the upper lobe sub-erect, slightly hairy outside; stamens (D, $\times 2\frac{1}{2}$) 4, two longer, all well exserted from the corolla; anther-loculi 2, separate; ovary (E, $\times 2\frac{1}{2}$) on a large fleshy disk, deeply 4-lobed, with the bifid style inserted between the lobes; nutlets smooth (family *Labiatae*).

The flowers are either bisexual or female, the former being larger. They are crowded into dense clusters, and they are much visited by insects. Stamens and style project from the corolla, but self-pollination is prevented by the anthers opening before the stigmas are receptive. The bodies of insects are dusted with pollen, thus effecting cross-pollination.

Erect-branched perennial up to about 2 ft. high, very minutely hairy all over; stems 4-angled, hollow between the nodes, and here and there tinged with purple; leaves opposite, in 2 rows, stalked, widely heart-shaped at the base, broadly ovate, very coarsely and bluntly toothed, strongly nerved; flowers in axillary stalked clusters gradually formed into oblong spikes with the upper leaves reduced to narrow green bracts; calyx (B, ×2) tubular, 5-toothed, with 15 green ribs, softly hairy; corolla (A, ×2) white to pale blue, with crimson spots on the limb, the upper lobe bifid, 2 half-moon side-lobes and a broad semicircular lower tip (C, ×2); stamens 4, exserted from the tube; anthers purplish; ovary (D, ×3) of 4 separate carpels with the style between them (family *Labiatae*).

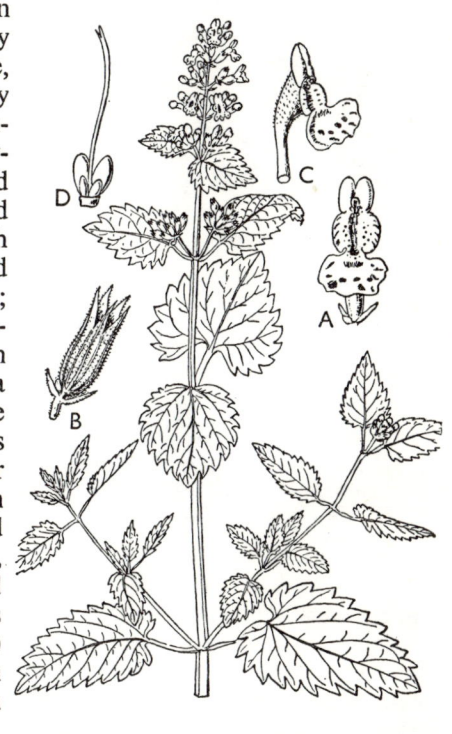

Grows in hedges, by roadsides, and in waste places, smelling rather like mint when bruised. Owing to this it has a strange fascination for cats who will destroy any plant of it that may happen to be bruised. It was formerly used for making tea.

The flowers of this species may be either bisexual or female. The females occur as a rule on the same plant as the others or rarely on separate stocks.

GROUND IVY
Nepeta hederacea (L.) Trev. ($\times \frac{2}{3}$)

Perennial with stems creeping at the base and rooting at the nodes; stems 4-angled, very minutely hairy, green and dull-purplish; lower leaves on long, upper leaves on shorter stalks, all opposite, often tinged with dull purple, broadly ovate-rounded, rather widely cordate at the base, coarsely toothed with rounded teeth (crenate) the terminal 'tooth' the largest with about 7 main nerves radiating from the base, very minutely hairy above, finely pitted with gland dots below; leaf-stalks connected at the base by line of long slender hairs (A, $\times \frac{4}{5}$); flowers (C, $\times \frac{4}{5}$) axillary, about 3 in each leaf-axil, the middle one flowering first whilst the other 2 are still tiny buds; stalk very short; calyx (B, $\times 1\frac{1}{4}$) dull crimson and green, tubular, 15-ribbed, shortly hairy, 5-lobed, the lobes ovate, very acute and nearly equal-sized; corolla blue, blotched inside the tube with crimson, twice as long as the calyx, 2-lipped, the two upper lobes forming the upper lip, with the forked style sticking out between them, two lateral rounded lobes, the lowermost lobe forming the lower lip and rather widely notched, with numerous stiff rod-like hairs across the mouth of the tube; stamens 4, in pairs under the upper lip, the upper pair the longest filament produced beyond the gaping anther (D, $\times 3$) ovary (E, $\times 2$) deeply and vertically lobed; style not hairy; fruit of four 1-seeded nutlets (family *Labiatae*).

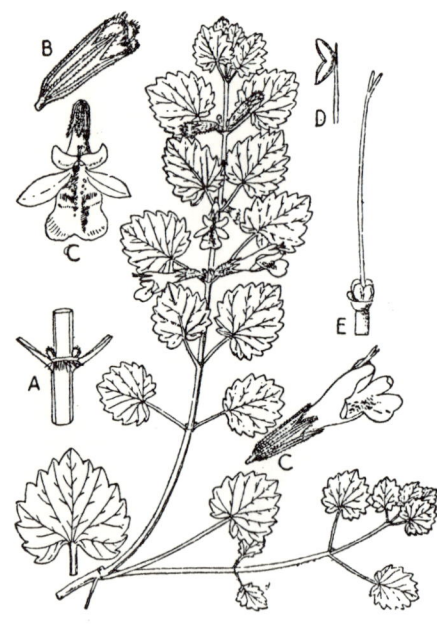

A very charming little plant, the great beauty of whose flowers is best seen with a strong hand-lens; blooms in early spring, and widely distributed in north temperate regions; nectar is secreted at the base of the ovary. Another name is *Nepeta glechoma* Benth.

Leonurus cardiaca L. ($\times\frac{1}{3}$)

Nettle-like perennial herb with square often reddish violet stems, the angles covered with very short downwardly directed hairs;

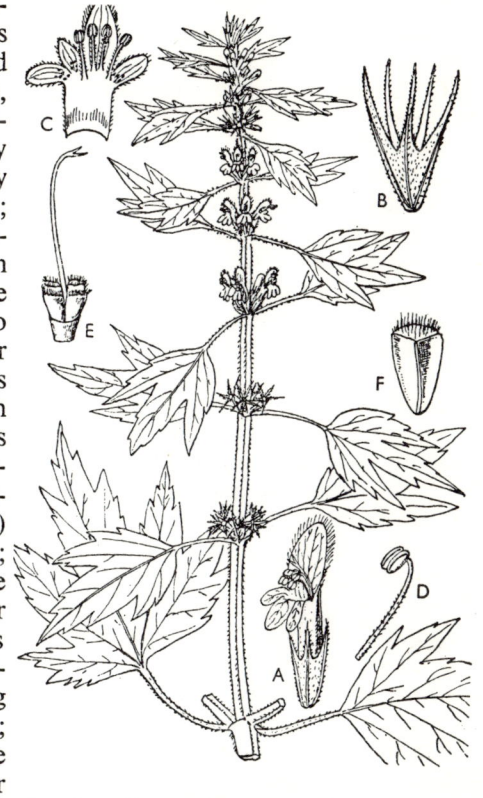

leaves opposite, petiolate, the lower ones digitately 5-lobed and 5-nerved at the base, those above only 3-lobed, lobes coarsely toothed, hairy mainly on the nerves below; flowers (A, $\times1\frac{1}{4}$) numerous and sessile in axillary clusters, the lower clusters well into fruit whilst the upper still in bud, the buds densely villous with long white hairs; bracts subulate and sharp-pointed like the calyx-lobes; calyx (B, $\times2$) 5-lobed and 5-ribbed; corolla (C, $\times3$) pale rose, 2-lipped, upper lip erect, very villous outside, lower lip 3-lobed, tube with a ring of hairs above the base; stamens (D, $\times4$) 4 the upper 2 with shorter filaments; anthers 2-locular, loculi parallel; ovary (E, $\times2$) of 4 free carpels flat and hairy on top and with the style inserted between them; fruiting carpels (F, $\times3$) triangular, the outer side rounded, hairy on the flat top (family *Labiatae*).

An introduced plant escaped from gardens and as such found naturalized, especially in Cornwall and in the Channel Islands, flowering from June to September; widely distributed in Europe.

DEAD NETTLE
Lamium album L. ($\times \frac{1}{2}$)

Perennial with a creeping rhizome and giving off stolons; stems up to about $1\frac{1}{2}$ ft. high, bearing whorls of flowers at each node almost to the base, square in section, pale green, slightly pubescent, especially in the upper part, hairs spreading; leaves opposite, in 2 ranks (decussate), stalked, broadly ovate, rounded to slightly cordate at the base, acutely acuminate, up to about 2 in. long and $1\frac{1}{2}$ in. broad, coarsely crenate-serrate, pale green, bullate-reticulate, very slightly hairy on both surfaces; leaf-stalks connected across the stem by a narrow ridge; flowers (B, $\times 1\frac{1}{2}$) axillary (pseudo-verticillate), about 7–8 in each leaf-axil, sessile, those towards the middle of the stem opening first; bracts very small at the base of each flower; calyx (A, $\times 2$) green, striped with brown at the base, campanulate, lobed to the middle into 5 narrow awl-shaped segments slightly hairy on the margin; corolla pure white, about 1 in. long, markedly 2-lipped, the upper lip hood-like and wrapped over the other in bud, hairy, the side lobes with a small tooth, the lower lip broad and rather deeply split in the middle; tube with an oblique ring of hairs towards the base inside; stamens 4, hidden under the hooded upper lip, the two anther-lobes (C, $\times 4$) opening by a continuous slit, hairy and black on the margins; style white, 2-lobed between the anthers; around the ovary (D, $\times 3$) a fleshy disk; ovary divided into 4 separate green lobes, with the style inserted between the lobes (gynobasic); fruit of 4 small truncate nutlets (family *Labiatae*).

Found in fields and waste places, but rare and local in Scotland and Eire, flowering from March to December; widely distributed eastward to north Asia and in north Africa; introduced in North America.

Nectar is secreted by the base of the ovary and stored at the bottom of the corolla-tube. The oblique ring of hairs described above acts as a nectar-cover. The upper lip shelters the anthers and stigma, and the lower lip forms a convenient alighting platform of insect visitors. On account of the length of the corolla-tube the nectar is only accessible to long-tongued humble-bees and bees.

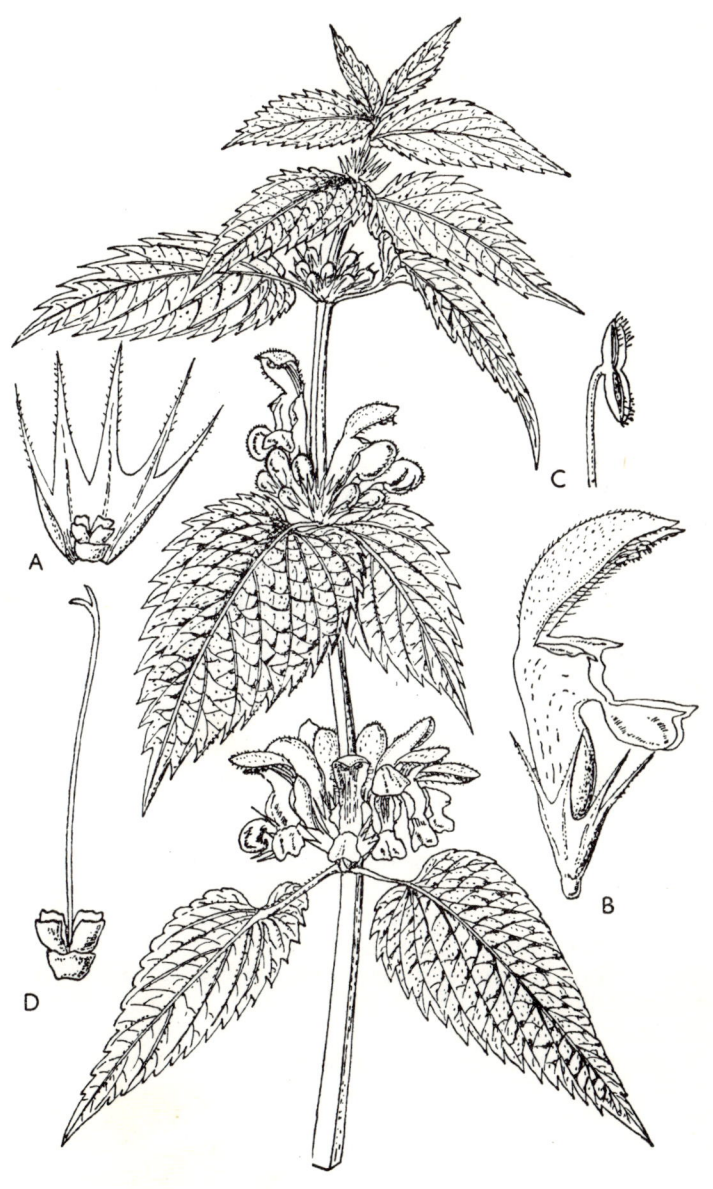

795

Lamium purpureum L. ($\times \frac{1}{2}$)

Annual or biennial, flowering more or less the whole season, usually found as a garden weed and in waste places; stems spreading and ascending, square in section, pubescent with short reflexed hairs; leaves opposite, the lower on stalks longer than the blade and fringed with rather long weak hairs, the upper with very short stalks; blade ovate, rather widely cordate at the base, coarsely toothed (crenate-serrate), very undulate (bullate) on the upper surface and coarsely reticulate; stalks connected across the stems; calyx (A, × 3) equally 5-lobed to about the middle, tinged with crimson, the lobes awl-shaped (subulate), shortly hairy; corolla (B, × 1½) 2-lipped, deep mauve-pink, the upper lobe undivided and forming a hood over the 4 stamens (C, × 4) with deep orange pollen, the 2 side lobes very small and narrow, the front lobe deeply split into two parts and mottled with deep crimson like the spotted orchid; anthers hairy; ovary (D, × 6) deeply divided into 4 parts with flat (truncate) tops, with the style arising from the base (gynobasic); fruit composed of 4 similar little nuts, each with a single seed.

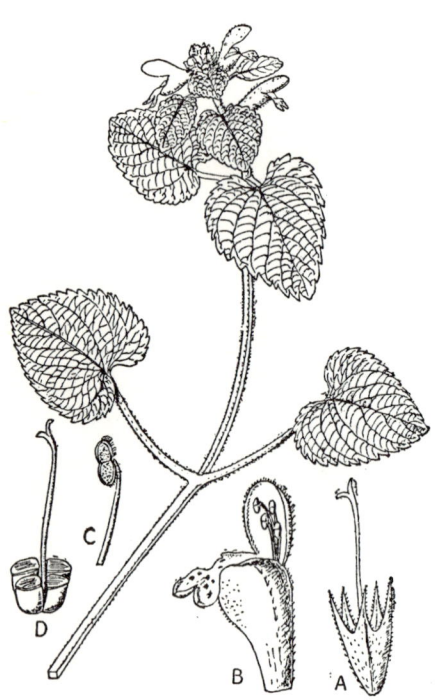

There are four other species of this genus in Britain, *Lamium album* L. (fig. 687) with white corolla, *L. amplexicaule* L., with purplish red corolla with a slender tube, *L. maculatum* L. (fig. 690) resembling *L. album* but with a red corolla and a ring of hairs in the tube, and *L. galeobdolon* Crantz, with a yellow corolla (fig. 689) (family *Labiatae*).

796

Perennial with somewhat tuberous rootstock and long stolons; stem simple, leafy, up to about $1\frac{1}{2}$ ft. high, square in section, covered with short deflexed hairs (A, × 2); leaves opposite, connected at the base by a narrow rim, shortly stalked, the lowermost ovate and slightly heart-shaped (cordate) at the base, gradually narrowing upwards, coarsely toothed, bullate, thinly hairy above and mainly on the nerves below; stalks clothed with slender hairs; flowers (C, × 2) in dense axillary whorls, sessile; calyx tubular, almost equally 5-lobed, lobes very acute; corolla yellow, 2-lipped, upper lip hood-like and hiding the stamens and style, lower 3-lobed and mottled with brown; stamens 4; anthers (D, × 5) with 2 divergent loculi, 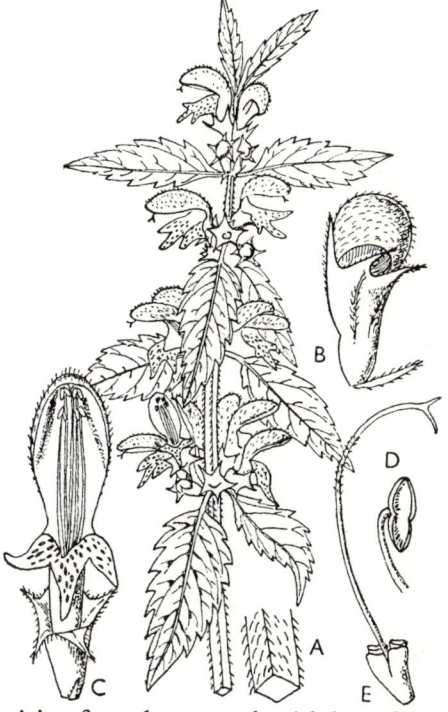 not hairy; style crimson, arising from between the 4 lobes of the ovary (E, × 2); fruit of 4 nutlets, very blunt (truncate) (B, flower bud, × 3) (family *Labiatae*).

A distinctive species, and very similar to the White Dead Nettle (fig. 687), but the corolla yellow and the anthers not hairy; grows in woods and shady places, ranging to western Asia, and flowers in late spring and early summer.

Some botanists regard this as a separate genus, *Galeobdolon* (*G. luteum* Huds.) or *Galeopsis* (*Galeopsis galeobdolon* L.). There is no *correct* genus name, because it is just a matter of opinion, though young and inexperienced botanists sometimes think otherwise.

Perennial with a creeping rhizome; stem 1–1½ ft. high, bearing whorls of flowers in the upper leaf-axils, square in section, green or tinged with dull crimson, covered with downwardly directed (deflexed) hairs; leaves opposite, in 2 ranks (decussate), the lower fairly long-stalked, broadly ovate, rounded to slightly cordate at the base, broadly pointed, up to about 2 in. long and 1½ in. broad, coarsely serrate, dull green except a broad nearly white band up the middle, shortly setulose on the upper surface, thinly hairy below on the nerves and veins; leaf-stalks connected across the stem by a narrow hairy ridge; flowers (A, ×2) axillary (pseudo-verticillate) about 7–8 in each leaf-axil, the middle ones opening first; bracts small and hairy; calyx 5-lobed, lobes awl-shaped (subulate), the back (adaxial) lobe a little longer than the others, all fringed with short hairs; corolla mauve, about 1 in. long, markedly 2-lipped, the upper lobe hood-like and wrapped over the others in bud, covered outside with very short white hairs; lower lip 2-lobed, mottled or streaked with dark mauve, the side-lobes reduced to fine points; tube with a ring of stiff hairs inside above the base and above them scattered stiff papillae; stamens (B, ×4) 4, hidden under the hood, the 2 anther-lobes hairy on the dark brown margins; filaments hairy, white; ovary surrounded by a thick fleshy disk, 4-lobed; style inserted between the lobes (gyno-basic); fruit of 4 small nutlets (family *Labiatae*).

This species is very similar to the common *Dead Nettle* (fig. 687), but with a peculiar almost white band down the middle of the leaves, a beautiful mauve corolla with mottled lower lip, and the hairs inside the base of the tube in a horizontal (not oblique) ring. It is not considered to be a truly wild species, having escaped from gardens and become naturalized, though it is comparatively rare.

Nectar is secreted by the fleshy base of the ovary and stored at the bottom of the corolla-tube. The hairs at the base of the tube serve as a nectar-cover. The helmet-like upper lip shelters the anthers, and the lower lip forms a convenient alighting platform for insect visitors. On account of the corolla-tube the nectar is accessible only to long-tongued bees. Humble-bees with pro-boscides too short to reach the nectar perforate the corolla-tube and steal it.

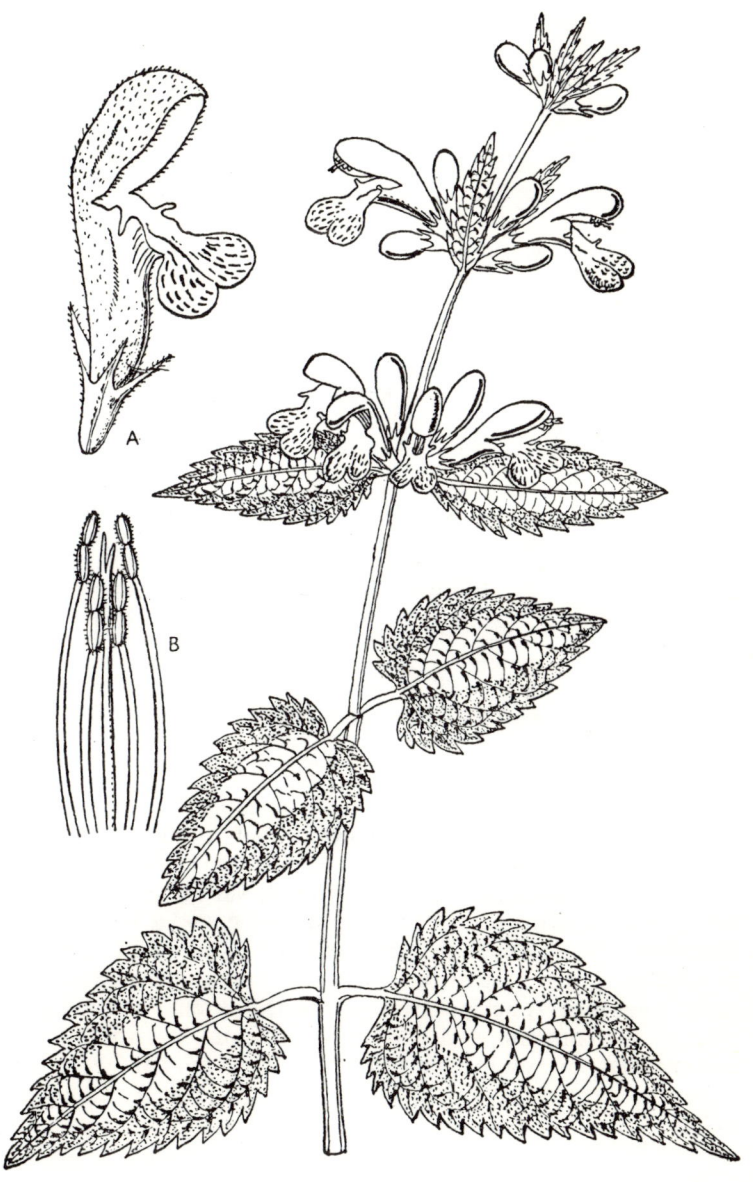

A strong-growing rather densely leafy and hairy perennial; stems square in section, purplish, clothed with short white reflexed hairs; leaves (A, × 1) opposite, petiolate, ovate, coarsely toothed, the teeth with little blunt tips, undulate (bullate), shortly hairy mainly on the nerves below; flowers (B, × 2) in axillary clusters, the clusters very shortly stalked, each flower with 2 or 3 long sharp very narrow bracts (C, × 2) at the base; calyx (C, × 2) green-crimson, funnel-shaped, 5-toothed, 10-ribbed, the teeth ovate, with sharp tips; corolla mauve-purple, 2-lipped, the upper lip at length recurved and villous, the lower 3-lobed, the lateral lobes small and bifid; stamens (D, × 4) 4, a little shorter than the back lip; anther-

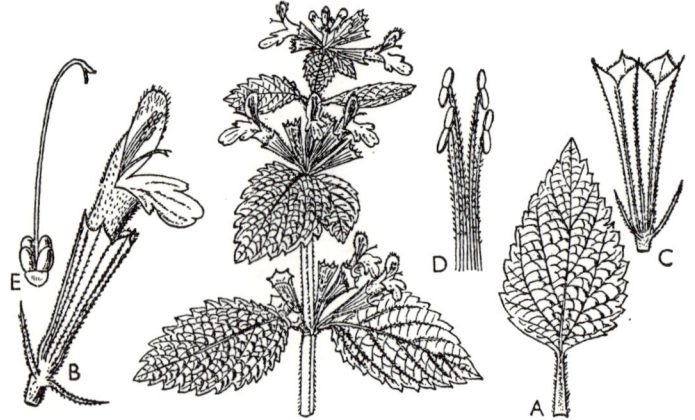

loculi divergent (D, × 4); ovary (E, × 2) deeply 4-lobed with the long slender style between the lobes; nutlets obtusely 3-angled, smooth (family *Labiatae*).

The corolla has a nectar-guide on the lower lip in the form of white lines pointing towards the corolla-tube, and a longitudinal furrow on the lip serves as a guide for the proboscis. The nectar is secreted by the base of the ovary and stored at the bottom of the corolla-tube. A nectar-cover is provided by stiff hairs as a protection, not from rain, as the flower is horizontal, but from nectar-seeking flies, preventing their broad proboscides from entering. After the anthers have shed their pollen the style bends downwards away from them.

Stachys sylvatica L. ($\times \frac{1}{2}$)

Perennial; rootstock with stolons; stem stout, quadrangular, up to 4 ft. high, rather densely hispid with whitish stiff hairs; leaves very much like those of the common stinging nettle, the basal ones sometimes as large; stem leaves opposite, stalked, broadly ovate, cordate at the base, with a broad triangular apex, averaging about

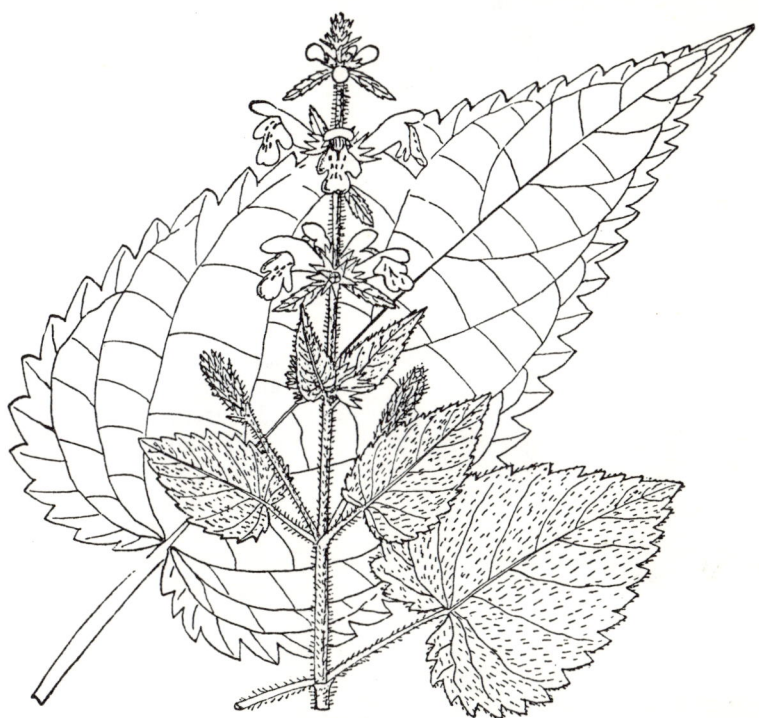

$2\frac{1}{2}$ in. long, very coarsely toothed (dentate), clothed with rather long stiffish hairs; flowers in whorls of about 6 to 10, the upper becoming more crowded, the leaves gradually reduced to bracts; calyx equally 5-lobed, lobes triangular, acute, glandular hairy outside; corolla dark reddish-purple, 2-lipped, upper lip forming a hood over the stamens and undivided, lower lip 3-lobed, the middle lobe notched; tube contracted and with a ring of hairs inside near the base; stamens 4, under the upper lip; filaments hairy; ovary deeply 4-lobed, with the style between the lobes; nutlets smooth, rounded at the top (family *Labiatae*).

A nettle-like perennial herb with tall stout quadrangular stems clothed on the angles with short reflexed hairs; leaves sessile or

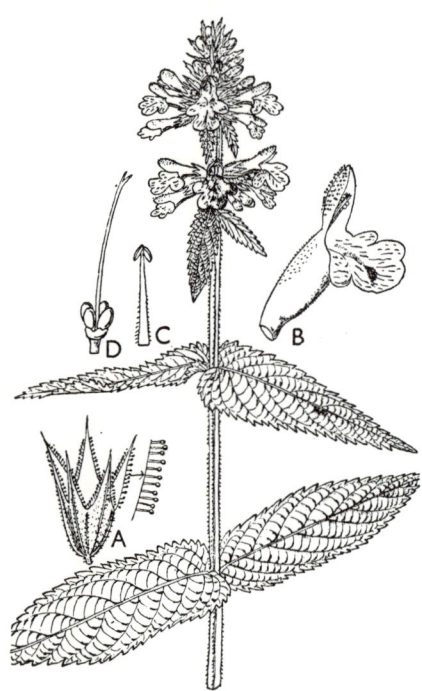

nearly so, oblong-lanceolate, rounded at the base, with a narrow triangular point, crenate-serrate, slightly bullate, covered with soft short hairs on both surfaces; lateral nerves about 6 pairs, prominent below; flowers collected at the top into a short pyramidal spike with reduced bract-like leaves, about 3 or 4 in the axil of each bract and sessile; calyx (A, × I) top-shaped, equally 5-lobed, lobes very sharply pointed and margined with gland-tipped hairs (A, ×6); corolla (B, ×1) mauve-pink mottled with crimson, 2-lipped, the upper 'ip with gland-tipped hairs on the back, the lower lip 3-lobed; stamens (C, ×1) 4, surrounding the stigma under the upper lip; style (D, ×1) inserted between the 4 lobes of the ovary (gynobasic); nutlets obtuse (family *Labiatae*).

Grows in ditches and on moist banks, flowering in summer and autumn; widely distributed in the north temperate zone.

Nectar is secreted by the base of the ovary and stored in the smooth lowest part of the corolla-tube. The upper lip not only shelters the anthers and stigma in bad weather, but also protects the nectar from rain. A circlet of hairs inside the corolla-tube just above the base also protects the nectar, and keeps away unbidden guests, such as flies. The lower lip provides a convenient platform.

Stachys officinalis (L.) Trevis (×⅓)

Perennial; stems 1–2 ft. high, erect, obtusely 4-angled, hairy, the hairs curved downwards; basal leaves on long hairy stalks, lanceolate, cordate at the base, averaging about 4 in. long and 1½ in. broad, bullate, rather coarsely toothed, the teeth rounded, hairy mainly on the nerves below; stem-leaves opposite, in 2 rows, the uppermost nearly sessile, smaller than but otherwise similar to the basal leaves; flowers densely crowded in the axils of the uppermost pair of leaves and the remainder crowded into a bracteate oblong spike; calyx equally 5-lobed, lobes crimson with sharp points, hairy on the ribs (A, ×2); corolla (B, ×2) 2-lipped, dark magenta, upper lip ovate, lower with 2 short side-lobes, not spotted; stamens 4, the anthers shortly exserted from the tube

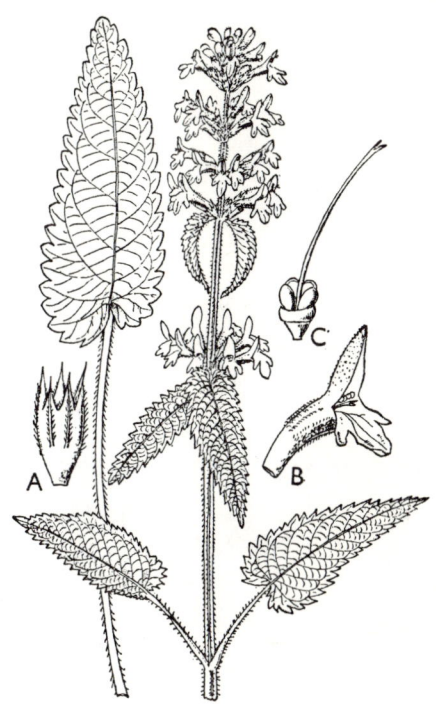

and sheltered by the upper lip; style shortly 2-lobed; ovary (C, ×2) of 4 separate lobes with the style between them (gynobasic) (synonym *Stachys betonica* Benth.) (family *Labiatae*).

This species flowers about the end of June and grows in woods, except in northern Scotland.

Betony was once the sovereign remedy for all kinds of maladies, and a weak infusion is said to form a very acceptable substitute for tea. A pinch of the powdered herb will provoke violent sneezing, and it was formerly used in snuff.

Marrubium vulgare L. ($\times\frac{1}{2}$)

Perennial with short stout rootstock; stems several, 1–1½ ft. high, covered with short woolly hairs; leaves opposite, stalked, ovate,

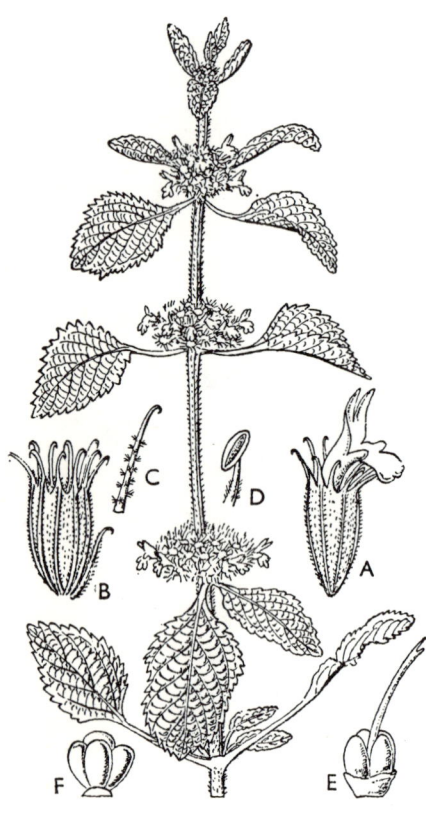

shortly wedge-shaped at the base, reticulate and crinkly (bullate), with rounded teeth, the lower nerves ascending to about the middle of the blade, shortly woolly-hairy on both surfaces; flowers (A, $\times2$) crowded and sessile in clusters at the nodes and forming balls; bracts subulate, with a hooked tip; calyx (B, $\times3$) tubular, 10-ribbed, covered with short clustered hairs outside, fringed with slender hairs inside the mouth, with 10 subulate teeth each ending in a hook (C, $\times4$); corolla white, of united petals and 2-lipped, the upper lip rather deeply cleft (2-lobed) at the apex, the lobes directed vertically upwards, the lower lip unequally 3-lobed, the middle lobe broad and notched; stamens (D, $\times3$) 4, the anthers situated about the middle of the tube; ovary (E, $\times3$) of 4 separate lobes with the short style between (gynobasic); nutlets (F, $\times2$) blunt, smooth (family *Labiatae*).

Waysides and waste places, and locally common; a very distinctive plant recognized at once by the 10 awl-shaped calyx-lobes with hooked points (a unique feature in our native *Labiatae*), and by the white corolla, the upper lobe of which is deeply cleft.

Perennial, with slender creeping rootstock; stems annual, up to about a foot high according to situation, sometimes only a few inches, decumbent at the base and rooting at the nodes; stems square in section, often crimson-tinged, more or less hairy; leaves opposite, shortly stalked, ovate-lanceolate, not pointed at the apex, rather broadly wedge-shaped at the base, with about 3 pairs of lateral nerves and entire or obscurely toothed, thinly covered on both surfaces with several-celled hairs; flowers in short terminal spikes which often lengthen considerably, subtended by a pair of almost sessile leaves, each whorl of flowers in the axils of very broad largely leafy pointed bracts; calyx (A, × 2) 2-lipped, crimson, the upper lip flat and broad, 3-toothed, the lower lip deeply 2-lobed and smaller, with a few longish hairs; corolla (B, × 1$\frac{3}{4}$) violet-purple, 2-lipped, the upper lip erect and hood-like, almost entire, the lower lip spreading and unequally 3-lobed, the middle lobe toothed; stamens (C, × 3) 4, in pairs under the upper lip, each filament produced into a tooth beyond the anther; ovary (D, × 3) vertically and deeply 4-lobed; style slender, shortly 2-lobed; fruit of 4 angular nutlets (family *Labiatae*).

Flowers from late spring until the autumn and grows in fields, banksides, etc.; one of the most widely distributed of our native species, even being found on some of the mountains of the tropics, and showing considerable variation in the size and colour of the flowers.

BASTARD BALM
Melittis melissophyllum L. ($\times\frac{1}{2}$)

Perennial with pale stout roots; stems up to 2 ft. high, square in section, stout, covered with spreading or slightly downwardly directed whitish hairs; leaves opposite, very like those of the common Nettle, ovate, coarsely toothed, wrinkled (bullate), about 3 in. long and 2–2$\frac{1}{2}$ in. broad, with short spreading hairs only on the nerves below, nearly glabrous above; stalks up to 1 in. long, with long hairs; flowers 2–3 in each leaf-axil, shortly stalked, maturing from below upwards and soon forming fruits; calyx (A, $\times1\frac{1}{2}$) 5-toothed, but the upper 2 teeth more or less united, all broadly triangular, clothed outside with long hairs and short papillae, green or tinged with crimson; corolla white except the pale purple lip which is margined with white; tube 1$\frac{1}{2}$ in. long, lip $\frac{3}{4}$ in. long; stamens (B, $\times5$) 4, anthers under the corolla-hood, pale cream, 2-locular, two halves unequal-sized, bearing rows of pearl-like bodies in bud; ovary (C, $\times3$) of 4 white nutlets which are 3-sided, rounded and hairy on the back; style reaching to the anthers (family *Labiatae*).

Specimen drawn from steep roadside east of Looe, in Cornwall, early in June, very local and apparently wild.

The flowers of this plant are very fragrant and markedly pro-tandrous, self-pollination being generally excluded. The corolla-tube is narrowed by two longitudinal folds, to which the filaments are united, and two narrow entrances are formed situated one above the other. Nectar is secreted in a cylindrical swelling under the ovary in such abundance that the corolla-tube is filled with it to a height of 7–10 mm. Visitors are humble-bees and hawk-moths, and there is a white variety, var. *albida* Guss. which seems specially adapted for pollination by hawk-moths.

During dehiscence of the anthers, which are situated in the upper part of the entrance to the flower and open downwards, the style is so short that the still immature stigma lies between the anthers of the short stamens or a little above. Usually it is only after dehiscence or towards the end of it, that the style elongates and curves slightly downwards in such a way that the now mature stigma is brought under the anthers of the longer stamens or a little in front of them.

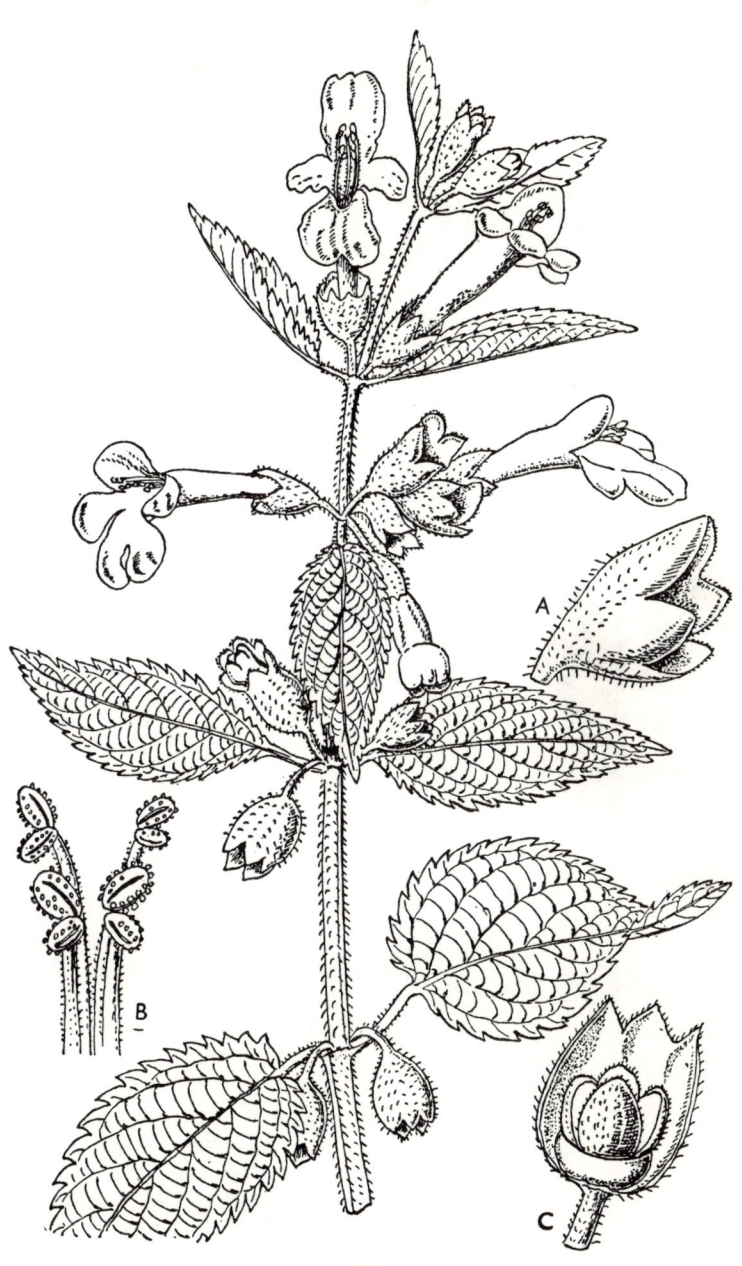

Acinos arvensis (Lam.) Dandy ($\frac{1}{2}$)

Annual in waste places and amongst crops, up to about 9 in. high; stems only slightly angular, covered with recurved hairs; leaves

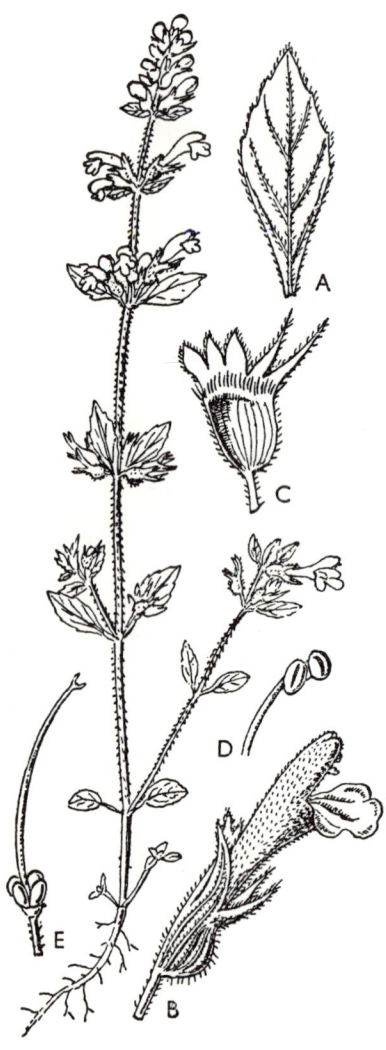

(A, $\times 1\frac{1}{2}$) opposite, ovate, wedge-shaped at the base, slightly and distantly toothed, hairy on the margin and midrib below, with about 3 pairs of lateral nerves, shortly stalked; flowers (B, $\times 2\frac{1}{2}$) about 3 in each leaf-axil, appearing whorled, shortly stalked; calyx (C, $\times 2\frac{1}{2}$) with a fat pouch on the lower side, strongly 10-ribbed, 2-lipped, the upper lip with 3 broadly triangular short lobes, the lower with two slender awl-shaped lobes, all fringed with hairs; corolla violet-mauve, white at the base of the lower lip, up to twice as long as the calyx, upper lip slightly 2-lobed, lower lip broadly 3-lobed, with two lines of hairs on the 'tongue', hairy all over the outside; stamens (D, $\times 2$) 4, the anthers hidden by the upper lip; style (E, $\times 2\frac{1}{2}$) inserted between the 4 lobes of the ovary seated on a nectary; nutlets smooth (family *Labiatae*). *Calamintha acinos* Scheele

This is a bee-flower with nectar secreted and stored within the base of the corolla-tube. The anthers are mature before the stigmas are receptive.

Clinopodium vulgare L. ($\times \frac{1}{3}$)

Perennial with annual stems up to 2 ft. high and a slender creeping rootstock; stems square in cross-section, densely covered with

soft reflexed or spreading hairs; leaves opposite, shortly stalked, ovate to triangular-ovate, obtuse at the apex, rounded at the base, obscurely toothed, loosely covered on both surfaces with soft spreading hairs; flowers in axillary shortly stalked clusters, each short flower-stalk with a pair of very narrow (subulate) hairy bracts at the base (A, × 2); calyx tubular, with 5 very narrow hairy subequal lobes and about 15 ribs, these clothed with gland-tipped hairs; corolla (B, × 1½) purple-red, nearly twice as long as the calyx, unequally 4-lobed; stamens 4, exserted; ovary (C, × 2) deeply 4-lobed, on a fleshy disk, with the style between the

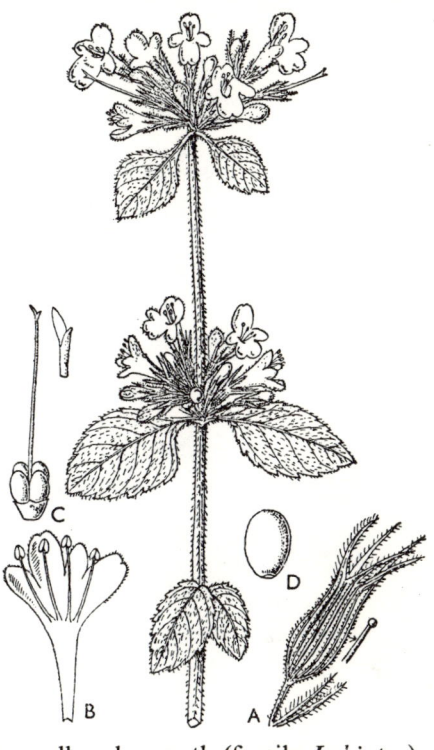

lobes; nutlets (D, × 4) very small and smooth (family *Labiatae*).

This is a bee or humble-bee flower with abundant nectar secreted by the base of the ovary and stored in the base of the corolla-tube even to a height of 3 millimetres. There are 2 kinds of flowers, bisexual and female, sometimes on the same plant (described as *gynomonoecious*!) or on different plants (*gynodioecious*!).*

---

* When first published under the title *Common Wild Flowers*, as few botanical terms as possible were used in the descriptions. However, one correspondent complained in an amusing letter that his enthusiasm for the study of the book had been completely shattered by the few which were introduced and which he could not find in the dictionaries in his local library.

BALM
Melissa officinalis L. ($\times\frac{1}{3}$)

Sweet-scented perennial herb up to 3 ft. high with long straggly branches; stems 4-angled, glabrous below, finely hairy towards the top; leaves long - stalked, ovate, rounded to slightly cordate at the base, the largest about 3 in. long and $2\frac{1}{2}$ in. broad, with numerous smaller cuneate leaves amongst the flowers, all coarsely serrate, thinly hairy on both surfaces or soon glabrous; nerves much branched; flowers in dense shortly stalked axillary clusters accompanied by large leafy bracts; calyx (A, $\times 1$) persistent, tubular, 13-nerved, 2-lipped, upper lip 3-toothed, lower lip bifid; corolla (B, $\times 2$) at first yellowish, afterwards pale-rose or white, 2-lipped, with a few hairs inside, upper lip erect, bifid, lower spreading, 3-lobed; stamens (C, $\times 6$) 4, shorter than the corolla; anther-loculi divergent; ovary (D, $\times 2$) deeply 4-lobed, the style inserted between the lobes; fruit of 4 nuts, these narrowly obovoid, brownish, convex outside, nearly smooth (family *Labiatae*).

Usually found as a garden escape and naturalized in some places; a native of central and south Europe, western Asia, and north Africa.

Slender perennial herb usually about 6 in. high, but occasionally stems a foot long, with rounded angles, glabrous; leaves opposite, shortly stalked, ovate or ovate-oblong, rounded to shallowly cordate at the base, rounded at the apex, at most about 1 in. long and $\frac{1}{2}$ in. broad, entire or with a few teeth towards the base, very slightly hairy; flowers (A, $\times 2\frac{1}{2}$) axillary, solitary; calyx bell-shaped, 2-lipped, lobes rounded, pubescent, the tube with a hump

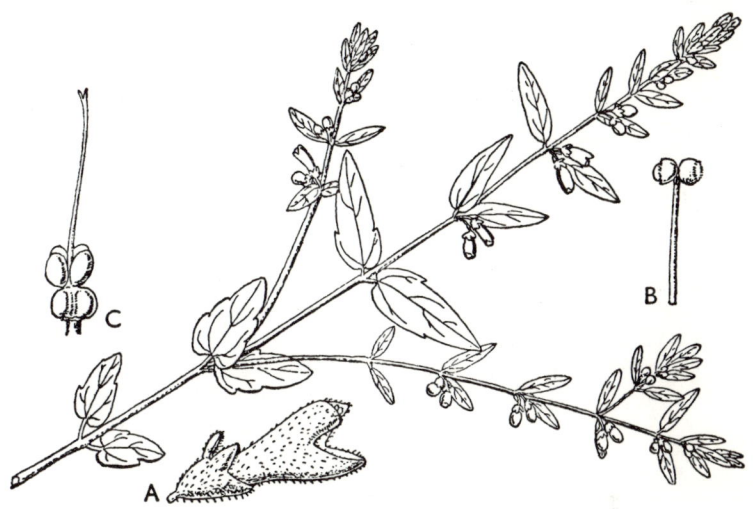

on the back; corolla pale pink or violet, about $\frac{1}{3}$ in. long, 2-lipped, hairy outside; stamens (B, $\times 2\frac{1}{2}$) 4, the divergent anther-loculi hidden under the upper lip of the corolla; ovary (C, $\times 3$) deeply 4-lobed, inserted on a rounded nectariferous disk, with the slender style between the lobes (family *Labiatae*).

Grows on moist heaths and in boggy places, sometimes penetrating into woods.

The genus *Scutellaria* much resembles some members of the family *Scrophulariaceae*, but the deeply lobed ovary and gynobasic style serve at once to distinguish it from that group. The second British species is shown in fig. 702.

SKULLCAP
Scutellaria galericulata L. ($\times \frac{2}{3}$)

Perennial with creeping rootstock, flowering from July to September; stems usually about 9 in. to 1 ft. high, erect, square in section,

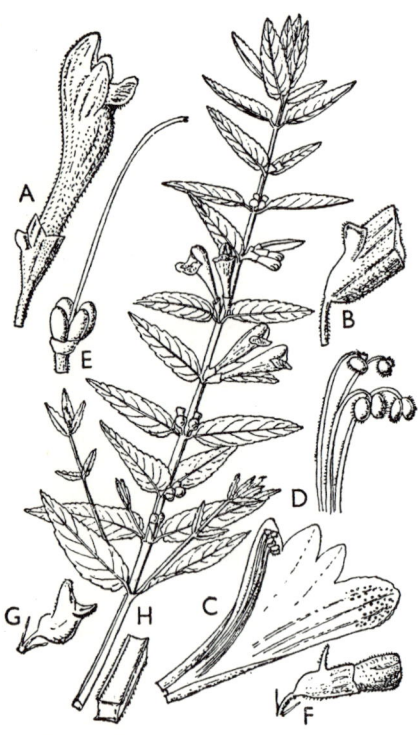

the edges covered with minute downwardly directed hairs (H, $\times 2$); leaves opposite, very shortly stalked, lanceolate, heart-shaped (cordate) at the base, $1-1\frac{1}{2}$ in. long, rather wrinkled (bullate), crenate, very minutely hairy on the margin and nerves below; a distinct ridge between the leaf-stalks; flowers (A, $\times 2$) borne towards one side of the stem, solitary, axillary, only a few out at one time, stalks with 2 very narrow bracteoles near the base, shorter than the tubular slightly 2-lipped calyx, the latter with a large leafy outgrowth on the back (B, $\times 3$); corolla mauve-blue, $\frac{1}{2}$ in. long, covered with soft white hairs, 2-lipped, the upper lip concealing the stamens, the lower forming a platform and beautifully mottled with deep-blue spots (C, corolla opened out, $\times 2$); stamens (D, $\times 3$) 4, the longer 2 with only 1 perfect anther-lobe (loculus), the shorter 2 with 2 perfect lobes, lobes hairy; ovary of 4 rounded separate lobes (E, $\times 2\frac{1}{2}$), supported on a fleshy disk; style slender; nutlets granular, enclosed in the calyx (family *Labiatae*).

In the bud stage the flowers recall an old and very short blunderbuss or highwayman's pistol, the process on the top of the calyx representing the hammer (F, $\times 2$). In the fruiting stage the calyx assumes the shape of an ugly duckling (G, $\times 1\frac{1}{2}$).

A familiar waterside plant, generally distributed in England and Wales; locally common in Scotland and rather local in Eire. It also grows in shady places in damp woods and in bogs and marshes.

Teucrium scorodonia L. ($\times \frac{2}{3}$)

Perennial with a creeping rootstock; 4-angled softly hairy stems up to 2 ft. high; leaves shortly stalked, ovate to oblong-lanceolate, cordate at the base, with a short triangular apex, $1\frac{1}{2}$–2 in. long, coarsely toothed, markedly wrinkled (bullate), hairy, closely and minutely glandular below; flowers (A, $\times 1\frac{1}{4}$) in slender terminal

racemes, all forming a loose panicle with the flowers all to one side; upper leaves gradually reduced to bracts; each leafy bract with a single flower in its axil; stalks very short; calyx (B, $\times 1\frac{1}{3}$) unequally 5-toothed, the upper tooth broad and ovate, turned back, strongly nerved in fruit, with a ring of long deflexed several-celled hairs inside (F, enlarged); corolla yellow (C, $\times 1\frac{1}{4}$) 1-lipped, lip unequally 5-lobed folded over the stamens within the tube; stamens (D, $\times 10$) 4, inserted half-way down the tube, anther-lobes opening by one continuous slit; ovary deeply 4-lobed; nectariferous disk large and cupular (family *Labiatae*).

COMMON BUGLE
Ajuga reptans L. (×⅖)

Perennial, the rootstock producing elongated runner-like stolons; flowering stems erect, unbranched, pubescent with weak white hairs, especially in a line below and between the leaf-bases; lower leaves obovate to oblanceolate, rounded at the apex, and with wavy margins, very slightly pubescent; upper leaves becoming sessile and gradually shortening into coloured bracts, obovate to

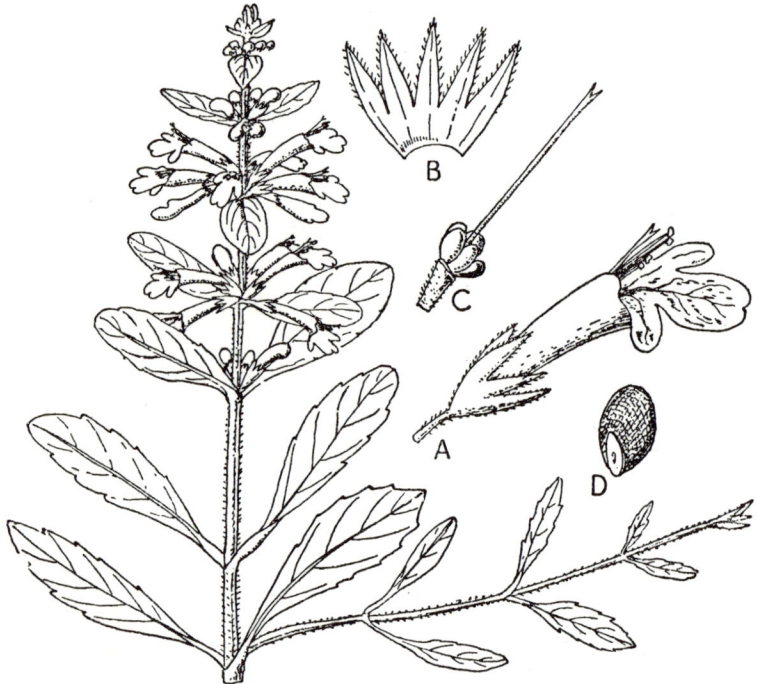

oblanceolate, with wavy or obscurely toothed margins; flowers (A, × 3) in close whorls in the axils of most of the leaves, nearly sessile, the upper ones forming a slightly interrupted spike-like inflorescence; calyx (B, × 3) equally 5-lobed to about the middle, fringed with jointed hairs; corolla blue, or rarely pink or white, marked with brighter coloured lines, 1-lipped, lip spreading and 3-lobed, the middle lobe largest; stamens 4, anthers exserted; ovary deeply lobed, with a large fleshy gland in front (C, × 3); style exserted, 2-fid; nutlets reticulate, with a large lateral scar (family *Labiatae*). Grows in fields and grassy open spaces in woods, sometimes in deep shade.

A coarse-growing annual up to about $2\frac{1}{2}$ ft. high, with a succulent stem thickened below the nodes, more or less branched, and clothed with very stiff jointed bristly hairs especially below the nodes, and with here and there a few shorter gland-tipped hairs (A, $\times 1\frac{1}{4}$); leaves fairly long-stalked, ovate to ovate-lanceolate, rounded to wedge-shaped at the base, broadly pointed at the top, coarsely

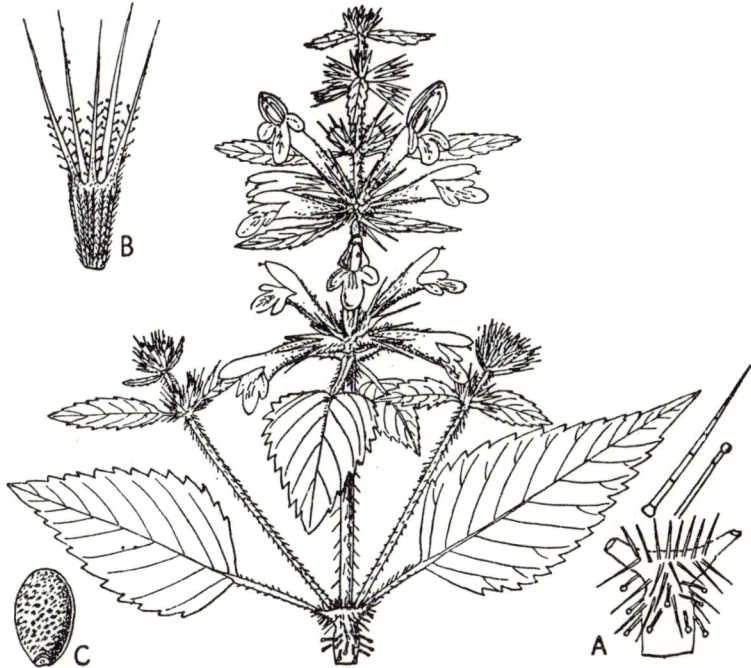

toothed (crenate-serrate) (except the rounded base), clothed with scattered long stiff hairs especially on the upper surface; flowers arranged in dense clusters in the axils of the upper leaves and leafy bracts, sessile; calyx (B, $\times 2\frac{1}{4}$) ribbed, divided into 5 equal long very sharp prickle-like lobes, pubescent outside; corolla pale purple or white, with a narrow very pubescent tube and markedly 2-lipped, the upper lip suberect, entire, the lower lip spreading and 3-lobed; stamens 4, in pairs under the upper lip; anthers bordered with minute hairs; ovary deeply lobed; nutlets (C, $\times 2\frac{1}{4}$) obovoid, brown, sprinkled with a paler lace-like layer (family *Labiatae*).

Galeopsis speciosa Mill. ($\times\frac{1}{3}$)

A coarse-growing annual with nettle-like leaves, up to $2\frac{1}{2}$ ft. high; stems erect, clothed with downwardly directed bristly hairs; leaves opposite, stalked, ovate-elliptic, broadly wedge-shaped at the base, pointed at the apex, about $3\frac{1}{2}$ in. long and 2 in. broad, serrate, with about a dozen pairs of lateral nerves, pilose all over the upper surface but mainly on the nerves below; flowers in clusters in the upper leaf-axils; bracts leafy; calyx (A, $\times1$) tubular, with 5 long spine-like lobes; corolla 2-lipped, yellow with a violet lower lip, upper lip forming a hood over the stamens and style, hairy; stamens (B, $\times2\frac{1}{2}$) 4; anthers with 2 ovate loculi opening by a horse-shoe-shaped slit; ovary (C, $\times2\frac{1}{2}$) of 4 separate carpels with the style between, and expanded at

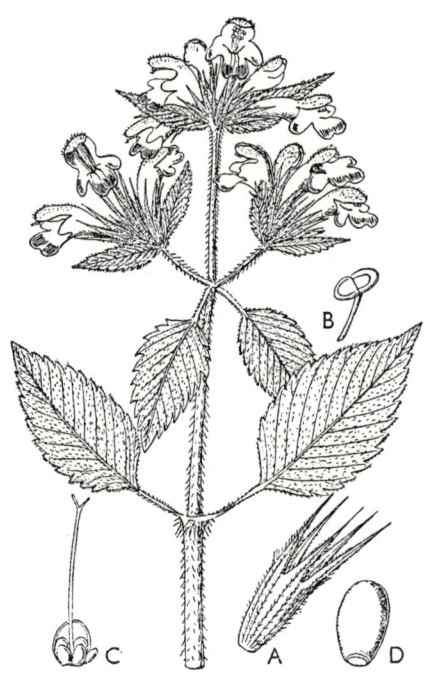

the base into a very large rounded nectary; nutlets (D, $\times3$) obovoid, brown, smooth (synonym *Galeopsis versicolor* Curt.) (family *Labiatae*).

Closely related to *Galeopsis tetrahit* (fig. 705), but flowers yellow with a dark violet lower lip. The upper lip of the corolla forms a roof over the anthers, while the lower lip makes a platform and is provided with 2 lateral lobes which guide the head of a bee visitor. Nectar is secreted in a broad rounded scale at the base of the ovary (C, $\times2\frac{1}{2}$).

Annual herb up to about 1 ft. high and branched in the lower half; stem obtusely 4-angled, with brown tumor-like swelling at the lower nodes, clothed with short white downwardly directed hairs; lower leaves stalked, upper less so, all lanceolate, narrowed to each end, about 2 in. long and $\frac{1}{2}$ in. broad, with two or three blunt teeth on each side, or the upper ones entire or nearly so, shortly hairy mostly on the margin and nerves below; flowers (A, $\times 1$) densely clustered in the leaf-axils (about 8–10 in each axil in the middle of the stem) but not all out at the same time in each cluster; bracts leafy and recurved with sharp tips; calyx nearly $\frac{1}{3}$ in. long, tube with 5 green ribs and several more obscure intermediate ribs; teeth 5, almost equal, very sharply pointed; corolla mauve or purplish mauve, more than twice as long as the calyx, 2-lipped, lower lip 3-lobed and broadly streaked with white, tube hairy outside; stamens 4, the outer two longer than the inner and partially hidden under the corolla-hood; anthers opening by transverse slits, with hairy 'tongues' inside (see figs. B, C); ovary of 4 separate carpels (D, $\times \frac{2}{3}$) with a slender style from their middle; nutlets (E, $\times 2$) 3-sided in fruit (family *Labiatae*).

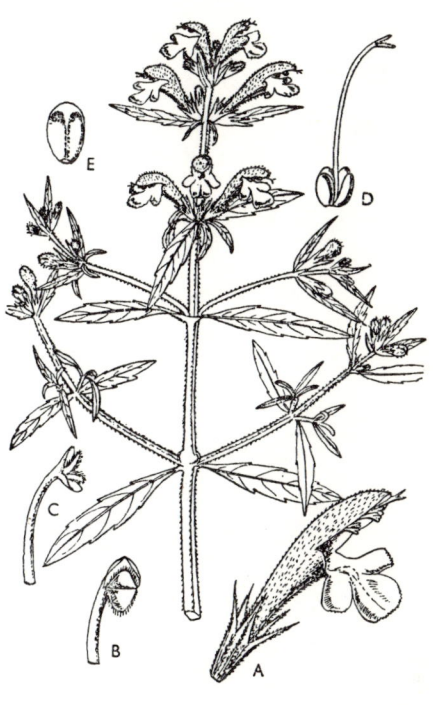

Sometimes common in arable land; widely distributed in Europe.

Lycopus europaeus L. ($\times\frac{1}{2}$)

A tall perennial with the habit of mint; rootstock creeping; stems up to 3 ft. high, erect, very slightly hairy; leaves nearly sessile, op-

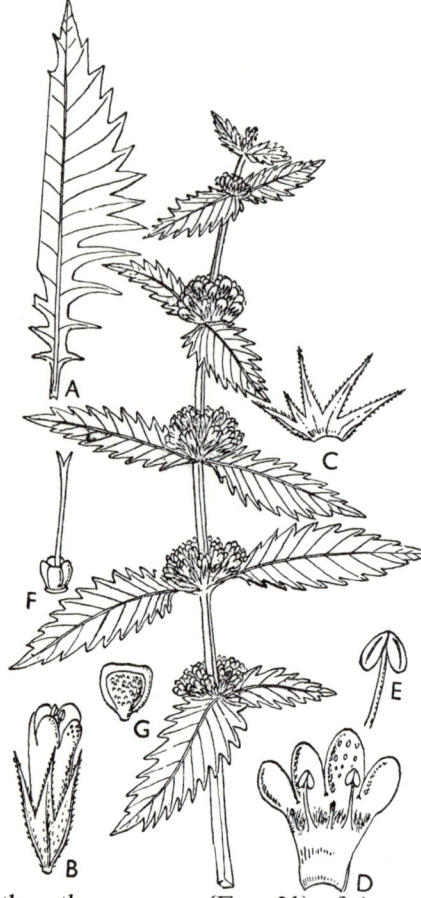

posite, all coarsely tooth-ed or lobulate, the lower pinnately divided near the base almost to the midrib (A, $\times\frac{1}{2}$), glandular-pitted on the lower surface, otherwise nearly glabrous; lateral nerves several, prominent below, ending in the teeth; flowers (B, $\times 2\frac{1}{2}$) bisexual or female, numerous, sessile, in dense axillary clusters; calyx (C, $\times 2$) 5-lobed, lobes narrowly triangu-lar, with rigid very sharp points; corolla (D, $\times 2\frac{1}{2}$) bluish-white, dotted with purple, scarcely longer than the calyx-lobes, nearly equally 4-lobed and almost quite regular (actinomorphic), the inner surface of the tube cov-ered with vertical hairs protecting the nectar from rain; stamens 2, shortly exserted from the corolla; anthers (E, $\times 7$) with 2 divergent loculi; vestiges of two stamens between the others; ovary (F, $\times 2\frac{1}{2}$) of 4 very blunt lobes; style inserted between the lobes of the ovary (gynobasic), 2-lobed; nutlets (G, $\times 2\frac{1}{2}$) truncate with thickened margins (family *Labiatae*).

The flowers may be bisexual or female, the latter generally be-ing smaller. Nectar-guides in the form of red spots on the lower lip are provided, the nectar being secreted by the large fleshy base of the ovary. This is accessible to very short-tongued insects, as the corolla-tube is short and wide.

Salvia verbenaca L. ($\times \frac{1}{3}$)

Perennial, with a woody rootstock; stem up to about 2 ft., erect and rigid, square, softly pubescent; lower leaves long-stalked, ob-

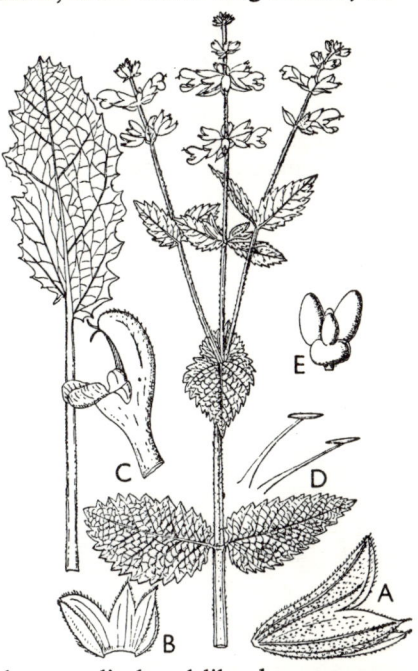

long or elliptic, irregularly serrate or sometimes coarsely pinnately lobed; stalks tinged with crimson; stem-leaves opposite, sessile, ovate, rounded or slightly cordate at the base, triangular or ovately pointed, coarsely dentate with ovate teeth, bullate - reticulate above, very veiny beneath and paler, glabrous or nearly so; upper leaves reduced, acuminate, each with 3 flowers in its axil, forming a whorl of 6 flowers at each node; calyx (A, $\times 2\frac{1}{2}$) 2-lipped, the upper lip of 3 united sepals, the lower of 2 united sepals, but split to the middle (B, $\times 1\frac{1}{2}$), strongly ribbed, gland-dotted between the ribs; corolla (C, $\times 2\frac{1}{2}$) bright blue, 2-lipped, upper lip hood-like, lower scoop-shaped, side-lobes ovate; stamens (D, $\times 3$) 2, hidden under the hood; anthers 1-locular; style with 2 blue exserted branches; ovary (E, $\times 4$) deeply 4-lobed, sometimes 2 of the lobes not bearing seeds, lobes inserted in a large fleshy disk (family *Labiatae*).

Clary grows in dry fields, by the roadsides, and in waste places; fairly common in England, but rare in Scotland, and in Eire is confined to the south; it flowers from late spring until autumn. It is widely distributed into north Africa and western Asia. The seeds when soaked in water form a thick mucilage, which was formerly used as an eye-wash.

An aquatic perennial with a thick horizontally creeping rootstock
and numerous rather thick fibrous roots; leaves long and narrow,
and narrowly sheathing at the base, closely lined by slender nerves
lengthwise and with a distinct thicker midrib; flowering stem leafless, up to 4 ft. high, bearing at the top and high above the water
an umbel of 20–30 pretty pink flowers; umbel with an involucre
of 3 large triangular pointed bracts, slightly ribbed by several
nerves lengthwise; a few smaller bracts among the flower-stalks;
flower-stalks (pedicels) 3–4 in. long; perianth of 6 parts in 2

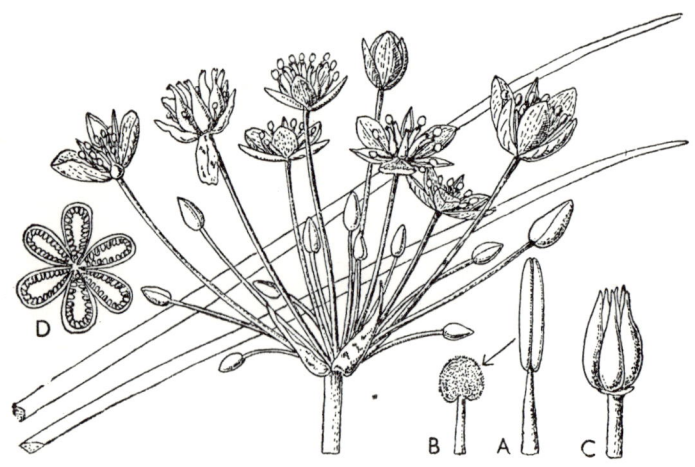

whorls, all petal-like, overlapping in bud; stamens (A, × 2) 9,
with long anthers in bud becoming rounded after opening (B,
× 2); carpels (C, × 2) 6, free, narrowed into a short style, each
with numerous ovules spread over the inside of the carpellary
wall (D, × 4); seeds numerous and very small (family *Butomaceae*).

The stamens as well as the carpels are red and help to make the
flower conspicuous. Of the 9 stamens, 6 not superposed on the
petals open first, and their filaments at the same time bend backwards and outwards. When the 6 have withered, the anthers of
the other 3 open, and their filaments remain nearly erect. The carpels now mature and become dark red, the stigmas appearing in
the form of slits, which expand gradually below the pollen-
covered anthers of the 3 stamens. Thus cross- or self-pollination
may take place.

Floating aquatic plant with runners giving off here and there a cluster of leaves and flowers; roots long and submerged, covered with long hairs towards the tips; leaves long-stalked, orbicular or kidney-shaped, deeply cordate at the base, up to about $2\frac{1}{2}$ in. diameter, with a few main nerves converging from the base to the top, glabrous; flowers dioecious, the males 2–3 from a pedunculate spathe, the females solitary from a sessile spathe; sepals 3, pale green, shorter than the 3 free white broadly obovate petals each with a nectariferous scale on the inner surface at the base; stamens (A, $\times 2$) varying in number from 12 to 3; anthers 2-locu-

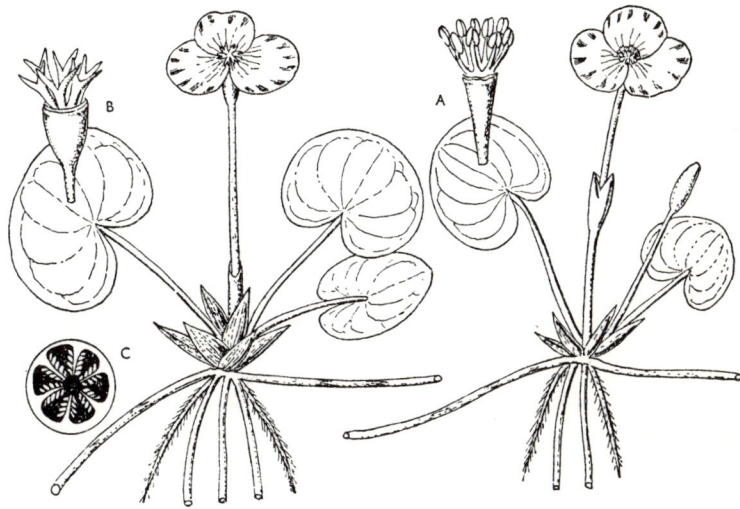

lar; female flower similar to the male but without stamens, and with an inferior partially 6-locular ovary and 6 bilobed styles (B, $\times 2$); ovules (C, $\times 5$) numerous on the dividing walls which do not reach the middle; fruit rather fleshy, not opening, with several seeds (family *Hydrocharitaceae*).

In ditches and ponds, widely distributed in Europe and Asia, flowering in summer. Though the flowers are of one sex, each kind sometimes shows vestiges of the opposite sex, i.e. in the male the rudiments of a pistil, in the female rudiments of stamens. The pollen grains are yellow and beset with spines which cause them to cling to one another and to the walls of the anthers for a time. Honey-bees visit the flowers.

Vallisneria spiralis L. ($\times\frac{1}{2}$)

Perennial aquatic herb rooting in the mud and sand, bearing stolons; leaves grass-like, floating, narrowly linear, thin, 5-nerved, obtuse, sometimes serrate near the apex, the two marginal nerves faint; male flowers (A, $\times\frac{1}{2}$) with a 2–3-lobed spathe on a short scape, numerous, nearly sessile; perianth 3-lobed; stamens 1–3, usually 2; female flowers (B, $\times\frac{1}{2}$) on a very long flexuous or spiral stalk, with a tubular 2-cleft 1-flowered spathe; calyx-tube adnate to the ovary, 3-lobed and with 3 small petals; ovary inferior, 1-locular, with 3 parietal placentas; stigmas 3, nearly sessile, short, broad, 2-toothed; ovules numerous, borne all over the ovary-wall; fruit elongated-cylindric, crowned with the persistent calyx (*Hydrocharitaceae*).

Widely spread in the warmer parts of the world; introduced into some of the western counties of England.

An aquatic plant which grows in still waters and is widely distributed in southern Europe. It lives under the water, with creeping stems attached to the mud by root-fibres. The flowers are unisexual (dioecious), the males numerous in each spathe, the female solitary in its spathe. The male flower-buds become detached from their stalk at the bottom of the water, and float to the top by means of the three concave segments of the calyx. There, when open, they come in contact with the stigmas of the female flowers already elevated to the surface by long peduncles, and pollination is effected. After pollination the female flower is drawn down by the spirally coiled peduncle and the fruit is then developed a little above the muddy bottom of the water. (The interested student should read the detailed account of this wonderful plant in Kerner's *Natural History of Plants* referred to on p. 742.)

Stratiotes aloides L. (×⅓)

Aquatic floating stoloniferous herb much resembling a small *Aloe* (hence the name) or more so the tuft of leaves at the top of a pine-apple; leaves in a rosette, broadly linear, acute, up to 1 ft. long and 1¼ in. broad, with 3–5 parallel main nerves and with sharp teeth on the margin; flowers dioecious or very rarely bisexual, sometimes all male in one district and sometimes all female in another; peduncles axillary, elevated above the water at flowering time, bearing 2 free bracts at the top about 1 in. long; male flowers (A, ×⅓) several within

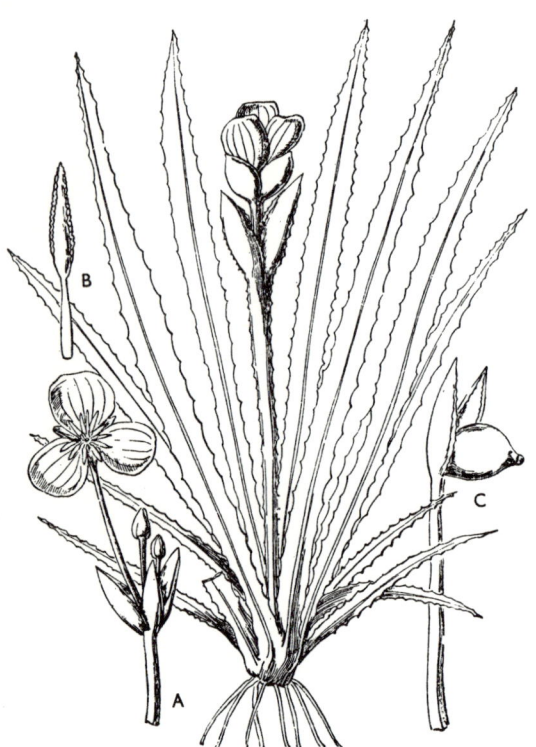

the bracts, stalked; sepals 3, green; petals 3, white, suborbicular; stamens (B, ×2) 12, with about 15–30 nectariferous staminodes; female flowers like the male but sessile within the bracts, without stamens but with similar staminodes; ovary inferior, partially 6-locular, each placenta with several ovules; style short, stigmas 6, each bifid; fruit (C, ×⅓) (not known to be produced in Britain) ovoid, bent at a right angle from the stalk; seeds few (family *Hydrocharitaceae*).

This interesting plant grows in fens, ponds, and ditches, especially in chalky districts. Plants sink to the bottom of the water in autumn, where they pass the winter safe from frost, suckers rising from it in spring.

Damasonium alisma Mill. ($\times \frac{2}{3}$)

Annual, often growing in small clumps, up to 1 ft. high; leaves all basal, long-stalked, the blades oblong-elliptic, cordate at the base, rounded at the apex, traversed lengthwise by 3 parallel nerves; flowers (A, $\times \frac{4}{5}$) in several whorls at intervals on the main stalk (peduncle); pedicels up to $1\frac{1}{2}$ in. long, each cluster of flowers subtended by 3 membranous bracts lined with parallel nerves; sepals (B, $\times 2\frac{1}{2}$) 3, green, nerved, hooded at the apex; petals (C, $\times 1\frac{1}{2}$) 3, white, yellow at the base, rounded-obovate; stamens (D, $\times 2$) 6; anthers light green; carpels (E, $\times 1\frac{1}{2}$) normally 6, free, each with 2 ascending ovules from the base (F, $\times 2$), in fruit (G, $\times \frac{4}{5}$) united at the base, spreading star-like and

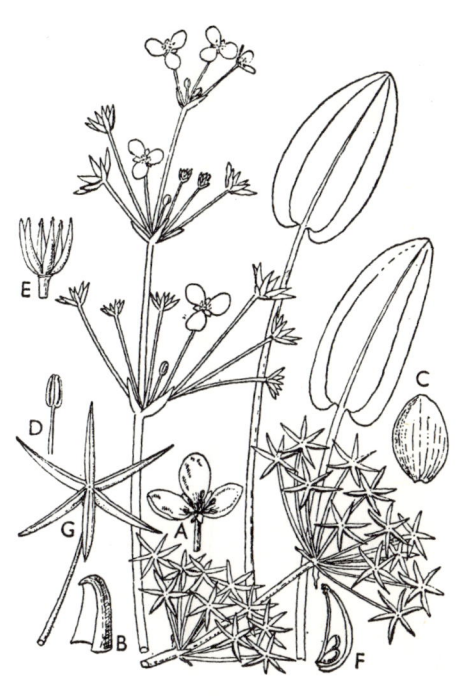

sharply beaked (synonym *Damasonium stellatum* Pers.) (family *Alismataceae*).

The flowers of this distinctive and interesting plant are very similar to those of *Alisma plantago-aquatica* L. (fig. 715) but with only 6 carpels, which become united at the base in the fruiting stage. It is found in south-eastern England, and is diminishing; elsewhere distributed south through Atlantic Europe into north Africa and east to Syria and Egypt.

Damasonium is one of the most advanced (highly evolved) genera of the family, which is closely related to the Buttercup family *Ranunculaceae*. This is because the carpels in *Damasonium* are united into a single whorl and not free and in several whorls as in the others, such as *Baldellia* shown in fig. 717, which looks quite like a 3-petalled buttercup.

Alisma plantago-aquatica L. ($\times \frac{2}{5}$)

Aquatic herb, erect and growing in the mud at the bottom of the water; rootstock perennial, bulb-like with the thickened bases of the leaf-stalks; leaves all from the base but with their blades mostly clear of the water, long-stalked, the normally well-developed more or less elliptic-ovate, bluntly pointed at the apex, mostly rounded and somewhat unequal-sided at the base, entire, with a broad flat midrib and 3 or 4 marked longitudinal nerves running parallel from the base to the apex; transverse nerves numerous, conspicuous, rather oblique; flowers small and numerous in a large lax much-branched pyramidal panicle; bracts lanceolate, acute, in whorls; stalks slender, in little clusters; sepals 3, green; petals 3, quite distinct from the sepals, a delicate pale rose colour; stamens (A, $\times 1\frac{1}{4}$) 6; carpels (B, $\times 2$) numerous, small, and 1-seeded, arranged in a single ring on a broad flat axis (C, $\times \frac{3}{4}$) (family *Alismataceae*).

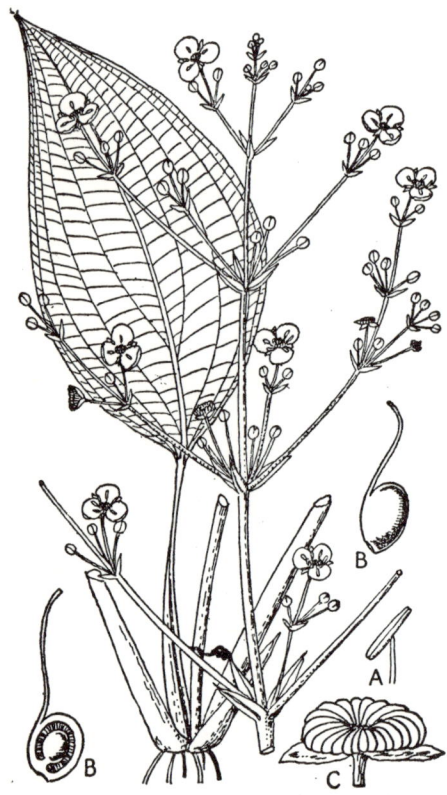

Attention is called in the description of the Spearwort Buttercup (fig. 226) to the close relationship between the family *Alismataceae* and the *Ranunculaceae*. This is evident if the flowers and fruits are compared, in both families there being free sepals, petals, and stamens, and several or numerous free carpels. *Alismataceae* is therefore of great botanical interest as it shows a link between the two groups, *Dicotyledons* and *Monocotyledons*.

Aquatic perennial with milky juice and with creeping rootstock, with bulb-like tubers; leaves rising above the water on long 3-sided stalks, arrow-shaped (sagittate), the 2 'barbs' almost as long as the end lobe, the latter with 3 main parallel nerves; flowers arranged in distant whorls of 3, each pedicel with a thin triangular bract at the base, upper flowers usually male, lower female on shorter stalks; sepals 3, ovate, deeply saccate, rather crimson and lined with closely parallel nerves; petals 3, broad and rounded, white, crimson at the base; stamens (A, ×4) about 25; anthers dark brown, sagittate; carpels (B, ×7) few in the male flowers, very numerous in the females, free from one another (apocarpous), arranged on a large fleshy axis (C, ×1), each with a single erect ovule (family *Alismataceae*).

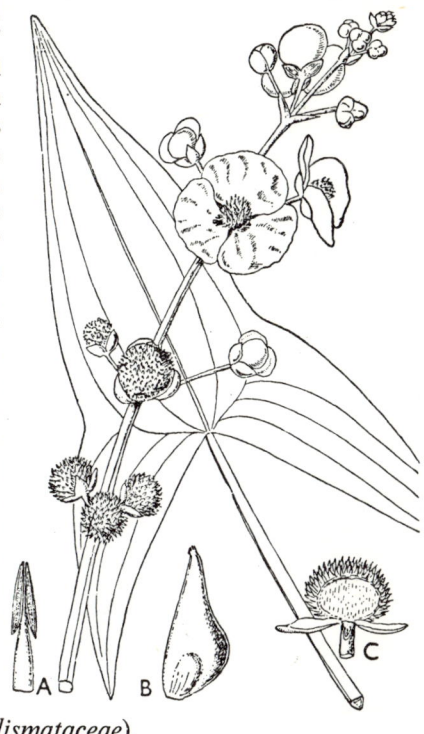

This water-plant is easily recognized by its handsome white flowers over an inch in diameter, the upper ones being male, with numerous stamens and few abortive carpels; the females have much shorter stalks and very numerous carpels. When the individual flower-stalks are cut, a white juice exudes from parts of the section.

The flowers are unisexual, but both sexes are found on the same plant. The females are smaller than the male, and the white petals have a red nectar-guide at their base. The females are mature before the males. The anthers of the latter are of a beautiful dark-brown colour and open at the side.

Baldellia ranunculoides (L.) Parl.($\times\frac{1}{2}$)

Herb with slender fibrous roots; stems up to about 1 ft. high; leaves few and all radical, long-petiolate, the petiole marked with transverse veins, the blade narrowly lanceolate, narrowed to each end, about $2\frac{1}{2}$–3 in. long and up to $\frac{1}{2}$ in. broad, with 3 parallel nerves lengthwise and a few side nerves between them; flowers several in a terminal whorl or sometimes 2 whorls, with slender stalks up to 3 in. long, nearly 1 in. in diam.; sepals (A, $\times$2) 3, rounded, greenish; petals (B, $\times$2) 3, very broadly obovate, white tinged with pink and a basal yellow blotch; stamens (C, $\times$2) 6, free; anthers ellipsoid; carpels (D, $\times2\frac{1}{2}$) numerous, free, irregularly arranged on a large globose axis, beaked (E, $\times$6) and with 4 or 5 strong nerves; seed (F, $\times$6) brownish, muriculate, with a large much bent embryo but no endosperm (family *Alismataceae*). – Synonym *Echinodorus ranunculoides* (L.) Englem.

In wet ditches and marshy places, flowering in summer and autumn; widely distributed in temperate regions of the northern hemisphere.

If insects visit the flowers, cross-pollination may be effected, but if this fails automatic self-pollination is ensured, the six short stamens projecting beyond the stigmas, which mature simultaneously with them and release the pollen.

As noted under *Damasonium* (see fig. 714), the family *Alismatacese*, which belongs to the large group of plants with only one seed-leaf (Monocotyledons), is closely related to the Buttercup family, *Ranunculaceae*, belonging to the group with two seed-leaves (Dicotyledons).

Baldellia is one of the more primitive of the genera of *Alismataceae*, having bisexual flowers and numerous carpels arranged inordinately (no doubt spirally) on a large globose receptacle, after the manner of *Ranunculus*. The genus *Sagittaria* is more advanced with its unisexual flowers, whilst *Luronium* and *Alisma* have the carpels on a very small receptacle, and in the latter they are reduced to a single whorl. *Damasonium*, as already mentioned in fig. 714, is the most advanced genus, at any rate in respect to its carpels, these being also in a single whorl but united at the base.

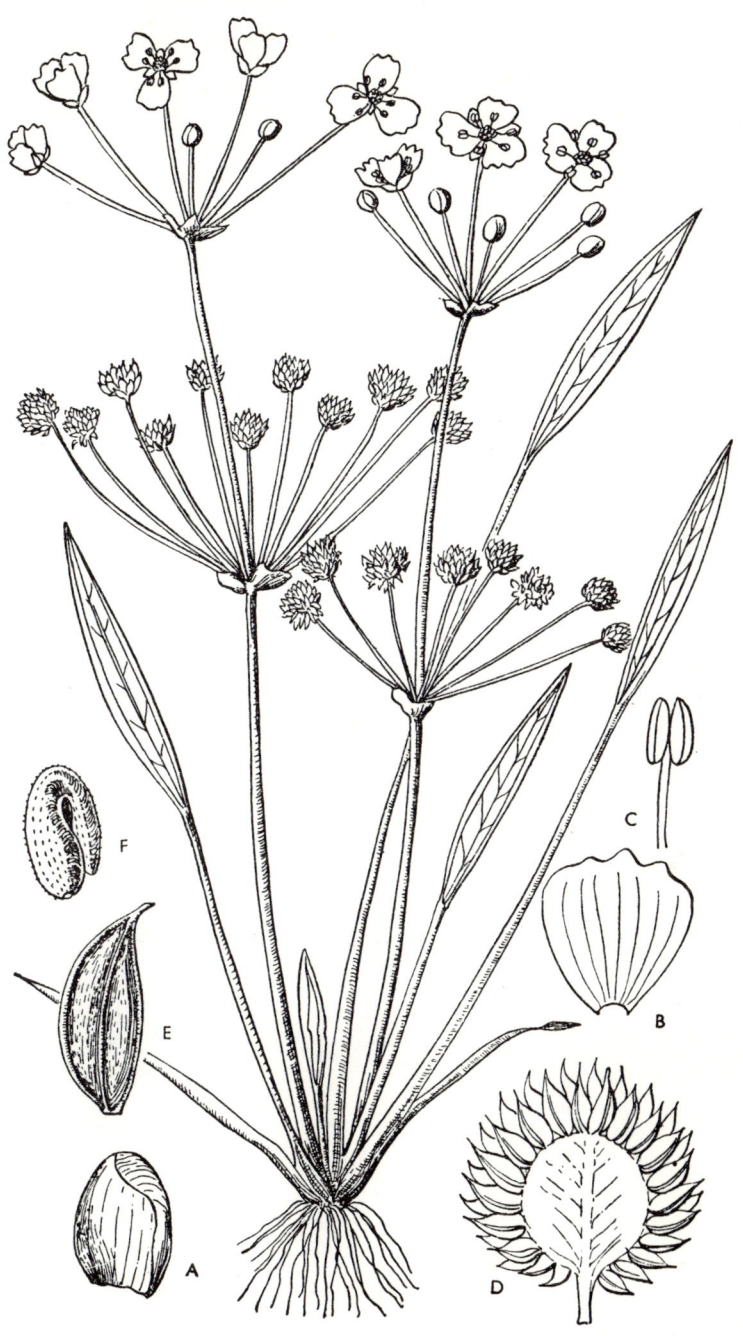

A small rush-like perennial herb up to about 1 ft. high, with a creeping rootstock covered with the membranous sheaths of older leaves; leaves few, grass-like, linear from a long broad membranous sheathing base; bracts about as long as the pedicels; flowers (A, ×2) very few in a loose terminal raceme; perianth slightly coloured, of 6 spreading free segments, the inner three narrower; stamens (B, ×5) 6, anthers large, erect, 2-locular, apiculate; ovary (C, ×5) of 3 or 4 united carpels, 1-locular, ovules few, basal, erect; stigmas as many as carpels, sessile, oblique, papillous; fruit (D, ×½) composed of divergent loculi, dehiscing by the inner margins (family *Scheuchzeriaceae*).

Widely spread across the northern hemisphere, but only in northern Britain, flowering rather early in summer.

830

A tufted herb with a few slender creeping runners; roots slender; leaves several from the base, linear, semi-cylindric, rather succulent, up to about 9 in. long, dilated and rather grass-like at the base, glabrous; flowers (A, ×3) yellowish-green, numerous on a slender raceme up to 1½ ft. high; bracts absent; pedicels very short at first, lengthening in fruit; perianth of 6 nearly equal ovate segments, the outer spreading, inner erect; stamens (B, ×3) 6, opposite the segments; anthers nearly sessile, ovoid, 2-locular; ovary superior, composed of 3 united carpels, with 3 sessile feathery stigmas, 3-locular, with one ovule in each loculus; fruit (C, ×2½) a capsule splitting from the base upwards, the valves hanging from the central axis like the ribs of a half-opened umbrella with sharp tips; seeds (D, ×2½) linear (family *Juncaginaceae*).

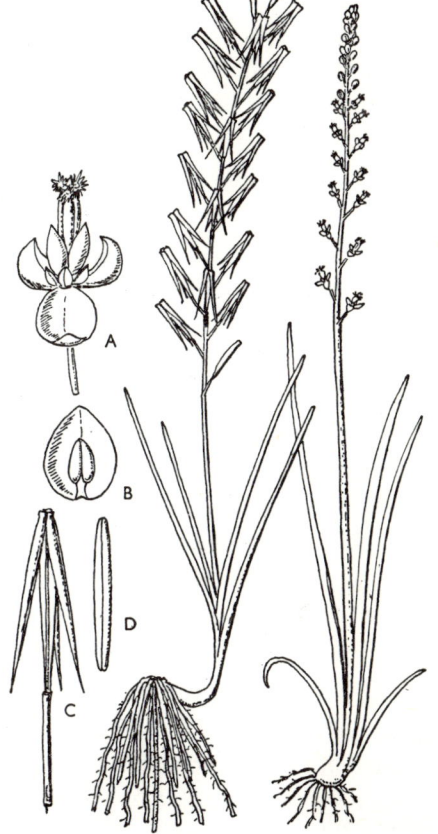

Widely distributed over Britain, in wet meadows and in marshes and by streams, especially in coastal districts; extensively spread in the northern hemisphere.

A second species occurs in Britain, *T. maritima* L., with a 6-locular ovary and fruit, the latter ovoid and oblong.

Potamogeton natans L. ($\times\frac{1}{3}$)

Perennial aquatic herb with a thick rootstock giving off stolons; stem often unbranched; lower submerged leaves linear, gradually passing into broader floating leaves, the latter broadly elliptic, rounded or slightly narrowed into the petiole at the base, rounded or slightly pointed at the tip, $2\frac{1}{2}$–$3\frac{1}{2}$ in. long and $1\frac{1}{2}$–$2\frac{1}{2}$ in. broad, with several principal nerves especially prominent below, these with 2–3 intermediate slender nerves between; stipules often longer than the internodes, with numerous close fibre-like nerves; peduncles longer than the spike, the latter cylindrical densely

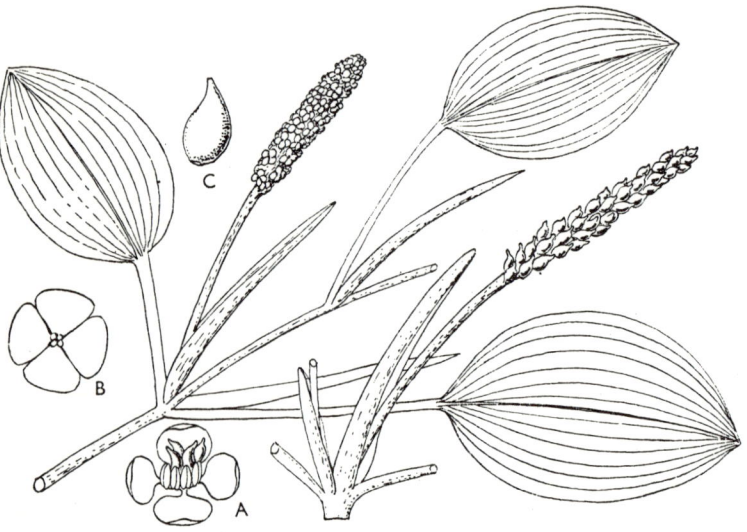

flowered, $1\frac{1}{2}$–2 in. long; flowers (A, B, $\times4$) small; sepals 4, clawed, at first spreading over the adnate sessile anthers and stigmas; carpels (C, $\times2\frac{1}{2}$) 4, obliquely ovoid (family *Potamogetonaceae*).

Widely distributed in temperate and subtropical regions, often common in ponds and backwaters; when in shallow water liable to be dried up in summer, land-forms are produced with a short stem and a tuft of broad leaves with a pair of narrow leaves below.

Potamogeton is the only genus of the family, after which it is named. Most of the species are aquatic, and the bisexual flowers are arranged in pedunculate axillary spikes devoid of bracts except for a sheathing bract at the base of the spike.

Eriocaulon aquaticum (Hill) Druce (× ¾)

Perennial herb with a slender rootstock creeping in the mud under water and giving off tufts of linear leaves (A, ×¾) with sharp points and dilated at the base, up to 3 in. long; flowerheads about ⅓ in. diam., terminating a peduncle enclosed at the base by a long sheath; bracts of the involucre dull in colour; flowers (B, ×4) numerous and minute, unisexual, the central ones mostly males, the outer mostly females, all intermixed with small bracts; perianthsegments (C, ×4) 4, with a minute black gland on the inner 2; stamens in the males 4; ovary shortly stipitate, 2-lobed, with 2 stigmas (family *Eriocaulaceae*).

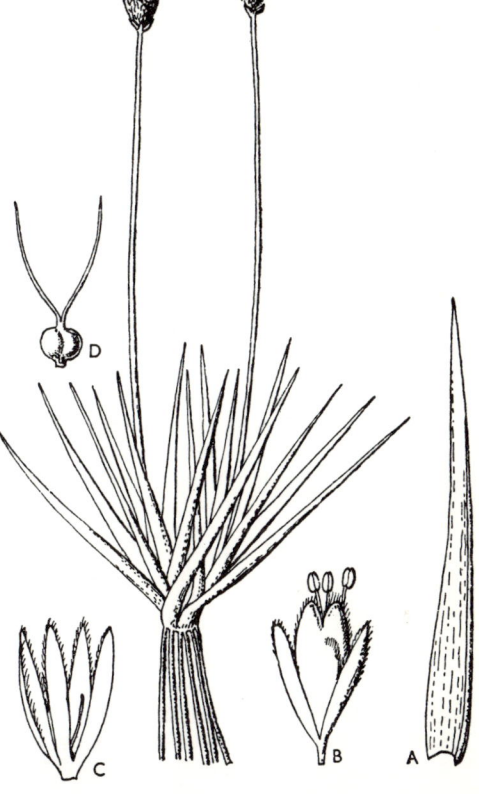

Of exceptional geographical interest, being found only in some islands on the west coast of Scotland and the west of Eire, as well as in North America, but nowhere else in Europe. Synonym *E. septangulare* With.

HERB PARIS
Paris quadrifolia L. ($\times\frac{1}{3}$)

Perennial herb with a slender creeping rootstock; stem un-branched, up to about 1 ft. high, bearing at the top a single whorl of 4 (very rarely 5–7) leaves, these widely obovate, rounded to a pointed tip, narrowed to the base, up to $3\frac{1}{2}$ in. long and $2\frac{1}{2}$ in. broad, with 3–5 main nerves from the base, and with a very lax venation, glabrous; flower solitary in the middle of the whorl of leaves, stalked; sepals (A, $\times1$) 4 (rarely 5), broadly lanceolate, pointed, nearly 1 in. long, 3–5-nerved; petals (B, $\times1$) as many as sepals but very narrow and more yellow; stamens (C, $\times2$) 8 (or

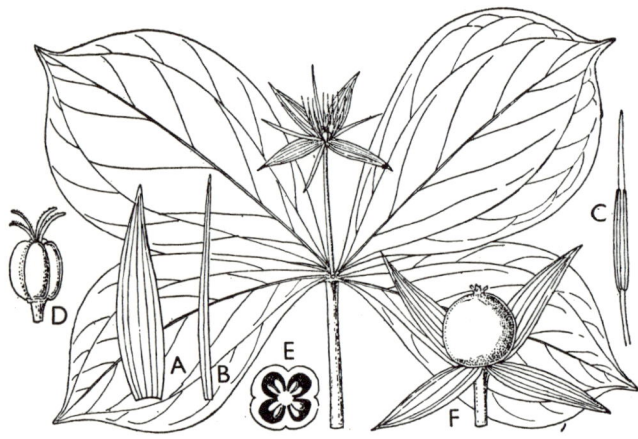

10); anthers 2-locular, with a long-produced connective at the top; ovary (D, $\times3$) superior, 4-locular (E, $\times4$), 4-lobed (rarely 5), and with as many styles free nearly to the base; fruit (F, $\times\frac{2}{3}$) globose, fleshy, bluish-black, about $\frac{1}{2}$ in. diam. (family *Trilliaceae*).

A most distinctive plant, growing in woods and very local, flowering in spring and early summer; extends through Europe to Siberia, south to the Caucasus.

The flowers have a foetid odour, and attract carrion flies. The berries are poisonous to man and poultry. In fact the whole plant is emetic, purgative, intensely acrid, and narcotic. Occasionally a flower is female, the stamens being devoid of anthers which then resemble the petals in form and colour.

Tofieldia pusilla (Michaux) Pers. ($\times \frac{3}{4}$)

Small perennial tufted grass-like herb with a creeping rootstock; leaves crowded at the base of the flowering stem, with broad sheathing overlapping bases, shortly linear, 1–1½ in. long, about $\frac{1}{10}$ in. broad, prominently 3–5-nerved lengthwise, glabrous; flowering stem nude except for 1 or 2 leaves near the base, up to 6 in. high, bearing at the top a short raceme of shortly stalked flowers (A, ×9); pedicels with a 3-lobed bract near the base; perianth yellow-green, composed of 6 free broadly oblanceolate persistent segments; stamens (B, ×15) 6, opposite the segments; anthers short and rounded, opening inwards; ovary (C, ×15) 3-lobed at the apex and ending in 3 short free styles with rounded stigmas; ovules (D, ×20) several in each of the 3 loculi; fruit (E, ×6) a small 3-lobed capsule opening between the loculi (septicidally); seeds oblong, very small, brown (family *Liliaceae*). – Synonym *T. palustris* of British *Floras*.

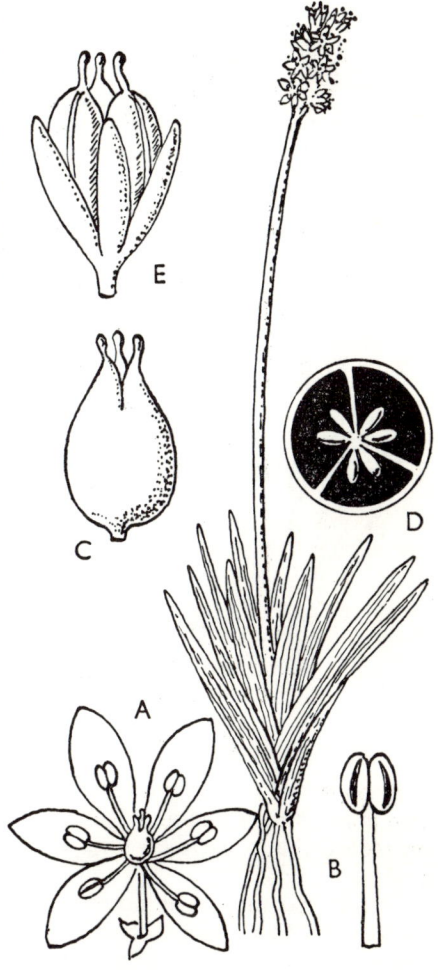

This is the smallest member of the family *Liliaceae* represented in Britain, with a wide circumpolar distribution and in the high mountains of central Europe; in Britain found only in northern England and in Scotland.

BOG ASPHODEL
Narthecium ossifragum (L.) Huds. ($\times \frac{1}{2}$)

Perennial with short creeping rootstock; stems up to about 1 ft. high, leafy at the base and with 2 or 3 much-reduced higher leaves; basal leaves sheathing at the base and encircling the stem, arranged in 2 opposite rows like those of an Iris, broadly linear, very acute at the apex, strongly ribbed (A, × 1) lengthwise with about 5 or 6 nerves; flowers (B, × 1) fragrant, arranged in a short terminal raceme; bracts narrow, a little shorter than the flower-stalk when the flower opens; perianth-segments 6, bright yellow but green on the back, spreading, broadly linear; stamens (C, × 2½) 6, shorter than the segments; filaments densely covered with yellow woolly hairs; anthers red; ovary above the perianth; fruit a capsule splitting from the top into 3 parts; seed-body (D, × 4) small, with a long narrow tail at each end (family *Liliaceae*).

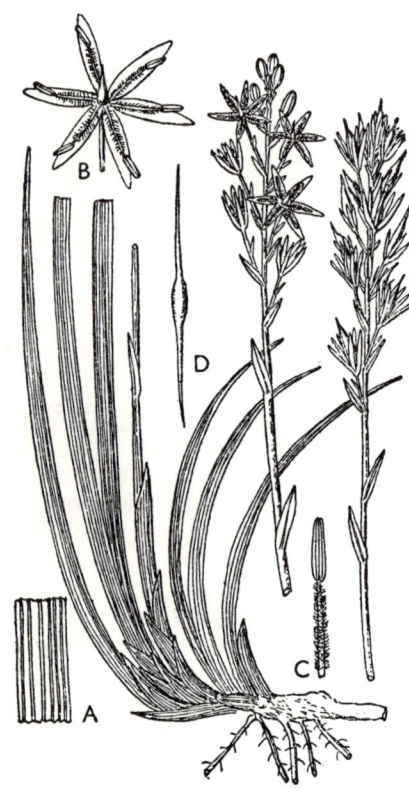

In bogs and wet moors in acid soil, flowering during summer. The plant is regarded as poisonous, especially to cows, and it is on record that a cat died after drinking the milk of an affected cow.

Two of the most striking features of this interesting plant are the densely hairy filaments of the stamens and the remarkable seeds (see fig. D). The latter have a small ellipsoid body with a long tail at each end. Certain epiphytic Rhododendrons have somewhat similar seeds. Cross-pollination mainly takes place through insect agency.

Simethis planifolia (L.) Gren. & Godr. ($\times \frac{1}{3}$)

Perennial herb about 1 ft. high; rootstock short, with several narrow fleshy tuber-like roots; base of stem covered by numerous fibrous remains of leaf-bases; leaves linear, flat and grass-like, as long as or longer than the inflorescence, 5-nerved, glabrous; flowering stem leafless, bearing a cyme at the top; bracts linear, up to $\frac{3}{4}$ in. long; flowers (A, $\times 1$) purple and white, on slender pedicels up to nearly 1 in. long; perianth-segments 6, spreading but closing up in young fruit, oblong-oblanceolate, strongly 5-nerved lengthwise; stamens (C, $\times 3$) 6, opposite the perianth-segments; filaments free, densely villous except towards the base and apex; anthers oblong, versatile; ovary (D, $\times 2$) 3-locular, slightly 3-lobed; style undivided; ovules (E, $\times 4$) 2 in each loculus, superposed; fruit (B, $\times \frac{1}{2}$) a subglobose capsule; seeds black and shining (family *Liliaceae*). – Synonym *Simethis bicolor* (Desf.) Kunth.

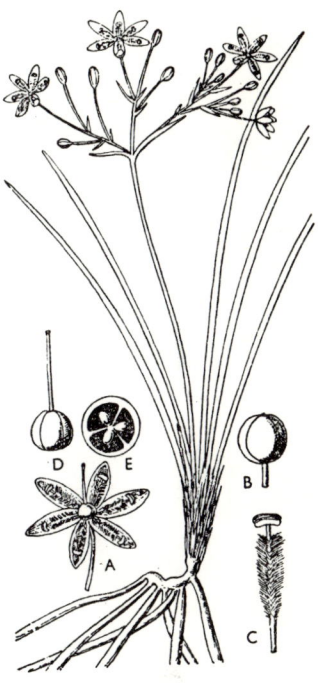

In England only found wild in pine-woods in Dorset; occurs also in south Kerry in southern Eire; otherwise distributed from France to Italy and in northwest Africa.

Easily recognized among the British *Liliaceae* by the cyme of purple and white flowers with densely villous filaments.

Convallaria majalis L. ($\times \frac{2}{5}$)

Perennial herb; rootstock slender, creeping, with numerous bunches of fibrous roots; leaves usually 2, rarely 3, with sheathing bases from scaly sheaths without blades; sheaths thin, marked with parallel nerves, glabrous; leaf-blades elliptic, narrowed at each end, usually about 5–6 in. long and about $2\frac{1}{2}$ in. broad, lined with numerous parallel nerves; flowering stem leafless, arising separately from the leafy shoot, slender, shorter than the leaves, bearing at the top a one-sided raceme about $2\frac{1}{2}$ in. long; bracts lanceolate, with thin margins, $\frac{1}{3}$ to $\frac{1}{2}$ as long as the pedicels; flowers white, very sweet-scented, nodding; perianth (A, $\times 1\frac{2}{5}$) bell-shaped about $\frac{1}{4}$–$\frac{1}{3}$ in. long, shortly 6-lobed; stamens (B, $\times 4$) 6, hidden in the tube and inserted at its base; anthers large, facing inwards; ovary (C, $\times 2\frac{2}{5}$) 3-locular, with 2 ovules in each on axile placentas (D, $\times 5$); style short; fruit a red globose berry

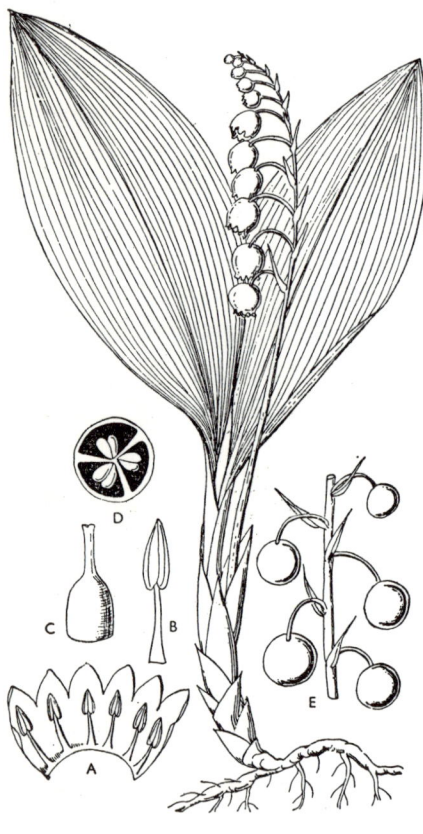

(E, $\times \frac{2}{5}$) with rather large seeds (family *Liliaceae*).

This delightful little plant, with its delicious scent, is so well known to everyone that it hardly needs a description. It is abundant in woods in many counties of England but very local in some and absent from others, flowering in spring. In a wild state it stretches from Europe to eastern Asia, and from the Arctic Circle to the Mediterranean.

Polygonatum multiflorum All. ($\times\frac{1}{3}$)

Perennial herb with a thick horizontal rootstock marked with circular scars of the fallen long membranous scales; stem erect or inclined, up to 2 ft. high, not angular; leaves alternate, shortly stalked, elliptic, 3–3½ in. long and 1½ in. broad, with numerous parallel nerves, a few of them more prominent than the others; flowers axillary, all growing to one side, 2–3 on a common stalk about ½ in. long, the individual stalks as long; perianth (A, ×1¼) about ¾ in. long, white, with greenish tips, lobes 6; stamens 6, included in the perianth; filaments hairy; ovary (B, ×1¼) 3-locular with 2 ovules in each loculus on axile placentas (C, ×5); style slender, hairy; berries (D, ×½) globose, ⅓ in. diam., dark blue (family *Liliaceae*).

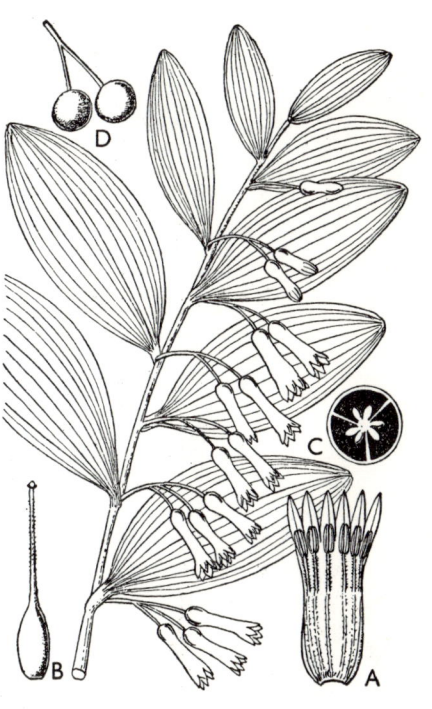

Grows in woods and shady places in various parts of England and southern Scotland; flowers in spring and early summer; extends into Asia.

The flowers are adapted for pollination by humble-bees. Nectar is secreted by the 3 septal glands of the ovary and stored at the base of the perianth.

Other two species are found in Britain, *P. odoratum* (Mill.) Druce, the 'Angular Solomon's Seal', with an angular stem, alternate leaves, only 1–2 flowers together in each leaf-axil, a longer perianth not constricted in the middle, growing in limestone woods in western districts; and *P. verticillatum* (L.) All., also with angular stems, whorled leaves, 1–4 flowers on a common peduncle, very rare from Northumberland north to Dumfries and Perth.

MAY LILY
Maianthemum bifolium (L.) Schmidt ($\times\frac{1}{2}$)

Rootstock very slender and branched, with numerous small roots; stem single, erect, bearing a few long ribbed sheaths at the base, glabrous; leaves usually 2, rarely 3, alternate, very shortly petiolate, ovate, deeply cordate at the base, 2–2$\frac{1}{2}$ in. long 1$\frac{1}{2}$–2 in. broad, arcuately several-nerved from the base, often minutely and sparingly setulose on the nerves on both surfaces; flowers (A, $\times4$) small in a terminal raceme about 1 in. long; axis of inflorescence slightly scabrid; pedicels 2–3 together; perianth-segments 4, white, spreading, oblong-ovate; stamens (B, $\times8$) 4, opposite the segments; ovary (C, $\times7$) 2-locular; style shortly bifid; ovules (D, $\times10$) 2 in each loculus; fruit ($\times\frac{1}{2}$) a small subglobose pulpy red berry; seeds pale brown (family *Liliaceae*).

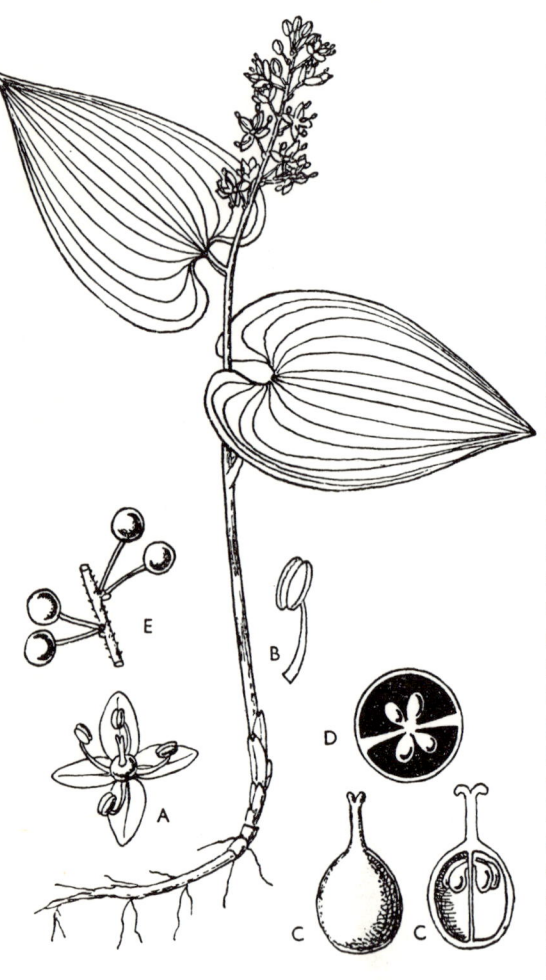

Grows in woods in a few counties of England, widely spread to north-east Asia.

Asparagus officinalis L. ($\times \frac{1}{2}$)

Perennial herb with a creeping matted rootstock and annual stems, these erect and much branched, up to 2 ft. high in wild plants, more or less flexuous, glabrous; real leaves very small and bract-like, triangular, scarious, with several linear leaf-like cladodes (modified branchlets) in their axils; flowers small and scattered in the branch-axils, on slender pedicels jointed about the middle, greenish white, some only with stamens; perianth (A, $\times 1$) of 6 free segments; stamens 6, opposite the segments; ovary (B, $\times 1$) 3-locular, with 2 superposed ovules in each loculus (C, $\times 2$); style solitary; fruit (D, $\times \frac{1}{2}$) a small red globose berry; seed with endosperm and straight embryo (family *Liliaceae*).

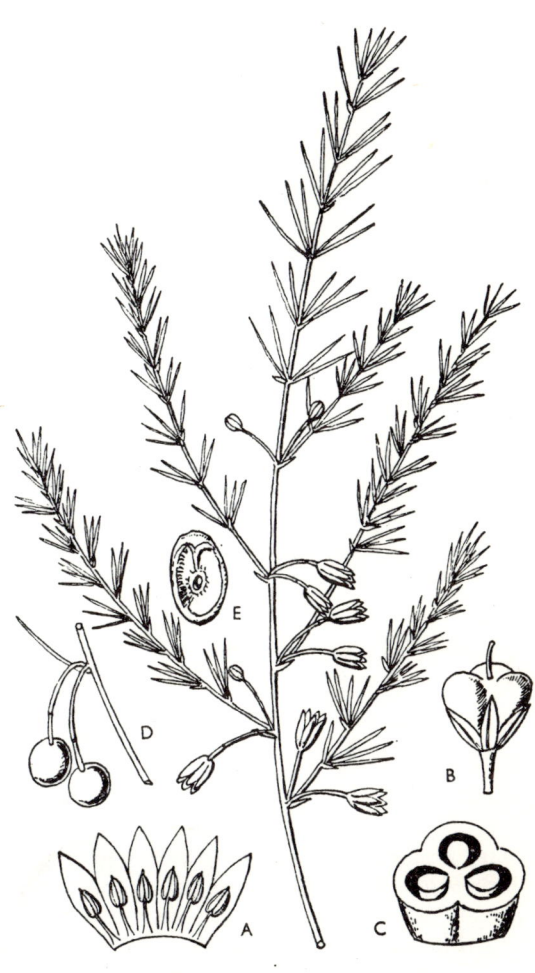

This is the wild Asparagus from which the cultivated plant was derived; occurs in maritime sands in west and south-west Britain and in southern Eire.

SNAKE'S HEAD
Fritillaria meleagris L. ($\times\frac{1}{2}$)

Herb with a bulbous base, the bulbs (A, $\times\frac{1}{2}$) sometimes clustered; scales few and thick; stem single, bearing a few scattered alternate

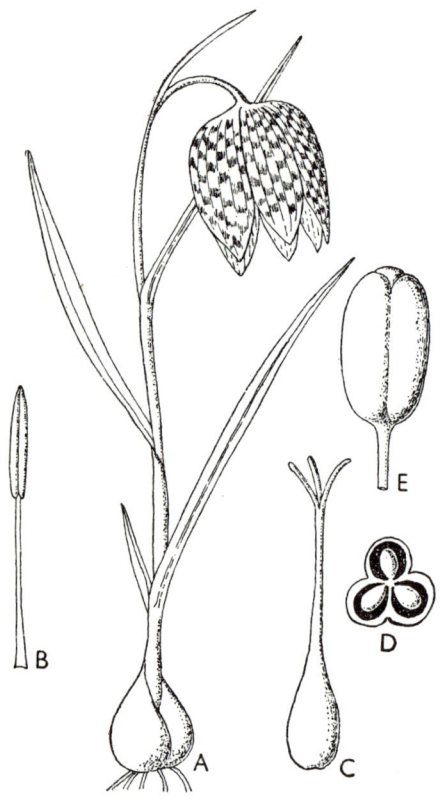

leaves, these linear, blunt and curved at the apex, about 4 in. long, closely and faintly nerved longitudinally; flowers single (rarely 2), terminal, drooping, bell-shape, composed of 6 free, broad segments about 1½ in. long, tesselated with dull purple, rarely white or yellowish; stamens (B, $\times1\frac{1}{2}$) 6, inserted at the base of the perianth; anthers ½ in. long, yellow; ovary (C, $\times1\frac{1}{2}$) long, triangular, 3-locular; style with 3 stigmas; ovules many on axile placentas (D, $\times1\frac{1}{2}$); capsule 3-valved, the valves hairy on the margin; seeds compressed (family *Liliaceae*).

Grows wild in moist meadows only in some southern counties, but with a wide distribution ·as far east as the Caucasus, flowering in spring,

The bell-shaped flowers are pendulous and mottled, with small light and dark purple squares on a reddish-white background. Pure white flowers sometimes occur. The flowers are protogynous, i.e. the stigmas are receptive as soon as they open and whilst the anthers are still closed. If cross-pollination has not occurred, one of the stamens usually elongates so that its anther is at the same level as the still receptive stigmas, the other 5 having shed their pollen.

Tulipa sylvestris L. $(\times \frac{1}{2})$

Perennial herb with an underground ovoid-globose bulb $1-1\frac{1}{2}$ in. long; stem about 1 ft. high, bearing usually a single terminal yellow flower (A, $\times\frac{1}{2}$); leaves 1–3, strap-shaped, gradually narrowed to the sheathing base, up to $\frac{3}{4}$ in. broad, with several close parallel nerves; perianth-segments 6, free, broadly oblanceolate, $1\frac{1}{2}-2$ in. long, up to 1 in. broad; stamens (B, $\times1\frac{1}{2}$) 6, opposite the perianth-seg-ments; filaments densely villous just above the base; anthers $\frac{1}{3}$ in. long, attached at the base, opening at the sides; ovary (C, $\times1\frac{1}{2}$) 3-locular; stigmas 3, sub-sessile; fruit (D, $\times\frac{1}{2}$) $1-1\frac{1}{2}$ in. long (family *Liliaceae*).

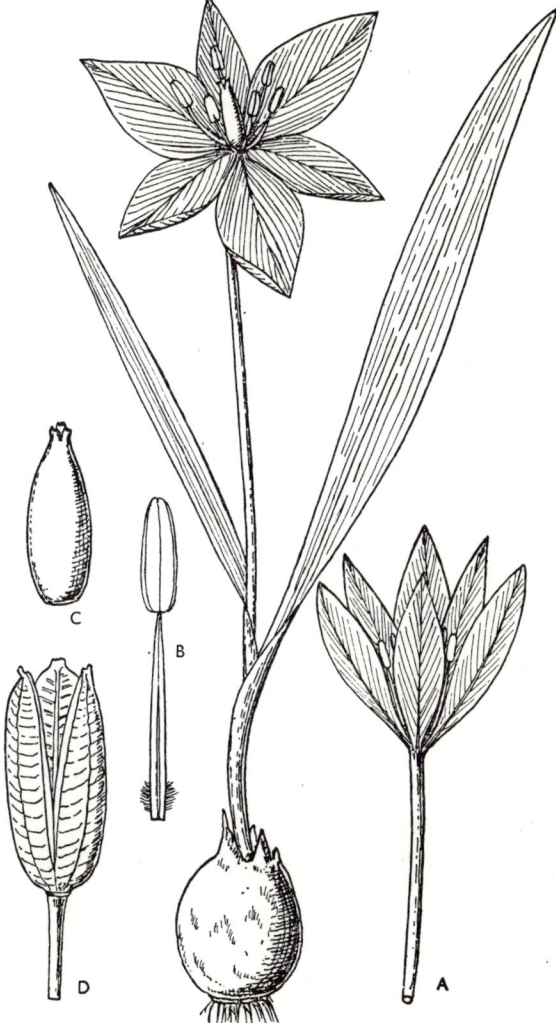

Possibly wild in some of the eastern and southern counties of England, flowering in late spring; native of central and southern Europe eastwards to the Caucasus.

Lloydia serotina (L.) Rchb. ($\times\frac{2}{3}$)

Tiny herb with a small bulbous rootstock with numerous thread-like roots; leaves 2–3, linear-filiform, up to 4 in. long, glabrous;

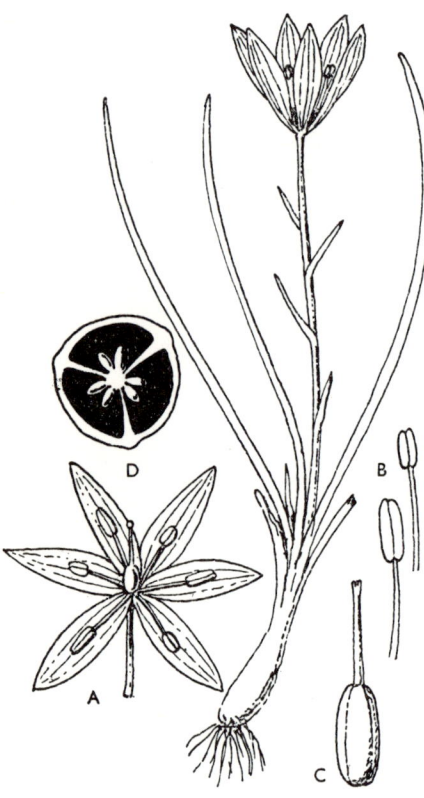

stem slender, bearing a few rather large leafy bracts and a single terminal flower (A, $\times 1\frac{2}{3}$); perianth of 6 free white segments with a small yellow spot at the base, the segments obovate-oblanceolate, $\frac{2}{3}$ in. long, 3-nerved, nerves reddish; stamens (B, $\times 2\frac{1}{2}$) 6, opposite the segments and inserted at their base (almost free); filaments glabrous; anthers oblong, alternately longer and shorter, opening by slits at the sides; ovary (C, $\times 3$) oblong-ellipsoid, slightly 3-lobed, 3-locular; style slender, a little longer than the ovary; ovules several in each loculus on axile placentas (D, $\times 8$); fruit a turbinate capsule opening into the loculi, 3-lobed; seeds numerous in 2 rows in each loculus, faintly margined, dusky brown (family *Liliaceae*).

As this is one of the rarest plants and found only in the mountains in Wales, it should on no account be disturbed by plant hunters. It flowers from late June until August. Otherwise the species enjoys a very wide almost circumpolar distribution from the Arctic and the mountains of southern Europe to eastern Alaska, and as far south as the Himalayas.

Perennial herb about 6–9 in. high, with a small ovoid-globose bulbous rootstock well below the level of the soil; basal leaf solitary, strap-shaped, longer than the flowering stem; $\frac{1}{2}$–$\frac{2}{3}$ in. broad, with about 12 parallel nerves; flowering stem nude except for 2 smaller unequal-sized leaves as long as the pedicels and below the corymb of yellow flowers; pedicels up to $1\frac{1}{2}$ in. long; perianth of 6 free segments (A, $\times 1\frac{1}{2}$) about $\frac{2}{3}$ in. long, spreading, three of them 3-nerved, the other three 5-nerved, yellow above, green below; stamens (B, $\times 2\frac{1}{2}$) 6, opposite the segments, free, flattened with fine tips; anthers oblong, equal-sized, opening at the sides; ovary (C, $\times 2$) ellipsoid, 3-locular, with numerous ovules in each loculus on axile placentas; style erect, longer than the ovary; fruit a capsule opening into the loculi; seeds numerous (family *Liliaceae*).

Grows in woods in several parts of England, Wales, and Scotland, usually rare, flowering in spring; distributed from Europe into temperate Asia.

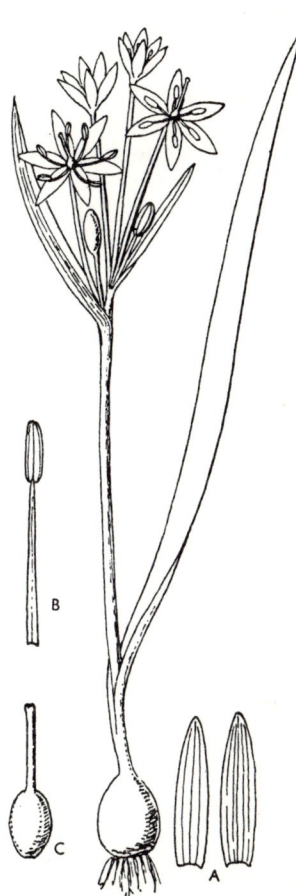

MARTAGON LILY
Lilium martagon L. ($\times\frac{1}{2}$)

Bulb ovoid, $1\frac{1}{2}$–2 in. long, yellowish, scales lanceolate; stem simple, up to 6 ft. high, green or spotted with purple, glabrous or pubescent; leaves in whorls of up to 15, the lower up to 6 in. long and $1\frac{1}{4}$ in. broad, with up to 5 nerves on each side of the midrib; racemes lax, up to 20-flowered; bracts lanceolate; pedicels nodding, 1–3 in. long; perianth wine-purple, spotted, sometimes white, segments reflexed from the middle, about $1\frac{1}{2}$ in. long; stamens (A, $\times\frac{3}{4}$) 6; anthers nearly $\frac{1}{2}$ in. long; pollen reddish; ovary oblong, style slender, $\frac{3}{4}$ in. long, curved from the base, 3-fid at the apex; capsule top-shaped, acutely angled, about 1 in. long (family *Liliaceae*).

This species has been cultivated for a very long period and if found apparently wild may have escaped from a garden. My drawing was made from a living specimen which grew in a wood by the North Tyne near Wark, Northumberland. It was indeed a thrill to find a little colony of this lovely plant so near my own birthplace, and I hope it will long remain undisturbed by vandals in what seemed to be a wild state, far from any habitation. The species is distributed from western Europe east as far as the Ural mountains.

847

Scilla verna Huds. ($\times \frac{1}{2}$)

Bulb about $\frac{1}{2}$ in. diam., ovoid; leaves radical, appearing in the spring before the flowers, linear (very narrow) and rather grass-

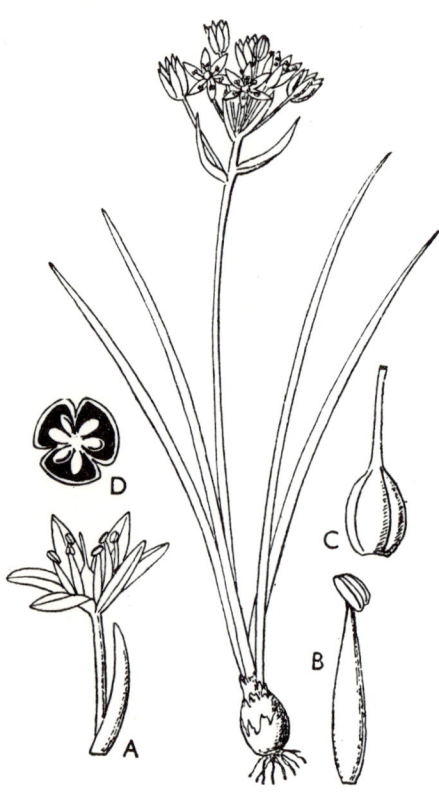

like, as long as the ped-uncle, scooped out (concave) on the upper side, shining, white towards the base; flowers (A, $\times 1\frac{1}{2}$) on a stout stalk and forming a corymb-like raceme, bright blue, fragrant; bracts single below each flower and nearly as long as the flower-stalks, pale except for the green midrib; flow-er-stalks pale green; flower-parts (perianth-segments) 6, free from one another and spread-ing, equal-sized, $\frac{1}{4}$ in. long, the midrib darker blue on the lower side; stamens (B, $\times 6$) 6, op-posite the floral parts; filaments expanded to-wards the base; anthers dark blue, with yellow-ish-green pollen; ovary (C, $\times 6$) a beautiful blue, deeply 3-lobed and 3-locular, with 2 rows of ovules in each loculus (D, $\times 6$); style prism-like; capsule 3-angled, 3-valved, $\frac{1}{6}$ in. diam.; seeds black (family *Liliaceae*).

A very local species and found mainly in the western counties; locally abundant on cliff pastures among bracken and the common Bluebell near Tintagel, Cornwall.

Meadows in that district are sometimes blue with this lovely little plant during April and May. The second British species is *S. autumnalis* L., the Autumnal Squill, which flowers from July to September, and which has no bracts to the flowers.

Bulb white, full of juice; leaves several, basal, linear, up to a foot long and ½ in. broad, bright green and shining, widely V-shaped and with a rather broad prominent midrib below; flowering stem leafless, varying in height according to exposure to light, normally about 9 in. to a foot high, very juicy, glabrous and shining, bearing at the top a raceme of about a dozen beautifully sky-blue nodding bell-shaped flowers opening from below upwards; at the base of each stalk a pair of unequal-sized narrow bracts, bluish purple; buds at first erect and almost stalkless, the stalk elongating to about ½ in. long in the mature flowers, these about ¾ in. long and composed of 6 perianth segments (A, × 1¾) arranged in 2 series, free to the base and with recurved tops;

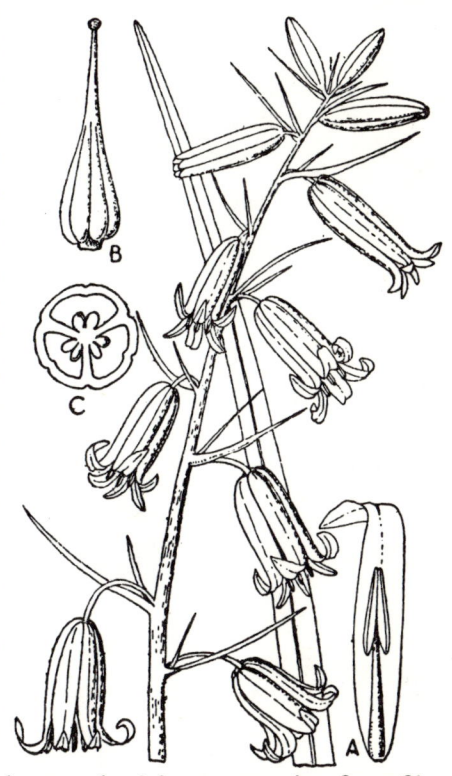

stamens 6, 3 long and 3 shorter, the 3 longer opening first; filaments attached above the base of the segments, blue; anthers white and rather large; ovary (B, × 2) above the perianth (superior), blue like the perianth, 3-locular and 3-lobed, in each compartment 2 rows of ovules attached to the central axis (C, × 4); fruit a capsule; seeds black (family *Liliaceae*).

Kew Gardens is justly famed for its bluebells which are usually at their best about the first week in May. Large areas are planted with this beautiful flower, and the sea of colour beneath the beech and birch trees just breaking into leaf is worth travelling a long way to see. The species is found wild only in the western part of Europe, extending east along the Mediterranean to Italy.

Perennial herb with a bulbous rootstock; bulb ovoid, about $1\frac{1}{2}$ in. long; leaves few, long and narrow, not sheathing at the base, weak, closely parallel-nerved; flowering stem up to 18 in. high, bearing at the top a lax ccrymb-like raceme, the lower pedicels the longest and up to $4\frac{1}{2}$ in. long; bracts rather large and conspicuous, linear-lanceolate, thin and membranous; ·perianth segments free, spreading, $\frac{3}{4}$–1 in. long, green outside with white margins, white above, the middle portion with several distinct parallel nerves; stamens (A, $\times 2$) 6, opposite the perianth-segments, nearly half as long; anthers cordate at the base; ovary (B, $\times 4$) slightly lobed, 3-locular; style shorter than the ovary; fruit (C, $\times 4$) a membranous capsule with a few black nearly globose seeds (family *Liliaceae*).

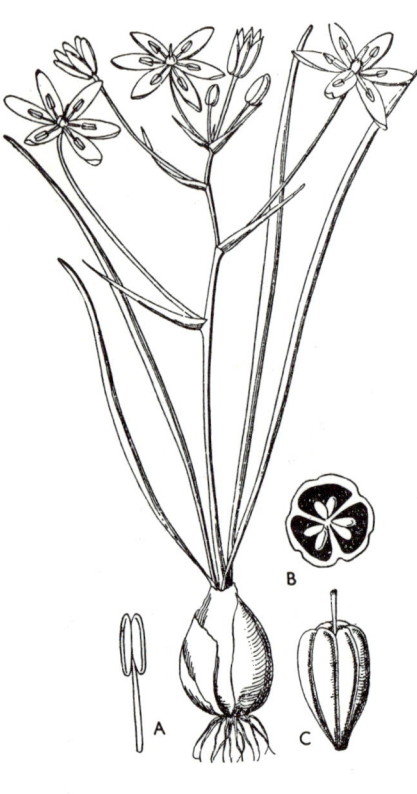

Grows in waste and grassy places, flowering in spring and early summer; extends through Europe to the Caucasus.

Other two species are found in Britain, one introduced from Europe, *O. nutans* L., the 'Drooping Star of Bethlehem', the flowers in a one-sided raceme with rather large flowers 1–$1\frac{1}{4}$ in. long and the filaments with 2 teeth at the apex; and *O. pyrenaicum* L., known as 'Bath Asparagus', with more numerous flowers also in a raceme and the filaments without teeth.

Bulb ovoid-globose, about 1 in. diam.; leaves few, elongate-linear, rather thick but flaccid, up to 1 ft. long, glabrous, about 7-nerved; flowering stem leafless, usually shorter than the leaves, rather fleshy, bearing at the top a raceme or head of small dark-blue nodding flowers with a musk-like scent, these when in bud looking like small berries or grapes; bracts short and broadly ovate, bluish; perianth (A, B, ×8) ellipsoid, with 6 short recurved teeth or lobes; stamens (C, ×8) 6, inserted in 2 series about the middle of the tube, enclosed; anthers blue, rounded; ovary superior, ovoid-globose, 3-locular, with 2 ovules in each loculus attached to the central axis (D, ×12); style slightly 3-fid; fruit (E, ×$\frac{1}{2}$) a 3-lobed (almost winged) capsule, with a few ellipsoid coarsely pitted blackish seeds (F, ×8) (family *Liliaceae*).

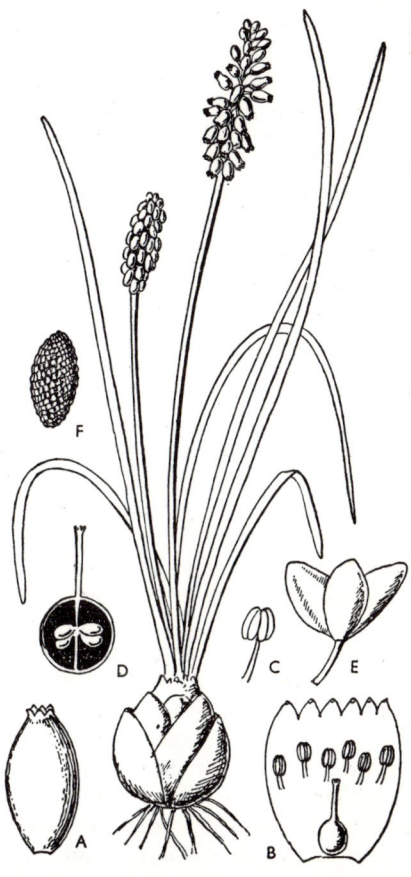

Confined in Britain to dry grasslands of Norfolk, Suffolk, and Cambridge, and also much cultivated; distributed eastwards through Europe to south Russia. Synonym *M. racemosum* (L.) Mill.

739 AUTUMN CROCUS, MEADOW SAFFRON
Colchicum autumnale L. ($\times \frac{1}{2}$)

Perennial with a preference for limestone soil, with a deeply placed narrowly ovoid acuminate corm covered with a thin, shining, chestnut-brown coat lined with parallel nerves; flowers and leaves produced at different times of the year, the flowers in early September, the leaves and fruits in late spring; leaves several, linear-lanceolate, up to about 9 in. long, sharp-pointed, green; in the middle of the leaves 1 or 2 fruits (F, $\times$ 1) produced in May or June and soon ripening; these narrowly ellipsoid and tipped by the bases of the styles, about 2 in long; flower long and tubular, pale purple or deep mauve, arising from near the base of the corm; perianth-segments 6, in 2 whorls, the outer slightly wider than the inner; stamens (A, $\times$ 2) 6, opposite the segments and inserted in the throat; anthers long, facing outwards, arrow-shaped at the base, attached near the middle; ovary superior, 3-locular (B, $\times$ 2), with numerous ovules inserted on the central axis; styles (C, $\times$ 1) 3, free from the base, longer than the tube, the exserted parts (D, $\times$ 2) coloured like the filaments of the stamens; seeds (G, $\times$ 1$\frac{1}{2}$) rounded, brown (family *Liliaceae*).

This lovely plant is sometimes called Naked Ladies, and occurs in meadows in many districts of England and Wales. Where stock are likely to browse, it should be rooted out because all parts of the plant are very poisonous both in the green and dried state and when mixed with hay. Domestic animals have been lost after eating it, and even calves and infants have died through drinking the milk from cows which had eaten the plant a short time previously. A case is recorded of the death of a woman at Covent Garden who ate the corms in mistake for onions.

From a biological point of view the Autumn Crocus is one of our most interesting native species. Unlike most bulbous or cormous plants, it flowers in the autumn. The styles are very long and free from one another, and the pollen tubes do not reach the ovules until the beginning of November. But the ovary remains dormant, and the embryo is not formed until the next May, when the fruits are developed, being then carried above the surface in the middle of a bunch of green leaves. In the wild state, like many ground orchids, the position in the soil of the corms may indicate how deeply in a given neighbourhood the ground is usually frozen, for they are imbedded just far enough to avoid injury.

740   BUTCHER'S BROOM
Ruscus aculeatus L. ($\times\frac{1}{3}$)

Evergreen undershrub growing in shady places in woods; root-stock creeping, woody, scaly at the top; branches more or less in whorls, closely ribbed; true leaves very small and scale-like, with leaf-like branchlets (cladodes) in their axils, these ovate-elliptic, sessile, about 1 in. long and $\frac{3}{4}$ in. broad, thick and leathery and with long hard sharp points, with several parallel nerves; flowers (A, B, C) unisexual and bisexual; yellowish green, solitary or paired on the 'midrib' below the middle of the cladode, surrounded by a subulate bract and 2 broad overlapping bracteoles; perianth of 6 free parts in 2 whorls, the outer larger and broader;

stamens 3, united into a tube; anthers rounded; female flowers without stamens; ovary (D, $\times 5$) ovoid, 1-locular, stigma discoid, nearly sessile; fruit (E, $\times\frac{1}{2}$) a globose bright red berry, nearly $\frac{1}{2}$ in. diam.; seed with hard endosperm (family *Ruscaceae*).

Occurs in the southern counties north as far as Norfolk and naturalized in other places; western Europe, Mediterranean, Azores.

The popular name was derived from the fact that the plant was at one time made by butchers into brooms to sweep their wooden blocks.

In a family tree of the Lily family (*Liliaceae*) and its near relatives, the genus *Ruscus* would occupy the tip of a branch, whence no further evolution has taken place or could possibly take place.

Perennial twining herb; rootstock a rounded-ovoid deeply buried tuber narrowed at the top, the skin clothed with root-fibres; stems angular, as long as 6 ft.; leaves alternate, stalked, broadly ovate or triangular-ovate, widely and deeply cordate, narrowed to an acute apex, at most about 3 in. long and $2\frac{1}{2}$ in. broad, glabrous, several-nerved from the base; stipules small, reflexed; flowers unisexual, dioecious, the males (A, $\times 1$) in slender axillary

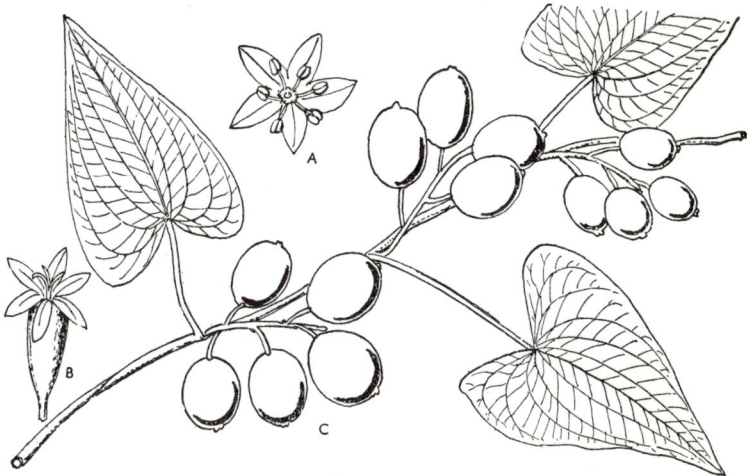

racemes, the females (B, $\times 1$) fewer in shorter subsessile racemes; bracts very small; pedicels about as long as the flower; perianth of the male greenish, deeply divided into 6 oblong spreading parts; stamens 6, anthers introrse; ovary rudimentary; female flowers similar to the male but stamens rudimentary and the ovary attached to the perianth-tube; style 3-lobed; fruit (C, $\times\frac{2}{3}$) ellipsoid-globose, about $\frac{2}{3}$ in. long, scarlet-red (family *Dioscoreaceae*).

Grows over hedges, bushes, nettles, and other weeds, the leaves making a splash of yellow colour in the autumn, accompanied by the lovely red berries, which, however, are poisonous; England and Wales, south and west Europe east to the Caucasus, and in North Africa.

SWEET FLAG
Acorus calamus L. (×⅓)

Perennial strongly aromatic herb with creeping branched root-stock, covered with the fibrous remains of the old leaf-bases;

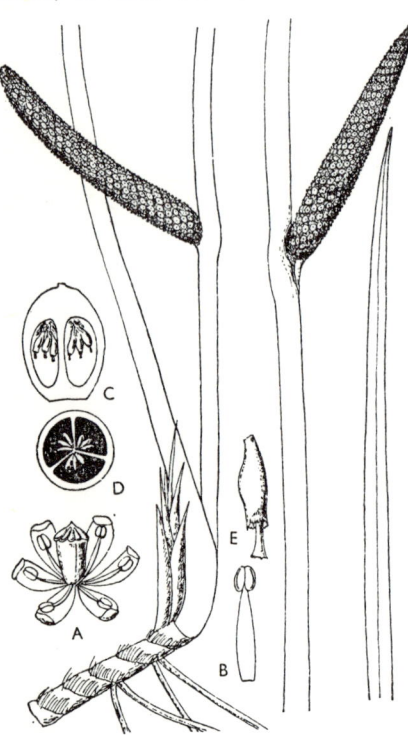

leaves sheathing at the base, erect, linear, with closely parallel nerves, up to 3 ft. long and ½–¾ in. broad; sheath with broadly membranous margins; flowering stems un-branched, erect, bearing two or three sessile spikes of dense spirally arranged flowers, ending in a leaf-like spathe forming a flattened continuation; spikes cylindrical and cigar-shaped, 2–3½ in. long and about ½ in. diam.; flowers (A, ×2) bisexual, densely packed in spirals, yellowish green; perianth-segments 6, free, oblanceolate, apex broad and inflexed; stamens (B, ×4) 6, opposite the segments but shorter; anthers rounded; ovary (C, D, ×5) superior, 3-locular, with a cap-like hardened top and minute sessile stigma (see fig. A); ovules (E, ×10) several, pendulous, the outer coat fimbriate around the micropyle; fruit an oblong reddish berry (family *Araceae*).

Flowers during summer and grows in wet places, often in shallow water of rivers and ponds. The leaves have an agreeable aroma when bruised, hence the common name.

Acorus represents rather a primitive type of the family *Araceae*, especially with regard to the leaf subtending the inflorescence of bisexual flowers, which is not modified into a protective spathe. In this it resembles *Lysichitum*, a genus from northern Asia, to be seen in some gardens, with a spathe not much modified from the foliage leaves except in colour.

Rootstock a white tuber; leaves long-stalked, ovate, arrow-shaped at the base, dark shining green, often spotted with purple or streaked with lighter colour; flowers arranged on a long fleshy axis (spadix) enclosed in a large green and purple sheath (spathe) folded over the edges and 6 or more inches long, tapered at the top; upper part of the axis barren and bright purple; lower part bearing the flowers which are unisexual, the upper cluster being male and crowded in a dense mass, each consisting of a single stamen, the lower flowers female, each of a single carpel; above each cluster are a few abortive flowers reduced to hair-like structures, those above the male being longer and directed downwards; berries red (family *Araceae*).

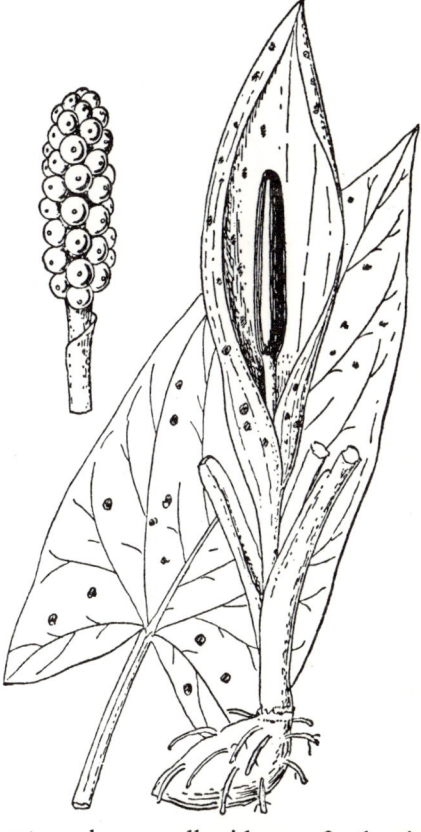

The spathe and the dark red upper end of the spadix attract small insects such as small midges, a further inducement for them being the decomposing, urinous smell. These small creatures creep down between the downwardly directed stiff hairs mentioned above and are trapped by them for a time. They thus deposit pollen from another spadix upon the already receptive stigmas of the female flowers at the bottom. Whilst they are trapped, pollen falls in a shower from the stamens above and dusts the insects with a fresh supply.

Sparganium emersum Rehm. (⅓)

Perennial aquatic herb with erect stems; leaves erect and partly out of the water, completely encircling the stem at the base and  with membranous margins in the lower part, flattened upwards but keeled below, narrowly linear, bright green and with about 3 longitudinal nerves on each side of the midrib; flowers unisexual, crowded into globose heads on a simple main axis, the upper male (A, × 1) and sessile, the lower female (C, × 2) and pedunculate, or sometimes the peduncle adnate to the axis (extra-axillary); male flowers consisting of slender stamens surrounded by free yellowish - green perianth - segments; anthers (B, × 2) linear-oblong, opening at the side; female flowers of a single long - beaked carpel surrounded by jagged scales, with 1 pendulous ovule (D, × 2) (family *Sparganiaceae*).

This is a very advanced (highly evolved) kind of Monocotyledon, with the male and female flowers in separate heads, and a single pendulous ovule in the solitary carpel of the female flower. Synonym *S. simplex* Huds.

Bulb ellipsoid, about 2 in. long; leaves very shortly sheathing the flowering stem at the base, long-stalked, flat, and broadly lanceolate, about 8 in. long, and 3 in. broad, contracted at the base, with several parallel nerves running from the base to apex, and with oblique secondary veins between (A, $\times$ 3); flowering stem up to about a foot high, leafless, bearing a loose umbel of about a dozen white flowers; bracts rather large and lanceolate, soon withering and falling off; flower-stalks up to about 1 in. long, slender; perianth segments (B, $\times\frac{4}{5}$) 6, lanceolate, acute, spreading; stamens (C, $\times 1\frac{3}{4}$) 6, shorter than and opposite to the segments; anthers (D, $\times$ 3) ovoid; ovary (E, $\times$ 2) above the perianth (superior), 3-lobed, with a rod-like

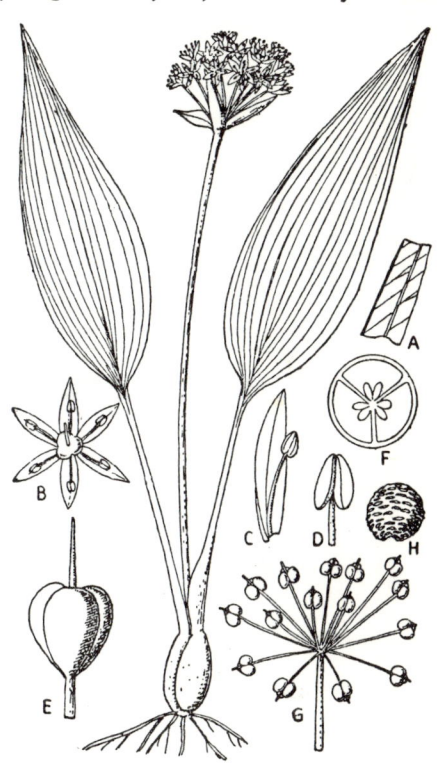

simple style, 3-locular, with several ovules in each compartment arranged in 2 rows on the central axis (F, $\times$ 2); fruit (G, $\times\frac{4}{5}$) deeply 3-lobed, with a black rounded transversely pitted seed (H, $\times$ 3) in each lobe (family *Amaryllidaceae*).

This plant is often very abundant in woods and shady places. It flowers in spring and early summer. Readers may wonder why it is placed here in the *Amaryllis* family instead of in the Lily family. The only difference between these two families as hitherto defined was that the ovary in the former family is inferior, and in the latter superior. The author, however, considers the nature of the inflorescence a better character, that of the *Amaryllis* family being an umbel, and of the Lily family a spike, raceme, or panicle.

Allium triquetrum L. (×⅓)

Bulbous plant with leaves and flower-stems about equal in length and up to about 1½ ft. high; each leaf sheathing those within towards the base; leaves flat

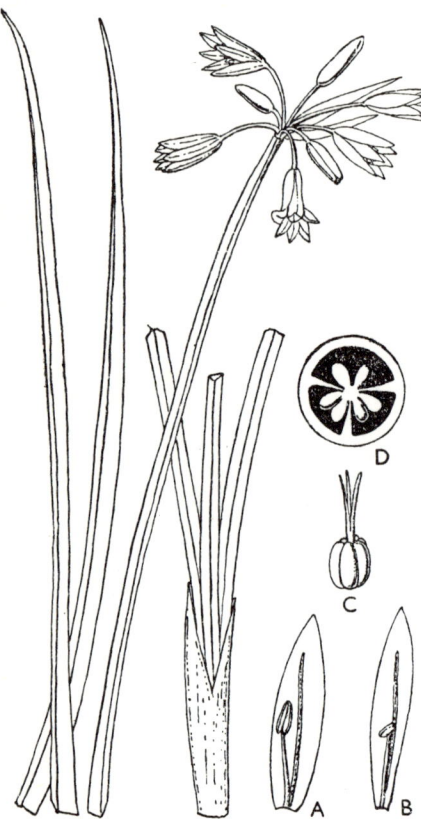

to concave on the upper surface, sharply keeled below, nearly ¾ in. broad, with about 10 slightly darker green parallel nerves; flowering stem (peduncle) sharply triangular in cross-section, bearing at the top 2 equal or unequal-sized membranous white bracts as long as the longest flower-stalks (pedicels), the latter up to 1 in. long, glaucous-green; floral envelope (perianth) of 6 free parts in 2 whorls (A, B, ×1⅓), each part (segment) nearly ¾ in. long and ¼ in. broad, with a green midrib not extending to the tip; stamens 6, opposite the segments, the pale yellow anthers of those opposite the inner segments opening first; filaments not toothed at the top; ovary (C, ×3) globose, green, slightly 6-lobed, 3-locular, each loculus with 2 rows (D, ×12) of large fat ovules; capsule as big as a small pea (family *Amaryllidaceae*).*

Formerly found only in Cornwall and the Channel Islands but now naturalized in several counties.

    * According to the present author's classification.

Allium schoenoprasum L., var. *sibiricum* ($\times\frac{1}{3}$)

Bulbs narrow, covered with more or less crimson sheaths; stems up to 15 in. high, often growing several together and forming a dense clump; leaves usually 1 or 2, sheathing the flowering stem for more than $\frac{1}{3}$ of its length, rounded in section and hollow (A, ×2), glaucous-green and lined with numerous parallel nerves, tapered to the tip; flowers in a dense umbel, enclosed in bud by 2–3 broadly-ovate, shortly pointed bracts (spathes); flower-stalks about $\frac{1}{2}$ in. long; floral parts (perianth) of 6 free segments (B, ×1$\frac{1}{4}$), pale purple with a deeper coloured midrib, oblong, shortly pointed; stamens 6, about half as long as the segments; anthers light-brown before opening; ovary (C, ×2) rounded, 3-lobed, 3-locular; style undivided; capsule globose, small (family *Amaryllidaceae*).

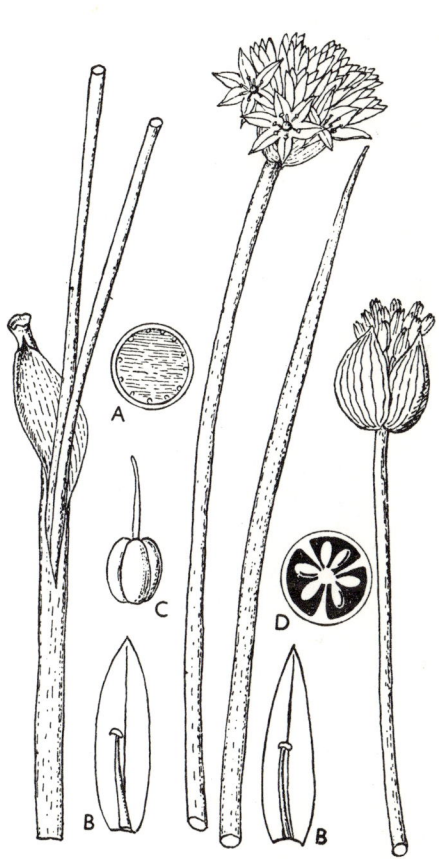

A rare plant found in a wild state in Britain in a few maritime counties.

SNOWDROP
Galanthus nivalis L. (×0)

Bulb white, ovoid, about ½ in. diam., usually 2–3 in. below ground; leaves and flowers appearing nearly together, in mild winters about

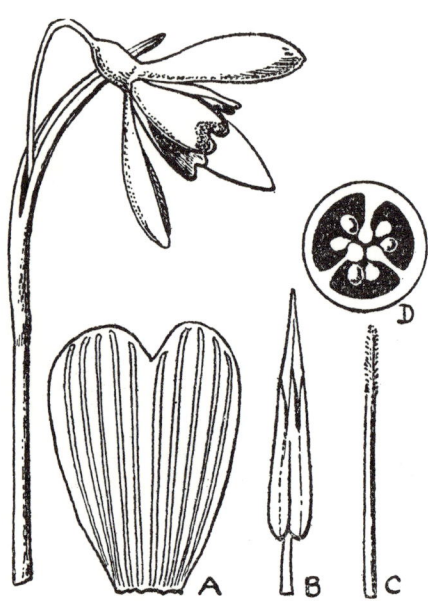

Christmas or soon after, often amongst snow, hence the common name; leaves 2 or rarely 3, linear, glaucous-green, with a blunt whitish tip, and a keel-like midrib below; flowering-stem exceeding the leaves, bearing at the top a single drooping flower, the stalk clasped for some distance by a large thin bract with green margins; ovary inferior, bell-shaped, green, 3-locular, with numerous ovules on axile placentas; perianth composed of 2 whorls, 3 parts in each whorl, the outer white, broadly oblanceolate with a narrow lower part, up to 1 in. long, the inner row (A, ×3) half as long, obovate, streaked with broad bands of green and with a V-shaped top and a similar shaped band of green; stamens (B, ×4) 6, erect, with orange-yellow anthers opening towards the top and with sharp tips; style (C, ×3) awl-shaped (family *Amaryllidaceae*).

A much-loved flower but probably not a native of Britain, naturalized in many places; native of central and southern Europe east to the Caucasus.

If plants could tell us their past history, this dear little flower would be able to show a very long pedigree, for it is indeed a *multum in parvo*. It would be a tale of how it has managed to acquire the habit of flowering in the depth of winter, often whilst snow is still upon the ground, how it produced its bulbous rootstock, and especially the reduction of the inflorescence to a single flower from an ancestral stock with several flowers in an umbel within the spathe such as shown in *Leucojum* (fig. 749).

Leucojum aestivum L. ($\times\frac{1}{2}$)

Bulbous herb up to $1\frac{1}{2}$ ft. high; bulb rather small (about 1 in. diam.), ellipsoid-globose, with a white covering; leaves and peduncles embraced by a few truncate sheaths; leaves several, broadly sheathing at the base, broadly linear, about $\frac{1}{2}$ in. broad, lined with about 20 parallel nerves, green, appearing before the flowers; peduncle stout, bearing at the top a 1-valved spathe about 2 in. long, and 2–6 flowers; pedicels about 2 in. long; ovary inferior, 3-locular with numerous ovules on axile placentas; perianth-segments 6, sub-equal, obovate, nearly 1 in. long, white with a green spot below the apex on both sides; stamens (A, $\times 1\frac{1}{2}$)

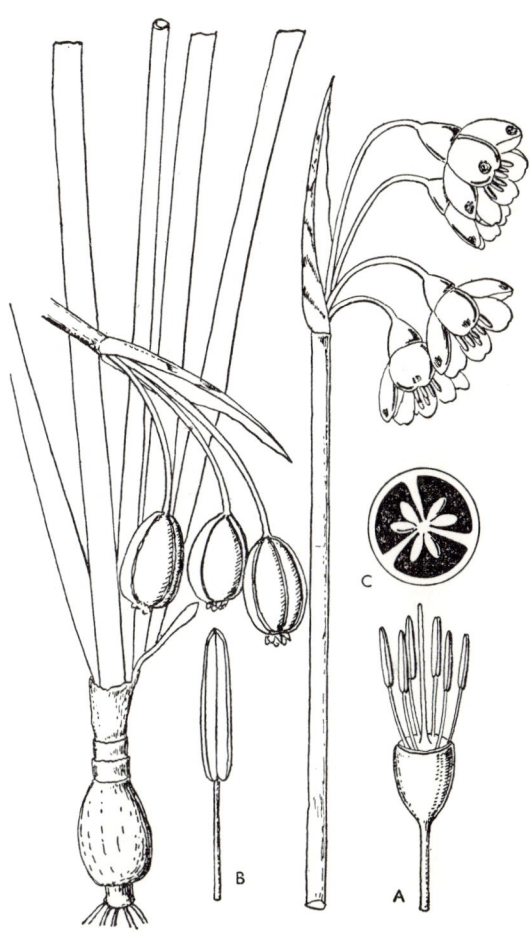

6; anthers (B, $\times 4$) yellow; ovary (C, $\times 3$) 3-locular; fruit a capsule, $\frac{3}{4}$–1 in. long; seeds whitish (family *Amaryllidaceae*).

Flowers in early summer in wet meadows and among willows. Found only in the southern counties of England and in Eire, but commonly cultivated and naturalized; extends to the Caucasus.

DAFFODIL, DAFFY-DOWN-DILLY

Narcissus pseudonarcissus L. ($\times \frac{2}{5}$)

Perennial herb with a fairly large bulb; leaves usually 2 or 3 or 4, at first stiff and erect, at length spreading, linear, $\frac{1}{3}$–$\frac{1}{2}$ in. broad, bluish green, with 2 main nerves up the middle which form a groove below; flowering stem erect, ending in a single flower, the latter subtended by a mémbranous faintly nerved bract (spathe) (A, ×1) split down one side and enclosing it in bud; perianth (B, ×1) tube about 1 in. long, 6-lobed, lobes 3 outer and 3 inner, ovate to oblong-lanceolate, acute, longer than the tube; corona trumpet-shaped, crinkly waved or lobulate on the margin; stamens (C, ×3) 6, inserted near the base of

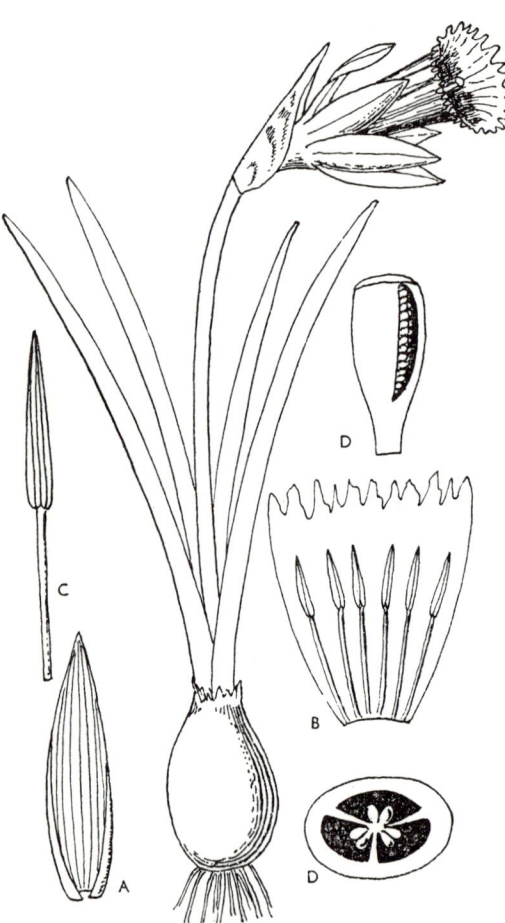

the corona but hidden within; anthers $\frac{1}{2}$ in. long, ovary below the perianth (inferior), 3-locular (D, ×3), with numerous ovules on axile placentas; style stout, stigma flat on top, minutely lobed; fruit a capsule with many seeds (family *Amaryllidaceae*).

Flowers in early spring in meadows and mountain pastures; widely distributed in temperate Europe.

Sisyrinchium angustifolium Mill. ($\times \frac{2}{5}$)

Rootstock tufted with several slender roots; leaves narrow and grass-like, sheathing at the base, shorter than the flowering stem, the latter narrowly wing-ed, merging into the leaf subtending the flowering branch; flowers blue, usually 3–4 in a terminal cluster, the slender pedicels almost hidden by a pair of acute lanceolate bracts; perianth-segments 6, nearly equal, spreading, tube short and broad; stamens 3, united into a short column, the anthers oblong and crowded at the top; ovary inferior, 3-locular; style divided into 3 filiform stigmas; fruit (A, $\times 1\frac{3}{5}$) a small oblong-globose capsule opening into the loculi; seeds (B, $\times 4$) rounded, coarsely wrinkled, blackish (family *Iridaceae*). – Synonym *Sisyrinchium bermudianum* L.

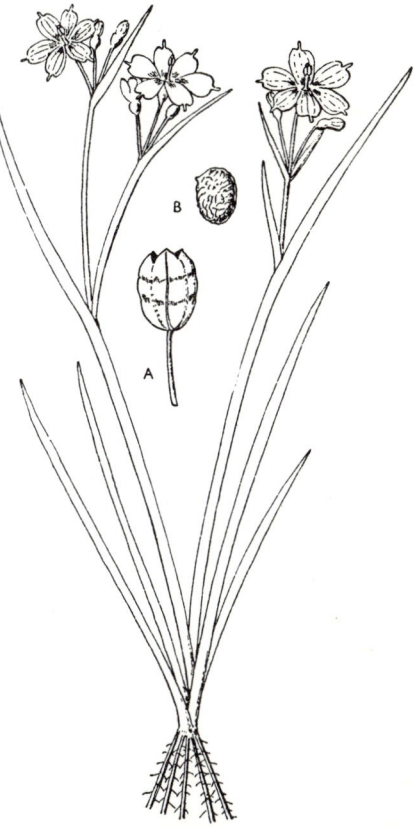

Considered to be native in western Eire from Cork to Donegal, and naturalized in several counties in Great Britain and elsewhere in Europe; also indigenous in eastern North America.

A second species, *S. californicum* (Ker.-Gawl.) Ait., a native of the south-western United States of America, is sometimes found in Eire, with yellow-orange flowers and a longer capsule.

Corm globose or ovoid-globose, $\frac{1}{2}$–$\frac{2}{3}$ in. diam., new growths produced from the corm in July long and stolon-like and 2–4 in.

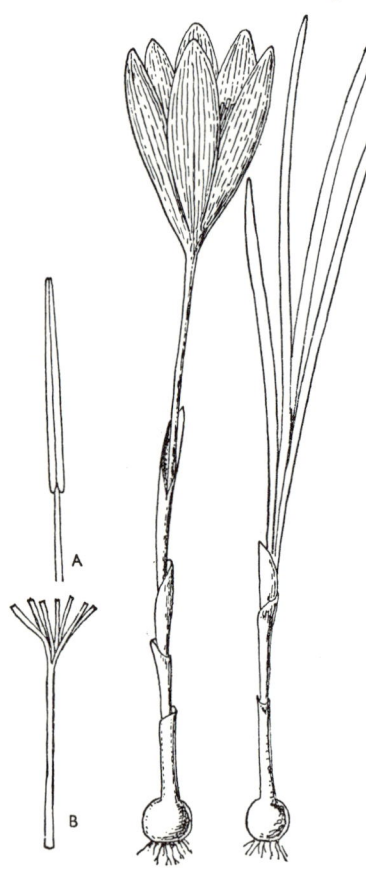

long, forming separate corms on the decay of the parent; tunic a rich brown membrane with parallel fibres; leaves dormant at flowering time, 3–5, linear, up to 1 ft. long, glabrous, margins revolute, keel prominent; leaves sheathing the flower about 5 without a blade, the uppermost reaching up to about $\frac{1}{2}$ the perianth tube, the latter up to about 7 in. long, slender; throat not bearded; segments 6, 2–2$\frac{1}{2}$ in. long, about 1 in. broad, rich bluish purple or rarely white; stamens (A, $\times 1\frac{1}{4}$) 3; anthers about $\frac{3}{4}$ in. long, pale orange; style with several rich-orange stigmas; capsule narrow, about 1 in. long (family *Iridaceae*).

Naturalized in meadows and pastures, native of south-west Europe, flowering in autumn. There are two so-called 'Autumn Crocuses', the real *Crocus* here figured, which has an inferior ovary and 3 stamens, and belongs to *Iridaceae*, and the other a *Colchium*, which has a superior ovary and 6 stamens and belongs to *Liliaceae*.

Perennial, with a thick horizontal rootstock; flowering stem up to about 2 ft. high; lower leaves often longer, up to 2 in. broad, all in one plane (equitant), pale green, the upper leaves becoming much shorter; flowers large and bright yellow, 2–3 at the top of each stem, appearing one at a time from a sheathing bract; outer perianth-segments recurved, broadly obovate, narrowed to the base, with a deeper band across the middle, the inner segments oblong-lanceolate, erect, very much smaller than the outer; stamens (A, $\times 1\frac{1}{2}$) 3, opposite the petal-like stigmas and hidden by them; anthers large; ovary below the perianth (inferior), 3-locular (B, $\times 1\frac{1}{2}$), with numerous ovules attached to the middle; stigmas petal-like, alternate with the inner perianth-segments, split into 2 at the top, with a short scale-like appendage inside; fruit a capsule up to 3 in. long; seeds numerous, pale green (family *Iridaceae*).

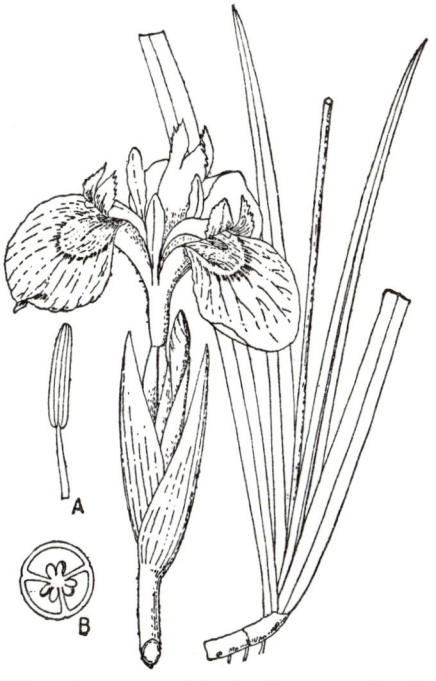

This beautiful plant grows in wet places and by the side of watercourses and is widely spread in Europe and Russian Asia. It flowers in summer and is one of the most handsome of our wild flowers and worthy of a place in a bog garden. A second species, *Iris foetidissima* L., is much less common and mostly found in southern counties. Its flowers are violet-blue or whitish, the capsules with their bright orange or scarlet seeds being very conspicuous and ornamental during the autumn.

Gladiolus illyricus ($\times \frac{2}{5}$)

Corm ovoid-globose, densely covered by fine fibres; stem up to 2 ft. high, with a few linear-lanceolate sharply pointed leaves up to 9 in. long, with 2–3 main nerves between the midrib and margin and fainter nerves between them; spike of up to 8 red flowers, all turned towards one side, with a long-pointed lanceolate bract on the side of each; perianth (A, $\times \frac{2}{5}$) about 1½ in. long; segments clawed, oblong-oblanceolate to obovate, the uppermost broader and a little longer than the others; stamens (B, $\times 2$) 3, ascending under the uppermost segment; anthers large, deeply sagittate at the base; stigmas (C, $\times 2$) expanded at the apex, entire; capsule (D, $\times \frac{1}{2}$) ellipsoid, 3-lobed, ¾ in. long, reticulate; seeds compressed, broadly winged (family *Iridaceae*).

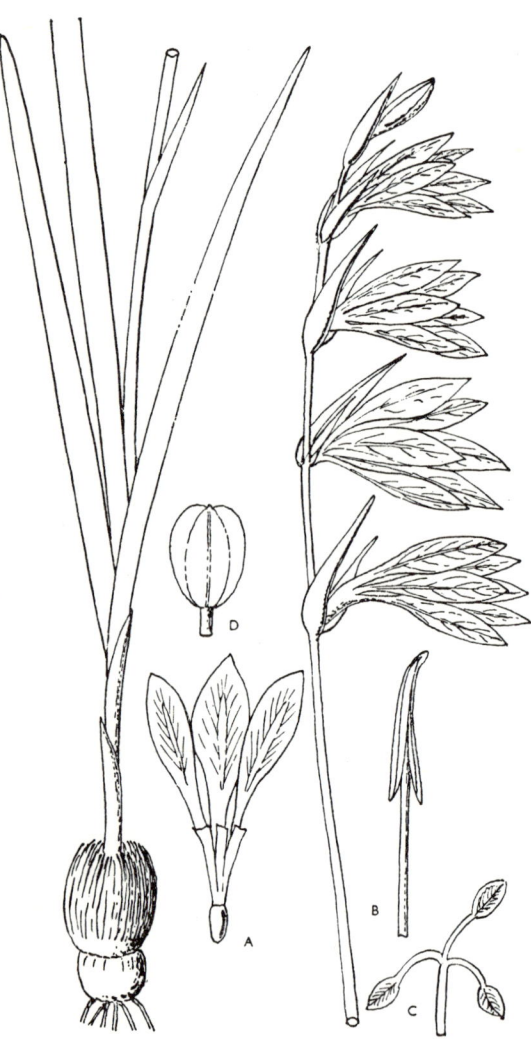

Formerly and probably still found in the New Forest, Hampshire, distributed in central and southern Europe.

ORCHIDS

Orchids are particularly fascinating to many people, and in response to requests from several correspondents drawings of all the native genera are included.

According to Summerhayes (*Wild Orchids of Britain*, 1951) there are 54 species of wild orchids in the British Isles, representing 21 genera. In the following pages I have given a drawing of at least one species of each genus, and from these the beginner may not find much difficulty in determining at least the *genus* of any of the species he may find. Eleven of these 21 genera are represented by a single species and these should be fairly easy to identify from the figures and descriptions. In many cases the habitat, i.e. the particular kind of locality or special type of soil in which the plant is found, will often be of great assistance, some growing exclusively or mainly in woods, some in open meadows, others on chalk-downs or in limestone soil, whilst a few grow only in acid swamps or heath land.

Some orchids have a spur at the base of the lip, which usually secretes nectar; others have no spur.

Of the spurless orchids, the extremely rare Lady's Slipper, *Cypripedium calceolus* (fig. 755), cannot be mistaken for any other, whilst some are distinguished by their mode of growth, being saprophytes without any normal green leaves and devoid of green colouring matter (chlorophyll). These are *Corallorhiza* and *Neottia*, the former with yellowish green flowers, few in a spike, and a coral-like network root-system, the latter with dull brown flowers, numerous in the spike and normal slender roots.

The remainder of the spurless orchids are easily recognized, *Listera* (fig. 758) by the seemingly opposite broad rounded leaves borne well up the stem, whilst *Hammarbya*, to be looked for amongst Sphagnum in acid bogs, produces each year a single pseudo-bulb at the base, and often little bulbils at the tips of the leaves. *Liparis* (fig. 765) has also this pseudo-bulb habit, and a character shared by both is that the lip by a double twist of the stalk is carried around to the *top* of the flower.

Two of the other genera of spurless orchids stand out from the remainder by their root-system, all bearing tubers as well as normal roots, except *Goodyera*, *Cephalanthera*, and *Epipactis*. These are shown in figs. 763, 756, and 759, 760 respectively. Those spurless genera with tuberous roots are not at all difficult to recognize, the Man Orchid, *Aceras anthrophora*, with a lip like a human figure dangling from a gibbet, the side-lobes representing the arms, the deeply bilobed tip its legs. The flowers of *Ophrys* (figs. 777, 778) resemble bees or flies, whilst in *Spiranthes* they are spirally arranged on the axis, which leaves only *Herminium*, with a closely set pair of lanceolate leaves and close spike of small yellowish-green or green sweetly scented flowers and a trilobed lip, bearing no resemblance whatever to either bees, flies, or spiders.

The largest genus of spurred orchids is *Orchis*, with 17 species (and numerous hybrids). The figures of the Common Spotted Orchis, *Orchis fuchsii* (described in most older Floras as *O. maculata*), and of the Military Orchid, *O. militaris*, should provide a clue to other members of this genus. All its species have a distinct spur at the base of the lip, and the only other genus likely to be confused with it is *Anacamptis* (also described in most books as *Orchis*), which too has a spur but with a markedly top-shaped inflorescence. Other genera with a spur at the base of the lip are *Epipogium*, *Platanthera*, *Gymnadenia*, *Himantoglossum*, *Neotinea*, and *Coeloglossum*. Of these *Epipogium* is a leafless saprophyte and exceptional in having the lip at the top of the flower and not at the bottom; *Himantoglossum* has large flowers with a long strap-like lip coiled spirally in bud; *Gymnadenia* (fig. 768) and *Platanthera* (fig. 770) have long conspicuous spurs, whilst *Neotinea* (fig. 773) and *Coeloglossum* (fig. 769) have very short blunt spurs, the former with a deeply trilobed lip, the latter with a shortly 3-toothed lip.

Cephalanthera damasonium (Mill.) Druce ($\times\frac{1}{2}$)

This species, especially when the flowers are in bud, may easily be mistaken for a member of the Lily family (*Liliaceae*); rootstock fibrous; stem up to 1½ ft. high; lower leaves broadly ovate-lanceolate and rather like those of Lily of the Valley (fig. 726) with numerous parallel nerves and few irregularly spaced cross veins; upper leaves gradually becoming narrow and bract-like, but the lower ones longer than the flowers; flowers often up to about 8 (rarely up to 16), pure white or creamy white except for deep orange ridges on the lip; sepals about ¾ in. long, the petals rather shorter; lip small, of 2 distinct parts, the lower part embracing the column, the upper part recurved at the tip (family *Orchidaceae*). – Synonym *Cephalanthera latifolia* Janchen. – A, column and anther, ×3; B, fruit, × 1. Grows in woods in south and south-

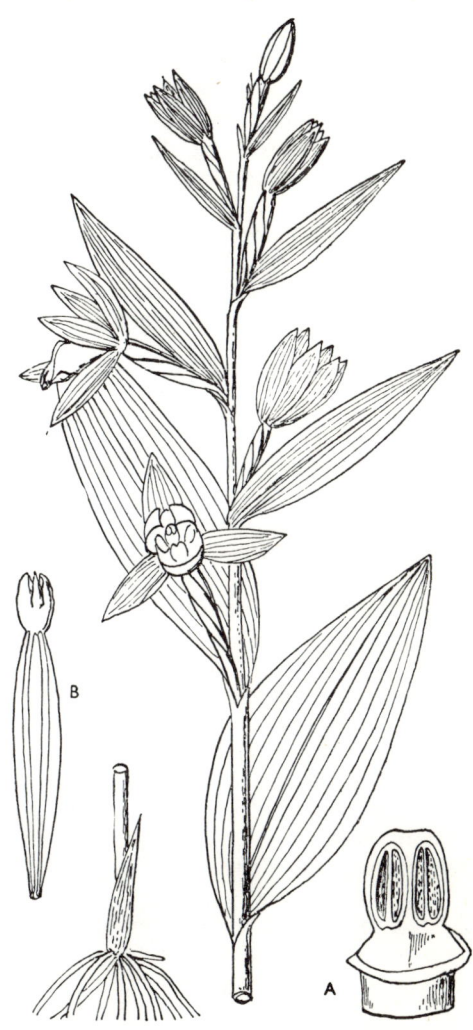

east England and the Midlands. The floral parts keep well together and give the flower the appearance of remaining in bud; they appear at the end of May and during the greater part of June.

Cypripedium calceolus L. ($\times\frac{1}{2}$)

Rootstock a creeping fibrous rhizome without tubers; stems un-branched, up to about 1 ft. high, bearing up to about 5 ovate-elliptic leaves very like those of the Lily of the Valley (fig. 726) with numerous parallel nerves; flowers one or two at the top of the stem, nodding, subtended by a large leaf-like bract; upper sepal opposite the lip, ovate-lanceolate, the two lateral sepals united nearly to the tip and below the large pouched lip (slipper); lateral petals narrow, spreading, lip large and pouched, yellow and spotted, the sepals and petals more or less purple; stamens 2, one on each side of the column which is dilated into a thick petal-like lobe (family *Orchidaceae*). – A, column, $\times 2\frac{1}{2}$; B, ovary and column, $\times 1$; C, fruit, $\times\frac{3}{4}$.

This is both the largest flowered and rarest of our British wild orchids, and is now seldom seen except in cultivation. Formerly it was found in carboniferous limestone woods in Yorkshire, Durham, and Westmorland.

As long ago as 1782 botanists were already concerned with its probable extinction as a wild plant, for Curtis in a leaflet accom-panying the first edition of the *Flora Londinensis* made the following statement:

'The beauty and extreme singularity of the blossoms of this plant, joined to its great scarcity, have occasioned it to be univers-ally sought after by Botanists and others; who, not content with contemplating its beauties in its native soil, are anxious to see it grow in their gardens, in which, however, they are generally dis-appointed, as it very rarely thrives on transplanting. We saw, indeed, a few instances to the contrary in some gardens in York-shire. To this rage for the Lady's Slipper we may attribute its present scarcity in Helk's wood, near Ingleton, where it used to be found in plenty. We were fortunate enough to discover this plant in considerable plenty in the neighbourhood of Kilnsay, not only in the woods with its usual attendant, the Red-flowered Helleborine, but also in hilly pasture ground, with the Ophrys ovata; but as some gardeners in the neighbourhood had dis-covered them, and were unremittingly employed in digging up every one they found, we may venture to prophesy, that in a few years they will be rarely found here also.'

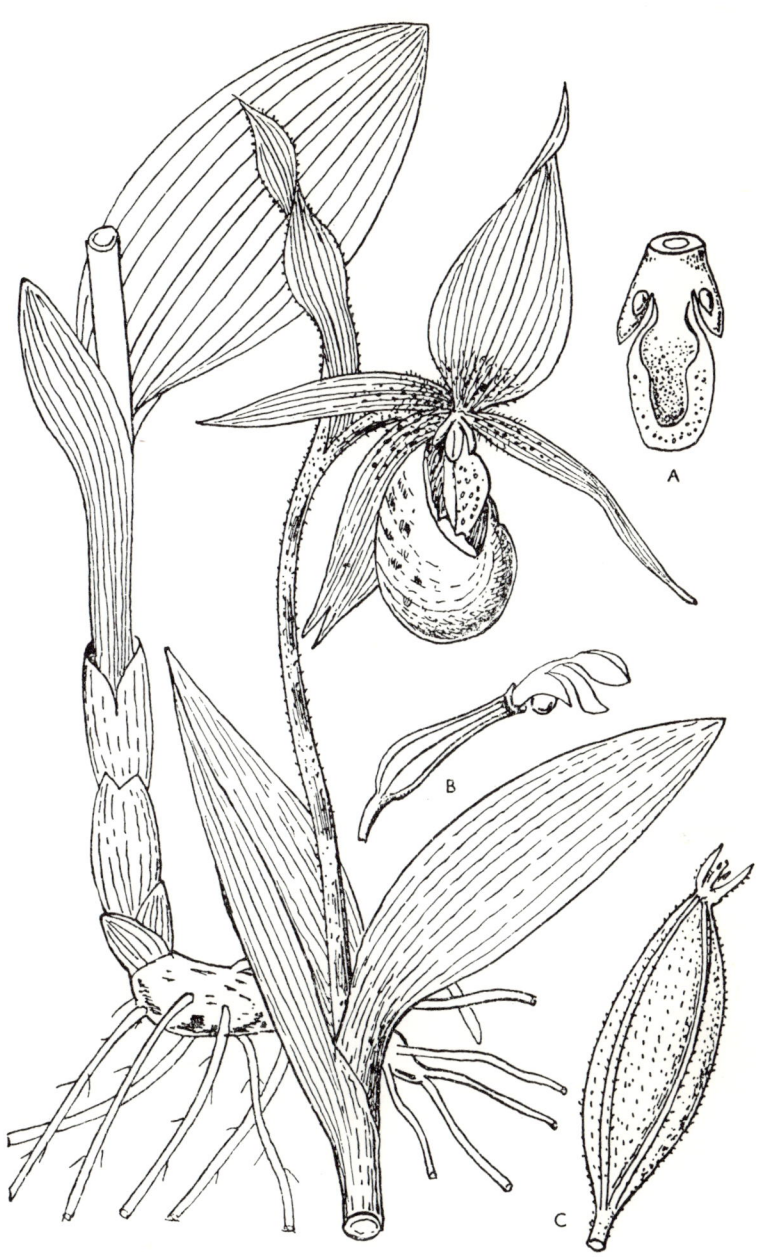

Neottia nidus-avis L. ($\times\frac{1}{2}$)

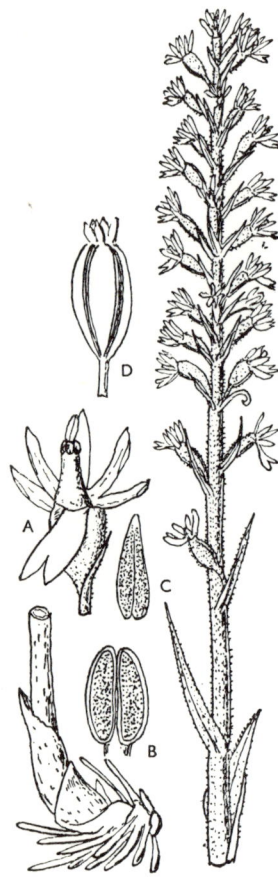

Leafless brown saprophyte growing in dark places in woods, especially Beech; rootstock a dense mass of fleshy cylindrical almost worm-like roots; stem up to $1\frac{1}{2}$ ft. high, stiff and erect, covered towards the base by pale fleshy scales, these becoming longer and thinner further up the stem, the latter clothed with very short thick hairs; raceme 3–4 in. long; floral bracts linear-lanceolate, 1-nerved, those of the lower flowers nearly as long, those of the more densely arranged flowers shorter; flowers numerous, the perianth dull brown, the ovary and short stalk pale dull cream and minutely hairy; sepals and petals very similar, narrow; lip curved downwards, deeply 2-lobed, with a wide cup-shaped saccate base; anthers hinged on to the cylindric free column; pollen masses 2, powdery; glands connate; stigma distinct; rostellum tongue-shaped (family *Orchidaceae*). – A, flower, $\times1\frac{1}{2}$; B, anther, $\times3$; C, pollinia, $\times3$; D, fruit, $\times1$.

Flowers in spring and early summer; extending northwards to central Scotland, and eastwards to Siberia; nowhere common and often difficult to find because of its peculiar habitat and colour.

Slender herb up to about 1½ ft. high; stem with 2 or 3 sheathing scale-leaves in the lower part, and higher a pair of nearly opposite very broadly elliptic-rounded spreading green leaves up to about 6 in. long and 4 in. broad, with a few conspicuous parallel nerves and finer parallel nerves between them; raceme long and slender, bearing numerous loosely arranged green flowers about ½ in. long; pedicels longer than the ovary; sepals ovate; petals narrow, dull green, sometimes tinged with brown or red, the lip pendulous, deeply 2-lobed and of a bright rich yellow-green, the central groove and base glistening with nectar; anthers attached at its base at the top of the short column (family *Orchidaceae*). – A, flower, ×1; B, top of column, ×2½; C, lip, ×4; D, pollinia; E, fruit, ×1⅓; F, cross-section of ovary.

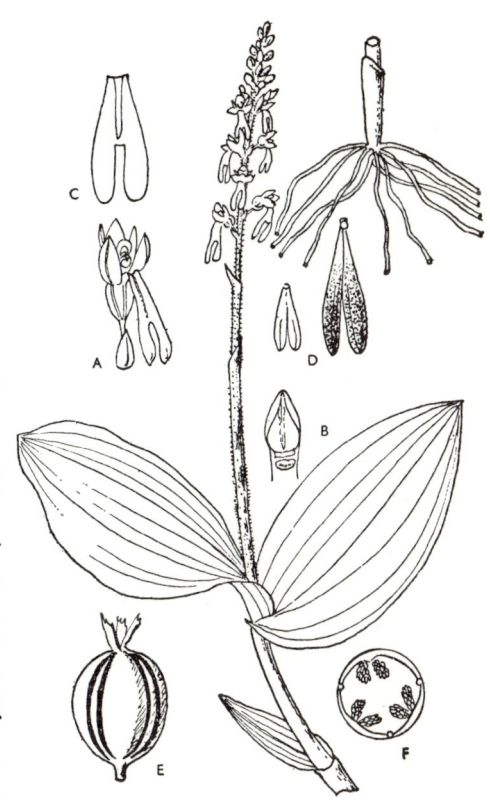

Often to be found in shady places in woods, but with a wide range of habitat, flowering from the middle of May until July; occurs almost throughout the British Isles, but more common in chalky or limestone districts; it has a wide distribution from Europe to Siberia south to the Himalayas.

There is a second species of *Listera* in Britain, the 'Lesser Twayblade', *Listera cordata*, with much smaller ovate-cordate leaves.

Epipactis purpurata Smith (×⅓)

Perennial herb with a vertical rather deep-seated rootstock, the roots sometimes penetrating the soil for as much as 3 ft.; stems

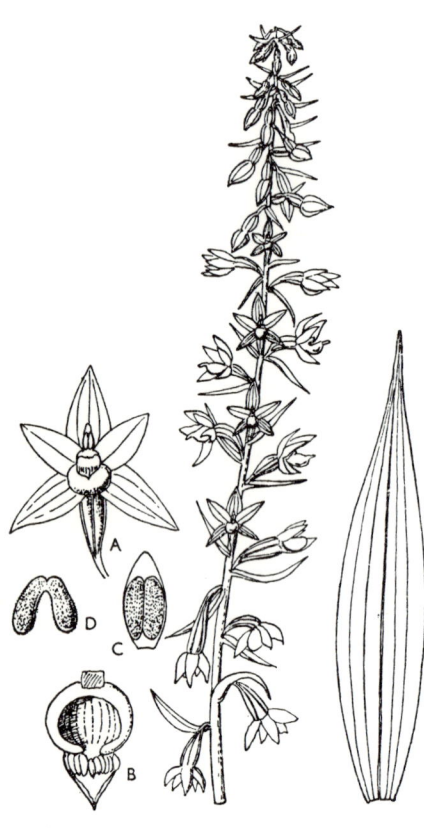

on older plants often clustered, up to nearly 3 ft. high, greyish-purple, puberulous; leaves several on each stem, the lower ones ovate to ovate-lanceolate, sessile and clasping the stem, very acute at the apex, about 4 in. long and 2 in. broad, with numerous prominent and less prominent parallel nerves; upper leaves gradually narrowed into linear-lanceolate bracts; spike up to 15 in. long, with many flowers rather closely arranged; sepals and petals acute, spreading widely, pale whitish-green, the lip pale green with the basal cup more or less purplish inside, the epichile pink or white with pink edges, hypochile pale inside; column short; anther terminal (family *Orchidaceae*). – Synonym *Epipactis violacea* Druce. – A, flower, ×1; B, lip, ×1½; C, anther, ×2½; D, pollinia, ×2½.

In woods, mostly in beech-woods on limy soil, where it pushes up through the deep layer of dead leaves, flowering from early August until September or sometimes earlier; generally distributed in southern England, becoming rare northwards as far as Perthshire; extends from Portugal through middle Europe to western Siberia.

Perennial herb with creeping rootstock; stem purple at the base, erect up to $1\frac{1}{2}$ ft. high, glabrous in the lower, shortly pubescent in the upper part; leaves several, the lower narrowly elliptic, the middle (the longest) oblong-lanceolate, the upper gradually narrower and becoming leafy bracts about as long as the flower-stalks and ovary combined; middle leaves about 3–4 in. long and $1–1\frac{1}{2}$ in. wide, with about 7 parallel nerves and fainter intermediate nerves; flowers fairly numerous (often about 12–15), spreading but soon pendulous; sepals spreading, obliquely lanceolate, $\frac{1}{2}$ in. long, yellowish green, keeled; lateral petals the same shape as the sepals, white streaked with dull crimson; lip divided into two parts the lower half scoop-like and lined with crimson, the upper half white with crinkly margins and a yellow-margined crest at its base; anther sessile, hinged on the top of the column; pollen masses powdery; rostellum short, erect; fruit a pendulous capsule (family

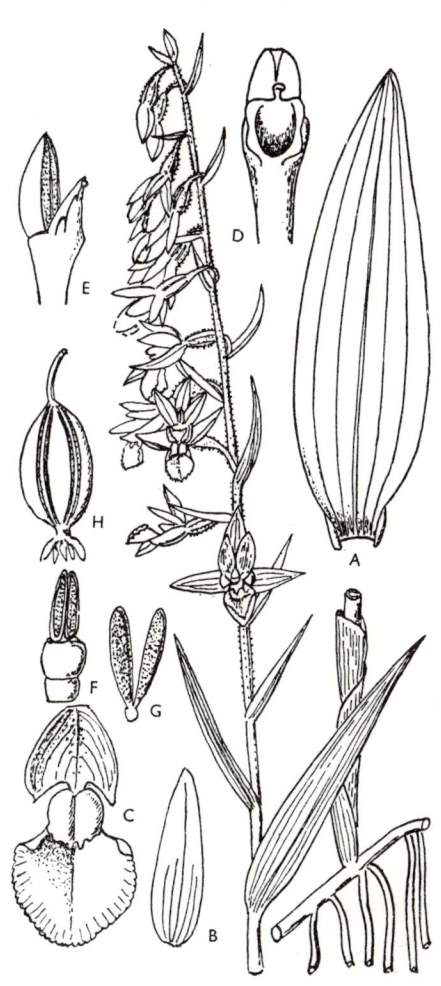

Orchidaceae). – A, leaf $\times\frac{1}{2}$; B, petal, $\times1\frac{1}{2}$; C, lip, $\times2\frac{1}{2}$; D, column from front, $\times2\frac{1}{2}$; E, same from side; F, anther, $\times2\frac{1}{2}$; G, pollinia; H, fruit, $\times1$. In fens and low places amongst dunes, northwards as far as Perth and in the Inner Hebrides.

Rootstock with several short thick fleshy branches; plant leafless, the stem about 6 in. high, swollen at the base, pale in colour, with

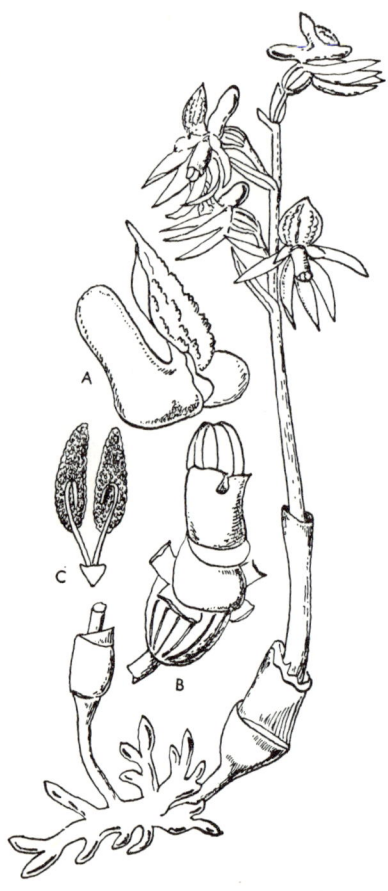

a very few short sheathing bracts; flowers pinkish, 1–5 in the raceme, pendulous on short pedicels, with the lip at the top and with a short blunt spur at its base; sepals and petals narrowly lanceolate; lip large, ovate, marked with raised dots on the surface, with an oblong lobe on each side at the base; column short, with a shortly stalked terminal anther (family *Orchidaceae*). – Synonym *Epipogium gmelinii*. – A, lip, $\times 2$; B, ovary and column, $\times 2\frac{1}{2}$; C, pollinarium, $\times 4$.

An extremely rare species growing among decayed leaves in woods in Herefordshire, Shropshire, and Oxfordshire; although so rare in Britain the species has a very wide distribution from Europe across Asia to Japan, south to the Himalayas.

A characteristic of this species is its sudden appearance after long periods during which it has seemed to be extinct. All that can be found during these periods is the underground stem or rhizome which consists of a much lobed flattened whitish or brownish coral-like structure, to which are added fresh lobes or branches from year to year. There are no true roots, but the rhizome is sparsely covered with long hairs by which it is infected by the usual mycorhizal fungus and through which it obtains its food from the dead and dying plant-remains in which it is buried.

This is the latest orchid to flower in Britain, during September and October; like *Hammarbya* (fig. 764) it is very small and incon-spicuous; it has also a curious mode of growth; a rosette of leaves is produced in the autumn, they last through the winter and die away in late May or June, the 6–9 in. high hairy flowering spike developing later from the middle of these withered leaves alongside a new rosette of newly developed lanceolate leaves; tubers usually 2 or 3, $\frac{1}{2}$ to 1 in. long; bract-like leaves in the spike long and narrow, very acute; flowers white, spirally arranged, all facing to one side of the axis with the bracts facing the other way, sweet-scented during the day-time; lip broad, not lobed but distinctly crenulate; column arching, with the anther attached at the back (family *Orchidaceae*). – Synonym *Spiranthes autumnalis* L. C. Rich. – A, flower, $\times 1\frac{1}{2}$; B, ovary and column, $\times 1\frac{1}{2}$; C, fruit and bract, $\times 1\frac{1}{2}$.

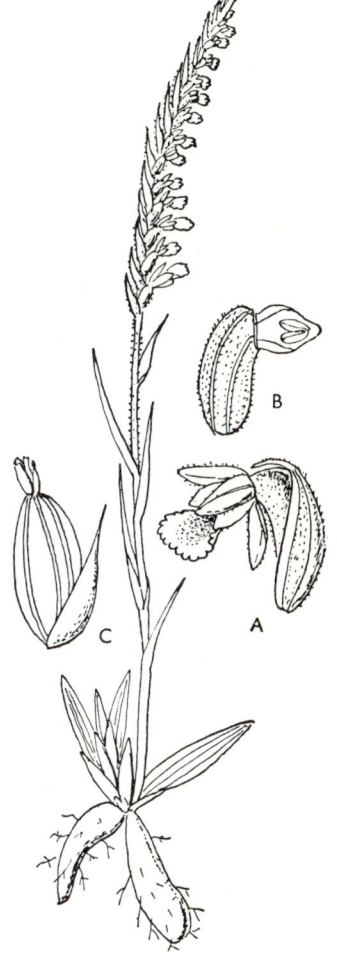

There are two other species of *Spiranthes* in Britain, both distin-guished by the leaves borne only on the flowering stem, the 'Sum-mer Ladies' Tresses' (*Spiranthes aestivalis* (Poir.) L. C. Rich.), a very rare plant, flowering during July and August; the third species, the 'Irish Ladies' Tresses' (*Spir-anthes romanzoffiana* Cham.) is found only in Eire and in the southern Hebrides, but is also widely spread in North America; its flowers are arranged spirally in three rows and not only in one as in the other two species.

Herb up to 1 ft. high; stems spreading horizontally, slender; no tubers, mature stems becoming erect and bearing a few (up

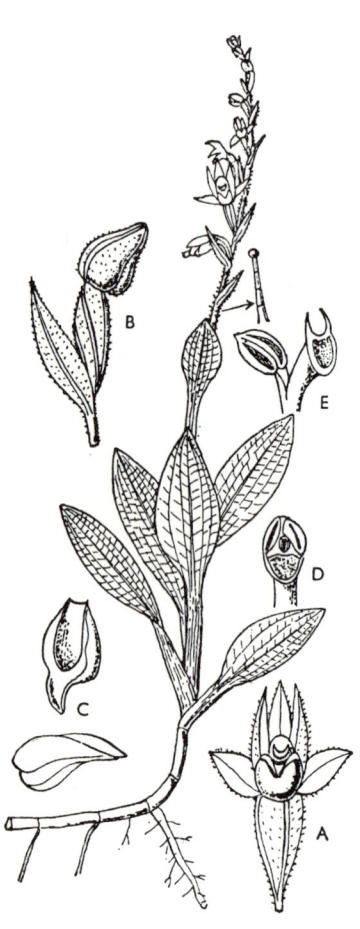

to about 7) lanceolate broadly stalked leaves 1–1$\frac{1}{2}$ in. long and dark green with paler green marblings; transverse veins very distinct; spike one-sided, with a few scattered scale-leaves below the flowers, the latter in a single row, sweetly scented, white; bracts lanceolate, acute, longer than the ovary; axis of spike clothed with numerous several-celled gland-tipped hairs; sepals ovate, obtuse concave, white or tinged with green, glandular-hairy outside, 1–2-nerved; petals lanceolate, narrow, 1-nerved; lip boat-shaped, with a spout-like tip; column short; anther stalked, brownish, hood-shaped, 3-toothed in front, resting on the upper surface of the rostellum; pollinia 2, short, yellow, ovoid, without caudicles; fruit $\frac{1}{2}$ in. long; ovary compressed laterally, glandular-hairy, with 3 ridges (family *Orchidaceae*). – A, flower, ×2; B, same in bud with bract, ×2; C, two views of lip, ×2; D, top of column, ×3; E, same with pollinia separated, ×3.

Generally distributed in Scotland, south as far as Yorkshire and probably introduced into pine plantations in Norfolk.

Hammarbya paludosa (L.) O. Kuntze $(\times\frac{1}{2})$

A tiny herb up to 5 in. high but sometimes not more than 2 in., growing amongst Sphagnum in acid soil in spongy bogs; rootstock producing 2 small solid ellipsoid pseudobulbs below the basal leaves; leaves 2–4, ovate-elliptic, up to 1 in. long and $\frac{1}{2}$ in. broad, often bearing a few tiny bulbils at the top; flowers yellowish green in a lax raceme up to 2 in. long; bracts almost as long as the pedicels which are doubly twisted to bring the erect lip at the top of the flower; sepals ovate, 2 erect alongside the lip, the third turned downwards; petals smaller, spreading laterally; pollen masses club-shaped, in 2 pairs suspended from a gland which terminates the column (family *Orchidaceae*). – Synonym *Malaxis paludosa* (L.) Swartz. – A, tip of leaf with bulbils; B, flower from front, $\times 3\frac{1}{2}$; C, flower from back, showing double twist, $\times 3\frac{1}{2}$; D, column from front; E, same showing anther from back; F, pollinia.

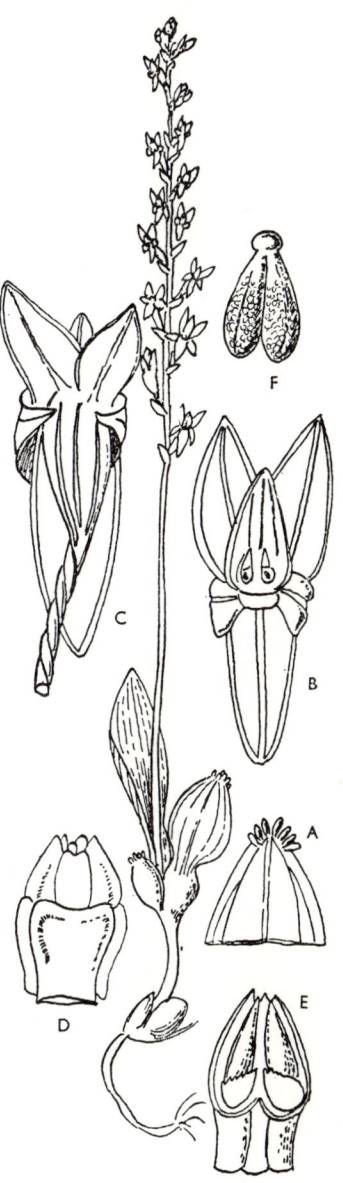

A rare plant in its boggy habitat, where it flowers about the end of July and early August; widely spread in Britain and Eire, extending eastwards into Russian Asia.

The flowers of this tiny plant are exceptional among British orchids in that the flower-stalk is twisted through a complete circle (360°) instead of only 180°, thus bringing the lip erect at the *top* of the flower.

FEN ORCHID
Liparis loeselii Rich. ($\times \frac{1}{2}$)

Herb up to 6 in. high; rootstock bearing a small ovoid-globose bulb by the side of the stem which develops into a new plant;

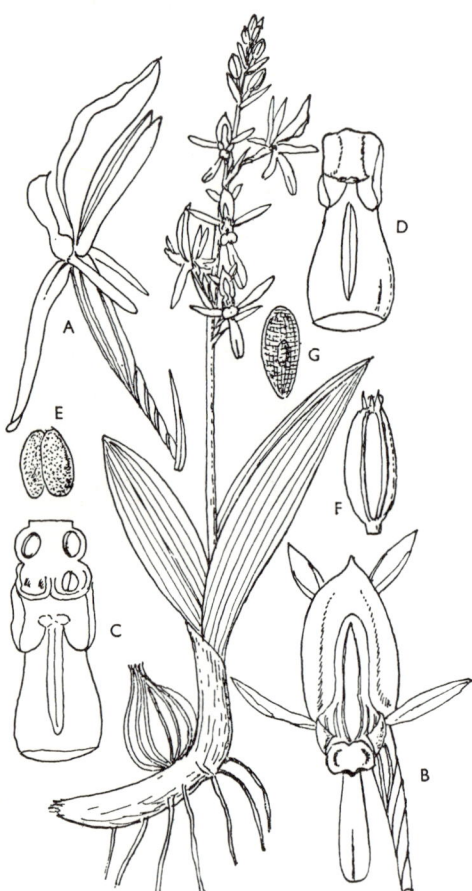

leaves 2, broadly lanceolate, sheathing at the base, with several parallel nerves; flowers dull yellowish green, up to about 10 in a raceme; sepals and petals very narrow, spreading; lip placed uppermost by a double twist of the pedicel, broadly ovate; column much shorter than the lip (family *Orchidaceae*). – A, flower and bract, $\times 3\frac{1}{2}$; B, same from front, $\times 3\frac{1}{2}$; C, column from front; D, same from back; E, pollinia; F, fruit, $\times \frac{1}{2}$; G, seed.

One of the rarer of our native orchids, found only in East Anglia and south Wales; elsewhere it occurs in Europe from southern Norway and Sweden, south to northern Italy and the northern parts of the Balkan Peninsula. It favours the edges of lakes and pools, flowering in June and early July. Unlike most other British orchids, the lip is uppermost owing to a double twist of the pedicel.

Herb up to about 10 in. high, without green colouring matter (chlorophyll), of a light brown or pale yellowish green colour; stems with 2–3 sheathing scales in place of leaves; rootstock consisting of a network of thick fleshy branches forming a coral-like cream-coloured structure (hence the name); raceme short, few-flowered; flowers yellowish-green, very shortly stalked, with a small bract below each; sepals and petals very similar; lip white and hanging, with 2 lateral rounded lobes near the base and 2 raised parallel ridges on the surface; column short, with a terminal lid-like anther and two pairs of globular pollen-masses; fruit ellipsoid, about $\frac{1}{2}$ in. long (family *Orchidaceae*). – Synonym *Corallorhiza innata* R. Br. A, flower, $\times 3$; B, column; C, pollinia; D, cross-section of ovary; E, fruits; F, seed.

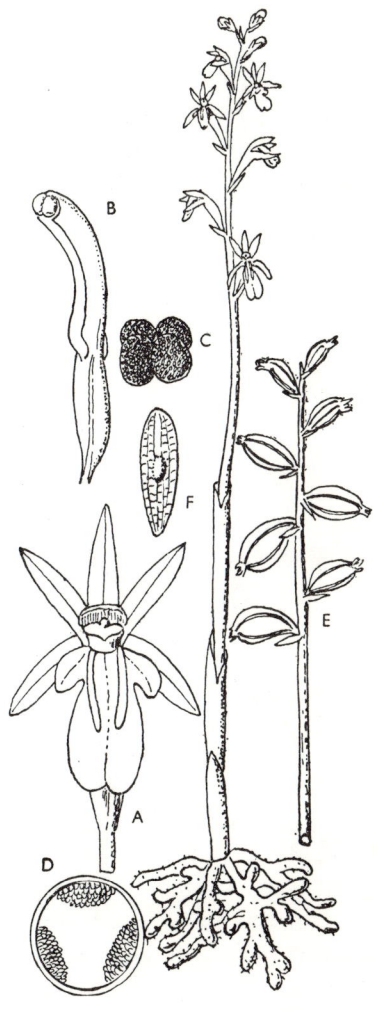

This species has a northern distribution, not being found south of Lancashire, Cumberland, and Northumberland. It grows in pine-woods or pine- and birch-woods rich in humus, and even in damp marshy places among sand dunes near the sea, flowering in June and July. It has a wide range from Europe to Siberia and northern China. The rootstock is heavily infected by a mycorhizal fungus which absorbs food from the decayed plant-remains in the soil and passes it on to the host plant.

Herminium monorchis (L.) R. Br. ($\times \frac{1}{2}$)

Small herb usually up to about 6 in. high but in more favourable habitats nearly 1 ft.; tuber rounded, at the base of the stem, the

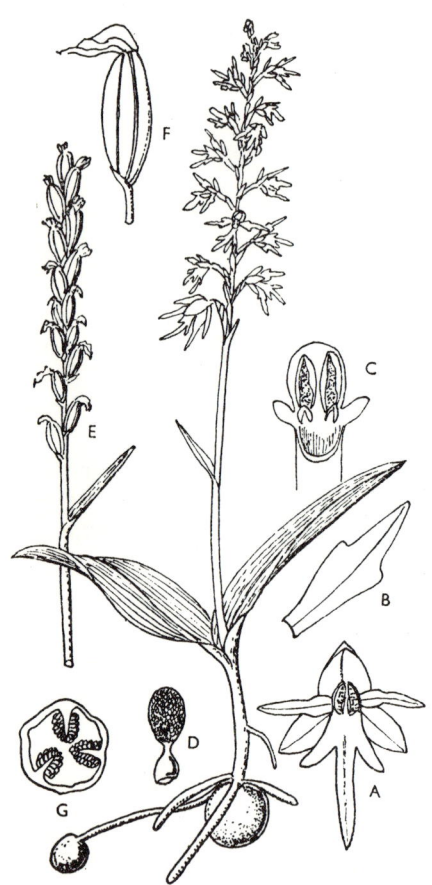

young tuber produced at the end of a stolon; normal roots very few; leaves oblong-lanceolate, usually 2, rarely 3, towards the base of the flowering stem, with 1 or 2 bract-like leaves between them and the flowers; flowers yellowish green or green, sweetly scented, set rather close together; sepals and petals narrow, more or less connivent; petals often with a tooth or angle on each side below the middle; lip narrow with a short spreading lobe on each side near the middle; no spur; pollinia ellipsoid, each attached to a rather large rounded viscidium; fruit about $\frac{1}{3}$ in. long (family *Orchidaceae*). – A, flower, $\times 2\frac{1}{2}$; B, petal, $\times 2$; C, column, $\times 5$; D, pollinarium; G, section of ovary; E, fruits, $\times \frac{1}{2}$; F, fruit.

Flowers during summer in chalky and limestone soils in the southern parts of England, as far north-east as Hunstanton in Norfolk, and Gloucestershire in the west. It ranges from Europe east to Japan.

Rootstock tuberous, the tuber forked for about half its length; ordinary roots very few; flowering stem up to $1\frac{1}{2}$ ft. high; leaves few, linear to narrowly lanceolate gradually decreasing upwards, the latter finely pointed and often as long as the flowers; flower-spike oblong; flowers rosy red or pink often with a distinct lilac or bluish tinge; bright magenta and pure white flowers sometimes occur; sepals ovate-lanceolate; petals erect, semilunar; lip broad, 3-lobed, with a long slender curved spur at the base; lobes oblong - deltoid, obtuse; anther loculi converging at the base; stigma with a rostellate pro-

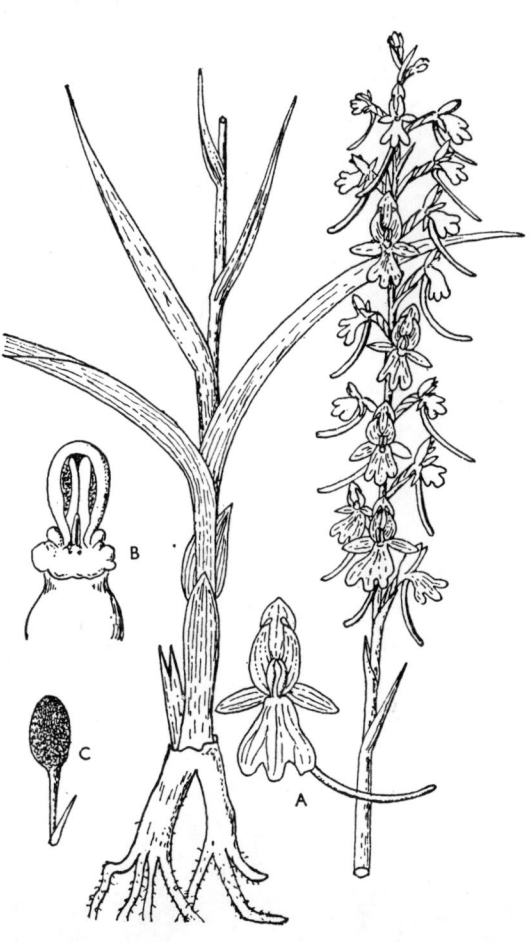

cess extending between the base of the anther-loculi (family *Orchidaceae*). – Synonym *Habenaria conopsea* L. – A, flower, $\times 2\frac{1}{2}$; B, column; C, pollinarium.

Found throughout the British Isles, on a variety of soils, but more especially in chalky or limestone districts.

769   FROG ORCHID

Coeloglossum viride (L.) Hartm. ($\times\frac{1}{2}$)

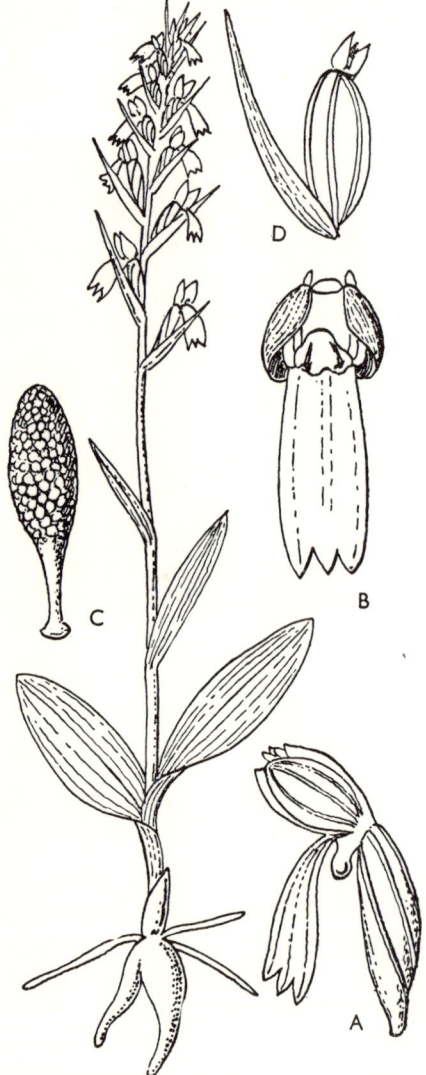

Flowering stem variable according to habitat, in tall grass or in bushy places up to 1 ft. high; tubers forked; lower leaves 2–5, more or less elliptic, up to 2½ in. long and about 1 in. broad; a conspicuous feature of the loose spike of green, brownish green, or reddish-tinged flowers are the large bracts which are sometimes much longer than the flowers; sepals and upper petals forming an almost globular helmet, below which hangs the much longer pendulous 3-toothed lip, the latter with a very short blunt spur; pollinia club-shaped (family *Orchidaceae*). – Synonym *Habenaria viridis* (L.) R. Br. – A, flower, $\times2\frac{1}{2}$; B, flower, front view, $\times6$; C, pollinarium; D, fruit.

Widely distributed in the British Isles and across the northern hemisphere; flowering in a variety of habitats in Britain from June until August; flowers faintly honey-scented.

Platanthera chlorantha (Custer) Rchb. ($\times\frac{1}{3}$)

Root tubers 2, ovoid; stem up to 18 in. high, pale green, ribbed; leaves 2 (rarely 3) at the base of the stem, appearing to be opposite, obovate-elliptic, narrowed to the base, glossy below with about 7 parallel nerves on each side of the midrib, the latter keeled towards the base; remainder of leaves alternate, few, linear-lanceolate, subacute, the uppermost about 1 in. long; flowers about 1 in. diam., white, slightly tinged with green, in a loose spike 3–8 in. long and about 2 in. diam., the very long spurs crossing the axis; bracts lanceolate, nearly as long as the ovary; ovary green, twisted, $\frac{3}{4}$ in. long, ribbed; upper (dorsal) sepal broadly ovate, arching over the lateral petals and column; lateral sepals spreading obliquely ovate-lanceolate, $\frac{1}{2}$ in. long; lateral petals narrow, forming an arch beneath the margins of

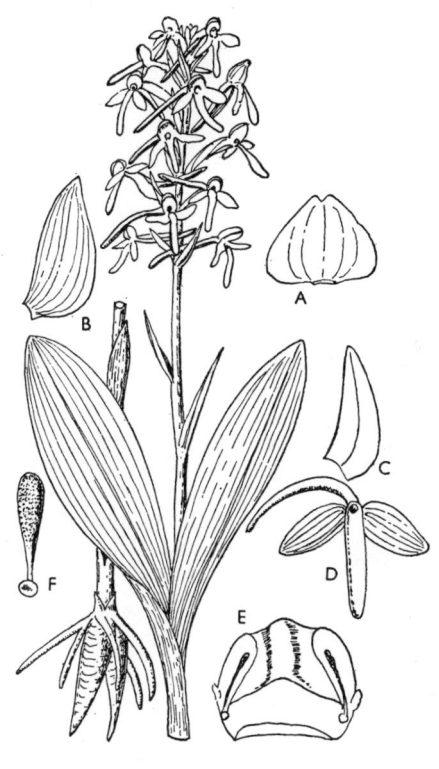

the dorsal sepals; lip $\frac{2}{3}$ in. long, broadly linear, tinged with green towards the tip; spur slender, nearly 1$\frac{1}{2}$ in. long, tinged with green towards the end; anther-loculi divergent downwards; column broad (family *Orchidaceae*). – A, dorsal sepal, $\times1\frac{1}{3}$; B, lateral sepal, $\times1\frac{1}{3}$; C, petal, $\times1\frac{1}{3}$); D, lip and lateral sepals, $\times1$; E, column, $\times4$; F, pollinarium.

The flowers are pollinated by moths attracted by the nearly white flowers which give off a strong odour like that of pinks, especially at night. In woods and grassy places especially in chalky soils, widely distributed throughout the British Isles except Orkney and Shetland; extends eastwards to Siberia.

LIZARD ORCHID

Himantoglossum hircinum (L.) Spreng. (×⅓)

A very striking orchid up to 5 ft. high; tubers 2, ellipsoid, with a few spreading roots above; stem leafy, leaves scattered, up to about 8 in. long and 2 in. broad, gradually decreasing upwards and becoming bracts, the latter narrow and longer than the ovary; flowers large, in spike up to 1 ft. long, grey-ish-purple green, with a strong smell of goats; sepals and pe-tals forming a darker coloured hood cover-ing the column; lip long, about 2 in., nar-row and ribbon-shaped, whitish to-wards the base, with small red spots or blotches, the rest be-ing dull green, the shorter side-lobes more or less purple; the middle lobe of the lip is spirally coiled in bud and remains more or less twisted when expanded; base of lip with a very short spur;

pollinia attached to a single viscidum; fruit ¾ in. long (family *Orchi-daceae*). – Synonym *Orchis hircina* (L.) Crantz. – A, petal, × ¾; B, column; C, pollinarium; D, cross-section of ovary; E, fruit, × ⅔.

Flowers in late June and in July, in chalky or limestone dis-tricts from southern England to Yorkshire, in bushy places among shrubs or in tall grass; distributed as far east as the Balkans and Asia Minor. The common name refers to the resemblance of the flowers to a lizard, the sepals and petals being like the head and body, the side lobes of the lip the hind legs, and the long twisted middle lobe of the lip the tail of this animal.

Anacamptis pyramidalis (L.) L. C. Rich. (× ½)

One of the best known of our British orchids and often abundant in limestone districts particularly in maritime counties; tubers 2,

ellipsoid, with a few fleshy ordinary roots; stem up to about 1 ft. high; leaves (often partly withered at flowering time) very narrow (linear - lanceolate) and sharply pointed, gradually reduced to bracts; flowers slightly fragrant, in a dense pyramidal spike up to 3 in. long, from pale pink to purplish red, rarely white, with a slender spur longer than the ovary; sepals lanceolate, spreading; upper petals narrow and converging over the column; lip broad, 3-lobed; pollinia 2, indian-club-shaped, joined to a single narrow strap-like viscidium; fruit ⅔ in. long (family *Orchidaceae*). – Synonym *Orchis pyramidalis* L. – A, flower from front, × 1½; B, same from side; C, pollinarium; D, fruit and bract, × 1½.

Flowers from mid-June until the end of July.

Neotinea intacta (Link) Rchb. f. ($\times \frac{1}{2}$)

Tubers 2, egg-shaped; roots few, fleshy; leafy shoot produced in October and persisting throughout the winter; stem up to 7 in.

high; leaves sometimes with small reddish or purplish spots, oblong-lanceolate, the upper two or three reduced to sheaths; spike of flowers up to $1\frac{1}{2}$ in. long, to 2 in. in fruit; flowers often facing in one direction (secund), whitish or pink; sepals and petals forming a hood; lip unequally 3-lobed, the middle lobe longer and broader with a short tip, a very short blunt spur at the base; stigmas 2, one on each side of the mouth of the spur; fruit nearly $\frac{1}{2}$ in. long (family *Orchidaceae*). – Synonym *Habenaria intacta* Benth. – A, flower and bract, $\times 2$; B, lip, $\times 5$; C, pollinarium; D, fruit and bract, $\times 2\frac{1}{2}$.

Found only in barren limestone country in western Eire, in counties Clare, Galway, and Mayo, flowering in May and early June; elsewhere it occurs in Portugal and Spain, eastwards as far as Cyprus and Asia Minor, as well as in Algeria and Morocco, Madeira, and the Canary Islands.

Rootstock tuberous, tubers flattish and divided into 2 or 3 finger-like lobes; stem erect, up to 1½ ft. high, rounded in the lower part, ribbed towards the top; lower leaves oblong, with irregular dull purple spots on the upper surface, pale and glossy below, and with about 6 parallel nerves on each side of the midrib; stem-leaves gradually narrower and shorter upwards, often with narrowly purplish margins; bracts as long as the flowers, slightly overtopping the buds, lanceolate, acute, green; flowers in a dense pyramidal spike up to about 3 in. long and 1½ in. diam., mauve or sometimes white, the lip lined or spotted with crimson; spur shorter than the ovary, the latter much shorter than the bract; dorsal sepal arched over the 2 lateral petals; lateral

sepals ascending; lateral petals arched over the anther; lip spreading or decurved, 3-lobed, lobes toothed or jagged; anther purple, the loculi pointed and convergent at the base; ovary twisted (family *Orchidaceae*). – Synonym *Orchis maculata* of many authors, not of L. and *O. fuchsii* Druce – A, flower, × 1½; B, flower bud and bract, × 1½; C, anther; D, pollinarium.

Grows in moist meadows and open woods, fairly common, flowering from late May to June.

This is the largest genus of orchids in Britain, and we can only figure two of the fifteen or so species, besides hybrids, for the determination of which Summerhayes' book is necessary (see p. 869).

Herb up to 2 ft. high; tubers 2, ellipsoid, entire; normal roots few; leaves 4–5 in the lower part of the stem, oblong-elliptic to oblong, 3–5 in. long, to $1\frac{1}{2}$ in. broad, with numerous parallel nerves, often with only one sheathing leaf above them and encircling the peduncle; bracts small, about $\frac{1}{3}$ as long as the twisted ovary; flowers fairly numerous in a dense oblong spike; sepals ovate, usually pale pink or whitish forming a hood over the petals and column; lip descending, bright red or violet, spotted, with 2 lateral spreading lobes near the base, and divided into 2 at the apex with a tooth between them; spur relatively short; anthers on the face of the column, with 2 erect loculi; pollen masses on a slender stalk (family *Orchidaceae*). – A, flower, $\times 1$; B, column; C, pollinarium. – A very rare plant flowering in May and June.

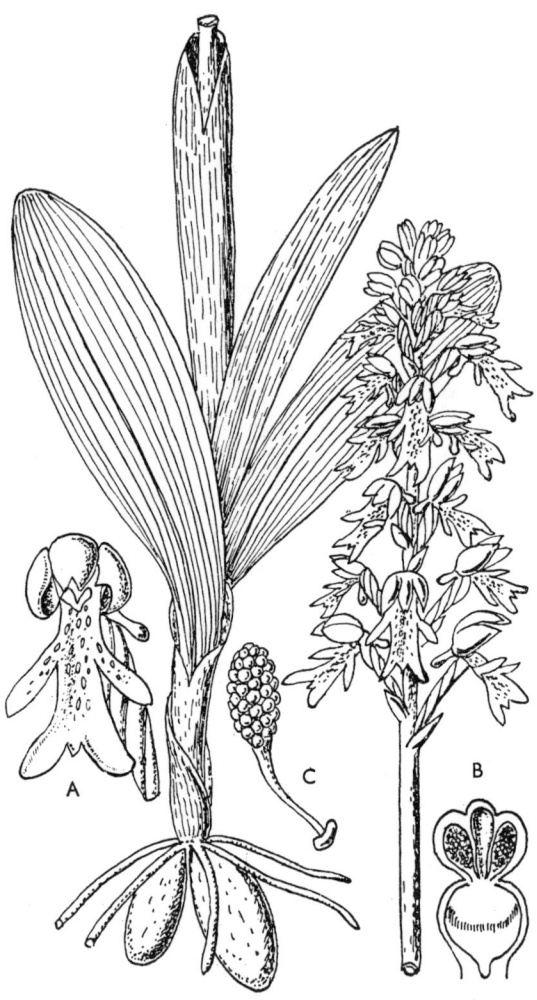

892

Aceras anthropophorum (L.) S. F. Gray ($\times\frac{1}{2}$)

Erect herb up to $1\frac{1}{2}$ ft. high; tubers 2, ellipsoid or globose, $1–1\frac{1}{2}$ in. long, entire; roots several, spreading from the base of the stem; leaves few towards the base, oblanceolate, up to 6 in. long and 1 in. broad, with 2 or 3 shorter leaves above and closely clasping the stem; flowering part of the spike up to 7 in. long; bracts short; flowers a dull greenish-yellow, often reddish on the edges of the sepals and petals, bearing some resemblance to a hanging human figure, the sepals and petals representing the head, and the lip the arms and legs; spur absent; sepals and lateral petals similar, but petals narrower; lip about $\frac{1}{2}$ in. long, hanging, 3-lobed; ovary twisted, green; seeds loosely

reticulate (family *Orchidaceae*). – A, flower, $\times 1\frac{1}{2}$; B, pollinarium.

Found among grasses in soil rich in lime in the south-eastern half of England.

Ophrys insectifera L. ($\frac{1}{2}$)

Tubers ovoid to subglobose, up to as large as a plum; stem up to 2 ft. high, but often about 9–12 in., glabrous; leaves few (3–5), oblong-lanceolate, with 3 principal nerves, shining on both surfaces, bright green; uppermost leaf smallest and embracing the stem; flowers 3 or more to a stem, sessile; bract about twice as long as the ovary, slightly keeled; ovary faintly ribbed, narrow; sepals green, oblong, 3-nerved; lateral petals very narrow and purple, like two horns, shortly pubescent; lip hanging down, about $\frac{1}{2}$ in. long, maroon purple, paler in the middle, with two oblong deflexed lobes, terminal lobe widely notched at the apex, two glass-like knobs in the middle (family *Orchidaceae*). – A, flower, $\times$ 1$\frac{1}{2}$.

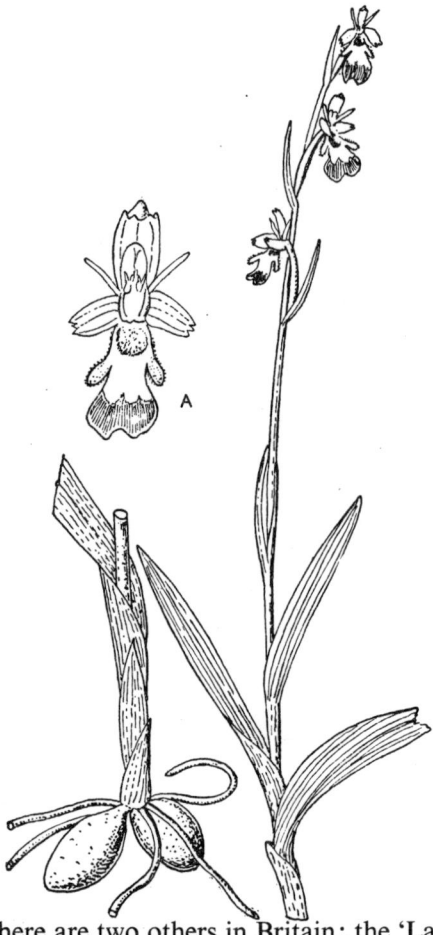

On chalk downs and towards the edge of beech woods, flowering in early summer.

This should be compared with the figure of the Bee Orchid (fig. 778). Besides these two species there are two others in Britain; the 'Late Spider Orchid', *Ophrys fuciflora* (Crantz) Rchb., with a more or less flat lip ending in an often cordate appendage, 3-lobed, the sepals rose pink; and the 'Early Spider Orchid', *Ophrys sphegodes* Mill., sepals green and herbaceous, the lip subentire, purplish-brown with yellow markings. All the species favour chalky soils. Synonym *O. museifera* Huds.

Herb up to about $1\frac{1}{2}$ ft. high; rootstock with 2 ovoid to globose tubers; leaves scattered on the stem, lanceolate, many-nerved, gradually reduced upwards to bracts; spike few-flowered (flowers 2–8); bracts lanceolate, acute, as long as or longer than the flowers; sepals spreading, finally reflexed, oblong, petaloid, pink or violet rose, rarely white, with 3–5 green nerves; petals about half as long as the sepals, linear with rolled back edges, green or brownish or reddish purple; lip bag-like but really 5-lobed, velvety, rich brown or dark purple edged with yellow or white, often with 2–3 yellowish spots near the apex and sometimes a yellow blotch on each side; lobes of lip strongly curved back behind the lip; column green, at right angles to the lip; pollinia yellow, pear-shaped, on long slender thread-like caudicles; fruit oblong, $1\frac{1}{2}$ in.

long, with prominent nerves (family *Orchidaceae*). – A, pollinarium, twisted over for self-pollination; B, fruits, $\times\frac{1}{2}$.

The Bee Orchid is so called because of its great resemblance to a bee; the male bee mistakes it for a female of its own kind, though the flowers are normally self-pollinated (for accounts of this remarkable flower see Godfrey, *British Orchidaceae* (1933), and Summerhayes, *Wild Orchids of Britain* (1951)).

Luzula campestris L. ($\times \frac{2}{3}$)

Perennial herb, up to about 1 ft. high, with rather slender root-stock; old leaf-bases persistent; leaves linear, 1-nerved, mostly at

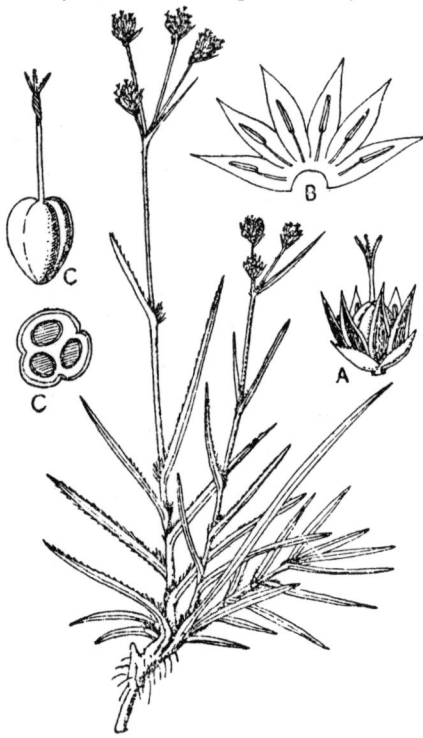

the base of the plants, the margins fringed with long weak hairs, completely sheathing around the stem at the base and with a bunch of long hairs at the top of the sheath; flowers (A, $\times 1\frac{1}{2}$) collected into head-like clusters, usually from 3–6 together at the top of the slender stems; the middle cluster very shortly stalked or almost sessile, the others on much longer stalks; bracts below each flower rather large, membranous, triangular-ovate, fringed with hairs; perianth-segments (B, $\times 2\frac{1}{2}$) 6, rich dark brown with pale thin shining margins, ovate-lanceolate and very acutely pointed; stamens 6, opposite the perianth-segments; anthers linear, attached at the base, opening inwards (introrse); ovary (C, $\times 4$) 3-lobed, 1-locular with 3 erect ovules attached at the base; style divided into 3 greenish white hairy stigmas which twist together into a spiral after flowering; capsule triangular, with 3 erect seeds (family *Juncaceae*).

A very common plant, flowering in spring, in rather dry fields, woods, and heaths, and widely distributed in temperate regions all over the world. A very similar species is *L. spicata* DC., but this has smaller flowers in *sessile* clusters, collectively forming a spike, is a mountain species from northern districts, and flowers in summer. Flowers of this family are anemophilous, i.e. the pollen is blown about by the wind, though they are not unisexual.

A small annual plant often growing in dense tufts like a perennial, with numerous stems up to nearly 1 ft. high; leaves very few, mostly from the base, much shorter than the flowering stems, very narrow; flowers (A, ×1) solitary or rarely 2–3 together at the main forks of the branches, sessile or nearly so, each subtended by 2 small ovate very thin bracts; perianth (B, ×1) of 6 unequal segments, the outer 3 longer and very sharply pointed, the inner 3 shorter and wider, and more membranous, but all longer than the capsule; stamens 6, opposite to the segments; ovary with 3 parietal placentas nearly meeting in the middle; capsule (C, ×2) splitting into 3 boat-shaped parts, 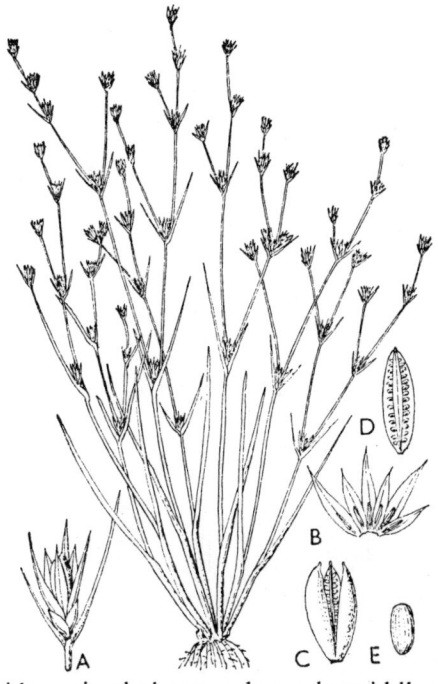 each part (D, ×2) with a wide parietal placenta down the middle; seeds (E, ×6) very minute and numerous, pale brown, faintly lined (family *Juncaceae*).

This species is very abundant in Britain, and is widely spread over many parts of the world. It flowers during the whole of the summer.

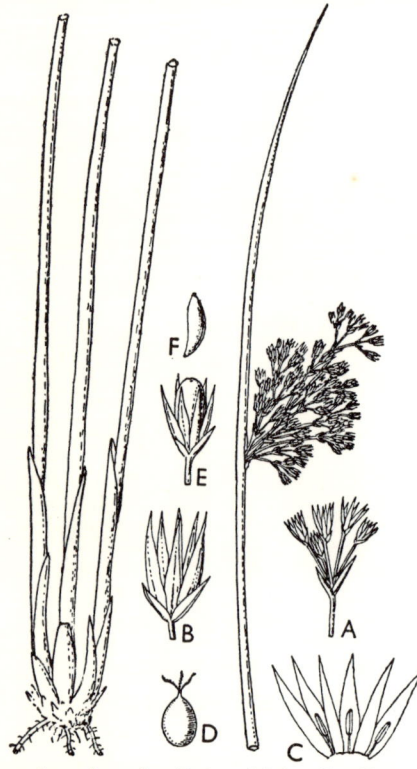

Perennial with closely matted rootstocks bearing dense tufts of rounded leafless stems 2–3 ft. high, clothed at the base with rather long brown sheaths and full of soft pith; only some of the stems bear a bunch of flowers about 6–8 in. below the tip; flowers (A, $\times 1$) in much-branched loose cymes varying greatly in number, sometimes quite few; each flower (B, $\times 2\frac{1}{2}$) with a pair of thin lanceolate bracts at the base; perianth-segments (C, $\times 2\frac{1}{2}$) subequal, very sharply pointed, about as long as the fruits (E, $\times 1\frac{1}{2}$); stamens 3, opposite the outer segments; ovary (D, $\times 4$) ovoid; styles 3; capsule rounded at the top, with numerous very small yellowish seeds (F, $\times 5$) (family *Juncaceae*).

This is very common in Britain, and grows in moist places in woods and on heaths. It is widely distributed in Asia and in both North and South America.

Perennial with short knotted rootstock; stems slender, crowded in tufts; leaves with long open sheathing bases and ligule-like at the top of the sheath, the blade cylindrical upwards and hollow, but divided inside by cross partitions of pith giving a knotted or jointed appearance; flowers (A, $\times$ 2) in small dense 'prickly' clusters arranged in panicles; lowermost bract of each cluster sheath-like and shortly pointed; smaller bracts lanceolate, acute; perianth (B, $\times$ 3) of 6 free segments, these lanceolate, acute, keeled; stamens 6, opposite the segments and about half as long; ovary (C, $\times$ 3) ellipsoid, with 3 short styles; capsule (D, $\times$ 2) 3-angled, splitting into 3 valves (E, $\times$ 2), each with seeds arranged down the middle; seed (F, $\times$ 6) faintly striate, with a dark brown tip (family *Juncaceae*).

This species is very easily recognized by its distinctive leaves, which are described above. It is very widely distributed in various parts of the world, and is sometimes split up under several names.

Juncus bulbosus L. ($\times\frac{1}{2}$)

Perennial herb with tufted stems about 6 in. high and the root-stock sometimes tuberous; leaves shorter than the flowering stems, needle-like, sheathing at the base and with a large membranous ligule-like appendage at the top of the sheath; flowers (B,

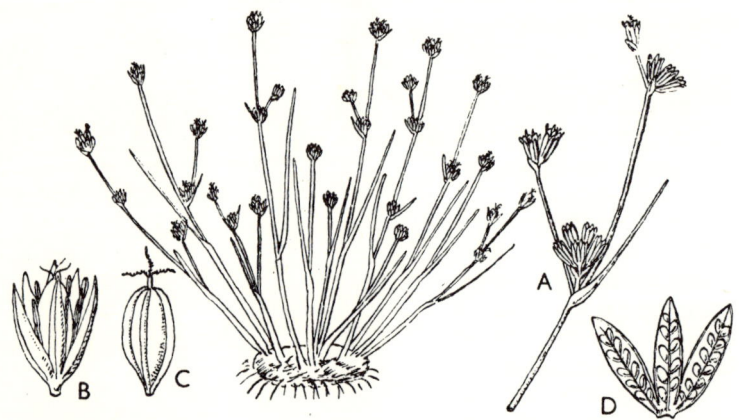

$\times$ 3) in a few small sessile or shortly stalked clusters (A, $\times$ 1) the lowermost with a leaf-like bract at the base, the others with much smaller membranous bracts about half the length of the perianth; perianth of 6 free lanceolate segments tinged with brown or reddish; stamens 6, opposite the segments; ovary (C, $\times$ 3) 3-sided, winged; capsule (D, $\times$ 2$\frac{1}{2}$) as long as the perianth, opening into 3 valves, each with 2 rows of seeds up the middle (family *Juncaceae*).

A common dwarf species in bogs, and especially in acid soils.

A perennial with a bunch of numerous leaves from the base, and these broadly sheathing in the lower part; leaf-blades stiff and spreading, very narrow, rounded below and grooved above, usually about as long as the flowering stems; the latter usually 2–3 to each plant, 9 in. to 15 in. high, very rigid, ending in a shortly branched cyme-like panicle; flowers (A, $\times 1\frac{1}{2}$) separate, though crowded, sessile or shortly stalked; bracts paired below the flower, ovate, short; perianth-segments (B, $\times 1\frac{1}{2}$) 6, equal in length, lanceolate, glossy, with a broad middle and thin chaffy margins; stamens 6, opposite the segments; ovary (C, $\times 3$) with a short style and 3 stigmas; capsule (D, $\times 2\frac{1}{2}$) about as long as the segments, obovoid,

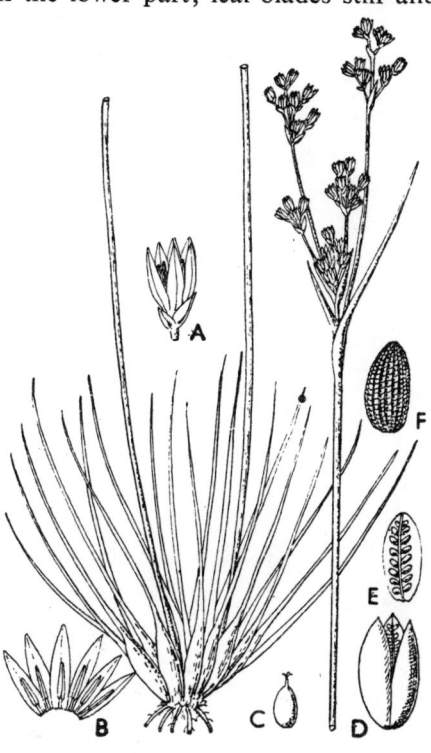

shining, splitting into 3 parts, each part (E, $\times 2$) boat-shaped, with a placenta in the middle and numerous, brown, closely pitted seeds (F, $\times 10$) (family *Juncaceae*).

This species grows on moors and heaths, and is found in drier places than most other rushes. The seeds (fig. F) are very distinctive. It flowers in summer, and is widely distributed in Europe and Asia.

BULRUSH
Scirpus lacustris L. ($\times \frac{2}{3}$)

Perennial with creeping rootstock covered with brown closely ribbed scales; stems erect, even up to 8 ft. high, cylindrical at the base and embraced with a few overlapping narrow pointed leaf-sheaths, the latter thin and closely marked with numerous parallel nerves; the stem towards the top becoming obtusely triangular; flower-spikes (A, $\times 3$) 3 or more together in sessile and stalked clusters, ovoid, $\frac{1}{2}$–$\frac{3}{4}$ in. long; outer bract stiff and continuing the stem and 1–2 in. long; flowers (B, $\times 4$) bisexual; floral bracts (glumes) numerous, overlapping all around the axis, ovate, acute, jagged at the margins; hypogynous bristles (C, $\times 10$) 5–6, shorter than the bracts, with numerous reflexed barbs; stamens (D, $\times 8$) 3; anthers apiculate, attached at the base; ovary (E, $\times 4$) obovoid; style divided into 2 arms; nut obovoid, smooth (family *Cyperaceae*).

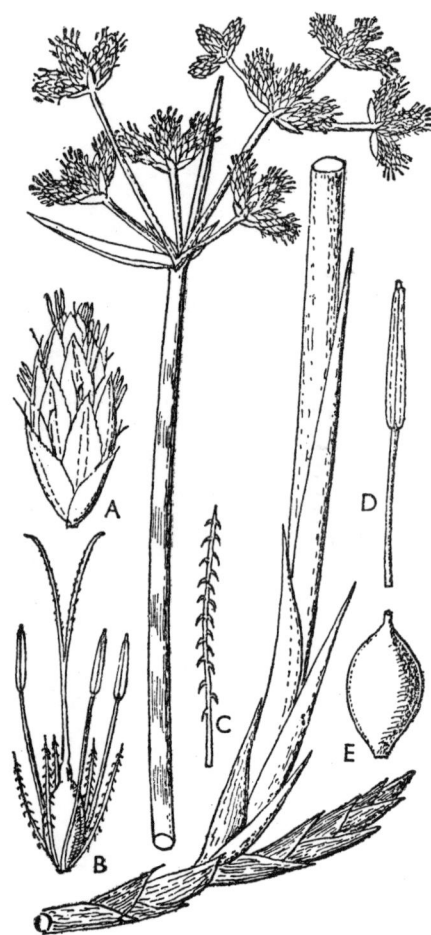

The Bulrush is very widely distributed, and is typical of the vegetation in almost every piece of water landscape, particularly in the Fen districts of East Anglia, reaching in some places up to 8 ft. high. It flowers in July and August. The leaves have been much used for matting, chair seats ('rush-bottomed chairs'), mats, and hassocks, and thatching. At one time pack-saddles were stuffed with bulrushes.

Scirpus setaceus L. ($\times \frac{2}{3}$)

One of the very smallest sedges growing in sandy or gravelly soil on the margins of ponds; plants forming dense tufts with matted roots; leaves very short and subulate, purplish at the base; flowering stems up to about 6 in. high, like fine wire, closely ribbed, smooth, bearing at the top 1–3 sessile spikelets (A, × 4), subtended by the shortly produced subulate bract-leaf; spikelets ovoid, about ¼ in. long; bracts (B, × 6) ovate, streaked with brown and with a green midrib; flowers (C, × 8) bisexual; no hypogynous bristles; stamens 3, anthers comparatively short; ovary smooth, with a slender 3-armed style; nut (D, × 12) very small, broadly obovoid, marked with several longitudinal brown ribs (family *Cyperaceae*).

Easily distinguished by its diminutive size, and differing from the rather similar *S. riparius* by the nut marked with longitudinal ribs, a feature only observable through a fairly strong lens.

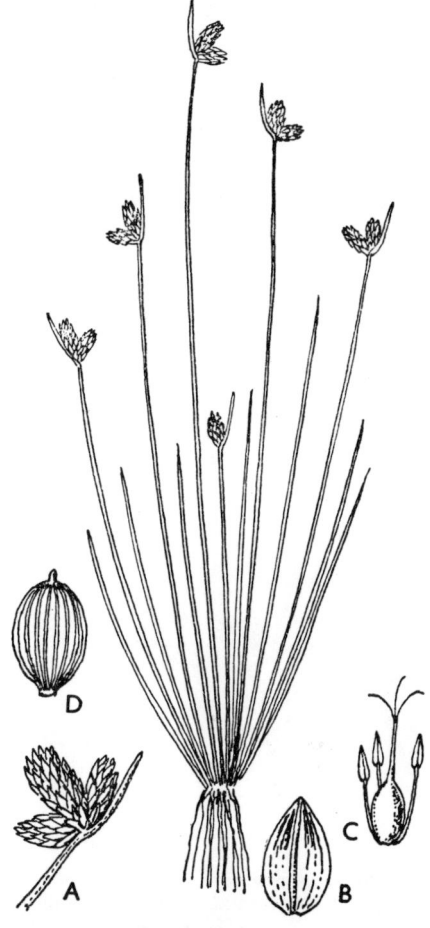

Scirpus caespitosus L. ($\times\frac{1}{2}$)

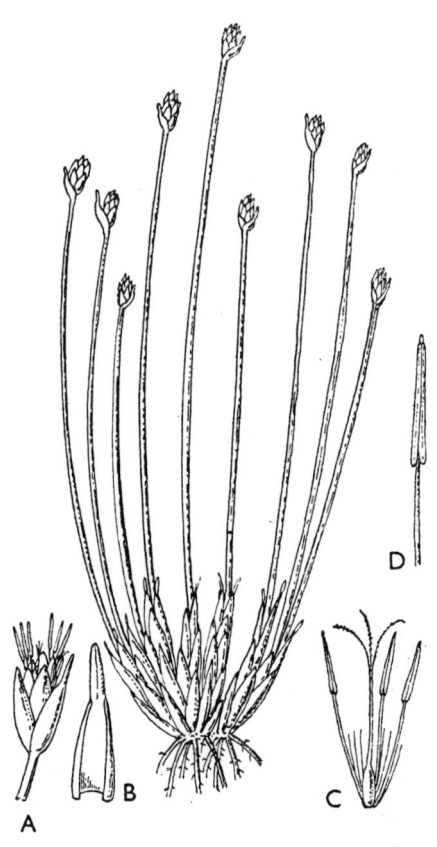

A very densely tufted perennial with numerous fairly thick roots; flowering stems up to 1 ft. high, covered with closely overlapping shining sheaths in the lower part, the lower brown, the upper green and with very short narrow leafy tips; spikelet (A, × 2) solitary at the apex of each stiff wiry peduncle, about ¼ in. long, ovoid, brown, the outermost bract the largest, but not exceeding the length of the spikelet, with a short leafy top (B, × 3); flowers (C, × 5) bisexual, about 6–8 to each spikelet; stamens 3; anthers (D, × 4) with a barren tip; hypogynous bristles about 6, very fine and hair-like and smooth; style with 3 branches; nut obovoid, 3-sided, pointed (family *Cyperaceae*).

Locally abundant in moorland and heath districts, but not found in cultivated land and areas with chalky soil. It is very widely distributed in the northern hemisphere.

Perennial with creeping blackish rootstock, on the edges of ponds, pools, and wet ditches; roots slender and fibrous; tufts of leaves and flowering stems numerous, often about 9 in. to 1 ft., but occasionally up to $2\frac{1}{2}$ ft. high; peduncles with a tubular sheath about 1–2 in. long at the base, the sheath truncate at the top, tinged with reddish-crimson; spikelets (A, $\times$ 3) solitary at the top of the peduncle, lanceolate in outline, composed of several spirally arranged imbricate reddish - brown bracts (glumes); lowermost bract (B, $\times$ 4) ovate, shorter and broader than the others and without a flower inside; other bracts all with a flower in their axils, broadly lanceolate, with green middle part, brown or reddish towards the membranous margin; stamens (D, $\times$ 10) 3; anthers basifixed, apiculate; hypogynous bristles 4, with reflexed barbs (C, $\times$ 6); ovary (E, $\times$ 6) obovoid, smooth, the base

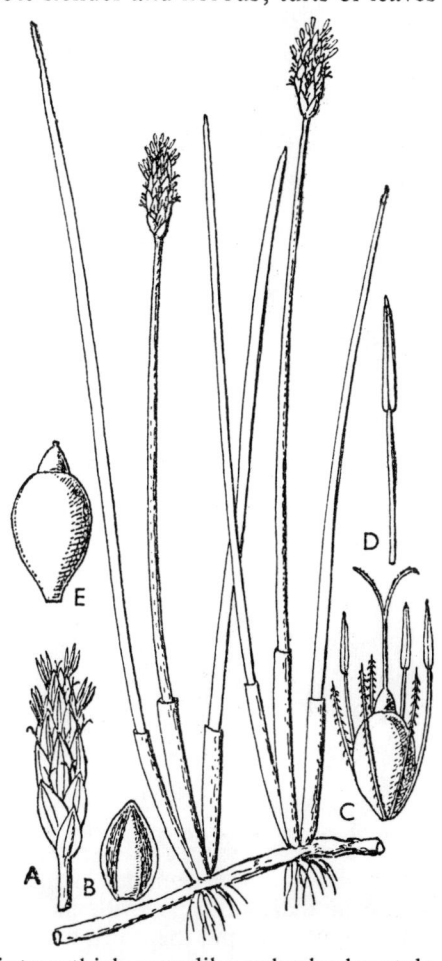

of the style much swollen into a thick cone-like paler body; style 2-lobed; nut obovoid, rather compressed, tipped by the swollen persistent base of the style (family *Cyperaceae*).

Like many other aquatic or semi-aquatic plants, this has a wide range of distribution, south to northern Africa, and in North America; it is common and widely distributed throughout Britain.

Eriophorum angustifolium Roth. ($\times \frac{2}{3}$)

Perennial with creeping rootstock covered with strongly nerved sheaths; leaves few from the base of the stem, very narrow and

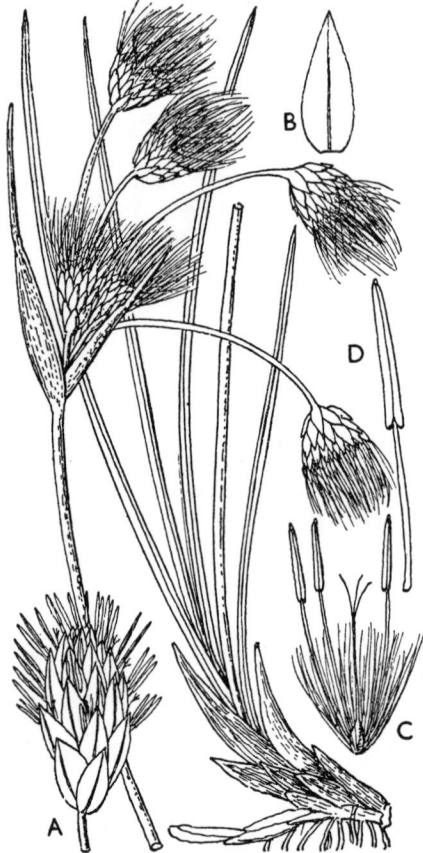

tough, closely ribbed when dry, glabrous; flowering stem about 1– 1½ ft. high, bearing at the top usually more than 1 spike of flowers arranged in an irregular umbel, some with longer stalks than others; spike (in flower) (A, × 1⅓) ¾–1 in. long, narrowly ellipsoid, with conspicuous long anthers projecting beyond the bracts (glumes); all the bracts (B, × 2) except the lowermost with a flower (C, × 2) in their axil, thin and membranous, with a very narrow midrib; stamens (D, × 3) 3; anthers very long, basifixed; hypogynous bristles numerous, very fine and hair-like, growing out in fruit and resembling cotton, hence the common name; ovary ellipsoid, with a slender 3-branched style; nut very small (family *Cyperaceae*).

Sometimes quite a common plant in marshes and bogs and a feature in the landscape, with its white cotton-like balls; it is widely spread around the north temperate zone.

Perennial herb forming dense grass-like
tufts, without a creeping rootstock;
stems up to 10 in. high, slender, glabrous, clothed at the base with short almost bladeless leaf-sheaths; other leaves
linear, a few up the stem, the lower ones
with a truncate sheathing base encircling the stem; spikelets nearly white, in a
small loose terminal cluster, often with
a secondary pedunculate cluster in the
axil of the uppermost leaf; spikelets
short, bearing 1 or 2 flowers and up to
about 4 empty pointed glumes; outer
glume (A, ×5) linear-lanceolate, pointed, 1-nerved, membranous; hypogynous bristles (B, ×6) up to 12,
shorter than the glume, slightly scabrid;
stamens 3; ovary shortly stipitate; style
swollen towards the base, stigmas 2;
nut (C, ×6) shortly stipitate, slightly
compressed with thicker margins, longer than the bristles (family *Cyperaceae*).

Flowers in summer and autumn in
bogs, generally distributed in Britain
and circumpolar.

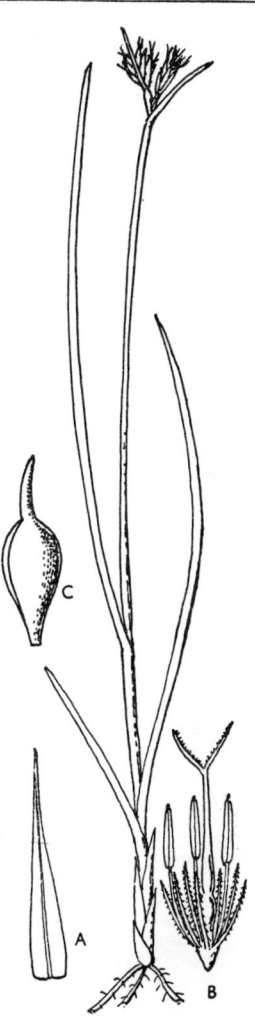

Blysmus compressus (L.) Link ($\times\frac{1}{2}$)

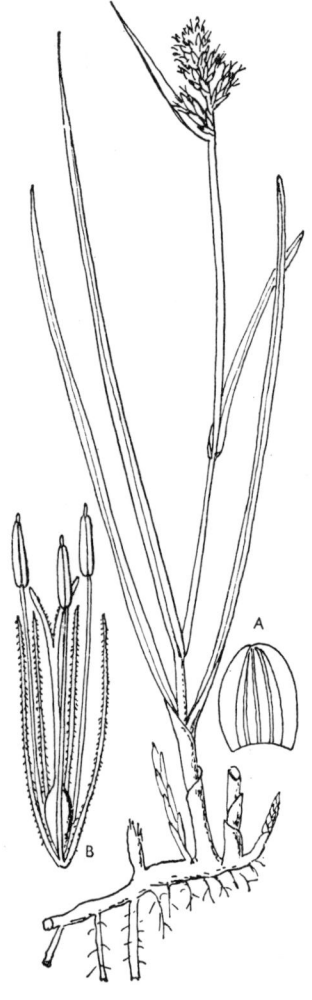

Perennial herb with a creeping root-stock; stems up to 1 ft. high, clothed at the base with 2 or 3 almost blade-less leaf-sheaths forming a 'collar' to the stem leaves which are few and rather crowded in a bunch; leaf-blades shorter than the flowering stem, flat and closely nerved; spikes terminal, about 1 in. long, consisting of 9–12 oblong spikelets sessile on opposite sides of the main axis, each spikelet $\frac{1}{4}$–$\frac{1}{3}$ in. long, the broad glume-like outer bract (A, $\times 2\frac{1}{2}$) much shorter than the spikelet and with broad margins and 3 median nerves; glumes imbricate all around the spikelet, the lowest often empty; stamens mostly 3, with 3–6 hypo-gynous bristles (B, $\times 3$) nearly as long; ovary shortly stipitate, style with 2 branches; nut slightly flat-tened, tapered into the style (family *Cyperaceae*).

Flowers in summer in southern Scotland and general over England; extends eastward into Russian Asia.

Cyperus longus L. (×⅓)

Perennial herb with stout triangular stems up to 4 ft. high and with a creeping rootstock; basal leaves few, mostly shorter than the flowering stem, about ½ in. broad, very closely lined with numerous parallel nerves, sharply serrulate on the margin; involucre of usually 3 leaves up to about 1 ft. long and very similar to the basal leaves; spikelets numerous in an umbel, the central ones on shorter peduncles; spikelets (A, ×1) several in a short raceme, linear, pointed, flattened, about ½ in. long; glumes numerous in 2 opposite rows, all nearly equal with one bisexual flower in each, bright chestnut in colour with a green keel; stamens (B, ×5) 3, exserted from the glume; ovary (C, ×4) gradually narrowed into the style, the latter deeply 3-lobed (family *Cyperaceae*).

Found only in southern England and south Wales, flowering in late July and August in wet meadows and pastures; extends from southern Europe to central Asia.

BLACK BOG-RUSH
Schoenus nigricans L. ($\times\frac{1}{2}$)

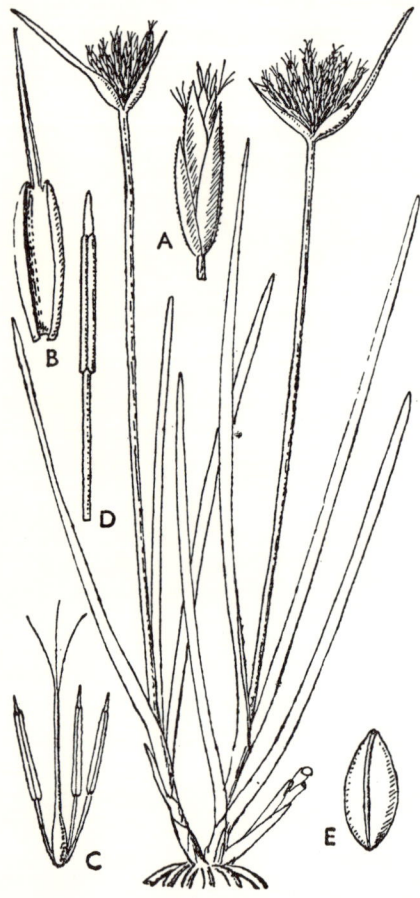

A densely tufted perennial with very numerous thick roots, up to $1\frac{1}{2}$ ft. high, but usually 9 in. to 1 ft.; leaves very narrow and rigid, their sheaths dark brown or reddish and shining, ribbed; flowers crowded in terminal heads subtended by a pair of opposite bracts (B, ×1), 1 or both with a leaf-like upper portion; spikelets (A, × 2) crowded together into a head, each spikelet shortly stalked and consisting of a few bracts (glumes) arranged in opposite rows, only the upper bracts containing bisexual flowers (C, × 4), the lower ones empty; bracts dark brown or nearly black, lanceolate, keeled, the keel slightly rough; stamens (D, × 8) 3; anthers with rather long barren tips; ovary ellipsoid, with a slender style and 3 slender style-arms; nut (E, × 5) triangular, pale-grey and smooth family *Cyperaceae*).

This is locally common and more frequent in northern Britain. It is a very widely distributed species in the northern hemisphere.

Kobresia simpliciuscula (Wahlenb.) Mackenzie ($\frac{1}{2}$)

Perennial herb very like some species of Carex but the fruit not enclosed in a utricle as in that genus; densely tufted, rarely more than 6 in. high; leaves all radical or sheathing the base of the flowering stem, ascending or spreading, linear, much shorter than the flowering stem, sheathing at the base; flowers unisexual, in sessile spikelets crowded into an oblong terminal spike, with a glume-like rounded, long-cuspidate bract (A, ×2$\frac{1}{2}$) under each spikelet (B, ×3); in each spikelet the lower flowers female (C, ×3), the ovary (D, ×4) with a deeply 3-lobed style; upper flower of the terminal spikelet and usually one terminal flower of the lateral spikelets male containing within the glume 3 stamens with long filaments and pendulous anthers; nut (E, ×4) 3-sided or compressed (family *Cyperaceae*).

Only found in the northern counties of England and in Scotland, flowering in late summer; widely distributed around the north temperate zone. Synonym *K. caricina* Willd.

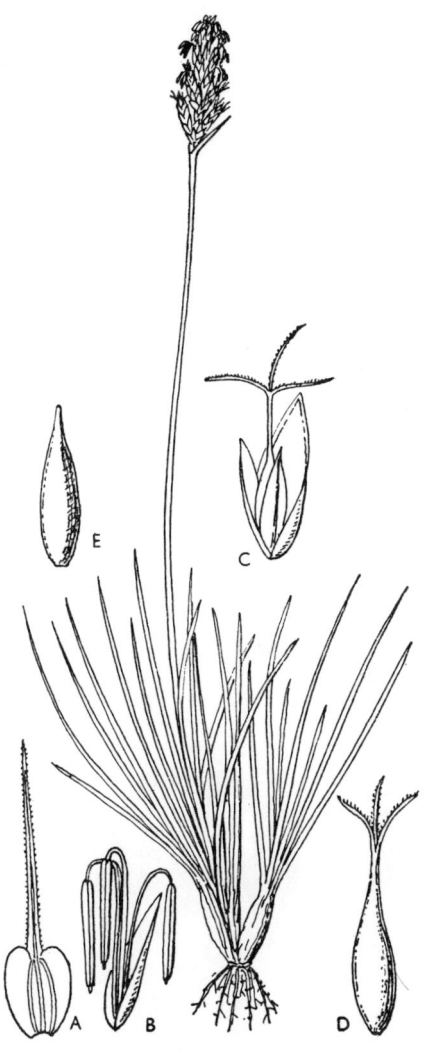

CARNATION GRASS
Carex panicea L. ($\times\frac{1}{2}$)

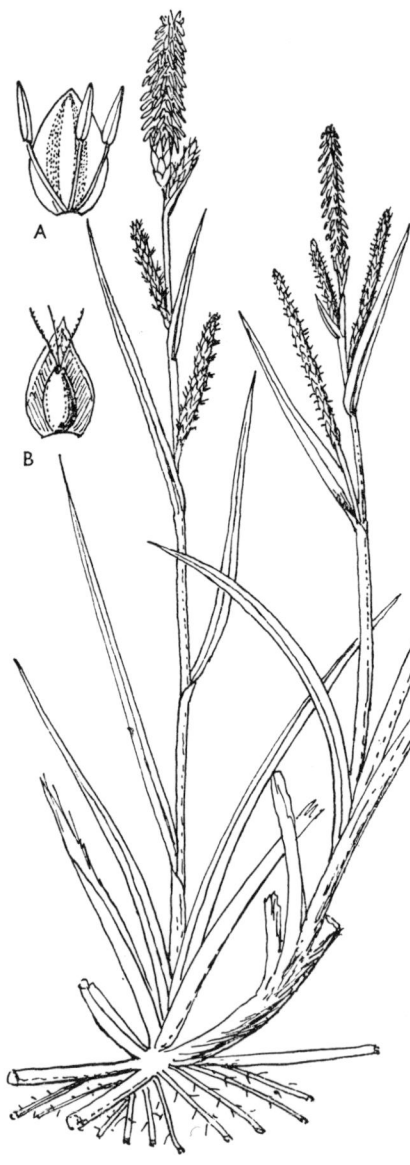

Herb with tufted smooth stems 1–1½ ft. high giving off creeping runners from the base; leaves suberect, much shorter than the stems, rather stiff, linear, flat, slightly rough on the margins, glaucous; spikelets usually 3, the terminal one male 1–1½ in. long, the others female about 1 in. long and distant except one just under the male, all except the end one in the axils of leafy bracts as long or longer than the spikelets; glumes (A, ×2) ovate, brown, with pale margins, and a green stripe up the middle; style (B, ×2) deeply 3-partite; fruits pale brown, ovoid, without ribs except the 3 angles, very shortly beaked (family *Cyperaceae*).

Common in Britain in meadows and moist pastures, flowering in early summer; widely spread around the north temperate zone.

Carex sylvatica Huds. ($\times\frac{1}{2}$)

Perennial herb growing in tufts up to 2 ft. high; rootstock with short thick branches, each producing several flowering stems and barren shoots; stem slender, weak, triangular, glabrous or slightly rough at the top; leaves linear, gradually tapered to the apex, sheathing at the base, flat, slightly rough on the margins, green, not glaucous; male spikelet (A, $1\frac{1}{2}$) terminal, $1-1\frac{1}{2}$ in. long, male flowers (B, $\times2\frac{1}{2}$) numerous, sometimes with a female flower (D, $\times2\frac{1}{2}$) in the lower part; lateral axillary spikelets female, slender, $1-1\frac{1}{2}$ in. long, on slender at length drooping stalks; glumes (C, $\times2\frac{1}{2}$) green, lanceolate, pointed; style (E, $\times2\frac{1}{2}$) 3-lobed; fruit pale olive, 3-sided, glabrous, ribbed, tapered into a long beak, closely covered by the utricle (family *Cyperaceae*).

In woods except in the north of Scotland; flowers in early summer.

In Bentham's *Flora* 47 species of *Carex* were described and in the latest *Flora* there are 77.

PANICLED SEDGE
Carex paniculata L. ($\times\frac{1}{3}$)

Perennial strong growing herb up to 4 ft. high forming dense large tufts; stems triangular, rough in the upper part; leaves in

luxuriant specimens as long or longer than the flowering stem, in poorer specimens shorter and narrower, linear, channelled, rough on the margins, not glaucous; spikelets numerous, brown, crowded into a compound spike or panicle, male at the apex and female below; outer bracts (A, $\times 2\frac{1}{2}$) scarious on the margins; ovary (C, $\times 4$) with a 2-lobed style; fruit (B, $\times 4$) ovate, beaked, marked towards the base on the inner face with several ribs (family *Cyperaceae*).

Widely distributed in the north temperate zone, generally found over Britain, in marshes and bogs, flowering in the early summer.

Carex nigra (L.) Reichard ($\times \frac{2}{3}$)

A perennial with long stoloniferous shoots, these clothed with fibrous leaf-sheaths; leaves few in the lower part of the stem, some as long as the flowering-stem, narrow, closely nerved, tapered to a fine point, the basal sheath with wide membranous margins; spikelets containing flowers of 1 sex only (unisexual) the terminal male (A), the others female (B, × 0); male spikelet narrow and slender, about ¾–1 in. long; bracts (glumes) (C, × 2) oblong-elliptic, rounded at the top; stamens (D, × 2) 3; female spikelets axillary, nearly sessile, about ¾ in. long in flower, or 1 in. in fruit; bracts (glumes) narrowly ovate, shorter than the utricle in fruit (E, × 2); utricle (F, × 2½) broadly bottle-shaped, shortly beaked,  ribbed lengthwise; style-arms 2 or occasionally 3; nut (G, × 2) somewhat flattened, beaked; bracts in fruit black or nearly so (family *Cyperaceae*). Male spikelets marked ♂, female ♀.

This species is usually called *C. goodenowi* Gay or *C. vulgaris* Fries in British *Floras*, but *C. nigra* is the name to be used according to the most recent research into the nomenclature. It is widely distributed in Europe, northern Asia, and in north-eastern America.

Carex rostrata Stokes (×⅔)

Tufted perennial up to 3 ft. high; leaves longer than the flowering
stem, ½ in. broad, tapered to a fine point, margins finely toothed,
the lower reduced to sheaths; spikelets with flowers of 1 sex only
(unisexual), 2–4 of the upper entirely male and sessile (A), the
remainder (D) female and more or less shortly stalked, the stalks

much elongating in fruit; terminal male spikelets (A) the longest,
about 2 in. long; bracts (B, × 2) narrow; stamens (C, × 2) 3;
female bracts also narrow (E, × 3), with a broad pale middle and
brownish margins; utricle (F, × 2½) longer than the bract in fruit
and beaked; style-arms 2; nut ellipsoid, smooth (family *Cyperaceae*). – Male spikelets marked ♂, female marked ♀.

In British *Floras* and lists this species is usually called *C. am-
pullacea* Gooden. It is widely distributed from Europe to Asia
Minor and as far east as Siberia.

Carex pulicaris L. ($\times \frac{2}{3}$)

A densely tufted perennial up to 9 in. high; roots very fine and fibrous; leaves very slender and wiry, some as long as the flowering stems; sheaths at the base narrow and strongly ribbed; spikelets (A, × 1) solitary at the top of each stem, $\frac{1}{2}$–$\frac{3}{4}$ in. long, bisexual, i.e. the upper slender portion with male flowers, the lower thicker half with female flowers; bracts ovate-lanceolate, with a green midrib and brown towards the thin margins, the lowermost bract like the others; each female flower (B, × 3) with a membranous brown bract; utricle (C, × 4) rather narrow and pointed; style with 2 branches; nut (D, × 4) oblong-ellipsoid, partly compressed, pale brown; fruiting spike (E, × 2) very loose, with the fruits spreading or drooping (family *Cyperaceae*). – Male part of spikelet marked ♂, female marked ♀.

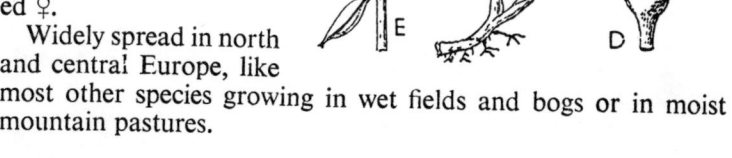

Widely spread in north and central Europe, like most other species growing in wet fields and bogs or in moist mountain pastures.

917

HAIRY SEDGE
Carex hirta L. (×⅖)

Perennial herb with long creeping rootstock covered with closely ribbed old leaf-sheaths and with very fine fibrous roots; stem slen-

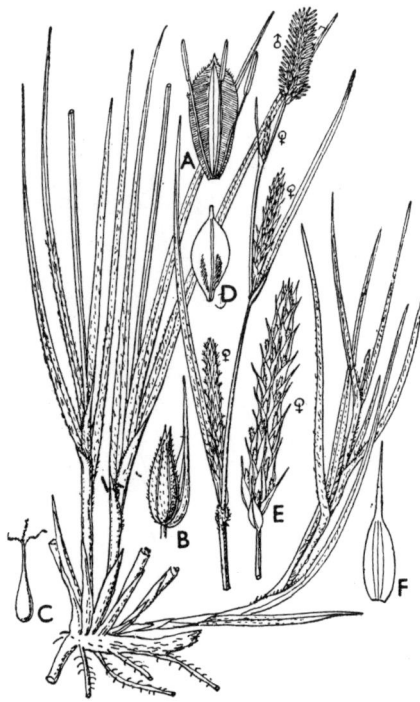

der, leafy throughout, rather sharply three-sided; leaves thinly pilose on both surfaces and very densely woolly-hairy on the margins towards the top of the sheath, the blade about ¼ in. broad and closely ribbed with nerves lengthwise; spikelets unisexual; male spikelets 1–3 at the top of the stem, the terminal about 1 in. long, the lower males shorter; glumes (A, × 3) oblong-obovate, shortly acuminate, pubescent towards the top; stamens 3, the anthers exserted; female spikelets 2–3, 1 in each axil of the leaves below the males, elongating to 2 in. long in ⁄fruit and stalked; glumes (B, F, × 1½) very long-pointed; utricle exceptional in being pubescent, beaked; ovary (C, × 3) narrow; style 3-lobed; nutlet (D, × 2) obovoid, triangular, pale, and smooth (family *Cyperaceae*). – Male spikelets marked ♂, female marked ♀ (E, × ⅘, fruiting spikelet).

This is one of the most easily recognized of the sedges because of the softly hairy leaves and leaf-sheaths and hairy utricles. It is very common in Europe, Asia Minor, and is also found in northern Africa.

Perennial with creeping rootstock; stems triangular, 2–3 ft. high; leaves very long and erect, densely overlapping at the base, and with thread-like margins, about $\frac{1}{2}$ in. broad, with sharply serrulate margins, and with nearly 20 close parallel nerves on each side of the midrib; leaf below the lowest female spikelet overtopping the terminal males; male spikelets usually 2 or 3 together at the top and nearly sessile, the end one the longest and about $1\frac{1}{2}$ in. long, covered with densely crowded exserted anthers; glumes (A, $\times 4$) oblong, not pointed; stamens (B, $\times 2$) 3; female spikelets (H, $\times 1\frac{1}{2}$) nearly sessile, lengthening to 3 in. in fruit; glumes (C, $\times 4$) elliptic, with an acuminate slightly hairy tip; utricle (D, F, $\times 2$) ellipsoid, shortly beaked, distinctly ribbed length-

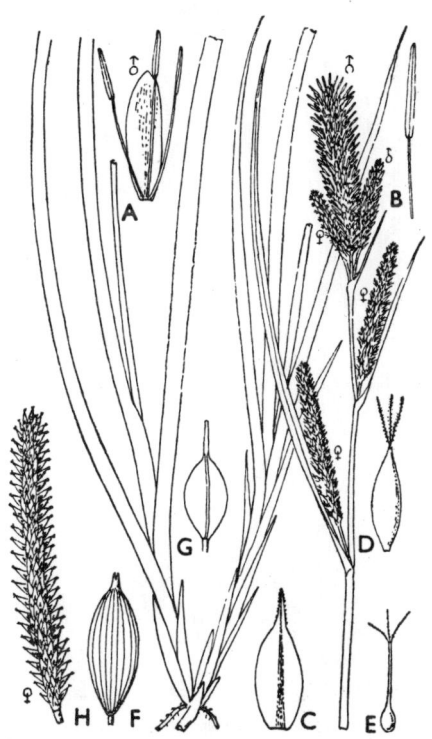

wise; ovary (E, $\times 2\frac{1}{2}$) ellipsoid, with a long 3-lobed style; nut (G, $\times 2\frac{1}{4}$) longer than the perianth, 3-angled beaked by the persistent style (family *Cyperaceae*). – Male spikelets marked ♂ female marked ♀.

This species flowers in May and fruits in June, and grows in wet meadows and marshes. It is widely distributed in Europe and central Asia to Siberia, and in north Africa. Another name for the plant is *C. paludosa* Gooden.

DISTANT SEDGE
Carex distans L. ($\times \frac{2}{5}$)

A slender perennial herb up to about 15 in. high; stems tufted from a creeping rootstock, leafy below the middle, the longest leaves up to about half as long as the flowering stems; lower leaves recurved, the others ascending, $\frac{1}{8}$ in. broad, glaucous-green; spikelets unisexual, the single male terminal, with usually 3 distant females, 1 in each of the upper leaf-bract axils, the lowermost bract sometimes reaching to the top of the male spikelet; male spikelet $\frac{3}{4}$–1 in. long; covered with overlapping brownish obovate glumes (A, $\times$ 2) with thin margins; stamens 3, the anthers exserted on very slender filaments; female spikelets shortly stalked, about 1 in. long; glumes (C, $\times$ 2) obovate, the lower (B, $\times$ 2) with a short hairy tip and green midrib; utricle bottle-shaped; style (D, $\times$ 2) 3-lobed, hairy; nutlet 3-sided, enclosed by the beaked utricle; fruiting spikelet fat, with a short stalk clear of the accompanying leaf-like bract (family *Cuperaceae*). – Male spikelets marked ♂, female marked ♀.

This very distinctive species has no other names to be recorded as synonyms. It is found throughout Europe and the eastern Mediterranean countries, in north Africa, and is also recorded from Madeira and the Azores.

Perennial with creeping runners from the base; leaves flat, with a prominent midrib, slightly rough on the margins, tapered to a sharp point; sheath truncate (abruptly cut off) opposite the base of the blade; flower spikelets of 1 sex (unisexual), the uppermost 2 male (A), the rest (usually about 3) female (B); male spikelets unequal in length, the uppermost longer and about 1 in. long; stamens (C, × 2) 3, the long yellow anthers long-exserted from the bracts (glumes); bracts (glumes) oblong-oblanceolate, with wide brown margins; female spikelets on slender stalks, $\frac{1}{2}$–1 in. long when in flower; bracts (glumes) (D, × 2) oblonglanceolate, with a green midrib and wide brown margins; utricle (E, × 2) not beaked; ovary (F, × 1½)

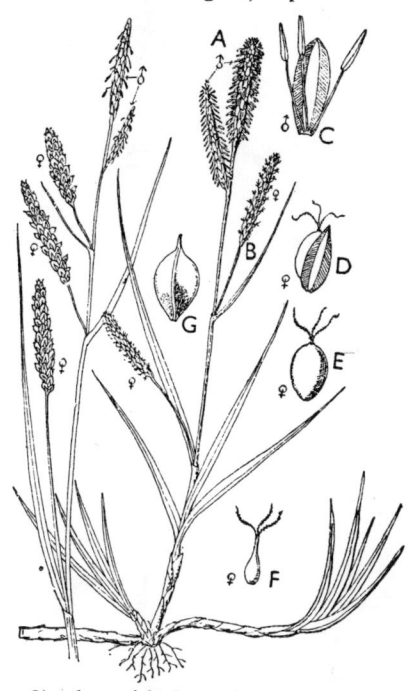

smooth; styles 3; nutlet (G, × 2) obovoid, 3-angled, pale straw-coloured (family *Cyperaceae*). – Male spikelets marked ♂, female marked ♀.

Another name for this species is *C. glauca* Scop. It is widely distributed in Europe and north Africa and in western Asia, and has been introduced into North America and a few other parts of the world.

PENDULOUS SEDGE
Carex pendula Huds. ($\times \frac{2}{5}$)

A tall perennial up to 5 ft. high with thick triangular leafy stems; leaves very long and about $\frac{3}{4}$ in. broad, keeled towards the base,

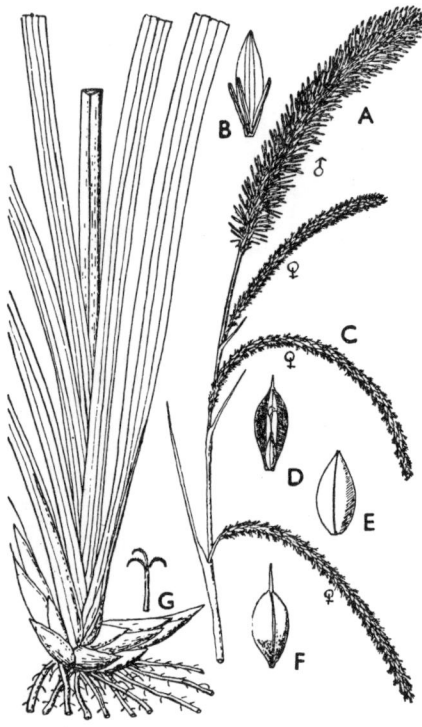

tapered to the apex, margins smooth, with 3 main longitudinal nerves and several close less conspicuous nerves; flowers in at length slender pendulous spikelets, the terminal spikelet (A) entirely male and about 3 in. long, with very conspicuous stamens within broadly oblanceolate acute thin bracts (B, $\times 1\frac{1}{4}$), remainder of spikelets entirely female (C), slender, often nearly 6 in. long, especially in fruit; bracts of female (D, $\times 1\frac{1}{4}$) obovate, acutely pointed, 3-nerved, brown between the nerves and the margin; utricle (E, $\times 2$) enclosing the ovary 3-sided; style (G, $\times 3$) 3-lobed; nutlet (F, $\times 2\frac{1}{2}$) 3-sided, pale, tipped by the persistent style (family *Cyperaceae*). – Male spikelets marked ♂, female marked ♀.

This species is easily spotted because of the long slender pendulous spikelets. It is not quite so widely distributed as most of the other species described in this book, being found in Europe, Asia Minor, and north Africa.

Perennial herb with a rootstock creeping for several feet in maritime sands; stems arising singly here and there along the rootstock, from a few inches up to $1\frac{1}{2}$ ft. high; rootstock covered with overlapping sheaths which soon split into threads, rooting at the joints, the roots covered with very fine much-branched rootlets; lowermost leaves reduced to sheaths, the few upper leaves linear and falling short of the spike; spikelets (A, $\times 1$) unisexual, arranged in a dense spike which becomes laxer in fruit, 3 or 4 of the lower spikelets entirely female, the remainder above male, all rather short and narrowly ovoid, about $\frac{1}{2}$ in. long; bract subtending the

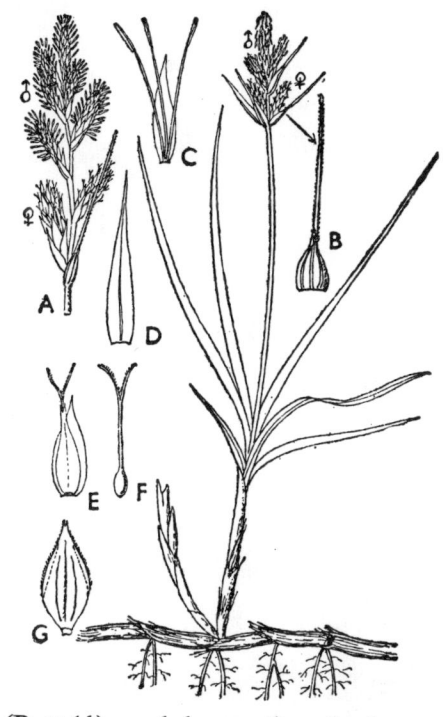

lowermost female spikelet (B, $\times 1\frac{1}{2}$) much longer than the latter, ovate at the base and 3-ribbed outside, shortly barbellate on the margins; bracts (glumes) of the male (E, $\times 1\frac{1}{2}$) broadly lanceolate, acute, very thin; stamens (C, $\times 2$) 3; lowermost bract (D, $\times 1\frac{1}{2}$) of the female spikelet lanceolate and long-acuminate; remainder ovate-lanceolate, shortly pointed; utrucle (G, $\times 1\frac{1}{2}$) flattened, ovate, barbellate on the margin; style branches (F, $\times 1\frac{1}{2}$) 2 (family *Cyperaceae*). – Male spikelets marked ♂, female marked ♀.

This species is widely distributed around Britain, growing in sandy places near the sea; common also inland in Breckland. It is useful as a sand-binder. As a native plant it is confined to Europe, but has been introduced into Atlantic North America.

OVAL SEDGE
Carex ovalis Gooden. ($\times \frac{1}{2}$)

Perennial growing in tufts, covered at the base with thread-like fibres of remains of leaf-bases; roots fairly stout; flowering stems up to nearly 2 ft. high; lower leaves quite short and sharp-pointed, upper leaves shorter than the flowering stems, ending in very fine points, microscopically serrulate on the margins; spikelets (A, $\times 1\frac{1}{2}$) about 4–7 and arranged in a close spike, each spikelet sessile, bisexual, a few male flowers (C, $\times 2$) at the base of each, the rest above female (D, $\times 2$), lowermost bract (glume) broadly elliptic-lanceolate, ending in a fairly long serrulate awn (B, $\times 2\frac{1}{2}$), but sometimes leaf-like and half as long as the spike; remainder of bracts ovate-lanceolate, acute; stamens of male flowers (C, $\times 2$) 3; utricle of female flowers (E, $\times 2$) flattened and lanceolate, shortly bristly on the wing-like margins; style divided into 2 branches (family *Cyperaceae*). – Male portions of spikelets marked ♂, female marked ♀.

In most *Floras* and lists of British plants this is called *C. leporina*, but the name used above takes precedence. The species is found in Europe, from northern Asia to Kamchatka, and in Atlantic North America.

A tufted perennial up to 1½ ft. high; stems very slender, bearing spikelets widely separated from one another and sessile; leaves very narrow, ending in fine thread-like points, minutely rough on the margins; spikelets (A, × 2) nearly as broad as long, about ¼ in., the lower half of each with male flowers, the upper half with

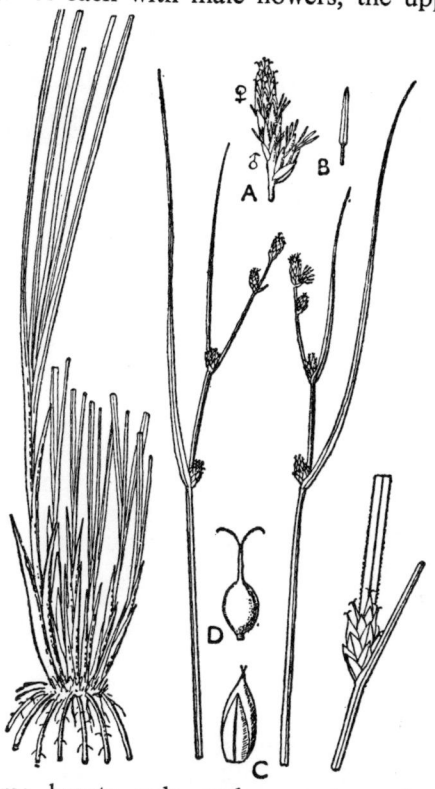

female flowers; bracts pale and ovate-lanceolate, 1-nerved; utricle (C, × 2) longer than the bract, tapered to a point; style with 2 branches; nut (D, × 2) ellipsoid, slightly flattened; the terminal spikelet often has more male flowers than the others, and the lowest placed spikelet is sometimes completely female (family *Cyperaceae*). – Male portions of spikelets marked ♂, females marked ♀ (B, stamen × 3).

In woods and moist places, widely spread in Europe, north Africa, and western Asia, flowering in early summer.

925

PRICKLY SEDGE
Carex echinata Murr. (×⅗)

A tufted perennial up to about 9 in. high; leaves shorter than the flowering stems or sometimes about as long, very narrow and rather rough on the edges, sheaths with membranous margins and a ligule-like top; spikelets (A, × 1¼) bi-sexual, collected into an interrupted spike in flower, but more crowded on the axis in fruit (D, × 1¼) and then 'prickly' with the spreading sharp-pointed utricles, the whole spike occasionally with a short leaf-like bract at the base; each spikelet male in the lower part, female in the upper part, ovoid, ¼ in. long in flower, a little longer in fruit, the terminal one narrowed to the base and with several barren glumes on the stalk; glumes ovate, at most subacute but not pointed; utricles (B, × 1½, E, × 2½) narrowly ovoid, beaked, hairy on the angles in the upper part; ovary (C, × 2) ellipsoid, with 2 recurved hairy styles; nut (F, × 2) ovoid and somewhat compressed, straw-coloured, beaked by a short portion of the style (family *Cyperaceae*). – Male portions of spike-lets marked ♂, female marked ♀.

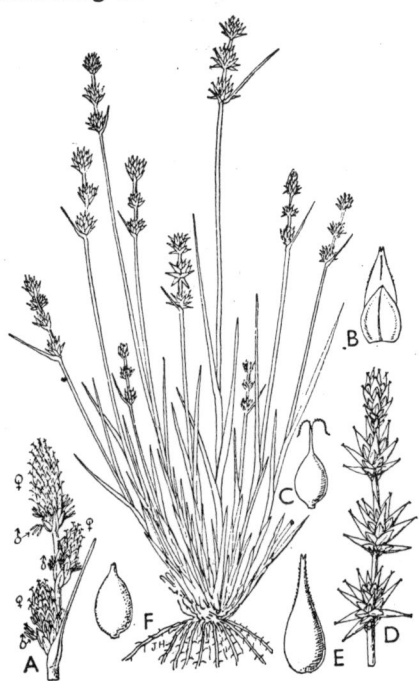

The usual name for this in British *Floras* and lists of species is *C. stellulata* Gooden. It has a wide distribution right around the north temperate zone, and, curiously enough, is also found in the mountains of south-east Australia and New Zealand, though not anywhere between these widely separated regions.

INDEX TO GENERA IN THE
TWO VOLUMES

(The numbers refer to volumes and illustrations)

INDEX TO COMMON NAMES IN THE
TWO VOLUMES

(The numbers refer to volumes and illustrations)